Special educational needs, inclusion and diversity:
a textbook

Norah Frederickson and
Tony Cline

Open University Press

Open University Press
McGraw-Hill Education
McGraw-Hill House
Shoppenhangers Road
Maidenhead
Berkshire
SL6 2QL

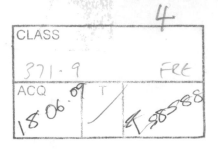
email: enquiries@openup.co.uk
world wide web: www.openup.co.uk

and
Two Penn Plaza
New York, NY 10121-2289, USA

First Published 2002

Reprinted 2003, 2005 (twice), 2006, 2007

A catalogue record of this book is available from the British Library

ISBN-10: 0 335 20402 3 (pb)   0 335 20973 4 (hb)
ISBN-13: 978-0-335 20402 1 (pb)   978 0 335 20973 6 (hb)

Library of Congress Cataloging-in-Publication Data
Frederickson, Norah.
    Special educational needs, inclusion and diversity : a textbook / Norah Frederickson and Tony Cline.
      p. cm.
    Includes bibliographical references and index.
    ISBN 0-335-20402-3 (pbk.)   0-335-20973-4 (hbk.)
    1. Minorities—Education—Great Britain. 2. Education, Bilingual—Great Britain. 3. Special education—~Great Britain. 4. Inclusive education—Great Britain. I. Cline, Tony. II. Title.

LC3736.G7 F74 2002
371.9´0941—dc21
                                                            2001021410

Typeset by Graphicraft Limited, Hong Kong
Printed in Great Britain by Bell & Bain Ltd, Glasgow

Contents

Acknowledgements

We would like to express our thanks to Professor John Morton and Professor Uta Frith for their very helpful comments on an early draft of Chapter 4.

The two cases featured in Activity 13.4 were taken from an advanced course which was run at University College London. The accounts were written by Ann Robson and we are grateful for her permission to use them here.

We would also wish to thank the many colleagues and students who provided source materials on which case studies and activities have been based.

Sections of the following chapters were adapted from earlier publications by the authors. We are grateful to the publishers and journal editors who have graciously given permission to use this material. Publishers and details of the original publications are as follows.

Chapter 6: Cline, T. (1998) The assessment of special educational needs for bilingual children. *British Journal of Special Education*, 25(4): 159–63; Cline, T. and Shamsi, T. (2000) *Language Needs or Special Needs? The Assessment of Learning Difficulties in Literacy Among Children Learning English as an Additional Language: A Literature Review* (Research Report RR184). London: DfEE. Authorized under individual licence from HMSO (no. C02 W0000128).

Chapter 7: Frederickson, N. (1992) Curriculum based assessment, in T. Cline (ed.) *The Assessment of Special Educational Needs: International Perspectives*. London: Routledge (International Thompson Publishing Services Limited); Cline, T. and Frederickson, N. (eds) (1996) *Curriculum Related Assessment – Cummins and Bilingual Children*. Clevedon: Multilingual Matters.

Chapter 8: Frederickson, N. and Cline, T. (eds) (1995) *Assessing the Learning Environments of Children with Special Educational Needs*. London: Educational Psychology Publishing; Frederickson, N. (1990) Introduction to Soft Systems Methodology and its application in work with schools, in N. Frederickson (ed.) *Soft Systems Methodology: Practical Approaches in Work with Schools*. London: Educational Psychology Publishing.

Table 9.1: Sternberg, R.J. (1985) *Beyond IQ: A Triarchic Theory of Human Intelligence.* Cambridge: Cambridge University Press.

Figure 9.2: Riding, R.J. and Rayner, S. (1998) *Cognitive Styles and Learning Strategies.* London: David Fulton.

Figure 9.3: Male, D. (1996) Who goes to MLD schools? *British Journal of Special Education,* 23(1): 35–41. Blackwell Publishers.

Figure 9.4: Guthke, J., Beckmann, J.F. and Dobat, H. (1997) Dynamic testing – problems, uses, trends and evidence of validity. *Educational and Child Psychology,* 14(4): 17–32, with acknowledgement to the British Psychological Society.

Table 9.4: Tomlinson, S. (1988) Why Johnny can't read: critical theory and special education. *European Journal of Special Needs Education,* 3(1): 45–58. Publisher: Taylor & Francis Ltd., PO Box 25, Abingdon, Oxfordshire, OX14 3UE.

Table 9.6: Molteno, C., Roux, A., Nelson, M. and Arens, L. (1990) Causes of mental handicap in Cape Town. *South African Medical Journal,* 77: 98–101, with acknowledgement to the South African Medical Association.

Table 9.8: Campione, J.C. (1989) Assisted assessment: a taxonomy of approaches and an outline of strengths and weaknesses. *Journal of Learning Disabilities,* 22(3): 151–65. Publisher: PRO-ED.

Figure 9.5: Byers, R. (1999) Experience and achievement: initiatives in curriculum development for pupils with severe and profound and multiple learning difficulties. *British Journal of Special Education,* 26(4): 184–8. Blackwell Publishers.

Figure 10.1: Crystal, D. and Varley, R. (1998) *Introduction to Language Pathology,* 4th edn. London: Whurr.

Figures 10.2 and 10.3: Bishop, D.V.M. (1997) *Uncommon Understanding: Development and Disorders of Language Comprehension in Children.* Hove: Psychology Press (International Thompson Publishing Services Limited).

Table 10.3: Baker, C. (1996) *Foundations of Bilingual Education and Bilingualism,* 2nd edn. Clevedon: Multilingual Matters.

Table 10.4: Skutnabb-Kangas, T. (1981) *Bilingualism or Not: The Education of Minorities.* Clevedon: Multilingual Matters.

Figure 10.6: Lees, J. and Urwin, S. (1997) *Children with Language Disorders,* 2nd edn. London: Whurr.

Table 10.5: Cline, T. (1997) Special educational needs and language proficiency, in C. Leung and C. Cable (ed.) *English as an Additional Language: Changing Perspectives* (pp. 53–64.) Watford, Hertfordshire: National Association for Language Development in the Curriculum.

Figures 11.2 to 11.4: British Psychological Society (BPS) (1999) *Dyslexia, Literacy and Psychological Assessment.* Leicester: British Psychological Society.

Table 11.5: Gregory, E. (1994) Cultural assumptions and early years' pedagogy: the effect of the home culture on minority children's interpretation of reading in school. *Language, Culture and Curriculum,* 7(2): 111–24, with acknowledgement to the Linguistics Institute of Ireland.

Figure 11.6: Palinscar, A.S. (1986) The role of dialogue in providing scaffolded instruction. *Educational Psychologist,* 21 (1 and 2): 73–98. Publisher: Lawrence Erlbaum Associates.

Table 12.1: Merttens, R. (1999) Family numeracy, in I. Thompson (ed.) *Issues in Teaching Numeracy in Primary Schools*. Buckingham: Open University Press.

Table 12.2: Shuard, H. and Rothery, R. (1984) *Children Reading Mathematics*. London: John Murray.

Figure 13.1: Ridley, J. (1991) The structure of the ear and the hearing system. *Education Guardian*, 25 June 1991: 10, with permission from Guardian Newspapers Ltd.

Figure 13.2: Watson, L. (1996) *Hearing Impairment*. Tamworth, Staffordshire: NASEN, with permission from the author and NASEN.

Table 13.6: Webster, A. and Wood, D. (1989) *Children with Hearing Difficulties*. London: Cassell (Continuum International Publishing Group).

Figure 14.7: British Psychological Society (BPS) (1996) *Attention Deficit Hyperactivity Disorder (ADHD): A Psychological Response to an Evolving Concept*. (Report of a Working Party of the British Psychological Society). Leicester: British Psychological Society.

Table 15.1: Caldarella, P. and Merrell, K.W. (1997) Common dimensions of social skills of children and adolescents: A taxonomy of positive behaviours. *School Psychology Review*, 26(2): 264–78. Sage Publications.

Figure 15.1: Dodge, K.A., Pettit, C.S., McClasky, C.J. and Brown, M.M. (1986) Social competence in children. *Society for Research in Child Development Monograph*, No. 213, Blackwell Publishers.

Figure 15.3: Frederickson, N. and Graham, B. (1999) Social skills and emotional intelligence, in N. Frederickson and R.J. Cameron. (1999) *Psychology in Education Portfolio*. Windsor: NFER-Nelson.

Figure 15.4: Oden, S. (1986) A child's social isolation: origins, prevention, intervention, in G. Cartledge and J.F. Milburn (eds) *Teaching Social Skills to Children*. Oxford: Pergamon Press (Pearson Education).

Figure 15.5: Shure, M.B. (1992) *I Can Problem Solve (ICPS): An Interpersonal Cognitive Problem Solving Program [preschool]*. Champagne, IL: Research Press, with acknowledgement to the author.

Figure 15.6: Salovey, P. and Sluyter, D.J. (1997) *Emotional Development and Emotional Intelligence*. New York: Basic Books (Perseus Publishing).

Part 1

Principles and concepts

Chapter 1

Children, families, schools and the wider community: an integrated approach

Objectives

When you have studied this chapter you should:

1 be able to explain the implications of describing special educational needs as one aspect of social and cultural diversity;
2 be aware of major changes that have affected the relationships between children, families and schools over recent years, and be able to outline some implications of these changes for work with children who have special educational needs;
3 be familiar with the way in which this book is structured and the main themes running through it.

Contents

Diversity in society

A changing society

We have written this book because almost all the books that we read about special educational needs (SEN) and inclusion did not seem to us to reflect adequately the rapidly changing, increasingly diverse nature of the society we live in. What was once a relatively homogeneous and stable population has been transformed. Every aspect of society that affects the treatment of disabilities and learning difficulties has changed radically and continues to evolve – the cultural, ethnic and religious profile, patterns of family organization, economic and occupational structures, the relative status of men and women, and the perception of human rights and social responsibilities.

We will illustrate the pace of change in the UK by outlining two of the dimensions of diversity that have particular implications for those working with children and young people who have SEN. The first dimension is ethnic background. In 1951 the non-white population of Britain was very small, perhaps less than 50,000 (Peach 1982). By the academic year 1996/7 there were just under three quarters of a million pupils in England alone recorded as having an ethnic minority background – about 11 per cent of all pupils in maintained schools. At the same time there were just over half a million pupils learning English as an additional language (EAL) – about 7.5 per cent of all pupils (Department for Education and Employment 1999a). While the great majority of ethnic minority children and children learning EAL live in urban areas, there has been a good deal of dispersal from the initial areas of settlement. In the local authorities in English counties in 1997, one in seven primary schools and almost one in five secondary schools had more than 5 per cent ethnic minority pupils (figures derived from Department for Education and Employment 1999a, Table E).

The second dimension is family organization. Fewer people than in the past spend the whole of their childhood with their biological parents and siblings in a household comprising a traditional nuclear family. Divorce is more common, and more men and women choose to cohabit without marrying. By the mid-1990s it was estimated that just over 1 in 14 of all families with dependent children in Great Britain were stepfamilies (Haskey 1996). Adoption by stepfathers is increasingly common: almost one half of adoption orders made in England and Wales each year are to birth parents (usually mothers) and their spouses (Batchelor 2000). O'Donnell (1999) reports that there has been increased appreciation in recent years within the law of different family structures and of functional parenthood. However she observes that 'lesbian and gay families present more of a challenge for this new approach to relationships with children than other forms of family diversity, because they are so clearly removed from the norm of the heterosexual ideal' (1999: 87). Many schools have felt confused about the extent to which they can acknowledge this aspect of the diverse family types to which their pupils belong. On the one hand Section 28 of the *Local Government Act* (Department of the Environment 1988) stipulates that a local authority shall not 'promote the teaching in any maintained school of the acceptability of homo-sexuality as a pretended family relationship'. On the other hand, Department of Education and Science guidance to schools advised that Section 28 does not affect the activities of school governors nor of teachers and does not prevent the objective discussion of homosexuality in the classroom, nor the counselling of students concerning their sexuality.

It is much more common than in the past for both parents in households with dependent children to be in paid employment (Ferri and Smith 1996), but the increasing numbers of lone parents find it difficult to obtain jobs and keep them. Parents of children with SEN find themselves under particular pressure. For example, Beresford (1995) found that in a sample of 1000 families of children with physical disabilities:

- household income tended to be lower on average than among families with non-disabled children (although they faced additional costs);
- fewer parents were in full-time employment;
- the family home was often unsuitable for the care of a child with disabilities;
- two thirds of the parents did not belong to a parent support group, though those who did found them helpful;
- almost half of the parents had not found their relationships with professionals supportive.

The arrangements for family organization and welfare support which meet the needs of most families in society appear to fall short in relation to families with children who have disabilities. There are good reasons to believe that the difficult-ies are exacerbated in lone parent families and among some ethnic and linguistic minority communities (Caesar et al. 1994). Any analysis of the education of children with SEN needs to take full account of the increasing diversity of society and the impact this has on the kinds of professional services and educational provision that are required.

Key concepts in charting diversity

As society becomes more heterogeneous, the terms that are used to describe its diversity become themselves a focus of debate and dissent. This applies equally to concepts that are associated with visible markers of diversity such as *race* or *ethnicity* (Ryan 1999) and to concepts that are associated with changing views on diversity such as *handicap* and *disability* (Corbett 1995, 1998). It is important to be explicit and clear about what one means when using such terms. We will attempt to clarify in Chapters 2, 3 and 4 how the concepts of SEN and *inclusion* are used in this book. At this point it is necessary to clarify how we intend to use the terms relating to racial, ethnic and cultural diversity. It is very common for terms in this area to be used loosely. At worst the effect is demeaning and racist. It may be helpful to have not only working definitions of some of the key terms but also observations on ways of using them that we have tried to avoid in this book.

Race was originally a biological concept categorizing a group of people who are connected by common descent or origin and have some common physical features. This term is often used in a metaphorical and over-generalized way in accounts of the speaker's own group or other groups. Talking in terms of race tends to reinforce traditional stereotypes.

Culture encompasses the learned traditions and aspects of lifestyle that are shared by members of a society, including their habitual ways of thinking, feeling and behaving. The use of this term is often based on an unjustified assumption that there is a high level of cultural cohesion and homogeneity in the social group that is being described (especially when it is a group of which one is not a member).

Ethnicity is a label that reflects perceived membership of, and a sense of belonging to, a distinctive social group. The crucial distinguishing features of an ethnic group vary between different contexts and change over time. They may include physical appearance, first language, religious beliefs and practices, national allegiance, family structure and occupation (Thomas 1994). A person's ethnic identity may be defined by their own categorization of themselves or by how others see them.

The use of terms such as *ethnic group* tends to focus attention on a particular aspect of an individual's identity. But in contemporary society everyone, whether adult or child, has multiple roles and complex identities. It is beyond the scope of this book to explore issues of cultural change and ethnic evolution in detail. We recognize that the definitions that are given here represent just one serviceable way of clarifying the scope of each concept. Fuller discussions of the implications of adopting different definitions may be found in Verma (1986, Ch. 2) and Hutnik (1992).

One reason why it seems important to highlight these dimensions of diversity in a book on SEN is that there is strong evidence of the operation of institutional racism in the delivery of services to children with SEN in many western societies. Institutional racism has been defined as:

> the collective failure of an organisation to provide an appropriate and professional service to people because of their colour, culture or ethnic origin. It can be seen or detected in processes, attitudes and behaviour which amount to discrimination through unwitting prejudice, ignorance, thoughtlessness, and racist stereotyping which disadvantage minority ethnic people.
>
> (Macpherson Committee of Enquiry 1999, para. 6.34)

When SEN provision began to expand in the West during the post-war period, once ethnically based statistics were collected, it became clear that there were higher than expected numbers of children from some minority communities in some forms of special provision. This was true both in the UK (Tomlinson 1984) and the USA (Franks 1971; Tucker 1980). For example, in England and Wales in 1972 children from the newly established West Indian communities in many cities constituted only 1.1 per cent of all children in maintained primary and secondary schools, but 4.9 per cent of all children in schools for the educationally subnormal (Tomlinson 1984: 21–2). Over the years in both countries the most dramatic forms of over-representation of black pupils in SEN provision were reduced, but there remained important areas where anomalies persisted. For example, African-Caribbean pupils continued to be over-represented in schools for pupils with emotional and behavioural difficulties (Inner London Education Authority 1984: 15) and among pupils who are excluded from school (Bourne *et al.* 1995).

Such findings reflect a more widespread phenomenon: SEN provision reflects a diverse society in uneven ways across a range of dimensions of diversity. For example, boys tend to outnumber girls by a large margin in schools for pupils with emotional and behavioural difficulties, but by only a very small amount in schools for those with profound learning difficulties and hearing difficulties (Riddell 1996). Similarly, children from working-class backgrounds are over-represented among those assessed as having moderate learning difficulties but not among those assessed as having severe learning difficulties (Inner London Education Authority 1984). These issues are discussed in more detail in Chapters 6, 9 and 14.

Sociologists of education have drawn a distinction between the forms of SEN that are usually identified in terms of apparently 'objective' criteria (e.g. the existence of visual impairment) and forms of SEN where subjective and relativistic judgement has a greater influence on diagnosis (e.g. emotional and behaviour difficulties). It seems likely that the risk of social bias affecting the processes of identification and assessment will be greater when teachers and other professionals are working with children in the second 'non-normative' category (Tomlinson 1982). As in the case of institutional racism, discrimination may occur through 'unwitting prejudice, ignorance, thoughtlessness, and . . . stereotyping'. Those insights and strategies that minimize the risk of institutional racism will also be likely to improve equity and effectiveness in relation to other dimensions of diversity.

Thus, although ethnic and linguistic minorities constitute a relatively small proportion of the country's population, an analysis of SEN in relation to these groups has a significance far beyond their numbers. A key question in every chapter of this book will be whether any analysis or intervention that is described can measure up to the diversity of those minorities and to the challenges of racism that they face. If they pass that criterion, they are likely to stand the test of time with the broader and less heterogeneous groupings that make up the rest of the population. As we saw above, these groupings are themselves becoming increasingly heterogeneous in many ways. We will employ an interactional model in order to ensure appropriate sensitivity to cultural context, and we believe that this will also enhance the analysis of SEN issues for *all* children within a range of educational contexts.

Children, families and schools

The key stakeholders in education are children, families and schools. If an integrated approach is to be developed towards SEN, it will need to take account of the individual perspectives of each of these stakeholders. Social changes and legal reform have affected their position *vis-à-vis* one another during the latter part of the twentieth century. Before introducing an interactional model and laying the basis for an integrated approach it is necessary to review those changes and consider their implications for practice.

The child's perspective – hearing the voice of the child

It might seem self-evident that children's views should be taken into account when decisions are being made about them. But this principle was not made explicit in English law until the Children Act 1989 which reformed legislation on children's welfare. The guiding principle in that Act was that local authorities and the courts should treat a child's welfare as the paramount consideration in any decision. The Act listed various factors that a court was to take into account in determining whether to make an order about a child. One of these factors was 'the ascertainable wishes and feelings of the child (considered in the light of his age and understanding)' (Department of Health 1989, Section 1).

Two years after that law was passed, the UK agreed to be bound by the United Nations Convention on the Rights of the Child. Article 12 of the convention states that:

> States Parties shall assure to the child who is capable of forming his or her own views the right to express those views freely in all matters affecting the child, the views of the child being given due weight in accordance with the age and maturity of the child. For this purpose the child shall in particular be provided the opportunity to be heard in any judicial or administrative proceedings affecting the child, either directly or through a representative or an appropriate body, in a manner consistent with the procedural rules of national law.
>
> (Newell 1991: 44)

At that time there was no statutory requirement in the education service to take children's views into account. It was after a further three years that the first Code of Practice on SEN introduced guidance on the issue, advising that schools should 'make every effort to identify the ascertainable views and wishes of the child or young person about his or her current and future education' (Department for Education 1994a, para. 2: 36). This guidance has been considerably strengthened in the revised Code of Practice in which one of five 'fundamental principles' is that 'the views of the child should be sought and taken into account' (Department for Education and Skills 2001, para 1.5). A whole chapter is devoted to pupil participation on the basis that children with SEN have a right 'to be involved in making decisions and exercising choice' (para 3.1).

What has led politicians, social workers and teachers to come to give such status to children's views on their own future after centuries in which children were treated legally as simply the possession of their parents? Two main arguments were set out in the first SEN Code of Practice:

- *Practical*: children have important and relevant information; their support is crucial to the effective implementation of any individual education programme.
- *Principle*: children have a right to be heard (Department for Education 1994a, para. 2.35; cf. Gersch 1992: 26).

Davie (1996) has argued that, when schools introduce arrangements for consulting and involving pupils, there is such immediate evidence of the value of the exercise that the principle has 'the characteristic of self-reinforcement'. It is increasingly common to seek pupils' views across a range of school situations (Cade 1989; Davie and Galloway 1996; Breen and Littlejohn 2000; Lewis and Lindsay 2000). Although they will not have a clear overall appreciation of the scope and structure of the curriculum, they may have a great deal to contribute to thinking on how it is presented and on effective conditions for learning (Rudduck and Flutter 2000). These are issues of considerable relevance to children with SEN. The question for the future is not *whether* or *why* educators should listen to the views of children with SEN, but *how*.

Gersch (1987) and Gersch *et al.* (1993) piloted a 'Student Report' as a framework for enabling children aged 10+ to present their views in a formal way as part of the SEN assessment procedure. It covers seven sections:

1 School
2 Special needs
3 Friends
4 Out of school
5 Feelings
6 The future
7 Anything else

Figure 1.1 illustrates how this framework is intended to work. A key advantage of a strategy of this kind is that, within the constraints of that structure, the communication is controlled by the children themselves. It seems important that, wherever possible, they should have direct access to the process and express what they wish to say without the 'support' of others. Figg *et al.* (1996) showed in a small-scale study that there are risks of distortion when children's observations are reported by others, such as educational psychologists. These investigators were particularly concerned that the risks appeared to increase when the child and the person describing the child's views came from different social or cultural backgrounds. Armstrong *et al.* (1993) showed how the failure to investigate a child's perspective in an SEN assessment may lead to misleading conclusions. For example, a child who did not want to transfer to a residential school refused cooperation in an interview with a psychologist about it but was not led to explain his reasons for not cooperating. The authors argue that, while training might improve professionals' skills in conducting such interviews, that would not on its own change how they decide their priorities. The dilemma of professionals such as educational psychologists is seen as arising from 'the demands of a complex situation in which the needs of competing clients (schools, parents, LEA and

Figure 1.1
Some examples
of entries made
on the 'Student
Report'
Source: Gersch
et al. (1993).

child) determine the extent to which the child's perspective is allowed to be relevant' (Armstrong *et al.* 1993: 130).

With increasing frequency, children with SEN are now invited to contribute their views on other occasions and not solely during the process of formal assessment. Morton (1996) described booklets entitled *My Learning Plan* in which children are guided through a process of setting learning targets. The series of questions that they answer enables them to specify the help they think they will need to achieve their targets and encourages them to specify success criteria by writing down (or dictating for an adult to write down) how they will know that they have achieved each target. Glenny (1996) has shown that exploring a child's own perspective can enhance the value of regular reviews of SEN Statements when progress on an Individual Education Plan is evaluated. Such reviews often rely on the collection of data on curriculum achievements and professionals' reports about children's work and behaviour. Jelly *et al.* (2000) point out that where SEN Statement annual review meetings are conducted in the absence of the pupil concerned and without consulting them, the pupil is likely to feel that such a review has little meaning for them. By contrast they describe a process, developed through an 'Involving Pupils' action research project in Essex local education authority (LEA) where pupils' active participation is supported. Prior to the annual review, pupils are provided with an opportunity in a one-to-one tutorial with an adult to contribute their views using the schedule shown in Figure 1.2. They also participate in most, if not all, of the annual review meetings held in the project schools. Jelly *et al.* (2000) report that pupils have responded

Figure 1.2
Annual review
schedule
Source: Jelly *et al.*
(2000).

Annual review: pupil views
This is a chance for you to say what you feel about your school and learning. Please tell us as much as you can. An adult or friend can help you if you wish.

A: Last year at school
What things did you most like doing?

What did you do best?

What improvements did you make?

What helped you to learn or get on better?

What things did you not like doing?

What things did you find difficult?

B: Next year at school
What things do you want to do better?

What things do you need help with?

Are you worried about anything? If so, what?

Would you like to talk to anyone else? If so, who?

Signed: Helped by: Date:

with enthusiasm and have often made perceptive and self-reflective contributions that have taken the adults involved by surprise.

Others have also found that when the children themselves are asked to say how they think others believe they are doing, the situation may be illuminated from a different angle:

> One hearing-impaired child . . . relaxed and opened up when asked about the view of his hearing-impaired teacher of whom he was very fond. This pupil's perception of an apparently well-organised and comprehensive procedure revealed that his mother was very unhappy about the process and that he felt that teachers other than his hearing-impaired teacher did not understand his difficulties.
>
> (Glenny 1996: 10)

A similar point was made by Sinclair Taylor (1995) after investigating the working of a free-standing SEN unit situated on the campus of a mainstream secondary school. She showed that it was only when the pupils in the unit expressed their views that it became clear that 'the unit, rather than promoting integration, fostered the marginalisation of its pupils' (1995: 263).

A range of methods may be used to empower children with SEN to articulate their perspective for themselves. Older children and young people may be able to respond to an invitation to give their views in writing or by speaking into a tape recorder. They are likely to appreciate the rationale for doing so and, even if learning difficulties sometimes set a limit on how clearly they can articulate their wishes and feelings, they are likely to be able to convey the main thrust of what they wish to say. Figure 1.3 shows a proforma developed by The Edith Borthwick School which uses the Widgit symbols programme to assist pupils who have communication difficulties to contribute their views to their annual review. Safeguards are required so that children are provided with a listener in whom they feel they can trust and in order to ensure that they do not simply say what they assume their listener wants to hear (Dockrell *et al.* 2000). It is important that their understanding of the situation is elucidated: do they feel that they are being interrogated because something is wrong? Do they understand what their views are being collected for and how their contribution will be used?

It has been shown that young people with severe disabilities can contribute to policy development in education and other fields if their contribution is facilitated in focus groups (e.g. Educable (Young People with Disabilities Able to be Educated) 2000) or through flexible communication methods (e.g. Morris 1998; Detheridge 2000). Children with less severe difficulties can contribute in larger numbers if questionnaires are adapted to their competence level and if researchers are prepared to read items aloud for them and act as scribes when needed. Wade and Moore 1993 used a sentence completion technique to give children the opportunity to offer open-ended comments on their views, even when they could not manage extended free writing. When the children were asked to complete the sentence 'I get worried in some lessons because . . .', they expressed their lack of confidence in completions such as:

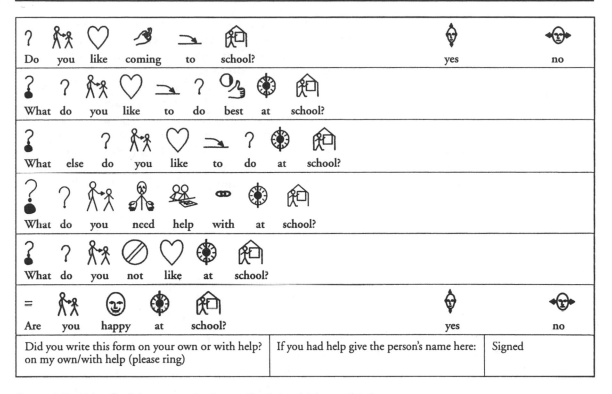

Figure 1.3 Using flexible communication methods to obtain pupils' views
Source: Jelly *et al.* (2000).

I can't do it very well (girl 7–11).
Sometimes I do not no how to do my work (girl 7–11).
I can't do a lot on my own (girl 12–16).
I think the teacher is going to tell me off (boy 12–16).

Techniques are needed for working with children who find it difficult to express their feelings and ideas verbally. Role-play methods may allow some to express their views indirectly (Sweeney 1995). For others a possible approach may be to elicit drawings in order to elucidate their attitudes. This approach has strong advocates (e.g. Dalton 1996) and severe critics (e.g. Dockrell *et al.* 2000). On the one hand, drawing may reflect 'aspects of knowing which exist at lower levels of awareness than that of verbal articulation' (Ravenette quoted by Dalton 1996). On the other hand, drawings are ambiguous and the factors that determine what a child draws are complex. It is not easy to decide unequivocally for any single drawing what message it conveys about the child's views of the subject: 'A child may draw a person crying for many reasons' (Dockrell *et al.* 2000: 57).

Those who think that problems of interpretation need not eliminate the use of drawing tasks for this purpose altogether, tend to emphasize the value of specific safeguards. These tend to be introduced to prevent investigators imposing their own projected ideas onto their version of what the child is communicating. Most commonly what is advocated is the principle of *triangulation* – seeking confirmatory evidence from other sources. Multi-method approaches to assessment are advocated throughout this book. Steps can also be taken 'within method' to provide checks on the reliability of the interpretations made. For example, Ravenette (1997, 1999) invited children to construct the opposite of a picture they had created in order to help them to explain or show what they thought the first picture signified. This strategy has its roots in Kelly's (1991) personal construct theory in which people's ideas about their personal world are represented as a continuum between opposites (cf. Salmon 1988; Stoker and Walker 1996). Ultimately, investigating the perspectives of children with SEN simply reflects in a particularly stark form the key dilemmas that face investigators with all children: how can adults learn what children think and feel without influencing and distorting the message?

The changing role and contributions of parents in schools

Over the last 40 years increasing emphasis has been placed on the value of parental involvement in the education of their children. Initially attention was primarily focused on the negative consequences of mismatches between home and school. For example, Bernstein's (1971) research showed that there were marked differences between classrooms and middle-class homes on the one hand and many working-class homes on the other in the way in which language was used. He argued that these differences could inhibit the school achievements of children from working-class homes. The Central Advisory Council for Education (1967) (the Plowden Committee) concluded that children's educational achievements could be significantly influenced in a more general way by parental attitudes to schooling. They were the first of a series of official committees and other bodies to stress the importance for schools of encouraging good working relationships with parents and their closer involvement in schools (Cullingford 1985; Vincent 1996, Chs 1–3).

By the end of the century, Kelley-Laine (1998) was reporting on an Organization for Economic Cooperation and Development (OECD) survey that showed widespread encouragement of parental involvement in education across nine countries, including the UK. The following reasons for increasing parental involvement were identified:

- *Democracy*. In some countries parents are considered to have a right to involvement in their child's education.
- *Accountability*. Parental involvement is seen as a means of making schools more accountable to the community that finances them.
- *Consumer choice*. Parents are encouraged to choose the education they want for their child and complain if it falls short of their expectations. This is seen as a mechanism for making schools more responsive to society's requirements of them.

- *Means of raising standards.* Research has shown that high achieving, well-ordered schools are characterized by good home–school relationships. It is hoped that improving home–school relationships will have a positive impact on standards.
- *Tackling disadvantages and improving equity.* Here the focus is on raising the achievements of individual children by helping their parents to support them more effectively at home. This is seen as particularly important where there are cultural differences between family and school.
- *Addressing social problems.* In some countries school–family programmes are being developed to tackle serious social problems affecting young people (e.g. targeting drug and alcohol abuse, teenage pregnancy or delinquency and violent crime).
- *Resources.* Parents are regarded as a source of extra funds for schools and of unpaid staffing for school trips, sporting activities and additional support in the classroom.

There is thus a wide range of reasons why schools and public authorities endorse effective partnership between home and school. But one goal in particular is emphasized more frequently than any other – the enhancement of student learning. With this goal in mind, Chrispeels (1996) presented an overview of those school practices that have been seen as most effective in this respect, especially in communities where families have few socioeconomic advantages and are likely to be helped by active outreach initiatives from their children's schools (see Figure 1.4).

Reporting on a study of Asian-American, Latino and European-American families, Okagaki and Frensch (1998) highlighted the need to be sensitive to ethnic

Figure 1.4
Effective school
practices for
reinforcing parents'
efforts to enhance
their children's
learning
Source:
Chrispeels (1996).

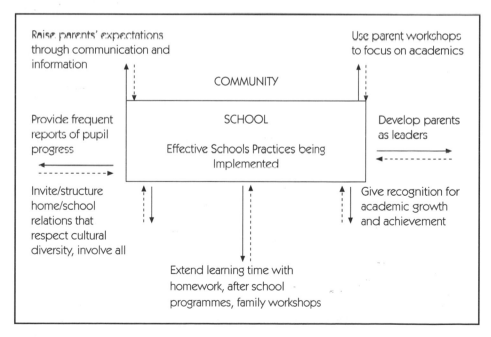

group differences in parents' beliefs about education and goals for their children. Working in the USA they pointed out that it cannot be assumed that what works in some family contexts will necessarily work in all. Huss-Keeler (1997) reported a case study in an urban primary school in the North of England where 80 per cent of the pupils were from Punjabi speaking Pakistani families. She showed that parents from this community were very interested in their children's learning but demonstrated their interest in different ways from middle-class white parents. This was misinterpreted by teachers in the school as lack of interest. De Abreu *et al.* (in preparation) carried out a series of case studies in a similar community in the South of England. They found that, where parents' own experience of mathematics learning had been different from their children's (e.g. in terms of the strategies they were taught for simple arithmetic), their success in supporting the children's learning of mathematics depended on how they negotiated the gap. This applied to both monolingual and bilingual parents, but for the latter group uncertainties about the use of language for mathematics were a central concern. As in Huss-Keeler's sample, it was noted that the children's teachers appeared not to be aware of how important this worry was to the parents.

Parents whose children have SEN

The involvement in education of parents whose children have SEN should be considered in the context of the general trends in parental involvement that were outlined above. The Warnock Committee suggested that the relationship between parents and professionals be conceptualized as 'a partnership and ideally an equal one' (Department of Education and Science 1978: 151). However almost ten years later Wolfendale was to reflect that partnership 'is a slippery concept, probably because it is rarely manifest' (Wolfendale 1989: 107). Cunningham and Davis (1985) suggested that the ways in which parent–professional relationships around SEN have been described over the years might be characterized in terms of three models:

- *An expert model* in which professionals are construed as the source of all knowledge about children who have SEN and where parents are cast in the role of passive recipients of advice from the experts.
- *A transplant model* in which professionals are regarded as the key decision makers and main source of expertise. However, parents are regarded as a valuable resource and source of active support and intervention for their child. Some of the professional's expertise can be transplanted to the parents who are taught to carry out programmes at home.
- *A consumer model* in which the parent becomes the key decision maker and the professionals offer information and services from which the parent can select according to their needs.

These three models are contrasted with a partnership model in which: 'teachers are viewed as being experts on education and parents are viewed as being experts on their children. The relationship between teachers and parents can then be a partnership which involves sharing of expertise and control in order to provide the optimum education for children with special needs' (Hornby 1995: 20–1).

Following on from the Warnock Committee's advocacy of the partnership model in their 1978 report, the 1981 Education Act on SEN appeared to place new power in the hands of parents of children with SEN. However a review of the implementation of the Act by the House of Lords Select Committee on Education, Science and Arts after six years highlighted a number of concerns:

Although the Act, and the climate of opinion behind it, enhanced the position of parents in a way which is welcomed by LEAs and teachers, nevertheless there are still situations in which parents feel their contribution to the process of assessment has been insufficient or ineffective. The most common difficulties experienced by parents are:

(i)   inadequate or unclear information about the local education authority's assessment procedures and about the range of special educational provision available;

(ii) insufficient help in completing the parental contribution to assessment;

(iii) a lack of weight being given to their views during the assessment process;

(iv) a lack of choice from a range of forms of provision.

(House of Commons 1987, para 16: ix)

There was evidence that the problems may have been even more acute for parents from black and ethnic minority communities. For example, research carried out by Rehal (1989) in one London borough highlighted particularly poor levels of communication with and involvement of Punjabi-speaking parents. Of the 14 parents interviewed only one was aware that their child had been formally assessed under the provisions of the Education Act 1981 and issued with a statement of SEN. Similar concerns were expressed at that time by agencies working with the Bangladeshi community in London (Chaudhury 1986), by investigators of South Asian communities in other cities (Shah 1992) and by researchers working with the African-Caribbean community (Inner London Education Authority 1985: 69–71). A case study by Grugeon (1992) illustrates vividly the way in which parents and professionals from different cultural backgrounds can misunderstand each other in the course of an SEN assessment. She shows in detail how 'the process . . . has not taken into account the evident disjuncture between the cultural norms of his [the Child's] home and community and those of the school' (1992: 92).

It appears that many authorities and schools ignored the official guidance that the formal notification to parents of SEN assessment and the subsequent reporting should be in a language they understood or for which they could obtain an interpreter (Department of Education and Science 1983). Over the years the guidance has been considerably strengthened. For example, where access to interpreters or translated information material is needed in the early years, the revised Code of Practice makes clear that it is for the LEA (and not the parents) to ensure that it is provided (Department for Education and Skills 2001, para 2.13). When such arrangements are made, it is essential that there is sensitivity to the position of the parents and children. In some (probably rare) situations what is required is exact, word-for-word translation, while in others the bilingual worker may need to take on a wider advisory and liaison function, helping both the family and the professionals to understand the social and cultural assumptions that each is making (Martin 1994; Shackman 1984).

In recent years the perception has grown that professionals and LEAs have generally been slow to embrace partnership in so far as it requires active sharing of information and control. Legislation has increasingly been used to attempt to level out the power imbalance in parent–professional relationships, ensuring that parents are empowered and are not denied their rights. This increasing emphasis on parental rights can be seen in the establishment of bodies independent of LEAs to which parents can appeal against LEA decisions and turn for information. The establishment by the Education Act 1993 of the SEN Tribunal was a major step in this direction. The *Special Educational Needs and Disability Act* (Department for Education and Employment 2001) outlines two steps (in Chapter 10, Part I, Sections 2 and 3) which it is hoped will prevent many cases from going to the SEN Tribunal by providing better information and opportunities for negotiation at an early stage. Information on these developments is provided in the revised SEN Code of Practice:

- All LEAs must make arrangements for parent partnership services and are encouraged to work together with voluntary organizations in doing so. The aim of these services is to ensure that parents of children who have additional needs (not just those with statements) 'have access to information, advice and guidance in relation to the special educational needs of their children so they can make appropriate, informed decisions' (Department for Education and Skills 2001, para. 2.19).
- All LEAs must provide arrangements 'which demonstrate independence and credibility in working towards early and informal resolution of disagreements (Department for Education and Skills 2001, para. 2.24) . . . Confidence in disagreement resolution arrangements will be greatest when all concerned consider that the service offered is genuinely independent' (Department for Education and Skills 2001, para. 2.26).

The changing situation of schools

Across the developed world the situation of schools has changed substantially in recent years. These changes are perhaps even more radical than the developments affecting the position of children and parents (McLaughlin and Rouse 2000). Previously in the UK the dominant voice in the development of policy on school management and the curriculum was that of professional educators. Schools in the public sector were accountable to governing bodies and subject to inspection, and they worked within a framework of law and regulation that was set by elected politicians. But the democratic touch on the tiller was a rather light one locally and nationally, and it appeared to many observers that the main consumers of the service – the children and their parents – had little influence.

Politicians of the right began to argue against the 'stranglehold' exerted by 'public monopoly' schools. Their case has been summarized as follows:

ACTIVITY 1.1   Parental diversity and principles of partnership

The following statement of key principles in partnership with parents is derived from a policy document produced by the National Association for Special Educational Needs (NASEN 2000). The last of these principles refers to 'diversity'. Consider each of the other bullet points. Can you identify how two aspects of diversity might impact on each of them in practical terms – (i) cultural diversity and (ii) lone parenthood?

- *Parental rights.* Parents have legal responsibility for the proper care and development of their children. They should therefore be regarded as having a major stake in the way education and other services are provided. For parents of children with SEN, this extends to the provision of a range of inputs from different agencies as well as formal schooling.
- *Parental responsibilities.* The rights and needs of children are fundamental and parents have responsibilities that arise from these. For parents of children with SEN these responsibilities extend to working constructively with other education and care providers and with relevant agencies that contribute to children's well-being and development.
- *Parity in partnerships.* Partnership between parents and professionals implies mutuality of respect, complementary expectations and a willingness to learn from each other. The fact that parents are experts on their child and can influence attitudes and attainment needs to be recognized, respected and acted upon. In best partnership practice, the process of decision making is most effective when professionals acknowledge and incorporate parental perspectives and seek constructive ways of reconciling different viewpoints.
- *Empowerment.* Parents should be encouraged and empowered to work with professionals to ensure that their child's needs are properly identified and met as early as possible. In order to play an active part in their child's development, parents should have access to all the information that is available and relevant to their child's education as well as to appropriate training that enables them to reinforce learning in the home.
- *Effective communication.* Parents are assisted in playing an active role if professionals communicate clearly with them and with other professional colleagues. Parents need to be able to understand any differences in professional opinion and the evidence on which these are based. Professionals should seek where possible to resolve such differences in a way that ensures more effective cooperation between all concerned.
- *Support.* It should be recognized that parents of children with SEN will at times have their own needs for emotional and moral support. Adequately addressing these needs will help ensure that parents can play a full part in planning for and responding to the needs of their children.
- *Diversity.* While there are some common issues for parents, they do not all have the same or similar needs. There is diversity not just in the culture and interests of different parents but also in the resources that they can bring to bear. Proper account should be taken of such differences to ensure that all parents can be supported in making as actively as possible a contribution to meeting their children's SEN.

- Financial support for schools (via taxation) was not linked directly to the satisfaction of their clients.
- The absence of profit or loss motives for school managers led to conservative, self-serving, minimalist, survival strategies.
- Schools' decision making was dominated by the pursuit of staff self-interest.

- There were inadequate checks and incentives to foster efficient administration or to force schools to be responsive to parental concerns.

It was argued that these features of the situation allowed educational standards to remain depressed and inhibited any urge to achieve excellence. Furthermore, the fact that schools in the public sector were designed to be similar and that there were restrictions on enrolment meant that parents effectively had no choice and that children's diverse needs could not be met. (This summary has been adapted from Ball 1993: 4.)

The reforms presented as a solution to these problems involved:

- enhancing quality by creating more competition between schools for resources and public support;
- encouraging greater diversity in the organization and funding of schools;
- enhancing parental choice by making enrolment more open and providing more information on which parents could base their decisions about which school would best suit their children;
- giving schools greater autonomy from LEAs in their day-to-day management while making them more accountable.

The overall effect of the changes was intended to be that individual parents would have greater responsibility for the quality of their child's education. There was certainly a considerable reduction in the powers of LEAs. Schools had greater freedom to compete for pupils, and since resources were linked to pupil numbers, a school needed to be popular in order to guarantee its income.

A key lever in the improvement in academic standards was the introduction of the National Curriculum. Schools maintained by LEAs were required to provide for all pupils of statutory school age a basic menu of three core subjects and six foundation subjects (seven in Key Stages 3 and 4 when modern foreign languages was added), plus religious education. Each core and foundation subject would have its objectives and programmes of study specified nationally. All pupils, including those with SEN, would share the right to a broad and balanced curriculum which would be designed to 'promote the spiritual, moral, cultural, mental and physical development of pupils' (Department of Education and Science 1989b, para. 16).

The national specification of the curriculum removed the substantial degree of control that teachers had previously had over what was taught in schools and how it was taught. The reforms went further. At fixed age points (the end of every 'Key Stage' of compulsory education) children's learning would be assessed, and the results for each school would be published. Teachers would thus be accountable for the delivery of the curriculum in a different way from before. The aims were to:

- give a clear incentive for weaker schools to catch up with the best while the best were challenged to do even better;
- provide teachers with detailed and precise objectives;
- provide parents with clear, accurate information;

- ensure continuity and progression from one year to another, from one school to another;
- help teachers concentrate on the task of getting the best possible results from each individual child.

Parallel changes took place in the Scottish education system, though sometimes with less constraining central control (Riddell and Brown 1995). In England and Wales there have been substantial developments in the working of the new curriculum arrangements since 1989, but the fundamental structure remains in place. (More recent initiatives such as the National Literacy and Numeracy Strategies will be covered in Chapters 11 and 12.)

What impact would these radical changes have on the experience of children with SEN? Official documents were optimistic, pointing out that:

the principle that pupils with SEN share a common entitlement to a broad and balanced curriculum with their peers has taken many years to gain acceptance . . . The right extends to every registered pupil of compulsory school age attending a maintained or grant maintained school, whether or not he or she has a statement of SEN. This right is implicit in the 1988 Education Reform Act.

(National Curriculum Council 1989b: 1)

At the same time it was acknowledged that:

the right to share in the curriculum defined in Section 1 of the Act does not automatically ensure access to it nor progress within it. Some pupils will have physical and sensory impairments which make access into a challenge; others have intellectual or emotional difficulties in learning. Some will meet attitudes and practices in schools which do not actively encourage full participation. Achieving maximum access and subsequent progress for pupils with SEN will challenge the co-operation, understanding and planning skills of teachers, support agencies, parents, governors and many others.

(National Curriculum Council 1989b: 1–2)

Commentators from the SEN field mostly adopted a more pessimistic tone and emphasized that many of the challenges in the new context arose from aspects of the new policies themselves. For example, Upton (1990: 4) reported that many were 'concerned about the relevance of traditional subjects to children who present severe learning difficulties and the effects which the introduction of an apparently narrowly conceived academic curriculum may have on the teaching of cross curricular issues such as social and life skills'.

In the event, many of the concerns about the curriculum were soon allayed, and resolute efforts have been made to ensure that there is meaningful access to an appropriate version of the full curriculum for all pupils. (See Chapter 9 for a discussion of what this means in the case of children with profound and multiple learning difficulties.) The most serious challenges for children with SEN and their parents appeared to arise not from the National Curriculum but from other provisions in the reform programme.

The arrangements for financial delegation to schools – 'Local Management of Schools' (LMS) – might, in principle, have enabled schools to make more flexible provision for pupils with SEN, because it gave them greater control over resources. But the allocation of funds depended on pupil numbers; schools were ranked on 'league tables' that were to be based on the overall performance of their pupils in National Curriculum subjects. If schools allocated resources to pupils with SEN whose performance might not raise the aggregate achievement level, they were making what would appear in an open financial market a risky investment. Another effect of LMS has been to force LEAs to delegate a steadily higher proportion of their funds to schools. LEAs are now smaller, leaner organizations, and hence cannot provide central services to support schools with SEN in the same way as in the past. Decentralizing such provision risks the advantages of scale being lost and other priorities swallowing up the available funding at school level (except where there is statutory safeguard – see Chapter 2).

Tomlinson (2000: 28) has argued that the new emphasis on market forces and consumer choice have operated to create new disadvantages for those cast as 'undesirable customers' by the system on account of 'social class, race and ethnicity, special educational needs and behaviour problems'. This is illustrated through discussion of failing schools. Research has indicated that the application of LMS has tended in practice to bring about a redistribution of resources from urban schools to rural and suburban schools. This exacerbates the difficulties of schools in deprived urban areas, which are disproportionately attended by minority ethnic and other socially disadvantaged groups, and contributes to their failure. It is of relevance that the 700 failing schools identified between 1993 and 2000 were concentrated in deprived urban areas. It is further argued that media coverage in which the ethnic composition of the population of these schools is often apparent 'perpetuates the xenophobic reaction that the very presence of minorities lowers standards in schools' (Tomlinson 2000: 32). Tomlinson (2000) argues that such disadvantages have resulted primarily from failure to consider or make reference to minority issues in constructing the new framework of educational legislation. While giving a tentative welcome to the establishment of the Social Exclusion Unit, designed to tackle low educational achievement and poor life changes of young people living in disadvantaged circumstances, questions are asked about the broader effectiveness of this initiative, given a continuing commitment to market principles in education. Nevertheless initiatives to date on school truancy and exclusions, in particular of black pupils, do appear to have had a positive impact in increasing inclusion.

With regard to the inclusion of pupils with SEN, this has slowly become a central goal of government policy and the rhetoric of inclusion is increasingly espoused at every level. But schools are still caught in a tension between the inclusion agenda and the education reform agenda (tighter curriculum control, the testing and inspection regimes, the pressure to improve 'standards', competition for pupils). There has been a shift of emphasis from some of the market principles that were enshrined in law in the late 1980s and early 1990s. But the pace of education reform has not slowed down, and key central features remain, such as aiming to improve standards by publishing assessment and inspection results and by encouraging competition for enrolment between schools. The impact on vulnerable children during much of the 1990s was charted in terms of increased rates of exclusion from school and an increased proportion of children being given a Statement of SEN. The first has the effect of enabling some schools 'both to rid themselves of "difficult" students and to demonstrate to potential clients that discipline and safety are taken very seriously' (Ball 1993: 8). The second enables schools to guarantee external provision to support their work with pupils who make considerable demands on resources. In Chapter 2 we will examine how the concept of SEN has evolved in response to these developments and how new guidance is intended to counteract the worst effects of the major reforms on children at risk.

The pessimism expressed by Tomlinson and Ball is to some extent countermanded by other observations about school trends. On the basis of research on school improvement and school effectiveness a number of investigators have

---

ACTIVITY 1.2   Collaboration between schools over pupils with SEN

The following extracts are taken from a 1993 news report (Pyke 1993):

> A grant-maintained school . . . has reneged on a 20 year agreement to take children from a nearby school for the partially sighted, according to the Royal National Institute for the Blind . . . For the past two decades the all-age JC School (which provides for pupils with visual impairment) has sent its pupils across the playing field to HP secondary for some lessons. A few partially sighted pupils have been fully integrated. In 1991 HP opted out of local authority control and became a grant maintained school. Now it is refusing to continue the arrangement unless it receives £26,000 from the LEA plus staff support from JC. The school says it cannot afford this and will have to send the pupils two miles to another secondary school. The RNIB added that HP has refused to integrate a wholly blind girl after a successful first year of partial integration. 'The head told me that, irrespective of financial considerations, he did not believe it right to educate a wholly blind child in a mainstream school,' said an RNIB spokesman. 'Given this comment and the amount of money the school is charging to take the other, partially-sighted pupils, I can only conclude that the head doesn't really want special needs children in the school.' The LEA's Chief Education Officer said: 'Arrangements had worked up to this point, and it's a great pity they are not working now.' HP's headteacher and the school's chairman of governors both refused to comment.

1 On the basis of this report would you agree with a teacher from another secondary school who said that the working relationship between the schools 'appears to be one-sided – not real collaboration'?
2 What features of the overall system might have led the headteachers of the two schools to adopt the positions attributed to them?
3 What changes in the law or in the approach of the LEA or the special school might lead the HP head to revise his view on the prospect of working with selected pupils from JC?

pointed out that some of the factors that are found in schools that achieve general improvements in standards are also found in schools with a strong record for inclusion: 'Put simply, this means that by improving overall conditions a school supports staff in developing a wider range of responses to pupils who experience difficulties in their learning. In so doing, it adopts a way of working that is essentially about the reformation of ordinary education, to make it more comprehensive' (Vislie 1994, quoted in Ainscow 1995: 153). 'Furthermore it seems likely that such moves will be to the benefit of all children in the school' (Ainscow 1995: 153). Such an ambitious goal can only be achieved if schools and other agencies develop an integrated approach in their work on SEN.

An integrated approach

This book seeks to promote an integrated approach to SEN along a number of dimensions:

- SEN and educational provision;
- theoretical approaches to SEN;
- research and practice.

These themes are introduced in this section and developed throughout the book. A major challenge in developing and sustaining an integrated approach in practice is that most children who have SEN require the support of professionals from many disciplines. In the next section we consider how effective multidisciplinary team work can be promoted.

SEN and educational provision

SEN are taken to be the outcome of an interaction between the individual characteristics of learners and the educational environments in which they are learning. This means that, if we are to fully understand the learning difficulties experienced by some children, we have to consider the curriculum and learning environment being provided for them. An analysis of learning difficulties in literacy or mathematics, for example, should incorporate a consideration of the curriculum demands and methods of teaching generally employed in these subject areas.

The importance of this sort of integrated approach is widely recognized and advocated. The Code of Practice on the identification and assessment of pupils with SEN advises: 'The assessment process should always be fourfold. It should focus on the child's learning characteristics, the learning environment that the school is providing for the child, the task and the teaching style' (Department for Education and Skills 2001, para. 5.6).

However, it appears that what has happened in practice has more often reflected a 'within-child' model of SEN. Goacher *et al.* (1988) reported that Statements of SEN and the professional reports on which they were based focused largely on deficits within the child in discussing their SEN. They found that very little attention was given to the learning environment. Seven years later a similar conclusion was reached by a working group of educational psychologists set up to review and develop approaches to assessing the learning environments of pupils who have SEN (Frederickson and Cline 1995). A recent small-scale study of teachers' views on emotional and behavioural difficulties suggests that many teachers continue to focus solely on within-child and family factors when seeking to explain such problems (Avramadis and Bayliss 1998).

Throughout this book we discuss ways of integrating SEN identification, assessment and intervention into an analysis of the educational curriculum and the learning environment that is provided. For example, two of the four chapters in Part 2 on approaches to assessment of SEN concern curriculum related assessment and the assessment of learning environments. This is line with the SEN Code of Practice (Department for Education and Skills 2001) which has made it clear that the learning environment, the learning task and teaching style should be assessed, as well as the learning characteristics of individual children. McKee and Witt (1990) have suggested that one reason why so much SEN assessment focuses on within-child factors is that professionals lack knowledge and confidence in other forms of assessment. We aim to support readers in developing the knowledge and expertise that are required.

Theoretical approaches to SEN

There are a number of theoretical approaches to SEN that start from different perspectives. Often, different theoretical approaches focus on different aspects so that it is difficult to integrate the insights and ideas that they offer. The definition and explanation of what children and teachers experience as 'learning difficulties' become a site for fruitless debates between theorists and practitioners who adopt incompatible terminology to reflect different perspectives and then cannot engage in a meaningful dialogue. This happened when sociologists of education and educational psychologists studied SEN assessment with different assumptions and when geneticists, neurologists, cognitive psychologists and teachers each tried to understand dyslexia by looking at a different aspect of the phenomenon. For many years the field of emotional and behavioural difficulties was the site of confused debates about the competing insights of behavioural, cognitive, psychodynamic and systemic theories.

In some respects the accounts offered by different theoretical approaches to SEN conflict with each other, but in other respects they may be considered to complement each other. It would appear desirable to be able to draw on different approaches in order both to ensure a comprehensive consideration of the area involved and to capitalize on the relative usefulness of different approaches for different purposes. Morton and Frith (1995) achieved a significant breakthrough in the integration of different theoretical perspectives on problems in child development and SEN. They developed a visual framework on which it is possible to represent different theories so that their commonalities and differences are readily apparent. The framework allows both difficulties of development and hypothesized causal influences to be described in terms of biology, cognition, behaviour and environmental factors or interactions. In this book we make considerable use of this framework to offer an integrated account of the diverse theoretical formulations that are available for many aspects of SEN.

Research and practice

A further theme that permeates this book is the interplay between research and practice. There has been extensive debate in recent years about the quality of much educational research and its relevance either to educational policy or classroom practice (Hargreaves 1996; Hillage et al. 1998; Tooley and Darby 1998). A central issue has been the extent to which practice can and should be based on research evidence. On the one hand Hillage et al. (1998: 60) recommend that 'more evidence-based decision-making should be encouraged where appropriate'. On the other hand, Hammersley (1997: 156) concludes:

> there is much wrong with the quality of teaching in schools . . . But it seems to me that educational research can only play a fairly limited role in resolving the problems. It can highlight and analyse them, and attempt to provide some understanding. But remedying the failings of schools is a practical business that necessarily depends on professional expertise of a kind that is not reducible to publicly available evidence, even that provided by research.

The proponents of evidence-based practice do not maintain that research evidence is the only knowledge base which will be drawn on in professional practice. However, they do highlight the extent to which other kinds of professional expertise also suffer from limitations. Hargreaves (1997: 411) draws an analogy with medicine which has been much discussed:

> Much clinical work depends on best practice (i.e. what works) derived from tradition and personal experience. Both are potentially deeply flawed, so must be subject to scientific test. When evidence is produced on whether one therapy rather than another makes for a more effective or speedier benefit to patients in certain categories or circumstances, it becomes a valuable component in the matrix of factors considered by a doctor in making a clinical decision. Research transforms individual tinkering into public knowledge that has greater validity and can be shared among the profession as the evidential base for better clinical practice.

Hargreaves argues that teachers also need to make complex decisions and that their decision making could be enhanced by the establishment of a more relevant research base in education. He also identifies a need to establish a culture of accountability in education and openness to new ideas wherein there is an expectation that the best available knowledge on 'what works with whom, under what conditions and with what effects' (Hargreaves 1997: 414) will be sought and utilized. This book aims to support teachers, educational psychologists and others who are seeking to update and develop their knowledge of the research base in key areas of practice for pupils who have SEN.

At the same time critics of an evidence-informed approach to educational practice have highlighted the dangers of a simplistic view, arguing that 'knowledge cannot be applied, like paint, to a blandly receptive body' (Edwards 1998: 89). In addition the relationship between research and practice cannot be a one-way street. Research findings may be generalizations drawn from work with representative groups. Or they may be insights drawn from case studies in which the researcher focuses on a unique individual or situation. 'Good practice' that is based on findings from either type of research will not be effective with every child. The only way to learn if an approach is successful in promoting the learning of an individual pupil is through the careful collection of data in monitoring their progress (Good *et al.* 1998). There are many parallels between the process of research and the approach to assessment recommended in the revised Code of Practice and adopted in this text. Such an approach involves:

- generating hypotheses about the difficulties being experienced by a pupil in a particular learning environment;
- collecting a range of data and information from different sources to test out the hypotheses being considered;
- giving careful attention to the reliability and validity of the information collected;
- drawing conclusions about the actions most likely to be effective in promoting the pupil's progress;
- monitoring changes in pupil progress in response to the action taken so that its effectiveness can be evaluated and any further assessment and intervention initiated.

Teachers who undertake extended and repeated cycles of assessment and teaching with pupils who have learning difficulties are actively engaged in a form of investigation of SEN that can contribute to enhancing how we think about the phenomenon in general as well as advancing an individual's learning. Edwards (1998) suggests that such activities can provide a basis for research that is reflexive and conducted on the analogy of a 'conversation' with its participants, where there is the potential for mutually illuminating outcomes. Other researchers who have investigated ways of increasing the contribution of research to the improvement of practice have reached very similar conclusions. Robinson (1993: vii) writes from a New Zealand perspective that:

Researchers must conduct . . . processes of problem understanding and resolution as a critical dialogue with practitioners, so that competing theories of the problem can be adjudicated and new theories of action learned during the course of the research itself, rather than left to some subsequent process of dissemination.

It seems that the different approaches to research which have been touched on in this section may each have a contribution to make to practice. Selection of strategies may valuably be informed by evidence about what generally is found to work in a specific kind of situation. The development of an application which is tailor-made for a particular context is likely to require the engagement of those involved in a problem solving process from which some more broadly generalizable learning is likely also to result. Finally there will be a need for systematic collection of data that will allow evaluation of the success of a particular application of a specific strategy in relation to the objectives identified for the pupil or pupils involved.

Multi-disciplinary teamwork

Organizational and individual issues

SEN are complex and heterogeneous: 'Meeting the special educational needs of children requires flexible working on the part of statutory agencies. They need to communicate and agree policies and protocols that ensure there is a "seamless" service' (Department for Education and Skills 2001, para. 10.1). Yet there are many obstacles to successful collaboration between colleagues from different disciplines. At an organizational level, 'fragmentation of services between different statutory agencies, competition and tight budgets' (Department for Education and Employment 1997: 71) have been identified as key problems. At an individual level other factors may impede successful collaboration between professionals from different disciplines:

- They have chosen to work in their field because it interests them and seems important to them. Such preconceptions are often reinforced during their training, so each professional may view the concerns of other groups as having lower priority.
- They are socialized during training to use a particular professional vocabulary. Differences in the use of language create problems of communication.
- They often work for different agencies which are funded in different ways and have different priorities. This sets up barriers, for example, to speech and language therapists working with teachers of children with language difficulties in mainstream schools – though such barriers are not insurmountable (Jowett and Evans 1996; Department for Education and Skills 2001, paras 8.49–8.53).
- Tensions may develop between professional groups because of differences in perceived status, management arrangements or workload.
- Some professional groups have strict codes of confidentiality which make it difficult to share records or information, even if the client agrees.

Some of the problems of communication arise not just between people in different professions but between people in different subspecialties in the same

ACTIVITY 1.3   Expectations and communication in multi-disciplinary collaboration

A team in Boston carried out a retrospective study of the work undertaken by medical consultants in a hospital over two separate one-week periods. They found that the physicians who referred patients and the consultants to whom they were referred completely disagreed on what had been the reason for the consultation in as many as 14 per cent of the cases. They concluded that 'breakdowns in communication are not uncommon in the consultation process and may adversely affect patient care' (Lee et al. 1983).

Review your own experience and consider whether you can recall problems arising in work with a child with SEN for a similar reason.

- What was the problem, and how did it arise?
- With the benefit of hindsight, what do you think could have been done to avoid it?

profession. In Activity 1.3 you are asked to review any experience you may have had of this in relation to work with children who have SEN.

Just as problems in multidisciplinary working may be identified at both organizational and individual levels, so too may positive influences on effective practice be identified at each of these levels. Problems will be less likely to occur if there are clear requirements for joint planning and provision. For example, sections 117–24 of the Schools Standards and Framework Act (Department for Education and Employment 1998d) established Early Years Development and Childcare Partnerships which have responsibility for the planning and provision of local services (education and care) for children aged 0–14 years. They include representatives of parents, LEAs, social services departments, health services and early education providers from the maintained, private and voluntary sectors, and have successfully forged effective partnerships in many areas.

It is often useful to identify a senior post in each organization as carrying the responsibility to liaise with other services and manage effective collaboration with them. For example, the medical officers designated by health authorities to work with LEAs on behalf of children with SEN have both strategic and operational coordination responsibilities across health authorities, National Health Service (NHS) Trusts, Primary Care groups and general practitioners (GPs). These are clearly detailed in Chapter 10 of the SEN Code of Practice (Department for Education and Skills 2001).

It is sometimes helpful to have written contracts between agencies that specify how collaboration between them will be organized and monitored. This is particularly important where jointly funded teams are established between agencies. A good example of such teams are those relating to the education of children and young people in public care that have been established by local authorities in response to the guidance on the education of children in public care (Department for Education and Employment/Department of Health 2000). This is typically a joint education department/social services department team whose main aim is to improve the educational experiences and achievements of children in public care. In one medium-sized county, for example, this team comprises a full-time team leader and four team members who each work half-time on the team: a reintegration officer, a senior educational psychologist, a liaison teacher and an administrator.

While good coordination at the systemic or organizational level is very important, at the individual level attention should be given to the knowledge and skills an individual needs in order to be an effective team worker. Barker (1989) led a working group which attempted to define the team working competencies required by social workers for this purpose. With minor adaptations the list appears to apply equally to professionals in the SEN field. The working group considered that the following were required in order to contribute effectively to a multidisciplinary team:

1 A distinctive discipline-based knowledge base:
   - being confident in one's own area of expertise without being arrogant;
   - being clear about the rationale, the scope, the boundaries and the limitations of one's own knowledge base.
2 Skills for collaboration:
   - partnership, e.g. identifying shared interests, stating agreed goals clearly, sharing/allocating specific tasks;
   - negotiation, e.g. making clear formulations of one's own view and the desired outcome, listening to and empathizing with the views of others;
   - networking, e.g. gathering and disseminating information about resources, linking individuals/agencies for reciprocal help;
   - communicating, e.g. writing reports for the team and for clients, using a common language (and avoiding specialist jargon unless it is genuinely necessary);
   - reframing, e.g. offering a different perspective on a problem discussed by the team or clients;
   - confronting, e.g. maintaining one's own integrity and being aware of one's own feelings and values, resisting being swamped by a dominant culture;
   - flexibility, e.g. having the ability and the humility to learn from the skills and working methods of others;
   - monitoring and evaluation.
3 Values:
   - client-centredness, i.e. putting the interests of the client or pupil first and not allowing oneself to give priority to scoring points off other disciplines, protecting one's own organization, etc.;
   - respect for colleagues and for service users;
   - openness.

Decision making at case conferences

When people from different professions have to take important decisions about children at risk, a common arena for enforced collaboration is a case conference.

A great deal of importance may be attached to the outcome of a case conference, but over an extended period there has been evidence of frequent weaknesses in the way they are run (Castle 1976; Hallett and Stephenson 1980). Cline (1989) drew up an observation checklist for participants that may be used in training and may be adapted to monitor effectiveness. It focuses on five basic processes in case conferences:

1 *Preparation*, e.g. was it clear before arrival why the conference was being held so that participants were able to prepare themselves adequately for the discussion that took place?

2 *Initiating the discussion*, e.g. were the objectives of the conference made explicit at the outset and agreed upon by all parties? Was the status of the meeting made clear and accepted by all (e.g. as to what it could take decisions about and what and to whom it could make recommendations about where it did not have executive powers itself)?

3 *Resolving the discussion and taking decisions*, e.g. did the discussion move towards a resolution too early (when the picture of relevant aspects of the current situation was still incomplete) or too late (when insufficient time was left to explore the available options fully)? Did any of the participants appear to have an interest in premature or delayed resolution?

4 *Observations of the process*, e.g. was any professional or specialist perspective overlooked or given less significance than you thought it deserved? Pay particular attention to professional groups who appear to be accorded low status in this context. Was any professional or specialist perspective given more significance than you thought it deserved?

5 *Parents, guardians and children*, e.g. were parents and children aware that the meeting was taking place? Did they participate for all or some of the meeting? What positive and negative effects did their presence or absence have? If they were not present at the end what arrangements were made to inform them of the recommendations made/decisions taken? Were they to be given any opportunity to comment on them and to influence the outcome?

Activity 1.4 invites you to consider this fifth point in more detail.

ACTIVITY 1.4   The changing role of parents

Consider the fifth point in the list concerning case conferences taken from Cline (1989) which concerns the involvement of parents, guardians and children.

Now look back at Activity 1.1 and consider the statement of key principles for partnership with parents that were set out by NASEN (2000).

What changes in the role and status of parents over the intervening 11 years are implied by the differences between the two?

Concluding comments about the structure of this book

Throughout this book we attempt to analyse SEN in a way that takes account of the diversity of modern British society and respects the range of individual perspectives and rights of different stakeholders in the education system. We argue for the integration of different strands of theory, research and practice. We also explore the implications of an interactional perspective which on the one hand considers the different layers of environmental influence that impact on individual functioning and, on the other hand, recognizes the extent to which such influences are mediated by the meanings that individuals ascribe to them. Ethnic and cultural differences represent important dimensions of diversity along which differences in the ways individuals interpret their worlds may be identified and environmental influences may vary.

Part 1, including this chapter, is concerned with key principles and concepts that influence work with SEN. Chapters 2 and 3 examine the key concepts of SEN and inclusion. The last chapter examines how SEN develop in children's lives and will introduce Morton and Frith's causal modelling framework which allows an integrated consideration of different theoretical perspectives on problems in child development and SEN.

Part 2 examines how SEN have been identified and assessed. Assessment is seen in its social and cultural context, and the contentious issue of bias is addressed. The last two chapters outline key approaches to assessment in educational settings that have particular importance when an interactional approach is adopted but which have often received insufficient emphasis in individually focused approaches to assessment – curriculum-based assessment and the assessment of learning environments.

Part 3 examines specific areas of SEN, including learning difficulties, literacy and mathematics. A book that attempts to address the challenges of SEN in a multiethnic society must take problems of communication very seriously. Part 3 includes extended chapters on language and on hearing impairment. The book ends with an examination of the area of need that possibly poses the greatest challenge to the goals of inclusion: emotional and behavioural difficulties and the development of social skills.

Chapter 2

Concepts of special educational needs

When you have studied this chapter you should be able to:

1 Define SEN and explain how they differ from special needs.
2 Evaluate the strengths and weaknesses of two major conceptualizations of SEN, with particular reference to a pluralistic perspective.
3 Consider the advantages and limitations of applying an interactional analysis to SEN and to special needs.
4 Outline the key legislative requirements governing assessment and provision for pupils with SEN.

Contents

Definitions

In the first section of this chapter we provide definitions of the terms 'SEN' and 'special needs'. SEN refers to children's learning needs in school. In Britain, as in many other countries, SEN is legally defined and this legal definition is used to decide whether *particular children* are eligible for special educational services.

Special needs is not a legally defined term. It is generally used to refer to the needs which may be experienced by pupils from particular social groups whose circumstances or background are different from most of the school population. We might think about children whose families are homeless or children who speak a language at home which is not the language of instruction at school. The needs of these groups of children are likely to require special consideration by their schools. Sometimes the term 'special needs' is used to refer to SEN and this can cause unhelpful confusion since individuals from groups which have special needs may or may not have SEN. Watch out for this sort of loose use of terms and consider carefully whether the author is in fact discussing SEN or special needs.

SEN

The past 15–20 years have seen parallel shifts in the UK and the USA in the concept of SEN and the legal framework surrounding its assessment. In the UK, SEN was introduced as a legally defined term by the Education Act (Department of Education and Science 1981), following the advice of the Warnock Report (Department of Education and Science 1978). Prior to 1981 the focus was very much on identifying and making provision for handicapped individuals. As can be seen from Table 2.1, there were 12 recognized categories of disability.

The Warnock Report recommended that the statutory categories of disabled pupils should be abolished and instead children who required special educational provision should be identified on the basis of a detailed profile of their needs following assessment. This change was recommended for a number of reasons; for example, it was recognized that:

- children often experienced a range of difficulties which meant they could not be fitted neatly into the categories in Table 2.1;
- children assigned to the same category of disability may have varied needs in terms of teaching approaches, classroom management etc.;
- particular children in different categories may have the same needs.

In addition the Report concluded that it was not appropriate to continue to focus attention on only a small proportion of children with severe difficulties and to perpetuate a sharp distinction between the disabled and the non-disabled. Using categories of disability, a yes/no decision would be made about whether a child should be assigned to a particular category or not. By contrast, SEN were conceived of as lying on a continuum with ordinary needs. It was proposed that provision too should be on a continuum, rather than segregated, in *either* special *or* mainstream schools.

Table 2.1 Children in England and Wales assessed to need special education in special schools, special classes and awaiting placement, 1 January 1982

Disability	Number	%
Blind	990	0.6
Partially sighted	2,065	1.3
Deaf	3,387	2.1
Partially deaf	4,261	2.7
Physically handicapped	13,999	8.9
Delicate	4,691	4.0
Educationally subnormal (moderate)	70,529	45.1
Educationally subnormal (severe)	30,503	19.5
Epileptic	975	0.6
Maladjusted	21,442	37.1
Speech defects	2,496	1.6
Autistic	1,028	0.7

Source: Inner London Education Authority (1985).

Figure 2.1
Legal definition
of SEN
Source:
Department for
Education and
Employment
(1996,
section 312).

A child has *special educational needs* if he or she has a *learning difficulty* which calls for *special educational provision* to be made for him or her.

A child has a *learning difficulty* if he or she:
(a) has a significantly greater difficulty in learning than the majority of children of the same age
(b) has a disability which either prevents or hinders the child from making use of educational facilities of a kind provided for children of the same age in schools within the area of the local education authority
(c) is under five and falls within the definition at (a) or (b) above or would do if special educational provision was not made for the child.

A child must not be regarded as having a learning difficulty solely because the language or form of language of the home is different from the language in which he or she is or will be taught.

Special educational provision means:
(a) for a child over two, educational provision which is additional to or otherwise different from, the educational provision made generally for children of the child's age in maintained schools, other than special schools in the area.
(b) for a child under two, educational provision of any kind.

The implementation of the Education Act (Department for Education and Science 1981) shifted the purpose of assessment from the diagnosis of disability to the identification of SEN. Figure 2.1 shows the definition of SEN introduced in the Education Act 1981 and maintained in subsequent legislation. It can be seen that the level of need experienced is understood to be the result of a complex interaction between the child's strengths and weaknesses, the level of support available and the appropriateness of the education being provided.

In legal terms, children are said to have SEN if they require special educational provision because they have a significantly greater difficulty in learning than the majority of children of their age or because they suffer from a disability which prevents or hinders them from making use of the educational facilities generally provided for children of their age (Department of Education and Science 1981; Department for Education and Employment 1996). In the USA legislation on SEN in the last quarter of the twentieth century also emphasized meeting the individual needs of children and focused on the provision of a match between these needs and the education offered. For example, the Individuals with Disabilities Education Act (IDEA 1997) defines a student as having a disability if he or she requires 'special education' – defined as 'specially designed instruction'.

The SEN approach has generally been welcomed as an improvement on the 'categories of handicap' approach which it replaced. However a number of criticisms have nevertheless been raised:

- The interrelationship between needs and provision embodied in these legal definitions of SEN, where one is defined with reference to the other, has been criticized as circular by Goacher *et al.* (1988) in relation to the British Education Act (Department of Education and Science 1981) and by Zigmond and Baker (1995) in relation to the US Individuals with Disabilities Education Act (IDEA 1997).
- More radically, Tomlinson (1982) has suggested that the real needs being served by this approach are the needs of dominant power interests in society, rather than those of children who experience difficulties in school, in that:

  state special education developed and took the forms it did to cater for children who had been categorized out of the normal education that was offered to the majority of children and that its development had more to do with the 'needs' of an industrialized society which was endeavoring to produce and train a stable, docile, productive workforce, than with the 'needs' of individual children. The smooth running of normal schools and, latterly, their examination-orientated, credentialling functions were impeded by troublesome children who could not, or would not, conform to the requirements of schools, particularly in terms of learning capabilities and appropriate behaviour. Humanitarian ideologies and Christian reformist principles were used to rationalize the removal of the defective, handicapped, or those in need to a special education sector which has expanded continuously.

  (Tomlinson 1982: 173–4)

Special needs

Pupils may exhibit special needs if they come from a social group whose circumstances or background are different from those of most of the school population.

In the case of black and ethnic minority groups, Robson (1989) has suggested four areas in which special or additional needs may be identified without any implication that individual pupils have learning difficulties in the same sense as those with SEN:

1 *language* – a particular need for help with English and, if possible, with the development and maintenance of their first language(s);
2 *culture* – a particular need for the school curriculum to include reference to and respect for a broad cultural range, including their own cultural heritage.
3 *overt racism* – a particular need for support from the school in opposing racist behaviour and in promoting a positive picture of other cultures.
4 *socioeconomic disadvantage* – a particular need for educational policies and provision that combat the negative effects of socioeconomic disadvantage on school achievement.

All of these special needs are group phenomena, widely shared by children in the same social situation. In this sense they are distinct from the individual experience of learning difficulty that is the foundation of SEN.

This distinction is recognized in one respect in the legislation on special SEN: 'A child must not be regarded as having a learning difficulty solely because the language or medium of communication of the home is different from the language in which he or she is or will be taught' (Department for Education and Employment 1996, Section 312). Deforges (1997) takes a broader view in making the distinction between individual SEN and group special needs. After reviewing the SEN classification system he points out that it

> does not directly address those differences that arise out of cultural values and beliefs, such as spiritual or religious values, or the importance of mother tongue, which will be common to a group and influence concepts such as the need to belong or to feel related to others. These are of key importance in whether individuals and groups from ethnic minorities will develop affiliation to the school as an institution and whether they will trust educational professionals to make decisions in the best interests of their children.
>
> (Deforges 1997: 37)

These two concepts – SEN and special needs – are still often confused in schools. When that happens, serious consequences may result:

- low expectations are held of all children from ethnic and linguistic minorities;
- discrimination against such groups is seen to be based on a valid set of assumptions;
- there is confusion in planning educational support – e.g. expecting the same staff to have expertise in teaching reading to children who are making slow progress and in teaching English as a second language.

A significant challenge in schools is to minimize the confusion between these two fundamental concepts and to prevent the negative consequences that arise when individual members of staff, parents or governors still confuse them.

At the same time schools which are committed to raising attainment will want to take account of special needs more generally and plan to address them. In some cases there are fairly clear implications for action. For example, during the summer holidays the achievement test scores of pupils from advantaged families continue to improve as they do during the normal school period, whereas the scores of children from disadvantaged backgrounds decline. Hence the gap between them and their advantaged classmates widens during this period. The organization of summer schools and play schemes which have a literacy component is likely to contribute locally towards ameliorating the effect of poverty on educational achievement in literacy (Cox and Jones 1983).

ACTIVITY 2.1   Special needs and SEN

1 Consider the brief case descriptions in the table below. Can you identify any SEN and special needs suggested by the descriptions?

Description	SEN	Special needs
Antonio (aged 8) has arrived recently from Spain after his father moved to the UK for work. He has a hearing difficulty and has learned little English so far.		
Jane (aged 14) is depressed, very dependent on her mother and cannot bring herself to get up and leave home in the morning in order to attend school.		
Louisa (aged 10) comes from a small local travellers' community. As with other members of her family, her school attendance is irregular and she never tackles the homework that is set regularly at the school near the site where she is living this winter.		

2 It is often claimed that there may be undesirable consequences if the terms 'SEN' and 'special needs' are confused. Reflecting on this Activity, or drawing on examples from your own experience, can you identify ways in which confusion between these two concepts may lead to low expectations of children, or to discrimination, or poor teaching?

Conceptualizations of SEN

Introduction

Definitions of SEN are based on individual deviation from normal expectation – on significant difficulties in learning compared to the majority of children of a given age. There are two conceptualizations of the nature of these difficulties which are often compared and contrasted. We first describe the view that SEN are best understood by looking at *individual differences* between children. We then describe an alternative approach which argues that SEN arise when inappropriate *environmental demands* are placed on an individual which exceed their current capabilities for meeting those demands. These two approaches are illustrated through the case study of Majid (see Activity 2.2, p. 43). Throughout it will be important for you to consider the sociopolitical context within which the conceptualization of SEN takes place and to ask questions such as, 'What is the purpose of defining SEN?' and 'Whose definition of "normality" is being used?'

Focus on individual differences

In this conceptualization the focus of causation is within the child. This was the view that was embodied in legislation prior to 1981, and the focus in the Education Act (1944) was on 'disability of mind or body'. Individual differences may be considered in a number of domains: biological (e.g. profound hearing loss, cerebral palsy); behavioural (e.g. the length of time the pupil can stay engaged in learning activities); or cognitive (e.g. poorly developed phonological skills, low self-esteem). Factors external to the individual (e.g. quality of teaching) are not considered. Issue has been taken with this approach for a variety of reasons. A number of key issues to consider are outlined below:

- *A focus on individual needs is often based on untested assumptions.* Solity (1993) outlines a number of such assumptions. For example, it is often assumed that children have had appropriate learning opportunities; that their learning experiences have been appropriately matched to their needs; that the teaching available has been effective with their peers but not them; and that the discrepancy cannot be attributed to starting school with lower attainments than peers or to widely differing preschool experiences. The appropriate evidence is rarely available to support these assumptions and yet, as Solity indicates, they are rarely challenged.
- *Social and educational contexts are important.* The first *Code of Practice on the Identification and Assessment of Special Educational Needs*, issued by the Department for Education in 1994, made this point:

  > Effective management, disciplinary and pastoral arrangements and policies in schools can help prevent some special educational needs arising and minimise others. Differentiation of classwork within a common curriculum framework will help the school to meet the learning needs of all children.

> Schools should not automatically assume that children's learning diffi-
> culties always result solely or even mainly from problems within the child.
> The school's practices can make a difference – for good or ill.
>
> (Department for Education 1994a, para. 2.19)

- *Where the educational context contributes to the problem, focusing on the
  individual will not make a broader contribution to improving the context.*
  Dyson (1990) argues that the education system is not equally favourable to
  every child who participates in it and urges that instead of asking how education can change the individual, we should be asking how the education system itself can be changed to accommodate the characteristics of all children,
  regardless of the degree to which they are atypical. Ainscow (1995) notes a
  growing recognition that the special needs agenda should be seen as an essential element in the drive towards effective education for all. Those seen as
  having SEN are coming to be recognized as the stimulus that can encourage
  developments towards a much richer overall environment for learning.

Focus on environmental demands

This approach is situation centred, rather than person centred. Proponents hold
that SEN 'can only be defined in terms of the relationship between what a person
can do and what a person must do to succeed in a given environment' (Deno
1989: 5). Solity (1996) presents an analysis which is based on the view that low
attainments which are different from those of peers do not imply a learning
difficulty. The assumption is that children's current attainments reflect the nature
and quality of previous learning experiences and that children will learn when
taught appropriately. At one extreme then, the environmentally focused approach
holds that there are no children with learning difficulties, only adults with teaching
difficulties. While a range of influences are acknowledged, it is typically argued
that the most pervasive cause of learning difficulties is that for some children 'the
curriculum moves too fast and demands too much in relation to their existing
skills. They get further and further behind and are entrenched in a failure cycle'
(Gickling and Havertape 1981: 376). The majority of school-related problems
are therefore regarded as being curriculum induced. It is also argued that even if
it sometimes is an oversimplification, the attribution of learning failure to factors
such as poor classroom organization, ineffective teaching strategies or inadequate
match between task requirements and learner skills, at least serves to emphasize
the power of the teacher in influencing educational outcomes.

Parallels can be drawn with the conceptualization of disability. Here a focus
on environmental demands leads to an analysis of disabling environments and
hostile social attitudes, rather than individuals and their different functioning and
abilities, which may be played down or even denied (Barnes 1996). Wheelchair
users would not be seen as people with a mobility problem. Instead they would
be seen as people whose mobility is often hampered by inappropriate building
design. Looked at in this way the individual's 'problem' is not their reason for

using a wheelchair, but that they are discriminated against in terms of access. Solity's (1991) view of SEN as a discriminatory concept would seem to reflect a similar approach. A number of key issues to consider are outlined below:

- *Individual differences matter too: different children will respond to teaching in different ways.* A focus on environmental demands attends only to features of the situation and ignores a child's characteristics that may be useful in explaining why they can or cannot perform. The emphasis is on adapting the child to the curriculum instead of vice-versa (Gickling and Thompson 1985). Frederickson *et al.* (1991) criticize the view that 'if a child can't read it doesn't matter why they can't read, what they need is to be taught to read'. This is problematic because once one moves on to asking *how* a child should be taught to read then an understanding of the particular nature of their difficulties, their areas of relative strength, their attitudes and interests becomes important.

  In eschewing individual differences, an environmentally focused approach also fails to account for variability, for the remarkable resilience of many children to learn in spite of teaching which is less than adequate, as well as the remarkable persistence of some children's difficulties in learning despite dedicated and skilful teaching.

- *'Within-child' factors can be influenced by teachers.* The argument that a focus on environmental factors is justified on pragmatic grounds because it encourages the view that teachers can affect outcomes would only be compelling if within-child factors could not be influenced by teachers. However it is not the case that nothing can be done about 'within-child' factors. To take one example, Frederickson *et al.* (1991) point to a range of intervention programmes which have powerful effects in improving children's self-esteem.

- *Teachers do not believe environmentally focused explanations of learning and behaviour problems.* A range of research indicates that an exclusive focus on environmental factors is likely to lack credibility with teachers. As shown in Table 2.2, Croll and Moses (1985) found that primary school teachers who were asked to give explanations for the learning and behaviour problems of children in their classes cited within-child or home factors in the vast majority

Table 2.2 Reasons identified by teachers for pupil learning and behaviour problems

Reason identified	Cases where reason was given (%)	
	for pupil behaviour problems	*for pupil learning problems*
Within child	32	69
Home/parent	67	30
School/teacher	3	4

Source: Croll and Moses (1985).

Table 2.3 Teachers' attributions about the origins of difficult pupil behaviour and reasons for improvement

Individual identified	Attributable cause of (%)	
	Origin of difficulties	Responsible for improvement
Pupil	45	36
Parent	33	8
Teacher	22	56

Source: Miller (1996).

of cases and rarely considered that teacher actions or school factors might be responsible. Frederickson (1998) uses these findings as an illustration of our well-established tendency to over-attribute the behaviour of other people to their personal characteristics and to underestimate the effects of the situation.

Attribution theory also predicts a tendency to take credit for successes while laying the blame for failures elsewhere and Miller (1996) reports an interesting example of this in teachers' attributions about children's SEN. He asked teachers who had implemented successful behavioural interventions with children about the original causes of the difficult behaviour and the reasons for the improvements which had taken place. Table 2.3 shows that the difficulties were most often seen as attributable to the pupil or their parent. However the percentage attributed to teachers is considerably higher than that reported by Croll and Moses (1985). This may relate to differences in methods and procedures between the two studies. However it may also be the case that teachers who have had experience of implementing successful interventions may be more aware of the impact they can have and may therefore be more willing to give attention to environmental factors. This research also leads us to consider teachers' causal attributions and beliefs as potentially influential aspects of the classroom environment for pupils with SEN. It highlights the importance of considering environmental factors which extend beyond a narrow focus on the curriculum.

An interactional analysis

An interactional analysis of SEN

An interactional analysis views the level of need as the result of a complex interaction between the child's strengths and weaknesses, the level of support available and the appropriateness of the education being provided. There is currently widespread support for this view and for the view that neither individually nor environmentally focused conceptualizations are adequate on their own.

ACTIVITY 2.2   Case study: Majid

Read the following case study and prepare to take part in a debate. If you have the opportunity to work with a colleague one of you can prepare notes on (a) below and the other on (b). You can then actually have a debate, where each person argues their case. If you are working on your own you should prepare both sides of the argument, (a) and (b).

(a) Prepare notes on the following case study that will enable you to present the argument that Majid's SEN can best be understood and addressed by adopting a focus on the individual.

(b) Prepare notes on the following case study that will enable you to present the argument that Majid's SEN can best be understood and addressed by adopting a focus on the classroom environment.

For the purposes of this activity be sure to focus on SEN rather than special needs (see the previous section for a discussion of this distinction).

Majid (9 years) is causing concern in his middle school due to his low attainments and generally poor progress. In the playground he joins in playing football happily, but in class his teacher describes him as being in a world of his own. He doesn't seem able to follow instructions given to the whole class, although he will usually try to do what the other children are doing. If the task is explained again to him individually he will sometimes seem to understand and be able to complete it. However in many cases he just doesn't seem to have the basic skills that would allow him to tackle the Year 5 curriculum successfully.

Majid attended a local nursery school for one year and then transferred to a nearby first school for a short time before going with his mother to live in Pakistan for 18 months. He attended school while in Pakistan, where his mother said he had some problems too, and returned to England in the middle of Year 4. Majid speaks Punjabi and English at home. His mother has expressed some concerns about his proficiency in Punjabi but considers that Majid is more competent speaking Punjabi than English. A bilingual assessment was completed six months after he started at middle school. It was reported that Majid answered most questions in English and did not talk with confidence in either language.

Majid's parents reported that he has had a lot of problems with his ears. He used to wake up at night in pain, he had constant ear infections and headaches and lost his appetite. Majid had grommets put in both ears about six months after he returned to England and his parents feel they have made a difference. Majid now turns around quickly when his name is called and is more attentive at home. Majid's teacher had not noticed much difference in the classroom but did say that Majid's attendance had improved as he used to have quite frequent absences with ear infections.

One lesson where Majid is doing better in school is in the Literacy Hour. His middle school sets the pupils in each year group. Majid is in the lowest set which is taught by the school's SEN coordinator (SENCO), supported by a learning support assistant. During the 15 minutes devoted to shared reading and writing at the start of the session the learning support assistant (LSA) sits with Majid's table. She prompts attention, checks understanding and provides additional explanation as necessary. During the word level work she reminds the group about work they have covered and encourages their participation. She then works with the group on catch-up programmes focused on objectives at earlier levels that they have not yet achieved.

Tomlinson (1982: 22) urges that neither 'fatalistic psychological views of individual causality or simple sociological views of environmental determinism' should go unchallenged. Gutierrez and Stone (1997), in discussing a cultural-historical view of learning and learning disabilities, argue that attention must be given to environmental *in addition to* individual variables, not *instead of* them.

An interactional position has been acknowledged in government guidance in the UK for over a decade. *Assessments and Statements of Special Educational Needs: Procedures within the Education, Health and Social Services* (Department of Education and Science 1989a, para. 17) stated:

> The extent to which a learning difficulty hinders a child's development does not depend solely on the nature and severity of that difficulty. Other significant factors include the personal resources and attributes of the child as well as the help and support provided at home and the provision made by the school and the LEA and other statutory and voluntary agencies. A child's special educational needs are thus related both to abilities and disabilities, and to the nature and extent of the interaction of these with his or her environment.

The National Curriculum Council endorsed a similar view: 'Special educational needs are not just a reflection of pupil's inherent difficulties or disabilities; they are often related to factors within schools which can prevent or exacerbate problems' (National Curriculum Council 1989a, para. 5). The *Code of Practice* on the identification and assessment of SEN points out: 'It should be recognized that some difficulties in learning may be caused or exacerbated by the school's learning environment or adult/child relationships' (Department for Education and Skills 2001, para. 5.6).

An interactional approach receives support from individual commentators across the world, drawing on their experience of a variety of different contexts:

- Booth (1993), writing in Britain, suggests that we should talk of children *who experience difficulties in learning* in schools to indicate that such difficulties arise in the context of a relationship between teachers, pupils and curricula.
- Keogh *et al.* (1997), in the USA, argues from a sociocultural perspective that it is impossible to separate the learning competencies of individual children from the contexts in which they live and function.
- In discussing the challenge of SEN in a rural community setting in India, Kaul (1992: 109) argues, 'To understand the special [educational] needs of children with disabilities we need to look at them as children with personal identities in a particular social milieu. We therefore need to examine not only the child but his or her particular social environment in order to understand his "special [educational] needs"'.

Dockrell and McShane (1992) outline a three-part framework for understanding learning difficulties which involves the task, the child and the environment. Assessment involves all three aspects and should include an analysis of:

- the tasks with which a child has difficulty so that the component skills necessary for successful performance can be identified;
- the child's current cognitive abilities and other relevant psychological attributes;
- the environment – the context in which the child and the task interact, aspects of which may be contributory factors to the child's difficulty.

The assessment of each of these aspects is outlined further in Chapter 5. In addition Dockrell and McShane discuss the interaction of the task, child and environment, and Chapter 5 introduces a fourth approach to assessment which is particularly relevant here – assessment which is focused on the *zone of potential development*. This involves identifying the improvement in task performance which can be achieved by a particular child given different levels of environmental intervention or support.

However, despite the fact that an interactional approach is widely espoused and advocated it cannot be assumed that it is widely implemented in practice. In discussing the operation of the Education Act (1981) (Department of Education and Science 1981) Goacher *et al.* (1988: 149) argue:

> though the definition proposes an interactive view of children's needs, the implications for the terms in which assessments of needs are made do not seem to have been grasped by many of those involved. Most of the Statements which we have seen in the course of our research concentrated their attention on deficits within the child which led to special needs, with very little attention given to the child's environment, whether at home or at school.

As you read accounts of practice in this book and elsewhere, consider the extent to which they reflect an interactional conceptualization of SEN. You may find more examples of individually focused or environmentally focused approaches than you expect. Activity 2.3 provides an opportunity to examine professional advice for evidence of individually focused, environmentally focused or interactional orientations.

An interactional analysis of special needs

In just the same way that the level of SEN experienced by an individual will depend on the responsiveness of the educational environment, so too will this influence the level of special needs experienced by particular groups. For example, the classroom is a unique context that requires special language and interactive skills, some patterns of which may be shared in home and community settings and some of which may not (Ruiz 1995). Whether children are judged to have adequate levels of communicative competence in the classroom will depend both on the opportunities which they have had to develop relevant skills in other contexts and on how classroom events are organized to enable or disable their participation. Children who have attended a well-structured playgroup may initially be more responsive to the style of teacher communication used in their Reception

ACTIVITY 2.3   Extracts from professional advice about two children's SEN

Below you will find extracts from the professional advice that was attached to the statements of SEN prepared for two quite different children. Can you identify phrases and sentences that:

(a) focus on the individual;
(b) focus on environmental demands; or
(c) are based on an interactional analysis of the child's difficulties?

You may find it helpful to tackle this activity with a partner. Make two copies of this Activity and start by working independently. You could each underline what you judge to be (a), (b) and (c) in different colours. Then compare your judgements and, where there are discrepancies, discuss why you each thought what you did. Can you reach a consensus on all the judgements in the end?

John (aged 7)

Extracts from a joint report by the headteacher and class teacher

John is a physically fit and healthy boy. He is tall for his age and derives pleasure from PE (physical education) activities especially when his height gives him an advantage. He generally works and behaves well both in and out of the classroom, he loves PE, games and using the computer. He attends school regularly.

Within the classroom he can be particularly tense when faced with a reading or writing task. He does try his best but his performance is well below average for his age. At the end of Key Stage 1 his SAT (Standard Assessment Task) scores were all at Level 1 apart from science which was at Level 2. Despite a great deal of work during the Literacy Hour his knowledge of phonics is very weak, and his written letters, particularly p, d, b are often confused. He still has difficulty remembering many letter sounds, and where he recognizes a letter he will often give the letter name rather than the sound. His unaided written work is now becoming more extensive, but it is still very difficult to understand, and even harder for him to read back. John can spell correctly a few key words and some two- or three-letter words (notably some of the words that are featured in a large display of 'Words we often need' that hangs across the top of the classroom wall above the teacher's desk). When this display was taken down during a test, he made serious errors in words that he has often spelled correctly in the past.

In mathematics John is a little more confident in his approach despite his performance being below average. In a secure, friendly atmosphere John responds well, especially when following predictable tasks. In a changing unfamiliar situation he quickly becomes unsure of himself and looks to others for help. When reassurance and support are quickly available he can usually tackle the task with some success. Otherwise, he tends to become anxious and tearful and unwilling to attempt the task. His approach to learning and his attitude to language work in particular have improved recently perhaps because of the amount of school-based support that is offered. However, he remains characteristically nervous and tense about his own performance. When he does a good piece of work and receives praise, he is reluctant to appreciate that the work is good.

John's needs are extensively related to his language development and his self-concept. He needs to improve reading and writing skills and to value himself more. He has a particularly weak memory for letter shapes, sounds and spelling. He has made most progress when given regular daily individual attention following a structured language programme in which he is required to over-learn everything. It is through this regular individual attention that some words have stayed in his memory.

John will require a greater access than other children to the computer, concept keyboard, language master and simple word games.

Peter (aged 6)

Extracts from an educational psychologist's report

I have been involved with Peter for three years since he was in day nursery. The staff there and his mother, Ms T, were finding it extremely difficult to manage Peter's behaviour. They reported that he was 'defiant', 'uncooperative in most adult-directed activities', and 'very distractible'. They felt that his short attention span and difficult behaviour were 'beginning to interfere with his general development and in particular with his learning'.

My most recent involvement with him began this year when he was referred by his school. He had started in a small class of 19 children but found it difficult to settle. His class teacher, Miss F, was concerned about his 'over-activity' from the outset and about his problem of concentration. She said that he seemed not to have difficulties understanding any of the work given, but that he rarely remained on task for more than one to two minutes. We discussed a reward system which involved gradually extending the length of time which Peter was required to be on task. Rewards included time on the computer (which Peter really valued) and extra time with Miss F (which proved to be quite difficult to implement because of the lack of any regular extra help in the classroom). Peter's progress was not consistent in that sometimes he remained in his seat and on task for the required length of time, but at other times he had difficulties doing so. Much seemed to depend on which other children were working at his table and whether they reacted to him in a way that calmed or provoked him. In addition, Miss F reported that his behaviour had rapidly deteriorated to include bad language, disobeying of instructions, fighting with other children, and 'high'/excited behaviour (e.g. screaming, 'karate' movements, etc.) in the playground.

A meeting was held in November with the headteacher, the class teacher, Miss F, and Peter's mother. We discussed a range of strategies for addressing Peter's behaviour. These included:

- the continuation of the reward system for on-task behaviour;
- explaining to Peter (and reminding him of) what was acceptable and unacceptable behaviour both within the classroom and in the playground;
- removing him (temporarily) from the playground or from one area of the classroom to another when conflict occurred or when he used bad language;
- planning activities in such a way as to try to minimize the possibility of conflict (e.g. placing him beside quiet children, making sure that he fully understood what he was required to do, etc.);
- establishing more regular liaison between his mother and the class teacher (i.e. every 1–2 days); and
- awarding him certificates for demonstrated effort to behave or to work well.

In January Miss F left, and over the following six months Peter's class had three changes of teacher. A number of supply teachers were also needed for various periods of time. A further 11 children joined the class, and a primary helper began to work in the classroom in the mornings. Peter's behaviour continued to cause concern, but it proved difficult to implement a consistent programme of behaviour management because of the high turnover of teachers. There were a number of other children in the class whose behaviour caused concern, including one child who was expelled from the school. Peter was suspended for three days in May because of aggressive behaviour towards another child (i.e. grabbing the child's balaclava and hair).

Strategies implemented by the various teachers in an attempt to manage Peter's behaviour included: praise for positive behaviour; giving stars for good work, effort or behaviour; reminding Peter to work and play nicely; giving him responsibilities (e.g. to distribute the milk); allowing him to take toys home; encouraging him to bring in work, drawings and models which he had completed at home; allowing him to stay at his desk doing drawing during storytime; rewarding him with time on the computer working with another child; certificates/letters home; 'time out' in other classes; working on his own in a corner of the classroom or close to the teacher; working with 'quiet' children; working with the primary helper outside the classroom; noting down his positive and negative behaviours in a 'behaviour book'; and asking Ms T to come into school to work with him in the classroom and to accompany the class on trips. It would appear from speaking to teachers and to Ms T that the most successful of these in terms of Peter producing work and not getting into trouble were the strategies that minimized distractions – that is, those which involved him working on his own or with an adult either within or outside the classroom. Ms T felt that a major deciding factor in Peter's behaviour was his perception of how the teacher viewed him – whether he felt she 'liked' him and treated him in a 'fair' manner, and whether she showed by her behaviour that she valued him as an important member of the class.

class than children who have started school from home without experience in a preschool setting. The clearer the expectations and the more predictable the Reception class routines the more quickly children without preschool experience are likely to learn about how to respond and communicate successfully in the Reception class.

The context profoundly affects behaviour, and that behaviour cannot be interpreted without taking into account situational factors. Cummins (1989: 111) argues that academic difficulties may be partially due to the reinforcement by schools of 'the ambivalence and insecurity that many minority students tend to feel with regard to their own cultural identity'. Pupils may become 'disabled' in a manner similar to that experienced by their ethnic communities as they become disempowered or 'disabled' by the dominant group. Adopting a sociohistorical perspective Cummins (1986) points out that internationally the minority groups who currently perform very poorly at school are those that have traditionally been discriminated against by the dominant group. He highlights two examples that are often quoted:

1 Finnish students have tended, in the past, to do poorly in Swedish schools where they are a low-status group, but have done comparatively well on average in Australia where their social status as a group is higher (Troike 1978).

2 In Japanese schools children of the outcast Burakumin group do poorly on average, but in the USA where the caste difference is not noticed by most people Burakumin children have done as well as other Japanese immigrants (Ogbu 1978).

Cummins (1986) identifies four characteristics of schools that are important in this context. These are:

- *cultural/linguistic incorporation* – the extent to which the language and culture of minority pupils are incorporated into the curriculum;
- *community participation* – the extent to which the community is involved in the school, such as parental participation and involvement;
- *pedagogy* – whether teaching is organized on a traditional transmission ('chalk and talk') model or is more representative of a reciprocal interactive model;
- *assessment* – the extent to which the purpose of assessment is to locate the problem within the pupil and legitimize their poor progress, or to advocate for changes to the social and learning context with the aim of promoting the pupil's progress.

Cummins argues that these characteristics should be examined along a continuum from an intercultural orientation at one end to an orientation stressing conformity to the majority culture at the other. This framework can be used to analyse the educational interactions that pupils have in order to understand where their difficulties may lie. It is argued that minority students can be empowered to the extent that patterns of interaction in school reverse those that prevail in society at large, promoting their confidence in their personal identity and ability to succeed academically.

Keogh *et al.* (1997) highlight some of the dilemmas involved in attempting to take account of cultural and ethnic diversity in education. They argue that 'on one level the issue is simple: Everyone's heritage is due respect and the ideal is to find strength in diversity and to capitalise on rather then stigmatise difference' (1997: 109). However there is often an unrecognized paradox in well-intentioned efforts to be sensitive to diversity in that individuals may be stereotyped and treated as if they share common traits with all others of a similar background. Ethnic group differences are often treated as markers of cultural differences, but this is usually an oversimplification. It is important to appreciate the social and cultural differences that may exist within groups that share the same cultural background.

Ethnic identity tends to persist though time, whereas culture changes as individuals and groups modify beliefs and practices over time. Consider the differences which may be observed between the lifestyles, expectations and values of new immigrants and those of the second generation to be born in the UK. Keogh *et al.* (1997) therefore argue for carefully distinguishing between ethnicity and culture in educational practice, which allows acknowledgement of variation at three levels: between ethnically defined groups; within ethnically defined groups; and between individuals within ethnic and cultural groups.

ACTIVITY 2.4

Imagine two schools that operate at opposite ends of each of Cummins' (1986) four characteristics (see Figure 2.2):

- Cultural/linguistic incorporation
- Community participation
- Pedagogy
- Assessment

You may find it helpful to recall schools that you know well and exaggerate the differences between them.

Consider each dimension in turn:

(a) What specific differences between the schools do you think a visitor might notice?
(b) What specific practices might show how the staff and pupils of the two schools differ in terms of their attitude, motivation and identification with the aims of the school?

The issues of group empowerment and group 'disability' analysed by Cummins (1986) and the concerns about group stereotyping highlighted by Keogh *et al.* (1997) arise in their most intense form when there are racial differences between groups that parallel (or partly parallel) ethnic and/or cultural differences. Black communities in Europe and North America experience special needs in schools to a marked extent. Racism is a key factor. In this book we will employ a simple educational framework for analysing perspectives on racism (Inner London Education Authority 1983). The model used as a reference point in the Inner London Education Authority covered both the content of the curriculum and the way schools and colleges were run. Three perspectives on racism were outlined. They were seen as developmental in character, the first being the earliest observed in the British education service and the last being the perspective to which the Authority now aspired. The implication was that the three perspectives were mutually exclusive. In fact, in most contexts they are likely to overlap to a considerable degree: each is a matter of emphasis, not a separate and exclusive category. The three perspectives highlighted in the model are:

1 a perspective emphasizing mainly assimilation;
2 a perspective emphasizing mainly cultural diversity;
3 a perspective emphasizing primarily equality.

These perspectives are illustrated in Table 2.4. In Chapter 9 you will find this model applied to different approaches to assessing intelligence and learning abilities.

The relationship between SEN and special needs reconsidered

While we have taken care to draw a distinction between SEN and special needs it follows that if SEN arise from an interaction between the child's difficulties and

Table 2.4 Three perspectives on racism

Perspective on racism	*Statements of education policy*
Emphasizing mainly assimilation	School curricula should help black settlement by reflecting British traditions, history, customs and culture. The first priority for black people is to learn and speak good English. Race relations are by and large good. It is counter-productive to try to improve them too fast. The main problems are caused by extreme right-wing groups. Racial and cultural differences should not be exacerbated by drawing attention to them.
Emphasizing mainly cultural diversity	Teaching about various cultures will promote a positive self-image among black people and tolerance and sympathetic understanding among white people. Educational establishments should make greater efforts to explain their policies and practices to black parents. Community languages besides English should be valued positively by schools. Bilingualism should be encouraged.
Emphasizing primarily equality	Black perspectives on world history should be introduced on an equal basis. Racism has a central and pervasive influence on all social systems. There should be continuous monitoring of policies and provision. Positive action is required on employment and appointments. Removing discrimination against black people should have a higher priority.

Source: Adapted from Inner London Education Authority (1983).

the educational environment in which they are placed, then assessing children's SEN must involve a detailed analysis of their learning environments. To take a single example of a group with special needs (children from a linguistic minority) one of the key elements in their performance in school will be the ethnic and language background of the pupil population of the school. Another will be the attitudes, skills and resources of the staff.

The Warnock Committee (Department of Education and Science 1978: 64) argued that 'any tendency for educational difficulties to be assessed without proper reference to a child's cultural and ethnic background and its effect on his education can result in a category of handicap becoming correlated with a particular group in society'. As there is evidence that certain groups in society are overrepresented in particular forms of SEN provision, does this mean that educational difficulties are typically assessed without proper reference to a child's cultural and ethnic background and its effect on their education?

The evidence comes from a variety of sources and, although conclusions differ somewhat, there is widespread agreement about the findings internationally. In the UK for example:

• Tomlinson (1982: 174) concluded:

> The majority of children categorised out of normal state education and into the MLD [moderate learning difficulties] and EBD [emotional and behavioural difficulties] categories of special education have always been working class children, particularly males who have been most trouble-some to schools in terms of their slow learning or disruptive behaviour. The difficulty of presenting these children as having special needs in the same terms as those with sensory or physical difficulties has been resolved by adding the ideology of cultural disadvantage and presenting special education as 'doing good' to working-class and, latterly, black children.

In support of this last comment she reports that in 1972, when the total proportion of the school population in schools for children with moderate learning difficulties (MLD) was 0.6 per cent, the figure for Caribbean children was 3 per cent. Over the next decade the overrepresentation of this group in provision for children with MLD in some areas was corrected, but its overrepresentation in provision for children with emotional and behavioural difficulties persisted (Inner London Education Authority 1985; Cooper *et al.* 1994). In contrast, there is evidence in some forms of SEN provision that enjoy higher social status (e.g. provision for children with dyslexia) of the under-representation of children from ethnic and linguistic minority communities (Cline and Reason 1993).

• When Croll and Moses (1985) examined the incidence of special needs in ordinary schools in their study they found that the ratio of boys to girls was almost 2:1 overall, although with discipline problems the ratio rose to almost 4:1. They also reported that more children from ethnic minority backgrounds were seen to have special needs than white children, the figure for both Asian and Caribbean children being 50 per cent more than for white children. When discipline problems are considered, the incidence for white pupils was twice that for Asian pupils and the incidence for Caribbean pupils more than three times that for white pupils.

Given the disproportionate number of ethnic minority students placed in special education programmes Artiles *et al.* (1997) identified a need to articulate conceptual frameworks that explain the interactions between certain sociocultural variables and disability. A major theme of this book is to explore these issues and provide practitioners with conceptual frameworks to guide work with children who have SEN which give consideration to sociocultural variables. Conceptual analysis will lead to, but go beyond, improvements that still support the current system of diagnosis, eligibility and placement. More radical proposals for system restructuring recommend eliminating the notion of eligibility and classification for mild disabilities. Referrals would become requests for assistance; school assistance teams would function to serve the needs of any teacher or pupil:

> The goal of these teams would be to assist *all* pupils without trying to validate their 'eligibility' for special education, thus a merging of ordinary and special education would occur. Educational psychologists would serve in a consultant capacity rather than a position of 'qualifying' pupils. Professionals from both special and ordinary education fields would, therefore, work together in a collaborative manner.
>
> (Graf 1992: 196)

It is interesting to note the many parallels which can be drawn with the proposals for change in special needs procedures put forward by the British government in their Green Paper, *Excellence for All Children* (Department for Education and Employment 1997). Specifically, there is a focus on policies aimed at raising standards for all pupils; on providing practical support in mainstream schools; and on different professionals working together.

The legal context

The National Curriculum requirements

The distinction that has been drawn in this chapter between SEN and special needs is reflected in recent statutory guidance which also highlights the importance of taking action to address the needs of groups and individuals. The National Curriculum handbooks for primary and secondary teachers (DfEE/QCA 1999a, 1999b) set out the legal requirements of the National Curriculum in English schools and offer guidance on its implementation. The statutory inclusion statements contained in these handbooks set out guidance for schools to assist them in meeting their statutory responsibility to provide a broad and balanced curriculum for all pupils. Schools are advised of a range of specific actions that should be taken in all teaching to respond to diverse pupil needs which may relate to gender, disability, social and cultural background, ethnic background (including travellers, refugees and asylum seekers), linguistic background and SEN. More detailed consideration is given to pupils who have SEN and to two groups of pupils with special needs – those who have a disability and those who are learning EAL. As was highlighted in Figure 2.1, the Education Act (1996) specifically states that learning EAL must not, of itself, be regarded as a special educational need. The National Curriculum handbooks make a similar point with regard to disability:

> Not all pupils with disabilities will necessarily have special educational needs. Many pupils with disabilities learn alongside their peers with little need for additional resources beyond the aids which they use as part of their daily life, such as a wheelchair, a hearing aid or equipment to aid vision. Teachers must take action, however, in their planning to ensure that these pupils are

enabled to participate as fully and effectively as possible within the National Curriculum and the statutory assessment arrangements.

(DfEE/QCA 1999a: 35)

The guidance offered on ways in which schools should respond to pupils' SEN observes that in many cases school-based intervention involving greater differentiation of tasks and materials will be effective in facilitating access to learning. A range of examples are provided to illustrate how help can be provided:

- with communication, language and literacy;
- through use of all available senses and experiences;
- through use of specialist aids and equipment;
- through support from adults and peers;
- through positive behaviour management and teaching skill for independent and collaborative working;
- through minimizing stress, building self-esteem and supporting the pupil in managing their emotions.

In some cases the school may itself need support in order to take further action:

A smaller number of pupils may need access to specialist equipment and approaches or to alternative or adapted activities, consistent with school-based intervention augmented by advice and support from external specialists as described in the SEN *Code of Practice*, or, in exceptional circumstances, with a statement of special educational need.

(DfEE/QCA 1999a: 33)

The SEN *Code of Practice*

The revised SEN *Code of Practice* (Department for Education and Skills 2001) provides guidance to LEAs, school governing bodies, early years' providers and health and social services on their duties under Part IV of the Education Act 1996. The *Code* also makes reference to provisions in the SEN and Disability Rights in Education Act, the revised Education (Special Educational Needs) Regulations, and the Education (Special Educational Needs) (Information) (England) Regulations.

The revised SEN *Code of Practice* identifies a number of fundamental principles (Department for Education and Skills 2001, para. 1.5):

- a child with SEN should have their needs met;
- the SEN of children will normally be met in mainstream schools or settings;
- the views of the child should be sought and taken into account;
- parents have a vital role to play in supporting their child's education;
- children with SEN should be offered full access to a broad, balanced and

relevant education, including the Foundation Stage Curriculum and the National Curriculum.

In accordance with the third and fourth of these principles, specific sections of the *Code* offer guidance on working in partnership with parents and on pupil participation in assessment and decision making.

Guidance on identification, assessment and provision is offered to early education settings and to primary and secondary schools. In accordance with the second of the principles outlined above it is emphasized that 'all teachers are teachers of children with special educational needs' (2000a: 27) and that SEN is a 'whole school' issue. The guidance in particular highlights the following aspects.

First, the importance of *early identification* and the role of class and subject teachers in monitoring performance in relation to level descriptions in the National Curriculum at the end of a Key Stage and National Literacy and Numeracy Strategy framework objectives.

Second, the importance for *children learning EAL* of considering the child within their home, cultural and community context and utilizing any available community liaison arrangements. Slow progress needs to be carefully examined and it should not be assumed that it can be attributed to the pupils' status as a learner of EAL. Early assessment should be made of pupils' past exposure to each of the languages they speak, their current use of them and their proficiency in them. This will provide a basis for identifying and evaluating both pupils' language needs and any SEN they may have.

Third, a *graduated response* is required to the continuum of SEN. Three levels are identified: *School Action*, *School Action Plus* and support provided by a statement of SEN. It is emphasized that pupils are not expected to progress through these levels. Indeed where interventions work successfully the expectation is that pupils will subsequently require *less* help rather than more help. Where teachers or others present concerns supported by evidence about pupils' progress, despite their receipt of differentiated learning opportunities, the SEN Coordinator (SENCO) should initiate further assessment to identify what school action is needed to help pupils progress. The SENCO is the member of staff within a school who has responsibility for coordinating SEN provision within that school (Department for Education and Skills 2001: glossary). School action may involve the deployment of extra staff to provide one-to-one or small group tuition or classroom support; the provision of different learning materials or special equipment; additional staff development and training on more effective strategies; or early advice on strategies or equipment from LEA support services. Parents have to be consulted and informed both about the action taken to help their child and its outcome. The provision made for an individual pupil which is in addition to or different from the differentiated curriculum plan for all pupils should be recorded in an individual education plan (IEP). The IEP should include information about:

- the short-term targets set for the child;
- the teaching strategies to be used;

- the provision to be put in place;
- when the plan is to be reviewed (at least twice-yearly);
- the outcome of the action taken.

Where pupils continue to experience difficulties despite an individualized programme and focused support under School Action, external support services may be consulted for more detailed advice through School Action Plus. This may involve external support services offering advice about new IEPs and targets, providing more specialist assessments, advising on specialist strategies or materials or providing direct support of various kinds. Although the expectation is that the delivery of the interventions recorded in the IEP will continue to be primarily the responsibility of the class or subject teacher and that the strategies should be implemented as far as possible in the classroom setting, external specialists may be involved in teaching pupils directly for part of the time or in partnership with their teachers.

Where a number of alternative intervention programmes have each been implemented for a reasonable period of time without success the head teacher may consider referring a pupil for *statutory assessment*, detailing information on their National Curriculum levels and attainments in literacy and numeracy, the evidence collected through School Action and School Action Plus, information from the involvement of other professionals and the views of the pupil and their parent. The pupil should continue to be supported through school action plus while the LEA is considering a request for a statutory assessment of their SEN.

Guidance is offered to LEAs on the statutory assessment of SEN. 'An assessment under section 323 of the Education Act 1996 should only be undertaken if the LEA believe that the child probably has special educational needs and that the LEA needs or probably needs to determine and provide the child's special educational provision itself by making a statement' (Department for Education and Employment 2000a: 51). A request for a statutory assessment may be made by a pupil's school, by their parent or by another agency such as an independent school, early education provider, health authority or social services department. Before deciding whether to make an assessment the LEA must notify and inform parents. If the request has not come from the pupil's school the headteacher must be informed and asked for written evidence about the school's assessment of the pupil's needs and the provision that has been made for them. In deciding whether to make a statutory assessment, LEAs are to pay particular attention to:

- evidence that the school has responded appropriately to the requirements of the National Curriculum, especially the section entitled 'Inclusion: Providing effective learning opportunities for all children';
- evidence provided by the child's school, parents and other professionals where they have been involved with the child, as to the nature, extent and cause of the child's learning difficulties;
- evidence of action already taken by the child's school to meet and overcome those difficulties;
- evidence of the rate and style of the child's progress;

- evidence that where some progress has been made, it has only been as a result of much additional effort and instruction at a sustained level not commensurate with usual provision through school action plus.

Guidance is offered on the type of provision that may be required to meet pupils' SEN in communication and interaction, in cognition and learning, behaviour, emotional and social development and arising from physical and/or sensory needs. Where the LEA judges that the child's needs can be met from the resources already available to mainstream schools in their area the decision will be taken not to make a statutory assessment. The LEA must explain the reasons for their decision to the pupil's parents and their school. Parents may appeal against the decision to the SEN Tribunal.

If the LEA decides to make a statutory assessment they must seek parental, educational, medical, psychological and social services' advice on the pupil's special educational needs plus any other advice considered desirable by the LEA or other relevant bodies. This may include the views of the child. The LEA will consider all this advice in deciding whether they need to make a Statement. The LEA has ten weeks from notifying parents that they intend to make an assessment to writing to parents letting them know the outcome of the assessment.

If, as a result of the assessment, the LEA decides that they do not need to make a Statement, they must present parents with a note in lieu, which gives the reasons for their decision, outlines the child's needs and offers guidance on the appropriate educational provision that might be made by the school, possibly with specialist advice, but without being determined by the LEA. Parents may appeal against the decision not to issue a Statement to the SEN Tribunal. The operation of the SEN Tribunal is governed by sections 333–6 of the Education Act 1996 and the associated regulations. Appeals to the tribunal are heard by a panel of three people, two of whom should have relevant expertise in SEN and/or local government and one of whom, the chair, will be legally trained. The SEN Tribunal's 'overriding aim is to consider the needs of the child' (Department for Education and Employment 1997: 29).

If the LEA decides they need to issue a Statement they will send a proposed statement to the parents. The Statement must be set out in the format shown in Figure 2.2 and all sections completed except Part 4, where parents will be invited to express their preferences about the school to be named. The *Special Educational Needs and Disability Act* (Department for Education and Employment 2001) places a duty on LEAs and schools to ensure that pupils with SEN are educated in a mainstream setting unless this is incompatible with the wishes of their parents or mainstream provision cannot be adapted to meet the pupil's needs without prejudicing the efficient education of the other pupils or incurring unreasonable public expense. If LEAs do not name the parents' first choice of school in the final version of the Statement they must explain their decision to the parents who have a right to appeal to the SEN Tribunal.

An *annual review* of each Statement must be carried out, involving the parents, the pupil, the LEA, the school and all the professionals involved. The purpose of

Figure 2.2
Format and
content of the
Statement of SEN
Source:
Department for
Education and
Skills (2001, paras
8.29–8.30).

The Statement of Special Educational Needs

Part 1. Introduction: The child's name and address and date of birth. The child's home language and religion. The names and address(es) of the child's parents.

Part 2. Special Educational Needs (learning difficulties): Details of each and every one of the child's special educational needs as identified by the LEA during statutory assessment and on the advice received and attached as appendices to the statement.

Part 3. Special Educational Provision: The special educational provision that the LEA consider necessary to meet the child's special educational needs.
(a) The objectives that the special educational provision should aim to meet.
(b) The special educational provision which the LEA consider appropriate to meet the needs set out in Part 2 and to meet the objectives.
(c) The arrangements to be made for monitoring progress in meeting those objectives, particularly for setting short-term targets for the child's progress and for reviewing his or her progress on a regular basis.

Part 4. Placement: The type and name of school where the special educational provision set out in Part 3 is to be made or the arrangements for the education to be made otherwise than in school.

Part 5. Non-Educational Needs: All relevant non-educational needs of the child as agreed between the health services, social services or other agencies and the LEA.

Part 6. Non-Educational Provision: Details of relevant non-educational provision required to meet the non-educational needs of the child as agreed between the health services and/or social services and the LEA, including the agreed arrangements for its provision.

Signature and date

APPENDICES
All the advice obtained and taken into consideration during the assessment process must be attached as appendices to the statement.
The advice appended to the statement must include:

A   Parental evidence
B   Educational advice
C   Medical advice
D   Psychological advice
E   Social Services advice
F   Any other advice, such as the views of the child, which the LEA or any other body from whom advice is sought considers desirable. In particular where the child's parent is a serving member of the armed forces, advice from Service Children's Education (SCE)

the review is to collect everyone's perspective on the child's progress, to ensure that desired outcomes are being achieved and, if necessary, to amend the Statement to reflect any new needs identified and provision required. The LEA may decide that the objectives of the Statement have been achieved and that they should no longer maintain the Statement. Where the pupil or their family have EAL the *Code* highlights the need to:

- translate any relevant documents into the family's mother tongue;
- ensure that interpreters are available to the child and family both in the preparatory stages to the review meeting and in the review meeting itself;
- ensure that any professionals from the child's community have similar interpretation and translation facilities in order that they may contribute as fully as possible to the review process;
- ensure that, if possible, a bilingual support teacher or teacher of EAL is available to the child and family (Department for Education and Employment 2000a: 91).

Any annual review held in Year 9 and subsequent years must draw up and review a *transition plan* in addition to reviewing the young person's statement. The aim of the transition plan is to prepare systematically for the young person's transition to adult life and ensure that they receive any specialist help they need during continuing education or vocational or occupational training. Any relevant agencies that may play a significant role in the young person's life during the post-school years should be invited and the 'Connexions' service must be involved.

Other relevant legislation and guidance

The Children Act (Department of Health 1989) is the most comprehensive piece of legislation on children enacted in UK to date. It brought together previously fragmented legislation about caring for, bringing up and protecting children. The welfare of the child is enshrined as the paramount consideration in all decision making. As noted in Chapter 1, children's ascertainable wishes and feelings are accorded importance in that courts must have regard to them. However the Act also emphasizes the importance of the family – the duty of local authorities being to provide support to children in need and their families. Children are defined as being in need if:

- they are unlikely to achieve or maintain, or to have the opportunity of achieving or maintaining, a reasonable standard of health or development without the provision of services by a local authority;
- their health or development is likely to be significantly impaired, or further impaired, without the provision of such services; or
- they are disabled.

In line with the distinction made throughout this chapter, the revised SEN *Code of Practice* acknowledges that 'a child with special educational needs will not necessarily be "in need" as defined in the Children Act 1989' (Department for Education and Skills 2001, para. 10.33).

The concept of parental responsibility was another central element of the Act. This applies even when children are unable to live at home, but must be looked after by the local authority. The local authority has a duty to ensure contact with the parents whenever possible for a child looked after by them and a duty to return the child to their family unless this is against their interests. While the interests of the child would require action by a local authority in cases of abuse or neglect in the family, the dangers are highlighted of unwarranted intervention in families which does not positively contribute to the child's welfare. The Act sets out a range of welfare duties for local authorities in looking after children and requires that account must be taken of the child's racial origin and cultural and linguistic background.

There are particular implications for education where a pupil is accommodated by a local authority, is subject to a care order or to an education supervision order (which can be made when a child of compulsory school age is not receiving efficient full-time education – for example through persistent poor attendance). The Arrangements for Placement of Children Regulations made under the Act require that the child care plan drawn up in these cases must include information about arrangements for the child's education (the personal education plan). The personal education plan should include information as appropriate from a Statement of SEN, annual review or IEP. The Department for Education and Employment/Department of Health (2000) *Guidance on the Education of Children in Public Care* suggests that LEAs and social services departments should consider the advantages of linking their reviews of a pupil's SEN Statement and child care plan in order to ensure an integrated approach to their needs.

The Disability Discrimination Act (Department of Trade and Industry 1995) introduced new measures aimed at ending the discrimination experienced by many disabled people. Circular 20/99 (Department for Education and Employment 1999d) entitled *What the Disability Discrimination Act Means for Schools and LEAs* informs schools and LEAs about their new duties. These are in three main areas: employing staff, providing non-educational services to the public (e.g. hiring school rooms) and publishing information about arrangements for disabled pupils. In this last area, governing bodies' annual reports to parents must explain their admission arrangements for disabled pupils, how the access of these pupils will be enabled and what will be done to make sure that they are treated fairly. The guidance points out that failure by the school to comply with their published policy in any individual case could be a central issue in a parental appeal under local admissions appeal arrangements or in an appeal to the SEN Tribunal.

Conclusions

In this chapter we have drawn a central distinction between the SEN of individual children and the special needs that may be experienced by particular groups of children whose circumstances or background differ from the majority of the school population. Changes over time in the conceptualization of SEN were tracked and approaches that focus on individual differences and on environmental demands were compared. The advantages of an interactional analysis that brings both of these approaches together was described.

The value of an interactional analysis of special needs also was discussed and approaches were identified that can be taken by schools to empower groups of students who have special needs. While maintaining the distinction between the terms 'SEN' and 'special needs', relationships that have been found to exist between them were described and possible reasons for these relationships explored. Finally, current legislation and guidance on identifying children's educational and other needs and on making appropriate provision for them was summarized.

Chapter 3

Inclusion

Objectives

When you have studied this chapter you should be able to:

1 Outline the range of educational provision which is described by different authors as 'inclusive' and identify common elements.
2 Discuss the main findings of the research which has been conducted in inclusive education.
3 Identify similarities and differences between the ways in which education for students with SEN and those learning EAL have developed.
4 Describe ways in which inclusion can be promoted and supported.

Contents

What is inclusion?

Segregation, integration and inclusion

'Inclusion' is often defined as a journey or movement away from the kind of segregation described by Bennett *et al.* (1998: 155):

> I arrived at the school at 8.45am. It seemed like a typical suburban primary school. The grounds and school building were well-kept. There was the usual scene of children playing in the yard and arriving at school. The principal had asked me to come to the school before the first class period so that he could introduce me to John's teacher and show me his classroom. He escorted me to a prefabricated building, physically separate from the rest of the school. It was the special class for ten children with mild mental handicap.

Traditionally, if children have particular difficulties in school they have been put together with other children whose needs are similar. It is argued that this allows special facilities and specially trained staff to be made available to children who need them. This solution has been applied not only to those with SEN needs but also to those learning EAL.

Putting together groups of children who are thought to have similar needs results in them being segregated from other pupils of their age. This can be stigmatizing; it can also restrict access to important educational opportunities. For example, pupils in a special unit in a mainstream secondary school that was studied by Sinclair Taylor (1995: 267) were in no doubt about their image in the school: 'They [mainstream] call us unit kids and provoke us and say we are spastics' (unit pupil, aged 16); 'Main school kids tease you, they see the unit as a place for mental people – less better than themselves' (unit pupil, aged 12).

The issue of restricted educational opportunities was highlighted when the Commission for Racial Equality (CRE) condemned the segregated arrangements that Calderdale Borough Council made for children who failed an English language screening test that was given to those applying for admission to local schools (CRE 1986). The formal investigation found that there was 'indirectly discriminatory practice contrary to the Race Relations Act 1976' (CRE 1986: 5). The investigators noted that 'children in both language centres have no access to a normal school environment' (CRE 1986: 9) and that even in school-based language units 'the range of subjects . . . was narrower than that covered by the mainstream classes . . . [they] had no practical classes, no music, no foreign languages and no specific periods for religious education' (CRE 1986: 12). Such concerns have been important in fuelling a movement away from segregated provision.

The metaphor of a journey is explicitly explored by Clark *et al.* (1999) in their analysis of the attempts of four comprehensive schools to develop in a more inclusive way. Other authors similarly focus on inclusion as a process of change. Reynolds (1989) suggests that inclusion is best regarded as a progressive trend for taking increasing responsibility for educating groups previously excluded from mainstream society. He sees social values about race, ethnicity, language or disability as key influences on exclusion. From this perspective the current debates that will be reviewed in this chapter are set within a historical context where moves in the 1950s to racially integrate schools in the USA had an important influence (Liu 1995). This is also made explicit by Booth *et al.* (2000: 14) writing in a British context: 'Racism, sexism, classism, homophobia, disablism, and bullying all share a common root in an intolerance to difference and the abuse of power to create and perpetuate inequalities. Making schools more inclusive may involve staff in a painful process of challenging their own discriminatory practices and attitudes'. This chapter will focus on inclusion in provision for pupils with SEN and provision for pupils who are learning EAL.

Parallels between provision for SEN and EAL

There are many parallels between systems of special education and systems for the education of pupils with EAL in terms of history, needs and purposes. Ortiz (1984) identified the following similarities between special and bilingual education in the USA:

- each has a population with unique specific characteristics;
- each has specially designed procedures for identification, assessment and placement;
- each has administrators, teachers and support staff with specialized training;
- each has unique teaching materials, techniques and methods;
- each has a separate earmarked budget;
- in each case significant levels of prejudice and bias have been directed against programme participants.

Not all these points would be universally accepted. In Chapter 2 we saw that there is a debate about the extent to which pupils with SEN can be conceptualized as a distinct group. Many would argue that SEN are most usefully thought of as a set of continua, with pupils showing different profiles of strengths and needs or, more radically, with schools showing different patterns of strengths and weaknesses in responding to the full diversity of educational needs in their local communities. The view that education for pupils with SEN utilizes unique teaching materials, techniques and methods has also been challenged, for example by Lewis and Norwich (2000), who failed to find evidence for distinctive SEN teaching strategies. They concluded that it was probably more useful to think about a continuum of adaptations to generally effective teaching approaches that were successful for all learners.

In recent years questions have been raised about the necessity and desirability of systems of special education and language support which are segregated from mainstream schooling. In particular it has been suggested that this segregation may be instrumental in contributing to prejudice and bias, in school and later in society. This is embodied in the Salamanca World Statement issued by the United Nations Educational, Scientific and Cultural Organization (UNESCO) (1994: 11) on principles, policy and practice in SEN: 'Inclusion and participation are essential to human dignity and to the enjoyment and exercise of human rights. Within the field of education this is reflected in the development of strategies that seek to bring about a genuine equalisation of opportunity'. The statement was signed by the representatives of 92 governments, including the British government, and 25 international organizations. It calls on governments 'to adopt the principle of inclusive education, enrolling all children in regular schools unless there are compelling reasons for doing otherwise' (UNESCO 1994: 44).

The Department for Education in London has expressed support for this principle. At the same time it has been made clear that the needs of individual children are considered to be paramount. Where individual needs cannot currently be met in mainstream schools, the government has made a commitment to maintaining specialist provision as an integral part of overall provision. However, alongside this, the stated aim is, wherever possible, to return children to the mainstream and to increase the skills and resources in mainstream schools. This shift in emphasis from an exclusive focus on the needs of individual pupils to an approach which focuses centrally on the skills and resources available in mainstream schools is an important difference between the earlier concept of 'integration' and the more recent concept of 'inclusion'.

The difference between integration and inclusion

Ainscow (1995) suggests that integration is about making a limited number of additional arrangements for individual pupils with SEN in schools which themselves change little overall. On the other hand, inclusion implies the introduction of a more radical set of changes through which schools restructure themselves so as to be able to embrace all children. Integration involves the school in a process of assimilation where the onus is on the assimilating individual (whether a pupil with SEN or a pupil with a different cultural and linguistic background) to make changes so that they can 'fit in'. By contrast inclusion involves the school in a process of accommodation where the onus is on the school to change, adapting curricula, methods, materials and procedures so that it becomes more responsive. Given an inclusive philosophy, those with SEN can be the stimulus to development of a much richer mainstream learning experience for all.

Despite this conceptual distinction between integration and inclusion, Thomas *et al.* (1998) point out that the terms are often used as synonyms. Where one term is used rather than the other, this may have more to do with the date of publication of the book or article in question than with the educational provision that is being described. Different authors are working to different definitions and the term 'inclusive education' does not currently appear in legislation in the USA or the UK.

Definitions of inclusive education

In their study of full inclusion models in five US states, Baker and Zigmond (1995) found that while the term 'inclusion' had different meanings for different people, what was common was the view of inclusion as a 'place' – a seat in an age appropriate mainstream classroom, where a child could have access to and participate fully in the curriculum. It also meant bringing the special needs teacher or assistant into that place to help make it work. In a national study conducted in 1995, the US National Centre on Educational Restructuring and Inclusion defined inclusion as:

> the provision of services to students with disabilities, including those with severe impairments, in the neighbourhood school in age-appropriate general education classes, with the necessary support services and supplementary aids (for the child and the teacher) both to ensure the child's success – academic, behavioural and social – and to prepare the child to participate as a full and contributing member of the society.
>
> (Lipsky and Gartner 1996: 763)

Sebba and Sachdev (1997: 9) writing in a British context likewise offer a working definition which is prescriptive in suggesting what is needed rather than being descriptive of current practice:

> Inclusive education describes the process by which a school attempts to respond to all pupils as individuals by reconsidering and restructuring its curricular organisation and provision and allocating resources to enhance equality of opportunity. Through this process the school builds its capacity to accept all pupils from the local community who wish to attend and, in so doing, reduces the need to exclude pupils.

The Index for Inclusion, which has been distributed to British schools, also emphasizes a process view of inclusion:

> in our view, inclusion is a set of never ending processes. It involves the specification of the direction of change. It is relevant to any school however inclusive or exclusive its current cultures, policies and practices. It requires schools to engage in a critical examination of what can be done to increase the learning and participation of the diversity of students within the school and its locality.
>
> (Booth et al. 2000: 12)

Within the Index for Inclusion the term 'barriers to learning and participation' is used instead of 'SEN'. This is intended to focus attention upon an interactional model of learning difficulties, and upon the role of the school in identifying barriers and minimizing them through provision of appropriate support.

Special educational provision

A historical perspective

In the mid-1800s the first special schools in Britain were set up. At that time only the children of the upper and middle classes received education. The special schools were intended to provide for children with severe hearing or visual

Thomas *et al.* (1998) argue that the market orientated education polices introduced by government in recent years (e.g. the publication of league tables of exam results) have made many schools wary of accepting children whose low attainment or disruptive effect on others' learning may depress examination or SAT scores. They also suggest that the significant increase in exclusions which has been recorded in recent years (Ofsted 1996a) has been strongly influenced by these new pressures on schools.

(a) To what extent can you see parallels between the factors reported to be influencing inclusion and exclusion in British schools in the late nineteenth century and those which seem to be operating today?

(b) Are there other important influences that affect inclusion today but do not seem to have been operating then?

difficulties who could not learn using the methods and materials available in ordinary schools. As more and more children were brought within the education system in the late nineteenth century, the schools of the day were faced with a wide range of learning and behaviour to which they were not accustomed and which they could not easily accommodate. Increasing numbers of children were excluded. Indeed there was no incentive to try to include them, rather the reverse. Each year examinations in the 'three Rs' (reading, writing and arithmetic) were conducted by Her Majesty's Inspectors and the performance of each child was combined to determine the bulk of government grant to the school for the following year. Payment by results meant that part of each teacher's salary depended on the rate of exam passes in their classes (Sutherland 1981). The rejection by mainstream schools of slow learning and emotionally disturbed children who were entitled to education under the 1870 Education Act led to the expansion of the special school sector (Department of Education and Science 1978). It has been argued that similar factors again influenced the inclusiveness of educational provision a century later.

The expansion of the special school sector in the early years of the twentieth century was entirely consistent with the concept of 'handicap' prevalent at the time. Handicap was understood in terms of defect, and physical and sensory impairments were thought to impose limitations on cognitive development. Handicapped children were seen as different in kind from other children, so it made sense to develop a different education system for them. Indeed it was argued that separate provision should be made in the interests of the children concerned. This view is seen in Cyril Burt's (1917: 38–9) 'tentative suggestions' for special classes for children with learning difficulties:

The ideal arrangement, therefore, would be a series of classes parallel to the customary series, where promotion was slower or the increase of difficulty less. Since backwardness affects scholastic and abstract work more than practical or concrete, the curriculum should include a large proportion of concrete and manual work; and the teaching methods should be similarly adapted . . . The classes should be small in number, not only because these children need more individual attention in their work, but also because each class needs close observation and enquiry. Conditions should be systematically analysed; progress systematically tested; and accurate records kept of both in terms of objective facts rather than personal impressions . . . Too often when discovered the backward child is merely ignored, or else passed on to another school or class where he is accepted, and his condition has once more to be slowly rediscovered. The feeling that he is not wanted, not understood, not like other children, in short, subnormal and a nuisance, damages the child far more than the subnormality itself.

This concept, of different kinds of education for different types of children, also underpinned the division of the mainstream population at 11 years of age into 'academic', 'technical' and 'manual' which was introduced in most parts of the UK following the Norwood Report (Board of Education 1943) and the Education Act (1944).

Prior to the 1960s in many other countries also the 'handicapped' were considered to be quite distinct from the rest of the population. Ordinary schooling was just not considered to be an option for them. For example, in Britain children with severe learning difficulties – then called 'educationally subnormal (severe)' – were not considered capable of benefiting from education (Hegarty 1993). They did not attend schools run by LEAs. Instead they were provided with 'training centres' run by local authority health departments.

Moves from segregation to integration

Moves to reverse the separation of 'handicapped' children gathered momentum from the mid-1960s. There was a change in the conceptualization of disability as the result of a broader rights movement in society towards 'normalization'. In this view people with disabilities should have access to the same opportunities and options as other members of society. At the same time, concerns were raised by researchers such as Dunn (1968) about the lack of evidence to suggest that disabled children who were educated in special schools did any better than those who were being educated in mainstream schools by default, due to lack of provision. It was argued that mainstreaming or integration of children with SEN into mainstream schools would facilitate their access to and participation in society, both as children and adults, and that continued segregation could no longer be justified, from either a 'research' or a 'rights' perspective. The relationship between rights and research is considered in more detail on page 73.

In Britain the Education (Handicapped Children) Act 1970 removed the legal distinction between those who were and were not educable in school. When this legislation was enacted all children, including those with severe learning difficulties (SLD), were entitled to education for the first time. The educational experience of children with severe and profound learning difficulties was rapidly transformed. Two key factors seem to have been a rapid growth in the skills of teachers in this field (Mittler 1986) and a strong commitment to curriculum development in the new special schools (Coupe 1986).

In the USA, similarly, PL94–142: Education of All Handicapped Act of 1975 established the principle of 'zero reject' or entitlement for all in public education. Normalization focused on commonalties between children with disabilities and other children, rather than differences. It was consequently argued that 'the aims of education for children and young people with disabilities are the same as those for all children and young people . . . Disabilities and significant difficulties do not diminish the right to and equal access to and participation in society' (Inner London Education Authority 1985: 4).

Mittler (1985) drew attention to the way in which the integration movement started as a rallying cry for those with a vision of change in education and within ten years it had become the 'new orthodoxy'. The Warnock Committee (Department of Education and Science 1978: 99) identified it as 'the central contemporary issue in special education'. The OECD (1981: 5) considered it 'the dominant policy relating to the organisation of schooling for handicapped children in most of the member countries'. A survey by UNESCO (1988) reported that in 75 per cent of the 58 countries responding, integration was a declared policy.

In the USA the critical concept with regard to placement was the 'least restrictive environment'. Martin (1997) argues that this relative concept referred to the educational setting that would best facilitate the educational development of a particular individual child. In order to ensure access for individuals to the least restrictive environment it was often considered important to ensure that a continuum of services was available. Figure 3.1 illustrates the importance that has been accorded to a continuum of special education provision both in the UK and the USA. On the other hand it has also been argued that all students with disabilities should be taught completely within mainstream classrooms through full inclusion (Lipsky and Gartner 1996). This later interpretation was reinforced by the Regular Education Initiative (REI) which was introduced in the USA by the Reagan administration in 1986 and called for mainstream schools to be more responsible for the education of children with SEN. Proponents drew attention to the stigma attached to withdrawal programmes and the fragmentation of the learning experiences offered to children receiving withdrawal, especially where communication and cooperation between mainstream and special needs teachers was limited.

Opponents of the REI (Kauffman 1989) criticized its proponents for naïvety in two respects. They first of all argued that a mainstream classroom might not be the least restrictive environment for all children, and that the objective of providing appropriate education should take precedence over that relating to the setting in which it is provided. Second they demonstrated that the REI could be perceived as being underpinned by a quite different set of values to those espoused by its proponents. Hence Kauffman (p. 273) argues that 'the belief systems represented by the REI are a peculiar case in which conservative ideology (e.g. focus on excellence, federal disengagement) and liberal rhetoric (e.g. non-labelling, integration) are combined to support the diminution or dissolution of a support system for handicapped students'. Goetz and Sailor's (1990: 335) paraphrase, 'REI is a

Figure 3.1
Special education:
a continuum of
provision?
Source: Mastropieri
and Scruggs (1997)
(left column).
Department of
Education and
Science (1978,
para. 6.11)
(right column).

Sample Continuum of Services Level 1: General education classroom Level 2: General education classroom with consultative services Level 3: General education classroom with supplementary instruction and services Level 4: General education classroom with resource room services Level 5: Full-time special education classroom Level 6: Special school Level 7: Special facilities, non-public school	(i) Full-time education in an ordinary class with any necessary help and support (ii) Education in an ordinary class with periods of withdrawal to a special class or unit or other supporting base (iii) Education in a special class or unit with periods of attendance at an ordinary class and full involvement in the general community life and extracurricular activities of the ordinary school (iv) Full-time education in a special class or unit with social contact with the main school (v) Education in a special school, day or residential, with some shared lessons with a neighboring ordinary school (vi) Full-time education in a day special school with social contact with an ordinary school (vii) Full-time education in residential special school with social contact with an ordinary school (viii) Short-term education in hospitals or other establishments (ix) Long-term education in hospitals or other establishments (x) Home tuition

Reagan–Bush plot to cut the costs of special education' was echoed in UK debates on integration and in-class support strategies (Dyson 1991). Kauffman characterizes proponents and opponents of the REI as espousing an opposing set of assumptions or beliefs, as shown in Figure 3.2.

Inclusion within a continuum of provision

Notwithstanding the different assumptions underlying inclusive provision on the one hand and special educational provision on the other, in Britain the commitment to a continuum of special educational provision has remained a consistent feature over the past 20 years. The Warnock Committee (Department of Education and Science 1978) described the continuum from non-segregation to segregation outlined in Figure 3.1. The Committee also distinguished between locational, social and functional integration. These are defined as follows:

- *Locational integration* refers to physical location and exists where special classes are located in mainstream schools or a special school is located on the site of a mainstream school.

Proponents hold that:	**While opponents believe that:**
• Pupils are more alike than different. The same basic principles apply to the learning of all, so no *special* teaching is needed by any.	• Some pupils are very different from most and special educational approaches are required to meet their needs.
• Good teachers can teach all pupils, using the same basic techniques but making some adjustments for individual differences.	• Not all teachers are equipped to teach all pupils; special expertise is required to teach pupils with special needs who are particularly difficult to teach.
• All pupils can be provided with a high quality education without identifying some as different and targeting funding separately.	• Pupils with special needs must be clearly identified to ensure that they receive appropriate services.
• All pupils can be taught and managed in the mainstream classroom. Segregation of pupils with special needs in any way is ethically unacceptable.	• Education outside the mainstream is sometimes required for part of the school day to: (a) provide more intensive individualized instruction; (b) provide instruction in skills already mastered or not needed by most pupils; (c) ensure the appropriate education of the other pupils.

- *Social integration* refers to social interchange between children with special needs and others and includes eating, playing and engaging in out-of-classroom activities together.
- *Functional integration* refers to joint participation in educational programmes which have been carefully planned to ensure that all the children benefit.

The Warnock Committee shifted the focus from separate or alternative provision to provision that was additional or supplementary to that normally available in mainstream schools. Since the implementation of the 1981 Education Act in April 1983 there has been a trend towards the greater use of mainstream placement. From their questionnaire survey Goacher *et al.* (1988) found that 76 per cent of LEAs reported an increase in the proportion of primary and secondary aged children with SEN receiving education in mainstream schools. The Audit Commission (1998) found that the proportion of pupils with SEN Statements nationally who were being educated in mainstream schools had risen since 1992 from 40 to 55 per cent.

Considerable variation between LEAs is reported and a national review of inclusive education in the UK carried out by Sebba and Sachdev (1997) was able to identify only one LEA in England that had adopted a comprehensive policy of inclusive education. Newham LEA state as their ultimate goal that every child, whatever their SEN, should be able to attend their neighbourhood school, have full access to the National Curriculum, be able to participate in every aspect of mainstream school life and attain their full potential. However, at present even in Newham many pupils with special needs are placed in one of a number of 'resourced' mainstream schools, rather than in their neighbourhood schools. Jordon and Goodey (1996: 6) describe the establishment of resourced schools as 'very much a compromise in response to parents' concerns about local schools not having developed sufficient experience and confidence to meet needs'.

Inclusion and the reform of mainstream education

Dyson (1991) has criticized the conception of the mainstream curriculum which underpins the Warnock Committee's thinking in that it assumes that certain children will fail without additional resourcing (which in turn is defined as that needed in order to prevent failure). He argues that this might be applicable to some children with sensory or physical difficulties, where they can be given clearly identifiable resources such as technological aids or large print worksheets to enable them to succeed in a unreconstructed curriculum. However for the large majority of children with SEN there is a need to look at the curriculum and the way in which it is delivered, and to make substantial revisions.

The Green Paper, *Excellence for all Children: Meeting Special Educational Needs* (Department for Education and Employment 1997) does attend to the need for mainstream school reform, while remaining committed to the concept of a continuum of SEN provision:

> We want to develop an education system in which special provision is seen as an integral part of overall provision, aiming wherever possible to return children to the mainstream and to increase the skills and resources available in mainstream schools. We want therefore to strengthen links between special and mainstream schools, and to ensure that LEA support services are used to support mainstream placements.
>
> (Department for Education and Employment 1997: 44)

It also encourages school adaptation in order to maximize functional, rather than social or locational, integration:

> We believe that – taking account of any normal arrangements for setting – children with SEN should generally take part in mainstream lessons rather than being isolated in separate units. But separate provision may be necessary on occasion for special purposes, and inclusion must encompass teaching and curriculum appropriate to the child's needs. Many schools will need to review and adapt their approaches in order to achieve greater inclusion.
>
> (Department for Education and Employment 1997: 44)

In the UK, current government targets encourage further development of in-clusive provision, while stopping well short of a commitment to full inclusion. Reviewing the situation in the USA Gerber (1995: 182) points to 'a discrepancy between inclusion rhetoric and reality' and suggests that the tide of inclusion may already have begun to ebb. He adds, 'If this is true, special educators will be left with what has always been the harder job – getting schools to progressively expand opportunities for students with disabilities, designing ways for these students to learn in ever more integrated settings without sacrificing the kind of intensive or extensive instruction that they require' (1995: 182). This concern with the instruction required by individual children mirrors the British government's primary focus on the educational needs of the child. The view that inclusion represents an unquestionable moral imperative has been challenged by those who argue that the rights of the child to have maximum access to mainstream education need to be balanced by their right to an effective education, appropriate to their needs. Whereas questions about inclusion as social policy tend to have been debated in terms of values and rights issues, questions about the effectiveness of education tend to have been addressed by research and evaluation studies. This has led to some argument at cross purposes, but also to the identification of some interesting issues concerning the relationship between rights and research, which will be outlined before the literature on integration and inclusion is reviewed.

Rights and research

Proponents of inclusion have concentrated on the human rights of children with SEN when arguing their case and have emphasized the social benefits they expect the children to experience (Stobart 1986; Roberts and Zubrick 1992). However, the social status and acceptance of mainstreamed children with learning difficulties in different national school systems has consistently been found by research studies to be low (Kaufman et al. 1985; Taylor et al. 1987 USA Roberts and Zubrick 1992 – Australia – Nabuzoka and Smith 1993 – UK). Stobart (1986) asked, 'is integrating the handicapped psychologically defensible?' Booth (1986: 141) in a rejoinder to Stobart draws the following distinction: 'The rationale for policies depends on an interplay of moral/political and scientific reasoning. Broadly speaking decisions about whether to advocate a policy depend primarily on moral or political reasons and knowledge about how to achieve a desired policy change may involve detailed factual considerations'. McLeskey et al. (1990: 322) argue along similar lines: 'Data can be used to evaluate progress towards the goals established by values, but data cannot alter the value itself'.

There appears to be some agreement at least for the importance of research in monitoring the outcomes of integration. Thomas et al. (1998: 5–6) point out that even if principles cannot be evaluated for their veracity, nor ethics for their truth, 'it is crucial that the principled policy decisions to provide inclusive education are rigorously monitored, especially as recent evidence concerning the academic, social and emotional benefits of integrative programmes are nowhere near as clear-cut as earlier evidence promised'. Martin (1995) describes his worst fear about inclusion as being that the value of programmes would be judged primarily by teacher and administrator 'feelings', with, in some cases, parent feelings being taken into account. He argues for the importance of careful systematic measurement of child achievement, progress in areas of difficulty, self-concept and socialization, and criticizes the omission in many initiatives of any formal, comprehensive evaluation plan to measure outcomes.

Concerns about outcomes may be challenged by those who argue that inclusive education is of value in itself. However there are other values which are espoused concurrently with a commitment to maximizing inclusion which may sometimes be in conflict. Hegarty (1987: 9) argued that 'What pupils who have difficulties need is education, not integration. Placing them in an ordinary school is not an end in itself but a means toward the end of securing them an appropriate education'. This would appear also to be the view of the British government: 'The needs of individual children are paramount. Where these cannot currently be met in mainstream schools, specialist provision should be available' (Department for Education and Employment 1997: 44). So the right of children to an 'appropriate' education appears to be being prioritized over their right to be educated in an inclusive school context. In addition, 'Parents will continue to have the right to express a preference for a special school where they consider this appropriate to their child's needs' (1997: 45).

The Education Act (1996) explicitly requires that these rights and others should be given consideration. Section 316 sets out the conditions for educating children with SEN in mainstream, stating that this should not be incompatible with:

- parental wishes;
- the children receiving the special educational provision which their learning difficulties call for;
- the provision of efficient education for the children with whom the children with SEN will be educated;
- the efficient use of resources.

The *Special Educational Needs and Disability Act* (Department for Education and Employment 2001) strengthened the endorsement of inclusion by revising Section 316 of the Education Act. The second bullet point is removed, so mainstream schools will no longer be able to refuse a place to a child with SEN on the basis that the school cannot meet the pupil's needs. In addition the section was rephrased positively:

> If a statement is maintained under Section 324 for the child, he must be educated in a mainstream school unless it is incompatible with:
> a. the wishes of his parent, or
> b. the provision of efficient education for other children.
> (Department for Education and Employment 2000: 1–2)

Gerber (1995: 189) considers that the place of special education in the USA 'in the social policy market-place . . . reflects a history of social regard for individuals with disabilities, regard that seems to ebb and flow with eerie cyclicality in a sea of changing and changeable values and priorities'. It would seem overly simplistic to suggest that there is a clear moral imperative for inclusion, irrespective

Table 3.2   Effects of inclusive placement

Author(s)	Carlberg and Kavale	Wang and Baker	Baker
Year published	1980	1985–6	1994
Time period	Pre-1980	1975–84	1983–92
Number of studies	50	11	13
Academic effect size	0.15	0.44	0.08
Social effect size	0.11	0.11	0.28

Source: Baker *et al.* (1994–5).

The efficient education of mainstream pupils

In the UK the law requires that the inclusion of pupils with SEN also take account of the need to provide efficient education for the mainstream pupils involved and to ensure that resources are used efficiently. With regard to the first of these requirements, Staub and Peck (1994) reviewed a number of studies in the USA that had examined the outcomes for mainstream students in classrooms where students with SLD were included. While it is acknowledged that the research base in this area is quite limited, none of the studies found any deceleration of academic progress for the mainstream students. The review also considered available research related to the concerns sometimes expressed, in particular by parents of mainstream pupils, that inclusion may lead to mainstream pupils losing out on teacher time and attention and that mainstream children will imitate or learn inappropriate behaviours from pupils who have SEN. Staub and Peck reported that in the small number of additionally resourced contexts that had been studied, teacher time spent attending to mainstream pupils was not found to be affected by the presence of students with severe disabilities and mainstream children did not pick up undesirable behaviour.

Manset and Semmel (1997) reviewed the learning outcomes achieved in a number of different well designed and evaluated inclusion programmes. Variable results were reported for the progress made by included pupils with MLD compared to pupils with similar difficulties who were educated in separate special education programmes. In two of the programmes the included pupils made significantly better progress in literacy, but similar progress in maths. In two of the programmes better progress was made in maths, but similar progress in literacy. In one programme better progress was made in both literacy and maths. In one programme similar progress was made in both literacy and maths and in one programme similar progress was made in literacy, but poorer progress in maths. However, all seven of the studies that compared the progress of pupils without SEN in inclusive classrooms found greater improvements compared to matched classes in the same school district where inclusion was not occurring. While reminding their readers of the methodological problems affecting these studies, Manset and Semmel (1997: 177) concluded: 'This suggests that the efforts to transform the mainstream into an effective environment for students with disabilities may also have a positive impact on normally achieving students, at least on measures of basic skills'.

The efficient use of resources

Turning to available research on the issue of the efficient use of resources, Affleck *et al.* (1988) in the USA demonstrated that an integrated classroom for special needs students was more cost-effective than a resource programme, while achievement in reading, maths and language was very similar in the two programmes. Crowther *et al.* (1998) examined costs and outcomes for pupils with MLD in 33 special and mainstream schools across eight LEAs in the UK. They compared pupils with MLD in different bands of need, from A (low) to D (high) and found that special school costs were consistently higher than costs in mainstream for pupils with similar levels of need. However, they encountered major problems in relating these costs to pupil outcomes because of the paucity of available data on outcomes: 'Despite a good deal of consensus around desirable outcomes, little evidence was found to indicate that either schools or LEAs had set up systematic procedures for monitoring outcomes from different types of provision' (Crowther *et al.* 1998: 3). Similarly, Hunt and Goetz (1997) highlight the importance both of carrying out a comprehensive analysis of costs, including for example transport costs, and of considering costs in relation to the outcomes for pupils with SEN. Simmons (2000: 264) reports a ruling made in a high court appeal against the outcome of the SEN Tribunal where decisions by LEAs and the Tribunal about the efficient use of resources in making a mainstream placement were to follow a two-stage process: 'first calculate the additional expenditure involved, then, second, consider the additional benefit that this additional expenditure might bring'.

It is important to acknowledge that there is likely to be a financial disincentive for LEAs to reintegrate pupils as, in the short term, they have to fund the empty special school place as well as the mainstream school place (Audit Commission 1992). Lipsky and Gartner (1996) report the following guidance from the US Department of Education for states attempting to revise their special education funding formulas to promote inclusion:

- fiscal incentives favouring restrictive and separate placements should be removed;
- states must make decisions about the extent to which they wish to encourage private special education placements;
- funding systems should be developed in which funds follow students as they move to less restrictive placements;
- states could enhance funding for local training;
- states could fund and encourage the use of appropriate interventions for all students.

Within a number of LEAs in the UK consideration has also been given to ways in which funding mechanisms for mainstream schools can be used to encourage the acceptance of responsibility for educating a wider diversity of pupils (Gray and Dessent 1993; Moore 1999). Moore suggests that a method of funding is required that reduces the current 'perverse incentive' where mainstream schools can be thought of as being rewarded with additional resources for demonstrating persistent lack of pupil achievement. Moore argues (1999: 177) that a method of funding is required that:

- replaces the perverse incentive with recognition of positive outcomes;
- reduces the tendency to label pupils;
- reduces the number of pupils 'registered' and therefore the level of bureaucracy;
- reduces reliance on statutory assessment;
- supports pupils more adequately at Stage 3 of the *Code of Practice*; and
- promotes responsibility at school/cluster level.

With regard to the first of Moore's points, the new emphasis in the revised *Code of Practice* (Department for Education and Skills 2001) on the crucial role of progress monitoring in SEN decision making offers a way forward. The 'perverse incentives' currently operating in this area mean that schools are often caught on the horns of a dilemma. Consider a young child who is making very slow progress but whose skill levels are not quite low enough to meet the current static LEA criteria for a formal assessment. What is the school to do? Should they allocate a maximal level of resource to support the child from the special needs funding devolved to them? This is not a straightforward decision if staff believe that allocating a high level of resource now will only delay the time at which the child's skill levels will meet the LEA criteria and gain them access to an even higher level of resource, more appropriate to their needs.

From the LEA point of view also the present approach lacks a certain logic, particularly where the outcome of the formal assessment process is that the child remains in their present mainstream school with a Statement. Essentially, this school has had to demonstrate that despite their best endeavours, the skills of their staff, the deployment of their devolved special needs budget and the advice of outside specialists, they have consistently failed to teach the child effectively. One wonders what grounds the LEA might have for believing that this unsatisfactory situation is likely to be remedied by the allocation of a further couple of thousand pounds to the school, particularly as such funds are typically used to purchase the time of an unqualified learning support assistant.

A focus on the rate of progress being made allows a more positive and coherent approach to be adopted. By using fine-grained, but time-efficient progress monitoring techniques, such as precision teaching (see Chapter 7) schools can provide evidence on the rate of progress made by a pupil given different teaching approaches and levels of resource. Over a period of two terms it would be possible to establish for most pupils what teaching arrangements and resources are needed in order for them to achieve particular rates of progress. The need for a Statement would be established where it has been demonstrated that the level of resource needed to achieve an adequate level of progress exceeds that which could be sustained in the longer term given the resources devolved to schools and where progress otherwise will continue to be inadequate and will ultimately trigger existing static criteria for formal assessment.

There is need for further work in a number of areas. For example, 'adequate progress' will need to be further defined as the revised *Code of Practice* is implemented. In other respects well-established processes already exist – for example for training teachers and support assistants in precision teaching techniques and for extra-polating from progress graphs generated by these techniques. However, this new focus on progress offers the possibility of creating a system where incentives are linked to success rather than failure, and where early intervention is facilitated rather than discouraged.

Factors in successful inclusion

Contemporary summaries of comparative research on inclusion parallel the conclusions drawn by Madden and Slavin (1983) and reported above, suggesting little advance over the period. Salend and Garrick Duhaney (1999: 123) highlighted similar methodological limitations to those identified in previous research and likewise urged caution in the interpretation of findings. They concluded that:

> the impact of inclusion programs on the academic and social performance of students with disabilities is varied. Whereas some studies suggest that inclusion more often results in positive academic and social outcomes for students with disabilities, other studies indicate that some students with disabilities benefit academically when they receive their educational programs through traditional SE [special education] service delivery models. Although several factors may contribute to this inconclusive finding, important variables seem to be the quality of the inclusion program and the extent to which the GE [general education] system accommodates the academic and social needs of students with disabilities in inclusion programs.

With the consistent conclusion that the quality of the inclusive programme seems crucial, the emphasis in research has shifted to identifying the characteristics of effective inclusion. In recent years a range of different studies, conducted in different countries and using different methodologies, have reported conclusions which show substantial overlap (see Table 3.3).

Ainscow (1995) drew on findings from the UNESCO Teacher Education Project 'Special Needs in the Classroom' in identifying conditions necessary within a school if it is to restructure so as to provide effective education for all. McLaughlin (1995) identified five areas necessary for building a flexible and unified restructured school system from interviews with educational administrators and teachers in 67 school districts in the USA that were actively engaged in educational restructuring. McLaughlin (1995) highlighted in addition the importance of flexibility in teaching and student grouping and pointed out that nothing in the vision of a unified school system precludes students from having individualized instruction at some times.

Table 3.3 Factors in successful inclusion

Identifying author(s)	Factors
Ainscow (1995: 152)	• Effective leadership, not only by the headteacher, but spread throughout the school. • Involvement of staff, students and community in school policies and decisions. • A commitment to collaborative planning. • Coordination strategies. • Attention to the potential benefits of enquiry and reflection. • A policy for staff development.
McLaughlin (1995: 206)	• Clear vision. • A set of learner outcomes that can be used for school-wide accountability. • Governance structures that promote collaboration and school level flexibility. • A curriculum that promotes high expectations for all students. • Professional development that builds collaborative work structures, joint problem solving and the sharing of expertise.
Lipsky and Gartner (1996: 780)	• Visionary leadership. • Collaboration: building planning teams and scheduling time for teachers to work together. • Refocused use of assessment – developing methods that allow all students to express their learning. • Support for staff and students. • Funding models where the funds follow the students. • Effective parental involvement. • Curricula adaptation and adopting of effective instructional practice.
Scruggs and Mastropieri (1994: 794–803)	• Administrative support. • Support from special education personnel. • Accepting, positive classroom atmosphere. • Appropriate curriculum. • Effective general teaching skills. • Peer assistance. • Disability-specific teaching skills (e.g. for children with hearing difficulties).

Lipsky and Gartner (1996) analysed the results of the second annual study of inclusive education programmes in the USA which was carried out by the National Center on Educational Restructuring and Inclusion and described factors which appear to be necessary if inclusion is to be successful. Scruggs and Mastropieri

(1994) carried out a fine-grained analysis of factors associated with mainstreaming success in primary science lessons for students with hearing, visual and physical difficulties. Over a school year evidence was gathered from classroom observation, videotaped records, student and teacher products, curriculum materials and interviews with students, teachers and administrators.

Do inclusion programmes really provide for individual needs?

Walberg (1993) highlighted a number of practices that research has identified as enhancing the education of students with learning disabilities: instruction closely matched to student academic needs; materials and procedures that allow students to progress at their own pace; increased student responsibility for their own learning; cooperation among students in working on learning goals. Baker and Zigmond (1995) provided illustrations of some of these factors in their case study descriptions of full-time inclusion models for primary aged children with specific learning difficulties in five different states in the USA. Their accounts serve to remind us that some changes may be more readily implemented than others. They also call into question the extent to which individualization and differentiation are really provided in inclusive education programmes.

Baker and Zigmond (1995) made a two-day site visit to a centre in each of the five states. They focused on two children selected by headteachers and special needs teachers. Classroom observations were carried out and semi-structured interviews conducted with the children, their parents, class teachers, special needs support teachers, heads of special needs and headteachers. Baker and Zigmond concluded that students with SEN in the models of inclusive education surveyed were receiving a very good general education from enthusiastic class teachers. Special needs teachers were playing roles as coordinator, co-planner and co-teacher and were making it possible for class teachers to feel adequately confident about working with SEN students and for the SEN students to feel adequately confident in their mainstream classes. In all schools teachers, parents and administrators acknowledged that some SEN students needed more than the in-class team teaching being provided. The schools tended to provide special opportunities where they considered them necessary by extending the school day, engaging peers, aides or volunteers in mediation or coaching, or making minor modifications in assignments. Mostly they avoided singling out students with SEN by making these opportunities available to all students in the schools involved who might need them.

Class teachers showed willingness to make changes to help students with SEN, although these consisted of changing an approach for the whole class with the needs of the SEN student in mind. However, Baker and Zigmond (1995) report rarely seeing adaptations directed at a single student and when these did occur they tended to consist of more explicit instructions repeated specifically to the student. Indeed some teachers expressed the belief that SEN students had to learn to cope with the world and therefore required them to take the same tests and complete the same assignments as the mainstream students, proudly asserting that they did not individualize or differentiate their work in any way. Similar conclusions were reached by Pijl (1995) who carried a study that compared the education of students in a highly segregated system (Netherlands) with that in four other countries (Denmark, England, Sweden and the USA). Data was collected from existing written accounts about the availability and use of resources, and interviews were conducted with experts from the first three more inclusive countries listed. From these investigations Pijl offered the tentative conclusion that teachers working in inclusive school systems did not differentiate between students more than Dutch teachers working in a largely segregated system.

However, this has not been the conclusion of other studies. In their comparison of eight different model inclusion programmes Manset and Semmel (1997) report that the programmes that were most effective in promoting the educational progress of pupils with SEN did incorporate curricular modifications, highly structured teaching (particularly of basic skills) and frequent testing. They also provided opportunities to individualize teaching and focus intensively on particular targets through reducing class size, providing additional staff in the classroom or incorporating peer tutoring. Where inclusion programmes depart from widely recommended practice it is particularly important to evaluate the educational impact through the ongoing assessment of student progress in relation to desired goals and objectives. Williams (1993) points to a further reason for monitoring and evaluating the progress of individual students with SEN in inclusive schools – namely that positive findings from group investigations rarely reflect positive findings for every child, some of whom will not respond well to an environment which suits the majority.

Williams (1993: 316) also highlights the growing political attention in a number of countries to educational effectiveness and argues against a narrow conceptualization: 'when effectiveness is measured mainly or even solely through achievement in traditional academic subjects, and when resourcing depends on this, rather than the social objectives encapsulated in the integration of children with learning difficulties, there are dangers'.

Nonetheless, taken too far this approach would trigger Scruggs and Mastropieri's (1995: 231) concern that 'full inclusion is a policy that suggests that students are in school primarily to be in the company of age peers, and not primarily to learn'. This brings us back to the conclusion of the previous section regarding the value of research in monitoring the achievement of educational outcomes and in identifying associated process variables which aid or impede their achievement. In this section we have seen that research has contributed much in these areas, while the social policy debate on the aims of education for students with and without special needs continues.

EAL teaching

A historical perspective

Britain has always been a multilingual country, but it is only since the 1960s that serious attention has been paid within the education service to the language needs of pupils learning EAL (Reid 1988). Section 11 of the 1966 Local Government Act empowered the home secretary to pay a grant to help minority ethnic groups overcome linguistic and other barriers that inhibited their access to mainstream services. Over a period of more than 20 years this provision was the main source of funding for the teaching of EAL in schools in England and Wales. In 1999 that grant (administered by the Home Office) was replaced in England by the Ethnic Minority Achievement Grant (administered by the Department for Education and Employment). This grant was to have a broader purpose: 'to provide equality of opportunity for all minority ethnic groups'. A letter to chief education officers in November 1998 (NALDIC/NASSEA 1999: 2) highlighted the government's intention that the grant should 'meet the particular needs of pupils for whom English is an additional language, and . . . raise the standards of achievement of those minority ethnic groups who are particularly at risk of under-achieving'. A key feature of the new arrangements is that there is much greater devolution of funding to individual schools. Though not without disadvantages, this strategy has the great advantage of emphasizing that the responsibility for raising the achievements of pupils from ethnic and linguistic minorities lies firmly with individual schools and their teachers. It is too early to evaluate this initiative, but guidelines on good practice have been developed (NALDIC/NASSEA 1999) and monitoring studies are in progress (Wiles 1999).

Since the 1960s a range of approaches have been adopted in the UK to meet the language needs of children who learn EAL. Initially little provision was made, and children were left to absorb English simply by participating in the life and work of the classroom 'with perhaps a little special attention from the teacher as the opportunity presents itself'. But it was soon realized that 'this process of learning can be speeded up and rendered more effective' with more focused arrangements for language teaching for at least part of the working week (Ministry of Education 1963: 14). In some areas it was hoped that enabling new immigrant pupils to attend a specialist off-site language centre together with others who were in the same situation would give them an increased sense of security which would promote confidence and enhance language learning. At the same time, many teachers and LEAs continued to recognize the value of integration and tried to make provision within mainstream schools (Townsend 1971).

One of the many problems with the full-time withdrawal arrangements was that there was some confusion between withdrawal for language teaching and withdrawal for SEN provision. The 'return criteria to mainstream' used by the language centres were often less stringent than those used by the mainstream schools, where demands made by the school organization and the range of the academic curriculum were also considered. These different expectations were often not appreciated, and mainstream teachers were inclined to regard continuing difficulties after discharge from a language centre as evidence of 'learning difficulty'. In Activity 3.3 you will be asked to consider how far arguments put forward in support of integrated provision for children learning EAL parallel those that have been made in relation to children with SEN.

ACTIVITY 3.2 **Arguments for inclusive EAL and SEN provision: are there similarities?**

A number of the arguments that have been advanced in favour of integrated EAL provision in mainstream by Deforges and Kerr (1984) are listed below. Consider which of these are similar to arguments made in favour of including children with SEN in mainstream and which are unique to children learning English as an additional language.

(a) There is a need to offer ongoing support over a five- to seven-year period to the development of language for thinking and learning, as opposed to language for social communication (Cummins 1984). This is too long a time period to consider withdrawal from mainstream.

(b) Mainstream placement provides exposure to a richer diversity of appropriate models of language.

(c) All teachers would have EAL support clearly in their brief as part of the whole school language policy. This should assist continuity for the child and prevent responsibility for the child's learning being passed from mainstream teachers to specialist teachers.

(d) If EAL support is used in helping to modify curriculum tasks and resources it is likely to benefit many pupils, rather than the few that might be placed in language centres.

(e) The motivation to acquire language necessary for academic progress and social integration is more likely to develop in a situation which requires it and where it has immediate use.

Steadily, withdrawal arrangements involving off-site centres lost support. While different demands were made of pupils by primary and secondary schools in terms of both curriculum and organization, by 1987 less than 5 per cent of the LEAs in one survey had full-time language centres outside schools for primary pupils, as opposed to 15 per cent which still had such provision at secondary level (Bourne 1989: Table 3.1). The publication of the CRE report on Calderdale's provision, which was quoted earlier in this chapter, led to a speeding up of the trend to close such centres (Bourne 1989). By 1992–3 when HMI (Her Majesty's Inspector of Schools) surveyed educational provision funded through Section 11 (S11) they found that:

14 The most common method of support in primary and secondary schools was by S11 staff working with small groups or individual pupils within normal classroom lessons taught by mainstream teachers.

19 In some cases the withdrawal of pupils to work outside the mainstream classroom was appropriate and successful. S11 staff in primary schools sometimes taught the pupils separately, working on the main class topic or subject but with heightened attention to developing the language of bilingual learners and dealing with the specific difficulties of under-achieving pupils. This withdrawal work was usually for quite brief periods of teaching (sometimes just part of a lesson) or of limited extent, for example, half a term, and it prepared pupils well for their subsequent work in the mainstream lessons. Withdrawal work was counter-productive

when it lacked a clear purpose and was unrelated to mainstream work. In those cases the pupils missed important aspects of the curriculum and fell even further behind when they rejoined their classmates. These pupils made minimal progress in the subject, and in their understanding and use of English.

20 Induction courses in secondary schools, where pupils were withdrawn for part of the day for up to half a term, helped early bilingual learners to settle more quickly and effectively into mainstream working practices. Some schools were experimenting with other approaches to meet clearly identified, individual, short term needs. For example in one school, pupils within a year group were able to leave normal lessons, as appropriate, for additional instruction in particular subjects in a learning base staffed by a team of subject specialists, as well as by S11 and special educational needs (SEN) teachers. This approach was very effective in assessing and meeting the needs of all the pupils.

(Ofsted 1994: 4)

Thus the focus had moved from arguments about where English language provision should be made to arguments about how it could be most effective when arranged in a mainstream school. For fuller accounts of the issues that are now in debate see NALDIC (1999) on the distinctiveness of EAL as a cross-curriculum discipline, Bourne (1997) and Green (1998) on strategies for managing partnerships between EAL and class teachers, Meek (1996) and Gravelle (2000) on curriculum planning, and Blair and Bourne (1998) and Ofsted (1999a) on the broader challenges of raising the achievements of ethnic minority pupils. (For discussion of work on children's first languages, see Chapter 10.)

Sleeter and Grant (1987) in reviewing multicultural education in the USA identify five approaches which can be seen as occupying different points on a continuum of inclusion, although they are all delivered within mainstream schools:

- *Teaching the culturally different.* This approach developed during the movement in the 1960s to end racial segregation in schools in the USA. The aim is to adapt instruction so that culturally different students can fit in and succeed within the existing system.
- *The human relations approach.* Here specific activities and information are added onto the mainstream curriculum with the aim of reducing prejudice and encouraging better relations between different cultural groups.
- *The single group approach.* Students are given the opportunity to undertake in-depth study of a particular oppressed group and the curriculum is reorganized to present a perspective from the point of view of that group. Black or women's studies programmes would be examples of this approach.
- *Multicultural education.* This approach calls for reorganization of curricula, materials, instruction and staffing to reflect the perspectives and knowledge of different racial, ethnic and social groups so that all students experience success, cultural pluralism and social equity in school.

- *Education that is multicultural and socially reconstructionist.* This approach goes beyond multicultural education in incorporating a more explicitly political focus on promoting equity and cultural pluralism beyond school into society generally.

For accounts of a similar range of approaches in the UK see Gill *et al.* (1992), Gaine (1995), Todd (1991) and Tomlinson and Craft (1995).

As with the education of children who have SEN there is considerable debate about the relative priority which should be given to different educational goals in the case of children who speak a first language other than English. Such goals include their maximal inclusion in school communities, their acquisition of EAL and their academic progress. Again research can contribute in assessing outcomes and identifying factors associated with successful outcomes in relation to any or all of these educational goals.

Effective EAL methods: theory and research

Comparative studies

Comparative studies have most commonly contrasted programmes which adopt a native or heritage language emphasis and those which are characterized as sheltered English/structured immersion programmes. Heritage language programmes involve instruction in the child's first language, particularly in cognitively complex areas of the curriculum where there is heavy emphasis on language as the medium of instruction. A historical concept which has to be described would be an example, as opposed to a science concept which could be largely demonstrated. This means that children can have access to other areas of the curriculum during the early years in which they are learning English. However, heritage language programmes are criticized for restricting students' exposure to English. Structured immersion programmes, by contrast, seek to maximize exposure to English. It is assumed that the learning of English and learning about other areas of the curriculum through English can occur successfully hand in hand provided that appropriate adaptations are made and context provided – for example, through the use of concrete materials. Immersion programmes have been criticized for often lacking structure and so providing little real assistance to acquire academic competence in the language of instruction, leaving students to sink or swim, and sometimes resulting in submersion!

Gersten and Woodward (1994) report that research contrasting the effectiveness of structured immersion and heritage language programmes has produced equivocal findings. In particular many longitudinal studies reported little or no difference between the two types of provision even when a wide range of outcome measures were used. One factor which may be relevant is the range of practice which actually goes on in classrooms labelled as operating structured immersion or heritage language programmes. For example, Tikunoff's (1985) observational research found that English was used 60 per cent of the time on average, irrespective of the label which the programme had been given. For both types of programme there were large variations both between schools and teachers. This parallels the finding that in studies of integrated and segregated placements for children with SEN, integration may be minimal in some cases whereas some special class 'segregated' children may spend some time each day in mainstream classes. There is a further parallel in Gersten and Woodward's (1994) conclusion that the type of teaching model selected may be less important than the quality of instruction provided. So, while more recent, carefully conducted research has slowly led to a firmer consensus that teaching in a child's first language strengthens their performance in their second (Thomas and Collier 1997), successful EAL provision appears to be influenced by a range of factors.

Factors in successful EAL provision

In discussing the quality of instruction which should be provided, Cummins and McNeely (1987) argue for the application of the 'comprehensible input hypothesis'. This hypothesis holds that acquisition of a second language depends on exposure which is modified so that it is comprehensible. Cummins and McNeely recognize that in many cases teaching of a child's first language may not be practicable, but highlight the importance in all cases of communicating to students and parents in a variety of ways the extent to which their language and culture are valued in school. They also highlight the importance of teachers working at the collaborative end of a collaborative-exclusionary dimension. This involves actively encouraging minority parents to participate in promoting academic progress at home and through involvement in classroom activities. It also requires a willingness to work closely with teachers or other workers who speak the first language of the child or family in order to communicate effectively with parents and children. This is recognized in the revised SEN *Code of Practice* (Department for Education and Skills 2001). Schools are given guidance on annual reviews for pupils with Statements of SEN that interpreters and, if possible, a bilingual support teacher or teacher of EAL should be available to help pupils and families who have EAL contribute as fully as possible to the review process.

A number of other studies have likewise moved beyond examining the efficacy of different approaches and instead focused on factors associated with successful provision. The following are reported by Lucas *et al.* (1990: 324–5) to be features of secondary schools in the USA that promote the achievement of pupils learning EAL:

1 Value is placed on the students' languages and cultures by treating students as individuals, learning about their cultures and languages, hiring bilingual staff, and encouraging students to develop their primary-language skills.
2 High expectations of language-minority (LM) students are made concrete by providing minority role models and preparing and supporting LM students for college.

3 School leaders make the education of LM students a priority. These leaders maintain high expectations of LM students, are both knowledgeable of and involved in strengthening curriculum for LM students, represent minority groups themselves, and hire bilingual teachers.

4 Staff development is explicitly designed to help teachers and other staff serve LM students more effectively. Schools and school districts offer teachers/school staff development programmes that include effective instructional approaches for LM students, principles in second-language acquisition, and cross-cultural counselling.

5 A variety of courses and programmes for LM students are offered. The programmes include courses in English as a second language and primary language instruction. They offer advanced and basic courses taught via bilingual and sheltered methods, and establish support programmes to help LM students in the transition from ESL to mainstream classes and then to college.

6 A counselling programme gives special attention to LM students through counsellors who share students' language and cultural backgrounds, are well versed in postsecondary educational opportunities for LM students, and believe in the academic success of LM students.

7 Parents of LM students are encouraged to become involved in their children's education. Schools can provide and encourage staff who speak their parent's language, hold on-campus ESL classes for parents, and involve parents in planning their children's course schedules.

8 School staff members share a strong commitment to empower language-minority students through education. This commitment is made concrete through staff who devote extra time to LM students, including extra-curricular activities; take part in political and community activities in which they act as advocates for minorities; and request training to help LM students to become more effective.

At the classroom level the following implications for classroom practice are based on Wiles (1985) and Cummins (1984) and have been supported by subsequent commentators:

• All communication must be for a purpose – making friends, constructing a model, explaining intentions etc. Discover and use the child's interests. Ask real questions; if complete sentence answers are desired, ask questions which will naturally elicit them. Respond to content not to form.

• Allow the child listening time and in particular a silent period of three to six months before expecting them to start speaking in English. Insistence on oral responses too early may hinder learning and be experienced as threatening.

• Consciously integrate language use and development with all curricular content, rather than teaching language and other content as isolated subjects. Within each curriculum area there should be a focus on developing higher order cognitive skills, in addition to any focus on factual recall.

• The degree to which language is embedded in a meaningful context can be increased by the teacher in a number of ways. For example, natural opportunities for repetition in rhymes and stories and in regular classroom activities can be used. Real objects, extra materials/visual aids and more gestures/demonstrations by the teacher are likely to help. The pupil can be helped to prepare for a lesson, for example by being provided with diagrams beforehand which can be studied in advance to provide a framework for the lesson content.

- Other children make excellent tutors and helpers. Peer reinforcement is one of the strongest motivations for learning, so classrooms should be organized to take account of peer-group talk.
- Parents should not be advised to switch to English in the home. Work by Cummins (1984) and others suggests that this is unnecessary because higher order cognitive constructs can be developed in either language. Furthermore if parents switch to English it may possibly be damaging on account of the lower quantity and quality of interaction which they are likely to be able to provide for the child in their less preferred language.

Promoting inclusion in a multiethnic society

Issues of common concern and principles for progress

The parallel development of special education and multicultural education is summarized by Ball and Harry (1993). Both fields developed in response to exclusion. In both cases the first steps towards integration focused on the 'remediation' of difficulties so that the students concerned could better fit into the mainstream. This was followed by a focus on school reconstruction in order to create learning communities for all. This is very much the emphasis in the Index for Inclusion (Booth *et al.* 2000) which provides materials designed to be used by schools in their development planning and outlines a process which can involve school staff, governors, pupils, parents and other community members in creating inclusive cultures, producing inclusive policies and evolving inclusive practices in their school. These are designed to minimize barriers to learning and participation related either to SEN or other special needs, and the range of prompt questions contained in the Index stimulates reflection across these diverse areas as the following extract from the Index illustrates:

INDICATOR A.1.1   *Everyone is made to feel welcome*

(i)   Is the first contact that people have with the school friendly and welcoming?

(ii)   Is the school welcoming to all students, including students with impairments and transient students such as travellers?

(iii)   Is the school welcoming to all parents/carers and other members of its local communities?

(iv)   Is information about the school accessible to all, irrespective of home language or impairment (e.g. Brailled, taped, large print, when necessary)?

(v)   Are sign language and other first language interpreters available as necessary?

(vi) Is it clear from the school brochure that responding to the full diversity of students and their backgrounds is part of school routine?

(vii) Does the entrance hall reflect all members of the school community?

(viii) Does the school celebrate local cultures and communities in signs, and displays?

(Booth *et al.* 2000: 49)

Ball and Harry (1993) also highlight a number of ways in which the fields of special education and multicultural education have traditionally diverged. In multicultural education there has been a strong focus on challenging school processes that reproduce inequalities, whereas the prevalent perspective in special education regards inequality as stemming from individual differences. Alongside this conservative perspective is a radical perspective which regards special needs as social constructions which scapegoat individuals while allowing schools to avoid self-examination and reform. In between these two views is the interactionist conceptualization of SEN adopted in this book which acknowledges individual differences in need while recognizing the role of the learning environment both in creating and in ameliorating these needs. This approach draws a distinction between special needs and SEN, while acknowledging the many common principles for progress which can be identified.

The divergence between the two fields is quite apparent from the isolation between them in the literature. In Sleeter and Grant's (1987) analysis of 127 publications on multicultural education only five articles directly included disability as a concern. Similarly, Bos and Fletcher (1997) report that only two of the 26 articles published on the inclusion of students with specific learning difficulties between 1990 and 1995 gave consideration to EAL in describing the students who participated. They argue that in order to better inform our understanding of

ACTIVITY 3.3   Factors associated with successful EAL and SEN provision: are there similarities?

What similarities and differences can you identify between the factors identified in the previous section as being associated with successful EAL provision and those identified in this section as associated with successful SEN provision?

Factors associated with successful SEN *and* EAL provision	Factors only associated with successful *SEN* provision	Factors associated only with successful *EAL* provision

successful integration of students with SEN, particularly for those who also come from culturally and linguistically diverse backgrounds, it is important to broaden the range of both student and contextual variables that are typically considered and reported.

Cross and Walker-Knight (1997) point out that inclusion does not involve simply placing children with disabilities in general education classrooms. Rather, those classrooms must be restructured to meet all children's individual needs: 'inclusive settings must emphasise building a community in which everyone belongs and is accepted and supported by his or her peers and other members of that community while his or her educational needs are being met' (1997: 269–70). Booth (1993) observes that while progress may have been made in some areas, we still have a long way to go before there is an acceptance of diversity in other areas – for example, the sexual orientation of students. Young people who grow up as gay or lesbian are more likely to experience bullying and may often feel a sense of exclusion which can interfere with learning and participation in school (see Rivers 2000; Robertson and Monsen 2001). An increased incidence of poor school performance, behavioural and emotional difficulties and truancy may result. Booth suggests that our concern should extend to all students who are devalued or insufficiently included within the curriculum or social life of the school.

Practical ways in which inclusion can be promoted at classroom level

As was evident in the review provided in the section on research evidence (see p. 75), research on organizational and teaching strategies is often focused on factors which have been found in successful inclusive provision. Only very rarely are practice guidelines based on intervention research. It is important to make this distinction between research which identifies factors present in successful inclusive provision, and intervention research which evaluates the success of introducing particular strategies into a setting in an effort to make it more inclusive. This is illustrated by the example provided in Figure 3.3.

The factors which have been found to be associated with successful inclusion are reported at the end of the section on research evidence. This may provide helpful guidance. However, in the absence of intervention research, it cannot be assumed that implementing the strategies suggested will necessarily promote inclusion. In the next section we describe the intervention research which has been conducted at the classroom level in two key areas. While recognizing that research is often limited in scope, it should have an important role in informing practice. Strategies that are supported by intervention research can be implemented with considerably more confidence than those that merely *appear* plausible. However, even if there is convincing research on the effectiveness of an intervention, it will always be important to evaluate individual progress. This will ensure the appropriateness of the approach for individual pupils and will allow fine-tuning where necessary to the needs of particular individual pupils in particular school contexts.

Figure 3.3
Associations do
not indicate causes

> Rutter *et al.* (1979) published *Fifteen Thousand Hours*, which reported the results of their survey research in London comprehensive schools. In this influential book they analysed the success of different schools by measuring outcomes such as examination results and attendance. They found a large number of factors which differentiated more successful from less successful schools. The factors associated with success varied from the total amount of teaching time and the setting of homework to the presence of pot plants in classrooms and whether the pupils were required to remove their coats in lessons.
>
> Shortly after the publication of the book apocryphal tales circulated of London comprehensive headteachers issuing edicts to staff that each classroom must be furnished with a pot plant and pupils required to remove coats in lessons in the expectation that these measures would boost attainment! Such tales are amusing because it is obvious that these actions could not cause an improvement in attainment. It is likely that they are associated or correlated with success because they are indicative of care for the physical environment of the school on the one hand and the existence of clear and agreed policies on pupil dress and behaviour on the other. However, we could not be sure about this unless these areas were targeted for intervention. Then we could see if a whole school drive to improve the physical environment and/or the agreement and implementation of clear policies on dress and behaviour did indeed lead to improvements in pupil attitude and motivation and, in turn, to improvements in outcomes such as attainment.

Cooperative learning

Cooperative learning models are among the best documented approaches for promoting successful inclusion in classrooms where there is substantial diversity in the student group. Cross and Walker-Knight (1997) review studies which have focused on inclusive provision for students who have SEN while Smith *et al.* (1993) review studies related to their own year-long cooperative group work intervention focused on improving social relations in the multiethnic classroom.

Cross and Walker-Knight (1997) describe the five attributes which Davidson (1994: 272) identifies as common to all cooperative learning approaches:

1 *Common task or learning activity suitable for group work.* The teacher structures a task or activity to accomplish as a group. All members of the group are aware of the task.
2 *Small-group learning.* Small groups (from 2–6 students), usually heterogeneous, are organized by the teacher.
3 *Cooperative behaviour.* Teachers directly teach students the skills they need to work and learn together.
4 *Positive interdependence.* Teachers structure tasks in such a way that students perceive that they can only attain their goal by working together. Often a team-scoring method is utilized.
5 *Individual responsibility and accountability.* Students are held individually responsible for the learning that takes place in the group.

It is clear from this outline that the teacher has a central role in directing the approach. It is suggested that the teacher should intervene both organizationally, in composing the groups to ensure diversity, and by providing additional instruction – for example, in skills necessary for effective group work, such as giving and receiving criticism, encouraging participation and seeking suggestions/assistance. Peer tutoring and support strategies, which are outlined in the next section, place greater emphasis on active involvement and initiation by students.

Peer tutoring and support

A wide range of studies support the effectiveness of peer tutoring and support in promoting inclusion (Eiserman 1988; Maheady *et al.* 1988). The essential feature of these approaches is that students are paired up, with one acting as tutor and one as tutee. Improvements have been reported in the self-esteem and academic achievement of both tutee and tutor and in their social interactions with others. The consistent finding that tutors also benefit (Cross and Walker-Knight 1997) is important in that concerns may otherwise be expressed by parents of tutors, or by teachers, that the tutors are being 'used' to the detriment of their own learning (Mallon 2000).

In some cases cross-age pairings are established where older students, sometimes students with SEN, tutor younger students. More commonly, in-class pairings are established. In some cases class-wide peer tutoring is routinely used to reinforce learning with members of the dyad taking it in turn to play the role of tutor. This may provide a helpful framework within which particular arrangements for individuals may involve only small modifications to existing practice for teacher and students. An example of the use of peer tutoring to enhance the reading skills and self-esteem of 13-year-old pupils who have physical and learning difficulties was described by Bagley and Mallick (1996). The students with SEN were found to have made better progress over a 12-week intervention than did a control group who did not have physical difficulties but who were matched with them in other respects.

While there is much agreement on the effectiveness of peer support in promoting inclusion, questions have been raised about the maintenance and generalization of the effects obtained. For example, Farrell (1997) reviewed a range of studies in which mainstream pupils had been trained to interact positively with integrated pupils with severe learning difficulties. Although improvements in interactions were found in most cases, these were rarely maintained over time or generalized to other settings. On the other hand, Ronning and Nabuzoka's (1993) small-scale exploratory study with children in Zambia who had mild to moderate learning difficulties reported both maintenance and generalization. They described the introduction of a 'special friends' approach which involved teachers first in discussing with their mainstream classes the likely effects on the children with SEN of inclusion and exclusion in play activities. The teachers then paired two mainstream children with each SEN child and encouraged interaction at playtimes at school. This occurred and there was generalization to a natural situation (when children were waiting to be collected at the end of the school day). The increased levels of interaction were found to be maintained in both contexts when follow-up observations were carried out after one month and again after six months. A further example of generalization, of a different (and very encouraging) kind was also reported. Whereas only half the children with SEN had been assigned special friends by their teachers, other mainstream children who had been part of the general class discussion made themselves special friends without having been asked to do so or given the instruction which was provided for the special friends selected by the teacher.

It may be that what makes specific strategies effective is the context within which they are implemented. For example, a peer tutoring or support programme may well have greater impact if it is introduced within an explicit classroom ethos of mutual help and support. While particular strategies may be helpful in promoting inclusion, no single specific strategy is going to provide 'the' answer. The danger of focusing too narrowly on specific strategies is that they become 'bolt-on' additions for the 'special' children. By contrast, in an inclusive school they will be seen as important ways in which access and participation can increasingly be achieved by all children and they will be used in a range of contexts. For example, Curtis (1992) outlined ways in which a well organized peer tutoring system can deliver support and facilitate curriculum access for new entrants to a school who are learning EAL. This may be particularly valuable where peer tutors are drawn from those who speak the same first language. Given this broader perspective, peer tutoring and support would be one of a number of strategies used when any children face particular challenges – for example, when children with EAL at an early stage of learning English cannot understand the instructions for a science experiment; when a child with SEN is first introduced to a mainstream class; when children whose literacy skills are advanced for their age embark on reading a new genre of text.

In-class support: extra adults in the classroom

Thomas (1992) identified a substantial movement over the previous decade of additional adults into mainstream classrooms, previously the preserve of a single teacher. This movement was partly influenced by an increased emphasis on parental involvement in schools. However, it was largely attributable to an increasing emphasis on providing for special needs and SEN in integrated settings. Hence, in addition to parents, the adults who could increasingly be found in classrooms included LEA peripatetic teachers, EAL and learning support teachers, teachers from special schools operating 'outreach' programmes and learning support assistants. In their review of the role, management and training of learning support assistants, Farrell et al. (1999: 1) describe their increase in numbers in recent years as 'dramatic'. An important factor in this increase was the role they began to play in supporting the education of pupils with SEN in mainstream schools.

It is not surprising then that Clark et al. (1999) identified in-class support as the most commonly used approach to facilitate inclusion in the four schools they studied. However, despite its popularity, a number of problems were reported. First, it was not possible to support each class attended by a pupil with SEN, as

Table 3.4 A comparison of pupil engagement with different models of in-class support

Condition	Mean level of engagement (%)	Standard deviation
A. The classroom functions normally with one teacher without additional adults	57.8	27.1
B. The same classroom functions with one teacher, a learning support assistant and two parents	69.1	25.3
C. The same classroom functions with the same adults as in B but using room management	90.2	11.0

would be possible with peer tutoring. Therefore, on its own, in-class support did not provide a comprehensive and holistic approach. Second, a variety of problems were identified in these four schools which have also been identified in other studies (e.g. Thomas 1992): 'relationships between class teacher and supporter were variable, with some teachers resenting the intrusion of the supporter; roles were frequently unclear; and effective planning of the support partnership was largely non-existent' (Clark *et al.* 1999: 163).

Do these problems influence the effectiveness of the education provided for pupils with SEN? A study carried out by Thomas (1992) suggests that at least some of them do. Thomas used video recordings to analyse the engagement in learning activities of a class of 10–11-year-old pupils. Engagement in learning is consistently found to be significantly related to pupil achievement. Table 3.4 shows the percentage engagement achieved under three different conditions, the last of which involves a version of 'room management'. Room management is an approach which gives each adult in the classroom a clearly defined role. In this study two such roles were specified in detail:

1 *Individual helper* who concentrates on working with an individual on a teaching activity for 5–15 minutes, allowing 4–12 individual teaching sessions to be provided in an hour.
2 *Activity manager* who concentrates on the rest of the class, who are normally arranged in groups of between four and eight pupils. The activity manager moves quickly round keeping the groups occupied and focused.

In Thomas' study the parents and learning support assistant worked as activity managers with particular groups of pupils while the teacher operated as an individual helper. In a given session therefore the teacher was not required to simultaneously manage the class and individualize the curriculum for particular pupils. Essentially the results of the study suggested that having extra adults present was better than not having them present, but that their effectiveness could be significantly enhanced by clearly defining their roles. Clear role definition has a central place in the set of recommendations for effective teamwork in the classroom produced by Thomas (1992):

- The shared classroom should express whole-school policies that all participants have been involved in developing (e.g. on parental involvement, community participation and SEN).
- There should be opportunities from the outset for team discussions of pedagogic, professional and affective concerns.
- The main focus of team discussions should be on clear definitions of the tasks and activities to be undertaken and of individuals' roles in tackling them.
- Planning should involve all team participants.
- Individuals' strengths and weaknesses ought to be identified during planning.
- Team composition needs to be considered carefully. Heterogeneous teams (e.g. teachers and learning support assistants) are often found to develop effective ways of working more easily than homogeneous teams (pairs of teachers).
- The team needs to meet regularly to discuss and evaluate the way they have been working. It will be important for these meetings to have an open and honest ethos where participants seek to identify ways of improving the work of the team.

Conclusions

Lipsky and Gartner (1996) argue that integration cannot be achieved by 'allowing' people of colour (for example) into existing white society, but only by transforming society so that diversity is genuinely valued and normal expectations are not defined by a single group. Inclusive education goes beyond mainstreaming which is founded on the assumption of two separate school systems – a general system and a special system. Also, a restructured inclusive system goes beyond a readiness model which requires that students with SEN prove their readiness to be in an integrated setting, rather than regarding integrated settings as the norm.

Whereas the focus of mainstreaming efforts has been individual students with SEN, the focus in inclusive schooling has been the creation of a school environment supportive of all students and including those at risk of school failure for a variety of reasons: SEN, poverty, homelessness, seasonal migration patterns or sociocultural and linguistic differences (Ball and Harry 1993). Unlike mainstreaming, inclusion is considered not a special education programme, but an outcome of school reform.

Where inclusion is embraced and educational provision carefully structured to meet a diversity of needs, research into social and academic outcomes for pupils with SEN has identified net benefits. Research has played an important role in identifying ways in which inclusion and learning can be promoted both for students with SEN and those with EAL. It will be important to monitor individual students' progress on an ongoing basis in order to ensure that they receive their full rights – an education appropriate to their needs as well an education in an inclusive setting.

Tom is a 7-year-old who has Down's syndrome. His parents are committed to him receiving his education in his local mainstream school. He has attended his local nursery/infant school since the age of 3. He spent the first two years in the nursery class. This year and last year he has been in the Reception class.

Tom's self-help skills (dressing, feeding, toileting) are similar to most of the other children in the Reception class. However, his language skills are more typical of a 3–4-year-old in that he will talk in short (on average 4–5 word) 'telegraphic' sentences which leave out connecting words – for example, 'Where Lego box?' He has no particular friends, but his classmates (especially Vikki, Emma and Sarah) will include him in their play. He clearly enjoys this interaction, although he is always given dependent and subservient roles – the baby, the patient. His teacher finds him a delightful, friendly child. He loves picture books and will join in appropriately with refrains – for example, 'I'll huff and I'll puff' when familiar stories are read to him. He does not seem to be aware of the function of print in conveying the story. However he can recognize his own name. He can also produce simple representational drawings; his 'people' have heads separate from their bodies, from which the arms and legs originate.

Currently his school receives 0.2 full-time equivalent specialist teaching time per week and 0.6 learning support assistant time, as stipulated on his Statement. He is maintained in the classroom for 0.8 of the week which includes the Literacy and Numeracy Hours. However, he has his own learning programmes in everything, except project work and PE/games. His teachers fear that he may not be able to make a successful transition to junior school next year. They feel that Tom is making some progress in the Reception class which would probably be disrupted if he were moved to the Year 2 class in preparation for transfer to junior school. They also fear that he may be bullied in junior school by children from the other (rather rough) local infant school. His teachers feel that his needs would best be met in the medium term through placement in a special school for children with MLD.

(a) Can you list Tom's special educational needs?

(b) Can you make suggestions about how support could best be provided to meet those needs?

(c) Draw up a balance sheet for the placement decision facing Tom's parents:

	Junior school	Special school
Potential advantages		
Potential barriers to learning and participation		
Ways of minimizing the barriers and realizing the advantages for Tom		

Chapter 4

Special educational needs: understanding pathways of development

Dimensions of development

In any culture, development for most children and young people proceeds in a predictable way that can be traced along five key dimensions: physical development, cognitive development, language development, social development and emotional development (Sharman *et al.* 1995). Table 4.1 shows typical achievements of a 4-year-old on these dimensions in a western, English-speaking culture. Clearly the precise expression of developmental achievements will vary with cultural and social context, but within each subculture it will be possible to establish norms of development along these dimensions.

Traditionally, SEN have been defined for each child in terms of the developmental dimension which is most obviously or severely impaired. Examples of lists of handicap categories used in the past in England and Wales, the USA, the Netherlands and New Zealand are given in Table 4.2.

This approach to categorizing SEN appeals to most people's common sense view of the situation. It seems obvious, for example, that a person with physical disabilities whose mobility depends on the use of a wheelchair will experience their physical impairment as the most salient aspect of their difficulties. Historically, in many countries charities and special provision have first developed to meet the needs of those with particular categories of handicap that were defined

Table 4.1 Typical achievements of a 4-year-old along five dimensions of development

Dimension of development	*Examples of typical achievements in this dimension of a 4-year-old in a western, English-speaking culture*
Physical	Climbs stairs and descends confidently one foot to a stair. Can dress and undress except laces, ties and back buttons.
Cognitive	Builds tower of 10+ bricks and bridge. Dramatic make-believe play can be sustained for an extended period.
Language	Speech intelligible but may still have difficulty pronouncing w – f – th. Continually asking questions: 'Why?', 'When?', 'How?'
Social	Capable of sharing and taking turns but may cheat in games in order to win. Shows sympathy for friends who are hurt.
Emotional	Becoming more independent and self-willed, which can lead to conflict. Has an increasingly confident sense of self as capable of challenging adults; can be cheeky and impertinent (rather than having temper tantrums).

Source: Adapted from Sharman *et al.* (1995).

Table 4.2 Official categories of handicap used in the past

England and Wales (Brennan 1982)	USA (Haring 1982)	The Netherlands (Den Boer 1990)	New Zealand (Department of Education 1981)
Blind Partially sighted	Visually handicapped	Blind Partially sighted	Sight
Deaf Partially hearing	Hearing impaired Deaf-blind	Deaf Children with impaired hearing	Hearing
Physically handicapped Delicate	Physically handicapped Multi-handicapped	Physically handicapped Children with multiple handicaps	Physically handicapped
Maladjusted	Behaviorally disordered	Severely maladjusted	Maladjusted
Educationally subnormal (severe)	Mentally retarded	Severely mentally handicapped	Intellectually handicapped
Educationally subnormal (moderate)	Learning disabled	Mentally handicapped Children with learning and behaviour problems	Backward pupils Educationally retarded
Speech defect	Speech impaired	Children with severe speech disorders	
Epileptic		Children in hospital Chronically sick children	

in this way. Examples include the Royal National Institute for the Blind in the UK, the precursor of which was established in 1868; and the Institution for Deaf, Dumb and Blind in Australia, which was established in Sydney in 1860. The lists from different countries in Table 4.2 differ in the language that is used but do not differ very much in substance.

However, in an individual case the picture is frequently more complex than the category labels suggest. Most importantly, children may have strengths and personal qualities that dwarf their primary disability. To define their identity in terms of that problem will be misleading as well as demeaning. Apart from that, children with physical or sensory disabilities may well show problems in other dimensions of development too. These may arise in many different ways:

• Problems in other developmental dimensions may be a direct consequence of the syndrome causing the 'primary' impairment. For example, surveys of children with cerebral palsy have shown that, in addition to their manifest physical difficulties, they tend to have a higher than usual risk of visual and hearing difficulties (Baird 1992; McCarthy 1992).

- Problems in other dimensions may also arise as a side-effect of the main difficulties. For example, the obvious problems that children with cerebral palsy experience with the control of movements may also show themselves in speech problems, fatigue and irritability. Speech involves complex motor coordination, and exceptional efforts of motor control exhaust children physically and emotionally.

- A key factor in additional difficulties may be the attitude of parents or families to the child's difficulties. For instance, Stone (1995: 25) described a blind baby girl who, for her own protection, was kept by her parents within the confines of a playpen for most of the day: 'Opportunities to move and explore the environment were very restricted. This child became so fearful of moving that it was some years before she could walk by herself'.

For a teacher, such additional difficulties are of great importance. An educational programme will only be successful if it takes account of the full range of a child's strengths and needs. So it is important to identify each child's strengths and needs across all the dimensions of development.

ACTIVITY 4.1   Identifying dimensions of difficulty for children with SEN

For each child described in the next section identify the major dimension in which they show SEN and also the other dimensions in which they appear to show particular strengths or needs.

Case studies of exceptional development

John

John, who is 6 years old is described by his mother as 'driving me mad'. He is constantly restless and does not sit still even to watch noisy action movies which he loves. He is the youngest of three children, born when his two sisters were in their teens. 'We hadn't planned him,' his mother says, 'but we were delighted when he came, especially when he turned out to be a boy. My husband dotes on him. But then he's always away driving and doesn't have to put up with his noise and his clumsiness twenty four hours a day.' The family live in a neat, three-bedroomed house in a pleasant suburb of a small town in the south of Scotland. The parents both grew up in the town, and their parents live nearby. Their daughters are both now away from home most of the time, one in the armed forces and the other at university. When they come home for a few weeks at a time, they find John's behaviour wearing and frustrating, and the elder one is critical of her parents for not controlling him better. In school John is constantly in trouble with his peers for interfering in their games. The teacher comments that he seems to lack the social skills to negotiate his way out of trouble and that he does not mean any harm but 'somehow causes chaos wherever he is'. He is not aware of how he is seen by others and 'seems a happy child with good self-esteem'. However, he is beginning to be aware that he is falling behind in basic academic skills. His concentration is weak, and he does not appear to have benefited from the school's systematic teaching of literacy and numeracy.

Mirza

During a period when there was extensive fighting in Bosnia, Mirza and her mother arrived in the South-East of England as asylum seekers. After a short time they were placed in a hostel for refugees in a small coastal town, and Mirza was admitted to a school in the area at the age of 10. She had missed a great deal of schooling in the past because of the hostilities. She now appears to have considerable difficulties in settling down into the routines of her new school. She is seen as immature by her classmates and has made very slow progress in learning English, in spite of regular small-group teaching by a school-based teacher from the local English language support service.

The family's first language, which they use together and with one other Bosnian family in the hostel, is Serbo-Croat. Mirza has very poor eyesight, which was not treated until some time after her move to the UK. The cause of the difficulty was macular degeneration. Her mother reported through an interpreter that her vision had appeared normal during her early years. But when she was about 6, it deteriorated first in one eye and then in the other. She could still see out of the corner of her eye quite well and managed without too much difficulty, except when she had to do close work. By that time medical services were limited in the area where they lived, and nothing was done about the problem. The family had other preoccupations when they first arrived in the UK but once Mirza was referred to a specialist clinic the diagnosis was made quickly and advice on management helped a good deal. The macula is a tiny area in the centre of the retina of the eye. It must have been destroyed by illness or an accident. The family cannot now say exactly when or how that might have happened. The effect is to impair Mirza's fine central vision. Good contrast in the stimulus she is looking at helps her to make it out. So she is not very good with newspapers but manages well with large print books at school. Her class teacher is now trying to ease her slowly towards using smaller print. But her poor progress in learning English as a spoken language inhibits advances in reading as well. The teacher finds it hard to decide whether her problems with books that have normal-sized print are wholly attributable to her visual defect or are partly caused by her limited English vocabulary.

Janet

Janet, who is 10 years old, lives alone with her unemployed mother. They moved a few years ago into a decaying post-war estate on the edge of a small industrial town in the North-East of England. A group of families arrived there together – rehoused from one street in Newcastle when it was demolished for redevelopment.

Janet, like her mother, appears overweight, slow-moving and slow-thinking. There is a question mark about her hearing, as she often seems to look vacant during whole class sessions in school. But her mother has failed appointments for hearing tests. In the Year 6 classroom Janet rarely speaks unless spoken to. She is teased by most children in her class but protected by a small, lively group of girls whose streetwise leader, Stephanie, is the daughter of a neighbour. In the company of this group, when Stephanie is present, Janet will participate clumsily in playground skipping games and suchlike. But, if Stephanie is absent (which is not uncommon), she will often be on her own in the playground.

She made good progress in reading with small-group help during Year 5, though her comprehension lags behind her ability to decode print and read aloud. At this stage most of her attainments are far behind the rest of the class. In maths and in any kind of project work she will sit passively and achieve very little output. Her teacher, an energetic and committed young man, pronounces himself at a loss as to how to break into what he sees as a cycle of self-reinforcing educational failure and increasing social isolation.

The interactive factors (IF) framework

As these case studies illustrate, SEN are diverse and develop in many different ways. The main questions to be addressed in this chapter are how individual patterns of SEN develop and whether there is a simple framework that can accommodate the different accounts and explanations that are given. Our starting point is a framework for *causal modelling* which was developed by Morton and Frith (1995). We believe that their approach has a particular advantage in the context with which we are concerned, because it aims to accommodate diverse perspectives on the pathways that development may take.

Morton and Frith aimed to create a simple visual aid to make it easier for people to communicate about developmental problems. Frith (1995: 6) suggested that their graphic schema can act 'as a map, largely white, in unknown territory' which will hint at where to look for landmarks. The framework can be used to represent all theories of development or difficulties in development in a neutral fashion. It has been employed by developmental researchers (Morton and Frith 1995) and educational psychologists (Frederickson 1997). The examples below focus on reading problems but the framework can be used for any type of difficulty.

Figure 4.1, which is reproduced from Frith (1997), shows a causal model of dyslexia (severe and persistent reading difficulties). It can be seen that the framework uses three levels of description to explain developmental problems: the

Figure 4.1
Causal model
of dyslexia as a
phonological
deficit
Source:
Frith (1997).

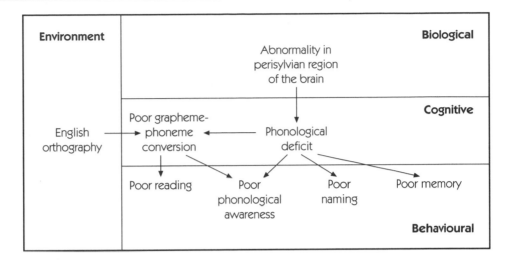

biological level, the cognitive level and the behavioural level. Arrows indicate a hypothesized causal chain. In addition, the framework recognizes the operation of environmental factors at all three levels, as 'this chain of causal links from brain to mind to behaviour has to be set within the context of environmental and cultural influences' (Frith 1997: 2). These influences may sometimes be of critical importance for exceptional children in a society that is ethnically and culturally heterogeneous.

Biological level

The biological level box can be used to record observations about the brain and about sensory processes such as hearing and vision. In Figure 4.1 an abnormality in the perisylvian region of the left hemisphere of the brain is represented at the biological level. If a brain abnormality is thought to be caused by a genetic factor, this genetic factor can also be shown in the biological level box, and an arrow drawn from it to the brain abnormality. Brain functioning may also be influenced by environmental factors such as quality of nutrition or levels of toxins, and by environmental interventions such as the use of a cochlear implant as an intervention for sensori-neural hearing loss.

Cognitive level

Where it is hypothesized that there are within-child causes of poor performance, they are placed in the cognitive level box. Cognitive skills or deficits cannot be directly observed but must be inferred from observed behavioural data. The inferred and hypothetical underlying cognitive deficits are different in different theories. Figure 4.1 shows the central explanatory role given in this theory of dyslexia to what is hypothesized to be a phonological deficit, where difficulties are experienced in identifying and manipulating sounds within words. Morton and Frith (1995) also included affective factors at the cognitive level. An argument could be made for placing affects in the biological level box (as physiological responses) or in the behavioural level box (as facial expressions, voice modulations, etc.). But the cognitive level is crucial in ascribing meaning to affects and explaining their influence on mental activities and behaviour. Again the environment plays an important role. Frith (1997) pointed out that whether a cognitive or affective difficulty will result in literacy problems will not just depend on the nature and severity of the problem but on interactions with environmental factors such as the complexity of the writing system involved. Hence dyslexia appears to cause fewer difficulties for individuals learning to read German or Dutch than for those learning to read English because the process of mapping sounds onto letters (establishing grapheme-phoneme correspondences) is more straightforward (De Gelder and Vroomen 1991; Landerl *et al.* 1997; Goswami 2000).

Behavioural level

Observations and facts about poor performance in reading and spelling activities and/or tests are represented in the behavioural level box. We can directly observe behaviour such as spellings written incorrectly, words read inaccurately or poor performance in naming and memory tests. Of course, any observations and data that are collected will be affected by a range of environmental factors (such as the work ethos in the classroom). In addition, within-child factors other than those directly related to literacy difficulties (such as motivation) are also open to environmental influences.

Environmental influences

Further examples of environmental influences are given in Figures 4.2 and 4.3 (reproduced from Frith 1995). These figures also illustrate the way in which the causal modelling framework can be used very simply to represent general ideas in outline, without including much detail. In Figure 4.2 you will see that the child had a cognitive deficit that was expected to lead to reading problems, but the provision of remedial teaching was successful and there was therefore no 'behavioural sign' of poor reading. Frith (1995: 8) described this as 'an example of compensation: here remedial teaching is shown to give a protective effect'. In Figure 4.3 a child who shows no problems at the biological or cognitive levels nonetheless is making poor progress in reading. Frith claims that 'more economically than I can do it in words, I can use the diagram to declare just what I assume the critical factors and relationships to be'.

Figure 4.2
Example of
compensation
Source:
Frith (1995).

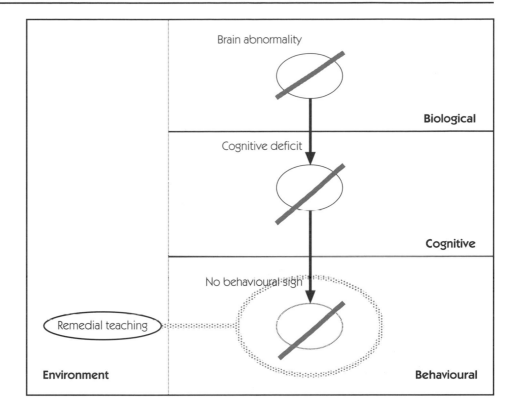

In these theoretical models produced by developmental psychologists and neuropsychologists the contribution of the environment is acknowledged throughout. But that contribution is often poorly specified because of the wide variability that would have to be represented. When one comes to look at individual differences and individual needs, that variability is of crucial importance. Morton and Frith (1995) suggested that these diagrams could also be used to describe particular individuals. Frederickson (1997) reported that this had been done successfully by educational psychologists in training. A couple of modifications had been made to the framework to facilitate the description of individual children.

Describing individual needs

An example of what was now called the interactive factors (IF) framework is presented in Figure 4.4. Instead of showing the biological, cognitive, behavioural and environmental factors that are characteristic of a specified developmental difficulty, the model for a particular individual represents what is known about the complexity of that individual's particular pattern of strengths and needs. It also shows the environmental and other factors which are thought to be influencing the individual's learning and development. It is often hard to be sure about

Figure 4.3
Example of poor
reading due to
emotional causes,
not dyslexia
Source:
Frith (1995).

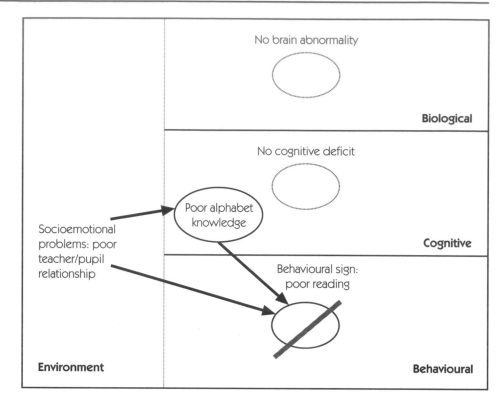

some of the influences that are identified because any ideas about them will typically be based on a limited amount of information. However, a hypothesis about particular influences can be used to guide intervention. Then an evaluation of the individual's response to intervention will show whether they are accurate and useful. For example, in Figure 4.4 the individual's literacy difficulties are thought to be exacerbated by high levels of off-task behaviour resulting from ineffective classroom management. An intervention to improve classroom management would be expected to reduce levels of off-task behaviour and improve performance on literacy tasks. If subsequent evaluation confirms that this is the case, then the accuracy and usefulness of the model would be supported. However if the predicted outcomes are not achieved, then further investigation is likely to be needed leading to a revision of the model.

By comparing Figure 4.4 with Figure 4.1 you can see the slight changes that have been made to Morton and Frith's framework. There is, first of all, much greater conceptual space given to environmental factors. This includes the recognition that the environment is also the source of all intervention and management efforts. Figure 4.4 shows that intervention and management strategies might be targeted at all three levels of the framework: decongestant medication at the biological level, instruction in memory strategies and teaching of letter-sound (grapheme-phoneme) correspondences at the cognitive level, and the introduction

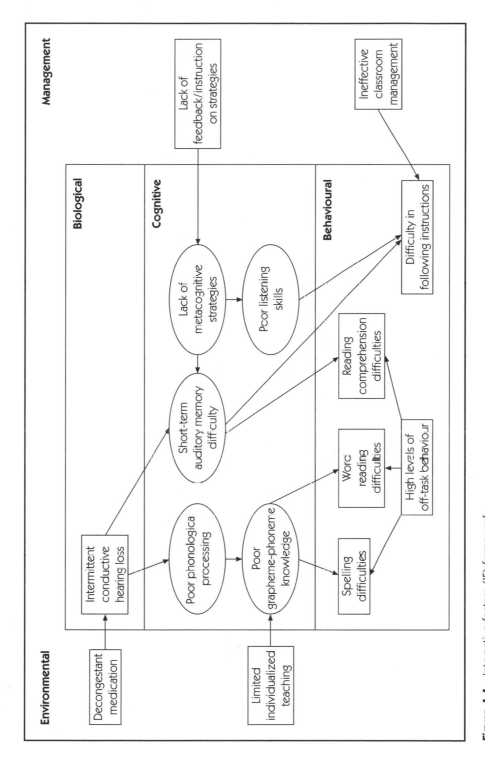

Figure 4.4 Interactive factors (IF) framework
Source: Frederickson and Cameron (1999).

of classroom management techniques at the behavioural level. Figure 4.4 represents an individual within their environment.

Just as Morton and Frith (1995) suggest that it is helpful to consider different levels of analysis of individual functioning, so Bronfenbrenner (1979: 3) has suggested that it is helpful to conceive of the environment as 'a set of nested structures, each contained inside the next like a set of Russian dolls'. Four levels are identified in this broader and more differentiated conception of the environment:

- A *microsystem* is a pattern of activities, roles and interpersonal relations experienced by a child in a given setting. The home, classroom and playground would all be examples of settings within which children actively participate.
- A *mesosystem* describes the relationships between two or more settings in which a child actively participates. For example, the relationships between home and school, between neighbourhood and peer group.
- An *exosystem* refers to one or more settings that do not involve a child directly as an active participant but which affect or are affected by what happens in settings that do involve the child. Examples of exosystems might be the work setting of the child's parent(s) or the LEA.
- The *macrosystem* refers to consistencies in the other systems that exist or could exist at the level of the subculture or culture as a whole, together with belief systems underlying any such consistencies. Within a given society (e.g. Britain, France, Japan) settings such as school classrooms, restaurants or home–school relationships will share certain features, along which the settings differ across cultures.

Gibbs and Huang (1989) point out that Bronfenbrenner's perspective is particularly relevant in analysing the influence of factors such as poverty, discrimination and immigration on the psychosocial development of children and young people from minority cultural groups. In addition, where families have recently moved to another country, the different sets of values and norms to which the child is exposed in different settings can be analysed and potential areas of conflicting expectations examined. For example, one source of stress for Mirza, who was described above, has been the different views on food and diet of her peer group at school and her mother at home.

A further difference between the two frameworks can be seen in the use of slightly different terminology such as 'interactive factors framework' rather than 'causal modelling framework'. While Morton and Frith had emphasized that causal links in the modelling process are not determinant, it was found that use of the word 'causal' could prove confusing when professionals were developing tentative representations of the factors thought to be affecting an individual child. In this age of acronyms, the title 'IF framework' seems particularly apt given that a major purpose is to represent working hypotheses about the nature of children's needs. Professionals working with an individual can ask '*If* the child's learning is being influenced in this way, what are the implications for teaching and management?' The evaluation of the intervention they design will show whether their working hypothesis is a useful guide to practice. The focus

---

ACTIVITY 4.2   Applying the IF framework to individual cases

(a) Reread the account of Janet in the previous section. Can you draft an IF framework to show what her current reading difficulties are and how they may have developed?
(b) Repeat the process for a child known to you professionally or personally.
(c) Show your two diagrams to a friend or colleague and ask them to tell you in words what they think is the nature of each child's difficulties and what lies behind them. Does their verbal account agree with what you would have said yourself?

---

on *interactive* factors is also important, given the points made in the opening section of this chapter about the complex and multi-faceted nature of individual children's needs. On the basis of Figure 4.4 we would not expect an intervention at one level alone to be enough to meet the child's needs. For example, the introduction of more effective classroom management techniques alone would not have a sufficient impact on the child's literacy skills in the absence of appropriately individualized teaching. Similarly, it is unlikely that individualized teaching of letter-sound correspondences on its own would result in improved reading and spelling performance in the classroom unless the ineffective management is also addressed.

In this book we will return to the causal modelling framework in describing different theories of particular developmental difficulties. We will also use the IF framework in describing the complex difficulties experienced by individual children and the ways in which professionals working with them can attempt to understand and meet their needs.

Further considerations in using the IF framework

Morton and Frith (1995: 359) argued that, when constructing a model of how a serious problem develops, it is essential to 'start with biology'. This will be important even if the precise disturbance to the brain system is not fully understood. For example, when childhood autism was first identified, an influential theory suggested that the family's style of interaction might be a key factor in the development of the symptoms. Over recent years evidence has accumulated that the condition in fact has a biological origin (Rutter *et al.* 1999). If professionals continue to suggest that a mother's manner in handling her child may be the cause of his or her strange behaviour and social isolation, it is not only misleading and unhelpful, but also potentially very damaging.

Another example is the group of children with problems of attention and activity labelled as ADHD ('attention deficit/hyperactivity disorder'). John, who was described earlier, is an example of a child with this pattern of difficulties. Some educationists treat ADHD as a wholly educational issue. They assume that, if appropriate classroom management strategies are adopted, the children's behaviour will be controlled and their attention will be focused (Cooper 1997). Unfortunately this is sometimes too optimistic: neuropsychological factors make it so difficult for some children to inhibit impulsive behaviour that changing the approach to classroom management will not on its own enable them to sustain concentration on schoolwork. If key factors are involved at the biological level it may not be effective to intervene solely at the behavioural or cognitive level.

However, saying that we should 'start with biology' does not mean that we should give attention only to biological factors. The intensity of a child's problems of attention with ADHD may be affected by what they or others think about the causes of their difficulties. So cognitive processes mediate the impact of biological factors. In turn, the views of the child and parents will be affected by external environmental factors such as social and economic pressures on the family and expectations about children's behaviour that are prevalent in the general community.

The impact of environmental factors may operate at a broader level as well as in the subtle ways implied in the example of ADHD. When socioeconomic differences within a society are extreme, the incidence of different types of mental and physical handicap will reflect this. For instance, in a series of studies in the area of Cape Town in South Africa, Molteno and his colleagues showed that the proportion of children developing severe SEN after birth was higher in the African population than in the coloured population and lowest among white children (see Table 4.3). The incidence of postnatal disabilities in the white group was comparable to what had been recorded in other developed countries. It was evident that the higher rates among the other groups in the same area were not linked to some ethnic disadvantage but were a consequence of their worse socioeconomic conditions. For example, children were more likely to develop diseases such as tuberculosis, pneumonia and measles in these groups, and also more likely, once they had these illnesses, to develop secondary cerebral infections leading to disability (Arens and Molteno 1989; Molteno et al. 1990; Donald 1994).

Thus environmental factors may influence development in a range of different ways. We will illustrate this further with an outline framework that was used by Cline and Baldwin (1994) to show ways in which selective mutism can develop in childhood. Selective mutism is the term used to describe a phenomenon in which children who are able to speak and do speak in some situations (e.g. home) persist in remaining silent in some other settings (e.g. school). It appears to

Table 4.3 Proportion of children in Cape Town with mental handicap or cerebral palsy for whom postnatal causes had been identified

Population	Mental handicap (%)	Cerebral palsy (%)
African	21.7	36.1
Coloured	13.6	24.0
White	9.8	13.2

Source: Donald (1994).

Table 4.4 A summary of how selective mutism may develop

Factors	The community	The family	The child
Disposing	Family is isolated or marginalized in the community.	Parents have personal experience and/or a family tradition of silence/ reticence.	
		Factors within the family encourage mutism as a reaction to challenge.	Factors within the child favour mutism as a reaction to challenge.
Precipitating			The child faces a challenging transition to the outside world (or other stressful challenge) and reacts by withholding speech.
Maintaining	Reactions from adults and peers reinforce mutism.	Reactions from family members reinforce mutism.	The child experiences reduced anxiety and secondary gains.

Source: Cline and Baldwin (1994).

develop most often around 3–6 years of age when children are moving out of their family homes into a different kind of setting outside the family, such as a playgroup or nursery or school. (For a fuller account, see Chapter 10.)

Table 4.4 presents a summary of how selective mutism may develop. Note that the community (including school) as well as the child and the family may play a part in the process. It is usual to distinguish between three ways in which factors may influence psychological events. We can differentiate between:

- *disposing factors*, which create a situation that is favourable to the development of the behaviour;
- *precipitating factors*, which trigger the behaviour on the first few occasions;
- *maintaining factors*, which encourage its persistence.

Tables 4.5, 4.6 and 4.7 list examples of disposing, precipitating and maintaining factors, showing how related features may occur at each level. It seems most likely that selective mutism will develop when some factors are present at each of the levels – the community, the family and the child. However, it may occur when only two levels (or even one level) are implicated. However, the development of a particular pattern of difficulty is often 'over-determined' – i.e. caused by several interacting factors (cf. Figure 4.4). The IF framework is helpful in not just depicting the status of each factor but attempting to show how they may have formed a causal chain.

Table 4.5 Possible disposing factors which may also later serve a maintaining function

The community	The family	The child
Social distance maintained between families or groups in a rural community or between ethnic or linguistic groups in an urban community.	A family history of shyness or mutism or social isolation.	A temperamental disposition towards shyness, timidity and fearfulness.
	Modelling/encouragement of shyness or mutism by family members individually or as a whole group.	Learning from family models.
Community pressures, such as racial harassment (or simply a failure to welcome newcomers), foster family's sense of threat and isolation.	Family ethos of group exclusivity and wariness in dealing with the outside world.	
	Anxiety about disclosure of family secrets.	A strong need to control.
	Family unable to face and resolve conflicts.	Negativism.
	Marital problems and a strong bond of interdependence between mother and child, excluding or distancing father.	Failure to develop age-appropriate independence from one or both parents.
Peers who tease and reject those who are different (e.g. in speech mannerisms and/or accent).	Intense sibling rivalry.	Speech difficulties.

Source: Cline and Baldwin (1994).

Table 4.6 Possible precipitating factors

The community	The family	The child
	Birth of a resented younger sibling (or their development of speech).	
	Family members cannot work through change or loss by sharing their feelings or open discussion.	Is thrust into a new domestic situation without adequate preparation (e.g. after bereavement).
Legal requirement that all children attend school.	Some family members find it extremely difficult when it is necessary for them or other family members to move outside the family circle.	Starts nursery, playgroup or school.
	Family moves to new (and strange) environment, e.g. as immigrants.	

Source: Cline and Baldwin (1994).

Table 4.7 Possible maintaining factors

The community	The family	The child
Adults and peers outside the home:	Family members:	
Treat the child as special and unusual.	Treat the child as special and unusual.	Relishes own uniqueness; gains privileges and attention.
Convey expectation that the child will remain mute.	Convey expectation that the child will remain mute.	Holds a self-image as a mute.
		Is fearful of consequences of speaking.
Reinforce non-verbal methods of communication and make them effective, even in school.	Reinforce non-verbal methods of communication and make them effective.	Finds that silence need not bring social isolation or academic failure.
	Experience reduced anxiety as the child's behaviour helps the family avoid having to resolve internal conflicts.	Anxiety is reduced.

Source: Cline and Baldwin (1994).

ACTIVITY 4.3   Analysing factors that underlie Mirza's difficulties at school

Re-examine the account of Mirza that was given on page 103 and decide what might appropriately be written in the cells of this table to summarize factors underlying her current difficulties at school.

	The community	The family	The school
Disposing factors			
Precipitating factors			
Maintaining factors			

Pathways of development

Over the last 50 years the prevailing climate of opinion among researchers has shifted more than once. During the period following World War II an image was presented of a high degree of consistency in personality: children were seen as being born with certain fixed characteristics which changed little over time, though very adverse factors in the early years, such as 'maternal deprivation', might impair development. This simplistic view was challenged during the 1960s and 70s when it became clear that the way people develop was more varied and unpredictable than had been thought (Clarke and Clarke 1976). Commentators such as Mischel (1969) highlighted evidence that behaviour is often situation-specific: a person will behave quite differently in different circumstances. Moss and Susman (1980: 590) summarized indications from longitudinal research as showing that some problems persist and others fade away:

> Severe disturbances tend to be long-standing, whereas isolated symptoms and mild reactions tend to be transitory. This difference in the persistence of severe and mild reactions may be based on the probability that severe disturbances are likely to reflect a fundamental and pervasive personality problem that is tied to the psychobiological history of the individual. Isolated symptoms are more likely to reflect temporary stress reactions to passing situations and ephemeral developmental demands.

In recent years evidence has accumulated that there are both continuities and discontinuities in development. There has been growing interest in analysing *pathways of development* in greater detail to show how both stability and change may be seen in individual cases. Rutter (1989) reviewed a number of factors that may affect vulnerable children over their life span. We will illustrate his analysis by examining one factor in particular – the effectiveness of the school the child attends in early adolescence. The criterion of effectiveness in these

Figure 4.5
Simplified pathway
from poor
schooling to poor
job success (Gray
et al. 1980), where
'2x' = twice as
likely to lead
to . . . , etc.
Source:
Rutter (1989).

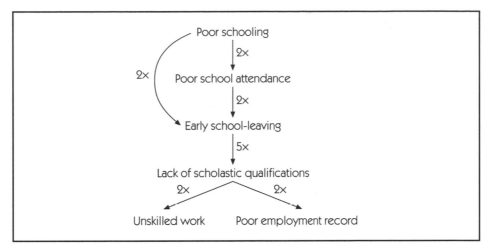

studies was not the school's success with a particular pupil but general outcome measures for all its pupils. Figure 4.5 presents a simplified summary of data on the employment record of young people one year after leaving school, studied by Gray *et al.* (1980).

There was no direct relationship between attending one of the less effective schools in their sample and moving into unskilled work or having a poor employment record. But if a child attended one of the less effective schools they were twice as likely to attend poorly, and if their attendance was poor they were twice as likely to leave school early without sitting national examinations. That had an impact on how well qualified they were, which in turn affected their work record.

Our second example is taken from a study of girls who were admitted to children's homes in the 1960s (Quinton and Rutter 1988). There was a policy in the homes to distribute children among many different schools in order to avoid concentrating too many institutional children in any one school. Figure 4.6 shows the enhanced likelihood of a chain of positive outcomes for those young women who had more positive experiences at secondary school.

Conclusions

The meticulous analysis of environmental factors which characterized much research in the latter part of the last century is now being complemented by increased interest in genetic factors. Improved techniques of genetic research are making it possible to analyse biological influences in much more detail. When Rutter *et al.* (1997) reviewed findings to date, they concluded, among other things, that:

- genetic factors have an influence on every aspect of development that has been studied;

Figure 4.6
Simplified
adaptive chain of
circumstances in
institution-reared
women (Quinton
and Rutter 1988),
where '3x' = three
times as likely to
lead to . . . , etc.
Source:
Rutter (1989).

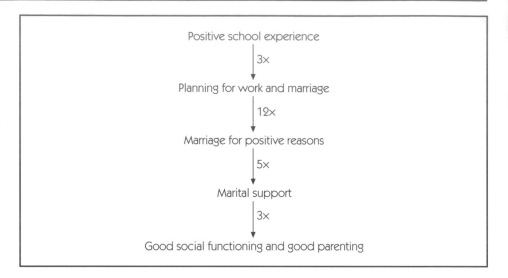

- most deviant or pathological development is influenced by a multiplicity of factors;
- several genes are involved in most mental disorders;
- some genetic effects do not operate through the genetic factor directly affecting the disorder but through an impact on the risk features that make a person more vulnerable to the disorder.

But they acknowledged that environmental factors too influence all aspects of development. In a subsequent article, Rutter *et al.* (1999) outlined the increasingly extensive findings available by then about the role of genetic factors in a number of specific conditions, including ADHD. They emphasized that it would be important that the pendulum should not swing too far: 'It will be crucial for genetic studies . . . to include adequate measures of environmental risk factors' (Rutter *et al.* 1999: 40).

A full analysis of the pathways of development of SEN for an individual child will need to take account of the whole range of possible factors that might play a part. It will have to give attention to the timing of significant events in a child's life and the interaction between them. It will also examine how biology, cognition, behaviour and the environment interact to produce the observed outcome. In the rest of this book we will return to these themes constantly as we examine different types of SEN and consider issues of education and management.

Part 2

Assessment in context

Chapter 5

Identification and assessment

When you have studied this chapter you should be able to:

1 Understand key principles and concepts that are used in discussing the identification and assessment of SEN.
2 Explain key requirements which all approaches to identification and assessment should meet, and analyse the extent to which any particular approach meets those requirements.
3 Critically examine the broad advantages and disadvantages of the most common approaches to identification and assessment.

Contents

Identification of SEN in the early years

In Chapter 2 you were invited to compare different ways of thinking about SEN. It will be obvious that, if professionals conceive of SEN as a permanent individual characteristic of a child, they will approach the tasks of identifying and assessing those needs differently from the way they would go about it if they had an interactional model of SEN. In this chapter we will consider various approaches to identification and assessment that relate to how SEN are conceived, and we will examine the practical implications of tackling the task in different ways.

It is conventional wisdom that SEN and possible educational disadvantage should be identified as early as possible: 'early diagnosis and appropriate intervention improve the prospects of children with special educational needs, and reduce the need for expensive intervention later on. For some children, giving more effective attention to early signs of difficulties can prevent the development of SEN' (Department for Education and Employment 1997: 13). On the face of it the logic is obvious. Children who are not given extra help at an early stage will fall behind their classmates at school and will then not be able to follow what is taught. They will be aware of the gap between what they can do and what their peers can do, and as a result may come to see themselves as incapable of school learning. Their motivation for classroom tasks will be undermined, their concentration will falter, and this will feed a negative cycle in which failure leads to further failure. Clearly, early identification of potential difficulties could help parents and teachers to halt this process before it starts.

However, the situation is more complex than that scenario makes it appear. With any system of screening or early identification it is inevitable that mistakes will be made. When children are young, their behaviour and performance are more variable than when they are older; they may underperform because of minor differences between the way a task is presented and the way they are accustomed to it at home; they may not be prepared by their early experiences for the activities that are used to assess them; children who are very familiar with the assessment materials may do relatively well initially because of prior practice. As a result, children may be wrongly identified as having serious difficulties when this is not the case ('false positives'); or they may not be identified as having difficulties when they really do ('false negatives'). The aim must be to maximize the number of 'true positives' and 'true negatives' – a task that is more challenging when the children involved are younger.

In many areas of the USA there is some kind of screening evaluation of children prior to school entry. Cannella and Reiff (1989) found that this was mandated in 16 out of 48 states they surveyed. It is not uncommon for large-scale kindergarten testing to be used in order to screen for SEN (Rafoth 1997). In the UK until recently greater reliance was placed at the preschool stage on surveillance by professionals in the health and other services. Before school entry this was seen as fairer, more efficient and more cost-effective. Strategies have included:

- health screening before and after birth and in infancy;
- monitoring by the health visitor service;
- use of developmental checklists in nurseries, playgroups and other preschool provision;
- priority admission of children at risk into 'opportunity playgroups' and similar facilities where additional support is available.

The problem with such a patchwork of arrangements is that it is not difficult for children to fall through the net (for example, if their family moves a great deal or does not make use of the services available because of fear or unfamiliarity). There is evidence that the factors that lead to underuse of the relevant services are more likely to impinge on families from ethnic and linguistic minority communities (Baxter *et al.* 1990; Shah 1992; Caesar *et al.* 1994). Efforts have been made to ensure that services are offered more consistently, are coordinated more effectively and are accessible to the most vulnerable families. In relation to SEN, a statutory requirement has been placed on health authorities and NHS Trusts. They must 'inform parents and the appropriate local education authority when they form the opinion that a child under the age of five may have special educational needs. They must also inform the parents if they believe that a particular voluntary organisation is likely to be able to give the parents advice or assistance in connection with any special educational needs that the child may have' (Department for Education and Employment 1996, Section 332).

It is no accident that that requirement places an emphasis on communication between agencies. The fragmentation of provision for children in their early years has been seen as a major weakness in the past (Bradley 1982; Pugh 1988). At the same time the statutory, private and voluntary agencies that are involved offer a rich variety of facilities to meet the complex needs of parents and children. They include maintained nursery schools, nursery classes in primary schools, independent schools, day nurseries, family centres, preschool centres, playgroups, childminders, and, for children with SEN, a variety of parent support schemes, including Portage schemes. Over the last decade local authorities have been required to develop Early Years Development and Childcare Partnerships in each area. These networks encompass all the providers of early years care and education – statutory, private and voluntary. Their aim is to try to tackle the problems of communication between agencies and to ensure that all children in target age groups have facilities available if their parents or guardians wish to use them. Those early education providers which accept any form of government funding are required to have regard to the SEN *Code of Practice* and to have a written SEN policy. They are expected to monitor individual children's progress and to make a graduated response to any difficulties that arise (Department for Education and Skills 2001, Section 4).

In the past some types of SEN have tended to be identified very early in children's lives and others not until they were well into their school career. As a result, when most children with severe or complex needs were placed in special schools and units, the age profile of these establishments varied markedly.

Table 5.1 Age of pupils in some* Inner London special schools and units in 1983

Type of school/unit	% pupils aged <11	% pupils aged >11	Total no.
Hearing impaired**	54	46	527
Motor impaired	49	51	472
Emotional and behavioural difficulties	13	87	1286
Moderate learning difficulties (MLD)	30	70	2516
Severe learning difficulties (SLD)	42	58	1378
Total (incl. provision omitted above)	34	66	8051

* Figures for groups of less than 400 are omitted from this table.
** Figures for special schools and units in mainstream schools combined.
Source: Kysel (1985, Table 3).

Table 5.1 shows that in a large metropolitan area pupils with special needs that are relatively easily detected, such as SLD, tended to be admitted to special schools and units earlier in their school careers, so that a higher proportion of them were in primary provision.

A distinction can be made between lifelong difficulties with physical manifestations that are typically identified before school entry and school-related difficulties that are typically identified at a later stage by teachers. Concepts such as 'hearing impairment' appear comparatively straightforward – a matter of medical diagnosis from the point when the impairment is established (which may be at birth or following a severe illness such as meningitis during childhood). On the other hand, the position is seen to be different when we consider those forms of SEN that were more strongly represented in secondary special schools and units in Table 5.1 – 'emotional and behaviour difficulties' and 'MLD'. These forms of SEN are often defined in terms of problems in school, so that they are identified later. Sociologists such as Tomlinson (1982) have pointed out that the categories of SEN that are seen as 'subjective' may be more prone to distortion than those sometimes described as 'objective'. (In fact, even apparently straightforward forms of SEN cannot be understood adequately through focusing on obvious impairments and their amelioration. See the discussion of a social/cultural perspective on deafness in Chapter 13.)

There may still be a problem if a child is correctly identified as having significant difficulties but an important aspect of those difficulties is overlooked. Consider the example of Steven who was identified at the age of 3 as having made a slow start in talking. He lived with his mother and two siblings in a run-down cottage in an isolated rural area. The family rarely left the immediate vicinity of their home, and the older children had a poor attendance record at school. Steven's problem was noted by an education welfare officer when he visited the home to follow up the attendance issue with the children's mother. He advised her to 'take the lad to your GP for a check-up'. But she could not afford the expense of having to make frequent bus trips to the local town. In addition, she was scared of getting involved in anything that might further overwhelm the family, especially if it required her to keep all three of her children under control in the presence of others. Steven had an intermittent hearing problem (glue ear) in a serious form, and it was not finally identified and treated until he started school two years later.

So there can be errors in early identification, and the consequences for some children are likely to be negative. What will make errors less likely or their impact less serious? Here are three suggestions that have received wide support:

- *Parents must be fully involved throughout.* Full involvement of parents from the outset will add a crucial dimension to the picture. The intimate knowledge that parents bring is enhanced by their emotional commitment to their child. Of course, if you stand very close to something, you do not always see it in the round. But you will still see things about it that nobody else notices.
- *Everyone who knows the child must collaborate.* Errors will be minimized where there is close cooperation and communication between any health and social services professionals who know a child and the teachers who have responsibility for him or her in school. If views from different perspectives are sought, listened to and reconciled, it is less likely that the child's difficulties will be misunderstood because of one person's (or one profession's) blind spots.
- *Intervention should have a low profile.* Low-profile helping strategies will build on the normal school routine of the child's class group and interrupt and disrupt them as little as possible. The effect will also be to reduce any potentially stigmatizing effect of labelling to a minimum.

These three imperatives are important well beyond the identification stage, and you will find that we come back to them again and again throughout this book. Each of them is emphasized in the revised SEN *Code of Practice* issued by the UK government (Department for Education and Skills 2001). In England all who work with children with SEN in mainstream or special settings are required to have regard to the *Code*. All teaching and non-teaching staff in schools and all those in early education settings who act as educators are required to be involved in the development of the SEN policy and be fully aware of the procedures for identifying, assessing and making provision for children with SEN (Department for Education and Skills 2001, para. 1.39). The *Code* requires professionals to work in close partnership with parents on the basis that they hold key information and have a critical role to play in their children's education. As noted in Chapter 1 it also requires professionals to enable children to participate actively in their own assessment and to contribute their views.

During the Foundation Stage of education for children aged 3–5 years, progress towards the targeted Early Learning Goals (QCA 2000b) should be monitored closely. It is pointed out in the *Code* that this will benefit a wider group of children and not only those with SEN: children making slower progress may include those who are younger, who are learning EAL or who have particular learning difficulties. It should not be assumed that children who are making slower progress must, therefore, have SEN. But such children will need carefully differentiated learning opportunities to help them progress, and careful monitoring of their progress (Department for Education and Skills 2001, paras 4.5–4.8). Both in the early years and during children's time at school a key requirement of the *Code* is that there should be graduated response so that the action taken is no more than what is required to resolve a child's needs. Only where progress continues to cause concern should additional action be taken (2001, paras 4.9–4.14).

Baseline assessment on school entry

In the UK pupils must now be assessed on school entry – normally within seven weeks of admission. Schools are required to use a scheme of assessment that has been accredited against national standards. These schemes must cover, as a minimum, aspects of language and literacy, mathematics, and personal and social development. In addition, all accredited schemes include guidance on assessing the attainments of children with EAL and on linking the results from the scheme to the more detailed assessments needed for children with SEN. On its own, baseline assessment does not provide enough evidence to enable teachers to decide whether to place a child on the school's register of children with SEN. But the results may lead to close observation of children's progress and specific follow up activities or further tests to check on their needs. For example, it may be appropriate to arrange for children's hearing to be tested in order to make sure that they can deal with the comparatively noisy conditions of a busy classroom. Or children from a linguistic minority background who do relatively poorly on the language-related section of the baseline assessment scheme when it is given in English might be assessed for their understanding and ability to express themselves in the language they use most often at home. This will enable their teachers to decide whether they have an underlying general problem with language or whether all that is required is normal provision for learning EAL (see Chapter 10).

The information that is collected shortly after school entry will provide a profile of individual children that should be useful in planning teaching and classroom organization. Longitudinal studies of educational progress during the primary school years have shown that children's assessed knowledge of reading, writing and maths on entry to school is a good predictor of their later educational attainments (Tizard *et al.* 1988). There is a strong tendency for those children who do least well at the outset to continue to perform poorly relative to their peers throughout the primary school. Arrangements for systematic and open assessment at the time of school entry can help teachers to plan the delivery of the curriculum more carefully to respond to the needs of individual children. It may also make it less likely that schooling will simply reinforce – by default – knowledge differences already developed and evident when children are first admitted (Blatchford and Cline 1992).

However, there are also risks in highlighting individual differences between children on school entry. What is noted by a teacher at that stage and placed on record may become a self-fulfilling prophecy. Children who do poorly on the baseline assessment scheme may be stigmatized as failures almost before they start. There is a good deal of evidence that children whose teachers expect little of them may be under-stimulated in the classroom, receive less positive feedback for what they do achieve, and ultimately obtain worse results than would otherwise have been the case (Tauber 1997; Brophy 1998). It will be more likely that this negative spiral of low expectations will be set up when children come from disadvantaged homes or from backgrounds that are culturally different from those of the majority at the school. If the approach to baseline assessment is designed to counteract these tendencies, it will support children and families at risk. One strategy is to involve parents and children actively in the process of gathering information. This can provide teachers with a rich picture of children's lives before starting school, and lay the basis for future parent–teacher communication about children's progress (Wolfendale 1990).

The problems described above that are endemic in any screening procedure inevitably affect these arrangements. There is also an additional risk of a 'false positive' in identifying SEN in young children from ethnic and linguistic minorities. Their preschool experience is less likely to have prepared them for the school curriculum, and pupils who are learning EAL often develop linguistic and other skills in English rapidly after school entry. This means that a very early assessment may soon be out of date. For example, Bartlett (1995) carried out an analysis of the baseline assessment results obtained by children admitted to Birmingham schools in 1994. He showed that children who had attended an LEA nursery class or school previously for at least one term did better, on average, in the baseline assessment results for English (see Table 5.2). The important point for the present argument was that this association was especially strong for children learning EAL. The implication must be that in the case of children learning EAL an emphasis on early identification may risk throwing up too many false positives – i.e. it would appear to show that children were in need of special help when what they really needed was a longer period of induction to school

Table 5.2   Baseline assessment results from Birmingham – English, 1994

	Pupils scoring 5 and above by first language (%)	
Language	Nursery	No nursery
Bengali	26.5	4.6
English	36.5	31.6
Punjabi	22.7	7.2
Urdu	18.5	8.8

Source: Bartlett (1995).

and to the use of English. (For a fuller discussion of this issue see Cline and Shamsi 2000, Ch. 4.)

Labelling children wrongly as having SEN will itself have a negative impact. If teachers believe that a child has serious learning difficulties they are likely to reduce their expectations of what he or she can achieve. The child may be offered a less stimulating curriculum and will then face reduced intellectual challenges in school. In the case of a child from a linguistic minority community a 'diagnosis' of learning difficulties may mask the need for additional language provision.

Initial assessment questions

When a child has been identified as being at risk or as experiencing difficulties, it is necessary to carry out a more detailed assessment. Harlen (1983) has suggested some initial questions that need to be considered when embarking on any assessment in school, whatever the focus. We have added a commentary below to highlight issues that arise in relation to work with different groups of pupils.

What is the purpose of the assessment?

For example, checking what has been learned; making comparisons; reporting achievements; diagnosing difficulties; evaluating teaching or the curriculum; monitoring at school, LEA or national level.

What information is required for that purpose?

For example, what learning outcomes are to be assessed – knowledge, techniques, problem solving strategies, creativity, confidence, ability to work autonomously, ability to work with others on solving problems and carrying out tasks? (In the case of children with EAL it may be important to assess their knowledge of the vocabulary for the subject.)

What methods will provide this information?

Any assessment method will have the following components:

- *Ways in which the tasks are presented*. For example, on paper; by demonstration; in a practical situation; through normal class work. (In the case of pupils with EAL the use of methods that place a premium on language proficiency may mean that they fail to understand the question or task properly, so that their knowledge of the target subject is not assessed at all.)
- *Ways in which pupils can respond*. For example, selection of correct answer from multiple choices; writing; drawing, etc.; constructing; speaking. Note

that pupils may differ in their success in responding through different media. For example, there is evidence that boys do better on a test in a multiple-choice format, while girls do better when their knowledge is assessed through an essay-writing task (Gipps and Murphy 1994).

- *Standards or criteria used in judging the response*. For example, comparing with others' performance; comparing with stated performance criteria; comparing with pupil's own previous performance.
- *Ways of presenting the results of assessment*. For example, number of correct answers; grade; qualitative comments.

Together these factors combine to determine whether a method of assessment is *reliable* (consistent, yielding the same results whoever administers it and whenever it is given), and *valid* (accurate, giving results that reflect the reality of the child's abilities or achievements). Specifically, we may want to know whether the assessment has:

- *Concurrent validity*. Indicates the current state of affairs accurately, would agree closely with other assessments carried out at the same time, and/or
- *Predictive validity*. Indicates accurately how the child will develop in the future, would agree closely with other assessments carried out at a later date.

It will always be important that a test or assessment is reliable. For different purposes either concurrent or predictive validity may be more important.

How will the results be interpreted and used?

While the purposes of assessment will not differ for different groups of children in the same situation, the interpretation of the results may be less certain and more sensitive. For example, if children from a minority ethnic group obtain a low score on average on an attainment test, this may be taken to mean that, as a group, their abilities are lower, or it may be taken to mean that the curriculum is ethnocentric or the test biased.

For pupils with EAL concurrent validity could be high if decisions made about the purpose, information and methods of assessment take account of their needs. But predictive validity could still be low. If the interpretation of their results takes account of their (possibly unusual) educational history, predictions about their future progress should be more accurate.

Tests for testers – what standards must assessment meet?

This section will highlight four reasonable expectations of the process of assessment: theoretical integrity; practical efficacy; equity; and accountability (Cline

Figure 5.1
Questions to be
asked about the
process of
assessment

Theoretical integrity

? Is the approach to assessment based on an acceptable model of SEN (or is the model on which it is based reliant on outdated or misleading categories of handicap)?
? Does its implicit model of human development incorporate all aspects of development (or is it based on a narrow view of what is important in development – for example, focusing on intelligence to the exclusion of everything else)?
? Is it based on an acceptable model of the learning process that respects the autonomy and initiative of the learner (or does it appear to assume a top-down, highly structured process for all aspects of classroom learning)?
? Does it explicitly focus on aspects of development that are important for successful learning (or does it emphasise only weaknesses, limitations, gaps in knowledge and what might make for failure)?

Practical efficacy

? Does the assessment draw upon the richest sources of information available (or is it based on thin evidence that comes from a restricted perspective on what the child is like)?
? Does it produce information that can lead directly to improvements in teaching and learning (or is the information it yields of limited value in planning how the child can best be taught)?
? Does the way the assessment is conducted empower children, parents and teachers (or does it place them in a subordinate position so that their observations as stakeholders in the situation are ignored)?

Equity

? Are the rights of children and parents effectively protected?
? Does the process operate without bias with respect to gender, social class, ethnicity, language use and religion (see Chapter 6)?

Accountability

? Is the process and the information it produces open and intelligible to children, parents, teachers, other professionals and educational administrators?
? Are the agreed purposes of the assessment satisfied?
? Is the process cost-effective?

1992). The first two of these have regularly featured in accounts of SEN assessment. We will emphasize the equal importance of the last two – equity and accountability. As different approaches to assessment are introduced in this book, we will examine them in the light of the questions presented in Figure 5.1.

From time to time professional groups involved in SEN assessment have tried to define a set of principles to guide their assessment practice. The following

ACTIVITY 5.1   Defining principles of assessment for your own setting

Consider the principles of assessment agreed by the Southwark Educational Psychology Service. These are clearly based on the challenge of assessment as it is experienced by a group of people doing a particular job in a particular kind of setting. Do all the principles they described apply to the context in which you work? How would you adapt their statement for your situation?

statement was produced by a team of educational psychologists in the London Borough of Southwark (Shah *et al.* 1997):

> Assessment carried out in the Southwark Educational Psychology Service will be underpinned by the following principles:
>
> *Psychological*   The assessment will be informed by the testing of hypotheses which derive from current psychological theory.
>
> *Understandable*   The assessment will have a number of audiences. It must be understandable by those audiences and have value for all those audiences.
>
> *Beneficial*   The assessment must make a difference, and that difference must be a beneficial one, both in terms of the process and in terms of the outcomes.
>
> *Equity*   The assessment process must promote equity and address the issues of disadvantage and deprivation.
>
> *Parents*   The assessment should in the majority of cases take place only with the full agreement and involvement of the parents/ carers of the child or young person.
>
> *Contextual*   The assessment must be rooted firmly in a real life context and explore concerns in the context in which they occur. The assessment should acknowledge the maturational, developmental and pedagogical processes that children and young people undergo and take account of those processes.
>
> *Accurate*   The assessment should be based on fact, and opinion and interpretation presented in the report should be denoted as such.
>
> *Reproducible*   Another psychologist working with the same hypotheses should be able to reach similar conclusions provided no change has taken place.

Assessment and the delivery of the curriculum

When teachers assess SEN they work within the context of whatever assessment procedures a school has in place for all children. In the UK there is a national system of assessment at the end of each Key Stage – i.e. at ages 7, 11, 14 and 16. The results are published school by school, and these arrangements are seen as playing a central role in improving educational standards. Since everyone is able to examine the public 'league tables' of schools' results, there is a strong motivation for schools to present the best possible picture of their achievements. These requirements, which are a relatively new feature of the UK scene, reflect an international trend towards more systematic assessment of pupils' attainments in school and public dissemination of the results (Broadfoot *et al.* 1993).

The strategies of assessment employed to meet national requirements at the end of each Key Stage have been designed to enable broad-brush information to be obtained across the age group. They are not usually helpful in relation to children with SEN. But, although it is statutorily possible to exempt some children with Statements, teachers have considered it important that all children are included in the process wherever possible (Lewis 1995). Special arrangements may be made in order to enable children with SEN to participate. For example, they may be allowed additional time during the test session; material may be presented on audiotape or in Braille or enlarged print; they may use any mechanical and technological aids that they would normally use; an amanuensis or a reader may be employed. It is important to ensure that the operation of the assessment procedures is as equitable as possible. But this is not the only challenging issue that is presented by the national assessment regime in relation to children with SEN. It is equally important that those who are aware that they have under-performed on the assessments are not discouraged from future effort or made to feel that what they can achieve is of no worth.

The ultimate aim of all assessment in the classroom must be to enable teachers to match their delivery of the curriculum to the needs of each pupil – a process of *differentiation*. 'The purpose of education for all children is the same; the goals are the same. But the help that individual children need in progressing towards them will be different' (Department of Education and Science 1978, para. 1.4). When there is a mismatch between the help that pupils need and the help they receive, there will often also be a culture of blame. Stradling and Saunders (1991) described this in terms of polarized assumptions about low attainment:

Pupils failing school	*School failing pupils*
Poor basic skills	Inadequate diagnosis of need
Poor personal and social skills	Irrelevant curriculum content
Poor attendance and behaviour	Inappropriate pedagogy
Poor motivation and self-image	Low expectation (by teachers)
Low parental expectations	Unfavourable pupil–teacher ratio
Social deprivation	Lax discipline
Poor parental support	Non-conducive environment

In order to plan for differentiation at any level it is necessary to focus assessment on both needs and provision, both the pupil and the school. A typical outline paradigm involves these elements (Barthorpe and Visser 1991):

- assess the child's needs;
- prioritize the curriculum, setting achievable, short-term goals;
- match the teacher's delivery to the child's needs, ensuring access for all;
- evaluate lessons in terms of what both teacher and children have learned;
- keep careful records.

While this is widely accepted as a paradigm of good practice, it does not appear to be achieved consistently. For example, studies of primary teachers in England (Bennett *et al.* 1984) and Scotland (Simpson 1997) found that a substantial proportion of the tasks they gave their pupils did not match the children's assessed capabilities and attainments. In addition, Simpson and her colleagues found that the pupils often perceived the tasks differently from their teachers, experiencing tasks that were intended to offer practice or revision as introducing new learning and vice versa. Bennett and Cass (1989) reported similar evidence in a series of observational case studies of children with SEN moving from special schools to mainstream schools. In the chapters on curriculum related assessment, literacy and mathematics (Chapters 7, 11 and 12) we will discuss strategies of assessment for intervention that are intended to facilitate successful differentiation within an inclusive classroom.

Approaches to the assessment of SEN

In this final section of the chapter we will describe four distinctive approaches to assessment that have been or are likely to become influential in the field of SEN. They vary markedly in their value in enabling teachers to plan for differentiation. The approaches are outlined in Table 5.3 (adapted from Cline 1992). The table shows how these approaches relate to the different ways of conceptualizing SEN that were discussed in the first chapter. The methods adopted with each approach are summarized briefly here. You may read more about them in later chapters where each is featured and explained in detail. For the present what matters is to identify the major emphasis of each approach.

Focus on the learner

Traditionally the assessment of SEN has involved a detailed examination of the children with difficulties. The assumption was made that the source of any problems would lie within the children: they must suffer from a disability or impairment of learning ability compared to most children of their age. The assessment task was thought of as similar to medical diagnosis. The aim of assessment was to determine what category of disability the children suffered from. Their performance was compared to norms for their age group. There were a series of assumptions behind this approach. It was assumed that:

Table 5.3   Four approaches to the assessment of SEN

Approach	Focus on the learner	Focus on the teaching programme
Hypothesis	This child suffers from a disability or impairment of learning ability compared to most children of the same age.	The curriculum is not well suited to the learning needs of this child.
Aims	To determine what category of disability the child suffers from.	To match work on the curriculum very closely to the child's existing skills and knowledge.

Approach	Focus on the 'zone of potential development'	Focus on the learning environment
Hypothesis	The teacher is not making full use of this child's emerging skills and abilities – that is, the performance of which she or he is capable when given some assistance; his or her 'zone of potential development'.	The learning environment in which this child experiences difficulties fails to provide conditions that will facilitate success.
Aims	To identify the child's zone of potential development in a particular domain of activity so as to make instruction more responsive to her or his current strengths and needs.	To determine whether there are factors in the learning environment that may cause or exacerbate the child's learning difficulties.

Source: Adapted from Cline (1992).

- individuals' traits and abilities are relatively permanent characteristics;
- they show a pattern of strengths and weaknesses in learning resulting from these characteristics which can be identified through educational assessment;
- this pattern of strengths and weaknesses is the prime cause of the child's poor classroom performance with other factors having less importance;
- a teaching programme which remediates weaknesses and builds on strengths can lead to improvement in performance.

This approach has been particularly associated with arranging provision for children with SEN in separate schools or units. (Approaches to assessment within this paradigm will be discussed in more detail in Chapter 9.)

Focus on the teaching programme

Over the last 30 years assumptions relating to a focus on the learner have frequently been attacked, and other approaches have been explored. To some extent the new approaches have been associated with the parallel movement in the direction of inclusive education in mainstream schools. The first new approach to attract attention on a large scale as an alternative to the focus on the learner was a focus on the teaching programme. The underlying assumption here is that the curriculum presented in the classroom is not well suited to the current learning needs of the child. It is necessary to match work on the curriculum more closely to the child's existing skills and knowledge. The educators' task is conceived within a framework of classical learning theory. The immediate challenge is to analyse learning tasks within the curriculum into a hierarchy of component skill elements. Because these elements are thought to be organized hierarchically, it is assumed that they will best be approached in incremental steps. It is possible to determine which elements the child has mastered and which require further work. For children with SEN the incremental steps can be made smaller or otherwise modified so that the challenge that is faced at each stage is less formidable. Thus it is assumed that:

1 the school curriculum can be analysed into tasks that can be expressed in the form of behavioural objectives;
2 these tasks can be arranged into pedagogically viable sequences;
3 by checking frequently on a child's attainments within one of these sequences teaching can be matched closely to the learning stage the child has reached;
4 through a method of instruction that is very firmly under the teacher's control children can be led to:
   • acquire new skills
   • perform them with fluency
   • maintain them after teacher support is withdrawn
   • use them in new contexts
   • adapt them to different challenges (Solity and Bull 1987).

This approach to assessment will be discussed in more detail in Chapter 7.

Focus on the 'zone of potential development'

A third approach focuses on the 'zone of potential development' as conceptualized by the Russian developmental psychologist, Vygotsky (Daniels 1992). Suppose the performance of two boys on a traditional test is at the same level – for example, a level equivalent to an average 8-year-old's performance. They are then retested with some adult help – for example, in the form of standard questions prompting them towards the correct solution of problems they could not solve before. One child now attains a score that is just a little better than before while the other now reaches a level that is associated with much older children. Vygotsky saw the difference between what children can achieve by themselves and the level they can reach with adult help as an operational definition of the 'zone of potential development' (ZPD). Those two children have the same zone of actual development (ZAD) but a very different ZPD: the latent learning ability of one was markedly superior.

Supporters of this approach argue that traditional (static) tests establish current levels of performance but usually tell us little about the processes that underlie that competence. They also ignore functions that have not yet matured but are in the process of maturing. They focus on the 'fruits' of development rather than its 'buds' and 'flowers'. They are retrospective rather than prospective (Vygotsky 1978). Observing embryonic (nascent, emerging) skills closely would provide a better estimate of individuals' potential for proceeding beyond their present level of competence (Campione 1989) and would offer more useful guidance on the kind of teaching that will help them realize that potential. Children are invited to carry out standard tasks that are at the limit of their capabilities. They are given adult assistance to help them to success, and the assistance is monitored closely. Thus the focus of the assessment is on both the children's performance and on the amount and kind of help they required to achieve it. This approach to assessment is discussed in more detail in Chapter 9.

Focus on the learning environment

A fourth approach shifts the focus onto the learning environment provided by the school. The assumption is made that SEN are relative and that, for individual children, a full understanding of their SEN can only be developed if one evaluates the learning environment that is provided for them. Perhaps the learning environment in which a child experiences difficulties fails to provide conditions that will facilitate success. The assessment may involve classroom observation, diary records, questionnaires and/or interviews with both children and teachers. The purpose of the analysis is to determine whether there are factors in the learning environment that may cause or exacerbate the child's learning difficulties (Frederickson and Cline 1995). This approach to assessment is discussed in more detail in Chapter 8.

Activity 5.2 provides an opportunity for you to consider how these approaches to assessment might be employed in practice. This activity introduces another way of thinking about the process of assessment – as a hypothesis-testing process. Wright (1991) and her colleagues regarded assessment as being like a piece of detective work. There was a situation to be explained. They thought of various hypotheses that might provide a satisfactory explanation. In the activity you are asked to suggest what kind of evidence should be collected in order to decide whether any of these hypotheses is justified.

ACTIVITY 5.2   **Why is this bilingual pupil not making the progress I would expect? Evaluating some possible hypotheses**

The question you are asked to address in this task is: Which of the approaches to assessment featured in this section would be most useful to evaluate each of these hypotheses? Remember that they focus on a child who is learning to speak EAL.
The list of hypotheses were developed by a team of psychologists and teachers in Surrey (Wright 1991). They suggested different reasons why a bilingual child might be underperforming and examined the implications of each explanation for how teachers might aim to help. Indicate in the right hand column whether the focus of investigation should be:

(a) The individual learner
(b) The teaching programme
(c) The zone of potential development
(d) The learning environment

Hypothesis	Suggested focus for assessment
1 The child is learning more slowly than others because the ethos and curriculum of the school are experienced as challenging and alien, rather than welcoming and accommodating	
2 The child is not learning because the child's good level of conversational English has misled the teacher into setting tasks that are too abstract for the child's current language level	
3 The child is learning at an appropriate rate, and just needs more time to get used to the demands of working in their second language	
4 The child has not attained a basic language proficiency in any language, because neither language has been given adequate opportunities to develop	
5 The child is failing because of a preoccupation with stress that is affecting their family or their community	
6 The child has a general difficulty in learning compared to other children of the same age	
7 The child is failing because of a specific language disorder	

Conclusions

While much emphasis is placed on early identification and assessment of SEN, there can be dangers associated with this as well as benefits. We have reviewed a range of measures which should be taken to maximize the likelihood of positive outcomes. These include: parental involvement; multidisciplinary collaboration;

and utilizing the least intrusive intervention approach available. Issues and implications for action arising from the results of baseline assessment on school entry were discussed. In particular cautions were identified regarding the implications that can legitimately be drawn about pupils who are learning EAL.

A major focus in this chapter was on the critical examination of assessment practice. A guiding framework was proposed within which the purpose of any assessment is carefully considered as a first step. Thereafter the information required for that purpose and the methods that can be used to obtain the necessary information can be decided. It was suggested that a series of questions be asked about the proposed plan of the assessment – questions relating to equity and accountability issues as well as concerning the theoretical integrity and practical efficacy of the process. Finally, we considered four distinctive approaches to assessment which relate to the different ways of conceptualizing SEN introduced in Chapter 2. Each of these approaches will be described in further detail in later chapters and has both advantages and disadvantages in relation to the questions posed for a critical examination of identification and assessment practice.

Chapter 6

Reducing bias in methods of assessment

Contents

Introduction

In Chapter 1 we saw that on both sides of the Atlantic there has been a tendency for higher than expected numbers of children from some minority communities to be admitted into some forms of special educational provision. In England and Wales in the early 1970s there were over four times as many children of West Indian immigrants in schools for the 'educationally subnormal' as would have been expected from their overall numbers in the child population (Tomlinson 1984). Although the overrepresentation of African-Caribbean pupils in these schools has been reduced over the years, relatively high numbers continue to be admitted to schools for pupils with emotional and behavioural difficulties. In Chapter 1 we also drew attention to other group differences in admission to SEN provision – between boys and girls and between children from working-class and middle-class backgrounds. Such group differences in outcome must arise at some point in the process of identification and assessment. It could be that there are uneven patterns of referral that arise from real group differences in how many children require help and how severe their needs are. Many commentators, however, have argued that these differences most probably reflect biased referral processes and the use of biased tests during formal assessment.

For example, one of the writers who first highlighted the overrepresentation of black children in schools for the 'educationally subnormal' in England (Coard 1971: 15) wrote that, when IQ tests were used, a range of biases operating

> against the West Indian child . . . apply just as much to the *actual questions asked on the IQ test* administered to the children, and the very nature of *'the test situation'*. The vocabulary and style of all these IQ tests is white middle class. Many of the questions are capable of being answered by a white middle-class boy, who, because of being middle class, has the right background of experiences with which to answer the questions – regardless of his real intelligence. The black working-class child, who has different life-experiences, finds great difficulty in answering many of the questions, even if he is very intelligent.

The Californian federal judge, R.F. Peckham, who banned the use of IQ tests with black children at the end of the 1970s stated: 'We must recognise at the outset that the history of the IQ test and of special education classes built on IQ testing is not the history of neutral scientific discoveries translated into educational reform. It is, at least in the early years, a history of racial prejudice, of social Darwinism, and of the use of the scientific "mystique" to legitimate such prejudices' (Baca and Cervantes 1989: 16).

For Howitt and Owusu-Bempah (1994: 28) tests of intelligence were 'nothing other than weapons of subordination when used with society's disadvantaged'. Similar, though less extreme, concerns have been expressed about other forms of test. (For a full discussion see Gipps and Murphy 1994.)

There is, however, another way of looking at the situation. In this view an advantage of using tests for assessment is that the process of decision making is

Table 6.1 Proportion of secondary pupils from different ethnic groups allocated to remedial sets for English and mathematics in a Midlands town

	West Indian	Indian	Non-minority
Remedial English	17% (30/176)	12% (23/188)	5% (13/239)
Remedial maths	19% (42/216)	12% (26/224)	8% (25/304)

Source: Adapted from Scarr *et al.* (1983) and Roberts (1984).

transparent. If bias is operating in the content of the tests or in the use made of the results, at least it is possible to trace what is happening. Some decisions in education may be affected by bias in a way that is hidden from gaze. One example would be decisions on the placement of pupils when classes are streamed. An early analysis of the educational careers of the children of immigrants in a UK Midlands town showed that they were two to three times as likely as their white peers to be placed in the remedial stream of a secondary school (see Table 6.1). HMI have observed that it is still the case that, where schools emphasize tight setting, some groups learning EAL (notably pupils from the Bangladeshi and Pakistani communities) are likely to be placed disproportionately in low sets, especially in English (Ofsted 1999a).

Some schools employ standardized attainment tests to profile the educational achievements and needs of groups of children and use the results for planning purposes. The observations of HMI have suggested 'that it is in those schools with the best ethnic data that the performance of the minority ethnic pupils has improved most strongly' (Ofsted 1999a). Inspectors considered that analysing performance on a test such as the Cognitive Abilities Test (Thorndike *et al.* 1986) could assist teachers to plan the organization of a cohort of pupils into groups or to identify students with unused potential by comparing ability with attainment. Focusing specifically on the situation of bilingual pupils, Cline and Shamsi (2000) commented: 'It is common for pupils learning EAL to obtain scores for nonverbal reasoning that are higher than their scores on L2 language and attainment tests (Valdes and Figueroa 1994, Table 4.1). Analysing the profile of scores on this type of test battery can help to counter the low expectations that are sometimes held of children in the early stages of learning English'. But they added a note of caution:

> If standardised tests are used for guiding even minor decisions about individuals learning EAL, particular care will always be needed. The appropriateness of the decision may be monitored by seeking confirmatory evidence from earlier school records, if available, or by reviewing any new arrangements or provision after an agreed fixed period on the basis of further teacher observation.
>
> (Cline and Shamsi 2000: 39–40)

In this chapter we will examine definitions of bias, consider its sources at various points in the assessment process and outline strategies for reducing the impact of bias to a minimum. It cannot be expected that bias will be eliminated altogether. It is not possible (or desirable) to develop methods of educational assessment that are culturally neutral or entirely 'culture-free'. Child development and school education are embedded in a cultural context which is often unfair (DeBlaissie and Franco 1983). The result of any assessment is likely to reflect, in part, the pattern of opportunities that exists. Equity in the assessment of SEN requires the recognition and reduction of sources of bias, not the pretence that this area of education can operate independently of inequalities that characterize other aspects of society.

Bias in test content

What is *bias* and what is *fair assessment*? The answers to these questions are sometimes based on confused assumptions. It may be thought that, if, say, a test item is more difficult for boys than for girls, that item must be 'unfair to boys'. But an assessment may still be 'fair' even if, on average, one group of people consistently obtains higher scores on it than another group. The first group may really be superior at whatever task the assessment is measuring. Williams (1971, 1975) devised a vocabulary test that would be 'fairer' to black Americans living in northern US cities than the conventional vocabulary tests in published IQ scales. His 'Black Intelligence Test of Cultural Homogeneity' (the 'BITCH' Test) was a multiple-choice vocabulary test comprising 100 items drawn from urban black culture. It was a culture-specific test highlighting the world of the inner city and covering elements of black slang. Two items from the test are:

> *Boot* refers to (a) a cotton farmer, (b) a black, (c) an Indian, or (d) a Vietnamese citizen.
> *Yawk* is (a) a gun, (b) a fishing hook, (c) a high boot, or (d) a heavy coat.

Williams showed that this test favoured black children while conventional tests favoured white children. Both tests appear to be biased – *if* the criterion of bias is that tests should not discriminate between groups in terms of outcome. Jensen (1980) described this criterion as 'the egalitarian fallacy' – assuming that all human populations are essentially identical or equal in whatever trait or ability the test purports to measure.

The purpose of an assessment is to make predictions about the people who are being assessed. In relation to *bias* the key question then must be whether a test makes equally accurate predictions about all groups of children. In psychometric jargon, a test is biased if it is 'differentially valid for members of different groups' (Wood 1991). From this viewpoint what matters is whether a test predicts performance on a criterion measure with equal validity for each social or ethnic group: 'Bias is a kind of invalidity that harms one group more than another' (Shepard *et al.* 1981). Various technical methods are possible to investigate this. One example is the constant ratio model (Thorndike 1971). Suppose that children are given a test of motor response speed in order to select a group to train for a computer games championship. The assumption is made that those who complete the test of motor response speed most accurately and in the fastest times will prove to be the ones who do well in the computer games after training. Now imagine that, on average, a group of boys obtain better scores than a group of girls on this test so that 68 per cent of the boys reach the threshold for selection for training and only 26 per cent of the girls. Is the test biased against girls? Using the constant ratio model, the question to be asked is: if all the children were trained, would the proportions of boys and girls who eventually reached the final stages of the computer games championship be approximately 68:26? If that is the case, the test of motor response speed has no gender bias: it predicts performance on the criterion measure without discriminating against either group. It should also be noted that it has been shown that there are problems in the detailed statistical operation of the constant ratio model (Cole 1973; Petersen and Novick 1976). For a discussion of other ways of considering the relationship between bias and validity see Cole and Moss (1989) and Wood (1991, Ch. 14).

With children it is normally expected that test scores will increase with age. This has been the basis of a developmental version of the constant ratio model. The question asked is whether the relationship between test scores and chronological age is the same for children in different ethnic or social groups. This can be illustrated with data on one of the versions of the most widely used individual intelligence scale, the Wechsler Intelligence Scale for Children (WISC). Table 6.2 shows the correlation of IQ with age across ethnic groups analysed from the standardization data for the test by Reynolds (1980). If there had been an exact one-for-one matching between IQ and age, the correlations would have been 1; if there had been no relationship at all they would have been 0. All the correlations shown are much closer to 1 than to 0 (at a level that could not have arisen by chance alone). The correlations are no higher for the white children than they are for the black children. Reynolds concluded that the relationship between IQ scores and age was consistent across ethnic groups (even though the scores of black males were lower than those of other groups on average). As far as he was concerned this evidence 'fails to support armchair claims of test bias . . . with regard to intelligence tests' (Reynolds 1980: 378). His confidence was increased

Table 6.2 Correlation of IQ with age on WISC-R Scale

	White males	Black males	White females	Black females
No. of children (6–16 years)	938	137	927	153
Correlation of IQ with age:				
Verbal IQ	0.84	0.83	0.84	0.81
Performance IQ	0.81	0.81	0.82	0.82
Full-scale IQ	0.85	0.86	0.85	0.84

Source: Adapted from Reynolds (1980).

by evidence that the WISC-R predicted scores on tests of educational achievement equally well for African-American, Hispanic and white children (Reynolds
and Kaiser 1990) – a result that has been confirmed with the WISC-III, the latest
American version of the WISC (Weiss and Prifitera 1995).

This robust defence of a general intelligence scale does not address the criticism
that bias operates in the way such tests are *used* and *interpreted*. In addition, it is
important to recognize that the correlation of overall score with age is a broad-
brush measure of bias in test content. Problems may occur with a whole test
and the way it is conceived, but they may also occur at the level of an individual
test item or task. For example, Ribeiro (1980) found that some test items in
the WISC-R proved easier than expected for one particular minority group in the
USA. Portuguese children coped well with two questions in an advanced section
of a test where they were failing most other items: 'What is the meaning of
"migrate"?' and 'Why does oil float on water?' The explanations were simple:
migration was a feature of the recent family history of many of the children, and
they were used to seeing oil float on water in an altar lamp in their Catholic
church. On the other hand, Hannon and McNally (1986) found that children from
linguistic minorities and working-class monolingual children did less well than
a matched middle-class monolingual group on certain reading comprehension
questions. These were questions based on assumptions about social conventions.
For example, the children from socially less privileged groups made 'errors'
when they were asked what might be expected by someone who is a guest at
teatime. They were required to fill a gap in a sentence. In this case the sentence
was: 'Jimmy . . . tea, because he was our guest'. Four choices were available to fill
the gap (of which no. 3 is correct) (Hannon and McNally 1986: 238):

1 washed the dishes after
2 was late for
3 got the best cake at
4 could not eat his

In a classic study of O-level English language exams Wood (1978) found a
similar phenomenon in relation to gender differences. Boys did better than girls
on items relating to a passage about a man looking back to a boyhood spent
near a railway, while girls did better than boys on a passage about a girl's ordeal
at a dance. On another test he found girls doing better on a passage about a
14-year-old girl and boys doing better on a passage about the Crimean War
(Wood 1991: 169).

Responsible test developers make a formal commitment to addressing the issue
of content bias. For example, in its *Code of Practice for the Development of
Assessment Instruments, Methods and Systems* (1998) the National Foundation
for Educational Research (NFER) states that in order to produce fair assessments, NFER developers will:

• review and revise questions, items or tasks and related materials to avoid
  potentially insensitive content or language;

- enact procedures that help to ensure that differences in performance are related primarily to the knowledge, skills, aptitudes or attitudes being assessed rather than to irrelevant factors;
- investigate the performance of people of different ethnic, gender and socioeconomic backgrounds when institutions helping with trials are willing to provide this information and when samples of sufficient size are available;
- carry out the investigation of performance of different groups using data provided on the first actual administration of the assessment;
- provide (where feasible) appropriately modified forms of the assessment procedures for people with disabilities.

If a test or assessment task is developed within a school, it is possible to employ less formal, school-based review strategies for checking on possible item bias. The list of questions given here was adapted for an earlier report (Cline and Shamsi 2000) from Berk (1984) and from Tindal and Marston (1990). These authors designed a method of reviewing to assist in the identification of test items which may reflect gender, cultural, racial, regional and/or ethnic content bias and stereotyping. Although there is a form for this purpose, the essential process can be followed through without elaborate form-filling. It is most effective if a number of people examine the test with the checklist in mind and if they come from a range of backgrounds. The review team should include sufficient people from the target minority groups to enable it to predict significant patterns of response accurately. They should each complete the task independently and only compare notes afterwards. Their first task is to identify any individual items to which they feel they cannot give an unequivocal answer 'yes' for each of the following questions:

1 Is the item free of offensive gender, cultural, racial, regional and/or ethnic content?
2 Is the item free of gender, cultural, racial, regional and/or ethnic stereotyping?
3 Is the item free of language which could be offensive to a segment of the examinee population?
4 Is the item free of descriptions which could be offensive to a segment of the examinee population?
5 Will the activities described in the item be equally familiar (or equally unfamiliar) to all examinees?
6 Will the words in the item have a common meaning for all examinees?

Note that the questions that are to be asked are specific, focused and explicit. If a more general question is asked (e.g. 'Would this item be likely to favour white children over black children?') it is not likely that reviewers would accurately identify items that actually discriminate between ethnic groups (Hieronymous and Hoover 1986).

After looking at the individual items separately the reviewers should consider the test as a whole. Each item may have little wrong with it in itself, but the cumulative effect of the test as a whole may still be biased against a particular subgroup of candidates. So, when the task of examining the items separately has been completed, it is necessary to consider the overall balance of the paper or tasks as a whole. There may not be many individual items that cause problems. But what about the overall balance? Some researchers have argued that achieving a satisfactory overall balance and heterogeneous range in a test is much more important than eradicating individual biased items (Roznowski and Reith 1999). Sometimes test developers may retain items that they know to be biased because they appear to make a valuable contribution to the predictive validity of the test. For example, Smith and Whetton (1988: 257) wrote of a test they had developed to support occupational selection: 'Of the items used in the final test only three had any evidence of bias, and in each of these the evidence was only slight. These three were left in the test because their other psychometric properties were particularly valuable. Since each of them slightly favoured a different group (whites, non-whites, females), it is unlikely that any noteworthy bias was introduced by their inclusion'.

In addition to having groups of people from different backgrounds inspecting test items for content bias, a test developer can carry out a statistical investigation. This will aim to find out 'whether any questions are disproportionately difficult for a particular group once that group's overall test performance has been taken into account' (Gipps and Stobart 1993: 60). Other statistical checks are possible both on individual items and on the test as a whole (Reynolds and Kaiser 1990).

It is not only aspects of content such as offensiveness or stereotyping that can give rise to bias. Work on gender bias has shown that the format of a test or exam may also have a differential impact between groups. It has been found both in the UK and the USA that boys tend to do better on multiple-choice exams while girls tend to do better on exams that involve writing essays (Wood 1991; Gipps and Murphy 1994; Willingham and Cole 1997). Various explanations have been offered as to why this happens. Perhaps girls' essays are evaluated more favourably simply because they are more fluent in their writing and produce longer answers (Pomplun and Capps 1999). Perhaps girls underperform in the multiple-choice format because they are more likely than boys to omit an item when they are unsure of the answer, while boys tend to guess answers more often (Hanna 1986; Linn *et al.* 1987). Whatever the explanation, the most frequently recommended solution remains valid both for general educational assessment and for SEN assessment: use a variety of methods of assessment so as to minimize the

---

ACTIVITY 6.1   Evaluating a novel test

Du Bois (1939, cited by Norman 1963) developed a 'Draw a Horse' test for use with Pueblo Indian children. He had found that tests that involved drawing a person were not effective for measuring cognitive abilities with this population.

(a) What assumptions do you think he made when developing this test?
(b) How would you find out whether using it will lead to unbiased assessment?

bias associated with any one format (cf. Murphy 1982). At the end of it all an additional check is recommended by Watson *et al.* (1987) – carry out a post-test interview with the children to check on how they experienced the test's demands.

Other sources of bias

Discussions of bias in assessment usually concentrate on the content of tests. But test content is only one of many possible sources of bias. Testing takes place in a social context. Whether the child is in a classroom group or working on their own with an adult, it is possible to think about the situation in terms of one of three models. In the examples given below we have assumed that a specialist teacher is testing a child's educational attainments on their own in a quiet corner of a classroom.

- *A psychometric model.* The teacher proffers a test stimulus; the child responds; the teacher measures the child's response.
- *A psychological model.* The teacher explains the task and offers a test stimulus; the child makes sense of the task and responds; the teacher assesses the child's understanding of the task and also the child's response.
- *A social psychological model.* The child compares the situation she or he is in with other familiar situations. The teacher explores the child's understanding of the situation and observes his or her responses to it. The tasks that the teacher gives the child are seen by both as a special feature of their encounter but not its only feature.

The social psychological model seems to reflect what we know about this situation most satisfactorily. A key concept is 'intersubjectivity': speakers take account of what they think their listeners are thinking as they choose what to say and how to say it; they monitor their own speech to make sure that its content and form are such that their listeners can 'tune into' it; listeners try to reconstruct what they think the speaker is intending to make known. The conversation that is quoted in Activity 6.2 illustrates the importance of exploring a child's understanding of the assessment situation and addressing any misapprehensions.

In the light of the social psychological model it is necessary to examine the overall assessment process. Each phase of that process may be a source of bias:

- defining the purpose of the assessment;
- briefing the staff who undertake the assessment and deciding what preliminary information they require;
- selecting the activities that are to be assessed;
- choosing appropriate test materials, if required;
- interviewing, testing, examining or observing children;
- evaluating children's responses;
- interpreting their performance;
- deciding on the action to be taken as a result.

ACTIVITY 6.2   The thoughts behind their words

Here is an extract from a conversation between a teacher and an 11-year-old child who has reading difficulties. They do not know each other well. The teacher is in the SEN department of a large secondary school where the child is a new Year 7 pupil. How would you fill in the right-hand column?

What they say	*What they may be thinking*

T: Will you read something for me? I want to find out
    how well you can read it.
C: I suppose so.
T: It's not very long.
C: I'll try.
T: This is the picture that goes with it.
C: OK.
T: Now here's the page I'd like you to read.

[Child reads the first two sentences in a monotone
without stopping. Then he pauses.]

T: Is that name difficult?
C: I've never seen it before.
T: Can you work it out? It's a man's name.
C: I guessed that but the letters are funny.
T: That's because it's not an English name.
C: How could I get it then?

[The session continues.]

In addition, bias may affect the initial identification by teachers of pupils who may have SEN. For example, there are many more boys than girls identified as possibly having dyslexia (Riddell *et al*. 1994). It is often assumed that this is because biological factors predispose boys to be at greater risk for all language-related disorders. But there is some evidence that *schools* play a role in this outcome. In a study in Connecticut when teachers were asked to identify children with learning disabilities, there was a preponderance of boys in the sample they selected. When tests were used alone to identify children at risk and the opinions of teachers were not sought, this male preponderance was reduced (Shaywitz *et al*. 1990). Similar data were reported by Wadsworth *et al*. (1992) with samples of children with reading disabilities in other areas of the USA and in the UK. Cline and Reason (1993) noted that in Shaywitz's study children who were identified as having a reading disability by the schools but not by the research team's tests were more likely to show behaviour problems at school. The subgroup numbers in this study were small, and it would be wrong to place too much reliance on a single finding. But the hypothesis must be: if children are a bit of a

Figure 6.1

Interpretations
of the same
behaviour in a boy
and a girl

Condry and Condry (1976) had subjects (a sample of college students) view a videotape of an infant responding to emotionally arousing stimuli such as a teddy bear and a jack-in-the-box. They found that the students' ratings of the type and intensity of the emotions the child displayed varied depending on whether they had been told the child was a boy or a girl. All the students saw the same child responding to the same stimuli. But those who thought the child was a boy were more likely to rate an ambiguous negative response to one of the stimuli as anger, whereas, if the same child was thought to be a girl, 'she' was seen as displaying the emotion of fear in this situation.

In a later study by Condry and Ross (1985) another sample of students was shown a videotape of two preschool children playing roughly in the snow. Their snowsuits disguised their actual gender, and the investigators systematically varied the gender labels used to describe the children. The students were asked to rate the degree of aggression and affection shown by one of the two children. They tended to rate the target child as significantly less aggressive when they thought she or he was a boy playing with another boy than when they thought he or she was a girl or a boy playing with a girl. This effect was particularly strong among participants with more experience with children. It appeared that they probably expected a higher general level of aggression in play between boys than in the other conditions. Condry and Ross suggested that this may have led them either to discount the aggressiveness they observed on the videotape if they thought the participants were boys or to inflate it if they thought they were girls or both: 'It may not be fair, and it certainly is not equal, but from the results of this study it looks as if boys and girls really are judged differently in terms of what constitutes aggression'.

nuisance in the classroom, it will be more likely that any learning difficulties they have are identified and action taken. Hill (1994) has shown that, when teachers and others describe children in the formal SEN assessment procedure, there is a tendency for gender stereotypes to appear. As the studies summarized in Figure 6.1 illustrate, the same behaviour may be interpreted differently in a boy and a girl.

How can we reduce the risk of initial identification and assessment in schools being influenced by gender or other bias? Structured observation schemes with well-defined subheadings make it less likely that behaviour that is not expected will be overlooked. Schemes that ask specific questions about the frequency and severity of particular types of incident make it less likely that vague assertions about extreme behaviour will be made without qualification.

In this situation, as in others, there are many advantages to drawing upon multiple sources of evidence. Sometimes, for example, it can be helpful to have a second adult observing the work of the classroom for a short time with a specific brief to investigate what happens from the perspective of the target pupil. When this was arranged in a Year 5 class by Williams (1996), another teacher interpreted various episodes during a reading activity quite differently from the class teacher. The target pupil was Harry, a mainstream pupil with language-related learning difficulties. Here is a record of the same episode as seen by the class

ACTIVITY 6.3   Approaches to recording observations of children's learning style

Below are two examples of published frameworks for observation relating to learning style in the classroom. They contrast in that the first is intended solely to provide headings under which a teacher will record comments, while the second aims to help teachers discriminate between different levels of severity by suggesting specific mini-scenarios that illustrate each level.

(a) We think that the *format* of the first approach may be more liable to the risk of observational bias. What reasons might there be for that view?
(b) On the other hand the *text* of the second example includes many vague and value-laden phrases which could, in themselves, encourage a biased approach to the observation task. Can you suggest ways of rewording the two items in the second example so as to reduce that risk?

This extract is taken from an account by Reid (1997) of a strategy for the assessment of dyslexia in the classroom. This section concerns observational assessment. The framework is not intended to be a checklist 'but a guide to the type of factors which should be observed in identifying learning strategies, strengths and weaknesses' (p. 75).

Attention/concentration   *Comments*
Focus on task
Major sources of distraction
Concentration span in different tasks

These items are taken from a *Guide to the Learning Skills* developed by Stott (1978). For comparison with the extract above, items relating to concentration and distractibility have been selected.

E: He/she is easily distracted
   Somewhat: Allows himself to be distracted to the extent that he doesn't get on with the job in hand.
   Definite: Creates frequent distractions for himself and others; behaves in a silly clowning way or creates disturbances.
   Severe: Flits rapidly from one momentary interest to another without ever doing anything productive.

N: He/she seems to try to attend, and is not hyperactive or distractible, but cannot concentrate.
   Somewhat: Seems to try hard but cannot keep his mind on the task, and gets things wrong that he was getting right.
   Definite: As soon as he is asked anything his mind flies off at a tangent.
   Severe: Cannot be induced to focus his attention on anything.

teacher and by the colleague who had agreed to observe the lesson by 'pupil shadowing' (Galloway and Banes 1994):

> *Class teacher:* Harry was asked an open-ended question which he struggled to answer and he fidgeted. To avoid focusing attention on Harry's difficulty it was passed to another child in the group.
> *Observer:* Harry needed more time to answer an open-ended question. When someone else was asked to answer the question he was left muttering.

When observing and recording children's academic achievements, pupil profiling systems have many advantages over repeated testing on the one hand and unstructured observation on the other (Sheil and Forde 1995). A profiling system normally comprises three elements:

1 *Indicators*. Statements describing pupils' achievements that are normally linked to the objectives of the curriculum.
2 *Levels/bands*. Indicators are grouped together within what is thought to be the same broad developmental level or band of achievement. A pupil's performance is rated as a whole across indicators so that a summary statement can be made about the level reached.
3 *Assessment tasks and contexts*. Special assessment tasks may be set for the purpose or the assessment may be based on portfolios of pupils' work or notes of observations made by teachers during everyday classroom activities.

Where there are groups of children of whom teachers' expectations tend to be low (e.g. many minorities) or whose performance tends to be variable (e.g. recently arrived refugees), a system of this kind may have additional benefits, quite apart from any advantages that apply to all pupils. The significant advantage is that in these schemes performance is rated *over time* and teachers' judgements are made in *a range of curricular contexts*. The effect is that, if a child underperforms on one occasion because of problems with the language or content of a particular task, this will be compensated for on another occasion if the foundation of competence in the subject is really established at the target level. In relation to reading it was found in one study that teacher ratings on a reading scale of this kind were less affected by the fluency in English of children learning EAL than were scores on the London Reading Test given at around the same time (Hester *et al.* 1988).

When external specialists become directly involved in advising on a child, they will initially be reliant on the information supplied to them by those who have been working with the child previously, particularly teachers. Where schools have followed the procedures set out in the revised *Code of Practice* successfully, there will already be careful records of the child's earlier IEPs and response to them. It will be possible, in the words of the *Code*, for external specialists such as educational psychologists to look at 'the pupil's records in order to establish which strategies have already been employed and which targets have been set and achieved' (Department for Education and Skills 2001, para. 5.57). If they have not been involved previously, the first impressions that they gain from the records at this point may have a significant effect on their approach to the assessment process. How far will the reports they read give them a biased view of the situation? What range of information will they receive? How far will the discussions and the paperwork at this stage be open and accessible to the child and parents? What provision will be made for interpreters to attend meetings and for documents to be translated where the family will otherwise be excluded from the process? The answers to such questions will determine to what extent there are effective safeguards against bias during this phase of assessment. Activity 6.4 will enable you to evaluate some examples of the kinds of summary reports that have been written for such purposes in the past.

ACTIVITY 6.4   Analysis of teachers' reports on children causing concern

After reading these three reports carefully:

(a) Circle any phrases that seem to you to be based on a stereotype about the group to which the child belongs and therefore liable to contribute to a biased impression.
(b) Underline any information or description that seems to you vague or imprecise. Note how it might have been presented more exactly, taking into consideration whether the advantages for the SEN assessment process would justify the extra time that would be required of the person preparing the report.
(c) To what extent do these descriptions 'identify which strategies have already been employed and which targets have been set and achieved' (Department for Education and Employment, 2000a, para. 6.16)? What additional information would need to be obtained in each case?

Rushana (aged 8) is the eldest of four children in her household. She lives with her parents, who both came to the UK from the Sylhet area of Bangladesh a few years before she was born. She herself visited Sylhet once two years ago to see her family. I think her grandmother was ill at the time. She did not attend school there and missed two terms of Year 2 in this school. Otherwise her attendance has been regular since she was first admitted to the part-time nursery class at the age of 4. She speaks fluent English now, though her only language on entry to the nursery class was Sylheti. It is reported that she uses Sylheti in almost all conversations with her parents and adult relatives at home. At school she is seen as a successful English speaker who does not need support from the part-time teacher of EAL. She used to enjoy bilingual support sessions with a visiting Bengali teacher, especially traditional singing. But unfortunately these sessions are no longer available. Now in Year 4 she is presenting with serious learning difficulties in the classroom. She can make out most of the words in the readng book she has (which I would judge suitable for a Year 3 child), but her fluency is appalling, and she does not seem to take in much of what she reads. She lacks confidence as a writer and has very poor spelling. In cooperative group work she has a strong tendency to allow others to take all the initiatives.

Jean-Paul was 10 when he arrived in this country two years ago from Mauritius to join his mother here. I understand that he attended school there regularly, though he himself seems to have only very hazy memories of that (in contrast to his memories of his grandmother's home there which seem to be vivid and happy). He now speaks the French dialect of Mauritius at home with his mother and communicates with his white, UK-born stepfather in English, a language he is still learning. Because there are very few children from linguistic minority families in this area, the school has no extra provision for meeting his language needs. It is his second school in this country, and when he arrived here four terms ago he had enough English to get by in the classroom. There is increasing concern about his fighting with other children in school (where he says people call him names) and his bullying of his younger half-brother and half-sister at home. While he is certainly not making good progress in school subjects either, our primary concern is the problems with his behaviour. He has not responded well to a structured intervention by the Behaviour Support Teaching Service. We have not seen his mother at school. His stepfather seems to think we should take a stronger line with him and finds it hard to accept that we do not use corporal punishment at all.

Everton (aged 13) has been a cause of concern to us for about two years. He tends to be sullen and aggressive and disrupts lessons. He has a very violent nature and has been violent to other boys on several occasions. Recently he was charged with thefts outside school and is due to appear in court in a month's time. We estimate his general ability to be about average. He has shown some flair in English and gets on well with his English teacher. But other subject teachers say he could do well but spoils himself with bad behaviour. He is disrespectful to teachers and a bully with his classmates. The one subject he seems to find really difficult is mathematics, and he often skips maths lessons. Otherwise his attendance is very good. He is resentful of any kind of authority and hence finds it difficult to do the work that is set. I have written to his parents three or four times and sent them progress reports going back over a year. But in and out of class he constantly causes trouble – sometimes with violence. His father says that at home he is quick tempered and cannot have his leg pulled. Both parents are very concerned about him. They come from Jamaica and are leading members of the Pentecostal church on the High Street.

Who can be fair?

Some commentators have argued that all children should have professional support from the same background as themselves. For some black people it seems 'quite obvious that many black parents and pupils will be at a serious disadvantage . . . in the absence of black psychologists . . . and other black professionals' (HBPGE 1984: 9). During the 1970s there was some indirect research evidence that seemed to support that view. For example, Strickland (1972) found that black children in her sample trusted a black interviewer more than they trusted a white interviewer. However, it is impossible to rely totally on indirect evidence. When researchers tried to show directly that the race of an examiner would affect the scores children obtained in tests, their results were inconsistent (Jensen 1980; Graziano *et al.* 1982). Many other factors seem to be involved. For example, the age of the pupils, the region where they live and the nature of the assessment task may each affect whether or not performance changes with race of examiner.

In any case, in a multiethnic and multilingual society where children in a conurbation such as London may speak more than 150 languages at home it will never be possible to offer ethnic and linguistic matching to all children who may require SEN assessment. The matching would need to cover not just language but dialect, and not just ethnic background but culture and regional area of origin. This would be impossible. In addition, there is a danger of placing those psychologists and teachers who speak minority languages in a professional ghetto working mainly with people from the same communal background and having restricted opportunities for wider responsibility.

An alternative strategy (Cline 1998) is to lay an obligation on trainers, employers and the unmatched psychologists and teachers themselves to ensure that all professionals are competent to work effectively with all ethnic and linguistic groups in their area. There is a major challenge for services and for university departments in establishing the necessary training as a normal element of all initial and in-service professional training. In some LEA services a crucial contribution has been made by the creation of various kinds of liaison and advisory posts (e.g. Rogers and Pratten 1996). The role of workers from ethnic and linguistic minority communities remains critical. What is being argued here should not take away the pressure for trainers and employers to ensure that the personnel in professional services reflect the composition of the communities they serve more closely. The argument simply concerns what the personnel should be doing once they are appointed and how they should be trained to do it.

The following list of some of the key areas of expertise that are required is based on recommendations made by an American Psychological Association Task Force on Cross-Cultural School Psychology Competencies (Rogers *et al.* 1999). The text refers to psychologists throughout but would equally apply to all other advisers and specialists working with children with SEN, including specialist teachers. The expectations held up for school psychologists by this task force include the following elements.

Ethical issues

- They will be aware of the unique ethical challenges and complex ethical issues faced when delivering services to racially, ethnically, culturally and linguistically diverse individuals in schools.
- They will uphold ethical standards. The example is given that, if asked to assess the language and cognitive skills of a non-English speaking child without adequate resources, materials, interpreters or training, the psychologist will not personally fulfil the request. Instead they will seek out the assistance of an appropriately trained person who is skilled in the language and culture of the child.

School culture and educational policy

- They will be well informed and aware of the systemic issues associated with cases referred to them for services. So, in this case, they will be knowledgeable about institutional racism, cultural misinformation and other systemic issues affecting the education of students from culturally and linguistically diverse populations.

- They will provide advice and support to develop systems interventions to support the educational success of culturally and linguistically diverse learners.
- When working with racially, ethnically, culturally and linguistically diverse children and their families, they will have an ethical and professional responsibility to assess whether problems presumed to reside within the student may be manifestations of systemic biases in the institution(s) serving the child. So they will rule out systemic factors as causal influences in the student's situation before proceeding with individually-focused assessment or intervention.

Psychological and educational assessment

- They will ensure that the assessments in which they are involved comprise a comprehensive process of gathering information about students that explicitly takes account of the impact of sociocultural, environmental, political, experiential and language based factors.
- They will consider cultural sources of information about students and search for culture-specific confirming data. Thus, when conducting observations, they will use appropriate comparison group members so that, for example, a second language learner would be compared to another second language learner.
- They will develop expertise in assessing the student's biculturalism and will be supportive of it. When conducting an assessment, they will take into account language and other behaviour considered to be socially appropriate in the culture of the child.
- They will incorporate cultural and linguistic information in their verbal advice and written reports.
- They will recognize the limitations of standardized instruments and the ramifications of using such instruments in the assessment of racially, ethnically, culturally and linguistically diverse students. For example, if tests are used for a group or individual for which appropriate norms do not exist, they will report any findings in a descriptive and qualitative manner.

Consultation

- They will aim to become skilled in developing a multicultural consultation model which reflects an understanding of cultural values and the implications for working with culturally diverse families.
- They will develop culturally sensitive verbal and non-verbal communication skills and an awareness of how their own cultural background and biases may influence their ability to communicate effectively with culturally diverse students, school personnel and family members.
- They will learn about the characteristic family structures, hierarchies, values and beliefs of the communities with which they work. They will aim to be knowledgeable about the main features of the communities, their history and their resources. For example, where a culture structures social interactions

hierarchically and prescribes gender roles within the hierarchy, they will initiate working contacts with families taking these expectations into account.
- They will develop strong community networks with culturally knowledgeable
practitioners. They will be aware of institutional barriers that may prevent
minority group members from accessing services and will be prepared to make
different arrangements to facilitate access.

If all specialist teachers and psychologists in multiethnic communities can develop expertise along these lines, then calls for all children to be assessed by
professionals from the same background as themselves will be seen as unnecessary. The more desirable and practicable aim must be that, whatever their own
background, those responsible become knowledgeable about and sensitive to the
key features of the children's culture and languages. Similar principles apply also
when those involved in SEN assessment are working across other, less dramatic
gaps, such as those of social class and gender. The training requirements represent a major challenge. It is not just a matter of generating the accretion of some
new items of factual knowledge. A professional who will be sensitive across the
range of diversity found in contemporary schools is likely to have needed to go
through a process of restructuring many of their key attitudes and beliefs (Causey
et al. 2000). Ultimately, the key to reducing assessment bias in practice lies in the
principle set out by Watson *et al.* (1987): *Know yourself, and the task, so that
you can know the child.*

Conclusions

The population profile of SEN provision is quite different from the profile of the
child population as a whole. It is possible that some aspects of this mismatch
reflect the impact of genetic and environmental factors on the development of
SEN, as illustrated in Chapter 4. However, there is a good deal of evidence that
it may also have resulted from the operation of systematic bias in procedures for
the identification and assessment of SEN.

In this chapter we have examined different ways in which processes of bias can
affect the judgements that are made during assessment. Test bias is important
and can be reduced significantly, even if it cannot be altogether eliminated. But
test bias is not the only source of distortion during the assessment process. Testing takes place in a social context, and assessment involves several stages apart
from any testing that may be included. Each phase of the process may be affected
by bias. We gave particular attention to how bias can be reduced in initial identification processes in school. Ultimately the greatest safeguard against bias will
be if the assessment draws upon multiple sources of evidence. A form of *triangulation* is recommended in which the viewpoints of more than one observer are
taken into account.

In the last section of the chapter we asked the question that is implied by that strategy – *Who can be fair?* A response to the challenge must involve appreciating the areas of expertise that are needed in a diverse society and developing the necessary arrangements for initial training and continuing professional development. Working towards a reduction in the bias affecting assessment is a task for services and systems as well as for individuals.

Chapter 7

Curriculum-based assessment

Objectives

When you have studied this chapter you should be able to:

1 Explain why there has been increasing interest in curriculum-based assessment (CBA) in recent years.
2 Describe the components of a behavioural approach to CBA.
3 Discuss ways of minimizing the limitations of a behavioural approach to CBA and the challenges that may be encountered in implementing it.
4 Outline the key features of an integrated model of curriculum management and a multi-dimensional approach to CBA that is particularly applicable in multiethnic classrooms.

Contents

Introduction

In Chapter 5 the following distinctive approaches to the assessment of SEN were outlined: assessment focused on the learner; assessment focused on the teaching programme; assessment focused on the zone of potential development; and assessment focused on the learning environment. This chapter is devoted to assessment focused on the teaching programme. A number of different types of approaches have been developed and a number of terms employed, of which the following are most commonly used in Britain:

Curriculum-based assessment (CBA)
Curriculum-related assessment (CRA)
Curriculum-based measurement (CBM)
Assessment through teaching (ATT)

Definitions

We will use the term CBA and will adopt the definition proposed by Tucker (1985: 200): 'Curriculum based assessment properly includes any procedure that directly assesses student performance within the course content for the purpose of determining that students' instructional needs'. In CBA the pupil's performance is compared in an ongoing way to each new set of curriculum demands as they are presented in the classroom.

This contrasts with:

- norm-referenced assessment where the pupil's performance is compared to that of the group of pupils on whom the test was standardized;
- criterion referenced assessment where the pupil's performance in each area assessed by the test is compared to a stated criterion or level of mastery.

Sometimes people try to make assessments serve more than one purpose. Teacher assessments of pupil performance in the UK National Curriculum were introduced to serve a CBA purpose 'in order to clarify the next steps for individual and class planning' (SEAC 1990). However, they were also intended to serve a criterion-referenced assessment purpose – namely to assess pupils 'in relation to a criterion given by a Statement of Attainment'.

Key assessment questions which CRA techniques are designed to answer are:

- questions about changes in children's rate of learning progress over time;
- questions about children's differential responsiveness to different teaching interventions.

Increasing interest in CBA

There has been increasing interest in CBA in the last ten years. This has been influenced by:

- the implementation of the National Curriculum;
- changes in the concept of SEN;
- concerns about the validity of norm-referenced assessment approaches in multi-ethnic contexts.

The implementation of the National Curriculum

The National Curriculum introduced a framework of curriculum objectives within which each pupil's progress could be assessed throughout their school career, and each school's performance in promoting pupil achievement evaluated. For the first time all schools in the UK were working to an agreed curriculum which applies to all pupils unless aspects of it are disapplied or specifically modified.

New national assessments were introduced and expectations set about what pupils would be able to do at particular ages. Previously, parents might have been told that their child scored overall below the national average on a norm-referenced maths test but they would not know what skills the child already knew and what they needed to learn in order to score at an average level for their age. Now parents could be told whether or not the child had reached certain criteria set for pupils of their age (e.g. carry out calculations involving long division), and which of the national maths curriculum objectives the child would need to achieve in order reach this criterion. This set a clear context for a process of ongoing assessment based on the curriculum which could be used to inform parents about their child's progress through a system of annual reporting.

Changes in the concept of SEN

Following the implementation of the 1981 Education Act the purpose of SEN assessment changed from the diagnosis of disability to the identification of SEN. The level of need experienced is conceptualized as a complex interaction between children's strengths and weaknesses, the level of support available and the appropriateness of the education being provided. The assessment of the children's learning progress in relation to the curriculum being offered is, therefore, highlighted as an important aspect in the assessment of their possible SEN.

Gickling and Havertape (1981: 376) argue that the most pervasive cause of learning difficulties is that for some children 'the curriculum moves too fast and demands too much in relation to their existing skills. They get further and further behind and are entrenched in a failure cycle'. They present the primary goal of CBA as the elimination of this instructional mismatch through the identification of the child's entry skills in relation to the curriculum, which allows appropriate tasks and materials to be selected accordingly. Gickling and Thompson (1985) report that without CBA such adjustments are generally not made by teachers for children whose performance deviates significantly from the norm expected for their age. They argue that individualization and differentiation rarely happen and children, increasingly unable to do assigned work, tend to get further behind and become entrenched in a cycle of 'curriculum related failure'.

Gickling and Thompson (1985) pointed to the rapidly increasing numbers of referrals for special educational placement in the USA in arguing for the introduction of a requirement that CBA be conducted prior to a formal referral. This, they argued, would produce detailed information on pupils' responses to the range of different teaching programmes and approaches that had been systematically implemented. This could be used to differentiate between those pupils whose problems are curriculum and/or teaching related and those who appear to learn differently from their normally achieving peers. The extent to which a child's performance is discrepant from that of their classmates can be indicated by assessing the performance of a sample of classmates using CBAs in one or more curriculum areas.

The first *Code of Practice* (Department for Education 1994a) required that school-based stages of assessment and intervention, recorded through IEPs, should generally precede referral to specialist LEA services. However, records are rarely detailed enough to serve the purposes identified by Gickling and Thompson (1985). Solity (1995) criticizes the *Code* for not going far enough in requiring that pupils' attainments and their respective rates of progress be compared with those of their peers. He points out that a pupil who is some way behind but who is making excellent progress in response to teaching programmes being provided by their school is in a very different position from a child who is similarly far behind but who is not making good progress. This is particularly so where the rate of progress being made is such that the pupil might be expected to catch up and bridge the gap between themselves and their peers. The revised SEN *Code* and *Thresholds* document clearly identifies the adequacy of the progress being made as the key test of how far pupils' learning needs are being met (Department for Education and Skills 2001).

Concerns about the validity of norm-referenced assessment approaches in multiethnic contexts

Another important influence on the shift towards CBA has been a growing appreciation of the extent to which the norm-referenced tests most commonly used in making special education placement decisions are affected by cultural and social bias. The resulting misclassification of children from minority ethnic groups has for many years been a focus of substantial litigation in the USA (Galigan 1985) and concern in Britain (Department of Education and Science 1985). As illustrated in Chapter 6, cultural bias is apparent in tests where a significant proportion of the items may be outside the cultural experience, customs or values of particular groups of children. The use of norms is another contentious issue as few of the standardized norm-referenced assessment measures which are commonly used in the assessment of children's SEN report the systematic inclusion of minority children in their standardization samples. Even those measures which have been standardized on populations including proportions of children from ethnic minority groups may not be applicable in communities where there is a different ethnic mix.

Concerns have also been raised about the validity of substituting informal teacher observation and identification for standardized tests. This has led in some school districts in the USA (Louisiana for example) to a requirement for the systematic and structured data provided by CBA to be collected by teachers in order to counter discriminatory practices in referral to special education services. The attorney for the plaintiffs in an influential court case (*Luke* vs. *Nix*) quoted research which showed teachers to be biased in their judgements about children's attainment of teaching objectives in a way which underestimated the achievements of children from black and minority ethnic communities. In a scathing attack upon 'the subjective and chaotic referral methods of individual teachers' the attorney pointed out that 'evidence abounds that regular teachers initiate referrals without documenting that alternative instructional strategies have been attempted and evaluated', and concluded 'teachers have manifested a pervasive propensity to refer students who "bother them". The result is a haphazard, idiosyncratic referral method whereby different teachers refer different types of students because different student traits bother them' (Galigan 1985: 290).

ACTIVITY 7.1   Potential advantages of CBA

Here are some of the potential advantages claimed for CBA. As you read this chapter, note any evidence that supports these assertions and any conditions which appear necessary for the potential benefits to be realized. Any queries or further suggested modifications to the CBA procedures should also be noted.

Potential advantage	Supportive evidence (with page and paragraph reference)	Queries or suggested modifications
It is not necessary to take a lot of 'time out' for assessment since assessment, teaching and monitoring of progress are combined.		
It can provide information that is of direct and immediate use in the classroom on which specific skills and knowledge the child has and has not mastered.		
It offers an immediate check on the appropriateness of particular tasks and materials for particular children. Even 'graded' books and sets of worksheets contain substantial variation in level of difficulty from page to page and task to task. If a low-achieving child is performing erratically it may well reflect constant fluctuation between instructional and frustration level tasks.		

Potential advantage	Supportive evidence (with page and paragraph reference)	Queries or suggested modifications
It enables teachers to chart small steps in progress towards the achievement of major curriculum objectives or National Curriculum attainment targets. Step size and pacing of individual programmes can be justified.		
Progress can be communicated in a way which is comprehensible to parents and children.		
It generates detailed assessment information which can be readily appreciated by other professionals who may be consulted about a child's special needs.		
It fulfils the school's responsibilities for assessment, intervention and evaluation and will provide a convincing basis for any case made for the provision of extra resources.		
The approach is based on the optimistic assumption that all children can make learning progress given appropriate teaching. Where difficulties are encountered it is the teaching programme, not the child, that is labelled problematic and targeted for change.		

Key aspects of CBA

Components of a behavioural approach to CBA

The CBA procedures that have most commonly been used in Britain over the past 20 years are those based on approaches from behavioural psychology. As Figure 7.1 shows, these have typically incorporated the use of task analysis, behavioural objectives, precision teaching and direct instruction. The first stage involves the use of task analysis to express the curriculum, or a section of it, in the form of behavioural objectives which are then sequentially arranged in order of difficulty. At Stage 2 precision teaching techniques are used to identify which of the sequentially arranged objectives the child has already learned, so that they can be placed at an appropriate level on the curriculum. At Stage 3 the selection of teaching methods is informed by principles derived from direct instruction. Finally, repeat measures using precision teaching techniques allow evaluation of progress in relation to the curriculum, the teaching methods and the classroom

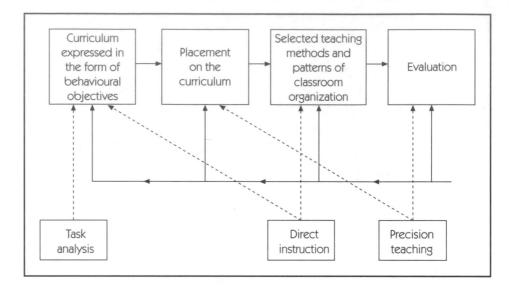

organization provided for the child. Each of the approaches underpinning this model will now be examined in turn.

The steps involved in *task analysis* are described by Solity and Bull (1987) as follows:

- *Step 1*. Describe the task – for example: names colours when shown an object and asked 'What colour is this?'
- *Step 2*. Identify and sequence component skills – for example, the following sequence might be identified for the 'names colours' task:
  Skill 1 – matches colours to a model
  Skill 2 – sorts objects according to their colour
  Skill 3 – recognizes colours (pointing to the appropriately coloured object when asked 'Show me a red one')
- *Step 3*. Slice tasks and skills – for example, if you have started with six colours and the pupil is experiencing difficulty at any stage, you can 'slice' the number of colours to three, or even two. Then when the skill or task has been securely learned with these, the other colours can gradually be introduced in ones or twos until the child can perform successfully with all of them.

The end product is a hierarchically ordered sequence of well defined learning outcomes expressed as behavioural objectives.

Behavioural objectives contain three essential components:

- A clear statement of what the child should do to show that learning has occurred. An active verb denoting observable behaviour should be used.
- A description of the conditions under which the behaviour is to be performed (e.g. teaching materials or teacher instructions).
- A description of the standard or criterion of performance required of the pupil before the next objective is taught.

Here is an example: Robert will *name* (active verb) colours when shown an object and asked 'What colour is this?': 9/10 correct (condition) on two successive days (criterion).

Direct instruction (see Solity and Bull 1987) provides:

- Full curriculum content consisting of sequential learning objectives, structured through analysis of the subject matter.
- A transmission model of teaching where the teacher leads and controls the lesson. Lessons are often scripted.
- Reinforcements (such as praise) and correction procedures (used when the child makes a mistake) are clearly specified and the teacher is cued to use them in the lesson scripts.

A closer look at precision teaching

The confusingly named precision teaching is not an approach to teaching but to monitoring and evaluation. It offers a set of strategies for carrying out brief, focused, daily assessments of pupil performance and for recording progress in a way that enables decisions about its appropriateness to be made on a very regular basis (typically weekly). This process is at the heart of CBA and will now be described in further detail.

In precision teaching the teacher records how quickly a child can respond to questions as well as whether or not the answers are correct. Thus precision teaching focuses on fluency as well as accuracy. Binder (1993) reviews evidence suggesting that establishing fluency in addition to accuracy is of great value. If a skill is well practised so that we can perform it without hesitation, we are less likely to forget it, are more likely to be able to perform it reliably in distracting or demanding situations and are better able to apply it flexibly in a range of contexts. This can be appreciated by comparing the gear-changing skill of a learner driver and an experienced driver. The experienced driver gives little conscious attention to changing gear, is unlikely to stall when the unexpected happens and quickly adapts to driving an unfamiliar car. When fluency is established as well as accuracy there are improvements in pupils' *resistance to distraction* when using a skill that they have learned; in their memory for and *maintenance* of the skill over time; and in their ability to *generalize* the skill and use it appropriately in a variety of circumstances.

Lindsley (1992) reports that *rate of response or fluency measures* (e.g. number of words read correctly per minute) are very much more sensitive to changes in environmental conditions or drug dosages than are *accuracy measures* (such as percentage correct). He also reports that involving the pupils themselves in daily assessment, marking and charting of performance increases the effectiveness of learning. By training pupils to work together in pairs, the time that needs to be spent by the teacher on the mechanics of monitoring can be greatly reduced.

Precision teaching involves five steps:

1 Specify the desired pupil performance in observable, measurable terms.
2 Sample and record the performance on a daily basis.
3 Chart the performance on a daily basis.
4 Record the teaching approaches in relation to pupil performance.
5 Analyse the data to determine whether:
   (a) the programme is satisfactory
   (b) changes are needed in the teaching approach.

Example: assessing Claire's reading progress using precision teaching

Claire is 7 years 3 months. Her class teacher, Mrs Wallace, has been becoming more concerned about her reading during the autumn term. She is in a reading group with five other children who were all behind at the end of Year 1. Whereas the other children in her reading group have been making steady progress and catching up on the group above, Claire seems almost to be going backwards and becoming more hesitant and less confident in her reading.

At Step 1 the desired pupil performance must be stated clearly – a behavioural objective may be used. The target or criterion level of fluency will often be identified by averaging the scores of two or three pupils who are performing at an expected level for their age or who are making satisfactory progress. In this case Claire and the two pupils from her reading group who are making best progress were asked to read for a minute from Claire's reading book. The number of words per minute they each read correctly and incorrectly was recorded. The scores of the other two pupils were averaged to produce the following objective, or statement of desired pupil performance, for Claire:

> Claire will read aloud from her reading book at a rate of 70 words correct per minute with no more than five errors.

At Step 2 the child's accuracy and rate of performance in the area being targeted is sampled on a daily basis using a short test that typically lasts for a minute. This allows the teacher to monitor progress towards the objective that has been set. The short test is called a 'probe' and these can take a number of different forms. A probe designed to monitor performance on a programme to develop sight vocabulary in reading might consist of a grid containing the ten new words being learned that week presented seven or eight times each in random order. However, probes can also be taken directly from learning resources used in class. Deno (1985) reviews extensive research indicating the reliability and validity of using extracts from the books being read by the child in their classroom reading programme as probes. Deno reports that the number of words per minute read correctly and incorrectly from reading scheme readers (using the kind of procedure shown in Figure 7.2) reliably and validly discriminates growth in reading proficiency through the primary school years.

So it seems that Mrs Wallace made a good choice in selecting this kind of probe for Claire. Deno reports that his data show a close relationship between

Figure 7.2
Administering a
probe from a
pupil's classroom
reading text

1 Select a passage which the pupil will read during their next session and make a photocopy for yourself.
2 Say to the pupil: 'When I say "start", begin reading aloud at the top of this page. Try to read each word. If you wait for a word too long, I'll tell you the word. You can skip words that you don't know. At the end of one minute, I'll say, "stop".'
  (Give pupil 3 seconds before supplying words.)
3 Turn on the stopwatch as you say 'Start'.
4 Follow along on your copy, circling with a pencil words that were read incorrectly (omissions, substitutions, mispronunciations, insertions).
5 At one minute, say, 'stop' and turn off the stopwatch.
6 Place a slash after the last word read.
7 Count the number of words correct and the number of errors.
8 Involve the pupil in recording both correct and incorrect scores on a graph.
9 Repeat steps 1–8 at least three times per week. A different passage can be selected each day as the pupil progresses through the book.

the number of words read aloud from the text in one minute and measures of pupil comprehension, but he does advise teachers that specific checks should also be made on children's comprehension. So this will be one of a number of aspects of Claire's literacy skills that Mrs Wallace will continue to monitor using the same approaches she uses for all the children. It is only Claire's progress on the specific reading accuracy and fluency objective that will be monitored using the precision teaching approach. Similarly, Claire will continue to participate in the same literacy programme as other members of her group while receiving some additional input focused on her specific reading accuracy and fluency objective. Typically a pupil would receive an additional 10–15 minutes per day structured teaching with two of those minutes being devoted to assessment of progress using the probe and graphing at Step 3.

Figure 7.3 illustrates the central role of graphing in this precision teaching approach with individual pupils. The number of words read correctly each day is charted with a dot and the number read incorrectly is charted with a cross. Techniques devised by White and Haring (1980) are used to make decisions about whether progress is satisfactory or when a change in the child's programme should be made. Initially, Claire read 37 words correctly and read 8 incorrectly per minute. The two classmates from her reading group averaged 70 words read correctly and 5 words read incorrectly. It was decided to aim to help Claire achieve this rate by the end of the spring term. An aim line was drawn by Mrs Wallace to help her monitor the rate of progress being made and decide whether or not it was on track. An IEP was drawn up and a specific teaching programme focusing on key phonic skills was devised. This was to be implemented by a learning support assistant during the Literacy Hour. A set of probes was developed to monitor Claire's progress in learning the phonic skills taught each week and the results plotted on her 'sounds chart' showed that the progress being made

Figure 7.3
Precision teaching
('reading book')
chart
Source: Adapted
from Deno and
Fuchs (1987).

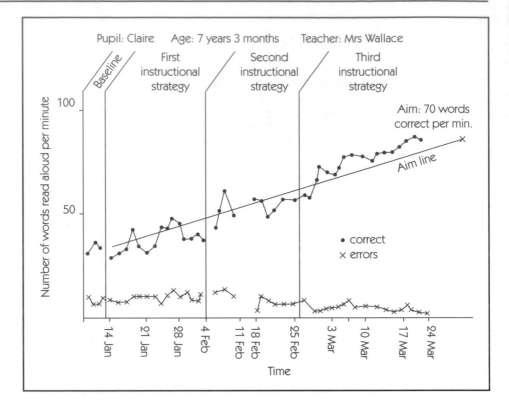

was very good. However, looking at Claire's 'reading book chart' (Figure 7.3) it can be seen that while some progress was made using this first instructional strategy her performance was quite variable. Nevertheless, the programme was applied consistently until the point in early February when Claire's perform-ance had been below the aim line for four consecutive days. Fuchs *et al.* (1993) advise that if four consecutive scores fall below the aim line a change in the pupil's programme should be introduced to try to increase their rate of progress.

Mrs Wallace planned the introduction of the second intervention. This in-volved, in addition to the session with the learning support assistant, a computer game which provided speeded practice in applying phonics skills to text. Claire was absent on Monday 11 February when this programme was due to start, as can be seen in Figure 7.3 by the break in the line joining the daily dots and crosses. Claire initially responded very well to the introduction of the computer programme but, after the half-term break she did not do so well when left to use the programme on her own. A further adjustment in her programme was required. Mrs Wallace included the second lowest performing pupil in Claire's reading group in the ten-minute daily computer session, after which the learning support assistant administered the probe with Claire. In addition, both Mrs Wallace and the learning support assistant made a point of reminding both pupils to apply the skills being practised in the computer sessions in their other reading activities.

Three weeks after the implementation of the third instructional strategy Claire attained her objective for the first time. The probe was administered and Claire's performance charted until the target rate of words correct and incorrect had been achieved for three consecutive days. Mrs Wallace planned to continue the programme after Easter for the first few weeks of the new term as performance typically shows a decline following a break of this kind. If Claire did not reach her objective by the target date, Mrs Wallace would have to decide whether to extend it. If steady progress was being made which could not be accelerated despite a variety of programme modifications then it would be likely that the initial target was too ambitious and that an extension to the time period was necessary. Alternatively, a less ambitious programme with smaller steps and a more modest target could be developed.

This example illustrates CBA's sensitivity to progress and indicates the way in which it can directly inform teaching decisions. It illustrates that the onus is on the teacher to find a strategy that works, and it can provide a very clear indication of the level and type of additional resources that a particular pupil requires to learn successfully. It also indicates how some meaningful norm referencing can be achieved. This is likely to take on particular significance in assessing children from minority ethnic groups in that a particular child's reading performance could be referenced against that of classmates having the same first language and similar educational histories.

For those children who are at a very early stage of reading development Gickling and Havertape (1981) describe the use of teacher generated story probes as an alternative to single word probes. Here children's own oral language is used to construct personalized 'books' which form the basis of their early reading instruction and sentences can be selected and adapted from these books for use as 'probe' stories. On the basis of their research findings Gickling and Havertape (1981) advise that teachers should ensure that known words make up at least 93 per cent of the words used in their stories. They regard this as an appropriate instructional level – so the probe has to reflect this aspect of curriculum delivery.

The use of precision teaching does not rely on the presence of a direct instruction teaching approach or the use of behavioural objectives. Lindsley (1992: 52) argues that precision teaching is compatible with a wide range of curricular approaches, 'except those so anti-structure that they cannot permit a counter, timer or chart in the classroom'. Booth and Jay (1981) point out that it is not necessary for behavioural objectives to be used provided that a specific and consistent task is given daily to the child.

The extent to which precision teaching is currently used by educational psychologists and teachers in Britain is unclear. In the 1980s many articles were published describing applications of the approach (Booth and Jay 1981; Raybould and Solity 1982; Williams and Muncey 1982; Booth and Jewell 1983). However Kessissoglou and Farrell (1995) observed that there had been very little recent British literature, although continuing active interest had been apparent in American journals. As British schools have become more structured, objectives focused and accountability orientated over the past 15 years it might be expected that precision teaching approaches would now be more congruent with general teaching practices and therefore more widely used today. However, it may be that the implementation of the 1981 Education Act led to some educational psychologists spending more time on the use of norm-referenced measures in statutory assessment activities and less time working with teachers on strategies to promote children's learning progress (Lokke *et al.* 1997). Whatever the reason for the apparent lower profile of precision teaching techniques in Britain in the 1990s, data reported from their application in the USA (Hasbrouck *et al.* 1999) suggest that they are very well suited to important aspects of the assessment needed to inform School Action and School Action Plus for pupils with SEN, as advised in the *Code of Practice* (Department for Education and Skills 2001):

- developing and modifying teaching programmes and evaluating programme effectiveness;
- monitoring pupil progress, the fluency of pupil's performance and the extent to which their difficulties persist across interventions and over time;
- generating the data needed by LEAs to ensure that additional resources are accessed in a fair and accountable manner (records such as the activity chart shown in Figure 7.4 would enable LEA panels to see exactly what had been done by schools and what the pupil's response had been).

The revised *Special Educational Needs Code of Practice* and SEN *Thresholds* (Department for Education and Skills 2001) place new emphasis on the crucial role of progress monitoring in SEN decision making:

The key test of the need for further action is evidence that current rates of progress are inadequate . . . Whatever the level of pupils' difficulties, the key test of how far their learning needs are being met is whether they are making *adequate progress.*

(Department for Education and Skills 2001, paras 4.13, 5.41, 6.48)

Where a request for a statutory assessment is made to an LEA . . . the LEA will seek evidence from the school that any action implemented for the pupil has been continued for a reasonable period of time without success and that alternatives have been tried. The LEA will need information about the pupil's progress over time, and will also need clear documentation in relation to the child's special educational needs and any action taken to deal with those needs, including any resources or special arrangements put in place.

(Department for Education and Skills 2001, para. 6.71)

Precision teaching is a well-researched and highly practical technique that could make an important contribution in addressing these requirements.

Figure 7.4
Precision teaching recording, using an activity chart
Source: Faupel (1986).

Programme Number:
Attained:
Not Attained:

ACTIVITY CHART
(MASTERY STAGE/FLUENCY)

NAME: ____________________

DATE STARTED: ____________ SCHOOL: ____________________

TEACHER: ____________

TEACHING TARGET
(Skills to be attained by the review date)

STANDARD OF SUCCESS
(Rates of correct responses per minute with specified rate of errors)

PREPARATION

NUMBER OF TEACHING/PRACTICE/ ASSESSMENT SESSIONS
(e.g. once daily)

MATERIALS
(Equipment worksheets needed to complete the teaching programme)

PLANNING

TEACHING PROCEDURES
(See over)

CORRECTIONS
(See over)

PERFORMANCE

REWARDS
(How will you convey to the pupil that he has been successful or has improved performance)

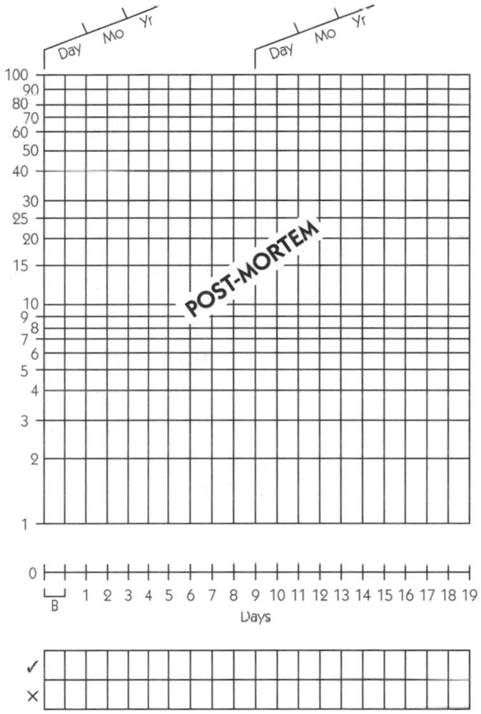

HOW TO RECORD (Plot • for number of correct responses;
Plot × for number of errors)

REVIEW DATE

CBA: challenges and limitations

A number of limitations of CBA's component processes have been identified in the literature and the approach overall has been challenged in several ways. These are described in this section, along with some improvement suggestions. In the following section we go on to describe more radical developments in which the whole approach has been reconceptualized.

Behavioural objectives and task analysis: concerns and limitations

A number of authors have highlighted concerns about behavioural objectives. They argue that the most trivial aims are likely to be the easiest to translate into specific behavioural objectives and that there is therefore a risk that these will be focused on, to the exclusion of more important aims. Some, such as Ainscow and Tweddle (1979), have attempted to minimize this risk through differentiating between the 'closed' basic skills curriculum which may be expressed in the form of behavioural objectives and the 'open' curriculum which may address creative, moral or aesthetic aims and which would not be dealt with in this way.

Cummins (1984) expresses concern that the prescriptiveness of behavioural objectives may restrict the recognition of cultural diversity. Behavioural object-ives attempt to spell out what is meant by terms such as 'understand' by giving an unambiguous description of the behaviour you can accept as evidence of a child's understanding. However, if we focus in on one, possibly ethnocentric, way of demonstrating understanding we may disqualify (or at least lose sensitivity to) different ways in which understanding may be expressed by children from different cultural backgrounds. For example, a teacher might be assessing chil-dren's performance on the 1999 version of the National Curriculum Attainment Target:

Science Attainment Target 3, Level 1 – Name external parts of the human body (for example, head, arm).

A relevant behavioural objective might be:

Pupils should be able to: Name arm, leg, head, stomach, hands, feet when the teacher points to part on their body and says 'What is this part of our body called?' Criterion: 6/6 correct, 2 consecutive days.

We need to consider whether this level of prescriptiveness might disadvantage a child with asthma who knows 'chest' but not 'stomach'. Or might it disadvant-age an Urdu speaking child who can name ten other body parts in English but has not yet learned that English (unlike Urdu) differentiates between 'arm' and 'hand'. Alternative approaches to setting objectives have been developed in response to these difficulties with behavioural objectives. The objectives setting process developed by Knowles (1990):

First →	Translates identified needs into general programme aims
and then	
separates →	1 the statement of relevant achievable learning objectives (in fairly broad terms)
from →	2 the establishment of specific evidence of accomplishment for each objective, for each learner if necessary.

Here is an example from Cline *et al.* (1990) of a secondary school where teachers had identified a need for pupils with dyslexic difficulties to be supported more effectively in mainstream lessons. Staff discussion yielded the following general programme aim: to enable subject teachers to modify the readability of teaching materials, pupil worksheets etc. This is not the only general programme aim which could have been selected in attempting to meet the identified need. Other general programme aims which were considered in the staff discussion included: to enable subject teachers to organize lessons so as to include some time when individual teaching is possible; and to enable subject teachers to effectively deploy and direct peer helpers/adult volunteers within the classroom.

From the general programme aim (to enable subject teachers to modify the readability of teaching materials, pupil worksheets etc.) the following objectives were then generated:

- to be able to determine the readability of any material using a computer-based readability index;
- to gain an understanding of the ways in which linguistic factors such as level of vocabulary and sentence length affect readability;
- to determine what worksheet formats containing simplified text would be acceptable to older pupils.

With regard to the third of these objectives the following evidence of achievement was specified: 'Eight out of ten dyslexic pupils in Years 10 and 11 will confirm that they would be happy to use the worksheets in class'.

Hence prescriptiveness is avoided at Stage 1 without clarity being sacrificed at Stage 2. This type of approach, which is highly congruent with the National Curriculum teacher assessment procedures, would seem to avoid the disadvantages of highly prescriptive approaches where 'the infinite variations of pupils' understandings in such methods are reduced to a limited number of can do/can't do categories which do nothing to recognise the context-dependent nature of children's performances' (Swann 1988: 93).

Cummins (1984), writing about bilingual pupils with SEN identifies further pitfalls associated with task analysis, 'at least in the way the procedure is usually interpreted'. He argues that the reduction in meaningful context which often results from breaking down knowledge or skills into less complex components that are taught, more or less in isolation, may well make learning more difficult. On the contrary, Cummins proposes that one of the best ways of assisting children to learn is to embed the knowledge or skill to be acquired as comprehensively as possible within a context which is meaningful to the child. In behavioural task analysis all of the emphasis is placed on the curriculum. Other approaches to CBA include a 'product' as well as a task analysis. This gives consideration to what is actually produced by the child in response to the task presented, and to how the child approaches the task. Attention to the task is balanced by equivalent attention to the child and the nature of his or her interaction with the task.

Product analysis is not a single approach but a set of techniques that involve:

- examining completed assignments;
- observing the child's work patterns;
- talking to the child about their work on the tasks;
- assessing the efficiency of strategies used by the child.

The purpose is to directly analyse the approaches children are adopting with their classroom tasks so that they can be helped to develop more successful learning strategies. Gickling and Havertape (1981) argue that in order to help children learn effectively teachers need to strive to understand children's understanding of their learning tasks.

Take Joe, for example, who produced:

$$3 + 6 = 9 \qquad 43 + 6 = 13 \qquad 7 + 4 = 11 \qquad 82 + 5 = 15 \qquad 73 + 8 = 17$$

A task analysis might suggest that we focus our teaching on problems of the forms:

$$11 + 3 = \qquad 13 + 2 =$$

which are the 'next step up' from the ones he got correct, given a logical analysis of the task. However, a product analysis should first of all alert us to look for *sense* in what Joe has produced. We might notice $6 + 3 + 4 = 13$ and $5 + 2 + 8 = 15$. We might ask Joe to tell us how he had done these (while recognizing that if he was following a one-off hunch he might not be able to remember). We might then want to see how he would go about adding 6 to 43, perhaps using money, before deciding where the teaching input needed to focus.

Direct instruction: concerns and limitations

A number of reservations have been expressed about the use of direct instruction programmes. It is argued that the approach is counter to research findings on how language and literacy skills are learned. Direct instruction embodies a transmission model of teaching which regards the teaching task as the imparting of skills and knowledge through interaction which is initiated and controlled by the teacher. Yet research on the acquisition of language and literacy skills highlights the importance of a reciprocal interaction model of teaching and learning where the learner is encouraged to enquire and initiate; to develop and test hypotheses about spoken and written language through their interaction with an adult guide. Webster (1987) argues that children with special needs do not require a different approach to the acquisition of language and literacy skills, as they too learn best if the teaching input is based on a reciprocal interaction model. He suggests that their progress might be substantially impeded if a transmission model of teaching is imposed instead.

It should be noted that these arguments are mainly based on studies of language development. It is now generally accepted (Adams 1990) that a more structured approach to literacy skills development is required than was previously suggested by influential researchers who advocated that reading be conceptualized as a 'psycholinguistic guessing game' (e.g. Smith 1973). However, Ainscow (1988) likewise expresses concern that concentrating on the teaching process may encourage teachers to see pupils as having a largely passive role in learning situations. He suggests that this could result in the design of learning activities that lack meaning and purpose from the pupils' perspective and so have negative effects on their learning motivation.

These concerns closely parallel those raised by Cummins (1984) in relation to bilingual pupils who have SEN. He argues that the use of scripted direct instruction programmes with bilingual special needs pupils may lead to a number of undesirable outcomes:

- they may decrease intrinsic motivation by establishing the teacher as the initiator and controller of linguistic interaction;
- they may focus teaching on superficial, low-level responses and skills which are easy to express as behavioural objectives, is in contrast to the more important higher order generalizable conceptual skills which Cummins has shown to be a necessary foundation for educational success;
- their emphasis upon teacher initiation and control may actually inhibit the active involvement of the child, which is necessary for the development of higher order cognitive and academic skills.

Overcoming challenges in implementation

In Hasbrouck *et al.* (1999) a teacher discusses frankly some of her initial concerns upon being introduced to a CBA approach and outlines her reasons for becoming committed to it. Initially she had taken it up reluctantly when the school district in which she worked made it a requirement that all special education teachers had to use CBA and graphing three times per week. One concern related to increased accountability where the graphs would offer concrete documentation of the effects of her teaching on the progress of those pupils with SEN with whom she was working. There was also an expectation that pupil's CBA graphs would be shared with parents, other teachers and the headteacher in informing decision making about the pupil.

Ainscow (1988) suggested that teachers may find it difficult to organize the implementation of the approach in large class situations and teachers in Hasbrouck *et al.*'s (1999) study reported that implementing CBA did reduce instructional time. However, they considered that the resulting greater efficiency in the use of instructional time outweighed the relatively minor cost in time and paperwork. They also identified the following specific advantages:

- the graphed results provide a powerful communication tool and evidence of positive progress – for teachers, pupils and parents;
- when progress is not being made teachers are alerted to this at once and can prepare to implement a programme modification to address the problem;
- the success of a programme change can be quickly evaluated.

Hasbrouck *et al.* (1999) also describe the implementation of precision teaching on a school-wide basis. In the autumn term all pupils are assessed three times on unpractised age appropriate reading passages and the median score is used as a baseline for comparison with a second assessment in the spring to see if the pupils are benefiting from the school's reading programme. Any pupils identified as being at risk of reading failure are assessed using weekly CBA measures, and graphs are kept of their progress. CBA only tells a teacher that the progress is not satisfactory, not why. A process analysis is then undertaken as the next step and the information used to design adaptations for the pupil. Sometimes the intervention may be as simple as a change in seating arrangements in the classroom to reduce distractions. At other times five to ten minutes daily on focused practice of a targeted skill with a learning support assistant may be needed, or the teaching session may need to be organized so that the teacher can spend a few minutes with the pupil previewing or reviewing the content of a lesson.

Challenges to the validity of CBA

A number of authors have argued that the behavioural approach to CBA needs to be broadened to take account of the cognitive psychology of the child and the social psychology of the context, as well as the instructional psychology of curriculum delivery. Ainscow (1988) suggested that a focus on analysing specific tasks for individual pupils may result in a narrowing of perspective so that insufficient attention is given to other important contextual factors that may be impeding learning – related, for example, to the curriculum in general, classroom organization or interpersonal relationships. Dessent (1992) argues for educational psychologists to work on 'connecting the individual and the system', while Mehrens and Clarizio (1993) argue that CBA focuses only on the curriculum and ignores a child's characteristics that may be useful in explaining *why* they may have difficulty with a particular task. They argue also that the data do not inform teachers about *how* to change the child's programme, only *when* to change it.

In summary, a narrow focus on the curriculum is considered inadequate. A meaningful CBA must take account of the child characteristics, including the meaning which the child makes of the curriculum, and of their contextually dependent interaction with it.

Developments in CBA

In this section we describe two examples of developments in CBA that attempt to modify the component processes in order to address the limitations described in the previous section and to respond to the challenge of embedding the approach within a broader, more ecologically valid model.

An integrated model of curriculum management in the classroom

The Educational Psychology Group at Southampton University has developed a curriculum management model which sets the CBM procedures in the context of whole-class planning, teaching and evaluation (Cameron 1988). It aims to aid the teacher in implementing the cyclical process shown in Figure 7.5 where they choose an appropriate level of curriculum planning, decide on the most relevant teaching methods, assess pupil progress and evaluate each aspect in consultation with the pupil.

The first stage of curriculum planning involves a choice between seven levels. At the broadest of these levels are teacher management objectives (e.g. to construct a wildlife pond; to stage a production of *Oliver*). The next three levels involve pupil objectives and curriculum content from the National Curriculum appropriate for the age range of the pupils in the class, and the more finely sequenced objectives characteristic of the Literacy and Numeracy Hours. The final three levels are ones that would be selected to assist with the more fine-grained planning needed for children identified as experiencing some level of SEN. Here it is recognized that children are likely to require that some priority objectives at least are task-analysed into smaller steps which may be written in the very precise behavioural objectives described in the section 'Key aspects of CBA' (see p. 164).

The model distinguishes between three levels of teaching:

- *Minimal teaching requirements*, where teaching strategies, pupil feedback and record keeping can generally be organized on a whole-class basis.
- *Structured teaching*, where particular pupils whose progress is being more closely monitored will have teaching strategies differentiated and be given systematic, individualized feedback.
- *Direct instruction*, where tightly scripted teaching input and pupil feedback procedures are designed to tackle apparently intractable learning difficulties.

The assessment carried out is curriculum related in that its main purpose is to describe what pupils know and can do in relation to the curriculum objectives on which they have been working. The model considers five levels of learning, the first two of which are incorporated in 'precision teaching': *acquisition* which focuses on accuracy, the number of correct and incorrect answers; and *fluency* which combines accuracy and speed. In addition, however, attention is given to the *maintenance* of learning over time; to *generalization* of taught skills (e.g. using the measuring skills that have been taught during maths lessons in an art

Figure 7.5
Curriculum
management
model
Source: Cameron
et al. (1986).

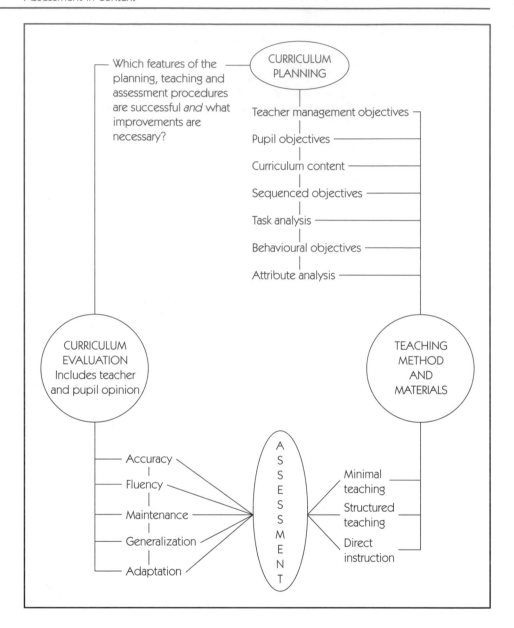

project); and to *adaptation*, where the skills that have been learned can be modified for use in solving new problems.

Finally, evaluation seeks to identify both assets of and possible improvements
to the curriculum planning, teaching method and assessment procedures. It is suggested that the pupils are involved in the evaluation and where learning support
assistants and parents have been involved in an individualized programme for a
pupil who has SEN, this could form a useful component of progress reviews.

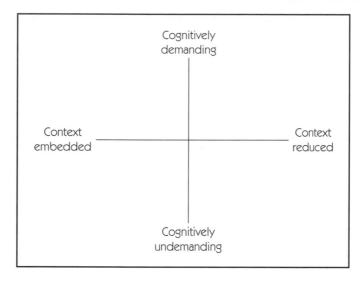

Multidimensional CBA in multiethnic classrooms

This kind of interactive, context-sensitive approach to CBA is illustrated by the approach developed by a working group of educational psychologists at University College London (Frederickson and Cline 1990). This working group focused on CBA with bilingual pupils but the principles are widely generalizable. The model has as its basis Cummin's (1984) theoretical framework which is illustrated in Figure 7.6.

In Figure 7.6 the *horizontal dimension* is used to indicate the degree of contextual support that is provided. At the context embedded end of the dimension language would be embedded within a meaningful context and gesture or expression cues would be likely to be present. On the other hand, at the context reduced end of the dimension the only cues to meaning would be linguistic ones. To provide a concrete example: if the child was asked to read the sentence 'Tom went to the shop' presented to them as one of the sentences in a sentence reading test, this would be an example of the use of written language in a context reduced situation. On the other hand, if the child was asked to read the same sentence just after it had been written by the teacher to the child's dictation under a picture which they had drawn of their brother, Tom, then this would be an example of written language use embedded within a context that was meaningful to the child.

The *vertical dimension* indicates the level of cognitive demand placed upon the child by language used in any particular task or situation. Cummins regards cognitive demand as depending on both external factors and internal factors. External factors refer to those such as task complexity – where one could agree for example that addition is an easier and less complex mathematical operation than is multiplication. Internal factors refer to the familiarity and acceptability of the task to the child as well as the child's current proficiency. This highlights the point that tasks which are relatively cognitively undemanding for a native speaker of English may be highly cognitively demanding for a second language learner. This model therefore attempts to incorporate knowledge of what the child brings to the learning situation over and above their entry skills on the task in question.

As Deforges and Kerr (1984) pointed out, the model also suggests how classroom activities may be modified in a way which maximizes the access of bilingual children to the curriculum. Typically, if a child is experiencing difficulty with a particular activity the teacher may respond by making that activity easier – i.e. by reducing the level of cognitive demand. However, second language learners may well be able to cope with the cognitive complexity of the task but simply not yet have developed the language skills necessary for access. To reduce the complexity of tasks in this situation would result in the children being provided with inappropriately easy work which does not stretch them intellectually. The Cummins framework suggests that as an alternative the teacher can facilitate the bilingual child's access to the curriculum by retaining the level of cognitive complexity involved in the task but embedding the task in a meaningful context so that the child is then able, despite their as yet rather limited linguistic skills, to understand the nature of the task and what is required from them.

In conducting a CBA it can be helpful to locate on the matrix those tasks where the child is able to succeed and those tasks where success cannot yet be achieved. It is then possible to build up a picture of the child's strengths and weaknesses in terms of the level of cognitive demand with which they can cope in particular curriculum areas, and to establish the level of contextual and other support required for success in a range of different situations. This framework can provide a useful basis for differentiating classroom tasks and designing particular modifications by level (vertical axis) or method (horizontal axis) in promoting maximum access to the curriculum by pupils having a range of SEN.

As noted above, the strategy outlined in this section was described in a set of 'working papers' published by the Department of Psychology at University College London (Frederickson and Cline 1990). A survey of purchasers of this publication (reported in Cline and Frederickson 1996) indicated the range of purposes for which it was considered useful:

- As a framework for topic planning   20%
- As a means of contributing to summative assessment   27%
- As a classroom observation tool   36%
- As a means of formative assessment   37%
- As a means of analysing curriculum content   42%
- To inform debate over bilingual children's perceived learning   70%
  difficulties

Cline and Frederickson's (1996) edited collection contains detailed accounts of the use of the model in primary and secondary schools by a range of education

ACTIVITY 7.2   Using the Cummins framework to map learning activities

Listed below are the learning activities included in the Key Stage 1 programme of study for English Attainment Target 1: Speaking and Listening. (You may wish instead to use the learning activities from a different programme of study if they are more relevant to your practice.)

(a) Consider how cognitively demanding and contextually embedded each of the activities would be for most 6-year-olds who have English as their first language. Locate each activity in the appropriate quadrant of the Cummins framework (see Figure 7.6). For some of the activities there may not be enough information for you to decide where they fit. In these cases you can add a phrase to them to make them more specific and then allocate them to one of the quadrants.
(b) Now consider a pupil of the same age who is in their second year of learning EAL. Would you want to change or query the location of any of the activities?

Speaking
  8 The range should include:
     (a) telling stories, real and imagined;
     (b) reading aloud and reciting;
     (c) describing events and experiences;
     (d) speaking to different people, including friends, the class, teachers and other adults.

Listening
  9 The range should include opportunities for pupils to listen to:
     (a) each other;
     (b) adults giving detailed explanations and presentations (e.g. describing how a model works, reading aloud);
     (c) recordings (e.g. radio, television).

Group discussion and interaction
  10 The range should include:
     (a) making plans and investigating;
     (b) sharing ideas and experiences;
     (c) commenting and reporting.

Drama activities
  11 The range should include:
     (a) working in role;
     (b) presenting drama and stories to others (e.g. telling a story through tableaux or using a narrator);
     (c) responding to performances.

service professionals with bilingual children working in a variety of community languages, including British sign language. The general conclusion is that it is an attractively simple as well as versatile model. However, a number of potential limitations have been identified. The most obvious of these is the assumption that the cognitive and contextual dimensions are distinct and readily separable. In observing and analysing classroom tasks, instructions and performances it has sometimes proved difficult to disentangle the 'cognitive' fully from the 'contextual'. In some cases, movement along the contextual dimensions has actually been represented on the model as a diagonal shift, as it was found in practice that making tasks or instructions more context embedded also made them somewhat less cognitively demanding. Similarly, changes in cognitive demand may result in tasks actually being presented which are embedded in context to a greater or lesser degree.

It is also important to remind ourselves of what the framework does *not* do:

- it does not analyse the child's cognitive strategies (e.g. preference for rote learning) nor his or her learning style (e.g. prefers to work independently);
- it does not provide the teacher with the information about the child's cultural background that is required to 'embed' the task.

Thus, ironically, the framework can only be meaningful for the teacher when it, too, is 'context embedded' – i.e. the teacher is clear about the aims of the lesson, knows the child's background well and has tried to match the task to the child's learning style and interest.

Solity (1993) has expressed concern that the classifications offered for determining task difficulty (cognitively demanding/undemanding and context embedded/reduced), and the way these are related to the cultural background of children make assumptions and predictions about children's learning which may create differential expectations based on ethnicity. While this is always a danger, the approach encourages teachers to consider for each pupil how their language proficiencies and their familiarity with particular materials and tasks may interact with the planned curriculum activities to increase or decrease the level of difficulty of these activities. The ultimate effect, therefore, should not be to create differential stereotypical expectations based on ethnicity, but to encourage those working with children in a classroom to be sensitive to the *individual* differences that are associated with linguistic and cultural diversity.

At worst, stereotypical under-expectation of children from minority linguistic and ethnic groups will lead teachers to substitute less cognitively demanding tasks (moving vertically in the framework) if difficulties are encountered, as is suggested by a traditional approach to task analysis. With this approach teachers are encouraged first to move horizontally (left across the model) to ascertain whether the child is able to demonstrate success when given greater contextual support to their developing proficiency in English. In this way the model based on the Cummins framework offers a new dimension to the CBA of bilingual children.

Using the Cummins framework in differential assessment

This section describes the use of the Cummins framework approach to CBA in addressing a key question in working with bilingual children for whom the language of instruction is not their preferred language: when does poor learning performance indicate a SEN and when does it indicate a need for further support in learning the language of instruction?

This decision between the identification of learning needs and language needs is often fraught with difficult political and ethical considerations. If it is mistakenly decided that a child has a learning need then the child may be provided with insufficiently challenging learning experiences and be subject to inappropriately low expectations. Decision errors of this type may also lay the professional involved open to charges of racism or of employing culturally biased assessment procedures.

However, difficulties are also created by mistaken decisions that a child has a language rather than a learning need. In this case the child is likely to receive a language support programme to which they cannot respond because its pace is too fast and it is structured in learning steps which are too large. In subsequent assessment therefore they will continue to present as having language needs, so it may be several years before it is finally recognized that their difficulties with learning language are not responsible for their slow academic progress but that problems in both areas reflect general learning difficulties. Maintaining the 'language difficulties' hypothesis until the evidence for 'learning difficulties' becomes overwhelming avoids the political pitfalls for professionals outlined above. However, it can present serious ethical problems if the children concerned do not receive the special learning support they need.

The CBA framework can be used to structure diverse assessment information, aiding its analysis and interpretation. Essentially the approach involves using the Cummins framework to map the tasks at which the child can succeed and those which they are unable to do. For the latter, further assessment involves increasing the level of contextual support as a first step. This may entail increasing non-verbal cues (such as those gained from demonstration) to support the verbal message. Learning experiences may also be contextually embedded by supplementing the language of tuition with explanation or examples in the child's preferred language.

Figures 7.7 and 7.8 provide schematic snapshots of the kinds of profile which may be interpreted as indicating learning and language needs respectively. Figure 7.7 shows a profile indicative of a child with learning needs. Providing increasing degrees of contextual embedding does not assist the child in achieving success. However, reducing the cognitive demand of the task (i.e. making it easier), does allow the child to succeed. By contrast, Figure 7.8 shows a profile indicative of a child with language of instruction support needs, for whom increasing degrees of contextual embedding allow success to be achieved. Typically however, those bilingual children who have learning needs will also present with language needs because their general learning difficulties will also affect their learning of the

Figure 7.7
A child with
learning needs
Source: Rogers
and Pratten (1996).

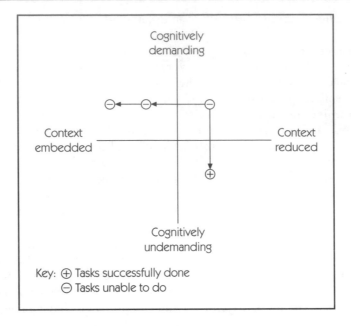

Figure 7.8
A child with
language of
instruction support
needs
Source: Rogers
and Pratten (1996).

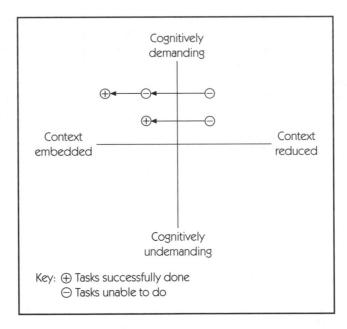

Figure 7.9
A bilingual child
with learning
needs
Source: Rogers
and Pratten (1996).

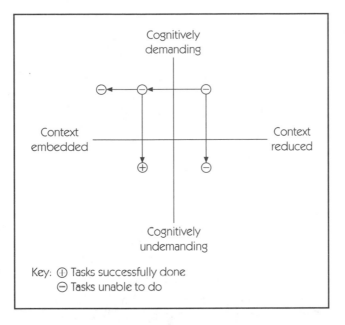

ACTIVITY 7.3   Differential assessment case studies

Read the following case studies (from Rogers and Pratten 1996) of children referred for
advice to an integrated LEA support service.

(a) For each child use a copy of the CBA framework to map the tasks which the child can
    and cannot do.
(b) Decide whether there is a closer match with Figure 7.7, indicating a learning need, or
    with Figure 7.8, indicating a language need.

Case study A
A 6-year-old boy from a Gujerati-speaking family who has no preschool educational
experience. Reason for referral: to establish whether the child has learning difficulties that
require formal assessment.
   Current targets:

● naming different rooms in the home
● three initial letter sounds to be taught
● drawing and naming shapes

The baseline is that the child only knows the initial letter sound 'a'.
   In the Cummins framework these targets would be cognitively demanding and not context
embedded. Working with the class teacher the bilingual support teacher observed that the
theme in the lessons was all about the home. The bilingual support teacher provided an
activity book with acetate peeling stick drawings. This was used as the medium to provide
context embedded experiences for the child to name the objects and to make him aware

of the initial letter sounds. In English, the bilingual support teacher found that the child did not know the word 'cooker'. In Gujerati, the bilingual support teacher found that the child identified the item from the question 'Where does your mum cook?' Only when she had made a home visit did the bilingual support teacher discover that the family used the word 'gas' to describe their cooking appliance. Many families would associate the word 'cooker' with a pressure cooker rather than a stove or range. In discussion with the mother, the bilingual support teacher now uses vocabulary used within the home setting. The work of teaching the initial letter sounds was reinforced at home by the mother using games such as 'I Spy'.

Having context embedded the material appropriate to the culture and environment, the bilingual support teacher was able to demonstrate that this child's rate of learning was such that he did not require formal assessment. The child was able to identify the common shapes found within his own home, name the different rooms and initial letter sounds, and therefore it was demonstrated that he did not have a significant learning difficulty.

Case study B

An 11-year-old boy from a Punjabi speaking family. Reason for referral: learning difficulties in the first year of secondary school. Previous experience: early schooling in India. Language of instruction, Hindi. Dropped out of school because of learning and behavioural difficulties. Mother remarried a Gujerati-speaking husband and the family came to England. The child had not spoken English before he was 11 years old. A bilingual teacher initially worked both in Hindi and Punjabi to establish the following targets.

Current targets:

- to write first name
- to develop work recognition skills
- to use common nouns in English

The last target was addressed first. Initially the child was taught solely in Hindi. Through stories from his own experience the bilingual support teacher introduced a basic vocabulary in English. After the teaching sessions it was demonstrated that the boy was capable of learning, though at a much slower rate than his peers even with a high level of contextual embedding. Use of the Cummins grid in this case indicated that it was not possible to ensure the child's success with an age-appropriate learning task simply by moving horizontally across the framework and providing more contextual support. Rather it was necessary first to move vertically down the framework in identifying easier small steps to the target. In addition it was still found necessary to ensure that these easier tasks were well embedded in context.

language of instruction – at least their acquisition of cognitive academic aspects of language proficiency (Cummins 1984). Hence, Figure 7.9 shows a profile likely to be indicative of a bilingual child who has learning needs. For these children to achieve success they will need to be provided both with tasks at an appropriate level of difficulty in respect of their learning needs and with tasks which are appropriately contextually embedded in respect of their language needs.

This points to the importance of learning and language specialists working effectively together.

Conclusions

In conclusion, CBA has often been defined in a narrow way which focuses on the content of the curriculum and excludes consideration of the meaning which it has for the pupil or the nature of their interaction with it. However, when CBA is defined more broadly as including *any* procedure that directly assesses student performance within the course content for the purpose of determining that student's instructional needs (Tucker 1985), it is possible to develop a range of strategies that overcome the difficulties associated with a narrow definition and so to realize many of the potential benefits claimed for the approach.

A final caveat remains. The approach relies heavily on the appropriateness of the curriculum and two aspects of curriculum appropriateness will now be considered. First, CBA can only be a non-discriminatory approach if the curriculum on which the child is assessed is appropriately multicultural and non-discriminatory. This needs to be evaluated, rather than assumed. McLaughlin (1985) points out that the developmental model of language used by schools tends to be based on white middle-class children's socialization experiences. The assumptions embodied in it about previous experiences at home and in the community are reflected in the standard monolingual curriculum as well as in tests. The ethnocentric character of the National Curriculum, particularly its earliest versions, has been criticized. However, descriptions have also been provided of ways in which teachers may try to offset some of the narrow aims and content through the strategies used in their teaching (Verma and Pumfrey 1994). For example, learning experiences may be selected to reflect the diversity of British society, to counter stereotypes of minority groups and to enable pupils with a different cultural background to pursue interests relating to that culture in cross-curricular topic work.

Second, Peverly and Kitzen (1998) argue that it is important to assess the quality of the curriculum as a potential cause of some pupil's learning difficulties and not just assess pupil's performance on the curriculum. For example, the reading curriculum should embody research findings on the cognitive processes involved in learning to read, such as findings which highlight the need for a balanced programme that incorporates both code-based (phonic skills) and language-based (reading for meaning) instruction. The curriculum cannot be taken as a 'given' against which children are assessed, but must itself be the subject of assessment.

Chapter 8

Learning environments

Objectives

When you have studied this chapter you should be able to:

1 Explain the reasons why a greater emphasis has been placed in recent years on assessing the learning environment.
2 Outline different theoretical models of the learning environment.
3 Describe the strengths and limitations of commonly used methods for assessing learning environments and designing interventions.

Contents

Introduction

In Chapter 5, four distinctive approaches to the assessment of SEN were outlined: assessment focused on the learner, assessment focused on the teaching programme, assessment focused on the zone of potential development and assessment focused on the learning environment. This chapter is devoted to assessment focused on the learning environment. Ainscow and Tweddle (1988: 18) wrote, 'In the 1960s we were preoccupied with analysing the individual child; in the 1970s the emphasis was switched to analysing tasks within the curriculum; and now we believe we should be focusing on the learning environment'.

Waxman (1992) argued that there are a number of advantages in focusing on 'at-risk school environments' rather than 'at-risk' students. Definitions of the at-risk student tend to focus on student characteristics, such as poverty, drug abuse, sexual activity, race, ethnicity, SEN, and first language other than English. There are concerns that this could be stigmatizing and may produce the 'Matthew effect'. The Matthew effect, a biblical reference, involves the rich getting richer and the poor poorer – or in this case, those who start off with advantages in learning making above average progress while those who start off with lower achievements than their peers falling ever further behind. There are a number of ways in which this effect might be magnified. For example, if Shama starts the year behind her peers in maths, her maths teacher may expect less of her, give her easier work or less of it and only call on her to answer low-level questions in class. These strategies effectively restrict Shama's learning opportunities and she falls further behind her peers who are being given a broader range of more challenging opportunities to develop their knowledge and skills.

Waxman (1992) argued that it would be more productive to identify those 'at-risk' school environments that:

- alienate students and teachers;
- provide low standards and a low quality of education;
- have differential expectations for students;
- have high numbers failing to leave school with a minimum level of qualifications;
- are unresponsive to students;
- have high rates of truancy and disciplinary problems;
- do not adequately prepare students for the future.

This kind of emphasis is apparent in the approach to school inspection introduced in Britain in the 1990s. A system of regular independent inspection of all schools was implemented with the purpose of reporting on the quality of education provided by the school, the educational standards achieved, the efficient management of financial resources and the spiritual, moral, social and cultural development of pupils (Department for Education 1992). Where a school is considered to be failing to give its pupils an acceptable standard of education it can be placed in 'special measures'. This is essentially an 'at-risk' designation and the school is required to produce an action plan to address the matters raised in the inspection report. The LEA is expected to comment on the school's action plan and to outline the steps it proposes to take to support the school (Department for Education 1993).

The focus on these 'at-risk' schools has steadily intensified. The ministerial letter introducing Department for Education and Employment Circular 10/99, *Social Inclusion: Pupil Support* (1999b) highlights that 'in a small minority of schools poor attendance and behaviour can have a depressing effect on the school as a whole. There is also widespread concern that bullying, including racist bullying, often goes unreported'. The letter continues:

> Even in the most difficult areas, schools can and do make a difference to the behaviour and attitudes of their pupils, especially when they are effectively supported by other agencies. Good teaching, sound behaviour management, effective anti-bullying policies, clear rewards, consistently applied sanctions and imaginative use of the curriculum all make a difference, and reinforce the message that all young people can achieve their full potential.

A number of other influences which have contributed to increasing interest in the learning environment can be identified, both from legislation and from research. These are discussed in the next two sections.

Influences from legislation

In the past, SEN legislation focused exclusively on disabilities within the child. Over the last 20 years more attention has been given to the learning environments of pupils who have SEN. The 1996 Education Act defines SEN needs in terms of the interrelationship between a child's learning difficulty and the educational support which they are receiving: 'A child has special educational needs if they have a learning difficulty which calls for special educational provision to be made for them' (Department for Education and Employment 1996, Section 323).

An interactional view of SEN was reinforced in the first edition of the *Code of Practice* on the identification and assessment of SEN, which was published in 1994. For example, it was advised that 'Schools should not automatically assume that children's learning difficulties always result solely or even mainly from problems within the child. The school's practices can make a difference – for good or ill' (Department for Education 1994a, para. 2: 19). The criteria for deciding to make a formal assessment which are detailed in Section 3 of the *Code of Practice* gave equal weight to evidence relating to the child's learning difficulties and their response to the special educational provision made by the school. The *Code* (para. 3: 50) advised:

> Bare facts of academic attainment will not be sufficient in themselves for LEAs to conclude that a statutory assessment is or is not necessary. Those facts must always be understood in the context of the attainments of the child's peers, the child's progress over time and, where appropriate, expectations of

the child's performance. A child's apparently weak performance may, on examination of the evidence, be attributable to factors in the school's organisation.

Other UK guidance also places emphasis on the importance of aspects of the learning environment: 'Many factors have a bearing on the behaviour of young people. The organisation and policies of the school, its physical environment and the overall ethos, can all have a strong influence on pupil behaviour' (Department for Education 1994b, para. 7). Similar views have been expressed by government bodies in other countries. The US National Academy of Sciences Panel on Equity in Special Education concluded that 'valid assessment of the learning environment is as critical as valid assessment of the individual' (Heller *et al.* 1982: xi).

The revised *Code of Practice* on the identification and assessment of pupils with SEN (Department for Education and Skills 2001) goes further. Rather than simply recognizing that the learning environment will have an influence and should be considered, the revised guidance requires the assessment of pupils who have SEN to include assessment of their learning environment. Likewise in devising interventions, changes to features of the learning environment should be considered (2001, para. 5.6):

> The assessment process should always be fourfold. It should focus on the child's learning characteristics, the learning environment that the school is providing for the child, the task and the teaching style. It should be recognised that some difficulties in learning may be caused or exacerbated by the school's learning environment or adult/child relationships. This means looking carefully at such matters as classroom organisation, teaching materials, teaching style and differentiation in order to decide how these can be developed so that the child is enabled to learn effectively.

Influences from research

School effectiveness research

School effectiveness research has had a major impact in education over the last 20 years. Prior to that there was a widespread belief that 'schools make no difference'. However, researchers in this area are now expressing the view that 'we have been instrumental in creating a quite widespread, popular view that schools do not just make *a* difference, but that they make *all* the difference', (Reynolds 1995: 13). In fact, Reynolds reports that only 8–15 per cent of the variance in pupil outcomes is usually found to be due to school and classroom factors – which are not therefore as influential as family and community factors. However, the influence of school factors is big enough to make the difference between educational success and failure for many pupils.

The following factors have been found to be associated with school effectiveness (Reynolds 1997):

- Leadership by the headteacher which is characterized by strength of purpose, proactive management and promotion of a consistent approach; involving staff in some decision making and leadership on key aspects of classroom practice, including the curriculum, teaching strategies and monitoring of pupil progress.
- Shared vision and goals held by staff, with a consensus on values, consistency of practice and effective collaboration.
- A learning context that is characterized by an orderly atmosphere and an attractive working environment.
- High quality teaching and learning which is generated by fostering an academic emphasis and extending pupils' opportunities to learn through ensuring broad curriculum coverage and maximizing the time devoted to academic work.
- High expectations of pupils – communicated and reinforced both at class and individual level.
- Positive reinforcement involving praise and appreciation within a framework of clear and fair rules.
- Monitoring of performance and progress effectively at pupil, class and school level.
- Pupil involvement in positions of responsibility within the school, and in out of school activities: in societies, teams, leadership and representative positions.
- Purposeful teaching, involving good planning and preparation and well organized and structured lessons, which allow a degree of pupil independence and responsibility within a well defined framework.

While these broad generalizations are well established, a number of questions remain:

- How consistent is school performance across different outcome measures? There appears to be considerable variation. Mortimore *et al.* (1988) found that those junior schools that came out high on academic effectiveness were not necessarily high on social effectiveness and vice versa.
- Are schools equally effective for all pupils or subgroups?

Nuttall *et al.* (1989) argued that there can be different school effects for children of different ethnic groups, ability ranges and gender within the same school. Using examination performance at 16 years as the outcome measure, a study conducted over three years revealed substantial differences between boys and girls, pupils of high and low attainment on entry to secondary school and pupils of Caribbean backgrounds, as opposed to those from English, Scottish, Welsh or Irish backgrounds. Doubts were raised about the meaningfulness of the concept of overall effectiveness and it was suggested that it may be more meaningful to describe differences between schools for different subgroups. This also seems to be the case in some primary schools. In a research study conducted by Mortimore *et al.* (1988) in London primary schools, gender differences in reading progress were compared. It was found that most schools were equally effective, or ineffective, in promoting the reading progress of boys and girls. However in 30 per cent of schools differences were found, and in 20 per cent of these, effects on reading were positive for boys but negative for girls.

Semmel *et al.* (1994) reported results from a longitudinal school effectiveness project focusing on primary and secondary schools in California. There was no evidence that schools that did well in terms of general academic achievement also did well with regard to the academic performance, self-esteem or school adjustment of pupils with SEN. Indeed, in primary schools a significant negative relationship was found between the reading performance on state assessments of a school's SEN pupils and school-wide reading achievement. The authors suggest that pressures on these schools to increase academic standards under conditions of reducing resources may have led to the development of strategies to improve reading performance over-all which had a negative impact on the reading progress of pupils with SEN.

Research on the classroom learning environment

Reynolds (1997) identified the study of classroom or instructional processes as a gap in current British research on school effectiveness. The same criticism was levelled by researchers in the USA at the research base in their country (Waxman *et al.* 1997). This is an important area for further work as many studies show that a great majority of the variance between pupils is due to factors at the classroom level, not the school level.

There is a substantial literature which demonstrates that characteristics of the classroom learning environment account for appreciable amounts of variance in a number of important outcome measures such as examination results, standard-ized test scores, inquiry skills, school attendance, attitudes, interest and anxiety (Fraser 1986). Haertel *et al.* (1981) conducted a meta-analysis of data from 12 studies involving 17,805 students in 823 classes across four countries and re-ported that better achievement was consistently found in classes perceived as having greater cohesiveness, satisfaction and goal direction and less disorgan-ization and friction. While it is acknowledged that much research has still to be done in this area, other researchers too have reported results which suggest that student attitude as well as student achievement might be improved by creating classroom environments with more of these positive features (Fraser *et al.* 1989; Burden and Fraser 1993).

An important aspect of research on classroom environments is its international and cross-cultural character. For example, the International Association for the Evaluation of Educational Achievement classroom environment study (Anderson *et al.* 1989) was conducted in eight countries: Australia, Canada, Hungary, Israel, Korea, the Netherlands, Nigeria and Thailand. This promotes confidence in the cross-cultural applicability of consistently emerging findings. However, to date much of the research has been descriptive or correlational in nature. Waxman and Huang (1996) highlighted the need for longitudinal and, especially, experimental studies which would be important in informing intervention. Urging researchers to examine specifically how aspects of the classroom learning environment can be changed in order to serve a protective function for pupils in at-risk school and community settings, they also argued for the importance of examining the data for differential effects of pupil characteristics such as sex, ethnicity and age.

Figure 8.1
Classroom
variables which
affect children's
learning
Source: Based on
a literature review
by McKee and Witt
(1990).

A. Physical setting of the classroom

1 Classroom design, furniture arrangement, seating positions
2 Spatial density and crowding
3 Noise and lighting

B. Classroom organization and management

1 Teacher's classroom management skills
   • 'With-itness'; overlapping; signal continuity; momentum
   • Group alerting and accountability in lessons
2 Procedures for establishing effective management
   • Rules and procedures for everyday classroom life
   • Procedures for student accountability
   • Managing inappropriate behaviour

C. Quantity and quality of instruction

1 Quantity or amount of instruction
   • Allocated time; engaged time
   • Time spent on tasks on which students have high success rate
2 Quality of instruction
   • Daily review and checking of homework
   • Presentation of material to be learned
   • Arrangements for guided student practice
   • Feedback and correctives on students' performance
   • Independent practice; periodic reviews

Figure 8.1 Classroom variables which affect children's learning. *Source:* Based on a literature review by McKee and Witt (1990).

Figure 8.1 shows the classroom-level variables which affect learning that were identified from a literature review conducted by McKee and Witt (1990). It should be noted that this review focuses on studies carried out with general populations of schoolchildren, rather than those with SEN. It cannot be assumed that the same variables will have equal salience for different groups of children. For example, Rossmiller (1982, cited in Berliner 1987) found that 'engaged time' had a different significance for high and low achieving pupils. Engaged time is the amount of classroom time during which pupils are engaged with instructional tasks. In this study, engaged time accounted for 10 per cent of the variance in reading and maths achievement for high achieving pupils but, in the case of low achieving pupils the percentage of variance accounted for was 73 per cent.

There is some further support for the view that the learning environment may play a different and relatively more important role in the educational progress of children with special needs as compared to their mainstream peers. Table 8.1 reports the findings from Kaufman *et al.*'s (1985) extensive evaluation of a major reintegration programme for primary-aged children with MLD in Texas. What emerges most strongly is the greater importance for both pupils with special

Table 8.1 Percentage of variance in academic achievement and anti-social behaviour attributable to individual and environmental variables for mainstream and integrated MLD pupils

		Type of variable (%)	
		Learner background (individual, family, home)	Environmental (classroom composition, socioemotional climate, instructional conditions)
Academic achievement	Integrated MLD pupils	13	27
	Mainstream pupils	33	45
Antisocial behaviour	Integrated MLD pupils	5	28
	Mainstream pupils	11	21

Source: Kaufman *et al.* (1985).

needs and their mainstream peers of a focus on environmental as opposed to individual variables.

There is evidence that pupils with learning difficulties are treated differently by teachers. However, this is not always advantageous for them. Slate and Saudargas (1987) found that teachers were more likely to leave pupils with learning difficulties alone when they were engaged in academic work than when they were engaged in other activities. On the other hand, teachers were more likely to interact with students with learning difficulties when they were out of their seats or interacting with other children. Teachers' differential attention to off-task behaviour was only found with pupils who had learning difficulties, not with their classmates. Alves and Gottlieb (1986) found that teachers directed fewer academic questions and less extended feedback towards pupils who have learning difficulties, although teachers did interact with them more frequently overall than they did with other pupils. The authors suggested that this evidence of lower academic input may reflect perceptions on the part of the teachers that socialization, rather than academic learning, represents the primary goal of mainstreaming for pupils who have learning difficulties. Cooper and Valli (1996: 156) argued that a very different approach is in fact required: 'classroom organization for poor children of colour and for children with learning difficulties must account for individual and cultural differences in knowledge construction by providing well-scaffolded, culturally responsive and socially mediated instructional activities'. Thus, those reporting and commenting on research have supported the official guidance emphasizing the importance of the learning environment of a child who has (or may have) SEN.

The learning environment: theory and practice

Theoretical models of the influence of the learning environment

There have been a number of influences on thinking about a systematic approach to the assessment of children's learning environments, most notably Lewin's (1936) field theory, Bandura's (1977) concept of reciprocal determinism and Bronfenbrenner's (1979) ecosystems approach. Lewin developed the formula $B = f(P, E)$ to represent the idea that behaviour (B) was a function of personal characteristics (P), environmental factors (E) and the interaction between the two. Bandura hypothesized that behaviour was determined by reciprocal interactions, continuously occurring between behavioural, cognitive and environmental factors. Bronfenbrenner developed a systems model of the multiple influences on child development that was introduced in Chapter 4. Figure 8.2 shows Knoff's (1984) ecomap representing, for the typical pupil, Bronfenbrenner's multi-level systems analysis of the environment.

From these theoretical approaches a number of specific models have been developed which outline the influence of the learning environment on pupil performance in school. Three of the most influential of these are outlined below.

Figure 8.3 shows Centra and Potter's (1980) model of school and teacher variables influencing student learning outcomes. The model makes a number of specific predictions about causal influences on student learning outcomes and behaviour.

Figure 8.2
Ecomap showing micro-, meso-, exo- and macrosystems in the environment of the typical pupil
Source: Knoff (1984).

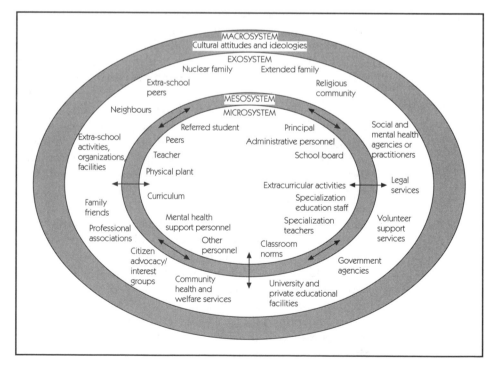

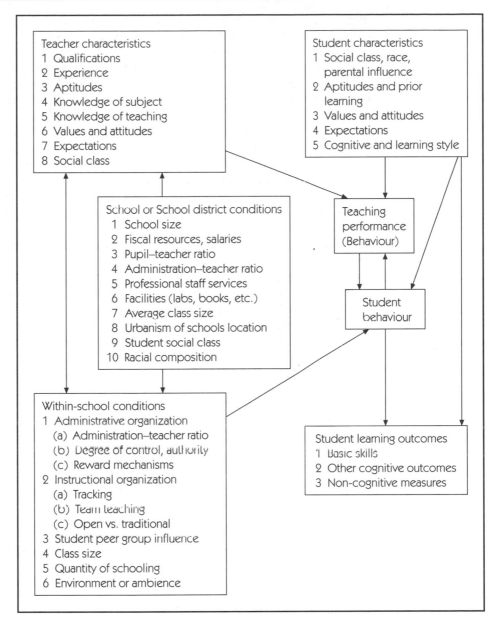

Figure 8.3
Centra and Potter's (1980) structural model of school and teacher variables influencing student learning outcomes
Note: Single headed arrows indicate predicted causal relations, double headed arrows represent correlations, but not causal relations.

Of particular interest is the prediction that the only sources of direct influence are student characteristics, teacher characteristics and within-school conditions. Other environmental variables, for example those related to catchment area, are not hypothesized to have a direct effect on student learning and behaviour, but are thought to exert an indirect effect through their influence on within-school conditions and teacher characteristics. This model would suggest that it will be important to focus directly on an individual child's immediate learning environment, whatever consideration may also be given to more global influences.

Of particular relevance to work with pupils who have SEN is the Project PRIME (programmed re-entry into mainstream education) taxonomic model (Kaufman *et al.* 1985). In this model, which was developed to guide a major integration study in the USA, competence is viewed as a function of the learner performing a specific role within an environment defined by a specific setting. In a clear parallel with Lewin's work, this function is represented mathematically by the equation $C = (Lr, Es)$, where (C) is competence, (L) is the learner, (E) is the environment, (r) stands for role and (s) stands for setting. The model analyses each term in the equation into subcomponents. For example, learner competence is further subdivided into academic competence and social competence. Learner background variables include: age, sex, socioeconomic status, IQ, attitudes and previous school experience. Aspects of the learning environment are considered under three headings: classroom composition, socioemotional climate and instructional conditions. These were used in the study to analyse three types of learning environment; mainstream class, segregated special class and a resource base (part-time withdrawal). A rationale is offered for focusing on the immediate classroom environment in this study: 'In a larger context the class is a sub-system of the school, school district and community. However, given the focus of the study is on programming and placement decisions for EMR (MLD) children, classes were considered to be the most critical and proximal unit of study' (Kaufman *et al.* 1985: 14).

Table 8.2 shows the third model, the student learning in context model (SLIC) produced by Christenson and Ysseldyke (1989) This model also emphasizes that the learning environment for a child in the classroom will be influenced by key features of the wider context, and, as Ysseldyke pointed out, the most powerful interventions will involve school and home collaboration as well as work at the classroom level. However, the SLIC model appears to ignore important and influential features of the wider environment – the subcultures of the child's neighbourhood and ethnic or linguistic community (Tharp 1994) which are represented in the other models.

Table 8.2   Student learning in context

School/LEA	Classroom	Home
Positiveness	Structure	Participation
Teaching resources	Expectations	Homework involvement
Order	Interaction	Consistent discipline
Inter-staff collaboration	Management	Educative environment
Leadership	Instructional match	Interest
Academic focus	Academic allocated time	Monitoring
Curricular decision making	Academic responding time	
	Evaluation	

Source: Christenson and Ysseldyke (1989).

The gap between theory and current practice

The research and theory outlined in the early part of this chapter have important practical implications for assessment and intervention practice with pupils who have SEN. Ysseldyke and Christenson (1987b: 20) urged teachers and educational psychologists to give more attention to environmental factors in their work with children who have SEN in order to improve outcomes:

> the purpose of any assessment is intervention. Since a student's performance is a function of classroom variables, it is necessary to analyze the learning environment to design effective interventions. We believe that educators should not categorize or label a student without considering the role instructional factors play in the student's learning difficulties. Both student characteristic data and learning environment data should be considered by child study team members engaging in educational and placement decisions.

Similarly, Sattler (1988) in his classic text on assessment of children and young people advocates environmental assessment as an important component of a comprehensive assessment and argues that it should be conducted prior to undertaking an individual assessment.

By contrast, however, the following quotations, taken from Department for Education and Employment sponsored reports, highlight attention to the environment as an area of weakness in Statements of SEN: 'Most of the Statements which we have seen in the course of our research concentrated their attention on deficits within the child which led to special needs, with very little attention given to the child's environment, whether at home or at school' (Goacher *et al.* 1988); 'Statements generally identify provision in such vague terms that, contrary to the intention of the 1981 Act, they cannot guarantee a specific level of provision' (Audit Commission 1992).

The existence of a gap between theory and practice was also identified by McKee and Witt (1990: 821) who suggested: 'There exists in school psychology a lack of congruence between, on the one hand, our data-based assumptions and beliefs concerning the importance of the environment, and on the other hand, our practice where environmental variables are seldom seriously considered for the purpose of designing interventions'. These authors went on to suggest that this discrepancy between educational psychologists' beliefs and behaviours may relate to two different sets of problems:

- *Social and political problems*: related to entering the teacher's domain and presuming to have the right and knowledge to target instructional variables for assessment/intervention.
- *Technical problems*: related to lack of knowledge about what to assess, how to assess it and how to communicate the information to teachers in a way that is helpful and enabling.

While social and political issues must be carefully considered, the introduction of the National Curriculum and regular school inspections has changed the construction of the classroom as the teacher's domain. In addition, accumulating research evidence on school effectiveness and the crucial effects on pupil learning of classroom instructional and environmental variables has altered perceptions about the need to target these variables in order to make a positive difference for the pupil. It is suggested that technical problems now represent the greatest impediment to developing approaches to assessment and intervention that more

ACTIVITY 8.1   How useful are accounts of the learning environment in Statements of SEN?

These extracts are taken from a selection of Statements of SEN. How useful do you think each of the accounts would be to parents, psychologists and future teachers of the children concerned?

Jonathan (aged 11) (specific learning difficulties in literacy)

Educational advice
'Reason for formal assessment': Although Jonathan has been supported by the literacy support service for five terms at B centre and four terms at H school his progress has been extremely slow . . .

'List strategies employed and outcomes achieved': The literacy support service has employed a multi-sensory approach to reading, writing and spelling. He has received individual and small-group tuition on a regular basis. This has resulted in limited progress in literacy but considerable improvement in self-organization and in his attitude to coping with difficulties. In the classroom Jonathan's programme of work is individualized with work supporting the literacy support programme.

Psychological advice
'Relevant information about this child and the learning environment': Jonathan has been supported by the literacy support service for five terms at B centre and four terms within H middle school.

Sharon (aged 10) (severe anaemia, problems of motor control, learning difficulties)

Educational advice
Sharon has been receiving support from a learning support assistant since September last year. The support has been either in class, helping her cope with instructions and develop some independence, or withdrawal support, going over curriculum content that Sharon has found difficult. She had use of a laptop computer and was given some instruction. The present programme of work is: (a) in close liaison with her class teacher, discussing objectives and targets, exploring the extent of her difficulties and planning future lessons; and (b) encouraging Sharon to talk about her work and explain what she has to do, and getting her to verbalize her ideas. The laptop computer was only a partial success as Sharon was only able to grasp and sequence the most simple of procedures. She was heavily dependent on the learning support assistant to check and print out her work. If she

was to have this facility again, she would need a teacher to be trained and designated 'on-site' as an adviser, maintainer and print operator.

(Support teacher)

'Brief description of school organization and child's place in it': National Curriculum year 5 mixed ability class in the first year of middle school.

'Has special attention already been provided in school, e.g. group teaching methods or remedial teaching in school or elsewhere?': Work in all subjects needs modification to meet Sharon's needs as she finds many concepts difficult to grasp even with extensive use of practical equipment. For example, she seemed unable to comprehend the idea of millilitres and litres even after considerable work with water and measuring equipment.

(Class teacher, SEN coordinator, headteacher)

Psychological advice
This advice refers to the learning support assistant support and to the provision of a laptop computer but gives no details or comment.

Adam (aged 8) (severe emotional and behavioural difficulties)

Psychological Advice (after a previous meeting)
Mrs L, Adam's class teacher, was advised to build on Adam's strengths in class – for example, his organizational ability and desire to help. Efforts were to be made to continue to give him 'important jobs' to improve his self-esteem and status within the class. I gave Mrs L details of self-recording as a means of boosting self-esteem and to modify Adam's behaviour. When a review was carried out a year later more concerns were being expressed about Adam's academic progress rather than his disruptive behaviour. The SEN support service team was then involved in providing support. Four months later the situation had deteriorated considerably and Mr R, the headteacher, requested 25 hours welfare assistance per week for Adam, as his attention-seeking behaviour was felt to be detrimental to the rest of the class: (I assessed Adam in school.) I observed him in class during a session where children share their 'treasures' with their teacher; when called out to show his valued object, he stood in front of Mrs L with his back to the children, physically blocking their access to the teacher. He was determined to have Mrs L's attention and was not interested in sharing with his peers.

I subsequently recommended Adam for attendance at the school D learning support department. Fortunately a place was available and he started almost at once. He also had psychotherapy involvement increased from one to two sessions per week. Although progress was made in the unit (e.g. in settling to simple tasks on his own), Adam still found it difficult to share. He continued to have considerable difficulties in the mainstream classes in School D.

I reviewed Adam's progress six months later. In the classroom, I noted that Adam would only work under the close supervision of his teacher. She had to physically sit at his table in order to keep him on task. At a meeting in school it was accepted that while Adam was calmer in school, his emotional needs were still such that he required a great deal of attention to stay on task, more than could be provided within the resources of a mainstream school.

adequately reflect the importance of the classroom learning environment and of individual/environmental interactions. Fraser (1987) suggested that measures of the classroom learning environment could be of value to educational psychologists in evaluating educational innovations, appraising the appropriateness of alternative placements and providing a basis for in-service work with teachers. Techniques that make it possible to assess participant's perceptions of teaching–learning contexts are seen as particularly important in supporting educational psychologists' greater involvement in prevention and early intervention, offering consultation and systems-based approaches (Burden and Fraser 1993).

Methods for evaluating learning environments and designing interventions

Frederickson and Cline (1995) identified the three most commonly used strategies as follows: (i) direct observation; (ii) investigating pupils' perceptions (e.g. through questionnaires); and (iii) investigating teachers' perceptions. Other approaches are: (iv) investigating parents' perceptions; (v) investigating the perceptions of support staff in the classroom; (vi) examining work completed by pupils and discussing it with them and with their teachers; and (vii) examining teachers' written lesson records.

Frederickson and Cline (1995) suggested that one perspective alone would provide a limited view and that exploring a number of perspectives on the learning environment would be more informative and valid. Fraser (1987), who has been very influential in developing pupil perception measures, acknowledged that the richest information about the classroom environment is likely to come from the use of both observational and student perceptual data, rather than from the use of either technique alone. Waxman *et al.* (1997: 57) also advise on the desirability of a multi-method approach: 'In order to capture all the processes and nuances that occur in classrooms, educators should use triangulation procedures to collect data from multiple perspectives'. They suggested using multiple measures of classroom processes, together with student and teacher self-report survey and interview data in addition to more qualitative ethnographic data from field notes. The next four sections examine in turn the following approaches: observational measures, pupil perceptual measures, multi-perspective measures and qualitative ethnographic assessment methods. Finally we will take a more detailed look at a methodology derived from systems theory that has been applied to issues in SEN by educational psychologists and teachers in Britain.

Observational measures

Frederickson and Cline (1995) summarized the relative advantages of observation as a method as follows:

- It is a very effective way to gather detailed information directly about how a child is interacting with the whole environment – teacher, peers, learning materials.

- Observation makes it possible to examine the teacher's expectations of the target child – in practice rather than theory.
- One can collect verbatim records of what the teacher, the target child and other children actually say to each other.
- A variety of structured techniques are available which allow detailed 'objective' information to be obtained which will assist in interpreting 'high inference' output such as individuals' accounts of how they see things.
- It is possible to analyse patterns across several situations – what is offered and the child's response to it.

It is important also to bear in mind some potential limitations of observational techniques. For example, there is a possibility that the very presence of an observer may affect the behaviour of teachers and pupils. This can result in reactive effects such as socially desirable responding. As observations are conducted for limited time periods it is also important to consider whether the periods used are sufficient to obtain a reliable and valid sample of the interaction(s) of interest. The collection of data may be time consuming. Isolated incidents may be focused on, without properly considering the preceding and subsequent events that may provide information about context and meaning.

Many observational techniques have been developed with the purpose of conducting research on features of classrooms and classroom processes. In this section we focus on observational approaches that can be used to assess the learning environment of a pupil who has SEN with the purpose of designing appropriate interventions. The Classroom Observation Schedule (COS) was developed by Waxman *et al.* (1988). It is a systematic observation schedule which is designed to record pupil behaviours with reference to a number of aspects of classroom learning environments:

- pupil interactions with teachers and/or peers and the purpose of these interactions;
- the settings in which observed behaviours occur;
- the types of material with which pupils are working;
- the specific types of activity in which they engage.

The COS has six headings:

1 *Interaction*: describes the type and purpose of any interaction a pupil may have with other pupils, the teacher or support staff.
2 *Selection of activity*: identifies who has decided that a pupil will be working on a particular assignment during the observation period.
3 *Activity types*: possibilities here include watching or listening, working on written assignments and social interaction.
4 *Setting*: identifies the grouping arrangements.
5 *Manner*: describes the pupil's behaviour in relation to the classroom context and activities being observed.
6 *Language used*: identifies the language(s) which the pupil is using for oral and written communication.

The COS, which has recently been published in Britain (Frederickson and Monsen 1999), has been used in primary and secondary schools in the USA, most notably as one of the key instruments in a five-year research programme being conducted by the National Research Centre for Education in the Inner Cities. In a number of recent studies the COS has been used to examine the classroom instruction and learning environment in effective and ineffective schools in the USA, for pupils generally and for African-American pupils in particular (Waxman and Huang 1997; Waxman et al. 1997). Waxman and Huang (1997: 10) argued that 'one of our most serious educational problems continues to be the underachievement of African-American students in urban schools' and reviewed research that suggested the importance of effective classroom learning environments in enabling African-American and other students at risk of failure to achieve success in school.

Waxman (1995) describes the use of the COS in a formative way to provide feedback to school staff and stimulate discussion about improvements. Observations were carried out across a whole school district and Table 8.3 shows an example of the profiles fed back to schools, allowing each school to compare their mean percentages on each category with the averages across the district. The profiles were considered at staff meetings and their implications discussed. In the case of the example shown in Table 8.3, Waxman reported that teachers' concern focused on the amount of time their pupils spent watching or listening (61 per cent), particularly as it was above the district average (53 per cent) and they discussed strategies for raising the amount of active pupil engagement in lessons.

The COS can also be used to monitor or evaluate the effectiveness of interventions or the effects of other changes by comparing differences between the percentage observations recorded in particular categories before and after the change was introduced. Particular teachers or groups of teachers may be interested in comparing the characteristics of the classroom environment they provide across different subjects (primary) or different groups of pupils (secondary). Teachers and schools may be interested in examining the data for any differences linked to gender, ethnicity or SEN.

The COS can be used to monitor and evaluate changes in aspects of classroom interaction, activity and organization where these have been directly targeted. For example, if a school decides to introduce more cooperative group work in order to promote the inclusion of pupils with SEN, the COS can be used to collect data on the amount of cooperative group work occurring before the initiative was introduced, and at various stages after its introduction. This data can be set alongside measures of the pupil's inclusion. The COS can also highlight other changes to the classroom environment that may not have been anticipated. The effects on the classroom environment and on pupil engagement in learning activities of changes in the deployment of special needs support staff could also usefully be assessed using the COS.

Waxman (1995) argued that many teachers, even those with substantial experience, are sometimes unaware of the nature of their interactions with individual pupils and that one of the most important purposes of systematic classroom observation is to improve teaching practice. There is growing evidence that feedback

Table 8.3 COS example feedback profile for a primary school

A Interactions

Variables	Your school mean (%)	All primary schools aggregated mean (%)
1 No interaction/independence	52.73	59.48
2,3,4 Interaction with teacher	39.07	33.40
5 Interaction with support staff	0.00	0.02
6,7 Interaction with other students	8.08	7.06
8 Interaction with others	0.10	0.01

B and C Activity selection and types

Variables	Your school mean (%)	All primary schools aggregated mean (%)
B1 Teacher-assigned activity	99.76	99.85
B2 Student-selected activity	0.23	0.34
C1 Working on written assignments	9.52	19.55
C2, C3 Interacting	5.00	6.74
C4 Watching or listening	60.83	53.03
C5 Reading	3.45	8.82
C6 Getting/returning materials	1.90	2.77
C7 Colouring, drawing, painting, etc.	1.07	0.46
C9 Working with manipulative materials/ equipment	10.83	4.55
C12 Presenting/acting	1.42	0.78
C13 Tutoring peers	0.00	0.18
C14 Not attending to task	3.33	4.08
C16 Other	4.04	3.21

Note: More than one activity may be coded during one observation.

D Setting

Variables	Your school mean (%)	All primary schools aggregated mean (%)
1 Whole class	80.23	78.19
2 Small group	13.09	12.20
4 Individual	6.66	9.60

E Manner

Variables	Your school mean (%)	All primary schools aggregated mean (%)
1 On task	95.11	94.48
2 Waiting for teacher	0.23	0.30
3 Distracted	2.97	3.45
4 Disruptive	1.19	0.84
5 Other	0.47	0.90

Source: Waxman (1995).

from systematic observations can be used to improve teaching (Stallings and Freiberg 1991). This may be particularly important where some groups of pupils are being treated differently. For example, many studies have reported gender differences in teacher–pupil interactions, with boys often receiving both more praise and more criticism in the classroom than girls (Brophy and Good 1974). Waxman (1995: 80) suggested that an important purpose for classroom observation is to investigate questions such as: 'Are some pupils being treated differently in the classroom, and does that explain why some pupils learn more than others?' The answers to such questions may have crucial policy implications for schools in raising the achievement of all pupils.

A number of studies have provided information on the validity of the COS categories in discriminating between effective and ineffective schools. Waxman and Huang (1997) designed a study to examine the classroom instruction and learning environment in effective and ineffective schools for African-American pupils. The primary schools studied were in urban districts that had predominately African-American students from economically disadvantaged families. Schools were classified as effective or ineffective on the basis of pupil scores on state-wide assessments of academic skills. Four schools were randomly selected from those classified as effective and four from those classified as ineffective. The COS was used in 15 randomly selected classrooms in each school during reading or mathematics classes.

The results of this study showed that pupils from the effective schools more often worked individually, whereas those from ineffective schools were taught as a whole class for a higher proportion of the time. Pupils from the effective schools also spent relatively more time interacting with their teacher and working on written assignments, while in ineffective schools more time was spent working with manipulative materials, reading and interacting with others. Although pupils in both types of school were on task for a very high proportion of the time (more than 90 per cent), the level of active involvement and intellectual demand was lower in the ineffective schools where a typical lesson would involve the teacher lecturing to the whole class and merely asking the pupils a few knowledge-type questions near the end of the lesson. Furthermore, students from the effective schools were observed interacting with their teacher almost twice as much as those from the ineffective schools.

The findings of this study are consistent with a range of other findings from the literature:

- That amount and quality of teacher–pupil academic interactions are two of the most important educational variables that promote student outcome (Wang *et al.* 1994);
- That over-reliance on whole-class instruction is detrimental to student outcomes because teachers often have difficulty in maintaining an instructional pace that is appropriate to all (Walberg 1995).

In addition it is reported that small-group instruction and cooperative grouping are especially effective for pupils from minority groups and lead to improved pupil outcomes (Allyn and Boykin 1992; Walberg 1995).

Thus the COS has been shown to identify dynamic influences in the classroom that are also revealed by other research methods. But all observation schedules have a degree of bias in that they concentrate on factors perceived to be important by their authors. Alternative classroom observation schedules with different emphases include the Immediate Learning Environment Survey (ILES) (Pielstick 1987) and the Instructional Environment System-II (TIES-II) (Ysseldyke and Christenson 1993).

The ILES is a survey instrument which covers four broad domains: physical conditions; social conditions; instructional materials and procedures; and psychological/learning factors. The full use of TIES-II involves four steps of which classroom observation is one, the others being teacher interview, student interview and parent interview.

Pupil perceptual measures

Some advantages of using pupil perceptual measures are:

- There is evidence that they account for more variance in achievement than directly observed (low inference) variables (Fraser 1991).
- They avoid giving inappropriate weight to events because of their frequency (quality or intensity may matter more than quantity).
- They are based on pupil experiences over many lessons rather than being restricted, as observation normally is, to a small number which may be atypical.
- With group methods the conclusions that are drawn are based on the pooled judgements of all pupils rather than data from a single (though trained) observer. With pooled judgements any individual biases are likely to cancel each other out.
- They directly assess learner perceptions of events which are as likely, if not more likely, to determine learner behaviour than the actual events. The classroom environment experienced by the student may be quite different from that which is observed or intended.
- This method facilitates the direct comparison of pupil and teacher perceptions. Fraser (1984) reported that teachers tend to perceive their classrooms more favourably than their pupils.
- Pupil perception measures respond to demands for accountability because information is obtained about the preferences and reactions of consumers.
- They are more economical than observation techniques.

A number of potential limitations should also be kept in mind. The following were reported by a group of British educational psychologists (Frederickson and Cline 1995), from initial trialling of one measure that had been developed by Fraser. First, some children seemed puzzled by the apparent repetition of questions (very similar questions typically make up each scale). Second, the reading level was too high for some pupils. Although this was overcome successfully by reading the items aloud to the children, this made the whole process less clearly 'private' between the individual child and the page. Third, some of the language used proved problematic for some pupils with learning difficulties (e.g. the use of double negatives). Finally, some children expressed uncertainty about generalizing on some questions (e.g. in response to 'In my class everybody is my friend' some children indicated that they would have liked to have had a midpoint between 'yes' and 'no' in the response options).

Fraser (1998) provided a review of available pupil perceptual measures and highlighted the strong influence on their development of the work of Moos (1973), who proposed that diverse psychosocial environments can be classified using three types of dimension:

1 Relationship dimensions which identify the nature and intensity of personal relationships, involvement and support within the environment.
2 Personal development dimensions which assess the directions along which personal growth and self-enhancement tend to occur.
3 Systems maintenance and systems change dimensions which refer to orderliness, maintenance of control and clarity of expectation.

The scales from the two measures described in detail in this section can all be classified according to Moos' scheme (Fraser 1998). The two measures that have been selected are those that have been most used and are readily obtainable in Britain. They both involve short pupil questionnaires which are easily scored and summarized in a diagrammatic form which teachers find meaningful and useful. The My Class Inventory (MCI) is designed for primary-aged pupils while the Individualized Classroom Environment Questionnaire (ICEQ) is designed for secondary-aged pupils and focuses in particular on aspects of the learning environment (e.g. individualization and differentiation) found to be particularly important in promoting the successful inclusion of pupils who have SEN (Madden and Slavin 1983).

Both measures are completed by pupil and teacher participants in the learning environments that are assessed and include an 'actual' and a 'preferred' form. The actual form asks students to rate aspects of their current learning environment while the preferred form asks how students would ideally like their learning environment to be. Item wording is almost identical in the actual and preferred forms. For example, the statement 'Different students do different work' in the actual form of the ICEQ is changed in the preferred form to 'Different students *would* do different work'. The questionnaires can be administered on a whole-class basis or individually to pupils and teachers. If there are concerns about the reading ability of members of the class it is acceptable for the teacher to read out the questions with time given for the children to mark their questionnaire.

The short form MCI (MCI-SF) consists of five scales, each containing five items. The meanings of the scales are defined as follows:

- *Cohesiveness*: the extent to which students know, help and are friendly towards each other.
- *Friction*: the extent of tension and quarrelling among students.
- *Difficulty*: the extent to which students experience difficulty with the work of the class.
- *Satisfaction*: the extent to which students like their class.

• *Competition*: the extent to which students perceive an atmosphere of competition in a classroom (Fraser 1982; Fraser *et al.* 1982; Fraser and Fisher 1986).

On the MCI-SF the children answer each of the 25 questions by circling YES or NO. The 'actual' and 'preferred' forms of the questionnaire are usually completed on the same occasion, with the 'actual' form being completed first.

The MCI-SF has been shown to be as reliable and valid a measure of classroom environment as more time-intensive and costly measures, such as direct classroom observations (Fraser 1991). Wright *et al.* (1991) conducted a study in ten primary schools in Surrey from which they reported that the MCI discriminated significantly among the classrooms surveyed and was considered to be useful by the teachers and educational psychologists who participated in the research. From their study of primary mathematics classes in Singapore, Goh and Fraser (1998) reported better student outcomes when classrooms were perceived as having more cohesion and less friction – a predictable finding that tends to support claims for the validity of the instrument.

The ICEQ was developed by Rentoul and Fraser (1979) to measure how secondary-aged pupil's perceptions of traditional classrooms differed from classrooms which included more enquiry-based and individualized approaches. Interest in these kinds of approaches originally came from research on investigator based science curricula. Their importance has also been highlighted by research showing that pupils who have SEN tend to make better educational and social progress in integrated mainstream school placements, but only if a suitable individualized or differentiated educational programme is offered (Madden and Slavin,1983). Fraser (1987) suggested that the ICEQ can also be completed by the teachers of the groups of pupils being surveyed and differences in perceptions between pupils and teachers examined.

The short form of the ICEQ was produced by Fraser and Fisher (1986) in response to research and teacher feedback that the original measure provided, a very useful assessment of the classroom environment but was time consuming to administer and score. The short form consists of 25 items, 5 items in each of 5 scales. The 5 scales are interpreted as follows (Rentoul and Fraser 1979):

1 *Personalisation*: emphasis on opportunities for individual students to interact with the teacher and on concern for the personal welfare and social growth of the individual.
2 *Participation*: extent to which students are encouraged to participate rather than be passive listeners.
3 *Independence*: extent to which students are allowed to make decisions and have control over their own learning and behaviour.
4 *Investigation*: emphasis on the skills and processes of enquiry and their use in problem solving and investigation.
5 *Differentiation*: emphasis on the selective treatment of students on the basis of ability, learning style, interests and rate of working.

Lim (1995) conducted a study using the ICEQ with students aged 15–16 years attending nine secondary schools in Singapore. As in most studies a gap was found between students' ratings of their preferred and actual classroom environments, with more positive and favourable ratings being given to the preferred environment. Fraser (1982) reports that a similar gap is also found in teachers' ratings of their preferred and actual classroom environments. In addition, teachers tend to rate the actual classroom environment more positively than the pupils. Lim found that in schools achieving better GCSE results, students generally viewed their actual classroom environment as having greater emphasis on personalization, independence and differentiation. Reliability studies in Australia (Fraser and Fisher 1983b) and England (Burden and Fraser 1993) have reported similar satisfactory data for the ICEQ.

A valuable feature of the ICEQ and the MCI is that they are intervention orientated. Pupil perceptions of both their actual and preferred classroom environments can be assessed in order to identify discrepancies and assist teachers in implementing strategies aimed at reducing them. Fraser and Fisher (1983a) reported person-environment fit research which suggested that students achieve better results when the classroom environment closely matches their preferred environment. Activity 8.2 provides an illustration of the way in which assessment information from these measures can be used as a basis for reflection, discussion and systematic attempts to improve classroom environments.

Burden and Fraser (1993) pointed out that as the feedback to teachers comes from the students themselves its impact is likely to be considerably greater than if it was provided by a detached observer. They described, as a development of this process, a case study where desired changes were discussed with a class of secondary school pupils and they were involved in the design and implementation of changes. Reassessment four weeks later indicated significant reductions in the preferred/actual discrepancy on four of the five scales.

Teachers could also use this approach to check whether pupils with SEN, those of different genders and those from different ethnic or cultural groups perceive their classroom environment differently and are affected in different ways by particular intervention approaches. Some initial research suggests that these might be relevant questions to address. Knight (1991) reported differences between African-American and Hispanic students in their perceptions of their classroom environment. Frederickson and Furnham (1998b) used the MCI among other measures to assess the extent to which environmental factors and individual characteristics each contributed to the social inclusion and peer group acceptance in mainstream classes of pupils who had moderate learning difficulties. They found that both sets of factors made an important contribution. In particular the perceived cohesiveness of the classroom peer group, as assessed by the MCI, had a significant effect both in supporting inclusion and preventing rejection.

Multi-perspective measures

A number of measures are available which collect information on the classroom learning environment from more than one source. TIES (Ysseldyke and

Fraser (1987) described a study involving a class of 31 boys aged 12–13 years who were studying English, maths and history with the same teacher. As you read about the study consider these questions:

(a) What interventions might be worth trying to increase personalization and participation?
(b) Can you think of any situations in your work where an assessment/intervention approach like this using the ICEQ would be useful?

The following steps were taken:

1 *Assessment*: administration of the actual and preferred forms of the ICEQ-SF.
2 *Feedback*: to the teacher of a profile showing the discrepancy between the actual and preferred class mean scores on each of the five scales. See Figure 8.4 where the 'pre-test' line shows the discrepancy between the actual and preferred class mean scores on each of the five scales of the ICEQ before the intervention.
3 *Reflection and Discussion*: as a result of which the teacher decided to introduce an intervention aimed at increasing the levels of personalization and participation.
4 *Intervention*: over the course of a month the teacher attempted to increase personalization by moving around the classroom more, making a conscious effort to praise students and demonstrate an interest in them. The organization of more group work and the reduction in teacher as opposed to student talk were the strategies adopted in an attempt to increase participation.
5 *Reassessment*: the actual form was readministered. The 'post-test' line in Figure 8.4 shows the scores after the intervention. The differences between the pre- and post-assessments suggested (and statistical tests confirmed) that success had been achieved in reducing the actual-preferred discrepancy, specifically in the aspects of the classroom environment that had been targeted by the teacher's intervention strategies.

Figure 8.4
Profiles plotted pre- and post-intervention to show the discrepancy between pupils preferred and actual classroom learning environment
Source:
Fraser (1987).

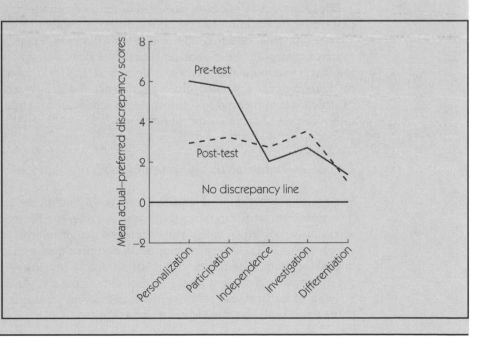

Christenson 1987a) obtains information through classroom observation and structured teacher and pupil interview. TIES-II (Ysseldyke and Christenson 1993) added a fourth source with the inclusion of a parent interview. The authors emphasized that their system 'is not a norm-referenced test or scale, but a set of tools to be used in a systematic way to gather descriptive information on the nature of a student's instructional environment' (Ysseldyke and Christenson 1993: 52).

The Student Classroom Environment Measure (SCEM), the Teacher Classroom Environment Measure (TCEM) and the Observer Classroom Environment Measure (OCEM) are three related measures developed by Midgley *et al.* (1991) which draw on the three most commonly used sources of information about classroom learning environments. These measures have the advantage that published data is available on their psychometric properties and interrelationships (Frederickson and Monsen 1999). They have been used to study the transition from primary to secondary school, so the SCEM is appropriate to older primary as well as secondary aged pupils. It is designed to sample students' perceptions of competition, social comparison among students, opportunities for cooperative learning, interactions among students, teacher fairness, friendliness and interest in class work. The TCEM and OCEM can be used by teachers and observers working across the primary and secondary age range. The TCEM is designed to sample teachers' perceptions of their general teaching and marking practices, discipline techniques, reward strategies, opportunities for student autonomy and cooperative interaction in the classroom. The OCEM is designed to sample observers' perceptions of aspects of task organization within the classroom, opportunities for student input, competition, cooperation and interaction among students, teacher fairness and friendliness and informal relations between teacher and students.

Educational psychologists have also developed a range of measures with which descriptive information can be gathered from a number of sources. Ford's (1995) Classroom Observation Guide, which draws on the research of Bennett (1991), involves classroom observation and pupil interview as well as planning and debriefing interviews with the teacher. Alders *et al.*'s (1995) instrument for assessing the learning environment from multidimensional perspectives, the development of which was influenced by TIES, includes schedules for child, parent and teacher interviews and for classroom observation.

Qualitative ethnographic assessment methods

Fraser (1998) highlighted the desirability of including both qualitative and quantitative strategies in the evaluation of learning environments. Used along with quantitative strategies, qualitative strategies can provide contextual information which assists in the interpretation of quantitative data and can help to generate hypotheses about influences and relationships in the situation. Fraser described the use of interpretative research methods involving classroom observation, interviewing of students and teachers, the construction of case studies, use of student diaries and analysis of students' written work.

Observation can also be used to collect quantitative data (as we have seen) and observation, interviewing and diary analysis can be used, albeit differently, in qualitative and ethnographic studies. What mainly distinguishes an ethnographic study is its purpose, described by Uzzell (1995: 303) as 'cultural description'. An attempt is made to understand and describe the situation from the perspectives of the participants. The focus is not on the researchers' questions or theories but on those elements which guide the actions of the participants in the environments under study.

Ruiz (1995) described an ethnographic study conducted as part of the Optimal Learning Environments (OLE) project, which aims to describe effective instructional contexts for bilingual students who have been identified as having general language difficulties. Students' language and literacy skills were observed over a period of 20 months and compared across different classroom events that ranged from teacher-structured formal class sessions to peer-structured sociodramatic play. Particular contextual factors were found to be associated with enhanced student performance while others were associated with communicative breakdowns and problems with literacy tasks. These are shown in Table 8.4.

Ruiz and Figueroa (1995) reported that at the start of the project teachers tended to see the source of students' academic difficulties as the result primarily of internal processing deficits, whereas towards the end of the study they appreciated the important role of the instructional context in producing effective or ineffective behaviour.

Soft systems methodology

Reynolds (1995) reported that schools have been slow to implement the findings from school effectiveness research, while Gallimore (1996) suggested that there may be important cultural forces operating to maintain the status quo:

Table 8.4 Contextual features of classroom events associated with the upper and lower ranges of children's language and literacy abilities

Upper range	Lower range
Emphasis on communication, not language forms	Syntactic and lexical constraints
Topic choice	Topic constraints
Increased student initiations	Few student initiations
Student directed discourse	Teacher-directed discourse
Functional use of language	Language use for teacher evaluation
Whole texts	Fragments of texts
Centred on students' experiences and knowledge	Centred on prepackaged curricular materials

Source: Ruiz (1995).

Lots of colleagues tell me that they've tried again and again to present to teachers research findings that could improve classroom practice. Many are frustrated that teachers do not share their enthusiasm. Even if told that other schools successfully tried new research-based practices, teachers may still reject what's offered. 'It's different at our school,' they'll say. 'Maybe it worked at those other schools, but your findings are not relevant to our situation, in our school, with our students.'

This insistence on the distinctiveness of the local situation is a tip off that cultural processes are at work. The local routine of classroom activities and how they are perceived are taken for granted as reality itself. They are the way things are, the way they are supposed to be. They are not recognised as evolved adaptations to the challenges of teaching at a particular school . . . If pressed, teachers defend them as unique, essential, and rational. Otherwise, they are so taken for granted they are seldom noticed and almost never examined. Asking that they be given up raises questions in the minds of teachers about the researcher's grasp on reality.

(Gallimore 1996: 234)

Frederickson (1993) argued that many problematic situations and issues in education are characterized by substantive differences in the perceptions and intentions of those involved. In these cases it is not possible to embark on a classical problem solving approach because it is not possible to agree on a definition of the problem or achieve consensus on the objectives of any change. In such situations there is a need for an explicit approach which can represent the range of views held without requiring that they be reconciled in order for progress to be made. 'Soft systems methodology' (SSM) is a systematic approach which can be used to guide intervention in the kinds of ill-structured real world problem situations common in the field of special needs. It aims to bring logical analysis to bear without oversimplifying the real complexities of the situations studied or underestimating the impact of human perceptions and interests in effecting or resisting change.

SSM was developed through a programme of over 100 action research consultancies in commercial and service environments, including health and social service contexts (Checkland 1981; Checkland and Scholes 1990). It does not focus on the problem but on the situation in which there is perceived to be a problem – or an opportunity for improvement. The initial task is not to converge on a definition of a problem to solve, but to build up the richest possible picture of the situation in question, drawing on the disparate perceptions of those involved. The essential nature of SSM is summarized in Figure 8.5. In overview, it consists of some stages which involve finding out about and developing a representation of reality, some stages which involve developing one or more models of systems which might be relevant to changing/improving reality and, finally, some stages where comparisons are drawn between the model(s) and the representation of reality in order to generate improvement suggestions/recommendations for action.

For descriptive purposes SSM consists of the seven stages which are represented diagrammatically in Figure 8.6. Stages 1 and 2 involve finding out about a

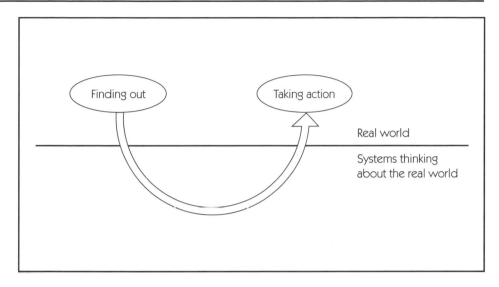

Figure 8.5
The essential
nature of SSM
Source: Checkland
(1986).

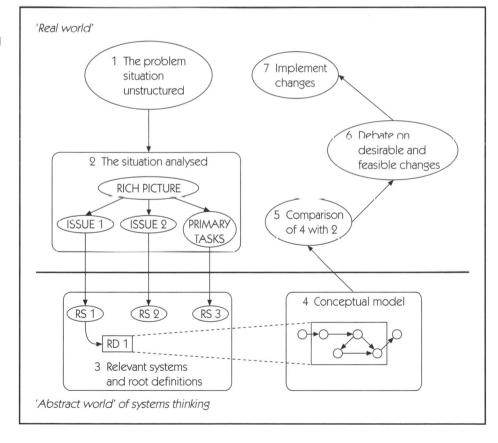

Figure 8.6
The conventional
seven-stage model
of SSM
Source: Adapted
from Checkland
and Scholes
(1990).

particular problem situation, collecting information and identifying important themes and issues. Information may be collected by a number of different means (e.g. interviewing, observation). These are practical activities where something is done in the real world.

In Stages 3 and 4 aspects of systems theory are used to analyse the problem situation and to build models of systems which may be relevant to improving it. Notice the words used. A model relevant to improving a problem situation does not purport to be a model of a problem or a problem situation. These activities are purely logical/theoretical. The defining characteristics of systems theories are explained in Chapter 14, while detailed discussion of different strands of systems theory and their application in schools can be found in Frederickson (1990a).

At Stages 5 to 7 possible changes to the real world situation are suggested so that those directly involved can debate the desirability and feasibility of the suggestions and, if appropriate, implement them. (The last three stages again involve practical activities, such as meetings and feasibility studies which would need to be carried out in the real world.)

Note the distinction which is drawn between Stages 3 and 4, the 'below the line' stages, and the other five stages, the 'above the line' stages. Stages 3 and 4 are theoretical in that they involve formal systems thinking whereas the other five stages are practical in that they involve activities which are carried out in the real world.

The information collected in Stage 1 is used in Stage 2 to express, represent or describe the problem situation – to build up the richest possible picture of the situation. This may be a 'pen picture' but it is often found to be more useful to express the information diagrammatically or indeed pictorially. A rich picture is defined as an evolving diagram that collects together and portrays key information and impressions about a complex situation in a loosely structured and evocative way. Figure 8.7 contains an example of a rich picture which was used by educational psychologists supporting a primary school in special measures, to collate and feed back information from staff interviews (Bettle *et al.* 2001). Figure 8.8 on the other hand, contains an example of a rich picture developed by a project group of secondary school staff working with two educational psychologists to consider how the needs of the large number of demanding pupils in the school could be addressed while ensuring that the rights of the majority of 'undemanding' pupils were also respected.

This kind of picture can helpfully highlight particular features of the environment under consideration and these can be selected as problem themes. Such a picture is also usually capable of being viewed from a variety of different perspectives. At Stage 3, consideration of these different viewpoints and problem themes, can help identify systems likely to be relevant to the debate about the problem situation, with a view to bringing about improvement. For example, consider the following notional systems which proved relevant to the resolution of a particular parent–school conflict over the school's homework requirements. The viewpoint which suggested each of these systems as potentially relevant is noted in parenthesis:

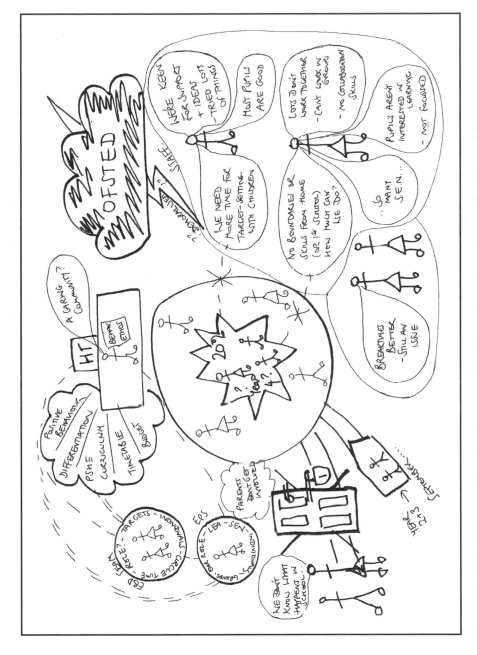

Figure 8.7 Rich picture used by educationa psychologists working with a primary school in special measures
Source: Bettle et al. (200˙).

Figure 8.8
Rich picture
developed by a
project group of
secondary school
staff

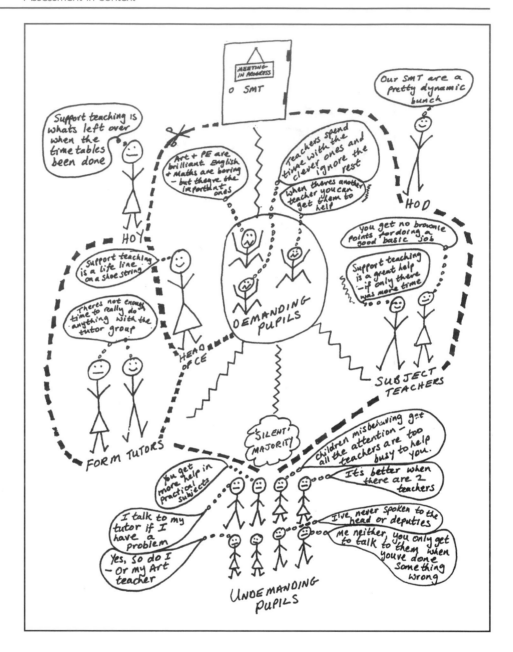

- A system to consolidate pupil learning (teachers).
- A system to enhance the school's academic reputation (headteacher).
- A system to cover exam coursework which isn't covered in class because the teachers can't keep order (pupil).
- A parent undermining system (objecting parent).

ACTIVITY 8.3   A rich picture

Choose a learning environment familiar to you where you feel there are problems or opportunities for improvement. Write a description of the situation that identifies key issues within it (maximum length: one side of A4). Now draw a rich picture to represent what you know about the situation and to capture key issues from your point of view.

Can you identify any differences between writing and drawing in:

- The clarity, accuracy and completeness of the representation produced?
- The amount of time taken to produce it?
- The sensitivity of the matters that can be represented?
- The number of different issues and their interrelationships that can be represented simultaneously?
- Sequences of events or changes over time?
- The sorts of issues that emerge?
- Your willingness to share your representation of the learning environment in question with a colleague?
- The ease with which colleagues can pick up key issues from the description/picture? (You might like to check out with a colleague your ideas about this.)
- Your willingness to share the representation with key staff in the learning environment in question?

In naming possible relevant systems there is no attempt to imply that any of these different perspectives is right or more accurate. In SSM a system is a hypothetical construct which is used to think about some real-world activity from a particular perspective (such as the four perspectives listed above). The purpose in naming relevant systems is to attempt to find some potentially useful or insightful ways of viewing the problem situation.

Having identified a number of relevant systems, some can be selected for further development. This selection is made on the basis of subjective judgement and experience. An element of trial and error is involved and the first attempt at analysis may fail to yield a useful outcome. It will usually be necessary to cycle through Stages 3, 4 and 5 a number of times in order to identify changes that are likely to bring about improvements in the problem situation. The rest of Stage 3 and Stage 4 involve the logical development of the relevant systems that have been selected. The relevant systems are first defined more clearly. This is done through producing a root definition of each, which describes its basic nature in a way designed to be revealing to those in the situation. The value of root definitions is not judged in terms of their correctness, but in terms of their usefulness in illuminating ways in which aspects of the problem situation can be helpfully changed.

In order to provide a clear definition of what the system under consideration is, the root definition should contain the following six elements:

C   Customers (victims or beneficiaries of the system)
A   Actors (who carry out the activities of the system)

T   Transformation process (what the system does to its inputs to to turn them into outputs)

W   *Weltanschauung* (the view of the world that makes this system meaningful)

O   Owner (who could abolish this system)

E   Environmental constraints (what in the environment this system takes as given)

Here is an illustration which is taken from Frederickson (1990b). One of the relevant systems selected on the basis of the rich picture shown in Figure 8.8 was: 'A system to provide effective access to the curriculum through support teaching in the school', The CATWOE analysis which was selected was as follows:

C   All pupils

A   Support teachers and subject teachers

T   Need for effective access to the curriculum – that need met through support teaching

W   'It's a good thing to maintain pupils with special needs in the mainstream, but important to ensure that the education of other pupils does not suffer'

O   Headteacher

E   School staffing levels, large proportion of pupils with special needs in a secondary modern school, attitudes of some staff, skills of some support teachers

The corresponding root definition (Root Definition 1) was: 'A headteacher-owned system, staffed by support teachers and subject teachers which provides for all pupils that support deemed necessary, to enable them to gain effective access to the curriculum despite the presence of a large proportion of pupils with special needs in the class and the constraints of current staffing levels, attitudes and skills'.

No root definition can claim to be objective. Rather, each is written from a particular viewpoint, which is largely reflected in the 'W' selected. However there are other components of the root definition on which opinions may differ. In this case there was much debate as to who should be considered to be the customer of the system – other candidates for the role being 'special needs pupils' and 'the subject teachers'.

The root definition describes what the system *is*. In order to describe what it *does* it is necessary to build an activity model of the system. This model will be conceptual in that you must strive to make it a purely logical representation of the activities which would necessarily have to happen in the system described by the root definition. No attempt should be made either to model what really happens or what might ideally happen. Your model is only a relevant intellectual construct to be used to help structure debate. In work at this stage, comments are often made about the advantages of involving an 'outsider' whose greater distance from the real-world situation helps to retain an appropriate focus on the logical and conceptual nature of the model building.

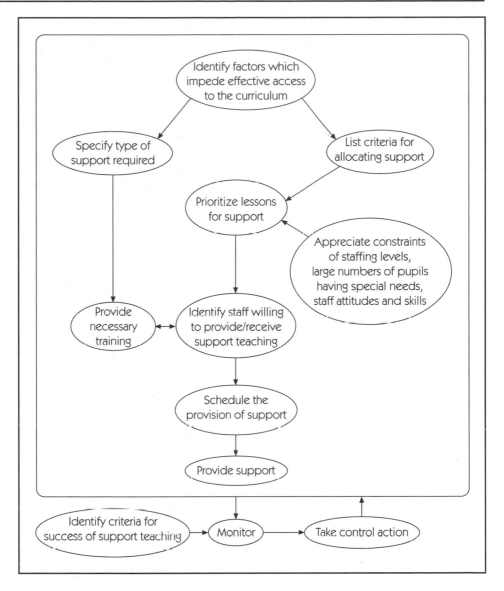

The crucial components of the model will be activities, represented on paper as verbs. The task is to assemble in a logical order the minimum number of activities required to operate the human activity system described by the root definition. The conceptual model shown in Figure 8.9 was developed from the root definition of the system to: 'provide effective access to the curriculum through support teaching in the school' which was described above.

In considering the issue of evaluation, Checkland argues that five different aspects need to be considered: efficacy, efficiency, effectiveness, ethicality and elegance (Checkland and Scholes 1990). In evaluating efficacy one needs to ask whether the system is in fact functioning, whether the transformation is being carried out, whether the means selected actually work. In evaluating efficiency one needs to ask whether the system is operating with minimum resources, including time. The evaluation of effectiveness involves asking whether the transformation at the heart of the system is the right activity to be doing in the first place. You should notice that questions about effectiveness can only be answered from outside the system in question, by reference to larger systems of which it is a part. Considerations of ethicality require us to consider whether the transformation is a moral thing to do, while the evaluation of elegance would focus on the extent to which the transformation is parsimonious and apt.

At Stage 5 the conceptual models which have been produced during Stage 4 are compared with the real world (the problem situations expressed in Stage 2). This comparison may reveal mismatches:

- Are some logically necessary stages simply left out of the process which operates in real life?
- Is operational effectiveness being reduced by the inclusion of unnecessary stages?
- Are activities happening in an illogical order?
- Are the activities being performed well?

In the above example the way in which support teaching was being provided differed radically from the conceptual model of the activity. The most obvious difference was the sequencing of stages. The conceptual model shown in Figure 8.9 indicated that prioritization of sessions for support should precede the deployment of staff, so ensuring that top priority sessions were effectively supported. In reality, however, support teaching had been described as 'what is left over when the timetable has been done'. Whatever their assessed need for support, sessions could only be allocated a support teacher if a teacher able and willing to provide support happened to be free at that time.

The identification of mismatches at Stage 5 is used at Stage 6 to structure a debate among those who inhabit the problem situation about possible changes which could improve the situation. The debate aims to identify changes which meet two criteria: they must be systemically desirable, as indicated by the outcome of the conceptual modelling activity; and they must be culturally feasible, given the characteristics of the situation and the people in it. As a result of the debate about support teaching a new approach to planning and prioritization was introduced so that support teaching for the top priority periods was formally timetabled for the first time, thus ensuring that it would in future be provided where it was most needed. The formal timetabling of support teaching had a positive effect on its perceived status. This was in addition to the practical advantage that support teachers were no longer called away at short notice to cover for absent colleagues. That had sometimes happened when they had essentially been using a 'free' period to provide support teaching.

The influence of *cultural feasibility* was seen in the decision for the SENCO to engage in a fairly time-consuming face-to-face process of liaison and consultation with department and year heads in identifying priority lessons for support. She could instead have drawn up a set of criteria and generated a list of prioritized sessions on this basis. Staff wished to avoid overtly listing criteria, as this would have involved formally recognizing, for example, that certain departments were more successful than others in supporting pupils with special needs, or that some staff had particularly poor classroom management skills. Such information was widely known informally, but it was felt to be culturally unacceptable to have it recorded formally.

Stage 7 involves the implementation of the changes which have been agreed. This may be straightforward or it may generate other difficulties which can in turn be tackled using the methodology in further cycles. Although the methodology has been described in stage by stage sequence, in the interests of clarity of exposition, Checkland (Checkland and Scholes 1990) emphasizes that much repetition of stages and flexible movement between them is expected and indeed desirable. For example, in selecting relevant systems at Stage 3 it may well be useful to test out various possibilities by quickly looking ahead to Stages 4, 5 and 6 and seeing what kind of models might follow from the root definitions considered and what kinds of changes are likely to be generated in the comparison stage. Also, at Stage 5, the attempt to make comparisons between the models that have been generated and the real world frequently highlights the need for more data gathering, where the information needed to make key comparisons is lacking.

Checkland points out that the methodology should not be regarded as a once and for all approach to something sharply defined as a problem, but as a general way of carrying out purposeful activity which gains from the power of some formal systems thinking and results in those involved 'learning' their way to the development of an improved situation. Hence the methodology deals with fuzzy real-world messes, whereas many alternative approaches require clearly defined problems/objectives. Such 'hard' approaches also typically produce ideal systems, modelled by experts, which are imposed on the situation and the people within it as solutions. Burden (1978), having applied the hard systems approach developed by Jenkins (1969) in a number of organizational-level projects in schools, questioned its appropriateness and suggested that a more flexible approach may be preferable. By contrast, SSM seeks to identify systemically desirable and culturally feasible changes to the existing situation, these changes having been selected by those who live in the situation.

Conclusions

The emphasis on assessing the learning environment has steadily grown in recent years. Research on school effectiveness and on features of the classroom environment that can facilitate learning has been influential. Legislation and guidance on the identification of SEN has increasingly incorporated a focus on the learning environment, alongside the traditional focus on the learner.

There are a number of well developed theoretical models of the influence of the classroom and/or school environment on student learning. However, practice with

ACTIVITY 8.4   A Classroom-level SSM case study

Figure 8.10 shows a rich picture that was drawn by the educational psychologist and SENCO shown in the top right hand corner of the picture. They were concerned about the learning environment being provided for Alex, a 9-year-old child with a Statement of SEN on account of his significant visual difficulties. Alex received additional provision of 10 hours per week from a visiting specialist teacher and had 20 hours per week from a learning support assistant. Alex only spent the first 40 minutes of each day in the class of which he was nominally a part. Once the visiting teacher for pupils with visual difficulties arrived at the

Figure 8.10
Rich picture of the learning environment being provided for Alex

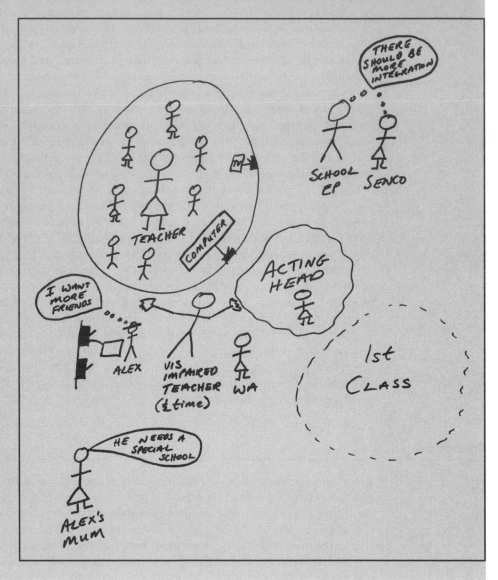

school, Alex was withdrawn to an alcove in the corridor outside the classroom where he worked with her in the morning and with the non-teaching assistant in the afternoon. This arrangement was said to be necessary so that Alex would have easy access to an electrical socket into which to plug his Brailler. The two sockets in the classroom were 'occupied' by the computer and the television! In addition, the noise of the Brailler was considered by the class teacher to be too distracting for the other children in the class.

Alex had joined the school at the start of the present school year, following a family move, and initially been placed in a parallel class. The teacher of this first class had been unhappy that Alex was notionally a part of her class but was withdrawn for so much of the school day. Four weeks into the first term, following a meeting between the visiting teacher and the acting head, Alex moved classes. Alex, who had been included almost full time in the classroom in his previous school feels very lonely and unhappy. His mother is upset by the change in him, as he used to be such a happy boy who loved going to school. Now he sometimes doesn't want to go. She has always feared that as he got older it would be harder for him to stay in mainstream school and wonders whether it would be better for him to go to a special school where he could at least make some friends.

(a) Make a note of any suggestions you have at this stage for ways in which the learning environment for Alex could be changed so that it meets his needs more fully.

(b) Look at the rich picture and consider in turn the perspective of each of those involved in order to produce a list of systems that might be relevant to improving the learning environment for Alex.

Among the relevant systems generated by the SENCO and the educational psychologist were:

- a system to help Alex find his way around familiar environments without assistance;
- a system to increase the time Alex spends in class.

The CATWOE analysis produced for the second of these was as follows:

C   Alex

A   SENCO, class teacher, educational psychologist, learning support assistant

T   Alex in class very little > Alex in class 50 per cent of school day

W   Alex's social and academic needs will be better met if he can spend time in the class

O   Acting headteacher

E   Noise of the Brailler? Availability of learning support assistant and other support time. Appropriateness of class lessons for Alex? Other needs specified on Alex's statement (e.g. learning to use the Brailler fluently)

Figure 8.11 shows the conceptual model produced for this system.

(c) Compare the conceptual model with the rich picture and make a note of any mismatches you can identify. Can you think of any systemically desirable changes whose cultural feasibility you would want to discuss with those involved? For example, have the use of other forms of recording in the classroom been considered? Could Alex use a pocket dictaphone some of the time?

(d) Finally compare the ideas you generated in (a) with those you generated in (c). What initial conclusions can you draw about the advantages and disadvantages of using SSM to structure thinking about the learning environments of pupils who have SEN?

Figure 8.11
A conceptual
model of a system
to increase the
time Alex spends
in class

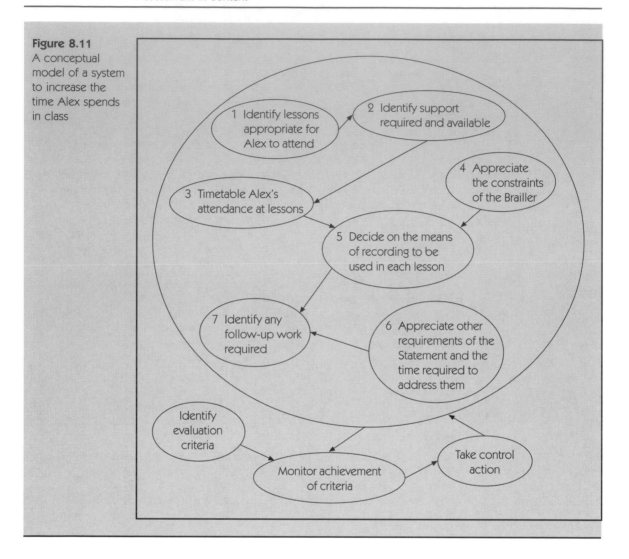

pupils who have SEN has lagged behind the theory and has tended to remain focused on the individual child. It was argued that many education service professionals need to develop their knowledge about assessment and intervention approaches that more adequately reflect the importance of the learning environment. Current lack of knowledge may represent one of the most significant problems to be overcome if the gap between theory and practice is to be closed.

A number of methods for assessing learning environments and designing interventions were described and their applicability to pupils who have SEN were illustrated. While multi-perspective measures and those involving direct observation typically involve a substantial time commitment, pupil perception measures may take little more than an hour to administer and score. The time taken to implement qualitative ethnographic approaches or SSM will vary with the scope of the investigation. However, all of these approaches offer a potentially high return on the time invested as environmental changes may have a broader preventative impact and benefit other pupils with similar difficulties. Evaluation of attempts to change the learning environment can readily be carried out and corresponding changes in the achievement of different groups of pupils examined. In this respect the approaches introduced in this chapter are likely to have relevance to many more aspects of schools' development plans than those relating specifically to pupils who have SEN.

Part 3

Areas of need

Chapter 9

Learning difficulties

When you have studied this chapter you should be able to:

1 Outline how thinking about intelligence, learning abilities and learning difficulties has developed over the last century.
2 Analyse the role of social factors in the development and definition of learning difficulties.
3 Explain the rationale for different approaches to the assessment of intelligence and learning abilities, and analyse their advantages and disadvantages.
4 Identify and evaluate a range of options in curricula and teaching methods for children with learning difficulties.

Contents

Introduction

The concept of *learning difficulties* is at the centre of the law on SEN. The relevant section of the Education Act 1996 opens: 'A child has "special educational needs" for the purposes of this Act if he has a learning difficulty which calls for special educational provision to be made for him'. The definition of a learning difficulty is that the child 'has a significantly greater difficulty in learning than the majority of children of his age' or 'has a disability which either prevents or hinders him from making use of educational facilities of a kind generally provided for children of his age in schools within the area of the local education authority' (Department for Education and Employment 1996, Section 312). Thus the definition is either normative (greater problems than the majority of age peers) or functional (needing special facilities). It is a broad and inclusive definition which embraces the whole range of SEN.

However, the theme of this chapter is *general learning difficulties* in the narrower sense employed in the *Thresholds* document issued with the draft revised *Code of Practice* (Department for Education and Employment 2000c). The scope of the term as we are using it here may be seen in Figure 9.1. *Specific learning difficulties* in which problems of learning are restricted to a particular area of development or the curriculum are discussed later (see Chapters 11 and 12). Here we are concerned with general problems that affect all aspects of children's learning at school or, in more severe forms, all aspects of their development. Work in this area has been strongly influenced by the way in which thinking about the nature of intelligence and learning abilities has developed over the years. The chapter opens with a discussion of these issues before turning to a detailed consideration of learning difficulties.

Learning abilities

Intelligence and abilities

The word *intelligence* has been used among professionals concerned with SEN as a convenient shorthand for describing a child's learning abilities. As a catch-all term it is intended to provide an overview of a person's mental abilities – conventionally summarized in the intelligence quotient or IQ obtained on a general intelligence scale. In relation to people with general learning difficulties, the IQ has been used traditionally as a simple indicator of an individual's overall level of intellectual functioning. As will be shown, it is now substantially discredited as a tool for that purpose, though its influence appears to linger on in many ways.

A general intelligence scale comprises a wide range of intellectually challenging tasks that are presented to the person being tested in a standard way. During the development of an intelligence scale for children a large, representative sample of children will have been given these tasks, and data will be available on the average scores of children at each age level and on the spread of scores around the

Figure 9.1
The nature and
range of general
learning difficulties
as presented in
official guidance

According to the *Code of Practice* (Department for Education and Employment 2000c: 13) general learning difficulties 'may show themselves' in the following ways:

- low levels of attainment across the board in all forms of assessment, including, for young children, baseline assessments;
- difficulty in acquiring skills (notably in literacy and numeracy) on which much other learning in school depends;
- difficulty in dealing with abstract ideas and generalizing from experience;
- a range of associated difficulties, notably in speech and language (particularly for younger children) and in social and emotional development.

Lower levels of difficulty may be indicated by:

- performance within the National Curriculum below the level within which most children are expected to work (i.e. Level 1 at the end of Key Stage 1; Level 2/3 at Key Stage 2; Level 3/4 at Key Stage 3);
- performance on measures of attainment and underlying cognitive skills which place the child in the lowest-attaining 10 or 15 per cent of the national population; this equates to a standardized test score in the low 80s;
- attainment in underlying skills (especially in speech and language, literacy and numeracy) which enables the child to function across the curriculum as a whole but which is beginning to interfere with their ability to progress as effectively as might otherwise be the case.

Higher levels of difficulty may be indicated by:

- performance within the National Curriculum outside the range within which most children are expected to work (i.e. Level W at the end of Key Stage 1; Level 1 at Key Stage 2; Level 2 at Key Stage 3);
- performance on measures of attainment and underlying cognitive skills which place the child in the lowest-attaining 1 or 2 per cent of the national population; this equates to a standardized test score of 70 or below;
- attainments in underlying skills (especially in speech and language, literacy and numeracy) which significantly interfere with their ability to learn effectively.

average. When individuals are given the scale subsequently, their performance can be compared to the norms for the original 'standardization' sample. Thus the IQ measure is norm-based. This is a quite different approach from that of CBA, which was described in Chapter 7. On the face of it, a norm-based measure seems suitable for use in identifying general learning difficulties, since they tend to be defined primarily in terms of a deviation from normal development. For example, the first items in each list in Figure 9.1 refer to a child's performance being lower than that of most children of the same age. But the use of a general, norm-based instrument to identify and differentiate among children with learning difficulties has been controversial for many years. Those who favoured this strategy tended to emphasize that, with the investment of very little time, it makes it possible to:

- provide a reasonably reliable estimate of general mental ability or potential which is stable over time;
- draw upon extensive normative information that cannot be accessed without the use of tests;
- screen for areas of weakness in thinking and information processing;
- provide a baseline index against which to measure future development or learning.

Critics of the strategy have argued that:

- the IQ is a less reliable measure than test constructors claim;
- it gives a misleading impression of scientific precision by presenting an individual's position on a distribution of summarized scores as a single summary number;
- Norm-based instruments are only valid for the population on which they have been standardized, yet they are often used for individuals who come from a different cultural or social background;
- knowing a person's measured intelligence does not give enough information on which to base a special education programme for them.

A fundamental problem with defining learning difficulties in terms of intelligence is that it is not clear what is meant by 'intelligence'. Different proponents of the strategy gave a different interpretation. Here are three early definitions of intelligence from Gross (1987, Table 27.1):

1 An individual is intelligent in proportion as he is able to carry on abstract thinking.
2 The aggregate of the global capacity to act purposefully, think rationally, to deal effectively with the environment.
3 Innate, general, cognitive ability.

It will be clear that each of the psychologists who wrote these definitions had something subtly different in mind when using the term. If the quotations are set in context, it is not difficult to see why they saw the concept in different ways. Lewis Terman, the author of (1) in 1921, was conducting a longitudinal study of talented and gifted people and emphasized the feature of their intellectual make-up that distinguished this group from others (Terman 1925). David Wechsler, the author of (2) in 1944, was employed in a veterans' hospital in the USA during World War II. He was responsible for advising on the rehabilitation and employment prospects of ordinary men who had been injured in the war. His concern, above all, was to help guide them towards independence in their everyday lives. Cyril Burt, the author of (3) in 1957, was involved in debates about the impact of heredity and the environment on children's development. He had advised the UK government committee that refined the use of intelligence tests for selection for secondary education (Hadow Committee 1924). Each of these pioneers in the scientific study of intelligence was influenced in his thinking about the concept by the purposes for which he was using the term and by the ideology prevalent in his society at the time.

Terman made his assumptions explicit as follows:

The essential difference, therefore, [between the moron and the intellectual genius] is in the capacity to form concepts to relate in diverse ways, and to grasp their significance . . . One may, of course, question our grounds for designating any kind of mental activity as 'higher' or 'lower' than another. Why, it may be asked, should certain types of mental processes be singled out for special worship? In fact, it is frequently intimated that the individual who flounders in abstractions but is able to handle tools skilfully, or play a good game of baseball, is not to be considered necessarily as *less* intelligent than the individual who can solve mathematical equations, acquire a huge vocabulary, or write poetry. The implication is that the two individuals differ merely in having different *kinds* of intelligence, neither of which is higher nor better than the other. It is difficult to argue with anyone whose sense of psychological values is disturbed to this extent.

(quoted by Heim 1970: 7)

As the twentieth century progressed, there was increasing support for the kind of 'disturbance' that Terman scorned. In theoretical work on intelligence, two developments in particular affected how theorists responded to diversity in the human condition.

The first development was the explicit recognition that there are cultural differences in what is judged to be 'intelligent'. For example, speed of response may be more highly valued in some cultures than in others. Also the context in which a task is presented will affect performance, depending on what is culturally familiar (Ceci 1996). The second development to challenge the values expressed by Terman has been the introduction of an explicit theory of *multiple intelligences* (Gardner 1993a). This approach places less emphasis on the fact that all measures of mental abilities correlate (suggesting that there is a general factor of intelligence). More emphasis is given to the fact that they do not correlate perfectly (suggesting that there are separate abilities that are best thought of as distinct from each other). For Gardner, intelligence is 'the ability to solve problems, or to create products, that are valued within one or more cultural settings' (Gardner 1993a: xiv). An ability could be described as an 'intelligence' if there was evidence that in some way it develops separately from other aspects of people's functioning. For example, there may be individuals who lose this ability after brain damage when other areas of functioning are unimpaired, or retain it when others are lost.

The exercise of the ability is likely to rely on an identifiable core mental operation or set of operations. Examples of what Gardner had in mind include:

- *Linguistic intelligence*: used in reading, writing, understanding what people say.
- *Logical-mathematical intelligence*: used in solving maths problems, checking a supermarket bill, logical reasoning.
- *Spatial intelligence*: used in reading a map, packing suitcases in a car so that they all fit.
- *Musical intelligence*: used in playing a musical instrument, appreciating the structure of a piece of music.

- *Bodily-kinesthetic intelligence*: used in imitating gestures, dancing, running.
- *Interpersonal intelligence*: used in relating to other people (e.g. in understanding another person's behaviour or feelings).
- *Intrapersonal intelligence*: used in understanding ourselves and how we can change ourselves.

This is not a definitive list. Gardner argued that 'there is not, and there never can be, a single irrefutable and universally accepted list of human intelligences' (Gardner 1993a: 59). He saw these distinct abilities as functioning somewhat independently of each other. But when we observe intelligent behaviour, it is usually the result of an interaction between intelligences.

Others have given more emphasis to this aspect of cognitive functioning. Sparrow and Davis (2000: 117) used the metaphor of a family to make this point:

Although these (cognitive) subsystems may differ in their degree of independence or coverage, it is suggested that each unit operates differently and through unique underlying principles. For example, as in a family, each individual member has unique characteristics. To fully understand the functioning of each individual, however, it is essential to learn about the family system. Similarly, to fully understand comprehensive cognitive functioning, one must comprehend the performance of the individual components as well as their integrated or gestalt functioning. Individuals may outperform the sum of their component processing abilities as they develop the capacity to compensate for relative weaknesses by relying on their areas of cognitive strength.

Gardner (1993b) suggested that his ideas could be the basis for an approach to the school curriculum that would take account of individual differences, allowing pupils to enter through what he called different 'doors or entry points'. He argued that it is necessary for teachers to combine different forms of experience and stimulation in order to meet the needs of pupils with a wide range of intelligences. It will be evident that a theory that emphasizes the possibility of developing distinct intelligences or areas of ability, if it is supported by research evidence over time, must become a threat to an approach to defining learning difficulties that relies on locating individuals along a single dimension of general intelligence.

Learning strategies and learning styles

Much of the passion in debates on individual intelligence has centred on claims that it is genetically determined and therefore fixed and unmodifiable. A proponent of this pessimistic view was Jensen (1969) who suggested that there are two main forms of intelligence: Level 1, involving simple mental acts of an associative and reproductive nature (e.g. learning the order of a series of familiar objects or pictures); and Level 2, involving complex transformational and abstract mental processes (e.g. learning new concepts, solving problems where the answer is not immediately clear). He argued that we will best educate those with Level 1 type intelligence if we teach to their particular pattern of abilities and, effectively, set them distinct and limited educational goals. A particular problem with his stance was that he appeared to accept that group differences in test performance meant that some groups, such as African-Americans, would be more likely to need to be treated in this way.

Opponents of that position argued that ability is modifiable and that any individual can develop a wide range of learning strategies if given appropriate support. They thought that 'it is more appropriate to regard genetic factors as producing variations in the level of responsiveness of the individual to learning situations that may require corresponding variations in the quality and quantity of investment necessary for growth' (Feuerstein 1979: 8). These authors do not accept any fixed limit on what learning can take place. They argue that it is necessary to examine the situation from the opposite perspective and ask how learning can best be facilitated. That may present a greater or smaller challenge to the teacher, depending on what the learner brings to the task. Even so, the conditions for learning, including the support available, will make a crucial difference as was pointed out in the SEN *Thresholds* consultation document: 'The wide range of strategies that skilled teachers can bring to bear is usually enough to meet whatever learning needs pupils may have. This is often true even where pupils have more persistent or serious difficulties. The more flexible and responsive the strategies are, the more likely it is that such difficulties will not hinder adequate progress' (Department for Education and Employment 2000c: 5).

In what he called a 'tri-archic' theory of intelligence, Sternberg (1985) attempted to describe how the human mind deals with the external world, ongoing experience and its own internal mental world. He stressed that people need both the ability to deal with the demands of novel kinds of task and situation and also the ability to automatize the processing of information. Thus children cannot read fluently unless they can both analyse new words when they come across them and process letter shapes mentally without conscious attention (see Chapter 11). In contrast to most of the theorists mentioned above, Sternberg was explicitly interested in the component, mental processes through which intelligence operates. He described three kinds of ability: analytic, creative and practical (see Table 9.1).

Table 9.1 Three types of ability comprising intelligence

Type of ability	Aim	Typical activities
Analytic	To solve familiar problems by using strategies that manipulate the elements of the problem or the relationships among the elements	Comparing; analysing; evaluating
Creative	To solve new kinds of problem that require us to think about the problem and its elements in a new way	Creating; inventing; designing
Practical	To try to solve problems that apply what we know to everyday contexts	Applying; using; implementing

Source: Sternberg (1985).

Our ability to undertake a task and complete it requires not only intelligence and abilities but also motivation, attention and an effective strategy. It has been shown that children who do not generally succeed with academic tasks can be taught more effective learning strategies (e.g. in relation to how they try to remember things – Male 1996). In some cases individual differences in *learning style* may be as important as differences in ability. A person's learning style is their characteristic ways of assimilating and processing information (Cameron and Reynolds 1999). A recent example of a model of learning style is the cognitive control model of Riding and Rayner (1998). They hypothesize that two key dimensions influence how a person approaches the task of dealing with information that is presented to them:

- the *wholist-analytic* dimension – whether they tend to *organize* information in wholes or parts;
- the *verbal-imager* dimension – whether they are inclined to *represent* information during thinking, verbally or in mental pictures.

Riding and Rayner also presented a model of how these dimensions might be related to other aspects of an individual's experience and functioning (see Figure 9.2). You will notice that they assume a person's memory of their past experiences plays a significant role in the development of their characteristic learning style. As might be expected, there is a good deal of evidence of cultural differences in learning styles (Hickson *et al.* 1994; Anderson 1995). It is not clear what implications this may have for teaching. Earlier research in this field has

Figure 9.2
Cognitive control model
Source: Riding and Rayner (1998).

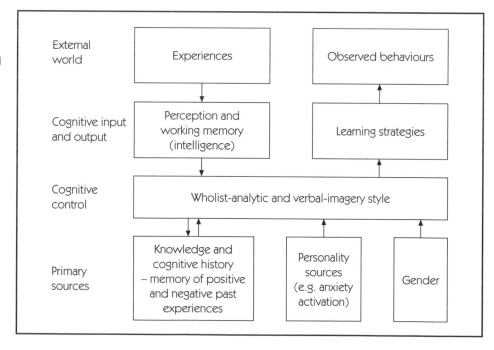

yielded inconsistent results when attempts have been made to evaluate the impact of matching teaching methods to pupils' assessed learning styles (McKenna 1990). Initial results with a questionnaire based on the cognitive control model have been more promising (Riding and Rayner 1998).

Learning difficulties

Historical background

When the Elementary Education Act 1870 established compulsory elementary education on a national basis, no children could be overlooked just because they found school work difficult. Within 20 years the Education (Defective and Epileptic Children) Act sanctioned the provision of classes and schools specifically for what were then called 'mentally defective' children. These were enabling powers, which could be ignored by local authorities and, in many cases, were. However, by 1913, without statutory compulsion, 175 education authorities had made some provision for 'defective' children, of whom there were 12,000 in 177 schools. But it was decided that a statutory duty should be placed on education authorities to ensure more even provision across the country. In a further revision of the law, education authorities were given the duty to ascertain which children in their area aged 7–16 were mentally defective. They also had to decide which of these were incapable of education in special schools. Responsibility for them was passed to medical authorities, while the education authorities had to provide schooling for the others. As Table 9.2 illustrates, the 1913 law introduced careful distinctions between three terms that had been used interchangeably up to the last decades of the nineteenth century – 'idiot' and 'imbecile', regarded as ineducable, and 'feebleminded', for whom schooling was to be provided (Pritchard 1963).

Children with moderate learning difficulties

At the end of World War II the 1944 Education Act placed special education on a firmer footing. LEAs were required to ensure that 'provision is made for pupils who suffer from any disability of mind or body by providing, either in special schools or otherwise, special educational treatment, that is to say, education by

Table 9.2 Official terminology for describing children with learning difficulties

Year	Notional IQ range		
	0–25	*26–50*	*51–70*
1913	Idiot	Imbecile	Feeble-minded or high-grade defective
1944	Educationally subnormal (severe)		Educationally subnormal (mild)
1981	Severe learning difficulties		Moderate learning difficulties

special methods appropriate for persons suffering from that disability' (Ministry of Education 1946). The regulations issued in connection with the Act included in the list of disabled pupils a category of the educationally subnormal 'who, by reason of limited ability or other conditions resulting in educational retardation, require some specialised form of education, wholly or partly in substitution for the education normally given in ordinary schools' (Ministry of Education 1945). The terms 'mentally defective' and 'feebleminded' were displaced. This 'educationally subnormal' (ESN) group was divided into a 'severe' category and a 'mild' category, abbreviated as ESN(S) and ESN(M).

Provision mushroomed in the period after World War II so that by 1963 special schools were catering for more than 37,000 ESN pupils – more than three times the number that had been identified 50 years earlier (Department of Education and Science 1964). However, this substantial expansion did not have the confidence of all commentators. When the Warnock Committee reviewed the position a decade later, they recommended, among other things, that the terminology should be revised again. They argued that the phrase 'educationally subnormal' was 'imprecise'. It assumed 'agreement on what is educationally normal with regard to ability and attainment', and 'suggests an intrinsic deficiency whereas often the deficiency has been in his [the child's] social and cultural environment'. They advocated the use of the term 'moderate learning difficulties' (MLD) because 'it gives more indication of the nature of the child's difficulties' and 'is less likely to stigmatise the child' (Department of Education and Science 1978, para. 3.26). A study by Hastings *et al.* (1993) showed that a sample of college students did indeed evaluate the term 'learning difficulties' less negatively than terms such as 'mental subnormality' and 'mental handicap'. Norwich (1999) obtained similar results when comparing it to terms such as 'deficit', 'impairment' and disability' with three professional groups in education.

Following the passing of the 1981 Education Act the term 'moderate learning difficulties' was adopted in official publications. The terms used in this field had thus changed three times in 70 years. In what ways, if any, had the concepts underlying the terms altered? Cline (1991) studied the SEN Statements of 26 children admitted to one inner-city MLD school over an eight month period. The analysis showed that, for professionals working in that area, measured IQ remained the crucial defining feature of children placed in an MLD school: 'the working model employed for moderate learning difficulties in the Statements is a version of the original model of educational subnormality that has been only partially reconstructed' (Cline 1991: 99). In spite of such doubts, the number of children assessed as having MLD has remained high. Children with MLD represent the largest single group with SEN. Some 45 per cent of pupils in special schools and units in England and Wales in 1982 were classified in the MLD category (Kysel 1985). In the 12 LEA areas studied by the Audit Commission (1992) the figure was 52 per cent of the special school population (Audit Commission 1992: Table 10).

A number of LEAs have closed or amalgamated special schools for children with MLD as part of their move towards a more inclusive SEN strategy. But the

Table 9.3 Numbers on roll of special schools for children with moderate learning difficulties

Numbers on roll	Fewer than 50	51–100	101–150	151–200	201–250
	2% (1)	35% (19)	50% (27)	11% (6)	2% (1)

% reporting changes in pupil numbers	Remaining the same	Increasing	Decreasing	Other
	39% (21)	46% (25)	9% (5)	5.5% (3)

Source: Male (1996).

schools that survive are not shrinking. In fact, a survey by Male (1996) of 54 special schools for this group indicated that their pupil numbers were tending to increase rather than decrease (see Table 9.3). However, the population of the schools is changing. Over 90 per cent of the headteachers in Male's sample felt that some of their pupils had SLD rather than MLD. She calculated that about 1 in 10 of the pupils in the schools were considered by headteachers to have SLD. One factor in the shift is parental choice (with parents of children with SLD preferring these schools to schools in which children with profound and multiple learning difficulties were placed). Such a choice was not available at all until a little over 30 years ago.

Children with severe learning difficulties

Until 1970 children with SLD were excluded from the education system altogether and were the responsibility of health departments. A very influential early physician in this field, A.F. Tredgold, had written that 'the essence of mental defect is that it is incurable, and by no "special" education, however elaborate, can a case of amentia [literally, mindlessness] be raised to the normal standard' (quoted by Potts 1983: 186). In the post-war period many children attended junior training centres run by local authorities. By 1967 there were over 18,000 children under 16 on the rolls of these centres (NAMH 1969). But there was increasing resistance to the exclusion of these children from the education system. Only 17 per cent of the staff in training centres had taken a short training course designed for the purpose, and just 2 per cent were qualified teachers. Over two thirds had no relevant professional qualifications at all (Kirman 1972: 128). There was an outcry against this form of provision as well as against the large hospital institutions in which many of the children lived.

In 1970 through the Education (Handicapped Children) Act responsibility for the education of *all* children passed to LEAs. This led to what Mittler (1986) called a 'radical transformation' in the education of pupils with SLD over the next 15 years. Teachers at that time wrote in terms that would have been unthinkable to Tredgold:

Of central importance is our emphasis on enabling a child to be capable of setting his own goals and having the necessary flexible adaptive behaviours to achieve them. We are concerned with the child's ability to create order from the chaos of the real world. A world which, unlike the classroom, is inconsistent and which brings a wide variety and differing intensity of stimuli and consequent demands on the child . . . The child must not be encouraged to view himself as completely dependent on other people, but to make choices and decisions and, hence, control his own environment. Because we cannot, and would not, wish to account for every situation that the child will encounter, achievement of the skill of generalisation is crucial. This is reflected in the need to avoid placing undue emphasis on the learning of specific skills, or indeed, even in sequences of behaviour, and instead to concentrate on providing learning strategies and opportunities for their use.

(Coupe and Porter 1986: 6–7)

This text and others like it expressed radically different ways of thinking about the educational potential of children with SLD. The terms of discussion had been transformed. However, the ideas of writers such as Burt and Tredgold and the preoccupation with a static, generalized notion of intelligence have continued to influence the way in which many contemporaries think about the education of children with learning difficulties. The tension between these two tendencies will be one of the themes of this chapter.

Issues of definition

The Warnock Committee's category label of moderate learning difficulties has been problematic. Traditionally, MLD was defined in terms of measured intelligence – those whose IQ falls within the range 50–69 (see Table 9.2). This approach was discredited at an early stage when studies of special schools for pupils with MLD during their period of rapid expansion in the 1960s showed that the IQ range of their pupil population was significantly wider than the official range. A substantial proportion of pupils had IQs of 70+ – for example, 25 per cent in a special school in the Isle of Wight studied by Rutter *et al.* (1970) and 38 per cent in schools in South Wales studied by Chazan (1964). When Yule (1975) analysed the Isle of Wight data more closely, less than half of those with IQs in the relevant range were actually to be found in the designated special schools (Yule 1975). What differentiated the children with low IQs who were in ordinary schools from those in special schools was that the latter had low reading ages. Similarly the children with relatively high IQs in special schools showed depressed reading skills. It appears that sustained low educational attainment may have been the key factor – a position with parallels in current practice. The revised *Code of Practice* (Department for Education and Skills 2001) has removed any categorical division between different levels of learning difficulties. The definitions in Figure 9.1 have the advantage of drawing on teachers' knowledge of expected levels of performance within the National Curriculum as a key reference point. Guidance is now available regarding a more detailed analysis of progress towards Level 1 (QCA 2001).

In the USA more attention was paid to children's *adaptive behaviour* – 'the performance of the daily activities required for personal and social sufficiency' (Sparrow *et al.* 1984). The authoritative definition of mental retardation put out by the American Association on Mental Deficiency (AAMD) referred to 'significantly subaverage general intellectual functioning existing concurrently with deficits in adaptive behavior'. But in the UK a notion of *curriculum need* was given more prominence. In line with official publications in the early 1980s, Fish (1985: 70) described the curriculum required by this group of pupils as:

> a curriculum similar in range to that taught in ordinary schools but modified in terms of objectives and pace. Such a curriculum . . . should be realistic in terms of what can be accomplished in the time available but have relatively high expectations. It should be much less dependent on literacy skills for access to the normal range of study areas than the ordinary curriculum.

In this argument the assumption is made that similar modifications to the ordinary curriculum are required by most or all members of a large group that is defined in terms of their moderate learning difficulties. Their curriculum needs could be differentiated from those of children with severe or profound learning difficulties, who would require a 'developmental' curriculum in which the range of content and the aims would be radically different from those of the ordinary school curriculum.

This approach to defining the children's needs in terms of a significantly different curriculum was, in fact, no more compatible with a trend towards inclusion than much of the earlier and more overtly segregationist terminology. If the aim is to provide full access to a broad and balanced curriculum (including the National Curriculum) for all pupils, any modifications should be the minimum that is required. The shift in fundamental educational aims can be illustrated most vividly in relation to children with SLD (see Figure 9.3).

Much of the language that has been used in defining learning difficulties throughout the period reviewed above has been based on a premise that the difficulty is *within the child*. Booth and Ainscow (1998: 239–40), among others, have argued that a *social* view of difficulties in learning would be preferable:

> On such a view learning difficulties are not something students have, but arise in a relationship between students and tasks and the resources available to support learning . . . the insights we gain in understanding the learning of some students, for example those traditionally designated as the ones with learning difficulties, can be applied to the learning of other students not so designated . . . We suggest that an emphasis on the social nature of difficulties in learning and disabilities can be signalled by the concept of 'students who experience barriers to learning'.

Hart (1996: 94) also rejected the terminology of 'learning difficulties'. Her concern was to empower teachers to make the adaptations that are needed to their own practices and their classrooms:

Figure 9.3
Stages in the
evolution of
thinking about the
aims of the
curriculum for
children with SLD
Source: Male
(1996).

Special training was the main remedy put forward when attention was first drawn to the requirements of the defective. In those days the problem seemed comparatively simple. We had only to count up the number of defectives and provide the requisite number of special schools; and the majority would eventually emerge, fitted and equipped for the duties of after-life. Further experience has revealed the error of these ingenuous hopes. We now realise that no amount of training will 'cure deficiency'. The special school may improve behaviour, implant decent habits, and teach the elements of useful knowledge; but it cannot convert a feeble-minded child into a normal adult.

(Burt 1937: 103)

The general aims of education and training for ESN(S) children with IQs roughly above 30 usually include enabling the children:

(a) to acquire certain self-care skills (e.g. dressing, eating, toileting);
(b) to protect themselves from common dangers in home and neighbourhood;
(c) to communicate orally in a limited way;
(d) to become socially adjusted at home and in the neighbourhood, learning to respect property and cooperate in the family unit; and
(e) to become economically useful at home or in the community, in many cases in a sheltered environment under supervision (Kirk 1957, quoted by Chazan 1974).

More specific curricular aims include the mastery of motor skills such as walking, running, climbing and dancing; developing visual and auditory discrimination; the learning of simple number concepts; learning to participate in group activity, for example of a musical kind; and the acquiring of certain occupational skills, such as running errands, using the telephone, setting the table, dusting and sweeping.

(Chazan 1974: 179)

The purpose of education for all children is the same; the goals are the same. But the help that individual children need in progressing towards them will be different.

(Department of Education and Science 1978)

The Qualifications and Curriculum Authority . . . has adopted five key principles which will underpin its work and promote the highest standards of achievement by all learners . . . By applying these principles, QCA aims to ensure that appropriate learning opportunities are developed for all, and unnecessary barriers to achievement are not created.

General principles
In all aspects of its work, including advice to the Government, QCA will seek to ensure:

• the appropriate inclusion of all potential learners at relevant levels of activity;
• opportunities for continuity and progression for all learners;
• the achievement of the highest possible standards for all learners;
• the recognition of the attainments for all learners;
• the provision of easily accessible advice and guidance relevant to all learners.

With the review of the National Curriculum . . . the intention is to enable teachers to provide appropriately challenging work for pupils with special educational needs within a new curriculum framework. The guiding principle will remain that the curriculum should represent real entitlement for all pupils.

(Wade 1999: 80)

prevailing ways of thinking about and making sense of children's learning – or failure to learn – undermine teachers' sense of their own power to make a difference to the outcomes of education. Determinist ideas about ability and educability continually present us with the possibility that limitations of existing attainment might be a reflection of ceilings of innate or acquired ability determined by factors largely beyond teachers' control. The language of learning difficulties and special needs creates the impression that there exists a distinct group of children whose capabilities and needs are different from those of the majority. They raise doubts in teachers' minds about the relevance of their own expertise and resources . . . That is why I believe that we need to set aside once and for all the language of learning difficulties and special needs if we are to become able to exploit more fully the scope available to us for enhancing children's learning.

Social ecology

There were, in addition, other disadvantages to some of the early approaches to defining learning difficulties. As noted in earlier chapters, the social profile of the special schools in this field gives cause for significant concern. Compared to ordinary schools and to special schools for children with SLD, special schools for those with MLD tend to have higher proportions of:

- boys;
- pupils aged 11+;
- pupils whose parents are in unskilled occupations;
- pupils whose parents are unemployed;
- pupils from families with 4+ children.

These characteristics of the population have been stable over an extended period (Stein and Susser 1960; Chazan 1964; Kysel 1985; Richardson *et al.* 1986; Male 1996). It is notable that the preponderance of lower socioeconomic groups is not found in those forms of special provision that carry less of a social stigma, such as classes for children with specific learning difficulties (Riddell *et al.* 1994).

Tomlinson (1988: 47) analysed this situation through the perspective of critical theory:

Critical theorists of education systems are concerned to map injustices and inequalities. They see a sharp contrast between liberal humanitarian rhetoric that education is a force for 'good', for progress, and for equality, and the reality that education systems often mirror, or contribute to, an unequal, competitive, uncaring society. They have noted the way in which education often helps to reproduce the children of minorities, the working-class, and handicapped children, into inferior, powerless social positions. They do not see terms such as 'ability', 'achievement', or 'failure' as objective or disinterested terms, but as social categories, socially constructed by groups who

Table 9.4 Why Johnny can't read

Level 1 Personal/interpersonal	Because he's thick He can't concentrate He doesn't like his teacher
Level 2 Environmental/institutional	He's got a disadvantaged background He lives in an inner-city area The school hasn't got the right staff/resources/ methods to teach reading
Level 3 Structural/societal	He's black and working class Schools help to reproduce cultural, social and economic inequalities

Source: Tomlinson (1988).

have the power to label others as failures, and they examine processes of labelling and categorisation, as events which usually serve the vested interests of particular groups.

In an earlier report Tomlinson had highlighted the lack of agreement among professional groups in education when asked to give an account of educational subnormality (1981: 10–11). Their disparate explanations were analysed using the framework that is shown in Table 9.4 (Tomlinson 1988). Tomlinson pointed out that teachers and psychologists have tended to use Level 1 and Level 2 explanations and that critical theorists have tried to move the focus to Level 3 'in which educational problems can be located in wider structural, historical and ideological contexts' (Tomlinson 1988: 49).

Even that sociological analysis cannot do justice to the global complexity of an outstanding major issue in the social ecology of learning difficulties – the impact of ethnicity. Coard (1971), who first drew attention to the issue in the UK, reported that Inner London's day special schools for ESN pupils had nearly 34 per cent immigrant children on roll at that time, while the ordinary schools in the area had only 17 per cent. When the Fish Committee reported on provision for SEN in the same area 14 years later, schools for children with SLD had been added to the picture (Inner London Education Authority 1985). The over-representation of African-Caribbean children had been substantially reduced (see Table 9.5). After a further decade, when Male (1996) surveyed 54 head-teachers of MLD schools, only one respondent considered that black pupils were overrepresented in their school. However, a quarter of the respondents expressed the view that Asian pupils were now overrepresented in their school compared to their numbers in ordinary schools in the area. This is a dramatic shift and will need to be monitored closely. It remains a highly sensitive issue. Male observed that 'this question, alone among all other questions in the survey, was the one that some headteachers (11%) chose not to answer. Of these, a number deleted the question and some inserted comments such as "not relevant" or "not

Table 9.5 Ethnic composition of schools for children with MLD and SLD
in Inner London

Ethnic background	Primary schools (%)	Schools for children with MLD (%)	Schools for children SLD (%)
African-Caribbean	16	17	20
Asian	11	6	9
White*	56	65	56
Other	17	12	15

Note: *The phrase used in the survey was 'English, Scottish, Welsh and Irish'.
Source: Kysel (1985).

known" . . . Clearly past evidence has indicated that such data *are* relevant and
should be known' (Male 1996: 40).

Analyses of the composition of 'remedial streams' and 'Statemented provision'
in secondary schools over the years have confirmed that similar patterns of ethnic
overrepresentation occur. Daniels *et al.* (1999a) investigated SEN provision in
35 primary and secondary schools in two LEA areas. In line with earlier work,
they found that black children (a group that included African-Caribbean and
'Black Other') appeared more likely to be allocated to the category 'general learning difficulty' than 'reading difficulty' when compared with their white peers. They
were particularly interested in gender and observed that gender differences varied
as a function of ethnicity. For example, the male/female ratio was close to 1.0 in
the African-Caribbean group and above 2.0 in the white English and Irish groups.
In addition, there was considerable variation between schools. Like Male (1996),
Daniels *et al.* argued for more detailed monitoring of the way in which resources
are allocated.

There has been some evidence that children from ethnic minority communities
are less likely to be overrepresented in provision for severe learning difficulties.
But Table 9.5 shows slight overrepresentation of African-Caribbean pupils in
Inner London special schools for this group in the mid-1980s. Curnyn *et al.* (1991)
found evidence of overrepresentation of Asian and Chinese pupils in this provision
in Glasgow later in the decade. It is necessary to look behind the overall figures
to appreciate the complex dynamics that can have an impact on the social ecology
of this type of special need.

The aetiology of SLD and profound and multiple learning difficulties (PMLD)
is complex (see Table 9.6). Problems may have a genetic basis and arise before
birth; they may develop perinatally as a result of problems during birth; and they
may emerge later as a result of serious illness or brain damage. In many cases the
problem is described as 'idiopathic' because no specific cause is identified. Within
any given population the relative importance of each type of cause in SLD/PMLD
is affected by social conditions as well as by environmental factors that have an
influence on general health. There is often, of course, a link between such factors
and ethnic background. In the recent past this has been seen in a particularly

ACTIVITY 9.1   Explaining the difficulties experienced by Ravinder and Paul

First, read the reports on Ravinder and Paul below and analyse what you learn about each of them and their situations in two ways:

(a) Draw a diagram using the IF framework (see Chapter 4, in particular Figure 4.4).
(b) On a separate sheet make three lists under the headings used to explain 'why Johnny can't read' (see Table 9.4). How would Ravinder's/Paul's situation be explained using Level 1, Level 2 and Level 3 explanations as described by Tomlinson (1988)?

Then review the two accounts you have produced. What does each tell you that the others do not? Do you agree with the view that both approaches contribute to producing a *full* account of an individual's SEN?

Extracts from a head of year's report from a girl's secondary school located on a run-down estate on the edge of a large industrial town

Ravinder (Year 8), whose first language is Punjabi, is the fourth child (second girl) in a large family. Her school attendance was irregular in primary school, we were told. It improved when she first started at this school but has not been good this year. Often she takes her younger siblings to school and is then late here. Her father speaks little English and her mother none. We usually communicate with the parents through her elder sister. We do not have many Pakistani families in this area, and there is no one on the staff who speaks their language.

Ravinder is functioning academically well below the level expected of her year, especially in maths. We have seen very little progress since she transferred here. She is receiving classroom support in subject lessons for nine hours a week along with other girls who have SEN in the class. She seems quiet and shy with everyone, except one other girl who I think is a member of her extended family. We have been told that she is uncooperative with her parents at home. Her father is a very strict Muslim who expects his children to keep themselves separate from pupils from western cultures. A medical report has indicated that her hearing is satisfactory, as is the vision in her right eye. The vision in her left eye is assessed as weak.

Extracts from the multidisciplinary advice attached to a Statement for a boy attending the reception class of his local primary school with additional support

Paul is a 5-year-old white boy both of whose parents are described as of limited intelligence. He is the third of four children in the family. Two others are attending special schools. They are both on the non-accidental injury register and are fostered out. Paul is not on the non-accidental injury register.

At a medical examination when he was 2 years old he presented as 'profoundly physically and mentally retarded'. He was admitted to an opportunity group for children with severe learning difficulties within a local day nursery where he made unexpectedly rapid progress. His general health was good, and he showed no sensory impairment. His physical development was slow but normal – though he was 'uncoordinated and unsteady on occasions'. There are inconsistent reports as to whether he was toilet trained by the age of 4. In the classroom he was 'very persistent and lively'. At times he would become uncooperative and have temper tantrums if prevented from continuing to do something he was enjoying. The teacher reported: 'He has made steady consistent progress in all areas of development. He is well motivated and seems to find activities interesting for their own sake and not to please others. He enjoys mastering a new skill and being given the opportunity to practise this new skill over and over again. His level of play has matured, and he is beginning to enjoy playing in the home corner cooperatively with other children, though finding it difficult to share toys'.

At the age of 4 and a half he was reassessed by an educational psychologist who used selected tasks from a developmental scale and stated that he was 'functioning generally at around the level of a typical 2 and a half to 3-year-old'. It was recommended that he be given a trial in the Reception class of the local infants school, where he receives ten hours' individual support each week from a special needs support assistant. The school has set out these educational goals:

- the continued development of language skills and attention control;
- helping Paul to improve his social skills in collaborative activities with other children;
- establishing closer home–school links and supporting his parents to ensure that Paul builds up age-appropriate self-help skills.

Table 9.6 Causes of mental handicap in Cape Town by ethnic group

	White (N = 122)		Coloured (N = 745)		Black (N = 267)	
	No.	%	No.	%	No.	%
Prenatal	57	46.7	289	38.8	60	22.5
Perinatal	26	21.3	97	13.2	54	20.2
Postnatal	12	9.8	101	13.6	58	21.7
Idiopathic	21	17.2	177	23.8	49	18.4
Unknown	4	3.3	76	10.2	45	16.9
Mixed	2	1.6	5	0.7	1	0.4

Source: Molteno *et al.* (1990).

stark form in South Africa. Table 9.6 presents data on the causes of mental handicap as reported by Molteno *et al.* (1990) for children born in the area of Cape Town between 1974 and 1986.

Molteno *et al.* (1990) observed that the number of children with mental handicap in the various ethnic groupings was in line with what would have been expected from the birth rates of these groups. However, the distribution of causes of mental handicap was quite different. As can be seen from the table, prenatal causes were identified far more often for the white children than for the black children. On the other hand, the handicap in black children was more often associated with a postnatally acquired disease, or else the cause was unknown. The profile of causes for the coloured children was somewhere in the middle between those for the white and black groups. Institutionalized racial discrimination may have an impact on the incidence of learning difficulties not just through assessment bias but also through the impact of broader socioeconomic factors.

However, this impact may be modest in societies where racial differences map onto social advantage in a less extreme way than in the South African regime of that period. When a research team working with the Fish Committee examined the interaction of social and ethnic background in the analysis of Inner London statistics that was outlined above, they found that differences in parental occupation, poverty (as indicated by take-up of free school meals), family size and single parent families did not explain the distribution of ethnic groups in schools for children with learning difficulties (Inner London Education Authority 1985).

Learning difficulties: assessment for intervention

Traditional approaches to the assessment of intelligence

We reviewed above and in Chapters 5 and 6 a number of damaging criticisms of such techniques, especially when applied in work with a multicultural population. Yet long after these criticisms were made, such tests have continued to be used regularly for SEN assessment both in the UK and the USA (Desforges 1995; Haney and Evans 1999). Those who see a continuing role for these methods have emphasised that:

1 While early intelligence scales such as the Stanford Binet and Wechsler series were developed pragmatically and not based on detailed theories of what intelligence and cognition comprise, a number of authors in recent years have produced tests that are carefully based on sound theoretical models. A short list of some major scales for which this claim is made can be seen in Table 9.7.

Table 9.7   Some recently published tests of intelligence and cognition that are claimed to have a strong theoretical base

Test	Theoretical base
Cognitive Awareness System (CAS) (Naglieri and Das 1997; Naglieri 1999)	The PASS theory of intelligence in which human cognitive functioning is seen to be based on four key processes: planning, attention, simultaneous processing and sequential processing.
Kaufman Adult and Adolescent Intelligence Test (KAIT) (Kaufman and Kaufman 1993)	The Horn-Cattell theory of intelligence which distinguishes between crystallized abilities (concepts and skills that are acquired through schooling and acculturation) and fluid abilities (involving tackling new and unfamiliar problems).
Universal Non-verbal Intelligence Test (UNIT) (McCallum and Bracken 1997)	A model in which reasoning and memory are seen as central features of intelligence that can be measured without the use of language, by either the examiner or the examinee.

2 Children's performance on a broad-based scale can be analysed to identify a profile of strengths and weaknesses rather than a single overall measure such as the IQ.

3 In clinical practice it is possible to draw upon recent advances in neuropsychological research in order to move beyond the simplistic models of cognition implicit in many traditional intelligence scales that just distinguish between verbal and non-verbal abilities. Sparrow and Davis (2000: 118), for example, advocate the 'independent evaluation of (1) attention; (2) auditory, visual, and tactile perceptual functions; (3) verbal and language functions; (4) spatial/constructional processing abilities; (5) memory and learning; and (6) executive functions (conceptual reasoning, problem solving, planning, flexibility in cognitive strategies and implementing cognitive plans)'. They argue that different rates of development across functional domains may 'lead to a wide range of configurations in the cognitive system. Such outcomes may have adaptive or maladaptive significance for a person's functional adjustment'.

4 The experience gained by regularly observing children carrying out standard tasks gives a psychologist a sound basis for noting and interpreting an individual's test-taking behaviour and problem-solving strategies during those tasks.

5 In schools the analysis of children's profiles of scores on verbal and non-verbal tests can help to counter the low expectations that are sometimes held of pupils in the early stages of learning English (Ofsted 1999a). They will often obtain scores for non-verbal reasoning that are higher than their scores on attainment and other tests using their second language (Valdes and Figueroa 1994, Table 4.1). A battery that is widely used for this purpose in secondary schools is the Cognitive Abilities Test (Thorndike *et al.* 1986).

Those who remain sceptical of normative approaches have replied to each of these numbered claims:

1 The new scales have not been standardized for use in countries outside the USA and do not directly relate to learning objectives in the school curriculum.

2 Many instruments that aim to make it possible to identify a profile of strengths and weaknesses are not sufficiently reliable for the purpose. Early reviews indicated that, when a profile is used as the basis of a teaching programme that is designed to remedy weak abilities, the results are generally unimpressive (Arter and Jenkins 1979). Recent reviews of attempts to use subtest analysis diagnostically (see Frederickson 1999) have drawn overwhelmingly negative conclusions. For example, 'this evidence, both historic and current, suggests that WISC-III subtest analysis should be abandoned' (Watkins *et al.* 1997: 317).

3 If the aim is to obtain diagnostic information on functions such as attention and perception in order to inform teaching methods and the planning of the learning environment, criterion referenced assessment and structured observation are likely to be more effective approaches to obtaining information than norm-based methods.

4 It may be possible to develop satisfactory levels of inter-observer agreement if a simple system is used for categorizing the observed behaviours (Douglas

et al. 1972). But reliability is not sufficient in itself. There is uncertainty about the validity of the procedure: observations in the setting of a test interview may not successfully predict children's behaviour style or problem-solving strategies in other settings (Glutting *et al.* 1989).

5 If standardized tests are used for any purpose with individuals learning EAL, particular care will always be needed. At the least confirmatory evidence should be sought from other sources. It will also be important to review any new arrangements or provision after an agreed fixed period on the basis of further teacher observation. As will be seen below, a cycle of assessment–planning–teaching–review is commonly advocated without the use of normative tests. If teachers were appropriately alert to the risks of developing low expectations of children from different backgrounds, there would be no need for this stage in the process.

There is one feature of normative methods of assessment that places an absolute limitation on their value in an educational context and cuts across the specific criticisms just listed. This is that the act of comparing children's performance to an age-related norm cannot help teachers to identify what they have already learned or what they need to learn next. So the information the tests give is of little value in planning an educational programme. The approaches to assessment that were described in Chapter 7 and most of the approaches described below attempt to address that challenge more directly.

Dynamic approaches to assessment

Dynamic approaches to assessment are based on a social constructivist view of child and adolescent development. In this view, deriving from Vygotsky's ideas, higher order mental processes develop on the basis of cooperating with other people, only later becoming 'inner, individual functions of the child itself' (Vygotsky 1978). Thus other people, notably parents, peers and teachers, are seen as playing a crucial mediating role in stimulating children's learning from infancy:

> In this view learning is constructed jointly through social interaction, and understanding can be enhanced by the appropriate amount of assistance, finely tuned to what children know and can do. The emphasis is on potential rather than maturation and readiness, and the role of the 'more knowledge-able other' person is immensely important.
>
> (Watson 2000: 135)

'Static' tests such as IQ tests evaluate what a child has learned in the past – their zone of actual development (ZAD). It is seen as more useful to assess what Vygotsky called their zone of potential development (sometimes known as the zone of proximal development or next development – ZPD). For this purpose 'dynamic' measures are required. Suppose the performance of two boys on a static test is at the same level (e.g. equating to the average for an 8-year-old).

They are then retested with some adult help (e.g. in the form of standard questions prompting them towards the correct solution of problems they could not solve before). One boy now attains a score typically associated with children aged 9 while the other reaches a level associated with 12-year-olds. Vygotsky saw the difference between the ZAD (what children can achieve by themselves) and the level they can reach with adult help as an operational definition of the ZPD. In this example one boy has markedly more extensive emerging skills and knowledge than the other: his assessed ZPD suggests that there is greater scope for immediately enhancing his attainments (Vygotsky 1978: 85–6).

With this perspective a further criticism is added to the list of concerns about static tests: they establish current levels of performance but usually tell us little about the processes that underlie that competence (Campione 1989). They ignore functions that have not yet matured but are in the process of maturing. To use a favourite analogy of Vygotsky's, they focus on the 'fruits' of development rather than its 'buds' and 'flowers'. Even if they are intended to form the base for prediction, the process of assessment itself is essentially retrospective rather than prospective. Observing embryonic (nascent, emerging) skills closely would provide a better estimate of individuals' potential for proceeding beyond their present level of competence and would offer more useful guidance on the kind of teaching that will help them realize that potential.

In the West particular claims have been made for dynamic approaches to assessment in relation to children from ethnic and linguistic minorities. Static tests are seen to penalize children who have had limited opportunities to learn whatever is being tested (Feuerstein 1979). By building coaching or training for the assessment task into the process it was hoped that dynamic assessment would offer a counterbalance to inequalities in experience and thus be less prone to bias (Hamers *et al.* 1996; Hessels 1997).

Different workers in dynamic assessment have different aims in view. For Budoff (1987) the main aim has been to classify children more accurately for special education placement. On the basis of a standard procedure he categorized children as:

- *High performers*: who perform well without support and improve their scores only marginally with coaching.
- *Gainers*: who initially perform poorly but make gains after coaching.
- *Non-gainers*: who initially perform poorly and gain little from coaching.

There was a particular interest in identifying children and adolescents who had been classified as of limited intellectual ability but proved to be 'gainers' in these tests. But it seems unlikely that reclassification is the best use of these methods. Higher priority might be given to a different goal – using dynamic assessment in order to plan instruction (or mediation) as effectively as possible.

There is a range of procedural options in dynamic assessment. The assessment may involve long-term learning with, say, daily training sessions over a week (e.g. Guthke 1993); or only short-term learning may be involved (e.g. when the pre-test, training and post-test phases all occur in a single session). The core of the method is the training phase. There are many different options possible for training:

- simple feedback on correct performance;
- demonstration of the correct solution to a problem (with or without an explanation of its rationale);
- prompts or hints in the form of questions.

Sometimes different forms of training will be combined in a standardized sequence.

A critical issue is whether or not the training is to be standardized and the same for all children or tailored to the needs of each child individually. Feuerstein (1979) advocated and practised a high degree of individualization of the training phase. So did Gallimore *et al.* (1989) in the Hawaii KEEP project in which reading skills were taught through an 'assisted performance' programme. Critics of individualized training highlight the risk that this strategy will make decision making subjective in both test administration and interpretation. It takes a long time to train in Feuerstein's methods; it takes a long time with each child to use them; inter-tester reliability is untested and suspect (Missiuna and Samuels 1988). One solution is to draw upon computer technology for adaptive testing. Guthke (1993) and Guthke *et al.* (1997) described a complex diagnostic procedure in which the kinds of error that a child makes determine both what kinds of prompt are given and which items are presented next. The key point in this strategy is that, while each child has a different experience, there are standard rules (embedded in the computer program) for determining what that experience will be. Inevitably it is an extremely complex procedure, as illustrated in Figure 9.4.

What exactly is measured in dynamic assessment? With a conventional intelligence test the final score recording an individual's performance is usually a quotient formed by comparing the sum of items passed with age norms. With learning ability or learning potential tests based on the dynamic paradigm there is a wide variety of possible ways of measuring performance.

Post-test score
Using this score (rather than a score on a one-off test) gives children the advantage of practice or training. It is thought to reduce the bias that might arise because they are unfamiliar with the task or with test procedures or solution strategies, or because their initial performance is depressed by fear of failure. Using this measure still involves focusing on achievement rather than ability to learn. In theoretical terms it represents an improvement within the conventional psychometric tradition rather than a radical departure. There are examples in the Kaufman Assessment Battery for Children (Kaufman and Kaufman 1983).

Difference score (sometimes called change score or gain score)
This is calculated by subtracting the pre-test score from the post-test score. This type of score presents many problems:

1 There is a negative correlation between score on the pre-test and gain score – an artefact that arises because it is statistically more likely that low scorers will gain. This is particularly important for those concerned with SEN because the

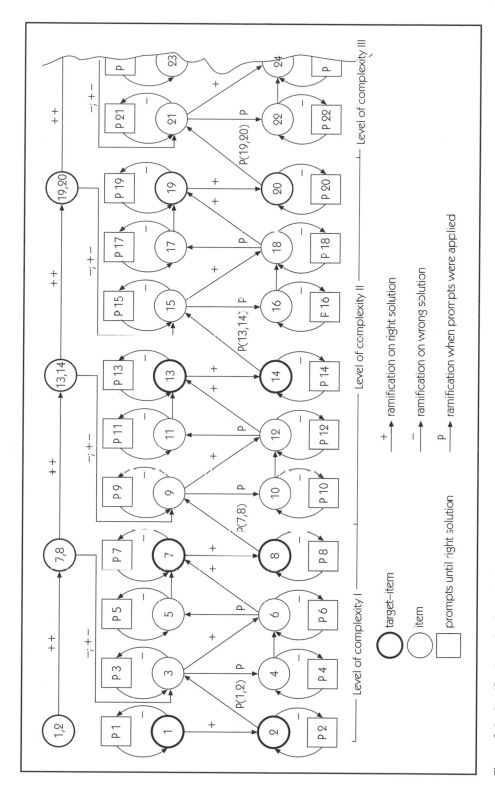

Figure 9.4 Ramification rules for adaptive computer-assisted learning test series of figures
Source: Guthke *et al.* (1997).

children they work with will often perform at a low level initially. So they will be more likely to appear to improve their scores, and their difficulties may be underestimated.

2 A difference score draws on two other scores. So, if it is to be reliable, it is essential that the pre-test and the post-test each separately have very high internal reliability (consistency). Otherwise any error component will be magnified.

3 Difference scores are confounded by memory effects (children may do better on the second test simply because they remember aspects of the task from their experience of the first), and by floor and ceiling effects (children may not have the scope to improve their scores with learning because the test overall is too easy or too difficult).

Some of these problems, but not all, can be overcome by constructing a 'residualized change score'. The statistical procedure to calculate this score takes pre-test score differences into account so as to eliminate problem (1). A more sophisticated solution is to apply item response theory (e.g. Sijtsma 1993).

Measures based on the training itself
Typically what is recorded is the amount and/or level and/or kind of training or help that a child needs to solve a problem or reach criterion performance on a task. Examples include:

- number of items in a standard set on which help is given;
- number or type of hints given at the child's request.

In this case it is the *cognitive process* that leads to difference scores that is of interest.

Which measure is chosen will depend on the aims of testing. It is suggested that in general, educationists will find measures based on the training itself more practicable and useful than difference scores. Campione (1989) has proposed a helpful way of classifying the range of approaches in dynamic assessment along three dimensions (see Table 9.8).

It has been argued that some of Vygotsky's concepts have been misunderstood in the West because of problems of translation and cultural distortion (Daniels 1992). A central notion in Vygotsky's thinking about dynamic assessment was '*Obuchenie*' which used often to be translated as 'instruction' but is more accurately seen as referring to both teaching and learning as part of the same interdependent process. For a successful outcome the learner must make active efforts of construction (what Valsiner 2000 calls 'the individual component') and others must guide those efforts in a desired direction ('the teaching component'). Psychological functions that are fully established are the basis on which new ones can emerge. Within the ZPD there is more than one way in which actual learning can occur. Valsiner shows the possibilities as branching routes out of the present: 'Which of these directions will actually be taken would depend upon the coordination of circumstances – the decision by the developing person, the guidance of "social others". It is here where social suggestions play their "guiding role"' (Valsiner 2000: 44).

Table 9.8 Classifying approaches to dynamic assessment

Dimension	Ranges between
The focus of the assessment	Assessing by direct observation of improvement and assessing the operation of processes that underlie the improvement.
The type of interaction during the assessment	Standardized interaction (measured quantitatively) and clinical interaction (perhaps measured qualitatively).
The target	Domain-specific skills (e.g. reading text) and general skills (e.g. non-verbal reasoning).

Source: Campione (1989).

Thus, in seeking to develop dynamic assessment, it may be necessary to stop thinking in terms of a paradigm that has been firmly established in SEN practice in the West in the past – the separation of the processes of teaching and of assessment, as exemplified by the IQ test. In this view, efforts to develop valid learning ability *tests* such as those of Hessels (1997) are unhelpful. Good practice in dynamic assessment will require a constant assessment–teaching–assessment cycle. An alternative view seeks to combine the advantages of assisted (dynamic) assessment with the psychometric standards of the best traditional tests. Ultimately the selection of an assessment approach for a particular purpose must depend on what will best inform intervention and lead to more successful learning.

There are practical issues too. Dynamic assessment takes longer than static assessment (and requires more extensive and sophisticated training). Are the improvements in the information that it offers sufficiently valuable in a particular case to justify allocating those resources? Can these methods be used cost effectively? Vye *et al.* (1987) have proposed a 'continuum of assessment services' in which assessment may begin with the simplest of screening procedures and continue through a graded series of methods to the most intensive of individualized dynamic methods.

How will the findings from such methods be followed up? Dynamic assessment with an individualized prompt procedure will lead to (or may be part of) an individualized teaching programme. Is it realistic to expect that such programmes will always be practicable in busy classrooms, granted the other pressures and demands made on teachers and the time and particular skills required to put such programmes into effect? Missiuna and Samuels (1988: 21) rephrase the previous point: 'Is the additional time and expense of a dynamic assessment only worthwhile if adaptive instruction is available?' Brown *et al.* (1992) showed that the potentially valuable information that is generated by dynamic assessment is not always utilized by teachers. Elliott (2000) observed that, in addition to the challenge of making time in a busy classroom, there is uncertainty over how much systematic knowledge teachers require of the underlying theory and associated concepts in order to make sense of the tasks they face with this approach.

At the same time, reports of work on *reciprocal teaching* (e.g. Brown and Campione 1996), *instructional conversation* (Tharp and Gallimore 1988), and *collaborative learning* (Meadows 1998) give ground for optimism. Watson (2000) summarized the advantages of these kinds of teaching approaches as promoting learning experiences in which:

- the learner is active;
- the teacher is responsive to pupils' interests and existing understanding;
- educational talk, focusing on the task in hand, is emphasized;
- social experiences are integral to learning and highly valued;
- teachers build on and extend pupils' thinking;
- through scaffolding and mediation, teachers encourage cognitive restructuring;
- pupils' awareness of their own learning is assisted;
- transfer is facilitated;
- challenging tasks indicate that teacher expectations are high;
- pupils are gradually helped to become self-directed, self-aware learners, who are in control of their own learning;
- confidence and self-esteem are raised.

Curriculum issues

As ideas about the nature of learning difficulties have changed, thinking about the aims of education has evolved. Figure 9.3 illustrates four stages in this evolution. What has this really meant for pupils with high levels of difficulty who need to develop basic skills as a central element of their learning at school? Sometimes working towards an inclusive ideal seems to have involved little more than a token attempt at 'redescription'. The teaching of developmental or functional skills that are relevant to the needs of the pupils was redescribed as teaching a National Curriculum subject. Grove and Peacey (1999: 83) parodied such attempts: 'Thus sensory exploration may be described as Science; eating skills as English or Personal and Social Education; tracking objects as Mathematics; and signs of anticipation as History'. An alternative approach which they recognized (and which Byers 1999a suggested is more commonly pursued in schools) is to take subjects as contexts of experience. With this approach a group of pupils with diverse needs and interests may participate in the same activity and take different things from it. Sebba *et al.* (1993: 21) illustrated the strategy with a piece of work designed to address what was then an attainment target in science at Key Stage 3:

> To illustrate some of these issues, consider an activity designed to address the effects of water on the Earth's surface (science, Key Stage 3). This can be successfully presented at a wide range of levels, through, for example, watering plants in the school grounds, observing hard rain on a mud slope compared with on the tarmac path, etc. Some pupils may learn something of this process and hence will achieve within this area of science even if the school staff could not have predicted they would do so prior to the session. Other

pupils may be able to work on current individual priorities within the context of this activity. For one pupil this teaching context might be used to practise wheelchair mobility skills while another is encouraged to produce the signs for 'rain', 'down' and 'on'. Hence, some pupils may achieve science skills, some mobility or communication skills and some nothing at all (but not necessarily predictably so).

What it means to achieve an attainment target is now widely understood, but 'experiencing' a learning activity is not as well defined. Byers (1999a) offered an example of a framework for clarifying this through plans for half a term's work on electrical circuits in Key Stage 1, developed by staff at Jack Taylor School in London (see Figure 9.5). Extending the work of Brown (1996) he proposed that there might be a continuum of pupil outcomes in relation to educational experiences. At one end this would involve *encountering* (being present during an activity) and *awareness* (noticing that something is going on); and at the other end would be *involvement* (active participation, doing, commenting) and *attainment* (gaining, consolidating or practising skills, knowledge, etc.) (Byers 1999a: 186).

Teaching methods and the classroom environment

For an extended period within the last half century teaching methods for children with learning difficulties were strongly influenced by behavioural principles. The adaptations that were made in order to respond to children's learning difficulties were a very considerable advance on earlier practice. For example, well-defined objectives were set for teachers and pupils, and systematic methods were available to work towards them. In schools which took these principles on board there was a purposeful ethos with a clear focus on the educational task (Ainscow and Tweddle 1979; McBrien and Foxen 1981). However, critics have argued that there were disadvantages too (list adapted from Watson 2000):

- *Teachers* became more directive, reduced their expectations of the pupils, set undemanding tasks and neglected to foster metacognition, learning strategies and generalization of learning.
- *Pupils* became more passive, showed low levels of engagement and low self-esteem, sought a good deal of reassurance and pretended to understand more than they really did.
- *Curricula* were highly organized and tightly planned, yet lacked intellectual coherence or intrinsic interest.
- *Tasks and activities* were often solitary with little demand or opportunity for joint or collaborative working.

With a shift towards inclusion there was a new emphasis on *differentiation*. This might mean grouping pupils on the basis of their past performance and teaching different versions or aspects of the curriculum to different groups of pupils (thus undermining the inclusive intentions?). Or it might mean teaching the same curriculum to all pupils and tailoring teaching methods to the different

Figure 9.5

Plans for work on
electrical circuits
in Key Stage 1
Source:
Byers (1999a).

Module Title: Electricity	Long-Term Map Reference: Science KS1 Summer A (a)	Subject Focus: Science	Links: Design and Technology

References to Programmes of Study: Science Key Stage 1 – Physical Processes

'Pupils should be taught:
– to construct simple circuits involving batteries, wires, bulbs and buzzers; – that electrical devices will not work if there is a break in the circuit.'

Objectives (What do I want pupils to learn?)	Key Activities, Experiences and Organisation (What will pupils do?)	Assessment Opportunities (How will I know when pupils achieve or make progress?)
Pupils should learn: • that sensory events occur; to respond to sensory events; and to focus on sensory events; • that lights and sounds can change – 'on/off, loud/soft, bright/dim'; • that events occur in time – 'Now it's on/off'; • that events occur in time and space – 'Look over there'; • that switches can be used to control events • that bulbs, batteries and wires can be joined to make circuits complete or incomplete; • to construct working circuits with bulbs, batteries and buzzers; • to 'name' (sign, symbol, eye point) sources of sound, light and movement.	*Use dark room/light and sound room* – regular sessions to explore lights and bubble tubes with small groups and/or individual pupils. *Explore switched equipment in and around classroom/school* – regular demonstrations and individual encounters with ICT, everyday objects, battery-operated toys, torches etc. *Use electrically powered toys and equipment and compare with non-electrical* – whole class activity with battery-operated toys, bells, buzzers, spotlights, tape recorders etc, and guitars, candles, clockwork toys, push/pull cars etc. *Visit 'Launch Pad' in Science Museum* – class outing with 1:1 volunteer helpers and use of minibus. *Construct circuits* – demonstration by staff followed by small group tabletop activity to replace batteries, join wires, use clips, bulbs, switches etc. *Extension* – some pupils may wish to draw/record their circuits (Key Stage 2).	Pupils may: • react to sensory outcomes – bulbs, lighting, flashes, buzzers, movement etc; • attend to sensory outcomes in a focused way – look, listen, track etc; • participate in controlling events – operate switches etc; • anticipate outcomes – respond before, during and after sensory events; • actively join in circuit making – joining components etc; • communicate a response to changes in circuits – bulbs, lights, buzzers etc – Level 1; • compare a working circuit with an incomplete circuit – Level 2.

Resources
(What will I need to use – what is available?)

Switch-controlled toys; battery-controlled toys; bulbs, wires, batteries, clips, buzzers; everyday electrical appliances, lights, torches, radios, tape recorders etc; soundbeam, keyboard, light and sound room, slide projector and OHPs; minibus for visits; variety of non-electrical sources of light, sound and movement.

learning needs of individual pupils (Stradling and Saunders 1991). Where the second strategy was adopted, teachers could consider a very wide range of options to improve access to the curriculum. It was necessary to analyse pupils' needs, the requirements of the learning task and the learning context. The following aspects noted by King (1989) might be differentiated:

- *General aspects* including aims, content, breadth, depth, pace or language.
- *Requirements for social interaction* including forms of teacher–pupil interaction, forms of pupil–pupil interaction and forms of pupil grouping.
- *Teaching and learning strategies* including teaching styles, reinforcement, forms of pupil recording, learning contexts, forms of classroom organization and use of support teachers.
- *Assessment strategies* including materials to get started on and resources for self-study.

Booth and Ainscow (1998: 229) observed that a great deal of time and effort is often put into the preparation of alternative study materials, 'whereas, in practice, the level of participation in classrooms was higher where the teacher adjusted the overall process of the lesson, particularly by utilising group work'. Simpson (1997) emphasized the value of finding out what pupils themselves felt about the tasks they were given and the support they received for completing them. She had a sample of teachers who were nominated for the purpose as 'good differentiators'. However, like Bennett *et al.* (1984) in a different setting, she found that there were serious discrepancies between what the teachers intended when they set work and how their pupils experienced it. In top groups, 50 per cent of pupils experienced as 'practice' tasks that the teachers had intended to be 'incremental', while 19 per cent of the bottom groups experienced the reverse. As a step towards trying to overcome this problem, Simpson proposed a partnership model. This was to involve 'a major change in the relationship between teacher and pupil, from one in which the teacher controls what is learned, how it is learned and how that learning is judged, into one in which learning goals are agreed between teachers and pupils and assessment is both shared and formative' (Simpson 1997: 100).

Hart (1996) analysed what she called 'differential thinking' as one of three possible types of response to children causing concern. The first approach she highlights is called 'diagnostic thinking' and is motivated by a perceived need to identify the source of the problem as a stage towards designing remedies or compensatory strategies. The second approach, 'differential thinking', sets out 'to look for ways to *match provision* more closely to the child's individual needs and personal learning styles'. She recognizes that there is a great deal that is positive about these two approaches, but nonetheless has reservations:

Both these first two approaches reflect a fundamentally positive stance on the part of those who adopt them. They start from an assumption that there is potential for enhancing children's learning to be found if we actively seek it out, and a commitment to finding ways of exploiting it in the interests

| ACTIVITY 9.2 | Differentiation in a history class |

This account is taken from HMI guidance for inspectors and schools on how educational inclusion should be evaluated (Ofsted 2000a). It describes a history class which the inspector clearly thought was well taught and met a range of SEN and EAL needs effectively. Can you identify which of the options listed by King (1989) (see p. 261) were employed by this teacher, and can you suggest why they might have appeared effective on this occasion?

Example of evidence about a Year 5, mixed-ability history class, concentrating on pupils with SEN and EAL

They make deductions about the coming of the railway, part of a series of lessons on the causes and consequences of changes brought about by the arrival and then closure of the railway in a small town. Pupils with EAL have been learning the language for two years and are confident speakers but, unlike other pupils in the class, their knowledge of the local area is limited. Pupils with SEN: speaking and listening skills are much in advance of their reading and writing skills and they have good knowledge of the local area from family working links in local industries.

Digital photographs taken on a recent walk along the disused railway track are used effectively to compare with old photographs. Effective questioning: How were goods transported before railways came? How do you know? In what ways was rail transport better? Did it have any disadvantages? helps pupils speaking EAL understand the importance of the railways to the history and wealth of the town and the importance of particular buildings, for example warehouses and other commercial buildings. Teacher ensures that all groups of pupils have an opportunity to contribute at their own level. Pupils with SEN are encouraged to demonstrate their knowledge of the town by short, focused questions that enable them to point out changes when the railways first came and since they closed. Lively discussions well directed by the teacher. Pupils have good understanding of the impact of railways. 'They were exciting and fast and made travel much easier'. 'Things that used to perish on a long journey could be transported now'. Pupils with EAL are given good support to write about the development of the railways, explaining how this brought changes; this activity is aided by written information in English and in Urdu about local industries of the past, and photocopies of old newspaper cuttings. They enjoy acting as 'historical detectives' and produce interesting and accurate notes on their findings. The teacher discusses words they have not encountered. Pupils with SEN produce a well organized, sequential taped 'BBC' report using the questions on cards provided by the teacher and photographs as prompts.

Commentary

This teaching is very effective because the objectives of the lesson are clear and the work is modified well to suit pupils with different prior knowledge and varying skills in reading and writing. The different strengths of the pupils are used to understand changes to the town and reasons for them. The provision of a variety of resources and carefully tailored support ensure that all pupils learn effectively. The diverse needs of pupils are known well by the teacher who modifies the tasks to maximise learning (Ofsted, 2000a: 16–17).

of learners. However, the kinds of thinking they encourage may well leave much of the potential that exists within mainstream education unexplored. Because the focus is upon the *child*, there is no guarantee that the analysis will open up to examination and reconsideration all, or indeed any, of the aspects of the situation – and practitioners' thinking – wherein that potential lies.

(Hart 1996: 110–11)

In place of these two types of approach, Hart proposes what she calls 'innovative thinking'. This involves a more reflexive process of examining concerns about children's learning. It should set in train 'a probing *analysis* of our *existing* thinking and understandings . . . going to work on our existing thinking in such a way as to generate *new* insight into what might be done, *beyond* what is currently being done or tried, to support and enhance the child's learning' (Hart 1996: 111). Thus the focus of assessment for intervention has moved from the learner viewed 'objectively' in normative assessment through the teacher–learner interaction in dynamic assessment to a new focus on the teachers themselves as well as the task, the individual and the context. This broader view is reflected in the *Code of Practice* (Department for Education and Skills 2001, para, 5.6) which advises: 'The assessment process should always be fourfold. It should focus on the child's learning characteristics, the learning environment that the school is providing for the child, the task and the teaching style'.

As we have noted throughout this chapter, low expectations that have deep historical roots continue to influence thinking about the education of children with learning difficulties. But there is an increasing tendency for their SEN to be discussed in terms of an analysis of their rights instead of an acceptance of their apparent limitations. Activity 9.3 gives you an opportunity to consider what that might mean in practice in the classroom.

Conclusions

There have been radical changes over time in the way in which learning difficulties are conceived. These changes have mirrored shifts in theorizing about the nature of intelligence and abilities. It is increasingly appreciated that successful performance may depend, in part, on effective learning strategies and on a learning style that is well matched to the way in which information is presented. This means that a learning difficulty is partly determined by the learning context and cannot solely be understood as a fixed characteristic of the learner. For some commentators this has led to the rejection of the term *learning difficulties* altogether.

Concerns about separate educational provision for children with learning difficulties were fanned by the recognition that those most likely to be identified tended to come from low status social groups and ethnic minority communities. The analysis of assessment techniques, curriculum issues and teaching methods

ACTIVITY 9.3   What have you done this week...?

The following list of questions for a parent, carer or teacher is based on a manifesto on the civil rights and responsibilities of those with learning difficulties developed in Wisconsin (quoted in Wood and Shears 1986). Imagine that you are the mainstream Year 3 class teacher of a child with SLD aged 8 who has recently been admitted to your class for three afternoons a week (spending the rest of her time in an SLD unit in a junior school nearby). At the end of one term you are asked these questions on a Friday afternoon. What would you hope to be able to answer?

(a) What have you done this week to convey to this young person that she is a valued member of the classroom community who is taken seriously?

(b) What have you entrusted her to do which challenged her sense of responsibility?

(c) How have you enabled her this week to demonstrate fresh self-confidence, courage and initiative?

(d) In what settings has she been enabled to cooperate actively on a valued task with others who have learning difficulties, and with others who do not?

(e) On what occasions over what issues have you sought her views and acted in a way that shows that you respect them?

(f) How has she been enabled to act unselfishly for the benefit of others?

each showed a shift over recent years in the direction of approaches that are compatible with inclusive principles. These principles pose new and uncomfortable challenges. The themes that have emerged as significant in relation to learning difficulties will reappear in various guises in the chapters that follow on other areas of SEN.

Chapter 10

Language

When you have studied this chapter you should be able to:

1 Describe the main areas of competence involved in language development for monolingual and bilingual speakers.
2 Recognize the possible impact of SEN on different aspects of language development.
3 Make decisions on when and how a full language assessment might be carried out with a child who has or may have SEN.
4 Analyse the implications for SEN of learning EAL.
5 Recognize and understand signs of specific language impairment that may be observed in the classroom

Contents

The knowledge and skills involved in language proficiency

Language and communication

Language is central to human experience – a key vehicle for thought and for social contact. Human beings are mutually dependent. Effective communication between them requires that:

- they know the forms of the language they share – how the words sound and how they go together (competence in phonology and syntax);
- they are able to use those forms to convey meaning and can understand what others mean when they use them (competence in semantics);
- they understand the social conventions that determine how people use language to each other, so that they appreciate another speaker's intentions in speaking and can communicate their own intentions to a listener (pragmatic competence);
- they can vary their style of communication and the language they use to suit the needs of different listeners in a conversation (conversational competence);
- they understand how language use and language conventions vary with the social and cultural context (sociolinguistic competence).

These competencies ensure that speakers can each play their full part in a complex 'communication chain'. This involves drawing on interdependent processes of decoding and encoding in which many areas of the nervous system are ultimately involved. Figure 10.1 shows a simplified form of the communication chain.

Children with SEN may have problems in mastering some or all of these areas of competence even when their difficulty is superficially not related to language at all. It is necessary to analyse individually for each child the challenges that are

Figure 10.1 The communication chain *Source:* Crystal and Varley (1998).

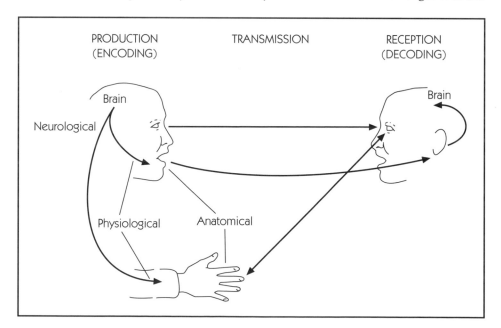

involved in the acquisition and use of language. Consider, for example, observations that have been made about the development of semantic competence by Susan who has been blind from birth and is now aged 4. When she adds to her vocabulary by learning new words for objects (nouns), she seems to be less likely than a sighted child of the same age to extend the nouns immediately to other situations (e.g. generalizing the use of the word 'soap' from the bathroom to the kitchen to the supermarket). Similarly, when she learns a new word for an action (verb), it will typically refer to an action which she has taken herself or an action by someone else that has directly affected her. She seems to be slower than most sighted children to use the new verb in an extended way to refer to an action by a third person that does not affect her (e.g. appreciating that an actor 'shouting' to another in a radio play is using the same action as a neighbour's child 'shouting' to her in the street). Some commentators have suggested that this slowness to generalize (which is not uncommon among children who have been blind from birth) implies that they show egocentricity and a lack of creativity (Dunlea 1989). More recent analysts have argued that it is simply that blind children need longer experience because they lack visual information regarding surrounding objects and events (Perez-Pereira and Conti-Ramsden 1999: 80).

It is possible to portray what happens when we listen to a statement such as 'The fish is on the table' as a sequential series of transformations of sound waves into meaning (see Figure 10.2). However, this model fails to take account of the way in which listeners' perception of the context and their general knowledge influence their interpretation of what they hear. Bishop pointed out that the statement 'The fish is on the table' will be interpreted differently in different circumstances. For example, the meaning will not be the same if it is uttered by the person doing the cooking at dinner time or by a child whose parent is letting the cat into a room when she is cleaning out a tropical fish tank (Bishop 1997: 14). Figure 10.3 illustrates a model of verbal comprehension that takes account of these effects.

In research and clinical work in the past, most attention was given to the first two types of competence (knowledge of language forms – phonology and syntax; and knowledge of its meaning – semantics). But it is increasingly being recognized that children who have problems in other aspects of language competence, such as pragmatic competence, are just as impeded in communicating effectively with other people as they would be if the sounds of their speech were distorted or their vocabulary was limited (Smith and Leinonen 1992). John, a London child who has been assessed as having an autistic disorder, illustrates this point. When he speaks, he uses the intonations and the words of his parents. But he rarely looks at the person he is talking to. In fact it is sometimes difficult to tell whether he is talking to another person at all. He seems to be choosing his words without reference to what people have said and without following any conversational thread. His mother reports that he constantly reverts to the same few favourite themes and often uses the same pet phrases to talk about them. He makes the journey to school each day by car, but when he arrives he usually lists a series of London Underground stations as though talking about the journey. The list

Figure 10.2
Model of the
stages of
processing
involved in
transforming a
sound wave into
meaning when
comprehending
the utterance 'The
fish is on the table'
Source: Bishop
(1997: 3).

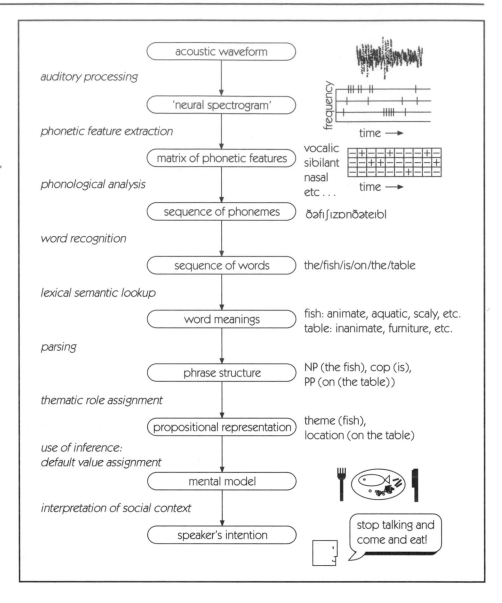

accurately reflects the route from his family home to his grandparents' house, but has nothing to do with the district where the school is located.

Language diversity

Difficulties may also arise not because a child has failed to acquire the language and social conventions to which they have been introduced, but because they

Figure 10.3
Modified model
of stages in
comprehension
from phonological
representation to
meaning, showing
top-down effects
of context and
general knowledge
on earlier stages
of processing
Source: Bishop
(1997: 14).

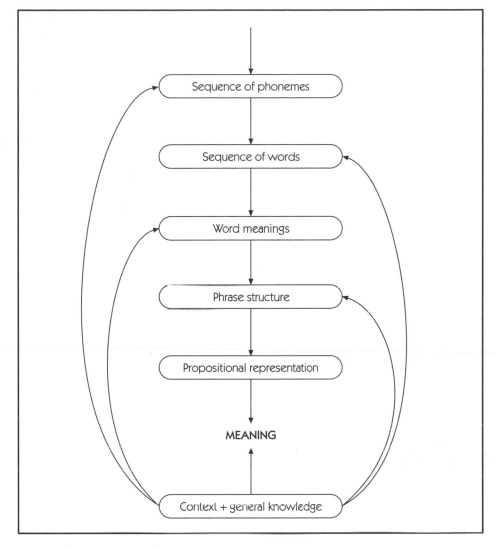

have grown up with a different set of conventions from those that they encounter at school. It may be that they speak a different language at home, or a different variety of the same language, or that they use different non-verbal signals for communication (e.g. when demonstrating agreement or deferring to another person). At school they are expected to comply with the social code of the classroom and to extend their linguistic repertoire to encompass the accepted standard language of their society (e.g. standard English). The curriculum goals of the school will prioritize that form of the language: 'In order for children to participate confidently in public, cultural and working life, pupils need to be able to speak, write and read standard English fluently and accurately. All pupils are therefore entitled to the full range of opportunities necessary to enable them to develop competence in standard English' (Department for Education 1995: 2).

In the UK, when working with children who make poor progress, this requirement has to be interpreted alongside an apparently unrelated principle in the law about SEN: 'A child is not to be taken as having a learning difficulty solely because the language (or form of the language) in which he is, or will be, taught is different from a language (or form of a language) which has at any time been spoken in his home' (Department for Education and Employment 1996, Section 312). This provision in the law is intended to provide protection so that children are not stigmatized as having SEN when they are simply in the early stages of learning EAL. This protection is important, but it has significant limits. For example, it does not mean that the language or dialect spoken in a child's home will necessarily be treated with respect in the classroom. The National Curriculum guidance that is quoted above continues: 'The richness of dialects and other languages can make an important contribution to pupils' knowledge and understanding of standard English. Where appropriate, pupils should be encouraged to make use of their understanding and skills in other languages when learning English'.

It appears that the value of having mastered another language is seen mainly as providing a route to learning Standard English. Monolingual teachers often feel ambivalent about their pupils using dialect or another language in the classroom to talk to each other. In Activity 10.1 you are asked to consider how your own experience bears on this issue. There is now good evidence that teaching in a child's first language strengthens their performance in school in their second language (Thomas and Collier 1997). Encouraging children to draw on the whole of their language repertoire in collaboration with others can improve their performance in tests and classroom-based Standard Assessment Tasks (SATs) (Pema and Pattinson 1991).

Among speakers of English, the majority of children – white and black – use different language registers or dialects in different situations (see Edwards 1986 for an illustration of this from the African-Caribbean community). It is possible for a range of dialects to be respected in the classroom while children are helped to access and use the standard version for some purposes. Problems arise when the privileging of the standard dialect is managed in a way that belittles others and when children's personal language difficulties make 'bi-dialectalism' a challenging goal for them. Grossman (1998) summarized US evidence about some of the difficulties associated with this approach, ending with a strong statement of the objections:

- Efforts to teach students to speak standard English are ineffective. For most pupils there are only marginal increases in their adoption of standard forms in the classroom, much less outside school.
- Teaching pupils standard English before they are completely fluent in their original dialect may stunt their language development.
- Disparaging non-standard dialects damages the self-esteem of those who speak them, and it is not possible to encourage the replacement of one set of forms with another without appearing to disparage the first.

ACTIVITY 10.1   Encouraging pupils to use additional languages in the classroom

In the two columns below we have set out arguments that are sometimes used in the debate about encouraging language diversity in the classroom. Discuss the arguments with a colleague one by one. What personal observations can each of you recall that either illustrate the validity of each assertion or suggest it is invalid?

Reasons given for insisting that only English is spoken in the classroom (teacher quoted by Ryan 1999)	Reasons given for encouraging pupils to speak together in other languages if they wish
It makes for better order and control and prevents covert subversion	When teachers affirm students' developing sense of their own identity and show respect for their home language and culture, it is more likely that they will apply themselves to academic effort (Cummins 1996)
It helps pupils for whom English is an additional language to learn it more quickly and successfully	When classroom activities on word-meaning encourage bilingual pupils to draw on their first languages, they learn the second language more effectively and are helped to gain a richer appreciation of ways in which they can make use of each language effectively in their own lives (McWilliam 1998)
	Children in the early stages of learning the majority language will suffer less stress and fatigue and will have better access to the curriculum (Skutnabb-Kangas 1981; Baker 1996)
It fosters ethnic and cultural integration by discouraging the development of separate, language-based working groups	It makes the break between home and school as small as possible (UNESCO 1953, quoted in Baker 1996)

According to Grossman (1998: 50):

> Teaching standard English to nonstandard dialect speakers is a form of cultural subjugation. Nonstandard English speaking students and their teachers often have different perceptions of the implications of standard English. Teachers tend to view it as a way to learn more effectively and get ahead in the real world; many students view it as talking white, denying their heritage, and giving in to the European American power structure.

Bilingual language proficiency

The term 'bilingual' is used in many different ways. Throughout this book a bilingual child is taken to be one who regularly needs to understand or use more

Table 10.1 Varied circumstances of bilingual learners

	Social circumstances	Typical motive for learning second language	Investment in learning second language
Elite bilingual	Parent works in high status occupation away from home country (e.g. diplomat, business person)	Cultural enrichment; communication with local people, including servants	Modest – success will bring some advantages, failure will incur few costs
Majority bilingual	Parents speak a high-status language in a country where a second language is widely spoken (e.g. English in Quebec)	Political requirement to be able to speak second language for entry into many occupations	Success will offer significant economic advantages and will have some social cachet
Family bilingual	Mother and father from different language backgrounds (e.g. father originally Greek-speaking and mother originally English-speaking)	Parents wish child to be able to communicate with all members of extended family	Success likely to be valued highly by family
Minority bilingual	Parents are refugees or immigrants from a developing country	Social and economic necessity	Failure will restrict employment opportunities and social status very considerably

Source: Summarized from Skutnabb-Kangas (1981).

than one language (e.g. at home and at school). There is no implication that the child is yet (or will necessarily ever be) equally competent in both languages. Bilingual status for educational purposes is taken to be regular exposure to situations where dual competence would be desirable. Children will develop different versions of that dual competence in listening, speaking, reading and writing depending on the demands made of them and their ability to learn. Table 10.1 outlines different reasons for developing bilingual language proficiency and suggests the implications they may have for the learner.

The proficiency of a bilingual speaker is best understood if all five of the aspects of language competence that were introduced at the start of this chapter are taken into account – they all complement each other. A speaker's proficiency is not made up simply of knowledge of their languages and skill in understanding and speaking them. It also involves attitudes and feelings about the situations in which each language is used: a proficient bilingual speaker requires not only competence but also confidence across a wide range of situations – a wider range than a monolingual speaker will normally face. This is ignored when bilingual language use is described simply as a technical task in terms of a cognitive dimension alone. This overlooks the emotional, social and cultural significance that is usually associated with becoming bilingual. A simple framework of three dimensions has been proposed for describing people's associations with the languages in their repertoire:

- *expertise*: degree of proficiency in a language;
- *affiliation*: affective relationship with a language;
- *inheritance*: membership, by birth, of a family or community with a particular language tradition (Rampton 1990; Leung *et al.* 1997).

Grosjean (1985) has emphasized the different views that are often held of bilingual language proficiency. Across the world, monolingual speakers are in the minority and in many societies bilingual proficiency, and even multilingual proficiency, is the norm. But traditionally in much of the West the monolingual nation state has become what most citizens see as 'normal'. What effect does that have? Grosjean analysed the assumptions behind the monolingual ('fractional') view which takes monolingualism as the norm and treats bilingualism as a possibly risky deviation. A bilingual speaker is seen simply as the sum of two monolinguals. Bilinguals are described and evaluated in terms of the fluency they have in their two languages and the balance they maintain between them. Language skills in bilinguals are appraised in terms of monolingual standards. Research focuses on what are feared to be the possibly negative effects of bilingualism. Will it damage a child's prospects of normal cognitive development? Will it lead to phonetic or syntactical confusion? The contact between the bilingual's two languages is seen as accidental and anomalous.

Grosjean contrasts with that set of assumptions a bilingual ('wholistic') view. From this perspective bilingual speakers are celebrated for maintaining a flexible communicative competence through different situations and in the face of changing demands on their two languages. There is more to bilingualism than understanding

ACTIVITY 10.2   Testing the value of Grosjean's (1985) analysis

Some examples are given in the text of how Francois Grosjean considers that fractional and holistic views of bilingual proficiency may differ.

(a) Can you think of any instances in your experience of practices or assumptions that reflect fractional or holistic perspectives in a school or a service?
(b) Where would the Department for Education guidance that was quoted on page 270 be located on the fractional-holistic spectrum?

and speaking two languages: bilingual people have a unique and specific linguistic configuration which combines their knowledge of each. The analogy Grosjean uses is of a high hurdler. A sprinter can run faster on the flat and a high-jumper can jump higher, but neither of them has the unique combination of skills that enables a hurdler to race so fast over obstacles. Bilinguals use their languages – separately or together – in different domains of life for different purposes with different people. They switch between languages flexibly to meet the needs of those with whom they are talking or to convey emphasis or intimacy or private meanings when talking to members of their own bilingual language community. Any evaluation of their proficiency needs to focus on this communicative competence rather than on mastery of the forms of each language. Language learning and language forgetting arise in response to new communicative needs. Grosjean suggested that if there were more bilingual researchers (and more bilingual teachers) the holistic view of bilingualism would have greater support.

Assessment of language proficiency

The importance of assessing language proficiency

Signs of language difficulties in the classroom
The need for early identification of speech and language difficulties has been emphasized in official guidance and in research reports and handbooks on professional practice (Department for Education 1994a, para. 3.85; Botting *et al.* 1998; Crystal and Varley 1998). Children with severe problems will usually be identified before school entry, but less obvious difficulties may only become apparent when a child is faced with the challenges posed by school. Simple delays in the development of language proficiency may reveal themselves if the pupil speaks like a younger child, or shows limited understanding of complex sentences, or uses a limited vocabulary compared to most children of the same age.

A less common phenomenon, 'specific language impairment', which is described in more detail below, leads to problems in processing grammatical forms and abnormalities in the way children speak as well as limitations in their vocabulary. In school the children may:

- have difficulty keeping track of conversations;
- produce odd grammatical structures when speaking or writing;
- fail to fully understand words that make logical connections such as 'because', 'so', 'if-then', 'however', 'although';
- have a poor memory for information that has been presented through speech or writing;
- talk in a roundabout or vague way, often not completing sentences and often repeating themselves;
- start to avoid tasks and situations that involve using language;
- appear slow to respond to instructions in a group and depend on seeing what other children are doing.

This list of signs has been adapted from more detailed lists presented by Beveridge and Conti-Ramsden (1987) and AFASIC (Association for All Speech-Impaired Children) (1990). When some or all of these signs are observed, it is essential that a full assessment is made of the child's development of language proficiency. Children showing such signs in severe form are unlikely to overcome their difficulties without additional support.

Children with EAL

Because the use of language is central to the educational process, the assessment of language proficiency will always be important in a full assessment of SEN. While this will be true for any child with learning difficulties, in the case of bilingual children it is obviously crucial. The draft revised Department for Education and Employment *Code of Practice* for SEN assessment (2001, para. 5.16) emphasizes this:

> At an early stage a full assessment should be made of the exposure they have had in the past to each of the languages they speak, the use they make of them currently and their proficiency in them. The information about their language skills obtained in this way will form the basis of all further work with them both in assessing their learning difficulties and in planning any additional language support that is needed.

It may appear self-evident that this would be important, but the few studies that have been conducted in the UK indicate that such information may often not be collected or recorded. This was indicated, for example, when Curnyn *et al.* (1991) studied the records of need for 35 children with MLD and EAL attending Glasgow primary and secondary schools in 1990. A content analysis of the case papers indicated that the assessment report completed by the school mentioned language in describing the child's difficulties in only about half the cases, and bilingualism was referred to in the language assessment in less than a fifth of the cases. One might expect the assessment reports of the psychologists to be more meticulous. But they mentioned the child's bilingualism or EAL status in only two thirds of the cases and they indicated that the child's first language had been assessed in only half of the cases. It might be expected that professionals would qualify their overall assessment in such cases by indicating that it should be interpreted in the light of the child's bilingual or bicultural status. That was done in less than a fifth of the cases examined. Findings of a similar kind were reported by Cline (1991) and Desforges *et al.* (1995).

It is easy to see that there was a deficiency in the professional practice covered in those studies. It is not so easy to determine the most effective way to put that deficiency right. Language competence is complex and multi-faceted. How can we best assess children's language development, and how can we report on that assessment most effectively – whether the children are monolingual, or bilingual, or multilingual?

Investigating a child's previous experience of language

The first questions to be resolved are not about proficiency but about opportunities. What exposure have children had outside school to the main language used for teaching and learning in school, and what exposure have they had to other languages in their homes or neighbourhood, or in a religious setting? In Activity 10.3 you will find a long list of questions that might need to be asked. This list was collated from a sample of booklets and notes of guidance issued by LEA staff to teachers and schools. (For a fuller analysis of the coverage of these documents see Cline and Shamsi 2000.) Activity 10.3 asks you to select from this list the questions appropriate to a particular situation. It is not suggested that an answer to each question is needed in every case.

ACTIVITY 10.3   Determining the information that is needed about a child's language experience in different situations

Below you will find a long list of questions that have been proposed in guidance notes about SEN and bilingualism. They are not given in any particular order.

Mark with *A* those questions that you think primary school class teachers and secondary school form tutors should know the answer to for *every* child in their class.

Mark with *B* those questions that you think these teachers should be able to answer in the case of all EAL pupils.

Mark with *C* those questions that you think should be checked if a child shows some of the signs of difficulty listed on page 275.

Mark with *D* those questions that you think need only be checked if a child has difficulties with literacy learning.

1 What language(s) are used by the child and to the child at home and in the community?
2 What is the family's religion? Do the parents wish their religious affiliation to be taken into account at school in connection with diet, religious education teaching, participation in acts of worship, participation in other activities?

3 In what ways is the language with which the child is most familiar different from English – the direction in which the script is written, the alphabet, the symbols used for numerals, intonation and stress patterns?

4 What language(s) are spoken by the child to

- Mother:
- Father:
- Siblings:
- Grandparents?

Do any of these family members use a different language some or all of the time when speaking to the child? If so, give details.

5 How long has the child been living in this country?

6 What moves, changes or interruptions might have affected the child's learning of each language to which they have been exposed?

7 Has the child attended school overseas? If so, where, between what ages, for how long, what kind of school and what language was the medium of instruction?

8 Does the child attend any school/class in the community? If so, is the focus of the work home language and/or culture or religious tradition and practice, or support for mainstream school learning?

9 What is the child's reported rate of progress in any community language class that they attend?

10 Is the child learning to read/write any language in addition to English? If so, give details of the language, any formal arrangements for teaching, and an estimate of the child's progress.

11 What access has the child had to first language support in school? What kind of support was provided:

- Exclusively with learning activities; exclusively with assessment activities; both?
- Through bilingual teachers, bilingual assistants, peer support, dual language materials?

12 Is an interpreter needed for effective communication with the parents about schooling?

The list of questions does not probe in detail about aspects of the *school context* that are particularly relevant to children from ethnic and linguistic minorities. Figure 10.4 lists some supplementary questions that may be relevant. The assumption here is that it is not enough to focus on questions about language provision. A full appreciation of the educational setting in which a child's bilingual communicative competence is being developed must go much further.

Approaches to language assessment

Once information has been gathered about a child's language background it is possible to place any findings about their use of language at school and at home

Figure 10.4
Relevant
information about
the school context
of bilingual pupils
Source: Cline and
Frederickson
(1991).

- Is their first language widely shared by other pupils at the school?
- Are there adults in the school who share their first language?
- Is there a whole school languages policy that covers bilingual pupils?
- What resources/teachers are available to meet unique needs of bilingual pupils?
- Are there books, tapes, posters and displays in their first language?
- What flexibility of provision is there beyond what they now receive?
- Is a multicultural approach to teaching emphasized and valued by staff?
- Is there an explicit and effective school policy on racism and on racial harassment that is known to all staff, including support staff?
- Is there effective liaison with parents from their community?
- Is spoken/written information available to parents in their first language if needed?
- What efforts are made to ensure that parents understand what the school is aiming to do for their children and to learn their views on what it ought to do?

in context. When it becomes evident that there is a significant problem, the first challenge is to determine how to sample children's use of language in more detail. Alternative options (starting with the most 'artificial') include:

- Set children a formal language test individually or in a group.
- Arrange meetings with children on their own and record the language they use. This may include creating a contrived situation designed to elicit particular types of language.
- Collect audio or video samples of the child's language (or written records) in everyday situations, repeating this over time to show progress or repeating it in different situations and with different company to show range.
- Make a written summary record of language use in an everyday situation, selecting only examples of particular interest or significance.
- Conduct enquiries through questionnaires or structured interviews with adults who live or work with the child to record their observations of the child's comprehension and use of language. (This may also involve asking children themselves for a self-report.)

Language tests

The first option in the list, language testing, appears to have many advantages. There is a standard setting and standard materials, making comparisons simpler and more objective. At best, tests can be more systematic, more focused, more transparent and quicker than alternative options. But for more than 30 years there has been widespread criticism of formal tests as a method of language assessment. The main criticisms are that tests:

- force the analysis of a rich, complex, context-dependent communicative competence into a simplistic framework of narrowly defined and unintegrated 'verbal skills';

- assess competence in phonology, syntax and semantics in preference to pragmatic, conversational and sociolinguistic competence;
- often privilege monolingual proficiency in a standard dialect as the ideal with which the performance of all speakers should be compared (Milroy and Milroy 1985, Ch. 8);
- often lack adequate standardization data for the youngest ages when systematic identification of language difficulties is particularly important (Howlin and Cross 1994);
- risk that numerical scores will be treated with undue respect because they appear precise;
- assume wrongly that language production and use in a highly structured exchange dominated by an adult will be a valid sample of how a child might use language in 'real communication' in everyday life.

But, in spite of all these criticisms, structured and standardized tests continue to be used extensively for the assessment of language proficiency in relation to SEN (Wright 1993). Some examples of tests that are commonly used with children in the UK are described briefly in Figure 10.5. They may be used in SEN assessment by speech and language therapists, educational psychologists or clinical psychologists. For all its limitations, test evidence has the advantage that it is cost-effective to collect and can readily be replicated. The most important question about test data is whether they are a valid reflection of what they claim to measure. The inferences that are drawn need to be checked against information from other sources. Are they compatible with the reports of parents and teachers and concurrent measures of educational attainment?

Figure 10.5
Selected examples of language tests used with children with SEN in the UK

General language scales

Reynell Developmental Language Scales III – The University of Reading Edition (RDLS III) (Edwards et al. 1997). While based on the earlier versions of the scale, this revision is effectively a new instrument. This is a norm-based test for children aged 18 months to 7 years comprising an expressive scale and a comprehension scale. Toys and a picture book are used in both scales. The comprehension scale examines a range from responses to single words (the child points to toys named by the examiner) to drawing inferences (the child points to people in a complex picture of a burger bar in response to questions such as 'Who's being naughty?' and 'Whose daughter is having a birthday party?') The expressive scale also starts with single words (the child names familiar objects which the examiner presents one at a time). The scale ranges up to advanced language skills where, for example, the child is required to retell a story and is scored for using complex sentences (i.e. at least one main clause plus one other clausal structure). The scales are intended to 'reflect current knowledge about normal language development and language impairment and the way in which language may be conceptualised' (Edwards *et al.* 1997: 2).

Other general language scales in use include the Clinical Evaluation of Language Fundamentals (CELF) and the Wechsler Objective Language Dimensions (WOLD). Both

Figure 10.5
(*cont'd*)

are based on well established American scales and have been standardized in the UK (Wiig 1988; Rust 1995). The WOLD is narrower in scope but includes a writing task and can be interpreted alongside other scales in the Wechsler family, including the WISC.

Speech development and discrimination

Auditory Discrimination and Attention Test (Morgan-Barry 1988). This test aims to assess the ability to discriminate between sounds. The child is presented with a series of pictures that illustrate pairs of words that differ in a single phoneme. After some preparation the examiner says one of the two words, and the child has to indicate the relevant picture.

Edinburgh Articulation Test (Anthony et al. 1971). This test aims to assess speech-motor articulation skills. Children aged 3–6 years name 41 familiar pictures such as 'bridge' and 'train'. Their responses are evaluated for articulatory accuracy. Errors are analysed quantitatively and qualitatively to produce a detailed analysis of the overall maturation of articulatory skills.

Listening (receptive) comprehension

British Picture Vocabulary Scale (BPVS) (Dunn et al. 1982). In this test of listening vocabulary the child is presented with a series of pages on which four line drawings are shown. For each page the examiner says a single word that names the object or action depicted in one of the drawings. The child is required to point to that drawing.

Test for Reception of Grammar (TROG) (Bishop 1989). Another test in which each item requires the child to select one out of four line drawings. The examiner reads a sentence, and the child has to understand a targeted grammatical construction in order to choose the correct illustration. The complexity and difficulty of the grammatical contrasts increases steadily across 20 blocks of items.

Expressive language

Renfrew Language Scales: Bus Story Test (Renfrew 1997). This is a norm-referenced, screening test for children aged 3–8 years. It evaluates children's narrative speech: 'the ability to give a coherent description of a series of events'. The examiner tells the child a story about a naughty bus which runs away from its driver, showing a booklet of pictures that illustrate the story. The child is then required to retell the story referring to the pictures as they go. A tape of the session is scored for information, sentence length and subordinate clauses.

Pre-verbal language development

Symbolic Play Test: Second Edition (Lowe and Costello 1988). This test is designed to assess early (pre-verbal) concept formation and symbolization by children aged 1–3 years. The child plays with miniature toys that represent everyday objects. An evaluation is made of their level of thinking about the symbolic meaning of the toys, and this is the basis of an estimate of their language potential.

Meetings and interviews
If meetings are arranged for the purpose of language assessment (the second option in the list at the beginning of this section), there are choices as to how they will be conducted. A meeting can be set up as:

- a 'natural' conversation;
- an interview in which the adult takes the initiative most of the time; or
- an examination in which there is a repeated pattern of the adult initiating, the child responding, and the adult evaluating that response.

It is often assumed that an unstructured interview will generate a more authentic sample of a person's language than a 'formal' or structured interview, or a test. However, it has been shown that even an unstructured interview obtains only a limited sample of a person's linguistic repertoire (Perrett 1990). It may sometimes provide satisfactory data for the assessment of a person's competence in phonology and syntax (though there is evidence that children may produce syntactically more complex language in other situations – e.g. Kenner *et al.* 1996). It may enable a judgement to be made about the ability to use words to convey meaning and to understand what others mean in a limited context (competence in semantics). But it is an atypical social situation, and it will not provide useful information about pragmatic competence, conversational competence or sociolinguistic competence. For example, it is not normally possible to use an interview to assess a person's ability to control conversation, to initiate topics or to assume responsibility for the continuation of a verbal exchange. Suggestions to interviewers about conducting the process more sensitively 'cannot address those unchanging and unchangeable characteristics of the interview as a cultural event in which there is an uneven distribution of power and control' (Perrett 1990: 236). Interviewing has a role in language assessment, but it is a limited role.

Observation and recording of the use of language in 'natural' settings
For the reasons given above, many researchers have advocated collecting language samples in 'natural' settings. There are then further issues to be considered about the context. Will it be the classroom, elsewhere in school, the neighbourhood or the child's home? Will it be a formal or informal setting? Will the conversant(s) be familiar or unfamiliar to the child, and will they be other children, or adults, or both? There is a good deal of evidence that contextual factors of this kind have a major impact on the amount, the quality and the maturity level of a child's expressive language (e.g. Kenner *et al.* 1996). Everyday classroom language is often dominated by the teacher and takes the form of a stylized exchange of questions and answers (Edwards and Westgate 1994; Jefferies and Donlan 1994). This tends to elicit a restricted sample of a child's language repertoire. For example, the length of children's utterances may be reduced by as much as two thirds (Shields and Steiner 1973). In an inner-city nursery class, Kenner *et al.* (1996) demonstrated that a 4-year-old girl whose first language was Gujerati showed a more mature command of language in 'pretend play' with a friend than in a conversation about a colourful picture book led by a familiar teacher. Similar

Table 10.2 The impact of different types of question or comment from a teacher on children's verbal responses

Type of initiation	Mean length in words of child's utterance
Asking children to project into situations or predict outcomes	2.3
Questions on the overt content of the material used (e.g. books, play materials)	2.4
Asking children to give information or knowledge from outside the class	3.2
Questions on the implicit content of the material used	3.3
Asking children to recall personal experiences	5.1
Asking children to clarify what they have said	5.1
Offering children an opportunity to contribute	6.1
Asking children to give an opinion	6.8

Source: Adapted from Jefferies and Donlan (1994).

findings have been reported by many other investigators (e.g. Tizard and Hughes 1984, who contrasted young girls' extensive conversations with their mothers at home with more restricted exchanges with adults in a nursery).

Two concerns seem to impinge on teachers, leading them to dominate and inhibiting them from creating a more productive/fertile environment for a two-way conversation. One factor is a concern to educate – to extend children's knowledge of the topic being discussed and to help them towards formal correctness. The other concern is to maintain control. A more open approach to classroom talk might, it is feared, put at risk the teacher's ability to deliver planned thematic material, to keep the session to time and to maintain expected forms of order within the group.

Working in six Primary 2 classes in Scotland Jefferies and Donlan (1994) have shown that even small changes in what a teacher says can lead to a doubling of children's verbal responses (see Table 10.2). However, some have argued that changes of this kind will not be enough. The development of a culture of conversation requires a more radical rethink of classroom conventions at least for some of the time (Clay 1998, Ch. 2). Some of the 'rights' that a teacher may choose to give up are suggested by Edwards and Westgate (1994):

- to begin and end the encounters;
- to ask the questions and evaluate the answers;
- to allocate all the turns at speaking which they do not claim themselves;
- to provide a framework within which both they and their pupils operate.

Their approach to the study of classroom talk envisages:

the possibility that more 'open', untraditional patterns of communication may be recognised in the extent to which they [children] move towards the conversational end of the continuum of speech systems. The point is not that classroom talk 'should' resemble conversation, since most of the time for practical purposes it cannot, but that institutionalised talk (such as talk for instructional purposes) shows a heightened use of procedures which have their 'base' in ordinary conversation.

(Edwards and Westgate 1994: 116)

One of the occasions when this approach will be desirable in a classroom will be when speech samples are being sought to evaluate the language proficiency of a child at risk.

The key principles are that:

- the language should be sampled as unobtrusively as possible in situations that occur naturally in the classroom (or, if necessary, in contrived situations that *feel* natural);
- the context and the participants in the conversation should be familiar to the child;
- the language that is used should relate meaningfully to the situation and conform to the manner in which that language is normally used.

As a result, the assessment will be based on the child's use of language for 'real, purposeful communication'. Working with young children, Kenner *et al*. (1996) recognized that large-scale taping and transcription would be an impossible addition to teachers' workloads. They advocated spending short stretches of time in the role-play area with a pocket audiorecorder. With this approach it is important to make brief notes of the context at the time, as the tape can be difficult to interpret without them. Those working with older pupils have recorded talk in working groups without an adult present (Edwards and Westgate 1994).

The collection of samples of children's language is only the first stage of assessment. It is then necessary to evaluate what these samples show about whether their language is developing uniformly and in line with their developmental stage. At best the analysis should provide a basis both for comparison with developmental norms and for identifying areas of difficulty and planning intervention. The Bristol Language Development Scales (Gutfreund *et al*. 1989) exemplify a (relatively) teacher-friendly approach to this task. The scales were based on longitudinal studies of the language at home of 128 children between the ages of 15 months and 5 years. The analysis requires a sample of about 100 representative utterances (e.g. 30 minutes' language in six 5-minute periods) with accompanying commentary on the ongoing situation in which they occurred. The analysis (which is supported by thorough guidance in the manual) covers pragmatic, semantic and syntactic competence. A more specialized approach to the analysis of children's syntactic competence may be found in the Language Assessment, Remediation and Screening Procedure (LARSP) (Crystal *et al*. 1989). Two questions arise with such materials:

- Is the model of language development that is used valid and relevant for the purposes for which the assessment is planned (e.g. will it lead to helpful suggestions for intervention)?
- Will the analysis be reliable (e.g. would two different examiners obtain closely similar results) (cf. Ball 2000)?

Drawing on the observations of those who live and work with the child
It seems then that for many purposes test situations elicit too limited a sample of a child's language repertoire, while the language recorded in natural settings offers so rich a sample that it is time-consuming and complex to analyse. Would it be a more effective and economical strategy if language assessment drew on the observations of those who live and work with the child? In this, as in other areas, it has been shown that parents can be reliable reporters about their children's development (Cunningham and Sloper 1984). The accuracy of the reporting of parents (and of those who work with a child regularly, such as care workers and class teachers) will increase if the questions they are asked are precise and systematic. The most effective strategy appears to be to use a structured interview that focuses on current developmental changes. An example is the Pragmatics Profile of Everyday Communication Skills designed for children aged 0–10 years (Dewart and Summers 1995). Separate sections concern:

- a range of communicative functions that children may express, such as requests for an object or for information;
- the way they react and respond to communication from others;
- the way they interact with other people and participate in conversation;
- the way their communication varies depending on context.

Bishop (1998) developed the Children's Communication Checklist for use with teachers and speech and language therapists. Her aim was to offer a tighter assessment framework than is provided in the Pragmatics Profile of Everyday Communication Skills, with full information on reliability and validity. Another example of a structured approach to collecting systematic information from those who live and work with a child is the Pre-Verbal Communication Schedule which focuses on the communication skills of children with SLD or PMLD who cannot speak (Kiernan and Reid 1987). It will be evident that all such materials depend crucially on the observation skills and memory of the informant and the interviewing skills of the individual who is collecting the information: the record is at two removes from the child.

Evaluating the language proficiency of children learning EAL

When a child is bilingual, the question arises: Which language is dominant – i.e. which one are they more proficient in or which one do they prefer to use? In some states of the USA questions about 'language balance' or 'language dominance' have had great practical importance, because there has been a mandatory requirement that a child should be educated through their dominant language at least for a transitional period. In these circumstances it has been common to use a test to determine language dominance. For example, investigators will try to discover whether children give word associations more quickly in one language than in the other. The major problem with such tests is that a person may be more proficient with their first language in some domains of conversation (e.g. talking about cooking or about family relationships) and more proficient with their second language in other domains (e.g. talking about science or national history). Particularly for children moving between one language community at home and another language community at school the concept of language dominance may oversimplify the picture of their use of languages across settings (Valdes and Figueroa 1994; Baker 1996).

It is possible to obtain a more complex picture of children's patterns of language use by making enquiries of those who live and work with them in different settings. It is also possible to ask the children themselves. Beech and Keys (1997) developed a Language Preference Questionnaire for research purposes, while Baker (1996: 20–1) proposed a more comprehensive set of questions which do not ask about the child's preferences but about what actually happens. He added friends to the list of family members who are commonly identified as potential informants (cf. Activity 10.3). He also discriminated among many different settings, as Table 10.3 shows. Note that, compared to the abridged version shown in Table 10.3, there are seven other categories of person and seven other categories of situation in the full tables. The language alternatives would be varied to suit the individual child.

How should such data be analysed? A simple counting approach can be misleading. Baker and Hinde (1984) pointed out that, even if many items are ticked for a particular language (Welsh, for example), that language might still be used infrequently. This could happen if, for example, the child's mother who is there all the time speaks English but her father who is regularly away at sea speaks Welsh, as do other relatives on his side of the family whom the child sees rarely. In the Bilingual Language Assessment Record, which was developed in Leeds, Haworth and Joyce (1996) focused on children's observed skills in using their two languages as well as the frequency of their exposure.

What is the most effective way of evaluating children's development of EAL? Some have argued for the use of English language scales that are specifically designed for this purpose. This is the norm in many states of Australia and the USA where more resources have been put into achieving consistency and clear links to the school curriculum and classroom practice (Leung 1996; Cameron and Bygate 1997). The official English view in recent years has been that it is possible and preferable to integrate the assessment of children learning EAL with that of all other children by assessing their progress in English within the framework of the National Curriculum English levels (Ofsted 1997a; QCA 2000a). Whatever strategy is adopted for pupils learning EAL in general may not necessarily fully meet the needs of those showing learning difficulties. In their case assessment has to be sufficiently detailed and precise to discriminate well within the early stages of progress and to highlight uneven patterns of development. The

Table 10.3   Extracts from Baker's Language Background Scale

In which language do the following people speak to you?

	Always in Spanish	*In Spanish more often than English*	*In Spanish and English equally*	*In English more often than Spanish*	*Always in English*
Friends in the classroom					
Friends in the playground					
Friends outside school					

Which language do you use with the following?

Watching TV or videos					
Religion					
Cassettes/CDs/ records/					
Earning money					
Shopping					

Source: Baker (1996).

information available through statutory National Curriculum English assessment and unstructured classroom observation is not likely to achieve these objectives. Cameron and Bygate (1997) have argued that the most effective strategy would be to construct SATs and procedures around regular classroom tasks. They consider that this would strengthen the relationship between assessment and classroom activities, and between assessment results and classroom performance.

A curriculum-related approach has many advantages over those approaches which explicitly or implicitly make comparisons with age-related monolingual norms. In Chapter 7 we introduced an approach to CBA that involves analysing, among other things, how far classroom talk is 'context-embedded' or 'context-reduced'. You can find examples of the application of this framework to evaluating children's responses to different types of linguistic demand in Godfrey and Skinner (1995), Robson (1995, 1996) and Barrados (1996).

If there is disagreement around the assessment of children's progress in EAL, the situation regarding the assessment of children's home languages is even more problematic. A recent review found that there is little published work on the assessment of home language for children learning EAL who have learning difficulties

(Cline and Shamsi 2000). There have been some descriptive accounts of approaches to assessment and recording that are adapted to the needs of those working with children who may have SEN (Mattes and Omark 1984; Hall 1995; Haworth and Joyce 1996). However, while these approaches have significant advantages over the casual methods that are more commonly used, none of them is based on a programme of systematic research, and none takes full account of the range of language varieties encountered in UK schools. In conclusion, the assessment of the full bilingual language competence of children with EAL who appear to have learning difficulties can be seen to have many facets. While progress has been made with some aspects of the task, there is substantial outstanding development work in other areas needed.

Problems that occur in the development of communication skills

There is no certainty about how many people may experience speech and language difficulties during childhood. A number of surveys have been carried out but they have used different definitions of what constitutes a problem, have surveyed different professional observers and have sampled different age groups (Webster 1988; Winter 1999; Law and Tamhne 2000). As a result estimates vary greatly. It is agreed that preschool children show a relatively high incidence of problems and that the rate drops by school entry. Law and Tamhne (2000: 42) concluded from an extensive review of the literature that:

- conservative estimates are that 1–2 per cent of children have communication difficulties at some stage, but 'well-designed studies suggest that as many as 7 per cent of children may have difficulties which warrant attention';
- children whose communication difficulties are still in evidence at the time when they start school entry are at risk of subsequent educational problems, but the position is much less clear for younger children;
- while it is true that a large number of children who show early speech and language difficulties overcome them without specialist intervention, early delays should still be considered 'a risk factor both for subsequent speech and language difficulties and for other schooling and social problems, a risk which needs to be taken seriously'.

Webster (1988) focused on the (less common) severe and specific language problems and concluded that they develop in about 1 child per 1000. Boys are twice as likely to experience problems as girls (Donaldson 1995). Possible sources of difficulty include physical impairment, neurological impairment and social and emotional factors. The potential problems are diverse, and there has often been controversy about how they can most usefully be classified (Crystal and Varley 1998, Ch. 5). For example, it is common to differentiate between *receptive difficulties* (where the problems mainly arise when children are trying to understand what is said to them) and *expressive difficulties* (where the problems mainly arise around speaking and writing). But these two major processes are

linked, and children with severe difficulties often have problems in both areas –
receptive and *expressive*.

In a recent study of professionals' perceptions of children attending language
units, Crutchley *et al.* (1997b) employed a simple strategy of functional description.
Teachers and other professionals who worked regularly with the children were asked
to state whether or not their pupils had each of the following types of difficulty:

- *Articulation*: problems with pronunciation which appear to have a physical basis
  (e.g. poor muscle control).
- *Phonology*: problems with pronunciation which do not appear to have a phys-
  ical basis.
- *Syntax*:* Problems in putting words together to form multi-word sentences or
  understanding complex sentences.
- *Morphology*:* Problems using inflections and forming a word by derivation
  from another word.
- *Semantics*:** Difficulties with word meaning.
- *Pragmatics*:** Problems over the use of language in social contexts.

In this section we will discuss three patterns of speech and language difficulty
in more detail:

- the difficulties that develop in association with other disabilities;
- specific language impairment;
- problems of communication deriving from emotional and social difficulties.

Difficulties of language acquisition that develop in association with other disabilities

Speech and language problems are often found when a child has another disabling condition. Infants learn language by hearing it used by others, seeing and
understanding the context in which it is used, and experimenting with the sounds
they can make themselves. In Chapter 13 we will discuss how that process is
affected when children cannot adequately hear what is said to them. The development of language will vary with changes in other elements in the process too.
Examples include:

- if the language input children receive is limited (e.g. in conditions of extreme
  deprivation or neglect);
- if they are congenitally blind and so cannot draw on the visual clues that most
  infants use to make sense of the speech they hear;
- if they have severe physical disabilities and so cannot use their vocal apparatus
  to make the sounds they wish to try out.

---

*   These two are often linked because it is thought that morphological difficulties are
    associated with a problem over semantics.
** These two are also often linked, and the term 'semantic-pragmatic disorder' is com-
    monly used.

Table 10.4 Errors in initial consonants of words spoken by young blind children

	Sounds with visible articulation	Sounds without visible articulation
% errors of 3 blind children	41	51
% errors of 3 sighted children	21	52

Source: Adapted from Mills (1993).

The variability in the process does not necessarily mean that children in these situations operate to a different set of principles of language acquisition. It may rather be that the normal processes of learning become adapted to meet their needs. They will exploit the resources and mechanisms that they have at their disposal (or are given by adults) and use them to compensate for any deficiency in the input they receive or in their ability to use the strategies open to most children. We will illustrate this with two examples from work with blind children and one example from work with children with physical disabilities.

The first example concerns research on delays in phonological development in some blind children (Mulford 1988; Mills 1993). The conclusions reached in this line of research have been summarized as: '. . . blind children may be slightly delayed in learning those sounds that have clear visual articulation. However, older blind children show normal use of speech sounds, suggesting that blind children in due course can make use of acoustic information to correct their substitutions and to achieve standard adult pronunciation' (Perez-Pereira and Conti-Ramsden 1999: 70) (see Table 10.4).

Consider a second example relating to blind children. A distinctive feature of the early language development of blind children is a tendency to imitate whole phrases from others and use them for some time in a stereotyped form before analysing and segmenting them into their constituent parts. All young children do this, but blind children appear to do it more often than most and for a higher proportion of the language input they hear. Some commentators (e.g. Brown *et al.* 1997) have interpreted their style as 'autistic-like' and have suggested that it may arise because congenitally blind children are denied visual clues to other people's attitudes towards the world they share. Unlike autistic children they do eventually overcome this obstacle, but it takes them longer to do so than most unimpaired sighted children. Other commentators have rejected analogies with autism and stressed that the children 'arrive at a similar endpoint following different routes' (Perez-Pereira and Conti-Ramsden 1999: 134). This highlights the challenge for researchers and teachers of interpreting differences between patterns of language development shown by children with SEN and the patterns shown by the majority of children.

For some children with very severe physical disabilities that option is not open. They do not have the necessary motor control to generate intelligible speech. There is a tendency for children in this position to slip into a role of a passive spectator and never learn to communicate actively with others. In recent years the development of *augmentative and alternative communication systems* (AAC) has created the opportunity to prevent this happening. Various codes such as Rebus and Bliss symbols have been evolved, and technological advances allow children who can manage only the slightest of movements under conscious control to communicate successfully. So there has been a tendency to think of the challenge simply as a physical one (what kind of apparatus can the child operate?) and an intellectual one (what kind of code can the child learn?). But, like other language users, those employing AAC need also to develop versions of pragmatic and conversational competence. Light (1989) suggested that AAC users need eventually to develop four aspects of communicative competence:

1 *Linguistic competence*: adequate mastery of the native language (vocabulary and grammar) plus the code (e.g. signs or symbols) required to operate the augmentative communication system.
2 *Operational competence*: mastery of technical skills required to operate the system – i.e. the motor and cognitive skills required to signal a message or to operate specific device features (pointing, signing, visual scanning, operating switches, controlling cursors, editing, etc.).
3 *Social competence*: knowledge and skill in the social rules of communication (e.g. making appropriate eye contact, sharing the balance of talking and listening) and using communication for a range of different purposes (social chat, making requests, responding to others, contradicting people, etc.)
4 *Strategic competence*: flexibility in order to adapt communicative style to suit the receiver (e.g. signing more slowly to strangers, turning up the volume on the communication aid in a noisy room) or learning how to correct misunderstanding or to extend the conversation (e.g. if a child cannot explain something clearly on his touch talker he might have a message that says, 'Please hold up my Bliss chart. I'd like to explain something').

MacDonald and Rendle (1994) summarized this communicative competence as encompassing knowledge and skills in the use of tools of communication together with functional knowledge and judgement in interaction. They provide a detailed account of a programme of intervention designed to help four cerebral palsied 2-year-olds to become effective communicators in a range of situations.

Specific language impairment

Some children achieve normal milestones in most aspects of development but show specific difficulties in relation to speech and language – specific language impairment (SLI) or language disorder. In the past this was often diagnosed by excluding other possible causes of language difficulty one by one. A child's difficulties might be described as SLI if it could be shown that they were *not* caused by:

Figure 10.6
Defining language
disorder by
inclusion
Source: Lees and
Urwin (1997: 15).

> A language disorder is that language profile which, although it may be associated with a history of hearing, learning, environmental and emotional difficulties, cannot be attributed to any of these alone, or even just the sum of these effects, and in which one or more of the following is also seen:
>
> 1 a close, positive family history of specific difficulty in language development;
> 2 evidence of cerebral dysfunction, either during development or by the presence of neurological signs;
> 3 a mismatch between the various subsystems of language in relation to other aspects of cognitive development;
> 4 a failure to catch up with 'generalized' language help.

- hearing loss;
- general learning difficulties;
- environmental factors;
- emotional problems (Lees and Urwin 1997: 14).

In this respect the category bore some similarities to dyslexia (see Chapter 11). For example, the operational criteria adopted by one research team included 'performance IQ of 85 or above' (Stark and Tallal, cited by Bishop 1997).

Recent studies have emphasized that SLI can be associated with a wide range of factors. The course of its development and the patterns of behaviour associated with it are both complex and heterogeneous. It has therefore been argued (as in the case of dyslexia) that it is more helpful to define it by inclusion. In the example given in Figure 10.6, Lees and Urwin (1997) build on their account of exclusionary definitions cited above.

Recent research has thrown doubt on the value of another distinction that was traditionally given weight in the analysis of SLI – the distinction between expressive disorders and receptive disorders. The problem is that, first, most children with SLI turn out to have comprehension problems if assessed carefully and, second, those comprehension problems turn out to be complex and heterogeneous. So distinguishing between children with SLI who have an expressive-type disorder and children with SLI who have a receptive-type disorder does not take one much further forward (Bishop 1997, Ch. 2). However, increasing attention is being given to a subgroup of children with SLI who present a distinctive profile in everyday life and appear to have distinctive outcomes in education and therapy – children with semantic-pragmatic difficulties (SPD). They speak fluently in sentences that are well-formed syntactically, using the phonological system accurately. Yet they do not communicate well, because what they say does not follow on from what came before in the conversation. When young they often simply echo what is said to them. They seem to understand short phrases and individual words but not connected discourse. This pattern of difficulties is clearly recognizable in the classroom but progress in response to therapeutic intervention is found to be very slow.

Speech and language therapists play a key role in interventions for children with SLI, often working closely with teachers. (For a discussion of strategies for collaboration see Wright and Kersner 1998.) Current educational provision (which generally caters for a heterogeneous group of children with language difficulties) ranges from integrated teaching in mainstream classes through part-time, on-site language units to residential special schooling. The latter option is now generally restricted to the children with the most extreme difficulties, and follow-up studies in adulthood show variable outcomes (Haynes 2000). For the children with less extreme problems who attend language units in main-stream schools the aim is usually to make a successful transition to full-time attendance in an ordinary class within a specified period. Yet in a recent survey, Botting *et al.* (1998) showed that nearly two thirds of monolingual children in language units in Key Stage 1 continued in a language unit after the end of Year 2. There is a need for longitudinal research to follow the educational careers of children with SLI who spend a period in a language unit. Meanwhile it is important to plan carefully for the transition from such units to full-time attendance in mainstream classes (Nelson 1998). Activity 10.4 gives you the opportunity to consider what plans you would make to prepare for a particular child's transition.

Language difficulties among children learning EAL

The only language difficulties experienced by most bilingual children arise simply because they are living in a mainly monolingual society. Their competence in their first language does not help them to communicate with most of the people whom they meet, yet there is only limited provision for supporting them to learn their second language. They do not have SEN, and readers who wish to learn more about how they can best be supported are referred to other texts (Gibbons 1991; Blackledge 1994; Gravelle 1996).

Even so, it is inevitable that just as some monolingual children have severe difficulties over speech and language, a small minority of bilingual children will experience similar difficulties. There would have been problems even if they had only been learning one language. Almost certainly there are significant problems in their first language as well as in their second. But in their case the recognition of the problem in a nursery or at school may be delayed because of confusion among those working with them (Ofsted 1997a). Ethnic differences in rates of referral for language delay have varied over time. At an early stage African-Caribbean children were overrepresented in such referrals (Roberts 1984; Inner London Education Authority 1985). Local surveys reviewed by Winter (1999) suggest that children from linguistic minority backgrounds now tend to be referred to speech and language therapists when they are older, on average, than monolingual children with the same problems (Winter 1999: 86). In a national survey of children in language units Crutchley *et al.* (1997a) found that bilingual pupils in the units tended to have more severe difficulties than their monolingual peers and to progress less quickly.

ACTIVITY 10.4   Planning the future of a child attending a language unit

Peter (aged 6) was born prematurely. His development has been normal except for language skills. His motor coordination is good, and he relates to other children and to adults in a friendly and trusting way. The only concern about his social adjustment is that, when he is frustrated over a communication problem, he will sometimes have a temper tantrum. Comparing him to his older sister and brother, his mother says: 'He is no different from them really. They used to have tantrums sometimes at his age. But he has them more often because he gets frustrated more often.' In the language unit the tantrums are closely monitored and controlled. The staff take avoiding action when they can see frustration building up. The learning support assistant says: 'We can usually head it off.'

The language unit is located in an infant school, and, like all the pupils there, Peter is a member of an ordinary class as well as of the unit. He starts each day in his Year 2 classroom where he sits quietly through circle time in a state that the class teacher describes as 'all right but disengaged'. He has made progress in comprehension and use of language since entering the unit. He now follows almost all procedural instructions from teachers without relying on checking what other children are doing. He will respond to questions with one- or two-word answers in a group setting and can often produce fuller sentences in conversations on his own with adults in the unit. He has a small word recognition vocabulary in reading and a basic grasp of number concepts. He has not participated in the Literacy and Numeracy Hour routines in the ordinary classroom.

Peter's parents wish him to transfer at the end of Year 2 to the school near their home which his siblings attend and where his mother is a governor. They do not want him to transfer to the junior school unit which is located in a school at the other side of town, distant from his home. It is planned that he will soon begin to spend each morning in a Year 2 class in the school requested by his parents. His time will gradually build up so that by the end of Year 2 he should be attending that school full-time with continued support from a speech and language therapist. At this stage funding has been approved for a learning support assistant to work with him each morning in his new school.

How would you suggest that the unit teacher, the class teacher and the new learning support assistant plan for these changes? What are the key challenges to be addressed? What preparations will facilitate a good start, and what continuing support will build on the progress that has been made at the unit?

There has been relatively little coverage of ethnic, linguistic and cultural diversity in the literature on language difficulties and disorders. An examination of the subject index in three recent UK textbooks failed to identify any entries for 'ethnicity', 'bilingualism' or 'culture' (Donaldson 1995; Lees and Urwin 1997; Crystal and Varley 1998). There is, however, increasing interest in the issue among speech and language therapists evidenced by conferences (Martin 1994) and surveys of professional practice (Winter 1999). Guidance on assessment is offered with increasing confidence (Madhani 1994), and the issue is beginning to be covered routinely in at least some texts (Martin 2000).

One source of potential confusion is that some children develop their first language (L1) normally until they start to learn their second (L2). There may then be arrested development of L1 or even some language loss as they use L2 more and more for everyday purposes as well as at school. Children can be misdiagnosed as having specific language impairment if they are then perceived as having difficulties in both languages. Schiff-Myers (1992) argued that this error will be avoided if enough is learned about their early language history. In line with commentators quoted above she suggested that this should include:

- a description of the form and nature of the language(s) used in the home both by caretakers and by the child;
- the age and conditions under which the child began to learn English (probing to check whether this might have occurred before proficiency in the L1 was fully established);
- the ages at which the child achieved linguistic developmental milestones in the L1 before being exposed to L2;
- family contacts with their country of origin;
- the motivation to become or remain proficient in each language (which will be affected by attitudes in the home, the school and the community towards the child's home language and culture).

A further source of uncertainty is that phonological and linguistic demands vary between languages. This means that something which would not be problematic if a child were learning one language may lead to difficulties if they are learning another. For instance, a Chinese child who confuses tones will experience semantic and syntactic confusions that would not occur in English, because Chinese is a language in which syntax is partly signalled by tonal variations, whereas English is not. For example, a tone can change a noun to a verb in Chinese (e.g. 'seed' to 'plant') or determine the direction of an action (e.g. between 'buy' and 'sell') (Zubrick 1992: 135).

The planning of provision for children with SEN who are learning EAL must take account of their language learning needs. For all children learning EAL, support for their language learning will always be crucial to future educational achievement. The need for support will be greater if the child's acquisition of a second language is impaired by SEN. In the past, IEPs have often overlooked this issue. Sometimes, in fact, the arrangements made for special educational provision have moved children away from those areas of the education service in which provision for the teaching of EAL was available. For example, the pupils may have transferred from a primary or secondary school with EAL provision to a special unit that does not have access to specialist EAL staff. It is essential that intervention for SEN is planned in such a way that a child's language needs and cultural needs are fully taken into account. A number of options are illustrated in Table 10.5.

Options C, E and F involve some teaching in L1 as well as L2. Option F, 'bilingual special education', has been developed in the USA but not in the UK. To date, options B and D are much more common, but, where a bilingual language assessment suggests that it is warranted, schools might reasonably aspire to provide options C and E – at least for children from their largest local community

Table 10.5 Additive and interactive teaching options

Option A (additive)	Teaching in L2 of the general school curriculum adapted to meet the child's SEN.
Option B (additive)	Teaching in L2 of the general school curriculum adapted to meet the child's SEN *plus* teaching of L2 on a withdrawal basis or through in-class support.
Option C (additive)	Teaching in L2 of the general school curriculum adapted to meet the child's SEN *plus* teaching of L2 on a withdrawal basis or through in-class support *plus* part-time teaching in L1 of one or more aspects of the general school curriculum.
Option D (additive)	Teaching in L2 of the general school curriculum adapted to meet the child's SEN *plus* teaching of L2 on a withdrawal basis or through in-class support with adaptations to meet the child's SEN.
Option E (additive)	Teaching in L2 of the general school curriculum adapted to meet the child's SEN *plus* teaching of L2 on a withdrawal basis or through in-class support with adaptations to meet the child's SEN *plus* part-time teaching in L1 of one or more aspects of the general school curriculum with adaptations to meet the child's SEN.
Option F (interactive)	Teaching of L1 and L2 through teaching in L1 and L2 on a systematic basis all aspects of the general school curriculum with adaptations to meet child's SEN.

Source: Cline (1997b).

language groups. Gadhok (1994) has argued that the choice of options for a particular child should take account of the *parents'* command of L1 and of English.

It should be recognized that all of the options in Table 10.5, except Option F, represent an 'additive' approach: something required by a minority of children with SEN is added onto the provision that is made for the majority with SEN as a separate extra. Cline (1997b) argued that there are significant risks that the children's experience of school will be fragmented and that opportunities for enhancing learning through consolidation and through the planned interplay of different elements of experience will be lost. The teaching of EAL generally takes that principle into account (Gibbons 1991; Blackledge 1994; Gravelle 1996). But the principle can easily be overlooked in work with bilingual children who have SEN because expertise is often not shared across the SEN and EAL fields. More joint training may overcome this, and structural changes in schools and LEAs may also lead to improved communication between the two groups. As a result it is to be hoped that other 'interactive' options will be developed to add to Option F – options that are practicable in the UK context and achievable by existing staff.

Problems of communication deriving from emotional and social difficulties

Children with SLI can find it extremely frustrating that they cannot communicate easily with the people around them. In the early years they present a higher incidence of behaviour difficulties (Drillien and Drummond 1983). It has been shown by Farmer (1997) and others that the problem is also reflected in difficulties in relationships with peers and that these are most acute in the children with the most severe language difficulties. Farmer (1997: 43) argued that 'children with lower levels of competence with language should be allowed to receive the benefit of positive social interactions in familiar situations and . . . there is a specific need for the development of programmes which concentrate on the development of language skills for social interaction with peers'.

In general, these are secondary difficulties that arise from the child's SLI. Some children, however, develop language skills successfully but are unable to use those skills in the expected way because of emotional and social difficulties. The most distinctive pattern of development of that kind is *selective mutism*. Selectively mute children are able to speak and do speak in some situations (e.g. home), but persist in remaining silent with some other people in some other settings (e.g. school). They often develop effective non-verbal strategies for communicating their needs and getting their own way. While some may appear shy and sensitive, they are often also seen by adults as watchful, stubborn and devious. It is possible to behave in an assertive, even a bold fashion while still not speaking. Adults, including teachers, quite often react with strong feelings of frustration and anger when children in their charge refuse to speak to them. Selective mutism is most frequently reported to develop around 3–5 years as children manage the transition from their family homes to organizational life outside the family in a playgroup, nursery or school. There is sometimes an insidious development of shyness from an early age culminating in persistent selective mutism.

This pattern of development is unusual among language-related problems in that girls become selectively mute at least as frequently, if not more frequently, than boys. However, the phenomenon is rare overall. The best estimate of incidence (Kolvin and Fundudis 1981) is 0.8 per 1000 children. The incidence is probably a little higher in urban areas where there is a high proportion of immigrant or ethnic minority families and in rural areas where there is a high proportion of families living in isolated situations (Cline and Baldwin 1994, Ch. 1). Early reports suggested that selective mutism is strongly resistant to traditional therapeutic strategies and classroom management strategies. But later case studies and reviews have indicated that behavioural methods have a much greater rate of success (Kratochwill 1981; Cunningham *et al.* 1983). 'Stimulus fading' appears to be of particular value (Labbe and Williamson 1984). For example, it might be used to help a young child who talks readily to her mother at home but not to her class teacher at school. She might be helped to develop communication with the teacher by playing with (or reading to) her mother in school. After a number of sessions in which she becomes used to communicating with a familiar person in an unfamiliar setting, the teacher may gradually be 'faded in', and eventually the parent may be 'faded out'. A full account of a linked strategy of assessment and intervention based on stimulus fading may be found in Cline and Baldwin (1994).

Conclusions

In this chapter we have analysed the knowledge and skills that are involved in language proficiency and shown that forms of SEN that are superficially unrelated to language may have a significant effect on how it develops. It is important to identify speech and language difficulties as early as possible, but, precisely because language permeates so much of our thinking and our social interactions, the assessment of language proficiency is a complex task and may proceed by a variety of routes. We outlined different ways in which the development of language and communication may go awry, including SLI and problems of communication deriving from emotional and social difficulties. Under each heading the challenges increase when a child comes from a multilingual background. In the case of children and young people with speech and language difficulties, as in the case of those with SEN generally, the learning environment at school may play a crucial role in facilitating or inhibiting progress.

Chapter 11

Literacy

When you have studied this chapter you should be able to:

1 Describe ways in which pupils with SEN and those learning EAL can derive maximum benefit from the National Literacy Strategy.
2 Appreciate the range of theories that have been developed to account for learning difficulties in literacy and evaluate different approaches to the identification and assessment of dyslexia.
3 Describe methods for assessing: reading accuracy and fluency; the appropriateness of the literacy learning opportunities that have been provided; and pupils' learning progress in literacy.
4 Outline strategies that may be of value for teachers and other professionals working with pupils experiencing learning difficulties in literacy, including pupils learning EAL.

Contents

The literacy curriculum

The National Literacy Strategy

The National Literacy Strategy (NLS) has been described as one of the most ambitious national initiatives for change that primary education in Britain has seen (Ofsted 1999b). It developed from dissatisfaction both with the standards being achieved by pupils and the methods of teaching commonly adopted in primary schools. Hearing individual children read was identified as the major approach used by many primary school teachers in the past to develop literacy skills. By contrast, the NLS requires teachers to place a major emphasis on teaching reading skills directly to the whole class and to small groups.

The NLS was implemented in primary schools in September 1998. Its declared purpose was to improve literacy standards so that by 2002 80 per cent of 11-year-olds would reach the level expected for their age in the Key Stage 2 National Curriculum tests. The NLS consists of two components:

- *The NLS Framework of Learning Objectives*: this provides details of *what* should be taught.
- *The Literacy Hour*: this specifies *how* teaching should be organized and delivered.

The Framework covers the statutory requirements for reading and writing in the National Curriculum. The relevance and contribution of speaking and listening are recognized, although these elements are not separately identified in the Framework. A major emphasis is placed on learning to use a *range* of strategies to access the meaning of a text. Four types of strategy are identified:

- knowledge of context;
- grammatical knowledge;
- word recognition and graphic knowledge;
- phonic (sounds and spelling).

It is suggested that teachers have often given less emphasis to phonic strategies and the importance of directly teaching these skills is emphasized in the Framework particularly in the early stages of learning to read and write (Department for Education and Employment 1998c). It is recognized that the balance between different strategies may differ at different stages of literacy learning. However, the need for pupils to be taught to use the full range of strategies at each stage is emphasized and teaching objectives relating to word, sentence and text level strategies are provided throughout. The importance of this kind of multi-level approach to literacy learning and teaching is now widely accepted following years of debate about the respective merits of top-down text-based approaches and bottom-up phonics-based approaches (Chall 1983; Adams 1990).

The purpose of the Literacy Hour is to promote the direct teaching of key strategies. Figure 11.1 shows the structure of the Hour. Two thirds of the available time is devoted to whole-class work and the teacher is engaged directly

Figure 11.1
The structure of
the Literacy Hour

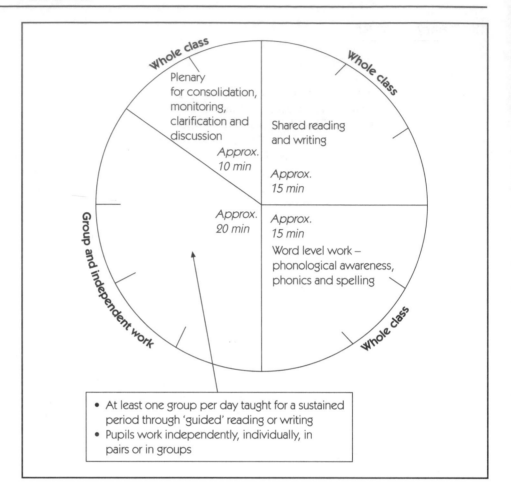

Figure 11.1
The structure of
the Literacy Hour

throughout in instructing pupils. Gross *et al.* (1999b) highlight the behavioural skills needed by pupils if they are to participate successfully in the Literacy Hour – skills such as maintaining attention, waiting their turn to speak, staying on task/ in seat, cooperating in a group. The requirement to be able to work independently for 20 minutes without direct recourse to the teacher demands considerable autonomy and self-discipline. Some have argued that such qualities are unlikely to be developed by an emphasis on direct instruction by the teacher. However, the Framework document states that the intention is not to advocate a simplistic transmission model of teaching but to encourage an interactive, well-paced, discursive style that engages the pupils and stimulates their learning. The wide range of different teaching strategies advocated by the Department for Education and Employment (1998c: 8) include:

- *Direction* (e.g. to ensure pupils know what they should be doing, to draw attention to points, to develop key strategies in reading and writing).

- *Demonstration* (e.g. to teach letter formation and joining letters, how to read punctuation using a shared text, how to use a dictionary).
- *Modelling* (e.g. discussing the features of written texts through shared reading of books, extracts).
- *Scaffolding* (e.g. providing writing frames for shared composition of non-fiction texts).
- *Explanation to clarify and discuss* (e.g. reasons in relation to the events in a story, the need for grammatical agreement when proofreading, the way that different kinds of writing are used to serve different purposes).
- *Questioning* (e.g. to probe pupils' understanding, to cause them to reflect on and refine their work and to extend their ideas).
- *Initiating and guiding exploration* (e.g. to develop phonological awareness in the early stages, to explore relationships between grammar, meaning and spelling with older pupils).
- *Investigating ideas* (e.g. to understand, expand on or generalize about themes and structures in fiction and non-fiction).
- *Discussing and arguing* (e.g. to put points of view, argue a case, justify a preference).
- *Listening to and responding* (e.g. to stimulate and extend pupils' contributions, to discuss/evaluate their presentations).

In September 1999 additional literacy support (ALS) materials were introduced. These are designed for pupils in Years 3 and 4 who achieved Level 1 or Level 2C in the SATs at the end of Key Stage 1. It is a catch-up programme comprising four modules, each of which is designed to be delivered in eight weeks. Each module contains lesson plans, guidance for classroom teaching and homework activities. Children start on Module 1 or 2 depending on their current skill level. The NLS focus on teaching the full range of reading strategies is maintained. While guided reading and writing sessions are commonly taught in the Literacy Hour, supported reading and writing sessions in groups with ALS-trained classroom assistants are often scheduled outside the Literacy Hour, so increasing the time these pupils spend on literacy learning. Initial examination of ALS implementation found that 'eight out of ten sessions led by teaching assistants were at least satisfactory and over half were good' (Ofsted 2000b: 22). It was considered to have had positive effects on reading but not as yet on writing.

Reports on the impact of the literacy strategy overall have been positive. For example, HMI pointed to significant overall improvements in reading standards during the National Literacy Project that laid the basis for the NLS (Ofsted 1998). After the literacy and numeracy initiatives were launched on a national basis a research team from Canada which was invited to carry out an external evaluation concluded that 'as an instance of large-scale reform NLNS [National Literacy and Numeracy Strategy] compares very favourably with other such efforts elsewhere' (Earl *et al.* 2000: 8). There is evidence that standards of achievement in English at Key Stage 2 are improving (Ofsted 2000b). But will the impact be positive for all pupils?

The National Literacy Strategy in a multicultural society

The philosophy of the NLS is that all pupils should be included within the normal structures of the class Literacy Hour. Ofsted (1999b) reported that teachers in most schools had been sympathetic to this, although there was still debate about how it could best be organized and available support deployed most effectively. The Ofsted report highlighted the importance of providing effective support for pupils learning EAL. This might include support with understanding vocabulary and accessing the meaning of the shared texts, sometimes making use of the pupils' home languages – for example, to illustrate features such as tenses. The use of dual language texts was also commended. However, further training needs were identified, with more extensive training on issues relating to EAL needing to be provided by LEA literacy teams. Only half of the EAL specialist staff surveyed had received any training on providing for the needs of EAL pupils during the Literacy Hour. This limited the extent to which their skills could be utilized.

The guidance provided in the NLS Framework document draws teachers' attention to the wide variety of skills and needs which pupils learning EAL may have. The importance in particular of obtaining information about pupils' educational history and their literacy skills in another language is highlighted. Available research evidence supports this advice. Most children who have learned to read beyond a basic level in one language are found to transfer some of their literacy knowledge to the task of learning to read in a second language and make quicker progress in learning to read their second language than would otherwise have been the case (Baker 1996). However, high levels of word reading accuracy in a child's first language will not necessarily mean that reading in English will come easily to them. In many languages the relationships between letters and sounds are more straightforward than they are in English. If a child has a dyslexic-type difficulty with phonological representations, they are likely to experience considerably greater difficulties with reading and spelling in English than in a more regular language such as German (Goswami 1997).

The Department for Education and Employment (1998c) NLS Framework document suggests that there are a number of features of the Literacy Hour that are likely to make it a valuable learning opportunity for pupils whose first language is not English:

- *Content features*: emphasis on careful listening, clear models of spoken English, supported reading and writing and access to formal styles of written English.
- *Process features*: participative emphasis in whole-class and group work, opportunities for intensive and focused teaching in groups or individual support from specialist staff, clear structure of the Hour and the shared context created by the whole-class work.

Cline and Shamsi (2000) suggested that for pupils at the very early stages of learning EAL, the regular Literacy Hour routines provide teachers with important opportunities to observe and evaluate in detail these pupils' strengths and difficulties.

Suggestions have also been offered about ways in which the NLS can be delivered so as to be maximally beneficial for pupils learning EAL. When the Literacy Hour was introduced, a working party of specialist teachers suggested that success in implementing the Framework with children learning EAL would depend on recognizing their need for the following:

- building on previous experience and experiences beyond school;
- comprehensible input with meaning supported by context, visuals and familiarity;
- a positive stress-free environment;
- plenty of active listening time, with respect for a silent period for new beginners;
- good peer role models for oral language and literacy;
- positive reinforcement and modelling of the target language;
- modelling, scaffolding and peer interaction to enable active use of new language as pupils become more fluent and confident;
- an emphasis on communication rather than correction until pupils are confident in English;
- an appropriate level of cognitive demand matched to pupils' abilities (not just their current achievement in English);
- repetition and revisiting language, making connections between different contexts (NALDIC Working Group 1998: 12).

The need for careful monitoring is highlighted by a number of studies which reported lower than average reading scores at the end of Key Stage 1 for children from the Pakistani community as compared to children from African-Caribbean, Indian or white backgrounds (e.g. Leeds City Council Department of Education 1992; Bartlett 1995). In relation to the NLS, HMI included a note of caution in their generally positive evaluation: 'All EAL pupils made progress over the life of the Project, but those who were just becoming familiar with English made less progress and needed more oral work within and outside the Hour; the needs of this group of pupils should be considered carefully when planning the Literacy Hour' (Ofsted 1998: 3). (The full data on this issue may be found in Sainsbury et al. 1998, Table A.2.8.)

Teachers are advised in Department for Education and Employment guidance that they need to distinguish between pupils who have additional language needs and those who also have SEN. Where pupils learning EAL also have SEN it is recommended that class teachers and specialist language staff should work closely with the SENCO to ensure that 'assessments provide opportunities for pupils to demonstrate their learning using all their language skills' (Department for Education and Employment 1998c: 107). This would seem to be an essential general principle of assessment which extends beyond literacy learning and might valuably be included in the revised Code of Practice (Department for Education and Employment 2000a).

The National Literacy Strategy and pupils with SEN

The NLS has a strongly inclusive philosophy for pupils with SEN:

> Many mainstream children with special educational needs, with help and encouragement, will be able to achieve at the level for their age in the National Literacy Strategy, and most will benefit significantly from being involved in classwork with their peers. Where children need to work to different objectives, they should nevertheless be taught with their own class and year group . . . Pupils with identified special educational needs should normally work with their peers within the Literacy Hour. They should only be taken out of the hour to work in parallel when extra support within the Literacy Hour or outside this time is not enough.
>
> (Department for Education and Employment 1998c: 115)

Guidance on teaching the Literacy Hour offers advice about adapting the level of complexity of the questions asked of different pupils so that all are stimulated and engaged. Guidance is also offered on the provision of extra support to help pupils access the lesson – for example, through specially designed materials or communication systems, or by using an assistant.

During the first year of implementation of the NLS, mainstream schools generally included pupils with SEN in the Literacy Hour, rather than withdrawing them (Ofsted 1999b). Targeted support was most often provided during the third part of the hour, when pupils are normally expected to work independently. This support was judged to be most effective when:

- the teaching assistants who provided it had been included in the school's literacy training and had been well briefed by the class teacher;
- the SENCO was involved in planning the work and monitoring pupil progress, providing intensive phonic work to particular SEN pupils and adapting IEPs to relate to NLS objectives.

Gross *et al.* (1999a) argued that the shared reading and writing in the first 15 minutes of the Literacy Hour is beneficial for pupils with SEN. Although the texts are likely to be at a level above that which these pupils can access independently, it was claimed that they can learn a lot from a well structured session where there is sufficient repetition and where teacher questioning directs their attention to aspects of the text appropriate to their current level of achievement and learning needs. Gross *et al.* also addressed a number of questions commonly raised by teachers about the Literacy Hour and pupils with SEN and concluded that:

- Independent activities in the group and independent work session do not have to link with the shared text, so that groups can work on reading schemes and structured catch-up programmes. It is however essential that the work is clearly focused on particular objectives from the NLS Framework. It is also recommended that all children should be as closely linked as possible with the main class topic themes and teaching foci.

- Programmes that take more than 20 minutes per day, such as reading recovery (involving 30 minutes' individual withdrawal work per day), or family literacy (where parents and children work together) can be scheduled in addition to the Literacy Hour. The same would apply to activities that would not fit easily within the Literacy Hour structure such as cross-age peer tutoring.
- While the aim is to teach to the objectives specified for the year and term of the child's age, pupils with SEN may work on objectives from earlier levels, even from a different key stage, so they can acquire a firm foundation of basic literacy skills. Pupils with SEN such as those in Key Stage 2 who still need intensive daily word level work (phonics) can therefore be accommodated.

The NLS has also been widely adopted by special schools, including schools for pupils with SLD and PMLD, with appropriate modifications to address pupil's specific needs (Berger *et al.* 1999). The modelling of strategies and provision of explicit instruction are features that would be expected to be beneficial to pupils who have SEN in both special and mainstream schools. Further discussion of the teaching of pupils with SEN during the Literacy Hour can be found in Hinson (1998), Byers (1999b), Dehaney (2000) and Pietrowski and Reason (2000).

ACTIVITY 11.1   Maximizing the value of the Literacy Hour for Pupils with SEN/learning EAL

In contrast to the optimistic and inclusive thrust of the government guidance, a number of authors have expressed reservations about the value of some features of the NLS. Consider each of the points listed below.

(a) To what extent do these concerns relate to your knowledge/experience of the operation of the Literacy Hour in schools?

(b) What implications would they have had for pupils with SEN and/or pupils learning EAl with whom you have worked?

(c) What might be done to overcome any difficulties identified?

- Solity *et al.* (1999) argued that research in instructional psychology indicates that teaching should initially focus on letter sounds, together with skills in segmenting words into phonemes and in blending phonemes into words. By contrast they pointed out that the NLS also teaches other things early on: letter names, initial and final consonant clusters and the segmentation of words into onsets and rimes (e.g. c/at, sk/ip). It is suggested that this is a lot of information to remember and that teaching different ways in which words can be segmented (into phonemes and into onset/rime divisions) is potentially confusing.
- Solity *et al.* (1999) also argued that research in instructional psychology indicated that it is more effective to teach children through distributed rather than massed sessions. They recommended 3 × 10–15-minute literacy sessions per day, rather than an hour-long session.
- After reviewing research evidence on the impact of teaching phonics, Wyse (2000) proposed that, while there is some justification for the work on phonics in Years 1 and 2, the NLS Framework should be rewritten 'to remove the phonics objectives from Years 3 and 4'. He pointed out that much of the evidence on the value of extended work on phonics 'has been collected in the context of struggling readers' (p. 362).

- Byers (1999b) highlighted a number of challenging questions that had arisen in discussions with teachers of children with learning difficulties. They included: 'Will the focus upon literacy and numeracy skills facilitate the process of inclusion (ensuring enhanced access, perhaps, to an increasingly inclusive society for school leavers) or lead to a hardening of the boundaries between those pupils who can "catch up", thereby helping the Government to meet its challenging literacy target, and those who cannot?' (p. 11).
- Pietrowski and Reason (2000: 52) suggested that it will be valuable that 'the common language of the NLS . . . enables class and support teachers to work together [as] support teachers now have a central role in preparing children for classroom activities through their assessments, targets and additional teaching as necessary. The information provided by support teachers enables class teachers to adjust their teaching to individual needs . . . This way of working assumes, of course, that we have the pre-requisite teacher time, expertise and resources'.
- 'Like their predecessors, they [New Labour] have repudiated all socio-economic explanations for low achievement in literacy, preferring to point to the variation between schools serving similar populations, rather than to the much more substantial variation between the mean scores of schools serving populations of different socio-economic levels' (Dombey 1998: 36).
- 'Why do we read and write? In addition to more mundane purposes, we read to enlarge our understanding of the world and our place in it, to explore other lives, to take pleasure in the virtual reality which we conspire with the author to create, and the language which gives it life. We write to shape our thoughts, to put them in a form which makes them communicable to others, to put our mark on the world. Such conceptions do not inform the Literacy Framework: formalism rules' (Dombey 1998: 39).

Learning difficulties in literacy

Learning difficulties in literacy were identified in the Department for Education and Employment (2000c) SEN Thresholds document issued with the consultation version of the draft revised *Code* as indicators both of:

- general learning difficulties (low levels of attainment across the board) – 'difficulty in acquiring skills (notably in literacy and numeracy) on which much other learning in school depends' (2000c: 13);
- and one of a number of specific learning difficulties (affecting only certain aspects of pupils' learning) – 'low attainment in one or more curriculum areas, particularly where this can be traced to difficulties in some aspect(s) of underlying literacy and/or numeracy skills' (2000c: 18).

Discussion in this chapter will focus on specific learning difficulties in literacy because general learning difficulties were discussed in detail in Chapter 9. Whether children have general or specific learning difficulties, the nature of their problems with literacy learning are found to be very similar (Stanovich and Stanovich 1997). While the literacy content of special programmes for these groups of pupils will be similar, the programmes will differ in other respects. For example, pupils with general learning difficulties will require differentiated work in most other curriculum areas, whereas those with specific learning difficulties are likely to be able to work at the same level as the rest of the class if provided with means of accessing the curriculum and recording their work that are modified to support their literacy difficulties.

Understanding difficulties in literacy

Hw cn u rd ths? 'It muts be fairyl obvouis to aynone rding ths lettre that raedres draw on thier konwledeg of how lagnuaege wroks, their abitily to recgonise wrods on sihgt and then capacity to ues contextual cleus to enabel them to maek senes of what has goen befor and perdict what is cmoing next.'

(Extract from a letter to the *Times Educational Supplement*, March 1991)

Reading the printed word involves working at many levels – at the level of the letter, the word, the phrase, the sentence, the paragraph, the text. For some readers there may be particular problems at word level (e.g. analysing and synthesizing the sounds that are signified by the graphic lines on the page). For others the greatest challenge may be making sense of the content of a text, linking it to earlier experiences and appreciating what type of text it is intended to be (Street 1995). A successful reader applies a complex combination of skills and knowledge to the task – including, at least, visual perception, auditory perception, linguistic knowledge, cultural knowledge, and knowledge about print and communication. But for fluent readers the process is not a conscious one. Learning to read is like learning to ride a bike. You become a skilled reader by automating some processes and carrying them out without conscious attention (e.g. recognizing all letters and most common words) so that you can pay attention to other aspects of what print conveys (e.g. the meaning of the message that the writer intended to communicate) (Oakhill and Garnham 1989). This acquisition of accurate and fluent word reading and spelling is what proves problematic for the majority of children identified as having literacy learning difficulties.

A wide range of different theories have been put forward to account for learning difficulties in literacy. A recent report by the Division of Educational and Child Psychology of the British Psychological Society on *Dyslexia, Literacy and Psychological Assessment* (British Psychological Society 1999) identified ten different types of hypotheses (see Table 11.1). Morton and Frith's (1995) causal modelling framework was used to represent and compare these different approaches. Some of the hypotheses included comprehensive description at each level in the framework and, in addition, modelled causal links between the features included at different levels. Others focused on description at one level of explanation only. A number of these will be discussed further to illustrate some of the most important general considerations in understanding learning difficulties in literacy. Information about the other hypotheses can be found in the British Psychological Society (1999) report.

Table 11.1 Understanding learning difficulties in literacy: theoretical accounts described in the British Psychological Society (1999) report on *Dyslexia, Literacy and Psychological Assessment*

Theoretical account	Reference source to consult for further information	Phonological difficulties implicated
Phonological delay/deficit hypothesis	Frith (1997), Snowling (1998), Stanovich (1988)	Yes
Temporal processing hypothesis	Tallal *et al.* (1997)	Yes
Skill automatization hypothesis	Nicolson and Fawcett (1995)	Yes
Working memory hypothesis	Rack (1994)	Yes
Hypotheses that involve visual processing	Lovegrove (1994), Stein (1994)	No
Syndrome hypothesis	Miles (1993)	Yes
Hypotheses involving intelligence	Turner (1997)	No
Subtype hypotheses	Boder (1973), Bakker (1979)	Yes
Learning opportunities and social context hypothesis	Solity (1996a)	No
Emotional factors hypothesis	Ackerman and Howes (1986), Rourke (1988), Biggar and Barr (1996)	No

The *phonological delay/deficit* hypothesis was identified in the British Psychological Society (1999) report as being particularly important, both because of the broad empirical support which it commands and because of the important role phonology is given in a number of the other hypotheses also. Figure 11.2 shows the core phonological delay or deficit hypothesis. Phonological processing is broadly defined as the ability to process sounds in spoken language. Phonology is that part of language that concerns the sounds of words, rather than their meanings or grammatical structures. The phonological hypothesis has gained particular prominence in recent years and many of its predictions are supported by a wide range of research evidence.

The hypothesis depicted in Figure 11.2 assumes a problem in some aspect of the way in which information is processed by the brain. Frith (1997) has suggested that the area affected may be the perisylvian region of the left hemisphere which is known to be involved in phonological processing (Galaburda 1989; Paulesu *et al.* 1996). At the cognitive level it is hypothesized that the processing problem will cause a weakness in a cognitive component of the phonological system. Frith (1997) points out that such a consequence, although likely, is not inevitable. There may be protective factors or redundancy in the system which allow normal phonological processing to be maintained.

If a weakness in phonological processing does result, this may affect aspects of speaking. Scarborough (1990) showed that children who were later identified as

Figure 11.2
Phonological
delay/deficit
hypothesis
Source: British
Psychological
Society (1999).

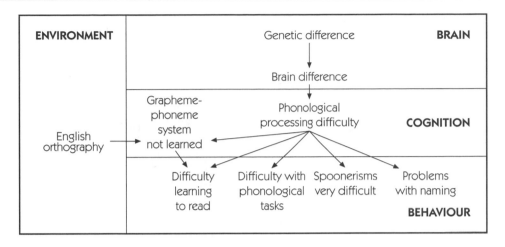

dyslexic showed subtle language difficulties when they were 3 years old. It is also likely to be more difficult for children who have phonological processing problems to establish grapheme-phoneme links and so their acquisition of literacy skills will probably be affected. This is represented at the behavioural level where the model predicts poor reading skills. However, phonological weaknesses are also found to have a number of other effects (see Snowling 1995 for a review). Some of these, like poor phoneme awareness (e.g. being able to tell which sound comes at the beginning of the word, 'cat' or in the middle of the word 'pig'), will also be influenced by knowledge of grapheme-phoneme correspondences and hence by reading skill. Other areas of poor performance resulting from weaknesses in phonological processing, such as poor rapid automatic naming and poor short-term auditory memory, are not likely to be directly influenced by reading ability.

A number of other influential accounts identify different types of difficulty and causative factors, while agreeing that the problems experienced with reading and spelling are due to phonological difficulties. A good example is the *skill automatization hypothesis* (Nicolson and Fawcett 1995). This hypothesis proposes that dyslexic children have difficulties across a range of skills, including phonological skills, when they are required to perform at a fluent, automatic level and are prevented from employing conscious compensation to overcome their difficulties (see Figure 11.3). For example, Nicolson and Fawcett (1995) reported that dyslexic children had difficulty in balancing without wobbling when they were prevented from consciously compensating for their difficulties (either by being given a distracting task or by being blindfolded). At the biological level Nicolson and Fawcett (1994) suggested that a cerebellar abnormality could give rise to a speech fluency problem that disrupts phonological processing, which in turn affects reading and spelling. They hypothesized that dysfunction in the cerebellum or its neural tracts can account for difficulties in areas as different as phonological processing, balance and estimating time.

Figure 11.3
Skill automatization
hypothesis
Source: British
Psychological
Society (1999).

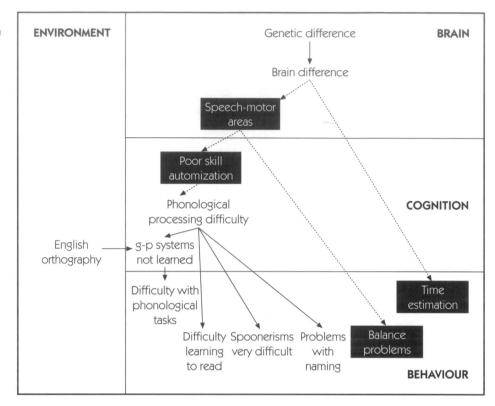

Given the strong evidence linking phonological processing problems with learning difficulties in literacy (Snowling 1998), it is worth noting that both the amount and quality of teaching that is focused on phonics and phonological awareness have been heavily criticized. Ofsted (1999b) reported that initial evaluation just after the NLS was introduced indicated that insufficient attention was being given to phonics teaching, particularly in Years 3 and 4, in as many as half the schools visited. A third of the lessons observed contained no phonics teaching at all. Furthermore, even where a significant phonics component was included, it was rarely taught well. Two terms later, following a major training initiative, overall improvements were observed in both coverage and quality of teaching. Even then, word-level work, of which phonics is a key element, emerged as one of the weakest elements of the NLS. Teaching of word-level objectives was rated 'good' in only half of the lessons observed and rated 'poor' in almost one lesson in five.

The 10 per cent of schools with the lowest reading achievement were identified to receive intensive support when the NLS was introduced. In these schools the phonics teaching was rated unsatisfactory or poor in a quarter of lessons observed, as compared with 1 lesson in 12 in other schools. While other factors may be involved, this data would be consistent with the hypothesis that ineffective teaching had been an important cause of low pupil achievement in these schools.

Figure 11.4
Learning
opportunities and
social context
hypotheses
Source: British
Psychological
Society (1999).

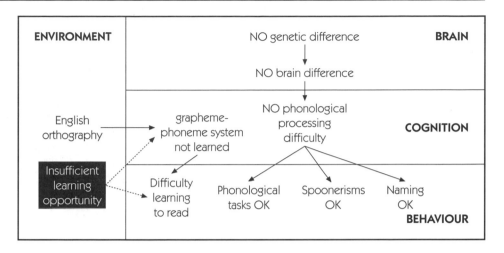

Indeed it was concluded that many teachers lacked the confidence to teach reading and spelling through a systematic phonics approach (Ofsted 1999b).

These findings would seem to relate in particular to the *learning opportunities and social context hypotheses* (see Figure 11.4). These are based on the assumption that poor literacy skills result primarily from limited or inappropriate learning opportunities and experiences, rather than individual processing differences (Solity 1996a). Poor learning progress is attributed to children's school and home-based experiences in learning to read, and attention is focused on environmental interventions which alter aspects of the social context, the learning opportunities and the instruction provided. The assumption is that, whatever their individual differences, children will learn given appropriate teaching.

It is argued that some of the individual differences that are ascribed causal significance in other theories may simply be indicators of consistent and important differences in children's social contexts. Solity (1996a) suggests that the preschool differences in phonological awareness may well reflect differences in parental input, while differences in progress with learning to read could also reflect differences in the effectiveness of the teaching received. While this hypothesis on its own would not be widely accepted as providing a complete account of available research findings, increasing importance has been given in recent years to evaluating the availability of learning opportunities both inside and outside school in understanding children's learning difficulties in literacy. This is particularly evident in the literature on dyslexia.

Defining dyslexia

At least one of the early exclusionary definitions of dyslexia (see Figure 11.5) did show rudimentary awareness of the need to consider the instruction received. The first of these definitions would 'rule out' a child who had never attended

Figure 11.5
Exclusionary
definitions of
dyslexia

A disorder manifested by difficulty in learning to read despite conventional instruction, adequate intelligence and sociocultural opportunity. It depends on fundamental cognitive disabilities which are frequently of constitutional origin.
(World Federation of Neurology 1968 in Critchley and Critchley 1978)

A disorder in one or more of the basic psychological processes in understanding or using language, spoken or written . . . does not include learning problems which are primarily the result of visual, hearing or motor handicaps, or mental retardation or emotional disturbance, or environmental, cultural or economic disadvantage.
(United States Education for All Handicapped Children Act, PL94-142 1975)

Table 11.2   Special classes for children with specific learning difficulties in Inner London in 1984

	No.	African-Caribbean (%)	Asian (%)	English, Scottish, Welsh and Irish (%)	Other (%)
All primary schools	131,415	15.7	11.1	55.9	17.3
Specific learning difficulty classes	300	19.0	2.3	64.7	14.0

Source: Inner London Education Authority (1985).

school, and clearly it would not be necessary to invoke a concept like dyslexia to understand why such a child might not be able to read.

However, both of these definitions also excluded sociocultural factors and this may have placed a hurdle in the way of bilingual children's access to specialist provision. A number of studies have drawn attention to the underrepresentation of bi/multilingual children in provision for dyslexic children. Some have argued that this might well be a consequence of the way in which dyslexia has traditionally been identified. Table 11.2 shows the results of a survey of children attending classes for pupils with specific learning difficulties in literacy in Inner London in the 1980s (Inner London Education Authority 1985). It will be seen that Asian children were underrepresented. The majority of the Asian children in London schools at that time came from families speaking one of the South Asian languages at home – estimated on the basis of Kysel (1986) to be approximately 55 per cent Bengali or Sylheti, 17 per cent Gujerati, 16 per cent Urdu and 13 per cent Punjabi.

Similarly, Curnyn *et al.* (1991) reported that children learning EAL were underrepresented in provision for those with specific learning difficulties in Glasgow during the period 1984–8. The authors pointed out that the data needed to be treated with some caution because of the relatively small numbers involved. However, a follow-up survey of Scottish schools across a much wider area confirmed the pattern of low identification of 'suspected dyslexia' in bilingual pupils (Deponio *et al.* 1999).

A variety of explanations have been advanced to account for this under-identification:

- distortions in the referral process (Graf 1992);
- sources of bias in the content of tests (Miller 1984; Lam 1993);
- inappropriate test administration and interpretation procedures (Desforges *et al.* 1995);
- failure to contextualize the assessment (Cline 1993).

Cline and Frederickson (1999) have argued that traditional ways of defining specific reading retardation and dyslexia may have contributed to the under-representation in provision for pupils with specific learning difficulties/dyslexia of children from minority linguistic or cultural backgrounds, not just through the use of sociocultural factors as a basis for exclusion, but also through the use of intelligence.

Both of the early exclusionary criteria shown in Figure 11.5 contain reference to general intellectual factors, one requiring 'adequate intelligence' and the other excluding children whose intelligence fell within the range designated as indicating 'mental retardation'. From this focus developed the approach to the identification of dyslexia which has been the most prevalent in the UK (Pumfrey and Reason 1991) and the USA (Frankenberger and Fronzaglio 1991) for almost a decade – the use of IQ-achievement discrepancies. It is possible to calculate the discrepancy between a child's actual reading test score and the reading test score which would be predicted for them on the basis of the correlation between reading and IQ test scores in the general population. Tables are available (e.g. Wechsler 1992) that show the statistical probability of different sizes of discrepancy and the percentages of the population in which discrepancies of different sizes occur. The use of various discrepancy criteria for the identification of dyslexia has developed in an attempt to make the deployment of limited public resources apparently objective and accountable through using measurable cut-off points (Ashton 1996).

However, the validity and utility of diagnosing dyslexia on the basis of a discrepancy between IQ and achievement has been heavily criticized and the role of IQ in defining dyslexia strongly questioned (Miles 1996; Share 1996; Stanovich 1996; Tunmer and Chapman 1996). Concerns have been identified in three main areas:

1 There is no clear conceptual basis for drawing a distinction between poor readers with and without an IQ-achievement discrepancy.
2 There are concerns that the discrepancy approach disproportionately disadvantages pupils who are learning EAL.
3 Research has not found empirical support for this distinction in studies of the reading performance, related cognitive skills or response to intervention of the two groups.

While there is a significant correlation between IQ and reading test scores among pupils in general the notion that an IQ score indicates a child's 'potential'

ACTIVITY 11.2   Problems with discrepancy definitions of dyslexia

(a) In this section on defining dyslexia a number of problems with discrepancy definitions of dyslexia are discussed. Summarize each of these in one sentence in the first column below.

(b) Ashton (1996: 134) defends the use of discrepancy definitions by some LEAs in identifying dyslexia on pragmatic grounds: 'the reality is that resources are limited and always will be. It would therefore seem constructive to tackle the issue of prioritising children in terms of severity of need and to try to find solutions to this problem which are seen to be fair . . . whereby LEAs can adjust their criteria for statementing to what they see as a reasonable level'. For each of the problems identified, consider whether or not they still apply if a purely pragmatic approach is adopted. Note your conclusions and reasons in the second column.

Problem identified   Is it still a problem from a pragmatic perspective?

for reading achievement has been challenged by studies of children with low IQs who are good readers (Siegel 1992). The positive response reported to the implementation of the NLS in schools for children with SLD (Berger *et al.* 1999) also suggests that assessed IQ should not be seen as having a causal relationship with reading achievement. While IQ may influence reading achievement, there is evidence of influence in the other direction also. Children with reading problems read less and are therefore less likely to gain the knowledge required by verbal IQ tests. Their verbal IQ therefore often decreases with age (Bishop and Butterworth 1980). By contrast Arnold *et al.* (1987) found that this drop in IQ could be prevented when an intensive intervention programme was provided. These results illustrate that the popular notion of IQ as a measure of innate potential that can set a level of expectation for reading achievement is not supported by the research evidence and may well have been damaging in setting inappropriately low levels of expectation for many children.

It is widely held that IQ scores based on a test administered in English lack reliability and validity for bilingual children whose language proficiency in English is still developing (Ashby *et al.* 1970; Figueroa 1989). When children born abroad were assessed on such tests, the gap between their mean scores and those of indigenous children became smaller the longer they had been in the UK (Ashby *et al.* 1970). Over the 5–7-year period required, on average, for the development of cognitive-academic language proficiency (CALP) in an additional language, IQ tests administered in English underestimate the cognitive skills of children for whom English is an additional language (Cummins 1984). Consequently these children may fail to meet criteria for access to additional resources where these are based on IQ-achievement criteria. Rueda (1989: 124) discussed the disproportionate exclusion of Hispanic students from special services in the USA despite the well documented low achievement of this group and concluded: 'These students may be unable to demonstrate a sufficient ability-achievement discrepancy on standardised norm-referenced measures to qualify for services partly as an artefact of the measurement tools (e.g. English-only IQ tests)'.

Stanovich and Stanovich (1997) review a number of studies which compare two groups of children who have learning difficulties in literacy: those with and those without significant IQ-achievement discrepancies. The two groups are found to have similar problems with non-word reading, with phonological segmentation skills and orthographic processing. They are also found to respond similarly to various educational interventions and show identical growth curves over time both for reading development generally and the component skills of word recognition. Velluntino *et al.* (1998) selected a large group of 6–7-year-olds whose reading test score placed them in the bottom 15 per cent of children of their age and who had a significant IQ-achievement discrepancy. After a term and a half of daily individual tutoring, only 1 per cent of these children were still scoring below the fifteenth centile. The children's IQ score or its discrepancy with their reading score had no bearing on their response to intervention. The results suggested that continuing reading difficulties were due primarily to basic deficits in phonological skills. Evidence from several countries, involving different research designs and age groups, leads to the same conclusion: children who have difficulties with literacy learning perform similarly on measures of reading, spelling and underlying cognitive processes, such as phonological skills, irrespective of the size of their IQ-achievement discrepancy. In other words, 'Individuals with dyslexia are distinguished by their phonologically based decoding disability, not by the presence or absence of a significant discrepancy between IQ and reading' (Moats and Lyon 1993: 289).

From IQ-achievement-discrepancy definitions to definitions based on phonological skills

A number of authors who have reached conclusions similar to those of Moats and Lyon (1993) have extended the argument by suggesting that phonological difficulties should form the basis for defining dyslexia:

> If we accept this characterization of reading disability as a result of a deficit in phonological processing and that this process is independent of intelligence (however defined), then logically we should not need IQ in the definition of reading disability. Instead, we should study phonological processing in the reading disabled and base the definition of reading disability on a measure (or measures) of phonological processing.
>
> (Siegel 1990: 124)

> I contend that reasonable reading of the state of the research evidence suggests that the most parsimonious conclusion is staring the field squarely in the face: If we have decided to keep the term dyslexia in our conceptual lexicon, then all children with problems in phonological coding resulting from segmental language problems are dyslexic.
>
> (Stanovich 1996: 161)

These reasons for adopting a definition of dyslexia based on phonological difficulties are based on conceptual arguments and research evidence. In addition, Frederickson and Frith (1998) hypothesized that an approach to identifying dyslexia which is based on phonological skills should prove to be less culturally biased than one based on IQ testing. They argued that phonological processing skills which are relevant to alphabetic literacy can be developed by exposure to any language and, as phonology is a surface feature of language, 'native-like' familiarity with the phonology of a new language should be developed within a much shorter period than is required to develop the deeper-level processing skills required for CALP (Cummins 1984).

DaFontura and Siegel (1995), working with bilingual Portuguese-Canadian children aged 9–12 years, reported that bilingualism *per se* did not have negative consequences for reading development. Rather, reading difficulties in both languages were strongly related to deficits in phonological processing. Frederickson and Frith (1998) report the results of a study conducted with two groups of 10–12-year-old children: a monolingual English speaking group and a group being educated in English whose first language was Sylheti. Phonological strengths and weaknesses were found to be very similar across the two groups, with bilingual children being neither more nor less likely than monolingual children to be identified as having significant phonological difficulties. In both samples the children whose phonological skills were weakest were the poorest readers.

It would appear that an approach to defining dyslexia which is based on phonology has a clearer theoretical basis, enjoys much stronger support from research and is less culturally biased than methods which involve the use of IQ tests. However, there are still two problems with the use of a phonologically-based definition of dyslexia. The first is that no account is taken of opportunities to learn either reading or phonological skills. Yet research has indicated that some phonological skills, such as the ability to identify the first sound in spoken words, appear to be developed by the process of learning to read. The second is that most, but not all, children who have severe and persistent reading problems show phonological difficulties. Frederickson and Frith (1998) report the results of a study of dyslexic pupils who had marked and long-standing reading difficulties where they identified a subgroup, comprising about 20 per cent of the sample, who showed evidence of unimpaired phonological skills despite below average reading performance. These children would not be identified as dyslexic if a purely phonological approach to classification was implemented.

Descriptive approaches to defining dyslexia

Observations such as these have led some to argue that identifying characteristics should be differentiated from causal factors and that the latter should not be included in a definition of dyslexia (Tonnessen 1997). This was the first condition for a working definition of dyslexia identified by the Netherlands Health Council's Committee on the definition and treatment of dyslexia. Gersons-Wolfensberger and Ruijssenaars (1997) proposed that a working definition should be:

- descriptive with no explanatory elements;
- specific enough to identify dyslexia within the whole of severe reading and spelling problems;
- general enough to allow for various scientific explanatory models and any developments they might undergo;
- operationalizable for the purposes of research;
- directive for statements concerning the need for intervention;
- applicable to the various groups involved.

The British Psychological Society (1999: 5) have proposed the adoption of a working definition of dyslexia which is closely based on that developed in the Netherlands and complies with these conditions:

> Dyslexia is evident when accurate and fluent word reading and/or spelling develops very incompletely or with great difficulty. This focuses on literacy learning at the 'word level' and implies that the problem is severe and persistent despite appropriate learning opportunities. It provides the basis for a staged process of assessment through teaching.

The report proceeds to spell out the implications – that the problem is severe and persistent and has resisted usual teaching methods and additional help at the school-based stages of assessment and teaching advised by the *Code of Practice*. As this definition of dyslexia requires persistent difficulties, notwithstanding appropriate learning opportunities, children whose reading problems are due to inadequate learning opportunities (Solity 1996a) would be expected to make progress when given appropriate help and therefore not be identified as dyslexic.

This working definition has no exclusionary criteria. Rather, positive identifying characteristics focus on severe and persistent problems with accurate and fluent word identification and spelling. It also allows for cases where literacy performance, particularly in older pupils, may appear relatively normal in some respects but where development is, or has been, achieved 'with great difficulty'. Where problems are identified, it is recommended that hypotheses are explored in areas involving phonological and orthographic awareness and memory and that account should be taken of compensatory styles such as heavy reliance on context when reading.

Literacy difficulties: assessment for intervention

It is widely advocated that assessment and teaching should be linked in a continuous cycle of action and evaluation in order to prevent reading failure (Clay 1987; Good *et al.* 1998). The British Psychological Society (1999) report on the identification and assessment of dyslexia recommends that assessment of learning difficulties in reading address the following questions:

- How well has the pupil learned accurate and fluent word reading and/or spelling?

- What possible hypotheses about the pupil's difficulties can be investigated to help understand their problems and how to help them?
- Have appropriate learning opportunities been provided?
- Has progress been made only as a result of much additional effort/instruction and does it show that difficulties are persisting?

A number of steps can be taken to collect appropriate assessment information in relation to each of these elements.

Assessing reading accuracy and fluency

The first question to address is: 'How well has the pupil learned accurate and fluent word reading and/or spelling?' In order to judge whether the pupil's learning has been 'very incomplete' or 'satisfactory', comparisons will need to be made between the levels achieved by the pupil and those required/expected of them.

The pupil's level of achievement may be compared to typical performance of other pupils of the same age. End of key stage tests serve this purpose. A number of standardized tests of reading and spelling are available which enable more detailed comparisons to be made as needed. Tests of reading accuracy are commonly of three kinds. Graded work reading tests (MacMillan Test Unit 1985; Elliott 1996) require pupils to read aloud a list of single words. Cloze tests (Hagley 1987) present pupils with sentences where a word is missing and a number of alternative words from which the pupil must choose the one that best fits. Prose reading tests (Neale *et al.* 1997) present passages of connected prose and count the number of words read incorrectly. The New Neale Analysis of Reading Ability also provides a measure of fluency as standardized scores can be obtained on the rate at which the prose passages are read.

Rather than comparing the pupil's level of achievement to that of other pupils of their age, it may be compared with performance criteria that define realistic accuracy/fluency levels for particular tasks. The objectives of the NLS Framework represent a set of performance criteria. Detailed observation and analysis of a child's reading performance on texts of known difficulty will indicate what levels of challenge the child can cope with. For this purpose teachers may record their observations using an informal reading inventory (Pumfrey 1985). As we showed in Chapter 7, CBA can help to establish whether knowledge in particular areas has been accurately learned and can be used fluently in reading and spelling. Good *et al.* (1998) explain how monthly measures of reading which require only 1 minute per child to administer can be used to chart progress at individual and class level across the school year.

There are advantages to drawing upon multiple sources of evidence, and reliable assessment of children learning EAL may require greater efforts to secure multiple sources of evidence than are needed with monolingual children. This may be done in a variety of ways: using multiple indicators to assess progress over time (Lacelle-Peterson and Rivera 1994; Carrasquillo and Rodriguez 1996);

or sampling the child's performance and behaviour in different roles and in different situations (Hernandez 1994). In complex or puzzling cases part of this process might usefully involve consulting any religious or community school that children attend (Cline 1995).

Testing hypotheses: phonological processing, attitudes and attributions

If the conclusion is reached that acquisition of accurate and fluent reading and spelling skills is not satisfactory, this will trigger an investigation of hypothesized factors that may be important in understanding the nature of the difficulties being experienced and in identifying ways of overcoming them. The report suggests that:

> observations start from a determination of the severity and persistence of problems with word reading and spelling. Reasons are then explored in areas involving phonological and orthographic awareness and memory and take account of compensatory styles, such as heavy reliance on context when reading, and coping strategies, such as the avoidance of frustrating learning opportunities.
>
> (British Psychological Society 1999: 53)

This is very similar to the approach recommended by leading researchers in the USA which also emphasizes an ongoing cycle of assessment, intervention and evaluation: 'Obviously assessment of reading skills would be the first order of business if one uses early intervention as a first cut approach to diagnosing reading disability. Assessment of cognitive abilities might then help to confirm or reject diagnostic impressions based on the child's ability to profit from remediation' (Vellutino et al. 1998: 392).

It is apparent from the variety of different theories outlined above that very many different hypothesized factors could be selected for investigation. In this chapter particular attention is given to two sets of factors: phonological skills, and children's self-perceptions and evaluation in relation to literacy. These have been selected because there is good research evidence on the effectiveness of targeting these variables in intervention programmes.

Several tests have been developed to assess phonological competencies shown by research to be closely associated with the development of literacy skills. Table 11.3 outlines the phonological processing skills assessed by standardized tests. Some of the tests listed also assess other cognitive abilities in addition to the phonological skills shown in the table. For example, the Dyslexia Screening Test, which was developed by Fawcett and Nicolson (1996), whose work was outlined above, assesses reading, writing and spelling fluency, motor skills, balance, temporal processing and semantic fluency in addition to the phonological measures. It should also be noted that, despite considerable overlap, no two measures assess exactly the same skills. Furthermore, it appears that performance on some measures, such as tasks involving phoneme awareness, is influenced by the pupils'

Table 11.3   Phonological processing skills assessed by tests standardized and published in the UK

Phonological processing skill	test
Alliteration detection	CoPS, PhAB
Alliteration production	PhAB
Auditory discrimination	CoPS
Naming speed	DEST/DST, PhAB
Non-word reading	GNRT, PhAB
Phoneme deletion	PAT
Rhyme detection	DEST/DST, PAT, PhAB
Rhyme production	CoPS, PAT, PhAB
Spoonerisms	PhAB
Speech rate	PAT
Word completion	PAT
Working memory	DEST/DST, CoPS
Auditory/verbal associative memory	CoPS
Visual/verbal associative and sequential memory	CoPS

Key:
CoPS: Cognitive Profiling System (Singleton 1995)
DEST: Dyslexia Early Screening Test (Fawcett and Nicolson 1996)
DST: Dyslexia Screening Test (Nicolson and Fawcett 1996)
GNRT: Graded Non-word Reading Test (Snowling *et al.* 1996)
PAT: Phonological Abilities Test (Muter *et al.* 1997)
PhAB: Phonological Assessment Battery (Frederickson *et al.* 1997)

reading skills – in this case their knowledge of grapheme-phoneme correspondences. It would therefore be possible for a pupil to be assessed as having phonological difficulties on one test, but not another. Even when the tests are assessing the same phonological skill, if they do so in different ways different results may be obtained. For example, if two methods of assessing the same phonological skill place different demands on memory, the child may be able to utilize compensatory strategies only when the assessment method having the lighter memory load is used. Highly relevant though they are, tests of phonological processing on their own are best regarded as indicative, rather than definitive.

It has been argued that finding out how children perceive the reading task and how they evaluate their own progress will be important in any assessment. The assessment should represent 'a vigorously active search for the child's best possible performance in relation to a particular learning objective and . . . therefore start from questions of what motivates a given individual to give her best' (Pema and Pattinson 1991: 41). When working with children learning EAL this is particularly important as there is more likely to be an initial mismatch between their perceptions and those of their teachers (Gregory 1994). The task is challenging, because 'far more effort has been put into the measurement of cognitive aspects of the reading process than has been spent on the measurement of attitudes towards reading' (Pumfrey 1986). Yet it is widely recognized that attitude and motivation have a major role in affecting children's progress.

The relationship between attitude and attainment is not a simple one and Pumfrey (1997) points out that in some cases pupils' attitudes to reading and their reading attainments are not found to be positively correlated. It is suggested that two kinds of threshold effect may be operating. First, children whose attitudes or motivation are below some threshold level may be prevented from engaging with the intellectual challenges of literacy learning and make poor progress. However, increases in enthusiasm and commitment above the threshold level may not automatically lead to improvements in attainment. Second, once children have attained a threshold level of basic competence in reading and writing they will not lose those skills, even if there is a loss of interest and reduced motivation as they move through school (Davies and Brember 1995).

Pumfrey (1997) has provided a short introduction to the range of techniques that are available for assessing attitudes to reading. Among others he lists:

- observations using checklists of reading-related behaviours from which the pupil's attitudes towards reading can be inferred;
- self-report techniques;
- scaling of various types (e.g. paired comparisons);
- projective techniques;
- semantic differential techniques;
- repertory grid techniques.

Other cognitive constructs that have been investigated in understanding reading difficulties are self-concept/self-perception and attribution. The Reading Self-Concept Scale (Chapman and Tunmer 1995) can be used by a class teacher or SENCO to explore with 5- to 10-year-olds their perceptions of reading competence and reading difficulty as well as their attitudes towards reading. The Burnett Self Scale (Burnett 1994) provides a global measure of self-concept and also assesses eight specific aspects including reading self-concept. The other seven areas relate to physical appearance, physical ability, peer relations, relations with mother, relations with father, mathematics and learning generally. The Reading Self-Concept Scale and the Burnett Self Scale are both widely available to schools in the Children's Self-Perceptions booklet of the *Psychology in Education Portfolio* (Burden 1999).

The Self-Perception Profile for Children (Harter 1985), which is described in more detail in Chapter 14, assesses a child's general self-worth/esteem and their judgement of their competence across a number of specific domains including scholastic competence – the others being social, behavioural and athletic competence, and physical appearance. Renick and Harter (1989) found that pupils with specific learning difficulties made fine distinctions between the items on the scholastic scale that were not made by normally achieving children. They subsequently produced an adaptation of the measure for children with specific learning difficulties (Harter and Renick 1988) where the scholastic scale was replaced by five separate scales assessing the following aspects: the extent to which the children perceived themselves to be smart; to be good readers; to be doing well at spelling; to be able to write good sentences to create a story; and to understand maths. Hence this measure can provide a differentiated picture of a pupil's self-perception across different aspects of literacy.

Where pupils are experiencing difficulties with some aspect of literacy it can be valuable to find out why they think they are having problems. Research has shown that the type of cause to which a child attributes their difficulties or their successes can have an effect on their motivation and subsequent achievement. Weiner (1985) suggested that common attributions made by children for success and failure in school could be classified along three dimensions – whether they are generally seen by children as internal or external to them, as stable or unstable and as controllable or uncontrollable. For example, if children think they did well in an examination because of luck with the questions (an external factor) rather than through their own hard work (a factor that is internal to them), it will make a difference to their future approach to school activities. Table 11.4 summarizes the research findings on these issues that apply to most children. But there are developmental and individual differences. For example, it is not until about the age of 9 that children begin to see effort and ability as distinct (Nicholls 1978). Also, some children who experience repeated failure can develop the perception that achieving success in learning is completely outside their control no matter what they do.

Weiner thought that stability was particularly important in influencing future expectations. He suggested that if a pupil attributed academic success to a supposedly stable factor (such as ability) and failure to a transitory one (such as use of an incorrect strategy), they would come increasingly to expect successful outcomes. On the other hand if a pupil attributed success to unstable factors and failure to stable factors this would be likely to lead to increasing expectations of failure and reduced motivation to engage in academic tasks. However, other authors have argued that controllability is more important than stability in influencing future expectations and motivation. The link between attributions and motivation is of particular relevance to pupils who experience difficulties at school. In one longitudinal study (Kistner *et al.* 1988) the progress of children with

Table 11.4 Attributions for success and failure in school

Attribution	*Dimensions*		
	Internal/external	*Stable/unstable*	*Controllable/uncontrollable*
Ability (> 9 years)	Internal	Stable	Uncontrollable
Effort	Internal	Unstable	Controllable
Task difficulty	External	Stable	Uncontrollable
Luck	External	Unstable	Uncontrollable
Poor teaching	External	Unstable	Uncontrollable
Strategy used	Internal	Unstable	Controllable

Source: Developed from Weiner (1985).

specific learning difficulties was monitored over a two-year period through use of achievement test scores and teacher ratings of classroom performance and behaviour. Those children who attributed failure to unstable, controllable causes, such as their own level of effort, made the greatest achievement gains and received the most positive behaviour ratings.

Promising results have been obtained from attribution retraining programmes involving children who have SEN. For example, Borkowski *et al.* (1988) designed and evaluated an attribution retraining programme on reading comprehension for older primary children with specific reading difficulties. Some children received attribution retraining alone, some received reading comprehension

---

ACTIVITY 11.3   Case study: Michael

Read the following case study and decide:

(a) What hypotheses might prove useful in understanding Michael's difficulties?
(b) What assessment approaches would you plan to use to collect more information and test out each of these hypotheses?

Michael (aged 14) is the second of two children of professional parents with high educational aspirations. He attends a successful comprehensive school in a prosperous suburb of a small county town in the South of England. He received speech therapy as a preschooler but now talks fluently and shows a lively curiosity, notably in relation to scientific topics. But, with the exception of mathematics, his educational attainments are poor because he is very slow at reading and has difficulty expressing his ideas in writing. In fact, his written work is so full of mistakes that some subject teachers underestimate his understanding.

As a small child he enjoyed being read stories at bedtime with his sister but took little interest in the books. In primary school he made very slow progress in reading, committing common words to memory but failing to develop strategies for working out words with which he was unfamiliar. He found this frustrating and began to use all kinds of tactics to avoid having to read or refer to books. His parents were not seriously concerned about this at first, because his father had been slow to learn to read as a child but had grown out of it and his paternal grandfather had a similar history. To some extent his parents' optimism was justified in that, with the help of an excellent learning support teacher, he did eventually learn how to overcome his problems with reading new material (though he still struggles sometimes when he comes across a text with a large proportion of unfamiliar vocabulary – e.g. in a new topic in history).

What is still undermining his educational performance (and his self-confidence) is that he can only write very slowly indeed, making many errors of spelling and syntax. He does not seem to recognize when he is going wrong, although his form tutor feels that he takes insufficient care in checking his work and could do better if he applied himself. Normally quite self-contained, he recently became angry when his history teacher criticized the amount of written work he had produced and its untidy presentation. An argument ensued with Michael saying that writing was a waste of time and that when he was a scientist he would talk into a computer and wouldn't be bothered with old-fashioned stuff like that.

strategy training alone and some received a combined programme of attribution retraining and reading comprehension strategy training. Only the combined programme group showed significant improvements in reading comprehension skills both on the special programme materials and on a standardized reading test. Borkowski *et al.* (1988) argue that teaching reading comprehension strategies alone or emphasizing the role of effort in isolation will be less effective than a systematically linked programme which can cue and motivate pupils to apply what they have learned.

Providing appropriate learning opportunities

The next question in the British Psychological Society (1999) sequence is, 'Have appropriate learning opportunities been provided?' 'Appropriate learning opportunities' can be defined as those approaches and methods known to be generally successful in increasing pupils' rate of progress in acquiring reading and spelling skills. Pietrowski and Reason (2000) reviewed theory and research on learning, literacy development and motivation and compiled eight questions that can be asked in assessing the appropriateness of the learning opportunities that have been provided:

- *A comprehensive model:* do the materials that are used in the classroom reflect a comprehensive model of reading and/or spelling development – e.g. including comprehension of the text as a whole and the anticipation of words and letter sequences as well as providing instruction in phonics?
- *Progression:* do the materials show a clear progression of targets – e.g. starting from phonological awareness and moving gradually to more advanced phonic structures?
- *Speaking and listening:* are children exploring and reinforcing the learning of phonological regularities through both speaking and listening?
- *Reading and writing:* are children exploring and reinforcing the learning of phonological regularities through both reading and writing?
- *Assessing to teach:* do the materials provide guidance on 'assessing to teach' – i.e. on assessing what the children know in order to plan, in appropriately small steps, what should be learned next?
- *Mastery learning:* are the materials based on 'mastery learning' – i.e. on planned repetition and revision that ensures retention of what has been learned?
- *Role of the learner:* in terms of motivational influences, is there explicit guidance on the involvement of the children themselves in setting their own targets and monitoring progress?
- *Home-school links:* is there clear guidance on how parents can help their children at home?

Pietrowski and Reason (2000) used these questions to compare three kinds of commercially published materials with a strong emphasis on the teaching of phonics. First, those that were developed for all children as meeting the require-ments of the NLS at the word level; second, those intended for learners making slower progress in literacy; and third, those targeted at learners regarded as having difficulties of a dyslexic nature. The comparison undertaken involved four programmes in each of the three categories. A number of interesting similar-ities and differences were reported. Explicit guidance for parents appeared in the text of only 4 of the 12 programmes – in 2 of the programmes for all children and in 2 of those for learners making slower progress. Possibly the dyslexia-orientated materials surveyed were considered too specialized for parental in-volvement? Likewise an explicit emphasis on the active involvement of learners in monitoring their own targets to enhance motivation was generally absent, only appearing in 2 of the programmes for learners making slower progress.

All programmes were reported to provide a progression of targets for teaching phonics. However, the materials developed for all children were more likely to teach through speaking and listening, whereas the dyslexia-orientated programmes were more likely to utilize repetitive reading and writing. Both the dyslexia-orientated programmes and those designed for learners making slower progress placed major emphasis on mastery learning. A focus on assessing to teach was also present in both these approaches, being particularly strongly emphasized in programmes for learners making slower progress. This was less likely to feature in materials that had been developed for all children.

It does seem that the provision of appropriate learning opportunities for pupils with learning difficulties in literacy can be assisted by the use of commercially developed programmes. However, on their own these are unlikely to address the full range of factors that have been shown to be important in enhancing progress and in most cases IEPs will need to incorporate other measures, depending on the programme used and the additional needs of the individual pupil. The preventat-ive impact of programmes developed for all children might be enhanced through incorporation of more emphasis on mastery learning. On the other hand, the materials developed for all children were more likely to fully incorporate a com-prehensive model of literacy. In many of the other programmes explicit links between text, sentence and word levels were not made and the need to attend to elements of literacy other than phonics was not clearly highlighted.

The implementation of a comprehensive model of literacy learning implies that attention should be given throughout to text-level work for all children. In addi-tion it should be recognized that children who have been struggling with print will have had fewer opportunities to develop comprehension-fostering strategies. Padron (1992) suggests that pupils who fall behind their peers for whatever reason may increasingly be denied the opportunity to learn higher-level thinking or comprehension skills, as effort is focused on skills assumed to be more basic, such as decoding skills. Indeed, in some cases they may have lost sight of 'getting meaning' from the text as a core purpose of reading. Explicit instruction in strategies for comprehension will therefore often be appropriate.

Reciprocal teaching (Palinscar and Brown 1985) is a well researched approach to the development of reading comprehension skills that has been successfully used in many classrooms. It involves a teacher working with a small group who are instructed in four specific comprehension monitoring strategies:

1 summarizing what has happened so far;
2 self-questioning about the passage before it is read, so that reading can be a purposeful seeking of answers to the questions posed;
3 clarifying and rehearsing any difficult, unusual or technical words in the passage;
4 predicting what is likely to happen or what information is likely to be gained.

The teacher begins by explaining what strategies will be learned, why, and when to apply them. The strategies are then modelled for the pupils through questions, generated initially by the teacher. The pupils summarize and add their own predictions, clarifications and responses to questions. The passage is then read (usually silently) by members of the group and the teacher leads a discussion, referring back to the questions asked before the passage was read. Through guided practice responsibility for leading the process is gradually transferred to the pupils who take it in turns to assume the role of the teacher and generate the questions while the teacher takes on a supporting role. Figure 11.6 provides an example of a teaching session from a reciprocal teaching programme involving 6–7-year-old pupils.

This process can be used by teachers and classroom assistants not only to teach generic comprehension skills but also to prepare pupils who have reading difficulties for particular lessons so that they are able to access meaning from curriculum materials with which they would otherwise have problems. Padron (1991) reports that this technique can also be very useful when teaching students who are learning EAL. If at the early stages of learning to decode the teacher reads the text aloud to the pupils, the process can provide opportunities to place emphasis on reading for meaning from the outset. The importance of this for promoting the reading progress of pupils learning EAL is discussed further in the final part of this section of the chapter.

Monitoring and evaluating progress

The final question to address is 'Has progress been made only as a result of much additional effort/instruction and does it show that difficulties are persisting?' Fine-grained progress monitoring can be carried out by means of well-established techniques such as precision teaching (Lindsley 1992) which is described in Chapter 7 on CBA. Such techniques offer opportunities to:

- fine-tune the learning opportunities offered to pupils within the context of general programmes such as the NLS so that they are as appropriate as possible to their assessed strengths and needs and consistent with research evidence on effective teaching approaches;
- monitor the fluency of pupil's performance and the extent to which their difficulties persist across interventions and over time.

Figure 11.6
Example of a
reciprocal teaching
dialogue
Source: Palinscar
(1986).

Text which the teacher read to the children: 'Behind the front legs, there are two odor glands. They look like two extra eyes. To protect itself, a daddy longlegs can give off a smelly liquid from these glands. Birds, toads, and large insects don't like it at all. It makes them feel too sick or too weak to try to catch the daddy longlegs'.

Child B is taking responsibility for acting as the teacher in this session and the group of 6–7-year-old pupils manage the dialogue independently for most of the time. The teacher mainly intervenes to restore direction when there is misunderstanding and the dialogue begins to go off course.

1 *Child B*: [question] What does the daddy longlegs do when something comes around it? J—?
2 *Child A*: Use that odor and . . . [not audible]
3 *Child B*: Yeah, C.
4 *Child C*: When an animal comes along, he puts out his odor and they get too sick to catch him.
5 *Child B*: Yeah, M.
6 *Child M*: Or too weak.
7 *Child D*: They feel too weak and too sick.
8 *Child B*: Everybody gave me good answers.
9 *Teacher*: Very good.
10 *Child B*: [summary] I will summarize. When an animal comes around, it gives out its bad smell, and they get weak and too old to catch it.
11 *Child A*: [clarification] Who does?
12 *Child B*: That's the daddy longlegs.
13 *Child A*: [clarification] Who does?
14 *Child D*: The animals.
15 *Child A*: [clarification] Which animals?
16 *Child D*: All kinds of animals.
17 *Child B*: Yeah, different kinds.
18 *Child A*: Different kinds of animals put out a spray?
19 *Child D*: [clarification] Um, it might be the same kind of animal as tries to catch the daddy longlegs.
20 *Teacher*: Okay, I think you are talking about two different things. He's talking about the animals that come around to the daddy longlegs and he's trying to get you to say who puts out the odor. Is it all animals?
21 *Child A*: No, the daddy longlegs.

In work on spelling, Brooks and Weeks (1999) showed how a precision teaching framework can be used to monitor progress on a daily basis for pupils with dyslexic difficulties. Each week for three weeks a different systematic teaching strategy was used to help the pupils learn ten new words. Each day a teacher, classroom assistant or parent tested pupils on the words. When an error was made, the pupil was taught by the strategy being used that week. The number of words spelled correctly each day was graphed. By comparing the graphs obtained in different weeks the most effective strategy for teaching that pupil spellings could be identified. Initial selection of the three strategies to try out was made by analysing the types of errors the pupil made when spelling, and/or drawing on research and experience of successful teaching of spelling. However, if none of the strategies that were trialled produced a satisfactory rate of learning then additional strategies would need to be tried out until this was achieved. The most important advantage of this kind of fine-grained progress monitoring for pupils who have learning difficulties in literacy is that it clearly shows which intervention strategies work best for each individual. Also, it quickly shows up whether a change in strategy is working and so avoids wasting teaching time on approaches that are not helping a particular pupil accelerate their rate of learning progress. As Adams (1990: 90) points out, 'For these children we have not a classroom moment to waste'.

The SEN *Code* document (Department for Education and Skills 2001) emphasizes that the key test of how far pupils' learning needs are being met, and whether further action is required, is whether they are making *adequate progress*. It is suggested that the adequacy of pupils' progress can be defined in a number of ways:

- against progress made by their peers (i.e. progress is adequate which closes the gap between them and their peers, prevents the gap growing wider or maintains their position relative to peers starting from the same attainment baseline);
- by comparing pupils' progress in areas of difficulty with their progress in areas of relative strength (i.e. progress is adequate if the gap between their areas of difficulty and strength is closing or is not widening);
- in terms of other success criteria for that pupil (i.e. it matches or betters the pupil's previous rate of progress, ensures access to the full curriculum, is likely to lead to accreditation and to participation in further education, training or employment).

It is suggested that different definitions will be appropriate for different pupils and that the preferred definition in any situation is one that is both realistic and ambitious.

The guidance makes it clear that action for pupils experiencing specific learning difficulties will be primarily taken by the class or subject teacher using the resources and strategies available in the ordinary classroom. Where pupils' progress is not adequate it will always be important to review the strategies currently being used. Where progress is still not adequate, schools are advised to consider a broad range of additional strategies for assessment, planning and review, for grouping for teaching purposes, for utilizing additional human resources and for selecting alternative curriculum and teaching methods. Schools are advised that overcoming specific learning difficulties may call for carefully targeted interventions using particular teaching techniques (such as multi-sensory approaches, a focus on phonological awareness, or motor programmes). Whether any of these approaches will be right for a particular pupil can ultimately only be determined by fine-grained monitoring of that pupil's rate or trajectory of progress. As Good *et al.* (1998: 68) argue, 'No matter how great an intervention sounds, no matter how much it costs, no matter how much research has been published, and no matter how many criteria or belief systems it satisfies, if the intervention does not change the child's trajectory, then it is not effective for that child and a change is indicated'.

Home–school support for literacy learning

There is evidence that the literacy needs experienced by pupils learning EAL are qualitatively different from those of pupils who have SEN (Cline and Shamsi 2000). Those pupils learning EAL who also have SEN are likely to require support in relation to both sets of needs. Frederickson and Frith (1998) studied the performance on reading tests and the Phonological Asssessment Battery (PhAB) of 50 children aged 10–12 years whose first language was Sylheti and who had been educated in English since the age of 5. They were compared with two groups of monolingual children – children assessed as having specific learning difficulties/ dyslexia and normally developing readers matched for age and IQ. The children with dyslexia showed considerable degrees of phonological impairment compared both to the normally developing readers and the bilingual pupils. The results suggested that the phonological skills assessed were similarly developed in bilingual children whose exposure to English has been sufficient to develop surface competencies, as in monolingual English-speaking children. The children learning EAL performed less well in reading comprehension than in reading accuracy, while the reverse was true for the children with specific learning difficulties. This was presumably because those with specific learning difficulties were able to use their semantic knowledge to compensate for their poor phonological processing and decoding skills, while those learning EAL were able to develop good decoding skills even when they did not understand what they were reading.

Cline and Cozens (1999) used miscue analysis to identify the sources of information children used when they found words difficult to read. They compared a group of monolingual Key Stage 2 children with a group of bilingual children from a Pakistani/Kashmiri community who were of the same age and level of reading achievement. All the children made most use of grapho-phonic cues and the two groups made equal use of grapho-phonic and syntactic cues. However the bilingual children made less use of semantic cues. The authors hypothesize that 'after struggling to read culturally unfamiliar material with a limited English vocabulary in the early stages, some of the children become habitual users of the surface and syntactic cues in print and, in effect, learn not to read for meaning' (Cline and Cozens 1999: 27).

So, available evidence suggests that most children learning EAL do not encounter particular problems in decoding print at the word level, even in their second language. Similar proportions of monolingual children and those learning EAL appear to experience the difficulties associated with phonological dyslexia (Frederickson and Frith 1998; Geva 1999). But children learning EAL do potentially face challenges with reading material at school at the sentence and text

Table 11.5 Learning to read in LEA primary schools and Bangladeshi community schools

LEA primary school	Community school
Extent:	
2–5 hours a week	6–9 hours a week
Length:	
20 minutes (often interrupted)	2–3 hours (usually without a break)
Purpose:	
To improve chances of employment (parents)	To strengthen cultural identification
To gain enjoyment (teacher)	To learn religion
To play (child)	To learn
Materials:	
Storybooks on high quality paper with coloured illustrations and complex language	Reading primers on low quality paper with black and white print and simple language
Can be changed when child pleases	Must be completed before changing
Bought by school and unfamiliar to parents	Bought by and familiar to parents
Method:	
Teacher reads to child, encourages, does not correct and does not test	Teacher demonstrates instructs, corrects, tests
Child experiments, 'pretends', guesses	Child repeats, practises, is tested

Source: Adapted from Gregory (1994).

levels as linguistic and cultural differences can become obstacles which they will need help to negotiate.

Schools need to give consideration to the severe cultural discontinuities that children learning EAL in the UK may experience between their home community and the local authority school over the development of literacy. In a typical study Gregory (1994) compared the experiences of children aged 5–7 from six East London Bangladeshi families in their local authority primary schools and in the community schools that they attended at the end of the day. Table 11.5 shows that children studied reading for longer in the community school, were expected to read for different purposes, used different types of reading material and were taught by different methods. For some children literacy practices in their LEA school may contradict expectations they bring from their experiences elsewhere, whether at home or in a community school.

An important implication for assessment is that if children who are learning EAL are making poor progress in learning to read English and are known to attend a religious or community class where reading is part of the curriculum, there are additional assessment questions to be addressed, such as: how do they respond to the different literacy demands made of them in that setting, and what impact does that experience have on their perception of the reading task in school? In general, teachers need to consider carefully how they can assess in an individual case of apparent learning difficulty whether discontinuities between home and school are inhibiting reading progress.

There are parallels here in terms of the successful outcomes that have been obtained through parental involvement programmes for pupils who experience literacy learning difficulties. MacLeod (1996: 382) had expressed concern about approaches where 'parents would be expected to accommodate to the school without the school being expected to accommodate to them'. She argued that parental involvement should build on parents' own resources and abilities rather than imposing school practices in an attempt to 'compensate for perceived deficits in community literacy practices'. Some of the approaches that have proved most successful are indeed characterized by attempts to accommodate to the needs of the parents involved. The PACT (Parents, Children and Teachers) project in Haringay produced gains in literacy learning which were still apparent three years later (Hewison 1988). In this project, where parents were asked to hear their child read on a regular basis, home visits from project staff were provided to offer support. Where children are experiencing significant literacy learning difficulties, where parents lack confidence and experience of educational success or where there are difficulties in the parent–child relationship, concern has been expressed that these additional parental needs will also have to be accommodated if a parental involvement programme is not to produce detrimental rather than beneficial effects.

A number of more structured methods were developed to support positive and failure-free parent–child engagement with books. Paired reading (Morgan and Lyon 1979; Topping and Lindsay 1991) is probably the best known of these techniques. It allows children to read at home with a parent whatever books interest them, provided that the books can be read by the parent who is working with them. If the text is too difficult for the child to read unaided they are supported by 'reading together' when parent and child read all the words out loud together. The parent adjusts speed to match the child whom they ensure says every word correctly. If the child makes an error, the parent simply repeats the word until the child reads it correctly. When the child comes to an easier section that they think they can read themselves, they give the parent some prearranged non-verbal signal, such as a nudge or a tap on the book, to tell them to be quiet. The child then continues reading alone until an error is made which is not self-corrected within five seconds. The parent then joins in again, says the word for the child to repeat, and they continue reading together until the child gives the next signal that they want to try reading alone. The parent gives the child lots of praise throughout for reading well, whether together or alone and for signalling to read alone. They also spend time with the child discussing the story or information about which they are reading.

Topping and Lindsay (1992: 222) report on a comprehensive review of the research on paired reading. They identified a number of criteria for community interventions against which paired reading could be evaluated.

It has been argued that community interventions should be: (i) simple, (ii) inexpensive, (iii) effective, (iv) compatible with the existing values and need structures of the population, (v) flexible, (vi) decentralised, and (vii) sustainable. The research on paired reading reviewed here is encouraging and suggests that the technique in the context of well-organized service delivery is capable of meeting at least requirements i–vi. Conclusions on the last requirement must await further longer-term follow-up studies.

Conclusions

In this chapter the discussion of SEN in literacy has been set within the context of the literacy curriculum. The NLS was briefly outlined and particular considerations relating to the participation of pupils who have SEN and who are learning EAL were discussed. The causal modelling framework which was introduced in Chapter 2 was used to represent the range of theories that have been advanced to account for learning difficulties in literacy. Recent research evidence has consistently supported the particular importance of problems with phonological processing in understanding difficulties with literacy learning.

Issues and problems in defining dyslexia were discussed. In particular, the problems associated with IQ-achievement discrepancy definitions of dyslexia were explained. These definitions are still used in some LEAs to make judgements about which pupils will have access to specialist support and resources despite the weight of research evidence against their use. The research evidence indicates that these definitions do not have a sound conceptual basis and do not identify children who have different needs or who respond differently to intervention. In addition, these criteria do not offer equitable access to specialist resources for pupils learning EAL who are experiencing significant literacy learning difficulties.

We suggested that the definition of dyslexia developed by the British Psychological Society (1999) was to be preferred. It separates description from explanation and provides a framework for assessment through intervention. Within this framework hypotheses about the reasons for a pupil's difficulties can be tested and we reviewed a range of assessment techniques which can be used to investigate two types of hypotheses in particular – hypotheses about a pupil's phonological processing skills and hypotheses about their attitudes to reading and attributions for success and failure.

We considered appropriate literacy learning opportunities that should be provided for pupils experiencing difficulties. The importance of monitoring and evaluating the progress in each individual case was highlighted. Finally the additional needs of those pupils who are also learning EAL were considered and parallels drawn between positive action to address home-school discontinunities and features of successful parental involvement in reading programmes for pupils who have SEN, including paired reading initiatives.

Chapter 12

Mathematics

Objectives

When you have studied this chapter you should be able to:

1 Outline in summary current issues relating to the mathematics curriculum and the social context of mathematics learning and teaching.
2 Explain how problems of understanding, procedural skill, anxiety and language may contribute to learning difficulties in maths.
3 Analyse the impact that specific learning difficulties and SEN may have on mathematics learning.
4 Describe the main approaches to assessment in mathematics and suggest what methods might be appropriate for different purposes.

Contents

The mathematics curriculum

The aims and scope of mathematics education

Following the Cockcroft Committee (Department of Education and Science 1982) successive official statements about the aims of education in mathematics emphasized that mastery of the subject:

- is needed for adult life and employment;
- is a valuable means of communication;
- is important as a tool for studying other subjects;
- can be an aesthetically pleasing element of our cultural experience.

For example, the report of the National Curriculum Council Working Group on Mathematics set out a vision of the nature of mathematics which at the time appeared to command a wide measure of consensual support (Department of Education and Science 1988, Ch. 2). This vision stressed that mathematics is a means of organizing, communicating and manipulating information with a language consisting of diagrams and symbols plus associated conventions and theorems. While it was to be taught because it is useful, the Working Group was also committed to the idea that it should at the same time be a source of delight and wonder. This might arise, for example, in discovering relationships or in achieving elegant solutions.

They saw it as important that pupils should master the special language of maths (including numbers, graphs and algebraic expressions) because this language is a powerful means of communication that can simplify and clarify a message. The use of symbols in maths makes for dense, concise and precise statements – a source of power but also, they pointed out, one reason why many children find it difficult.

'Arithmetic' or 'number' was even then seen as central and fundamental to school maths. While number was to be pervasive, maths was seen as much wider in scope. The National Curriculum for the subject at Key Stage 1 developed to include using and applying mathematics, number, and shape, space and measures. Handling data was introduced as a separate section at Key Stage 2 and algebra at Key Stage 3. The Working Group originally emphasized that the different areas of maths did not stand in isolation from each other. Maths was to some extent hierarchical, but 'it is more useful to see it as a network of ideas in which the various parts are interrelated to form a coherent structure' (Department of Education and Science 1988: 3). Teachers were not to concentrate too much on one part of the structure. A broad mathematical education was seen as essential for all pupils.

The balance of different aspects of the maths curriculum is subject to regular 'swings of the pendulum' (Brown 1999). In the early 1980s the Cockcroft Committee argued that at every level good practice in school mathematics should include:

- exposition by the teacher;
- discussion between teacher and pupils and between pupils themselves;

- appropriate practical work;
- consolidation and practice of fundamental skills and routines;
- problem solving and the application of maths to everyday situations;
- investigational work.

Through that decade many commentators, including HMI (1989), suggested that three of these elements were often missing from the classroom diet – discussion, practical work and investigational work.

Since 1988, political concern has been expressed about a perceived gap in maths attainments between children in the UK and in some overseas countries (Reynolds and Farrell 1996; Department for Education and Employment 1998a, paras 28–9). An increasing emphasis has been placed on teaching number and fluency in calculation. It was perceived that schools in countries with higher standards of performance in mathematics tended to give more time to developing oral and mental work at an early stage and to whole-class teaching. The National Numeracy Strategy (NNS) aimed to ensure that teachers would spend 'less time in mathematics lessons working and trouble-shooting with individuals' and would 'provide appropriately demanding work for pupils with limited differentiation around work common to all pupils in one class' (Department for Education and Employment 1998a: 22).

From the school year 1999/2000, as part of the NNS all primary schools in England have been expected to teach a daily maths lesson with a high proportion of the time devoted to numeracy. The legal position has remained that, while the Secretary of State determines the broad content of the National Curriculum, it is for schools and individual teachers to determine how it is taught. But in addition to setting out a detailed curriculum for each year group through Key Stages 1 and 2, the NNS Framework also specified additional requirements regarding the kinds of activity that should be organized by teachers and the amount of time to be devoted to them. While only the broader outlines are technically statutory, the Ofsted inspection regime puts schools under strong pressure to conform (Brown 1999).

The Numeracy Task Force stated that 'the national drive for early, high quality intervention in both literacy and numeracy is intended to reduce the number of children who need long term provision for SEN'. At the same time they acknowledged that including pupils with SEN in the daily maths lesson in mainstream primary schools would pose particular challenges for teachers (Department for Education and Employment 1998b, paras 122 and 124). In Activity 12.1 you are invited to reflect on the detailed recommendations that the Task Force made on this subject in the light of your own experience of work with children who have learning difficulties.

Multicultural mathematics

Maths is sometimes described as 'abstract' or 'international' or 'universal'. The implication is that there is one form of mathematical representation of human experience that is uniform across cultural groups. Such assumptions have been

ACTIVITY 12.1   Recommendations for work with children who have learning difficulties

Below you will find a number of statements about how pupils with SEN may be helped within the framework of the NNS. Where you have worked with children in the relevant age range and setting, reflect on your own experience with either one or two children who have experienced serious learning difficulties in school. Consider what aspects of the recommended strategies might work well with them and what aspects might present problems. How could those problems be overcome? Discuss these issues with a colleague.

> Our recommended strategy envisages that children would be taught together as a whole class right from the beginning of Year 1, and for some of the time in Reception . . . It is quite possible to accommodate a range of attainment at this stage, with children learning about mathematical ideas and language through a broad range of stimulating, interactive activities. The experience of the National Numeracy Project has been that children who know less about mathematics than others when they enter a Reception class can derive great benefit, and make considerable progress, by listening to, and watching, their peers engage in mathematical activities for part of their time. This is an important stage of learning, which gradually allows them to participate successfully in the activities.
>
> (Department for Education and Employment 1998b, para. 156)

> We have been particularly encouraged by the progress of pupils with SEN, including some with statements, in schools taking part in the National Numeracy Project. Teachers have generally aimed to keep children with SEN up with the general pace of teaching in the class, rather than to offer a high degree of differentiated work . . . There may, however, be a small proportion of children in mainstream schools who suffer from severe difficulties that seriously hamper their progress in mathematics . . . All these children should participate in at least part of the daily mathematics lesson with other members of their class. In the middle part of the lesson, children with severe difficulties with mathematics should follow an individualized programme with appropriate support, but would benefit from being included in the oral work with the whole class at the beginning of the daily lesson.
>
> (Department for Education and Employment 1998b, paras 122–3)

> Where special educational needs have been identified, it is important that the child's individual education plan (IEP) includes suitable objectives for numeracy, that are challenging but realistic. It is common at the moment for IEPs to refer to literacy only. If these numeracy objectives are linked to the school's framework or scheme of work, teachers can bear them in mind when planning lessons. Pupils with statements may to some extent be working on individual programmes based on their statements, but it would also be appropriate for their IEPs to mention numeracy.
>
> (Department for Education and Employment 1998a, para. 109)

> The National Numeracy Task Force expressed the hope that as many special schools as possible would be involved in the implementation of the National Numeracy Strategy. Indeed, aspects such as a high proportion of oral work, thorough consolidation of

learning, structured lessons, good diagnosis of children's misconceptions, and regular assessment and target setting for all pupils have long been recognised as best practice in special schools.

(Department for Education and Employment 1998a, para. 111)

Special schools will need to adapt these methods in some cases. Some pupils, for example, may find the physical and mental effort involved in concentration for, say, 50 minutes of mathematics, too great, and need a much shorter lesson of, say, 30 minutes, with a supplementary time later in the day.

(Department for Education and Employment 1998a, para. 111)

contradicted by research in both developing and developed countries over the last 30 years. For example, investigators have identified diverse skills and approaches to calculation among particular groups of workers such as weavers or market traders and among children in different countries. They have shown that the same children may adopt different approaches to mathematical tasks depending on whether they are working at school or in a family or street enterprise. The socio-cultural organization of the maths practices was a crucial factor (Nunes *et al.* 1993), as was the social value given to different forms of practice (Abreu 1995).

In a multicultural society it is beneficial if the school maths curriculum draws upon and refers to the diverse mathematical traditions that are represented in the cultural heritage of the various ethnic groups in the school population. This will enable maths teaching to contribute to the achievement of broader educational aims of inclusiveness, mutual respect and intellectual flexibility. An example of how that aspiration might be realized in practice is the SMILE scheme (Secondary Mathematics Individualized Learning Experience), a set of individualized materials that was developed originally in London and has been widely used in secondary schools. The materials have been created by many practising teachers over an extended period (Inner London Education Authority 1990). At an early stage the development team published an anti-racist policy for the scheme, which appears to have been generally followed by its authors over the years (Monaghan 1999). The policy makes a commitment to:

- teaching maths with a strong emphasis on its historical development, showing how at each stage mathematical developments have arisen as the response of different peoples to the problems they had to solve – be they Indian astronomers, Egyptian farmers, Spanish navigators or whoever;
- deliberately seeking out knowledge of the maths of the Developing World peoples and making it easily accessible to all children learning maths;
- making deliberate use of the different maths methods brought by children to the classroom (e.g. different counting systems);
- critically assessing the content of present maths from the point of view of its relevance to living in a multicultural society (Alladina 1985).

A fuller analysis of how the principles of multicultural maths might be realized in practice will be found in books by Shan and Bailey (1991) and Nelson *et al.* (1993). These principles will influence teaching methods as well as curriculum content. Monaghan (1999) observed that the SMILE materials did not just reflect a broad range of contributions to maths from other parts of the world and present Britain as a multicultural society. They also promoted inclusive, collaborative learning strategies. Joseph (1993: 20–3) set out four overlapping objectives in pursuing a multicultural approach to maths in the classroom:

- drawing on a child's own experience as a resource;
- recognizing different cultural heritages;
- combating racism;
- promoting 'socially desirable' attitudes.

When children from an ethnic or linguistic minority community experience learning difficulties in maths at school, one factor in the frustrations they encounter may be that the curriculum and the way it is taught are exclusive and narrow rather than inclusive and capable of responding to diversity. The perspective that is presented here may be contrasted with that of the working party who developed the original National Curriculum framework for maths who were sceptical of the value of such approaches (Department of Education and Science 1988, paras 10.18–23). See Activity 12.2.

School mathematics and home mathematics

There is general agreement that it is important to involve parents and carers in their children's education, including their maths education (Merttens *et al.* 1996; Department for Education and Employment 1998b, paras 172–8). This may require three kinds of activity on the part of the school:

- informing parents about their children's progress and about the maths curriculum and how it is taught;
- encouraging and supporting parents to engage in mathematical activities with their children at home;
- creating opportunities for parents to become actively involved in maths work with their children at school.

For practical suggestions under each of these headings see Burton (1994), Merttens *et al.* (1996) and Merttens (1999).

The task is not straightforward, as there is often a significant gap to be bridged between school and home. Table 12.1 shows Merttens' (1999) summary of the differences between 'school maths' and 'home maths'. These lists probably give too little attention to parents' participation in assisting their children at home with school maths – or with the best approximation they can make to school maths (Abreu *et al.*, in preparation). However, it is helpful that the lists highlight

Examine the quotations below and suggest three differences that you think might be observed between the classroom practices in mathematics of two teachers who adopt these contrasting perspectives. There will be differences in their work with all children, but you are asked to focus specifically on differences that might emerge in how they work with a child from an ethnic or linguistic minority with which you are familiar, who has learning difficulties in mathematics.

It is sometimes suggested that the multi-cultural complexion of society demands a 'multi-cultural' approach to mathematics with children being introduced to different numeral systems, foreign currencies and non-European measuring and counting devices. We are concerned that undue emphasis on multi-cultural mathematics, in these terms, could confuse young children. While it is right to make clear to children that mathematics is the product of a diversity of cultures, priority must be given to ensuring that they have the knowledge and understanding and skills which they will need for adult life and employment in Britain in the twenty-first century. We believe that most ethnic parents will share this view.

(Department of Education and Science 1988, para. 10.20)

That paragraph [i.e. Department of Education and Science 1988] should be replaced by: 'The mathematics curriculum must provide opportunities for all pupils to recognise that all cultures engage in mathematical activity and no single culture has a monopoly on mathematical achievement. All pupils must be given the opportunity to enrich their mathematical experience by selection of appropriate materials to stimulate and develop the knowledge, understanding and skills which they will need for adult life and employment in Britain in the twenty-first century. Mathematical experience may be enriched by examples from a variety of cultures – e.g. Vedic arithmetic enhances understanding of number, Islamic art patterns are based on complex geometric construction, and the Chinese had a rod numeral method of solving simultaneous equations that leads naturally to methods used in higher mathematics.

(Joseph 1993: 19)

Table 12.1   Differences between 'school maths' and 'home maths'

Maths at home	*Maths at school*
Occurs contingently, as a result of what is happening at the time.	Is usually planned, and follows the teacher's agenda.
Is often initiated by the child who is the prime mover in the questioning process.	Is often initiated by the teacher who is the prime mover in the questioning process.
Numbers are always in a real-life context, but are only occasionally matched to a physical representation.	The physical or concrete representation of numbers will often be emphasized.
Follows no formal curriculum and is bounded only by the child's interest and the parent's time/expertise.	Follows a formal curriculum and is bounded by professionally defined notions of what is appropriately taught at each stage.

Source: Merttens (1999).

basic differences in the way mathematics is generally practised in the two settings. These differences are associated with different perceptions of what tools are to be used and what skills are involved. More fundamentally, they are associated with different perceptions of the social value of what is done (Abreu 1995).

In a series of case studies of maths learning in multiethnic primary schools Abreu *et al.* (in preparation) found that in recounting their experiences with their own children, parents often described themselves as being confronted with alternative tools that could perform the same mathematical function:

> Some were faced with new strategies, others noticed different methods, and the bilingual parents were exposed to different linguistic codes. It was in these particular confrontations that we were able to see the emergence of issues that went beyond the negotiation of knowledge in purely technological terms. For instance, a difference in strategies could lead to debates about 'who owns the proper knowledge': was it the parent or the teacher? Or it might lead to parents questioning their own competence or to a child offering resistance to their parents' help, or to the parent being selective in what knowledge they presented to the child.
>
> In each case the basis of the action was a value judgement about home and school mathematics that was rooted in a wider set of values.

For example, a child might assert that they should not follow their parents' practices because they ought to give priority to what is contemporary and modern in mathematics over what is old and out-dated. Or a father who was a first generation immigrant might express confidence in the underlying efficiency of tried and tested approaches to life, even in a new environment.

This study corroborated others in finding that the patterns of parental response were similar across ethnic groups in the English context (cf. Sur and Sur 1997). However, parents from ethnic minority communities were not able to make effective use of the opportunities that existed for informal contact with teachers, in particular because of language differences and partly perhaps because of a sense of social distance (cf. Huss-Keeler 1997).

Where children learned maths in English at school and spoke a different language at home, parents were compelled to take a position regarding the role of language in their children's maths learning. Perhaps some parents who spoke the language of the school as their own first language faced a linguistic challenge in relation to changes in maths vocabulary since they were at school but did not recognize it as a serious problem. At least one white mother showed an awareness of the issue, calling for courses for parents on, among other things, the 'jargon . . . teachers use' (Abreu *et al.* in preparation). The importance of helping parents to bridge the gap between school and home was emphasized by the finding that across ethnic groups those who had a strategy for doing so were more likely to have a child who was succeeding in maths at school. One example was a mother who made it her business to ask in detail about the method taught in school for tackling a particular type of maths problem that featured in homework.

Another parent simply taught a different and parallel form of maths at home, making clear to the child that the school approach and the home approach were both valid but should be practised in the setting for which they were designed. It is necessary to challenge the notion that partnership with parents will always involve a one-way traffic in which professionals provide support. Many parents are the fount of hard-won wisdom on how to bridge the gap. Teachers will have much to learn from them, especially when the two groups come from different cultural backgrounds – 'Careful listening is the most critical aspect for anyone working with parents' (Wheale 2000: 2).

The learning environment in school

Research on school effectiveness has shown that performance in maths is more strongly influenced by differences between schools than performance in reading (Reynolds and Muijs 1999: 18). A full account of the evaluation of learning environments in school may be found in Chapter 6. There have been concerns about specific weaknesses in maths teaching for many years. In a review of 355 primary school visits between 1982 and 1988 HMI reported that shortcomings in maths teaching identified ten years before had persisted in many schools: 'It is evident and unsurprising that the children's confidence and competence in learning mathematics is closely associated with the confidence and competence of their teachers' (HMI 1989: 27) A key factor locally in England and Wales may have been the shortage of staff who were well qualified and confident to teach the subject (Straker 1988).

International comparisons of children's performance in maths are unflattering. For example, evidence from the Assessment of Performance Unit (APU) covering 1984–8 suggested that pupils in England and Wales underperformed compared with those in Northern Ireland (Foxman et al. 1989). The investigators found that the pupils in Northern Ireland had spent more time in lessons on maths (though this was not strongly associated with performance) and more time on homework. These may have been factors in their superior performance. But, in addition, more of their teachers had formal maths qualifications, and more of them had attended maths in-service education and training (INSET) courses within the previous three years. School inspections have continued to identify shortcomings in a significant minority of schools (Ofsted 1996b, 1997b). The National Numeracy Strategy represents an energetic attempt to address these issues (Department for Education and Employment 1998b). But for the foreseeable future staff shortages and the quality of maths teaching will remain possible contextual factors when seeking to understand children's learning difficulties in maths. A careful assessment of the classroom learning environment may be particularly important for this reason.

Media coverage of studies in which educational attainments have been compared across countries have tended to focus on mean levels of attainment. For example, such coverage has highlighted the finding that performance in mathematics in

England is relatively poor overall with 'some operations' (Reynolds and Farrell 1996: 52). Less attention has been given to another consistent finding in such studies – that English samples have a relatively wide range of achievements in maths and a greater proportion of low achieving pupils. The next section concerns children with learning difficulties in maths.

Learning difficulties in mathematics

Within the school curriculum learning maths is uniquely challenging in that it is highly organized, sequential and progressive. Simpler elements must be learned successfully before moving on to others: 'It is a subject where one learns the parts; the parts build on each other to make a whole; knowing the whole enables one to reflect with more understanding on the parts, which in turn strengthens the whole. Knowing the whole also enables an understanding of the sequences and interactions of the parts and the way they support each other so that the getting there clarifies the stages of the journey' (Chinn and Ashcroft 1998: 4). Because of the interrelating nature of the subject, children who have learning difficulties in maths may sometimes appear to feel even more lost and disempowered than those who encounter problems in other subjects.

In this chapter learning difficulties in maths will be analysed first in terms of what children understand about maths and second in terms of the emotional significance that the subject has for many children and adults. We will then examine the language that is used in maths and the challenges it poses for many learners. Finally, there will be short accounts of specific learning difficulties in maths (a complex topic that has received less attention than specific learning difficulties in reading), and of the learning difficulties in maths that are associated with other SEN.

Mathematical understanding

Skemp (1976: 20) pointed out that the word 'understanding' has been used in two different senses in relation to mathematics – *relational understanding* which means 'knowing both what to do and why' and *instrumental understanding* which means 'knowing rules without reasons'. As examples of 'rules without reasons' Skemp quoted the formulae for getting the area of a rectangle (multiply the length by the breadth), subtracting one large number from another (use the 'borrowing' method), and dividing by a fraction (turn it upside down and multiply). He argued that children's learning difficulties often arise because of a mismatch between what they are expecting (e.g. help towards instrumental understanding) and what the teacher offers (e.g. teaching of basic generalizable concepts) – or vice versa. Fashions in the teaching of maths shift over time between emphasizing procedures and emphasizing concepts (Hiebert and Lefevre 1986; Brown 1999).

Figure 12.1
Principles for
predicting the
order in which key
concepts and
procedures are
learned
Source: Rittle-
Johnson and
Siegler (1998).

Children will understand key concepts before they use target procedures if:

1 The target procedure is not demonstrated in the everyday environment or taught in school (e.g. single digit addition)

OR

2 Children have frequent experience with relevant concepts, either in their everyday environment or in the classroom, before the target procedure is taught

Children will use the target procedure before they understand the relevant concepts if:

3 The target procedure is demonstrated frequently, either in the everyday environment or in formal instruction, before children understand key concepts in the domains (e.g. counting, procedurally orientated instruction in multidigit addition and subtraction)

OR

4 The target procedure is closely analogous to a procedure in a related domain and can be induced from that procedure before children understand key concepts in the domain (e.g. multiplying fractions)

Research over the last two decades has suggested that children's understanding of mathematical concepts is positively correlated with their ability to execute procedures. On the basis of an extensive review of the literature, Rittle-Johnson and Siegler (1998: 105) have proposed four principles for predicting the order in which children learn key concepts and target procedures (see Figure 12.1). These predictions may be confirmed for children generally and still not hold true for those who find all aspects of mathematics challenging. For example, the learning of concepts through the practice of procedures may be disrupted. When children have difficulty with procedures for any reason, they work more slowly. This, in turn, prevents them from automatizing those aspects of the procedure that they have mastered, and this may create an obstacle to full understanding of more complex calculations.

It is commonly found that children who fall behind in maths across the board show a particular weakness in processes that are normally automatic. Examples of the processes involved are:

- recognizing small numerical quantities without delay (e.g. when 2–4 stars are displayed in an array on a screen – Koontz and Berch 1996);
- recalling basic number facts (e.g. 3×4, quickly – Russell and Ginsberg 1984);
- solving simple addition problems without a visual prompt (Ostad 1997).

The failure of automatic processes appears to have a further consequence. Ostad showed that the mathematically weak children in their sample did not broaden the range of strategies they used over a two-year period. Although the group was assumed to be heterogeneous in terms of intelligence, language skills, etc., there was a striking degree of similarity in the strategies used for these tasks across the group as a whole. In contrast the children they described as 'mathematically normal' continued to experiment with new strategies even after finding methods that were successful: their approach was seen as showing 'strategic flexibility'.

Anxiety and motivation

Many children and adults who take other intellectual challenges in their stride panic about maths. Buxton (1981) quoted adults saying things like 'A string of figures and my brain seizes up' and 'I can't think precisely enough for this sort of thing'. A survey carried out for the Cockcroft Committee (Department of Education and Science 1988) showed that such feelings were widespread in the adult population and that they were not without justification: many of those interviewed showed serious gaps in their competence when faced with mathematical problems in everyday life. Quilter and Harper (1988) interviewed a group of 15 graduates of other subjects who described themselves as having a negative attitude to maths. The reasons they cited most frequently were categorized by the researchers as:

• lack of relevance or applicability to real-world experience;
• exposure to instrumental learning at school leading to disaffection;
• personality characteristics and/or teaching style of maths teachers.

Thus the problems were attributed not to the subject itself nor to personal inadequacy but rather to deficiencies in the way maths was taught. A similar emphasis was found when trainee primary school teachers were interviewed about maths anxiety (Haylock 1995, Ch. 1).

Sepie and Keeling (1978) differentiated between anxiety about maths, anxiety about school and general (trait) anxiety. With a sample of 246 children aged 11–12 in New Zealand they showed that anxiety about maths correlated significantly with maths achievement, while the other two types of anxiety did not. Similar results were obtained by Suinn et al. (1988) and Gierl and Bisanz (1995) with North American groups that included younger children. In the second of these studies, maths anxiety was differentiated into *mathematics test anxiety* ('feelings of nervousness associated with past, present and future mathematical testing situations') and *mathematics problem solving anxiety* ('feelings of nervousness associated with situations both in and out of school that require students to solve math problems and use the solutions in some way'). They found that between the ages of 9 and 12 average scores on measures of maths test anxiety increased relative to average scores for maths problem solving anxiety. It seemed that, as children progress through school at this stage, they become relatively more anxious about maths testing than about using maths to solve problems in contexts other than testing.

That point may helpfully be kept in mind when examining the results of a systematic review of the effectiveness of various treatments for test anxiety. Hembree (1990) found that individuals who had scored high on measures of maths anxiety improved their scores on standardized maths achievement tests immediately after behavioural and cognitive-behavioural interventions that had brought down their levels of anxiety about the subject. This suggested to Ashcraft *et al.* (1998) that their abilities had previously been underestimated because anxiety had disrupted their test performance. Further work by that team indicated that anxiety disrupts maths performance selectively. The greatest impact is experienced when the maths tasks that are set involve close concentration and a challenge to working memory. In contrast, high levels of anxiety did not disrupt performance on the recollection of simple number bonds or the completion of straightforward addition and subtraction sums. When working with individuals who show high levels of anxiety about maths it is important to investigate how exactly their learning is affected. It may be that they will show depressed performance across the board, but they may only underperform on tasks that make high demands on working memory where their concentration is disrupted by thoughts of anticipated failure.

'Reading' mathematics

Some have argued that communication is at the core of the subject and that maths should be seen 'as a "language" in the same way that Italian is a language' (Rowland 1995: 54). But there are some important differences too. In everyday life many of the concepts we use most often are imprecise, contradictory and ambiguous. We tend to qualify what we say and put our thoughts forward tentatively. Mature adults like to express uncertainty and feel it is important to be able to tolerate ambiguity. When we talk, our comments are often repetitive, circular, imperfectly structured and full of redundancy. It is often claimed that mathematical thought is very different so that mathematical language is abstract, unambiguous, precise and without redundancies. This may be one reason why some people find the subject intimidating.

A specific source of difficulty in learning the language of maths is its reliance on special symbols. First, the speech forms used for '+', '−', etc. vary a great deal. Teachers have to decide when to employ one form consistently in order to aid understanding in their own classroom and when to vary the forms they use in order to aid generalization to other settings. (Misunderstanding is commonplace. Kerslake 1982 found that 29 per cent of a sample of 194 London pupils aged 12–14 had an accurate view of what $3 \div 4$ means, but 52 per cent read it the other way round – as 4 divided by 3.) Second, the same symbol may be used in ways that appear intuitively different. For example, the symbol '×' causes integers such as 3 to increase (as in $2 \times 3 = $) but fractions such as three quarters to decrease (as in $2 \times \frac{3}{4} = $). Third, the abstract character of mathematical symbols creates difficulties for children who may understand a concept in context but not when contextual cues are removed. In a useful chapter on the language of testing, Davis (1991) quotes the example of a 4-year-old boy who answered accurately the question 'How many is two elephants and one elephant?' but gave the wrong answer immediately afterwards to 'How many is two and one more?' Fourth, the organization of mathematical symbols in writing or print presents a challenge to children who are confused about left and right, or have problems over sequencing, or have visual-perceptual difficulties. For example, a child may read 34 as 43, or may tackle a decimal sum from the wrong direction, or may make frequent mistakes when reading down a column of figures.

Many of these problems arise because in a decimal system place value is crucial: the same digit (e.g. 3) means *three* if it appears in the right hand *units* column and *thirty* if it appears in the left hand *tens* column. Children in English-speaking countries often struggle to appreciate this (Jones and Thornton 1993). There is evidence that place value difficulties may be less acute for children in some other language communities, notably in Asia. Children appear to achieve higher standards of accuracy and speed in place value judgements in countries where the language reflects place value in a more systematic and consistent way than English (e.g. saying the equivalent of 'ten and four' instead of 'fourteen'). This has been shown in a number of comparative studies – for example, focusing on children from Japanese and Anglo-American backgrounds (Miura 1987; Miura and Okamoto, 1989) and children in Korea (Fuson and Kwon 1992). The language factor has been over-interpreted by some commentators to explain national differences in other aspects of maths achievement that almost certainly have a broader cultural basis.

In addition, Towse and Saxton (1998) have shown in a series of experimental studies that there may be non-linguistic explanations for some of the specific findings on place value. However, the fundamental conclusion remains in place: where the language of number is inconsistent in its structure, children are more likely to experience difficulties in learning to use it for maths and to transform it into its two written forms – number words and Arabic numerals. Fuson *et al.* (1997: 764) have proposed strategies for addressing the issue with Spanish-speaking children in the USA:

> . . . the widely reported gap in performance and understanding between East Asian children and children in the United States can be narrowed or eliminated, even in poor inner-city schools. Doing so requires a substantially more ambitious first-grade curriculum and active teaching that supports the children's construction of a web of multiunit constructions in which number words and written number marks (numerals) are related to ten-structured quantities.

Mathematicians' claims that the language of their subject is exact and concise appear to be undermined also by the ambiguous ways in which everyday terms are often used in maths education. An example of this was highlighted by Jones (1997) in a question he found in the 1993 National Curriculum Key Stage 3 tests. The topic was the price of popcorn containers. The illustration showed a plastic barrel that was 10cm high costing 22p, and another that was 30cm high

Table 12.2   Categories of words used in the teaching of mathematics

Words that have the same meaning in mathematical English as in ordinary English	Words that have a meaning only in mathematical English	Words that have different meanings in mathematical English and ordinary English
cat	hypotenuse	difference
dog	parallelogram	product
because	coefficient	parallel
it		odd
taxi		mean
shelves		value
climb		

Source: Shuard and Rothery (1984, Ch. 3).

costing £5.50. The maths question was: 'Is it true that the bigger container is better value? Explain your answer'. Jones argued that a reasonable answer could refer to how much popcorn the purchaser might actually want. But that was not allowed for in the marking scheme and would receive no credit. Students were expected to restrict themselves to an arithmetical interpretation of the word *value*. Shuard and Rothery (1984) analysed the problems posed by three categories of words that are used in maths (see Table 12.2). It is words in the right-hand column that cause most confusion (Otterburn and Nicholson 1976).

There is an additional dimension of linguistic complexity and ambiguity for bilingual children. In an earlier report on a GCSE paper set in Wales, Jones (1993) analysed the effect of translating the general English word 'similar' (in a phrase about 'similar triangles') into a Welsh word – cyflun, which is used only in maths. In a sample of Welsh and English speakers who were matched for overall maths achievement, the Welsh speakers did almost twice as well as the English speakers on that item. Wiliam (1994) showed how the technical and non-technical uses of terms for 'speed' and 'velocity' in the two languages could work in the opposite direction, making items more difficult in the Welsh version.

It is not just the vocabulary of maths that causes difficulty. The syntax in which mathematical ideas are expressed is often more complex than children are accustomed to in other areas of the curriculum. Examples include the use of the passive voice (as in 'Each side of the equation is divided by 3') and conditional clauses (as in 'if . . . then') (Shuard and Rothery 1984). Dawe (1983) showed that knowledge of logical connectives in English such as 'if' was a key factor in predicting the performance on maths tests of both monolingual English-speaking children aged 11–14 and bilingual speakers of Italian, Punjabi, Mirpuri and Jamaican Creole in the same age group in a sample of schools in two English counties. The bilingual children appeared to do less well overall, partly because of the difficulties they experienced with this syntactical construction in English. It was not clear how far the same would have been true if they had been tested in their first languages. On the basis of work with bilingual pupils in Bradford, Burwell *et al.* (1998: 22) advocated that teachers use the following checklist when communicating about maths to children, whether in written or spoken form.

Teachers should aim to use:

1 simple sentence structure;
2 one fact per sentence;

and ensure that:

3 any extra information given is useful;
4 questions are split into sections, as appropriate;
5 the first part of the question can successfully engage the whole group;
6 the question tests the mathematical skills of the child, not their English comprehension.

One initiative within the NNS has been to try to standardize the mathematical vocabulary that is introduced to each year group through Key Stages 1 and 2 (Department for Education and Employment 1999c). This will have many advantages, particularly when children move between schools. However, it will be important that teachers do not take it for granted that children with SEN and those learning EAL are familiar and competent with all the words listed for previous year groups.

Specific learning difficulties

It is relatively rare for a child to experience specific learning difficulties solely in maths – sometimes called 'dyscalculia' (Chinn and Ashcroft 1998). In the National Child Development Study of a large sample of children born in one week in 1958, only 1 in 100 met the criterion set by the investigators for 'specific mathematical failure' (Blane 1980, cited in Sutherland 1988). Surveys over the years have shown that it is more common for problems in maths to be associated with problems in literacy learning ('dyslexia') (Lewis *et al.* 1994; Light and DeFries 1995). For some children this may be because, as noted above, school maths tasks often make heavy demands on reading skills: the learning difficulties in maths arise from a cycle of failure based on learning difficulties in reading. Clements (1980) found that a quarter of the errors made in written mathematical tasks by low-achieving 12-year-olds were reading or comprehension errors. Average achievers made fewer errors overall, and a lower proportion of their errors were caused by problems of reading comprehension.

For some of the children who show difficulties in both mathematics and reading there may be a common underlying neurological deficit. For example, the same underlying problem that makes it difficult for a child to represent or retrieve phonological information while reading (see Chapter 11) may also make it difficult to represent or retrieve basic arithmetic facts in semantic memory (Geary 1993).

There is evidence that genetic and environmental factors both play a part when children have specific learning difficulties in maths alone or in reading and maths together (Light and DeFries 1995). A number of researchers in developmental neuropsychology have attempted to investigate whether different patterns of learning difficulties in basic school subjects are associated with different cognitive profiles. For example, Rourke and Finlayson (1978) suggested that children with problems only in arithmetic (Group A) may have right hemisphere dysfunction, while children with problems in both arithmetic and reading (Group R-S) may have left hemisphere dysfunction. In general, investigations of possible 'subtypes' of learning disability in maths along these lines have yielded inconsistent results (see Table 12.3). However, as techniques of investigation in neuropsychology and genetics become more sophisticated, it is possible that more consistent patterns will be identified among the many factors that contribute to learning difficulties in maths.

Learning difficulties in mathematics associated with other SEN

Children who have sensory or physical difficulties often experience related problems in maths. For example, a high proportion of children with cerebral palsy have oculomotor defects that affect the movement of the eye muscles. In addition, a substantial minority have impaired vision. As a result they may find it difficult to synthesize elements into wholes and to discriminate between background and foreground in what they see. There is a negative impact on the incidental learning of mathematical concepts in everyday life and on progress with formal mathematics in school (Chazan 1974).

At the same time many children with special needs will show compensatory strengths. For instance, some pupils with visual disabilities surprise their teachers in mainstream schools by particular success in mental computation. This appears to arise because they regularly rely on their memories rather than checking in books for what they need to know (Chapman and Stone 1988). But the same children will be handicapped if they are provided with the kind of textbook that is designed to make maths accessible and attractive for most children – visually stimulating in design, packed with illustrations, diagrams and graphs with fragments of text squeezed between them.

In the case of hearing impairment Nunes and Moreno (1998) have challenged the notion that the disability as such is a 'cause' of difficulties in learning maths because of the lack of some supposedly essential process in development. They pointed out that there is only a weak relationship between degree of hearing loss and maths test performance (Powers et al. 1998). Their investigations extended to exploring children's success and errors with materials designed to minimize communication problems. They found evidence that the hearing impaired and hearing children in their sample were progressing along the same developmental path. There was no sign of a qualitative difference in their approaches to learning how to tackle more difficult problems. They used 'schemas of action', including

Table 12.3 Some findings from neuropsychological research on correlates of learning difficulties in maths

		Children with low arithmetic scores and average reading/spelling scores (Group A)	*Children with low arithmetic scores and low reading/spelling scores (Group R-S)*
General cognitive skills*	Rourke and Finlayson (1978)	Poor performance on visuo-spatial, psychomotor and non-verbal reasoning tasks Arithmetic errors attributed to difficulty in spatial organization and grapho-motor output Left hemisphere dysfunction?	Poor performance on auditory-perceptual tasks Arithmetic errors attributed to difficulty with arithmetic facts and printed word problems Right hemisphere dysfunction?
	Share *et al.* (1988), Shalev *et al.* (1995)	Found evidence for the crossover effect between left and right hemisphere in boys but not in girls. Found patterns in the arithmetic errors of subgroups with left and right hemisphere dysfunction that were not consistent with Rourke and Finlayson's findings.	
Working memory	Siegel and Ryan (1989)	Poor memory for arrays of coloured dots that they had counted but not for a series of dictated sentences	Poor memory for both the arrays of coloured dots and the series of dictated sentences
	Swanson (1993) (cf. Hitch and McAuley 1991)		Failed to find evidence to corroborate subgroup differences. His results suggested instead that 'learning disabled children, regardless of their ability in math or reading, experience a generalised deficit in working memory' (p. 112).

* On distinct patterns of learning difficulty with dysfunction in left vs. right hemisphere see also O'Hare *et al.* (1991).

Source: Macaruso and Sokol (1998: 202–3).

counting, to analyse numerical situations. But there were extra hurdles for the children with hearing impairment. For example, they found it more difficult to learn the counting string and to use it to solve problems.

Research of this kind, which studies the thinking processes involved in maths performance, may lay the basis for developing effective intervention strategies. In their major review of the literature Powers *et al.* (1998) noted that there has been a shift in research focus away from factors pertaining to deafness as such to factors within the school environment. This had emerged earlier in research on other types of special need. For example, Bennett and Cass (1989) studied in detail the forms of support given in the classroom when five children transferred from special (ESN-M) schools to mainstream primary and secondary schools. They showed, among other things, that there was a lack of continuity between the two types of school. Three of the children experienced either totally novel work in their new school for which they were not prepared or repetitive work that took them back to a level they had already mastered.

A particular issue for many children with special needs in mainstream maths classes is the *pace* of teaching and learning. A visually handicapped pupil may have mastered the essential maths in a problem but may need longer than others to process the text and to produce a response (Mason and Tobin 1986). Altern atively, children with sensory disabilities may need more time (and more varied practical experience) to learn and consolidate a new concept in number or geo- metry. Careful planning of the use of learning support assistants may be a crucial step in ensuring success. If differentiation is to be effective, it needs to take account of children's specific needs in relation to particular tasks. There will be only limited benefits from an inflexible formula, such as 'teach key terms intensively before they are introduced in the general classroom'.

Learning difficulties in mathematics: assessment for intervention

Assessment in the context of educational reform

In most education systems, including the UK, systematic national or regional assessment arrangements are now in place that make it possible to monitor the overall progress of large groups of children on core elements of the curriculum, including maths. The introduction of a tighter testing regime is intended to ensure that schools and teachers are accountable for the results they achieve with their pupils. It is hoped that 'high-stakes testing' will improve standards by focusing instruction on the required curriculum and enhancing the motivation of both teachers and pupils. The evidence to support these aspirations is nebulous, and the impact on approaches to teaching may be more complex (and sometimes negative) than anticipated. For example, there may be excessive teaching to the test, resulting in a narrowing of the received curriculum, and there may be a lack of faith in the validity of the test, resulting in feelings of dissonance and alienation (Smith 1991, analysed by Gipps 1994, Ch. 3). However, there is an international trend towards this strategy, and it is likely to remain in place for some time before the usual cycle of further reform replaces or modifies it.

Large-scale systems of assessment are not usually sufficiently fine-tuned to make it possible to analyse the learning difficulties of individual children, but they provide a clear framework of expected achievement against which individual progress can be monitored. Traditionally this has led to detailed diagnostic assessment which underpins careful differentiation in teaching. However there is a tension between that approach and initiatives such as the NNS in England, which emphasize whole-class teaching and caution against excessive differentiation (Department for Education and Employment 1998a, 1998b). Within this strategy the Numeracy Task Force (1998b, para. 134) identified in particular the importance of:

- gathering information about each pupil's strengths and weaknesses, whether from formal or informal tests, responses in class discussions, performance in problem-solving or investigation tasks in which pupils apply their knowledge;
- agreeing personal targets with each pupil, and discussing and reviewing their progress towards them;
- giving constructive feedback, which will enable pupils to improve their strategies;
- using the information gained from assessment whether at the start of a topic, at the end or midway through to plan mathematics;
- meeting with other teachers at the school to assess and discuss pupils' work; and
- ensuring that systems for recording assessment information meet teachers' planning and reporting needs, and are easily understood, without becoming too time-consuming to maintain.

This guidance may well have a positive overall impact on school practices as they affect the achievement of most pupils without necessarily enabling teachers to identify and meet the needs of those children who are experiencing severe difficulties. Your response to Activity 12.1 above will have indicated how far you feel comfortable with the scope for differentiation in the Numeracy Task Force's prescription for practice. In the rest of this section we will describe strategies that are available to identify individual learning needs in maths. Many of the strategies are based on a teach–assess–teach cycle. With some children it will only be possible for teachers to follow through the implications of what they observe in such a strategy if the organization of the classroom and the school allows some degree of effective differentiation.

Assessment in the service of teaching

Traditionally children's mastery of mathematical knowledge and mathematical techniques has been the main focus of assessment. But, as noted earlier, there are other important aspects of performance that have a crucial impact on long-term results – thinking processes, problem solving strategies, creativity, confidence and attitudes towards maths. In the UK, work in the APU during the 1980s showed that assessment can be broadened to cover these features (Foxman *et al.* 1989). Classroom learning is a social process, and a rounded picture of the potential strengths and the learning needs of children with difficulties will also include observations on their ability to work autonomously and to work collaboratively in pairs or in teams. The guidance for the NNS takes account of these factors. It is essential that the detailed monitoring and assessment that is carried out when children are identified as being at risk investigates the possibility that problems in working autonomously or working collaboratively are exacerbating their learning difficulties.

A central aim of classroom assessment must be to help teachers to plan their teaching. This happens all the time, not just through formal testing. Throughout a lesson children will be observed closely to check their level of understanding. Teachers will look out for clues such as a change in demeanour, an ability to modify what has been heard rather than simply copy it, an ability to explain something to other children (Reynolds *et al.* 1995). The pace of the lesson and the use of concrete illustrations or textual materials will be adapted in the light of these insights. Unfortunately, sensitivity to relevant clues may be blunted when a pupil who comes from a different cultural background is not comfortable with the conventions of the classroom or gives non-verbal signals of comprehension or puzzlement that are unfamiliar to the teacher (Tharp 1989, 1994). In these circumstances the lesson may not be planned in an adaptive way that takes account of the pace of children's learning and provides scaffolding when it is needed.

In the past, formal assessment procedures have often consumed a great deal of resources and effort with remarkably limited feedback to those involved. The Numeracy Task Force was aware of the danger of this and gave more attention to what is to be done with the findings from assessment than to the detailed content of assessment tasks and tests. The justification for this was that evidence has accumulated that, when pupils are given frequent and detailed feedback about their learning, they often make substantial learning gains. In a thorough review of the available research Black and Wiliam (1998) showed that the nature of the feedback is crucial. They argued that feedback is more likely to have a positive impact on subsequent learning when, among other things, it:

- is designed to stimulate pupils to think further about the original learning task in the light of whatever additional information has now been provided (Bangert-Drowns *et al.* 1991);
- goes beyond informing pupils how far short their response was of a required standard and seeks also to suggest to them what they need to do to close the gap.

There are good reasons for believing that children with learning difficulties will be particularly reliant on feedback being explicit on such points.

Individual diagnostic assessment in mathematics

Ascertaining how the gap may be bridged requires *diagnostic* assessment. A variety of techniques may be employed:

1 the analysis of errors in written work;
2 published diagnostic materials;
3 informal observation;
4 questioning pupils and discussing their concepts and methods of work with them.

Often some combination of (1), (2) and (3) may be followed up by (4). These processes will generate hypotheses about what is going wrong, but the value of the conclusions that are drawn can only be assessed by implementing teaching strategies based on the information and evaluating the outcome.

In the past *analysis of errors* has often been advocated as the key approach. For example, West (1971: 467) wrote: 'Diagnostic teaching is teaching that looks at the errors children make and subsequently structures the learning experiences so that the errors will be eliminated'. When analysing errors in written work, West advocated that at the simplest level an attempt is made to distinguish between systematic (conceptual/process) errors and random (careless) errors. Is there any pattern to the careless errors? Do they occur in particular kinds of work or at a particular stage (e.g. after working for some time, suggesting a fatigue or boredom effect)? Where there are systematic errors, can one infer how they occurred – i.e. what misconceptions or faulty line of reasoning lay behind them? Stakes and Hornby (1996: 75) suggested that the key points in any assessment of difficulties relate to:

- What did the child get wrong?
- Why did they get it wrong?
- Is it a problem of the perception of how to address the task?
- Can children complete the task with the use of concrete examples?
- Can children explain the process which they are required to do? At which point are they not able to do this?

Teachers may attempt a more detailed categorization of the causes of a child's errors through inspecting written work and via structured questioning. Newman (1983) devised materials to explore whether errors chiefly arose during one of the following processes:

- reading the question;
- comprehending the question (specific terminology or general meaning);
- translating the question into an appropriate mathematical form (not all questions require transformation);
- process skills – i.e. working out the answer using an effective method (for numerical items errors might include random response, using an incorrect operation such as subtraction instead of addition, using the correct operation but in an incorrect way, faulty computation, no response);
- encoding the answer – i.e. writing it down incorrectly;
- carelessness (e.g. gives correct answer on second try and shows good understanding when questioned);

- motivation or attitude;
- task form (e.g. source of error appears to lie in ambiguous wording or poor presentation of the item).

Alternative approaches to categorizing children's errors may be found in Ashlock (1982) and Chinn (1985). It is possible for the analysis of errors to be carried out on computer. A computer-administered test can adapt its questions systematically to the child's responses, identifying and probing areas of difficulty as the test proceeds.

Such strategies develop hypotheses about children's difficulties solely on the basis of an analysis of their errors. But it may be worthwhile probing even when no error has been made. This can lead to a fuller appreciation of pupils' understanding of the task and the concepts involved in it (Foxman *et al.* 1989). It may enable the teacher to gain information about the methods pupils have used to reach their solutions and suggest the best way to help them develop further on the basis of their existing knowledge and problem solving style. Published materials designed to facilitate this process include the *Early Mathematics Diagnostic Kit* (Lumb and Lumb 1989), the *Quest* materials (Robertson *et al.* 2000) and a diagnostic procedure designed for children with dyslexia (Chinn and Ashcroft 1998).

Published materials such as these can make a significant contribution to diagnostic assessment in extreme cases, but the first and most important contribution will be made by *informal classroom observation* during the course of everyday maths sessions, including the Numeracy Hour. It is valuable to observe the child in a range of situations, both when maths is the ostensible subject and when mathematical concepts or procedures are being used in the course of other work. This is probably the most effective way of checking some hypotheses that you may have formed after examining children's written work and deciding that they are underperforming in maths (Charles *et al.* 1987; Sawyer 1995). You might check whether:

- they do not read the instructions fully before tackling a problem or they do not act on what they read;
- they do not take time to work out what a problem is about before starting work on it;
- they adopt ineffective strategies when attempting a new task or when faced with a task on which they have made errors previously;
- they employ unsystematic problem solving strategies when tackling a task or frequently change their approach without allowing time for one strategy to bear fruit;
- they stick to a single strategy and do not try a different approach when it is unsuccessful;
- they seek help appropriately when faced with a difficulty;
- they lose concentration quickly when they find something difficult;
- they work at a very slow pace, losing track of what they are doing;

- they race through their work making many careless mistakes without noticing that there are errors;
- they are frequently off task and take avoidance action such as making frequent trips to the toilet or interfering with other children;
- they do not check their work when it is finished;
- when working with others on a joint task, they adopt a passive role, contribute little to any discussion or wait for others to take the initiative and then follow;
- they could make effective use of concrete support materials such as interlocking cubes, a number track or a number line;
- they adopt a defeatist or hostile attitude when working in maths.

Informal observation will not be effective in facilitating pupils' progress unless the teacher's findings and conclusions are recorded systematically. This can be done with a minimum expenditure of time through the use of small 'free comment' cards that are prepared in advance, or structured checklists, or a simple rating scale (Charles *et al.* 1987). It is essential to minimize bias (see Activity 12.3)

There are some assessment questions which cannot be answered by examining children's test results or written products, or by observing them while they are working. For example, there are limits to what can be inferred about their thinking processes and about *why* they work as they do. So additional assessment information may be gleaned by *questioning pupils* about maths informally (and, in extreme cases, through a structured interview). It is helpful to have in mind the stems with which informal questions might begin. A teacher needs to be aware of what each type of question might achieve in terms of illuminating a child's areas

---

ACTIVITY 12.3   Minimizing bias in classroom observation

It is sometimes very difficult to avoid bias when observing children in the classroom. Bias reduces the accuracy and effectiveness of diagnostic assessment by distorting what one sees and records and by clouding one's judgement.

Examine the list of possible hypotheses on pages 355–6 and rate each of them on a scale of 1–5 on how far you think observations to check them are likely to be prone to bias in the case of:

(a) boys vs. girls;
(b) children from different ethnic groups represented in your area;
(c) children with physical or sensory difficulties working in a mainstream classroom.

A rating of 1 means that you do not think any form of bias at all likely, while a rating of 5 means that you think many teachers would find it difficult to avoid being affected by stereotyping or negative expectations when focusing on this particular aspect of a child's performance or behaviour with a child from this particular group.

When you have rated each of the statements for groups (a), (b) and (c), examine those to which you have given a rating of 3 or above. How do you think the likelihood of bias could be minimized in each case?

of mastery and weakness. Random questioning achieves little. Time is at a premium both because other pupils require attention and because the concentration span and length of recall of many children with learning difficulties is limited. So the aim should be to probe systematically in order to find out what a child has and has not mastered in the target area of maths. A further, and perhaps even more important, goal will be to identify the emerging skills and knowledge that they can only demonstrate securely with support from another person. Charles *et al.* (1987) suggested the following possible list of question stems:

1 How did you . . . ?
2 Why did you . . . ?
3 What did you try . . . ?
4 How do you know that . . . ?
5 Have you . . . ?
6 How did you happen to . . . ?
7 How did you decide whether . . . ?
8 Can you describe . . . ?
9 Are you sure that . . . ?
10 What do you think . . . ?
11 How do you feel about . . . ?

Questioning can explore these aspects of mathematical learning (Kerslake 1982):

- *Factual recall*: What are two threes? What is this shape called?
- *Application of facts*: What are all the factors of 24? Is this quadrilateral a rectangle?
- *Making hypotheses*: What does this suggest about the sum of the angles of a triangle?
- *Interpretation of results*: What does that tell us about the product of negative numbers?
- *Application of reasoning*: How do you know H is a subgroup of G?
- *Problem solving*: Can you suggest how to find the biggest volume we can enclose with this paper sheet?
- *Control*: Are you concentrating on this?
- *Genuine inquiry*: What do *you* think? How do *you* see it?

Foxman *et al.* (1989, Table 7.2) identified five types of response given by pupils in an APU study to the question 'How did you get your answer?'

1 No idea ('I guessed').
2 No indication of method ('I did it in my head', 'I worked it out').
3 General description ('I decided how many minutes to add on', 'I subtracted').
4 Detailed description, method partly correct ('It's 20 minutes from 9.40 to 10 and 12 minutes after, so add 20, 10 and 3 = 33 minutes').
5 Detailed description, method correct.

An example of the value of such questioning for the planning of future teaching may be seen in their study. When asked to find the time interval between

7.40 a.m. and 8.20 a.m., one pupil said: 'I imagined the face of a clock and worked out that 7.40 was 20 to 8, then up to 20 past is 40 minutes' (Foxman *et al.* 1989: 202). This pupil evidently found it helpful to use visual imagery to solve such problems. A teacher who was aware of this could suggest an imagery-based strategy when the pupil faced a mathematical problem they were finding very difficult.

Wiliam (1999: 18) has discussed the role of 'rich questioning' in work with a whole class (cf. Askew and Wiliam 1995: 12–13):

> it has become abundantly clear that students' naïve conceptions are not random aberrations, but the result of sophisticated and creative attempts by students to make sense of their experience. Within a normal mathematics classroom, there is clearly not enough time for the teacher to treat each student as an individual, but the good news is that the vast majority of the naïve conceptions are quite commonly shared, and as long as the teacher has a small battery of good questions it will be possible to elicit the most signific-ant of these misconceptions. If the teacher then does have any time to spend with individual students, this can be targeted at those whose misconceptions are not commonly shared. After all, teaching is interesting because students are so different, but it is only possible because they are so similar.

In a classroom where *all* pupils can expect to have their mathematical thinking probed in an exacting way, those who have learning difficulties are more likely to feel comfortable with an approach that focuses separate individual questioning on their particular areas of uncertainty and failure. The teacher's diagnostic information (as well as the pupil's confidence) will be enhanced if the questioning also probes how they achieve success in the tasks they complete satisfactorily.

Questioning strategies and other diagnostic procedures enable teachers to in-vestigate hypotheses about what a child who seems to have difficulties is doing. They can then develop inferences about the possible effects on the child's learn-ing of teaching them new strategies or employing different methods to teach the same strategies. To test out these hypotheses and develop an accurate under-standing of maths difficulties it would be necessary to undertake trial teaching along the new lines and evaluate its impact. This cycle of assessment, planning, action and review is in line with the general pattern recommended to schools in the draft revised *Code of Practice* (e.g. Department for Education and Skills 2001, para. 5.3). It was noted above that children with learning difficulties are particularly likely to benefit when any feedback they are given about the outcomes of assessment is explicit about what they need to do next. The same is true in relation to their teachers: an assessment–planning–action–review cycle will help them to set realistic but challenging targets for pupils with learning difficulties in maths and to develop clear ideas about how to work towards them.

Conclusions

Learning difficulties in maths must be seen in the context of the aims and scope of the school maths curriculum – which in the UK has evolved rapidly in recent years. In a multicultural society it is beneficial if the curriculum draws upon and refers to the diverse mathematical traditions that are represented in the wider society. When this is achieved, maths teaching can contribute to the achievement of broader educational aims of inclusiveness, mutual respect and intellectual flexibility. In maths, as in literacy, there is scope for deep misunderstanding in the interaction between home and school. But there is also the possibility of strong and mutually beneficial interaction and support. The NNS is transforming the learning environment for numeracy in Key Stages 1 and 2, but there are still significant weaknesses in the learning environment for maths in many classrooms.

We analysed learning difficulties in maths first in terms of what children understand about maths and second in terms of the emotional significance that maths has for many children and adults. We then examined the language that is used in maths and the challenges it poses for many learners, notably bilingual learners. Finally, there was a short account of specific learning difficulties in maths (less common than specific learning difficulties in literacy and also less well understood), and of learning difficulties in maths associated with other SEN. We highlighted that a particular challenge for many children with SEN in mainstream maths classes is the *pace* of teaching and learning. The essential maths may be within their grasp, but they may need longer than others to plan and produce a response or to consolidate a new concept.

The last section of the chapter concerned assessment for intervention. Assessment may take many forms and have many different purposes. Fullest attention was given here to individual diagnostic assessment and questioning. These processes are most effective when they occur within a well-established cycle of assessment, planning, action and review. Diagnostic assessment need not concentrate on failure and problems. It may also make a powerful contribution to the effectiveness of teaching when the teacher also explores how pupils achieve success in the tasks that they complete satisfactorily.

Chapter 13

Hearing impairment

When you have studied this chapter you should be able to:

1 Describe the main sources of hearing impairment and their impact on children's psychological development.
2 Explain the differences between a medical/deficit and a social/cultural perspective on deafness.
3 Discuss the implications for a child of the use of various systems of communication in the family and at school.
4 Analyse the particular challenges that face deaf people from ethnic and linguistic minorities.

Contents

Introduction

It was emphasized in Chapter 10 that children who are not proficient in their school's main language of instruction cannot easily access the full curriculum. This chapter concerns a group of children with SEN for whom the development of oral language is particularly challenging – those whose hearing is impaired.

Sound is a key channel of communication for human babies from birth. In daily activities such as feeding, bathing and dressing, adults interact with babies in a lively and structured way. They notice where the baby's attention is directed and comment on it, or they say something about what they think the baby is experiencing or feeling. For hearing babies, the sounds of the speech of those around them is a constant feature of their environment – a feature which, over time, reveals itself as having pattern and meaning. The speech they hear helps them to interpret regularities in their experience and make sense of them. At the same time the sounds that they themselves make, gurgling and babbling, are treated by others as a form of communication and reinforce those around them to maintain contact. The exchange of sounds plays a crucial role in infants' cognitive and social development. These achievements depend on a very fragile and vulnerable physiological system: the ear and the hearing system, illustrated in Figure 13.1.

In the outer ear soundwaves travel along the external auditory canal and hit the eardrum (the tympanic membrane) which lies across the canal, causing it to

Figure 13.1
The structure of the ear and the hearing system
Source: Ridley (1991).

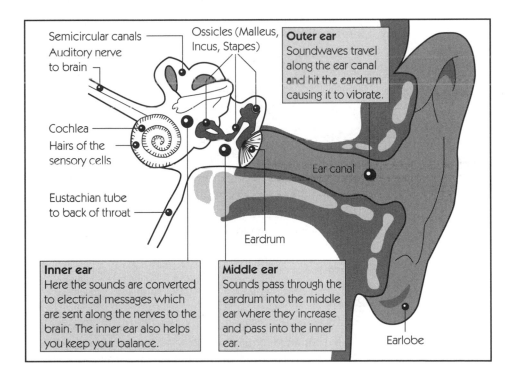

Semicircular canals
Auditory nerve to brain

Ossicles (Malleus, Incus, Stapes)

Outer ear
Soundwaves travel along the ear canal and hit the eardrum causing it to vibrate.

Cochlea
Hairs of the sensory cells

Eustachian tube to back of throat

Ear canal

Eardrum

Earlobe

Inner ear
Here the sounds are converted to electrical messages which are sent along the nerves to the brain. The inner ear also helps you keep your balance.

Middle ear
Sounds pass through the eardrum into the middle ear where they increase and pass into the inner ear.

vibrate. The vibrations are transmitted through the middle ear, an air-filled space, and greatly amplified in the process by the ossicular chain of tiny bones. The inner ear is a fluid-filled space containing the cochlea which turns the mechanical vibrations from the middle ear into electrical nerve impulses, activating fibres of the auditory nerve. Now that the sound has been detected, it must be processed and analysed in the central nervous system. The key tasks involved in auditory processing are:

Detection	Awareness	Is there a sound?
	Localization	What direction is it coming from?
Attention	Selective	Should I give it priority? Shall I focus on it?
	Sustained	Should I follow it over time?
Discrimination	Discriminate general features	Is it from a human voice? Is it meaningful in any way?
	Acoustic differentiation	What is its intensity, frequency, timing, rate?
	Segmental differentiation	If it is made up of words, can I pick up phonemic and syntactic patterns in the sound?
	Suprasegmental differentiation	What is the intonation and stress of the sound?
Organisation	Sequencing	Which sound came first and which afterwards?
	Synthesis	If they are put together, what do they sound like?
	Retention	What did I hear just before?

(Adapted from Lewis 1992)

Forms and causes of hearing impairment

In order to understand hearing impairment it is necessary to appreciate two key features of sounds and how they are measured – level and frequency. *Sound level* is the volume of a sound. It is measured in decibels (dB). At a standard distance of three feet:

Whispered speech = 30dB
Normal speech = 60dB
A loud shout = 90dB

Sound frequency is the main physical basis of our subjective impression of the pitch of a sound. Frequency largely determines whether we hear sounds as 'high' or 'low'. It is measured in hertz (Hz). The lowest C on a piano is 32Hz, the

Figure 13.2
Examples of pure
tone audiograms
Source: Watson
(1996).

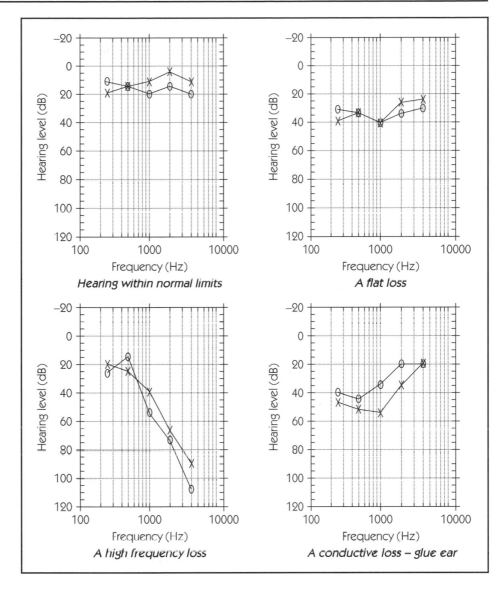

highest is 2000Hz (2KHz – kilohertz). The normal hearing range for human
beings is 18Hz–18KHz. The normal speech range is 100Hz–10KHz.

Hearing may be impaired in terms of the range of frequencies one can hear or
the volume of sound or both. As far as frequency is concerned, unless a person
can hear within the vital range 500Hz–2KHz, it is likely that their speech development will be affected. As shown on an audiogram (see Figure 13.2), a hearing
loss may be 'flat' – i.e. roughly equivalent for each frequency. Alternatively, it
may be uneven in one or both ears. For example, there may be normal hearing
for low frequencies but a loss for high frequencies (so that the graph on the right

Table 13.1 Impairment characteristic of particular levels of hearing loss

Decibel loss	Impairment	Understanding of speech
0	None	
Up to 40	Slight-mild	Some difficulties
41–70	Moderate	Difficulty with normal speech (41–55) and loud speech (56–70)
71–95	Severe	Limited/very limited understanding of speech
96+ (postlingual)		
96+ (prelingual)	Profound	Rarely show understanding of speech

hand side of the audiogram dips low). With that profile a child will hear vowel sounds clearly but will miss many or most consonant sounds – a pattern that may affect how they learn to read.

As far as volume is concerned, hearing impairment may involve a quite limited or very considerable level of decibel loss (see Table 13.1). It is typically described in terms of the average loss, even though the loss may vary between the two ears. A unilateral loss affecting one ear will be less severe in its psychological consequences than a bilateral loss affecting both ears. It should be noted, also, that the impact of any loss on development and psychological functioning will depend in part on the age of onset. A congenital loss that the child has from birth or a loss that occurs before language develops (say, before the age of 18 months) will have a greater impact than a loss that is sustained in the 'postlingual' period (i.e. after the person has developed speech and language). With all these provisos it remains helpful to be aware of the normal impact of a characteristic overall level of hearing loss.

It has been estimated that about a fifth of all children will experience some degree of fluctuating hearing loss during their first two to three years at school (Bamford and Saunders 1991: 78). Of course, the number with permanent and severe or profound hearing loss is much smaller. In the early 1980s it was estimated that approximately 1 in 770 children was born with significant hearing impairment, and for 1 in 2000 the loss was profound (Davis 1983). An estimate ten years later suggested a significant reduction in the incidence of profound loss to 1 in 2700 children (Davis *et al.* 1995). Advances in medicine were partly responsible for this. For example, it appeared that fewer children in western countries were becoming deaf as a result of their mothers contracting rubella during pregnancy. This was because of effective immunization campaigns. However, medical advances did not have an entirely positive impact on the statistics. Among the increased numbers of children who were surviving after very early premature birth there were a larger proportion who experienced serious hearing loss.

Hearing impairment is usually categorized in terms of the main site of the damage, as this is what normally determines the nature of the impairment:

- *Conductive*: physical transmission of sound in the outer or middle ear is interrupted.

Table 13.2 Main causes of hearing impairment

Type of hearing loss	Stage	Examples
Conductive	Congenital	Physical abnormality of the ear
	Acquired	Otitis media (middle ear infection)
		Glue ear
		Obstruction with wax or a small object such as a bead
Sensori-neural	Prenatal	Hereditary (e.g. Usher's Syndrome)
		Infections (e.g. rubella contracted by the mother)
	Perinatal	Lack of oxygen, jaundice
	Postnatal	Infections (of which the most common is meningitis)
		Damage from noise, accident, drugs and poisons

- *Sensori-neural*: damage to neural transmission in inner ear or auditory nerve. This is less common and more serious. It is also called perceptive or nerve deafness.
- *Mixed*: both conductive and sensori-neural loss are involved.
- *Central*: Damage to the auditory nerve in the brain stem or hearing centres of the cortex. This is also known as cortical deafness.

These forms of loss may be accompanied by:

- *Tinnitus*: noises without source 'heard' in the ear/head.
- *Recruitment*: sensori-neural sufferers may experience increased volume from loud sounds.
- *Vertigo*: giddiness experienced because the cochlea are linked to organs of balance.

The main causes of hearing impairment are summarized in Table 13.2. Overall in the past about 40 per cent of cases of hearing impairment have been linked to hereditary causes. But the relative importance of different causes changes over time. For example, as noted above, maternal rubella is now very much less common in the West as a prenatal source of risk leading to childhood deafness.

It has been estimated that 35 per cent of children with severe or profound hearing impairment have some form of impairment to their vision (Armitage *et al.* 1995). A small proportion of these will have Usher's Syndrome, a genetic condition which causes both sensori-neural hearing loss and progressive visual impairment. The eye condition is not evident at birth but becomes slowly worse as the child grows older. The outcome is variable with some adults losing vision totally and others retaining central vision throughout their lives. It appears that about 3 per cent of all children with sensori-neural hearing loss may have Usher's Syndrome (Lynas 1991).

The impression has been given so far that a hearing loss is a stable feature of an individual's experience and that, once a person's hearing is impaired, an assessment can be made and the position summarized in a single graphical representation as an audiogram. In fact, the most common form of hearing impairment in childhood, *otitis media*, fluctuates over time. If a child catches a cold with symptoms such as a runny nose, coughs and sneezes, the infection can spread into the middle ear via the Eustachian tube which leads there from the back of the throat. While the middle ear is affected, the mechanisms that enable it to conduct sound are blocked, so that the child's hearing is impaired (sometimes eventually becoming 'glue ear'). In most cases, as soon as the infection is overcome, hearing is recovered. Since some children have repeated infections, they can experience bewildering fluctuations in their ability to make sense of what is being said around them. Parents and teachers can find their behaviour puzzling; their language development and their educational progress may be affected (Haggard and Hughes 1991; Hind 1998). It can be easy for teachers to misinterpret the effects of intermittent hearing loss as chronic lapses of attention, emotional withdrawal or, when children become irritable because of it, disruptive behaviour. It is essential that teachers are alert to signs of unidentified hearing loss that they can look for in the classroom.

All such signs can have another explanation but they may indicate that a child has hearing difficulties. Some are particularly associated with 'glue ear'. The following list, which has been collated from a number of sources, including Webster and Wood (1989) and Watson (1996), may be helpful. It is worth raising a query about possible hearing loss if it is observed in the classroom that a child:

- is often slow to react to instructions or repeatedly asks what to do even though they have just been told;
- watches others to see what they do and then follows;
- constantly asks others to repeat what they have said;
- hears sometimes and not others, for example when standing on one side of the room and not the other;
- often misinterprets information and questions, or responds to only part of what has been said;
- is unable to locate a speaker or the source of a sound, especially in noisy conditions;
- has a tendency to daydream or shows poor concentration, especially during group discussions or when a story is being read aloud;
- makes inappropriate comments sometimes, as though not having followed the topic of conversation;
- has delayed language development (e.g. immature use of syntax, limited vocabulary);
- finds it difficult to repeat words or sounds or to remember the names of people and places;
- sometimes shouts without apparently realizing that they are being noisy;
- makes speech errors (e.g. omitting the consonants from the end of words, missing out s, f, th, t, ed, en);
- confuses words that sound similar (e.g. that, fat, vat);

- fixes their eyes on the speaker as though lip-reading;
- sometimes becomes disruptive during lessons in which children are required to listen;
- experiences difficulties with reading, spelling or writing;
- seems to have colds and coughs frequently.

Improving the conditions for effective hearing

There are three ways in which the physical conditions for effective hearing can be improved for children with hearing impairment.

First, better acoustic conditions can be created in the environment. For example, if a room has a carpet, curtains and soft furnishings, the amount of background noise will be reduced so that it is easier for a person with moderate hearing impairment to detect the sound signals they need to hear.

Second, children with many (though not all) forms of hearing impairment can be helped by wearing a hearing aid. Technical improvements to these aids are being achieved all the time. At present hearing aids comprise:

- a miniature battery that powers the system;
- a small microphone that collects sound and transforms it into electrical signals;
- an amplifier that increases the intensity of the signals;
- a receiver that converts the signals back into a (louder) sound.

It is possible to adjust aids to suit the individuals who wear them. For example, a child with high frequency hearing loss may best be helped by an aid that amplifies those frequencies more than others. There is usually a mechanism to cut out the loudest sounds that could be painful if amplified. Aids may be worn inside the ear, behind the ear or (for more powerful amplification) strapped onto the body. In use with children they require considerable care so that they work properly and so that the user gains the greatest benefit from them. Radio hearing aids are increasingly common. With these systems the teacher wears a transmitter which is turned on when addressing the class as a whole or a group with the target child in it. The child wears a receiver which is connected to their own regular hearing aid. A system of this kind reduces the problems caused by background noise.

The third (and newest) way of improving the physical conditions for hearing is a form of aid that can be fitted surgically for people with profound hearing impairment who cannot be helped with conventional hearing aids as they have irretrievable damage to their inner ear. A cochlear implant is an electronic device which bypasses the damaged area altogether, stimulating the nerve of hearing directly. For adults who have become deaf through illness or accident an implant can restore an auditory channel of communication which enables them to make use of their previously established language base. In working with most children the challenge is greater because the artificial channel of communication has to enable them to develop aural language from the fundamentals. Initially some critics argued that implants would give an impoverished auditory signal so that children's oral language development would not benefit: 'the human nervous system did not evolve to acquire language from cochlear prostheses' (Lane 1992: 225). Those associated with the medical centres providing cochlear implant surgery for children have attempted to offer very thorough selection, after-care services and school support (Archbold 1992; Gibbin 1992; O'Donoghue 1992). Some research has challenged the assumptions of the critics. For example, a follow-up study of 29 prelingually deaf children with three or more years of cochlear implant experience showed that their English language comprehension and production was superior to that of deaf children who had used hearing aids during the same period (Tomblin *et al.* 1999).

However, cochlear implantation remains controversial. A survey of a small sample of teachers of the deaf has suggested that, whatever the aspirations of most implant centres, the local experience is that there is little consistency in the follow-up and support services that are offered (Dryden 1997). Even when more positive views were reported from a survey carried out by members of a leading implant centre, a number of practical problems were highlighted (Archbold *et al.* 1998). A separate cause for concern has been expressed by some members of the deaf community. They were anxious not only that cochlear implantation programmes would raise false hopes for some parents and deaf teenagers but also that they would encourage the belief that 'getting rid of deafness' is a desirable objective (Lane 1992). This line of argument is based on a social/cultural perspective on deafness which is discussed in the next section.

A social/cultural perspective on deafness

The account of cochlear implants given above, which is based on advances in the medical understanding of hearing loss, inevitably makes it appear that what we are dealing with is mainly a mechanical problem. It arises because hearing is a rather fragile physiological system that can go wrong in various complex ways. As we have seen, some solutions and remedial approaches tackle the mechanical breakdown directly: a hearing aid or a cochlear implant aims to improve the efficiency of the impaired physiological system. The value of recent medical advances should not be underestimated. At the same time this should not lead us to assume that the medical perspective is the only one that has valuable insights and practical measures to offer. As with other forms of SEN, it is important to consider the role that social and communal attitudes play in the development of people with hearing impairment. In recent years increasing attention has been paid to a social/cultural perspective on deafness.

The medical/deficit perspective on deafness is based on the ideal image of an unimpaired, healthy person: to be deaf is simply to be without the ability to hear. An alternative perspective on what it means to be deaf focuses on the social and cultural status of the person in society as a whole and as a potential member of a community of deaf people. The central differences between these two perspectives

Table 13.3 Alternative perspectives on deafness

	Medical/deficit perspective on deafness	*Social/cultural perspective on deafness*
What are the implications of deafness for the individual's independent identity?	Deafness is an inherited or acquired deficit of the sensory apparatus which inevitably leads to dependence on the hearing.	Deafness gives a person the potential for autonomous membership of a community of deaf people with a shared language, culture and heritage.
What are the implications for the development of communication skills?	Attention is focused on limitations to communication through spoken and written English; the term 'bilingualism' is little used.	Attention is often focused on a form of bilingualism in which the individual makes use of a sign language as a first language with spoken or written English as an additional language.
What are the best conditions for effective communication with others?	Successful compensatory strategies are required to overcome the hearing impairment suffered by one party in a conversation (e.g. hearing aids).	Effective communication is achieved when both parties use a wholly visual mode of communication such as British sign language.
What are the implications for a child's cognitive development?	Deaf children have specific and important deficits compared to hearing children.	Deaf children will show the normal range of ability to learn if they are given an effective means of access to what other children access through hearing.

are summarized in Table 13.3 which is adapted from Cline (1997a) and draws on notes in Pickersgill (1994) and discussions in Gregory (1993) and Hindley (1997).

The value of the social/cultural perspective can be illustrated by considering the situation of those deaf children (5–10 per cent) who are born to parents who are themselves deaf. A research finding that has been influential in the development of current thinking has been the recognition that this small group of deaf young people fare better in their psychological development in many ways than the deaf children of hearing parents. Surveys have indicated that they tend to attain higher standards of academic achievement, report a more positive self-image and show greater self-reliance (Koelle and Convey 1982; Yachnick 1986; Marschark 1993).

One important factor in the more positive outcome for deaf children who are born to deaf parents appears to be that their family is likely to communicate using a sign language such as British Sign Language (Kampfe and Turecheck 1987). Deaf children of hearing parents will sometimes be well beyond the normal age of early language acquisition before they encounter a fluent speaker of a visual language – the only kind in which they can easily and quickly become fluent. This is bound to have a very adverse effect on the child's development of communication skills. Compared to hearing parents, deaf parents of deaf children may report a more positive emotional response when their child's deafness is identified (Gregory and Hindley 1996). They tend to:

- give more frequent positive facial expressions when interacting with the child as an infant, expressions that can be considered the visual equivalent of the warm tone of voice that hearing parents typically employ with their infants;
- ensure that their infant is located where they can see the parent's hands, face and eye gaze during conversation;
- maintain their infant's attention more effectively during joint play (Gregory and Hindley 1996; Hindley 1997).

Thus the parents' response to the child's deafness is a key factor in the early development of deaf children. At least in part this response is determined by general attitudes towards and awareness of deafness and sign language in society. Deaf parents are more likely to see their child as a potential full member of the community – the deaf community.

ACTIVITY 13.1   Case study: John

John is the only child (aged 5) of his devoted mother who is bringing him up alone after separation from his father when he was a year old. He had meningitis at two and became severely deaf. He attends a unit in an ordinary primary school where he spends about a third of his time in the mainstream Reception class. Many of the children there have learned that he is good at lip-reading and automatically turn towards him when they speak to him. But, while he understands spoken language quite well, John's own speech is halting and indistinct and his expressive language is limited. He lacks confidence in the classroom and is at his best when there are regular routines with which he is familiar. His command of number concepts is immature, and he tends to be restless during storytime. He has made only minimal progress in the underlying skills of reading.

Recently it has been suggested that he might be assessed for a cochlear implant operation. His mother is enthusiastic about this and is investing great hopes in it. The specialist teachers directly involved with John feel that she should move on from hoping for 'magical solutions'. The family doctor is cautioning her that most of the patients considered for the operation are found not to be suitable.

Draw up a balance sheet of the advantages and disadvantages of a cochlear implant operation for John from an educational and developmental perspective, assuming that the specialist advice is that the operation is medically possible.

Development of communication

Early years

There are differences in language development between deaf and hearing children from the outset. Although the speech sounds they make when babbling are initially similar, by 7–10 months of age the babbling of hearing babies has become significantly more complex while that of children with severe or profound prelinguistic hearing loss has become more limited (Stoel-Gammon and Otomo 1986). Their continuing development will be influenced by the forms of communication to which they are exposed. Within a deaf family where sign language is the normal mode of communication, they may develop simplified, playful hand movements with primitive elements of sign language – a form of 'manual babbling' (Petito and Marentette 1991). Within a hearing family, hearing mothers speak as much to their deaf child as they do to hearing children of the same age, and they modify their speech in similar ways (Gallaway and Woll 1994). In fact, they may adapt to the visual needs of their children, using visual communication more than mothers of hearing children and using touch more often to get the child's attention (Lederberg and Everhart 1998). But giving deaf infants this input does not mean that they understand it or even that they perceive it. The mothers in Lederberg and Everhart's study made little use of sign language with the children, even when they had attended signing classes. As is universally found in such studies, the deaf children's oral language development was severely delayed from an early stage.

Wood *et al.* (1986) analysed in some detail the preverbal stages of development that lead a deaf child to achieve effective involvement in a two-way conversation. They emphasized the changing nature of the child's participation and suggested strategies that adults can use to support a child towards fuller participation (see Table 13.4). Some of the points will not apply to children with the most severe degrees of hearing loss.

Hearing children acquire a significant proportion of their concepts, vocabulary and knowledge of the structure of language incidentally through overhearing adults and other children, through the media and through participating in group conversations. Opportunities for incidental learning of this kind are much more limited for those with hearing impairment (Gregory *et al.* 1995). All too often, deaf learners are in the position of asking what is being said in a group conversation (or a lesson) and being told: 'It's not important'. Subsequently, as with younger children, surveys of deaf adolescents have found that their oral language skills, use of syntax and vocabulary are depressed on average compared to those of hearing peers. For example, teachers of two samples of 16-year-old deaf pupils in mainstream schools in England informed Powers (1996, 1998) that almost one quarter of each group were unable to communicate easily through speech (while over 80 per cent were unable to communicate easily through sign language). The debate on school policies on sign language education and 'bilingual education' is discussed below.

Table 13.4 Preverbal stages to the beginnings of conversation in young deaf children

Stage of development	Patterns of interaction	Adult strategies
Disengaged	Child unaware of being addressed Looks fleetingly from place to place Conversation turns left unfilled Random vocalizations No synchrony between child and adult	Follow child's line of gaze and comment on what they are looking at Parallel play with commentary Use routines to encourage interaction, such as peek-a-boo, sharing a picture book, turn-taking games
Engaged	Child begins to look at object that adult is talking about Child attends partly to adult when talking Turn taking in a clear format	Create contexts for talk in the 'here and now' Encourage imitative play (play house, shop counter, dressing-up box)
Structured attention	Match between onset of adult's speech and child's attention Reads meaning or intention in social context Takes turns readily Vocalizes at appropriate point (words may not be clear)	Create opportunities for joint reference (finger puppets, small-toy play, construction toys) Adult responds contingently to child's glances, gestures or vocalizations
Structured vocalization	Few random vocalizations Vocalizations more word-like Conversational turns filled (even after not looking at adult) Responds to auditory information alone	Allow child to initiate, give time to respond Take up child's utterances and respond to intended meaning Listening activities such as listening for sound onset
Growth of autonomy and initiative	Equal conversation partnership Child actively initiates Child adds information Child interrupts, argues, teases and contradicts Child uses language to sustain social interaction, explore, question and fantasize	Facilitating strategies such as: paraphrase, expansion and clarification; personal contributions from adult; exchanges in which adult does not take control

Source: Adapted from Webster and Wood (1989).

ACTIVITY 13.2   Analysing a child's communication skills

Marschark (1993: vii) describes an incident when he was first becoming interested in the psychology of deaf children. A 4-year-old girl who was deaf visited the centre where he was working. He was asked to look after her for an hour or so in a preschool observation room while her mother and grandmother were taking part in a research project elsewhere in the building:

> My signing skills were just below beginner level then, and it did not take long for my companion to discover that fact. At one point we were looking through the observation mirror at a dramatic play center that included a 'kitchen'. My companion pointed into the room, turned to me, and made a sign. When I failed to respond, she took it (quite correctly) as a lack of comprehension. She then pantomimed putting bread into a toaster, pushing it down, taking out the finished toast, and taking a bite. Then she repeated the sign, TOAST. I was awestruck. . . .

Why do you think Marschark was awestruck? What might he have concluded from the episode about the child's communication skills?

School years

It is clear, then, that the primary challenge in educating deaf children lies in helping them to develop effective means of communication with others. A wide range of strategies has evolved for this purpose, and there has been intense controversy on the subject for more than a century. An influential International Congress for the Deaf in 1880 resolved that: 'considering the incontestable superiority of speech over signs in restoring the deaf-mute to society and giving him a more perfect knowledge of the language, the Congress declares that the oral method ought to be preferred to that of signs for the education and instruction of the deaf and dumb' (quoted by Markides 1991).

Very slowly over the last 30 years the downgrading of manual communication has been overturned. This has partly been because of convincing research evidence. Psychological studies have shown that the cognitive and social development of deaf children suffers if they are not given access to visually mediated forms of communication (Marschark 1993). In addition, linguists have recognized that the various national sign languages have all the main characteristics of an oral language (Kyle and Woll 1983, 1985). Finally, educational research has shown that oral methods do not enable most deaf pupils to keep up with their peers in basic aspects of the school curriculum (Conrad 1979).

At the same time, pressure from within the deaf community has built up to facilitate the official use of signing. A young deaf woman in an adult education group in Manchester expressed the feelings of many:

> My family don't like me to sign because they say I will lose my voice. They don't want me to go to the Deaf Club very often. My Gran thinks I have

wasted her time because when I was young she tried very hard to teach me...I know my Gran tried to do what's best for me, but she doesn't realise I need some friends who are Deaf. If I get friendly with hearing people we can understand each other but I often feel left out because hearing friends can talk to each other and not me. It feels like I'm wasting my time. I need to sign to talk to Deaf people. It can make me very happy and understand more. Sometimes I have fun with them and I am never left out with Deaf people.

(Cripps 1996)

Educators have not found it easy to develop an approach to the teaching of communication that takes account of all this evidence, builds on the skills of existing teachers and also meets the needs of the deaf community. American Sign Language, British Sign Language and other Sign Languages do not follow the structure of an oral language but have a completely different kind of syntax. This means that a child learning American Sign Language or British Sign Language is not at the same time directly laying the basis for oral communication in English. So a variety of supplementary communication strategies have been developed to support the learning of English by deaf people. These are shown in Figure 13.3.

Figure 13.3
Supplementary communication strategies to support deaf people in learning English

Cued speech	Many phonemes look similar when we mouth them. As a result, lip-reading is fraught with ambiguities and confusions. In cued speech different hand positions are employed together with speech to facilitate lip-reading.
Finger spelling	The 26 letters of the English alphabet are represented by 26 hand positions. These can be used (rather laboriously) to spell out words in English. This system appears to be used most often in schools for the deaf to support work on literacy skills (Baker and Child 1993).
Manually coded English (MCE)	American term for Sign Supported English (see below).
Signed English (SE)	A system that represents the English language grammatically in a manual, visual form. The signs for most words are based on signs used in British Sign Language, but these are supplemented by a set of specially devised grammatical signs and markers. The speaker speaks and signs simultaneously. SE is intended to help a deaf listener to interpret ambiguities in the oral language that arise because of limited hearing.
Sign Supported English (SSE)	SE without the grammatical markers. Only key words are signed in the expectation that this alone will be sufficient to facilitate comprehension.

Such approaches all emphasize the use of a visual/gestural system to facilitate an ultimate goal of using oral English fluently. Educational methods that employ visual and oral methods together with that aim ('Total Communication' methods) may be contrasted with 'oral' approaches in which language is developed through lip-reading and the use of residual hearing, together with amplification. Total Communication approaches became increasingly popular in UK schools for the deaf during the late 1970s and the 1980s compared to exclusively oral methods (Child 1991). But over the last 15 years there has been increasing pressure to take the possibility of bilingualism more seriously and to plan education on that basis. In this context bilingualism means teaching British Sign Language as a first language while English is taught as a second language. The education authority that pioneered this approach in the UK was Leeds (DAHISS 1995; Knight 1997). A teacher of the deaf there has described the policy as a variant on Total Communication:

> [The authority] employed deaf adults, trained as 'Deaf Instructors', to work alongside teachers of the deaf in the resourced primary schools. Deaf Instructors have BSL [British sign language] as their first language and thus are able to teach deaf children in BSL, while the teacher of the deaf continues to be responsible for teaching English, written and orally as appropriate and giving access to other areas of the curriculum. The policy is premised on the belief that deaf children must have access to their own language, BSL, especially those deaf children for whom it is the language most readily acquired, the preferred means of expression and the basis of cognitive growth. But they are also entitled to learn to speak English, and the teacher of the deaf provides opportunities for this.
>
> (Schmidt-Rohlfing 1993: 32–3)

After the earlier suppression of sign languages there has been an understandable reaction in the form of high hopes of bilingual education. It is not a panacea, and there are many outstanding challenges. For example, Gregory, Wells and Smith (cited in Gregory and Hindley 1996) found that deaf children in bilingual education programmes do usually become competent communicators in sign language. But the children in these programmes who develop relatively complex signing are mainly those with a signing background from a deaf family. The authors suggested that in such programmes children may sometimes receive inconsistent models of signing. Some of the hearing adults who work with them are still learning to sign themselves, and the deaf adults may modify their own language to accommodate the hearing people with whom they work. The passionate debate between those advocating oral methods and those favouring bilingual approaches continues.

In any case, bilingual approaches are only available for a minority. There is a much more powerful trend in deaf education, as in SEN provision generally, that has nothing to do with the development of language or communication *per se*. The trend is for an increasing proportion of the children to be placed in mainstream schools and for the pupils of special units to spend more of their time in ordinary classrooms. There is a risk that their particular communication needs will be overlooked in these settings. Observational studies have shown that there is a temptation for the children to adopt undemanding strategies in order to get by (e.g. copying another child or nodding instead of answering a question orally – Gregory and Bishop 1991). A major challenge for teachers is to ensure that a deaf child in a mainstream class is a full and active participant. In Activity 13.3 you are invited to consider alternative strategies for achieving this.

ACTIVITY 13.3   Teachers' conversation strategies – helpful or not?

The conversation strategies listed below are taken from a list prepared by Webster and Wood (1989: 200). They described ten of them as helpful and eight of them as less helpful.

Which ten strategies do you think would be likely to foster a deaf child's use of language in a mainstream classroom, and which eight do you think would be likely to inhibit it? Compare your ideas with a colleague and try to agree on a joint classification of the strategies into *helpful* and *less helpful*. You should also see whether you agree on the reasons for your decisions.

- Creating a context for conversation: sharing activities which are relevant and meaningful to children's lives.
- Enforcing repetition, asking children to imitate a correct model: 'Can you say *torn* not *teared*?'
- Commenting on the child's play or activity, showing an interest in what the child is doing and helping the child to explore a topic further.
- Talking with, not at, children – remember that the focus, at all levels, is the sharing of meaning.
- Deliberate teaching of vocabulary or grammar out of context: 'Today we're going to learn the names of things you find in a bathroom'.
- Using display questions: 'How many fingers am I holding up?'
- Encouraging the child to question and initiate dialogue.
- Stepping in to improve pronunciation: 'Make a better *ss* sound'.
- Talking for the child, not giving time to respond.
- Providing social oil to sustain interaction: 'Hm, that's interesting'.
- Expanding, clarifying and restating the child's intended meaning.
- Overusing two-choice questions: 'Is it blue or green?'
- Overusing wh-type questions: 'Where did you go at the weekend?'
- Incorporating some aspect of the child's contribution in the adult's response to ensure topical continuity across turns.
- Listening to what the child has to say, handing conversation back to the child each time and allowing time for a reply. Avoiding dominating the interchange.
- Using managerial, dominating and controlling comments.
- Giving personal contributions: 'I had a surprise today'.
- Using low-control moves to encourage spontaneous contributions from the child.

Deaf children from ethnic and linguistic minorities

The education of deaf children from ethnic and linguistic minorities presents particular challenges. This group is growing fast, but there has been relatively little systematic research on its size and characteristics. A National Deaf Children's Society (NDCS) survey in the mid-1980s suggested that about 18 per cent of special schools and just over 9 per cent of units and services in mainstream schools had pupils with hearing impairment from a non-European background. The community languages that were most commonly used by their families were Punjabi, Urdu, Gujerati, Bengali, Chinese and Hindi (Speedy 1986).

A later survey of children under 5 with sensori-neural hearing loss in England found that 18.8 per cent of that population were from ethnic minority backgrounds, of which the largest group (12.2 per cent) were from the Indian, Pakistani and Bangladeshi communities. In the area covered by the 12 Inner London boroughs over half the affected population was from ethnic minority backgrounds. These proportions are markedly higher than would be expected from the communities' numbers in the general population (Turner 1996). Overrepresentation was particularly marked in the case of children from South Asian communities. In studies in which the over-inclusive category 'South Asian' has been analysed further, it has emerged that it is the Pakistani and Bangladeshi groups who show the highest rate of overrepresentation (Parry 1996; Powers 1996).

There are serious concerns about the ability of existing services to respond to the specific needs of deaf children from ethnic minority communities (Sharma and Love 1991). Diagnosis may be delayed because professionals are reluctant to trust black parents' observations about their children or are confused about normal patterns of development in their community. For example, Sharma and Love (1991: 17) quoted an Indian parent who told how they took their son to the GP because his speech was developing slowly: 'His response was to say that our bilingual household was holding back his language development'. In the services covering the areas surveyed by Turner (1996) the number of qualified staff able to converse in a minority language was very small indeed. For example, 10 of the 12 Inner London boroughs had no such staff at all, although over half the children they served came from ethnic minority communities. This is an issue often highlighted by South Asian parents when asked to evaluate the services offered to them – for example, the parent interviewed by Meherali and quoted in Gregory and Bishop (1991: 58). Many teachers of the deaf share the parent's frustration and would like to see specialist interpreting services shared across local authority areas (Turner and Lynas 2000).

Surveys in both the UK (Powers 1996) and the USA (Holt and Allen 1989) have shown that deaf children from black and ethnic minority communities perform significantly less well on some measures of academic achievement than white deaf children. Powers' (1996: 114) analysis of English GCSE results suggested that it was 'not quite ethnic background itself that is the significant factor but rather the language used in the home'. But commentators have identified a wider range of factors that may disadvantage these groups of deaf pupils. In a later

ACTIVITY 13.4   Deaf children from ethnic minority communities

Zehra, aged 15

Zehra is 15 and comes from a Turkish-speaking Muslim family. There is no family history of hearing impairment. She is profoundly deaf and uses Sign Supported English in school. She is also exposed to British Sign Language which is used by the majority of her peers in school. She lives in a large city where she is able to attend a day school for the deaf and continue living at home. Her school employs a Total Communication strategy.

Recently the school staff and her parents identified small changes in the way Zehra performs everyday tasks. After a further medical examination she was identified as having Usher's Syndrome which means she is progressively losing her sight.

Zehra's parents do not speak English. They are described by a family member as a very traditional Turkish family with a strong Muslim faith. Zehra's older sister Sibel attends all the meetings in school regarding Zehra's progress. Sibel works in a bank and speaks fluent English.

At a recent review meeting in school all the professionals were concerned that Zehra should be helped to lead as independent a life as possible as a teenager for as long as her condition allows.

(a) Imagine that you are a teacher contributing to this review. How would you respond to the following questions and challenges?:

- What factors would you suggest need to be taken into account in planning Zehra's educational future?
- What further information would you seek during the review in order to ensure that any decisions that are made have a firm basis?
- Are there any stereotypes which you might expect to influence the views expressed by professionals or the family in this situation?
- What could you do to minimize the impact of stereotyped thinking?

Thaeba, aged 10

Thaeba comes from an Urdu speaking family. She has severe bilateral sensori-neural hearing loss which has recently been identified as having swiftly deteriorated to profound levels of loss in both ears. She is a member of a unit for partially hearing pupils using oral/aural approaches to communication. Her speech, which was previously quite good, is gradually deteriorating too. Thaeba has started to learn a few signs in Sign Supported English with her speech and language therapist to support her communication. It has now been agreed that Thaeba will transfer to a local school for the deaf at the start of the next academic year, where she will learn Sign Supported English as part of a Total Communication approach.

Thaeba attends a community school every Saturday to learn to read and write in Urdu, which is her family's first language. Thaeba's mother asks for your opinion as to whether she should let Thaeba continue attending Saturday school. She also wants to know what to do about learning to sign and if all the family should learn and attend classes.

(b) Consider the following:

- What factors do you think should be taken into account in answering the questions Thaeba's mother wishes to pose?
- What further information would be needed in order to give sound advice?

review Powers *et al.* (1998) highlighted three factors: the predominantly 'white' teacher population, the socioeconomic status of ethnic minority communities and language differences. In seeking appropriate measures to meet the challenge, analysts have drawn equally on insights deriving from specialists in deaf education and specialists in EAL and multicultural teaching.

In addition to tackling the staffing and discrimination issues noted earlier, the following elements have been suggested as important to a strategy for the future:

- measures to reverse negative teacher attitudes and expectations;
- improvements to parent/teacher communication as a basis for partnership;
- the introduction and celebration of the cultural traditions of ethnic minorities in the curriculum;
- the clarification of difficult issues in school language policy, such as whether greater emphasis should be placed on English or on a community language as a child's first oral language and what guidance to give parents on the use of language(s) with their child at home (Chamba *et al.* 1998);
- support for teachers to foster sensitivity and commitment in helping children to develop a strong dual personal identity as black *and* deaf;
- information materials on deaf education in community languages and information materials on minority religions and cultures in British Sign Language (Cohen *et al.* 1990; Meherali 1994).

The list focuses on school measures. There are many social factors outside school that may also have the effect of depressing the children's educational performance. The most important of these are probably the obstacles that deafness places in the way of what Meherali has called the 'immunization' provided by familiar and positive relationships within the family and immediate ethnic group against the threats posed outside in the broader society. Many children in ethnic minority communities experience sociocultural dissonance – stress and a sense of incongruity caused by belonging to two cultures: a minority culture and the dominant culture of the society where one lives (Chau 1989). For deaf children in hearing families in minority communities the balm of communicating about those stresses with others who share them may not be easily available.

Conclusions

In this chapter we have analysed a form of SEN in which the primary barriers to access to the curriculum are serious problems of communication. The most common forms and causes of hearing impairment were described, and we examined their potential impact on children's participation in school. A major challenge for architects, equipment designers and teachers is to find ways of improving the conditions for effective hearing while maintaining an appropriate learning environment for all children. Only if this is achieved will the majority of children with hearing impairment benefit from inclusive education.

The traditional medical perspective on deafness was contrasted with a social/cultural perspective. In illustrating this analysis we outlined some of the differences that have been identified between the experience of the 5–10 per cent of deaf children who are born to deaf parents and the experience of the majority of deaf children who have hearing parents. We outlined the development of communication by deaf children and discussed the passionate debate that surrounds the choice of a medium of communication for deaf children in school.

The last section of the chapter concerned the particular situation of deaf children from ethnic and linguistic minorities. It appears that a full response to the needs of this group of deaf children should have three prongs – respecting their hearing impairment, their family's cultural and religious values and language, and their unique and vulnerable identity as black and deaf, an identity that may be threatened by discrimination equally within the black community and within the deaf community. In every context educating for bilingualism must confront issues of personal and group identity. In the context of work with children who are black and deaf these issues are presented in an exceptionally complex and challenging form.

Chapter 14

Emotional and behavioural difficulties

Introduction

Definitions and distinctions

Department for Education Circular 9/94 (1994c) on the education of children who present emotional and behavioural difficulties (EBD) places these difficulties on a continuum (see Figure 14.1).

This continuum-based definition was supported by the EBD subgroup of the National Advisory Group on SEN and its continuing use recommended (Daniels *et al.* 1999a). However interviews with key staff in schools identified as having effective practice with pupils who present EBD (Daniels *et al.* 1999b) found that subject specialists and some heads of department did not make a distinction between EBD and general naughtiness in thinking about pupils presenting behavioural problems. By contrast this distinction was made by senior pastoral staff, SENCOs, headteachers and many staff in smaller schools. In discussing pupils known to them these staff described children who present EBD as engaging in difficult behaviour that is more persistent over time and pervasive across different

Figure 14.1
A Continuum of problem behaviour
Source:
Department for Education
(1994c: 7).

Behaviour that 'is simply disruptive or naughty'

- results from a child 'experiencing some emotional stress within normal and expected bounds';
- 'challenges teachers but is within normal, albeit unacceptable, bounds'.

Emotional and behavioural difficulties

- 'are persistent (if not necessarily permanent) and constitute learning difficulties';
- 'range from social maladaption to abnormal emotional stresses';
- 'may become apparent through withdrawn, passive, depressive, aggressive or self-injurious tendencies';
- 'may be associated with school, family or other environments or physical or sensory impairments';
- mean a child will 'generally behave unusually or in an extreme fashion to a variety of social, personal, emotional or physical circumstances'.

Serious mental illnesses

- 'may be episodic, but are generally indicated by significant changes in behaviour, emotions or thought processes which are prolonged and/or so severe that, taking into account the child's development and the social and cultural background, they interfere profoundly with everyday life and are a serious disability for the child, the family, friends or those who care for or teach the child'.

settings. Some reports also characterized it as more unusual for the child's age: odd or idiosyncratic. This is consistent with the further advice offered in Department for Education Circular 9/94 (p. 8): 'Whether the child is judged to have emotional and behavioural difficulties will depend on the nature, frequency, persistence, severity or abnormality and cumulative effect of the behaviour, in context, compared to normal expectations for a child of the age concerned'.

However, the distinction is not always perceived as relevant. Daniels and Williams (2000) question the value of distinguishing between behaviour problems felt to be due to naughtiness, as opposed to SEN. Their focus is very much on early intervention aimed at optimizing the learning environment to support positive behaviour. The crucial role of the environment in defining EBD is also recognized in current government guidance: 'Perceptions of whether a child's behaviour constitutes an emotional and behavioural difficulty are likely to differ according to the context in which it occurs as well as the individual teacher's management skills, tolerance levels, temperament and expectations (Department for Education 1994c: 9).

Earlier conceptualizations of EBD have frequently been characterized as exclusively 'within child', but there too there was some acknowledgement of the role of the environment in the definition. The 1944 Education Act introduced 'Maladjustment' to describe pupils who show evidence of psychological disturbance or emotional instability and who would require special education treatment to become readjusted – personally, socially and educationally. The Underwood Report on maladjusted children (Ministry of Education 1955) characterized them as follows:

- they are insecure and unhappy;
- they fail in their personal relationships;
- receiving and giving are difficult for them and they seem unable to respond to simple measures of love, comfort and reassurance;
- they do not readily improve in response to ordinary discipline.

Here, one of the defining characteristics of maladjusted, as opposed to naughty, children was seen to be failure to respond to ordinary discipline. This indicates that some weight was given to assessing the influence of environmental factors.

Circular 9/94 asserted that it is important to make a distinction between the three points on the continuum because each needs to be treated differently. This was reinforced in the Green Paper on meeting SEN (Department for Education and Employment 1997: 80) which stated that 'boundaries between EBD, ordinary unruliness, disaffection and various clinical conditions are not always clear cut but have a major bearing on the solution required'. Children who present EBD are regarded as having learning difficulties in terms of the SEN legislation in that they are considered to be experiencing barriers which cause them to have significantly greater difficulty in learning than the majority of pupils of their age. It is recognized that aggression, depression or hyperactivity may impede access to the curriculum. On the other hand, learning difficulties may undermine self-esteem or create frustration and so generate or exacerbate emotional and behavioural difficulties.

Incidence of EBD

Given the role of environmental demands and others' perceptions in defining EBD it is not surprising that both estimates of incidence and the ratings given to individuals will depend on who you ask. Rubin and Balow (1978) found that in any year 20–30 per cent of pupils were considered by teachers to present some problems of behaviour or attitude. Sixty per cent of children were considered a problem by at least one teacher during their time at primary school but only 7.4 per cent were considered a problem by at least three teachers and only 3 per cent were considered a problem by all their teachers.

Parents and teachers may have very different perceptions. In the Isle of Wight study (Rutter *at al.* 1970), parental completion of a schedule identified an almost completely different group of 'problem' children from that identified by teachers using the same schedule. For every six children identified by either parents or teachers, only one was identified by both. Tizard *et al.* (1988) reported an overlap of around 33 per cent between 7-year-olds identified as having a behaviour problem by parents and teachers. Similar results have been obtained in a number of studies carried out in different countries (e.g. McGee *et al.* 1983 in New Zealand; Verhulst and Akkerhuis 1989 in Holland), so indicating the cross-cultural applicability of these findings. Verhulst and Akkerhuis (1989) found low to moderate agreement between parent and teacher identification of EBD in children aged 4–11 years. Parents identified more problems and the highest agreement was generally reached for disruptive and other 'acting out' problems.

There are many important differences between home and school environments that might be expected to influence a child's behaviour. Furthermore, parents' and teachers' expectations are likely to differ in ways that will lead them to rate the same behaviours differently. A 6-year-old who finds it difficult to sit still and concentrate on a task for more than five minutes is more likely to be expected to do this regularly at school than at home and would therefore be more likely to receive negative ratings for these aspects of their behaviour from teachers than from parents.

Differences between teacher and parent expectations of behaviour and differences between children's behaviour at home and at school may also be culturally influenced. Keller (1988) compared parent and teacher ratings of the social behaviour of 7-year-old black, Hispanic and white children in the USA. As in other studies, significant low to moderate correlations were found between parent and teacher ratings. However, when the results for the three ethnic groups were analysed separately it was found that these conclusions only applied to the white pupils, as there were no significant associations between the behaviour ratings given by teachers and parents of the black and Hispanic children.

These studies suggest that great caution should be exercised in interpreting ratings of a pupil's behaviour when information is provided by a single rater in relation to a single setting. A much more complete picture of a child's emotional and behavioural strengths and difficulties will be provided by collecting information from different settings, both in school and outside. It has long been known that this is likely to be particularly important for pupils from minority ethnic groups (Rutter *et al.* 1974). Furthermore Keller's (1988) study suggests that parents and teachers each have even more unique and distinct information to contribute to the assessment process for pupils from ethnic minority groups than is the case for their white peers.

EBD are also reported to be more prevalent in inner cities, socially deprived families, boys, children who have other language learning, health or developmental difficulties, and among those who come from homes where there is or has been parental discord or divorce, mental health problems in the family, neglect, significant parental coldness or irritability towards the child (Department for Education 1994a).

Exclusion from school

The early 1990s saw a steep rise in permanent exclusion from school, from an annual rate of 2910 in 1990/1, through 3833 in 1991/2 to 11,181 in 1993/4 and 12,456 in 1994/5 (Parsons 1996). Only 27.2 per cent of the excluded pupils from primary schools and 14.8 per cent of those from secondary schools returned to mainstream schooling. Home tuition (for approximately five hours per week) was provided for 38.6 per cent of the primary pupils and 21.1 per cent of the secondary pupils, while 24.9 per cent of the former and 38.7 per cent of the latter attended pupil referral units where the education provided was often restricted to a narrow curriculum and was of poor quality (Ofsted 1995). Since then requirements have been placed on LEAs to ensure access to full-time education for pupils excluded for more than three weeks.

A number of possible reasons for the rise in exclusions have been discussed:

- Changes to school funding mechanisms have introduced a more market-based climate where schools compete for pupils and are very conscious of the need to maintain a positive public image with parents. It has been argued that schools may be less willing to retain and support pupils who present EBD, particularly if they would have to buy in support services. Parsons (1996) reports that exclusion rates in some LEAs were found to be as much as ten times higher than those in other, socioeconomically-similar LEAs, but it is not clear whether LEA exclusion rates are linked to the availability of behaviour support services.
- The demands of the National Curriculum may limit the flexibility available to schools to accommodate diverse pupil needs (Blyth and Milner 1993).
- The important role played by school organization and ethos is highlighted by sizeable differences in exclusion rates between schools having similar catchment areas (Ofsted 1996; Hayden 1997).

In 1999 the number of permanent exclusions started to fall for the first time since 1990, with government statistics showing a decrease of 15 per cent between 1998 and 1999. Possible reasons for this decrease, and potential repercussions in terms of teacher stress and discipline in schools, have been debated between ministers and teaching unions (Thornton 2000). Among the factors that would appear relevant to an examination of this fall in the number of exclusions are: the targets set by government, the identification of LEAs, which have been asked to produce action plans where particularly high numbers of black pupils are excluded, the requirements placed on LEAs to ensure that excluded pupils receive a full-time education and the provision of additional funding for school-based support for pupils at risk of exclusion.

Differences have been reported on the incidence of exclusion in different groups:

- *Exclusions and gender*. At secondary level around four boys are excluded for every girl, while in primary schools a ratio of 14 to 1 has been reported (Castles and Parsons 1997).
- *Exclusions and age*. Castles and Parsons (1997) reported that 12 per cent of those excluded were from primary schools and 5 per cent from special schools. Of the remaining 83 per cent excluded from secondary schools some 45 per cent were in Years 10 and 11.
- *Exclusions and race*. Gillborn and Gipps (1996) report that African-Caribbean pupils are between four and six times more likely to be excluded than are white pupils. Statistics for 1999 suggest that exclusions of black pupils are falling, although rates continue to be disproportionately high.
- *Exclusions and social disadvantage*. Children excluded from school are more likely to have experienced poverty, homelessness, parental illness and bereavement (Ofsted 1996a; Hayden 1997). Disproportionate numbers of children who were looked after by local authorities (in public care) were also excluded (Brodie and Berridge 1996).
- *Exclusions and SEN*. The rate of permanent exclusions is seven times higher for pupils who have a statement compared to those without Statements (Department for Education and Employment 1999b).

In considering the disproportionate number of black pupils who are excluded, Gillborn (1997) has hypothesized that teachers' stereotypes can lead to misperceptions and misunderstanding of black student's behaviour. In particular, teachers' perceptions of threat, described by Gillborn as 'the myth of a black challenge', may influence their interpretation of the behaviour of young black males. Particularly compelling was the fact that the teachers in this study were described as highly committed to the goal of equality of opportunity. It was suggested that only limited progress in improving the school experience of black students was likely to be made by focusing on the conscious intentions of teachers and that the focus should be shifted to a functional analysis of the consequences of their actions.

A similar emphasis on monitoring outcomes and taking positive action is apparent in recent government guidance:

Governing bodies and head teachers should monitor the use of sanctions against pupils of ethnic minority background and reassure themselves that the school's behaviour policy against racial prejudice and harassment is being fully enforced. Where there is unjustified over-representation of

Black-Caribbean pupils, a strategy should be implemented to address this. Staff need to take particular care if there is a possibility that an incident was provoked by racial harassment. Teachers also need to ensure that they avoid any risk of stereotyping and that they are alert to cultural differences in manner and demeanour. Good connections between schools and community groups can help in this process.

(Department for Education and Employment 1999b: 13)

In addition, the guidance seeks to make schools aware that 'so-called "colour-blind" policies can lead to the persistence of inequalities between ethnic groups' (p. 13). Among the measures advocated are: ethnic monitoring of achievement, community mentoring schemes, the development of a black perspective in the school curriculum and effective links between mainstream and supplementary schools. Grant and Brooks (1996, 2000) have emphasized the role that the black community can play and have described how an LEA can energize and support initiatives such as those advocated in the guidance.

When children in public care are considered it has sometimes been suggested that they may also be subject to disproportionate unofficial exclusion, justified on the grounds that they had access to full-time daycare (Department for Education 1994d). Brodie (2000) has highlighted a number of such unofficial pathways to exclusion including exclusion by non-admission, where schools refused admission to looked-after children living in local authority homes, sometimes explicitly because they were looked after. In other cases children were admitted following protracted negotiations between care staff and schools, which resulted in a considerable period of lost education. However, admission without adequate preparation was also problematic with some pupils being excluded within days of joining their new school. Best results were obtained when school and care staff worked collaboratively to devise admissions programmes, phased as necessary, to ensure the child was supported to succeed in school.

An examination of the increasing exclusion of pupils with Statements indicates that a large and growing number of these exclusions are from special schools for pupils with EBD. Schools are advised that, unless the circumstances are exceptional, they should avoid excluding pupils with Statements or those whose SEN are being assessed by the LEA. Where efforts to maintain a placement have been exhausted, schools are asked to liaise with the LEA to arrange an interim review of the pupil's Statement so that proper planning for their future education can take place. Government guidance (Department for Education and Employment 1999b) also alerts schools to consider whether difficult behaviour might be attributable to, or contributed to, by unidentified or unmet SEN.

Understanding EBD

There are a number of different approaches that can be adopted in understanding and managing pupil behaviour in schools. Given the range of the behaviour and the influences involved we will argue that a multi-level approach will usually be

Figure 14.2
The major
theoretical
approaches that
have been applied
to understanding
EBD

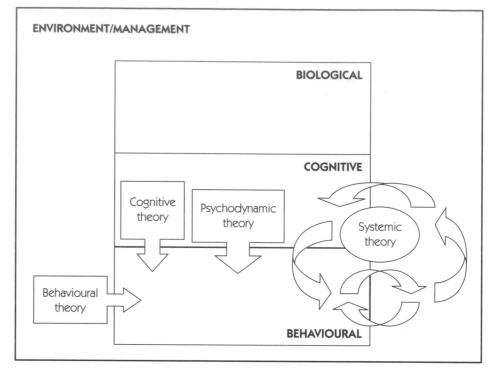

Figure 14.2 The major theoretical approaches that have been applied to understanding EBD

most useful. In the first part of this section the interactive factors (IF) framework, which is based on the work of Morton and Frith (1995) and was introduced in Chapter 4, will be used to summarize different theoretical approaches to understanding EBD. The IF framework uses three levels of description to explain developmental problems: the biological level, the cognitive level and the behavioural level and, in addition, the framework recognizes the operation of environmental factors at all three levels. At the biological level we record information about the brain and about sensory processes such as hearing and vision. Hypothesized within-child factors, including affective factors, are located at the cognitive level, while directly observable behaviours are placed at the behavioural level. The major theoretical approaches that have been developed to understand EBD are represented in Figure 14.2 using the IF framework which can help to clarify similarities and differences between them. Further information about these approaches and the assessment and intervention approaches developed from them can be found in Cooper *et al.* (1994) and Ayres *et al.* (1995).

Behavioural approaches

In behavioural approaches the primary focus is on behaviour that can be directly observed. It is assumed that behaviour is learned through what happens in a

Figure 14.3
A behavioural
approach

Consider the following example. A teacher consults an educational psychologist about a pupil's aggressive behaviour. Adopting a behavioural approach the psychologist would ask the teacher to specify what exactly it is about the pupil's behaviour which causes the teacher to call her or him aggressive (e.g. swearing at the teacher, hitting other pupils, knocking over chairs) and to identify a priority problem (in this case, swearing at the teacher) on which to collect further information about aspects of the environment surrounding the behaviour. The A (antecedents), B (behaviour), C (consequences) structure is often used to collect environmental information considered relevant. Using this, the teacher will note under B what happens on each occasion when the pupil swears at a teacher; will record under A what setting events or triggers have happened immediately prior to the swearing; and, under C, what happens as a consequence of it. This sort of pattern may emerge: A – teacher asks pupil to begin work; B – pupil swears at teacher; C – teacher sends pupil out of class to head of year who gives them a detention. Further analysis might focus on whether the work that was set was well matched to the pupil's current skill levels. For example, was it very much too difficult for them so that they had no prospect of gaining any satisfaction from attempting it? Alternatively, the analysis might focus on whether the pupil's actions bring them positive outcomes in terms of avoiding work and gaining personal time alone with the head of year.

child's environment, so that well-established patterns of behaviour can be changed by changing environmental consequences or other related events. There are a number of different learning theories – for example, Pavlovian classical conditioning, Hull's operant conditioning, Skinner's neo-behaviourism and Bandura's social learning theory. They all share the basic assumptions of the behavioural approach but differ in the detailed mechanisms through which behaviour is thought to be learned. Behavioural approaches make no reference to pupils' thoughts or feelings. The relationship between the environment and pupil behaviour which they embody is represented in Figure 14.2. In understanding emotional and behavioural difficulties the focus is on clarifying the specific behaviours regarded as undesirable and identifying the features of the environment that support the undesirable behaviour or can be used to help the pupil unlearn it. Figure 14.3 provides an illustration of the application of a behavioural approach.

From a behavioural perspective the undesirable behaviour characteristic of EBD develops when children learn to engage in it because it is associated with outcomes that are positive for them. For example, screaming in the supermarket may become associated with being given sweets. More worryingly, a child may learn that parental attention can only reliably be obtained by attacking a younger sibling. Even though they may not be able to articulate the relationships between their behaviour and contingent environmental events and conditions, children are sensitive to them from a young age, as are many animals. Screaming in the supermarket may occur with one parent, but not the other. It may not occur when both are there together as the child will have learned to discriminate the conditions under which screaming is associated with getting the sweets. The child may begin to generalize the behaviour – screaming in the supermarket to get other things, screaming at home to get sweets, screaming at nursery to get toys they want, etc. Whether the behaviour becomes established in each of these new situations will depend on whether or not it is reinforced by being linked with a desirable outcome. However, a child who screams in nursery when they don't get what they want is not necessarily one whose preschool reinforcement history has taught them this response. It might be that they have learned it in the nursery – they may have observed the screaming behaviour of another child being reinforced in this way, or their own screaming might have initially occurred accidentally – in response to a fall, for example.

In the behavioural approach intervention involves changing the environmental conditions to help the child unlearn the undesirable behaviour and learn desirable behaviour instead. The more securely learned the undesirable behaviour is the more difficult it is to unlearn. The consistency with which the new environmental conditions are applied will also influence the child's progress in unlearning the undesirable behaviour. For example, the parent with whom the child has learned to scream for sweets in the supermarket might try to help the child unlearn the screaming behaviour by not giving them sweets when they scream. If the parent sticks to this plan the child, although initially likely to redouble their efforts, will quickly learn that screaming no longer 'works' and will stop. However, if the parent gives in after a couple of visits the learning for the child will be that screaming still works, not every time, but sometimes, so it is always worth giving it a try. This is likely to make the behaviour even harder to unlearn in future as it will take much longer to establish that screaming really no longer works and that the parent really isn't going to change their mind again next time.

Cognitive approaches

In cognitive approaches the primary focus is on cognitive processes – how the individual perceives events, thinks about them, plans and problem solves. It is assumed that the relationship between environmental events and a child's behaviour will depend on the child's interpretation of events. If two children are reprimanded by the teacher they may each interpret this same event differently and attribute responsibility accordingly. One may feel that they deserved the reprimand and that they are to blame, while the other may feel that the teacher was picking on them unfairly and blame the teacher. An important factor in their response will be the way in which they *perceive* events. It is argued that in order to change the behaviour of children who present EBD it is important to help them change the way in which they think about themselves and the world. Different cognitive theories focus on different processes. Examples include:

- children's perception of themselves and their self-esteem;
- their attributions for the causes of their difficulties – for example, to themselves or others;

Figure 14.4
A cognitive
approach

> Returning to our example of the pupil who swears at the teacher when asked to begin work, an educational psychologist who adopts a cognitive approach will be concerned to investigate the pupil's perception of events and the meaning they have been given. In addition to considering whether the work presented is appropriate given the pupil's current skill levels, it will be important to determine whether the pupil believes this to be the case. Even if the work is well matched to their current skill levels, a pupil with a history of academic difficulties and low self-esteem as a learner may perceive the situation as threatening. Alternatively, such a pupil may perceive differentiated work as 'babyish' and attribute the teacher's gentle but public prompt to begin work as an attempt to draw attention to the work and show them up in front of their friends. When they get sent out of class the pupil may not attribute responsibility for this to themselves (as a consequence of swearing at the teacher) but interpret it as further evidence that the teacher hates them, has no interest in helping them and wants them 'out'.

- their attitudes and how they develop and change;
- their skills in problem solving, applied to situations that arise in their everyday interactions with other people.

Cognition can mediate the effects of events at the biological as well as the behavioural level. Mediation of biological-level influences is well illustrated by anger and anxiety management programmes where children are taught to recognize physiological indicators of these emotions at an early stage (e.g. pounding heart, sweaty palms) and to engage in re-labelling and other self-talk strategies in order to stay calm and not be panicked into 'fight' or 'flight' behaviour. For example, the following segment of constructive self-talk involves re-labelling: 'I am beginning to feel upset because they said I can't play and that might mean that they hate me. But it probably just means that they have got enough people for the game. That is disappointing, but is not something to get really upset about. I'll look for a game that hasn't got so many people and ask to play in it'. Figure 14.4 provides an illustration of the application of a cognitive approach to the example discussed in the previous section.

From a cognitive perspective the undesirable behaviour characteristic of EBD develops when children misperceive and misconstrue situations, so that they respond in a way that seems appropriate and rational to them, but inappropriate to other people who see the situation differently. For example, if a pupil is bumped into in a corridor by another, most teachers and pupils would regard a physical attack as an unreasonable response. Most people would not attribute negative intent to this action – we would assume that the pupil did not mean to bump into us, that it was an accident. However, if the pupil who was bumped into instead attributes hostile intent to the other pupil, assuming that it was done on purpose, this may make them feel angry and/or anxious. This may further generate the expectancy that if the perpetrator is allowed to 'get away with it' they are likely to do worse in future, and perhaps other pupils might see them as a soft target and join in. Given this kind of negative self-talk, panic can mount and lead to the pupil hitting out at their unwitting assailant.

Traumatic life events may predispose children to interpret the world as a hostile place. Dodge *et al.* (1995) followed up children who had suffered physical abuse in the preschool years. They found that these children were four times as likely to be rated as aggressive by teachers at 8–10 years of age. The children rated as aggressive were also found to be experiencing a number of associated cognitive processing difficulties. They misperceived social situations because they tended to focus disproportionately on any hostile cues that were present (a tendency that doubtless had protective significance in the past but which was counterproductive in the present). They also showed strong hostile attribution biases about the intentions of others and held beliefs that aggressive behaviours lead to positive outcomes for the perpetrator. Traumatic violence that can lead to hostile attributional biases is not confined to out of school contexts but can also be experienced in schools, as the literature on bullying illustrates (MacDonald 1996). Furthermore, vicious cycles are often set up where children who react in ways that seem unpredictable and unreasonable become rejected by the peer group and regarded negatively by teachers. In this way their belief that the world is a hostile place can become a self-fulfilling prophesy in each new situation they encounter.

Cognitive approaches to intervention involve working with the child or young person to challenge their misperceptions, faulty beliefs or attributions and to help them learn more adaptive ways of perceiving and interpreting themselves and their world. Pupils may be helped to improve their self-esteem by substituting rewarding and supportive self-talk for defeatist and undermining self-statements. A number of studies have found that attribution retraining can have a positive impact on the behaviour and motivation of pupils with SEN that leads to improved learning progress. For example, Reid and Borkowski (1987) carried out a study with three groups of hyperactive children. All three received training in the use of memory strategies. In addition, one of the groups received training in self-control strategies while the other received attribution retraining in addition to self-control training. At the end of six intervention sessions the children who received attribution retraining used more complex strategies, placed more importance on effort and showed reduced levels of impulsivity compared to the other groups. Their relative gains were still apparent when the groups were followed up ten months later.

The cross-cultural applicability of any intervention should not be assumed but must be specifically considered. The potential of attribution retraining in this regard is suggested by a series of studies with African-American 10–12-year-olds described by Graham (1997). Pupils labelled as aggressive by both peers and teachers were found to be biased toward perceiving peer provocation as intentional. Those aggressive pupils who received a 12-session school-based reattribution programme were compared with those who had received an attention skills training programme and those who had nothing extra outside the classroom. The pupils who received the reattribution programme were found to have altered their attributions and emotional reactions after the training. Compared to the pupils in the other two groups they were also rated as less aggressive by their teachers one month after the end of the programme. Graham notes that it has often proved difficult to demonstrate behavioural as well as cognitive changes resulting from attribution retraining. This is also true for other cognitive interventions where cognitive changes are not always accompanied by changes in behaviour. A pupil's difficult behaviour will often be well established and exacerbated by responses from peers which will not be changed by a cognitive approach that focuses on the target child alone. Cognitive interventions are therefore often combined with behavioural interventions to address other influences on the behaviour.

Psychodynamic approaches

Psychodynamic approaches are based on the assumption that many of the wishes, drives, anxieties and fantasies that determine our behaviour are unconscious. Children's behaviour problems are seen as 'outward and visible symptoms of internal and invisible conflict' (Davie 1986: 6). But the individual concerned may not be aware of the conflict that is expressed in this way, and they may simply have intense feelings for which they cannot easily find a cause. Perhaps, when their teacher sets them work that they find difficult, the scenario recaptures unconsciously a repeated sequence of events from earlier in their life. It may be that, whenever they tried to please one of their parents, there was a pattern in which whatever they did was not good enough and they were subjected to harsh criticism or punishment. Perhaps this did not always 'really' happen, but it seemed to them that this was how it was, because they came to expect to fail every time. Now, some years later, when work is set in the classroom the teacher is unconsciously treated as that parent through a process of *projection*. So the teacher too is seen to be expecting failure before they start.

Psychodynamic approaches focus on understanding and resolving such internal conflicts rather than working directly to reduce the undesirable behaviour that results from them. In fact, tackling the behaviour problem without resolving the inner conflict is seen as likely to have only a short-term impact. The underlying problem will manifest itself again in a different way. So psychodynamic approaches have a quite different focus from behavioural approaches. In Figure 14.2 they are shown as involving cognitive-level processes in the same way that cognitive approaches do. But, whereas cognitive theories focus on interpretations and perceptions of concurrent environmental events, psychodynamic theories focus on unconscious conflicts and fantasies that may have deep-seated roots in the early history of the individual concerned. These approaches thus give more attention to how a pattern of behaviour has developed. They are based on *developmental* theories in which emotional and behavioural difficulties are seen as emerging out of personal experience over time.

An important feature of psychodynamic approaches is that all of this is seen as applying not only to pupils and their parents but also to the teachers and carers.

Figure 14.5

A psychodynamic
approach

Returning again to our example of the pupil who swears at the teacher when asked to begin work, we can expect a different strategy for investigating the problem if a psychodynamic approach is adopted. Questions will arise such as: What does being set such work mean to the child? How do they feel about the situation? What ideas or images come to their mind spontaneously when they think about it? What events in their personal history, including their earliest childhood, might have left a residue of unresolved conflicts that have echoes in this situation? In this sort of context Holt (1996) suggested a number of functions that a pupil's behaviour might be interpreted as potentially serving:

- to increase interaction (albeit negative) with adults;
- to keep adults at an emotional distance;
- to vent pent-up feelings of anger and frustration that cannot be verbalized.

An important part of the investigation will be to identify psychodynamic factors that are interfering with the child's ability to learn (Wilson 1984; Barrett and Trevitt 1991; Greenhalgh 1994, Ch. 2).

The child will not be the only focus of attention. Questions will also arise about the teacher's feelings and their management of what is happening. How do they respond to the child's overreaction? What does it mean for them?

Just as a child may project unresolved and intense feelings onto adults, they may respond by becoming caught up in the distressing feelings themselves:

> Given the potency of some of the projections experienced when working with children experiencing emotional and behaviour difficulties, the adult needs to be keenly aware of the feelings aroused in him/herself, and what happens to those feelings. To what extent are we able to observe ourselves and recognise feelings being aroused by others? To what extent can we manage those feelings? To what extent do such feelings become unconsciously part of our interaction? Where the last of these happens, we lose the capacity to relate to the other person from the perspective of his/her own experience. Something as simple as an unconscious sigh may be experienced by the child as a further rejection, as further evidence of his/her hopelessness.
>
> (Greenhalgh 1994: 90)

Figure 14.5 describes how the case example discussed in the previous two sections would be approached from a psychodynamic perspective.

From a psychodynamic perspective the undesirable behaviour characteristic of EBD arises from intense internal conflicts over the expression or inhibition of basic impulses and needs. In the course of normal socialization children learn ways of satisfying basic biological and social needs that are acceptable in their sociocultural context. This involves learning to defer gratification of particular needs to socially approved times, places and situations. This socialization is accomplished through parental approval and disapproval, which is subsequently internalized by the child. Rizzo and Zabel (1988) outline a number of ways in which disturbances of these developmental processes may occur:

- where the intensity of needs or impulses is so strong (possibly due to some constitutional predisposition) that the child has difficulty learning to inhibit them appropriately;
- the caregivers fail to protect the child against the build-up of such intense needs, so that the child has difficulty learning to inhibit them;
- parental approval and disapproval are not expressed in the appropriate and consistent manner needed for the child to develop and internalize appropriate controls.

Psychodynamic approaches to intervention involve bringing to the child's conscious awareness unconscious defences and fantasies, interpreting them and building the child's positive resources and sense of security so that they feel strong enough to give up negative behaviour that was previously serving important purposes for them in defending the self. Individual psychodynamic psychotherapy with children is generally carried out by child psychotherapists employed by the NHS, and the work of art, music and educational therapists is often informed by psychodynamic perspectives.

Psychodynamic approaches were influential in the early development of special schools for children with EBD, a number of which aimed to offer a total therapeutic community, 'stressing mothering, regression, primary care and using the daily events of the residential community to repair and develop the incomplete egos' (Cole *et al.* 1998: 13). Psychodynamic ideas also influenced the development in the 1970s of part-time classes for children with EBD (Rabinowitz 1981). The focus of the work in these classes was educational but the provision had the key objectives of providing a safe place in which anxieties could be contained and children's emotional problems with relationships and learning explored. However, a later survey conducted by Wilson and Evans (1980) found little influence of psychodynamic ideas in most special schools and classes. Rather, the primary emphasis at that time seemed to be on cognitive-behavioural strategies within a humanist ethos to overcome children's expectancy of failure and boost self-esteem through ensuring success in educational and social activities.

Systemic approaches

In systemic approaches the focus is on reciprocal interaction between individuals' behaviour, thoughts and environment. The core features of a systems approach are summarized by Gorrell-Barnes (1985): 'Systems thinking derives principally from the concept of mutual causality and from the familiar notion that the whole is greater than the sum of its parts'. Two main strands of systems thinking may be identified. The first (general systems theory) stems from the work of von Bertalanffy (1968) and is derived from the study of biological organisms. Systemic family therapy (Palazzoli *et al.* 1978) and the joint family-school approach of

Figure 14.6
A systemic
approach

In the example of the pupil who swears at the teacher when asked to begin work a systems analysis, based on circular causality, might run as follows:

Teacher asks pupil to begin work, pupil swears at teacher, teacher sends pupil to head of year who gives them a detention, pupil feels resentful towards teacher. On the next occasion, teacher asks class to begin work, pupil feels unwilling to do anything for the teacher so doesn't start, teacher notices this and feels that their authority is being undermined, teacher asks pupil to begin work, pupil swears at teacher – and so the cycle may repeat itself.

Such an analysis would typically have been preceded by a holistic line of enquiry which would attempt to build up a picture of the behaviours, knowledge, feelings, beliefs and attitudes of both teacher and pupil that might be relevant to the problematic situations arising between them. Initial discussion with the teacher would not be narrowly focused on pupil behaviour. Rather, the emphasis is more likely to be placed on finding out on a broad level what the behaviours mean to all involved – both teacher and pupil. For example, in this case the teacher's use of the word 'aggression' appeared to signify a perceived threat to their authority. Pupil, teacher, parents, school senior management and LEA support staff will have perceptions and understandings of the situation that may overlap to differing extents.

Dowling and Osborne (1994) developed in this tradition. The second strand of systems thinking (systems analysis) was derived from the study of computer systems. Both 'hard' (Jenkins 1969) and 'soft' (Checkland and Schloes 1990) systems methodologies for addressing problems in organizations developed in this tradition and have been applied in schools (Burden 1981; Frederickson 1990a). Systemic theory is represented on the IF framework in Figure 14.2 which illustrates the reciprocal interactions and circular causality that are characteristic of this approach. The application of a systemic approach is illustrated in Figure 14.6.

From a systemic perspective the undesirable behaviour characteristic of EBD arises from mismatches in the goals and expectations of the different people who are involved. Even when the goals of different people and groups are not in conflict with each other, ineffective or inconsistent processes for achieving key goals may undermine, rather than support, pupils in learning socially acceptable behaviour.

Systemic approaches to intervention involve identifying and recognizing the different perspectives held by different groups and individuals in a situation and developing plans for improvement, usually involving interrelated action at a number of levels, that can be supported by all involved. A systemic approach to intervention will often utilize techniques and strategies from other theoretical approaches. What is characteristic is a recognition that both problem behaviour and intervention strategies have knock-on effects for everyone involved in the situation. Holt (1996) illustrates ways in which psychodynamic understandings can be embedded within a systems framework. If a behavioural intervention

focused on rewarding a pupil with praise when the
analysed from a systemic perspective the importance
impact on other members of the class group is lik
consequence, strategies may be incorporated to enc
pupil's appropriate behaviour. Similarly, recognizin
and pupil commitment to school and class rules ma
within clearly stated boundaries, in devising them.

Miller (1996) highlights the ways in which the inv
psychologist working with a teacher on a behavioura. p.~g.......... ... ~ p.p.
experiencing EBD can create a new temporary system. Such systems overlap the
boundaries of home and school and embody norms that allow pupils, parents and
teachers to construe each other in a different way from that usually dictated by
school policy and staff culture. Within such systems exceptions can be made and
flexible approaches adopted that allow participants to break out of entrenched and
unhelpful patterns of interaction. Teachers can also have a powerful impact on
the peer group ethos in the classroom through the use of systemically-orientated
strategies. The introduction of approaches such as 'circle time' (Mosley 1996;
Kelly 1999) can promote an ethos in which pupils are encouraged to openly
discuss problems and share responsibility with the teacher and each other for
promoting positive behaviour and a supportive climate in their class.

Biological-level influences

So far nothing has been said about biological-level influences on behaviour, or
about formulating and testing hypotheses at this level. While biological-level
influences will be important in some cases, their investigation is outside the
scope of the professional qualification and expertise of teachers and educational
psychologists. Close interdisciplinary collaboration with medical staff will be
important in these cases, of which attention deficit hyperactivity disorder (ADHD)
represents a good example.

Figure 14.7 uses the IF framework to summarize possible influences on ADHD
reviewed by a British Psychological Society working party (1996). From the
behavioural level we can see that children described as having ADHD tend to be
impulsive, overactive and inattentive to a degree that causes serious concern. At
the cognitive level are listed a number of the many psychological mechanisms
that have been put forward to understand the problems these children experience. At the biological level consideration is given to:

- factors that may result in types of neurological damage known to be associated with behaviour of this kind (e.g. head injuries, epilepsy, the metabolic
  disorder phenylketonuria);
- possible genetic factors which have been suggested in a number of studies
  carried out with twins (Pennington and Ozonoff 1996);
- neuroanatomical and neurochemical factors implicating reduced blood flow or
  levels of key chemicals in particular areas of the brain.

Figure 14.7
Possible
on the
ma

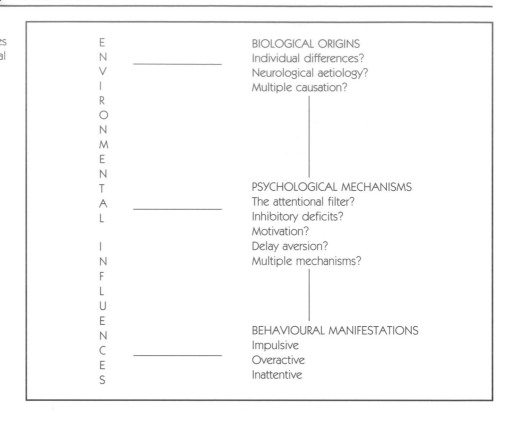

...nfluences ...e behavioural ...nifestations of ADHD
Source: British Psychological Society (1996).

BIOLOGICAL ORIGINS
Individual differences?
Neurological aetiology?
Multiple causation?

PSYCHOLOGICAL MECHANISMS
The attentional filter?
Inhibitory deficits?
Motivation?
Delay aversion?
Multiple mechanisms?

BEHAVIOURAL MANIFESTATIONS
Impulsive
Overactive
Inattentive

ENVIRONMENTAL INFLUENCES

It is recognized that there will be considerable individual differences in the effects such factors may have and that multiple influences may also be present.

There is positive evidence for the use of environmental interventions aimed at the biological level for some pupils with ADHD. These interventions include psychostimulant medication such as Ritalin and special diets. However the British Psychological Society working party report emphasizes that in addition psychological, educational and social support will always be required. Medication can help the child to be more receptive to learning and this is obviously important in preventing them from falling behind academically. However, to minimize damaging dependence on medication and maximize long-term outcomes for the child, advantage should be taken of this greater receptivity to teach strategies for managing impulsivity and developing attentional control. Specific interventions that have been found to be helpful in some studies include:

- behavioural management programmes at home and at school;
- parent or family training;
- modification of classroom antecedents to minimize distraction/support engagement with tasks;
- training skills for school success;
- self-instruction training.

ACTIVITY 14.1   Conceptualizations of EBD: trends over time

In this activity you will apply the IF framework to illustrative descriptions of behaviours characteristic of EBD. The first set are taken from *The Education of Children with Emotional and Behavioural Difficulties* (Department for Education 1994c), while the second set are taken from the SEN Thresholds consultation document (DfEE 2000c). Place on the framework each of the descriptive phrases used. For example, 'low self-image' is a within-child descriptor that cannot be directly observed, only inferred from aspects of the pupil's behaviour and what they say about themselves in everyday contexts and/or in response to assessment tools such as self-image questionnaires. 'Low self-image' should therefore be placed at the cognitive level. By contrast 'use of threatening language' would be located at the behavioural level. In some cases you may find that you cannot locate a phrase within a box but must place it across the boundary with the environment because it incorporates reference to environmental influences. In other cases you may consider that the phrase describes a complex interaction between different levels and environmental influences.

(a) What differences do you notice between the two sets of guidance in terms of the description of EBD?
(b) Which descriptions are likely to be more useful to teachers, and why?

The Education of Children with Emotional and Behavioural Difficulties

- Low self-image, anxiety, depression, withdrawal, resentment, vindictiveness, defiance.
- Refusal to speak, use of threatening language, frequent interrupting, arguing or swearing.
- Clingingness, truancy, failure to observe rules, disruptiveness, destructiveness, aggression, violence.
- Inability or unwillingness to work without direct supervision, to concentrate, to complete tasks or follow instructions.
- Difficulty/inability to trust or form relationships with peers or adults.

The SEN Thresholds consultation document

- Distractibility in the classroom that inhibits the progress of the pupil even with significant support and an increasingly individualized curriculum.
- Unpredictability and intensity of the pattern of behaviours which significantly disrupt the learning of peers and which are beyond what can be managed by the class teacher alone or by limited interventions from the SENCO and other specialists.
- Behaviour which is bizarre and/or self-injurious and/or endangers others and which leads to a significant level of rejection by peers, increasing the social isolation of the pupil.
- Evidence of significant unhappiness, stress and/or disaffection over a sustained period often accompanied by prolonged periods of absence often associated with an increasing awareness on the part of the pupil of their situation which may lead to a negative attitude towards education.

Although the extracts quoted from the guidance in Activity 14.1 are not comprehensive they do serve to illustrate the increasing influence of interactional or systemic approaches in understanding EBD. Rizzo and Zabel (1988) identify four guiding principles for work with pupils who present EBD in an educational context:

- commitment to an integrative framework;
- emphasis on an ecological/systemic orientation;
- belief in the necessity of interdisciplinary approaches in intervention;
- inclusion of parents as key resources in the educational process.

These principles are reflected in the following discussion of approaches to assessment and intervention with pupils displaying EBD.

Assessment methods

Different theoretical approaches lead to different questions being asked. The same assessment method may be used within different theoretical perspectives to collect different information. For example, the importance of involving the child's parents or carers has been highlighted. However, interviews with parents and carers conducted from different theoretical perspectives would seek different information, as shown in Table 14.1.

Often, because different information is considered relevant in different theories, different assessment methods will be used. Direct detailed observations in the situation where the problems occur will be considered very important from a behavioural perspective in order to identify the specific behaviour that causes concern and the environmental events that control its occurrence. From a cognitive perspective the actual sequence of environmental events will be considered less important than the pupil's perception and interpretation of what happened. So interviewing the pupil is likely to be prioritized over direct observation.

Table 14.1 Information collected in interviews conducted from different theoretical perspectives with parents/carers

Theoretical perspective	Information collected
Behavioural	Information about the frequency and duration of target problematic behaviours at home and the environmental events surrounding their occurrence. The child's 'reinforcement history' for similar behaviours.
Cognitive	Information about the parents' perceptions, interpretations and feelings about the child's behaviour and the actions being taken by the school.
Psychodynamic	Information about the child's early development and family relationships, paying particular attention to experiences that are seen as having had crucial emotional significance.
Systemic	Information about the parents' perceptions and their interpretation of the perceptions of others, such as the child and their teachers. Their hypotheses about ways in which everyone involved would be affected by particular changes.

Outlined below are some of the assessment methods most commonly used to gain an understanding of EBD and to guide positive action. The methods are categorized according to the theoretical framework with which they are most closely associated. Further details about many of these methods and their implementation in schools can be found in Ayres *et al.* (1995) and Cooper *et al.* (1994).

Behaviourally-based methods

Systematic observation may be carried out by teachers, the pupil or support professionals such as behaviour support service teachers or educational psychologists. Information may be collected on:

- the frequency and/or duration of identified problematic behaviour or of the positive behaviour which it is hoped to encourage;
- the events or conditions in the environment that occur prior to and following the behaviour and which may therefore be acting to encourage or reinforce it.

A number of systematic observation techniques are available. A crucial requirement of all of these is that the observer must define the behaviour they are observing clearly before they start. If an observer is not familiar with the classroom and pupil(s) concerned they are likely to need to spend some time talking with the teacher and/or conducting unstructured observations first.

Time sampling and interval sampling are two observational methods that are often considered together. For both you must first identify one or more target behaviours (e.g. working, sitting, calling out, inappropriate talking).

- *Time sampling* involves observing, say for 10 seconds and, on the tenth second recording whether or not the pupil at that moment is engaging in any of the target behaviours. The observation period might last in total for 20 minutes, with spot observations being made at the end of each 10-second period.
- *Interval sampling* involves observing for say 20 seconds and at the end of that time spending 10 seconds recording whether or not the pupil has engaged in any of the behaviours during the preceding 20 seconds. The observation period may last in total for 20 minutes with observations being made for the first 20 seconds of each half minute with the final 10 seconds of each half minute being spent recording those behaviours which had occurred at least once during the preceding 20 seconds.

Interval sampling makes good use of a visiting observers' time in that more time is spent observing than is the case with time sampling. However, the number of pupils that can be observed is limited and it is not really practical for teachers and pupils to use. With time sampling the use of a quiet timer can allow teachers and pupils to sample behaviours such as 'in seat' and 'on task' throughout a lesson at longer intervals, such as 1-minute intervals. Both time and interval sampling are appropriate only for behaviours that occur frequently. If the behaviour occurs less than once in 15 minutes event sampling (see below) should be selected.

ACTIVITY 14.2   Observation case study, Part 1

(a) Read the following account of an unstructured classroom observation.
(b) Write down clear descriptions of some behaviours you would like to observe using a structured method.
(c) Test whether your descriptions really are clear by asking someone else to 'act out' the description you have written down.
(d) As you read the descriptions of systematic observation methods in this section, consider which method might be most suitable for observing each of the behaviours you have selected.

A school consulted the LEA behaviour support service about Simon who was causing concern to his teacher because of aggressive behaviour (hitting, kicking, pinching) towards other children. Simon's teacher said that she used positive recognition with Simon in class but that it did not work.

Simon was observed for half an hour in the classroom. He and five other children were given the task of copying some writing from the board about a topic the class were studying. Simon started fairly well but after writing about five words in 10 minutes he began trying to make the other children laugh. He poked the girl sitting next to him and was reprimanded by the teacher. During the next 15 minutes he played with his pencil putting it down his back, looked around, played with his book and pinched the boy sitting next to him. He then started to write but after 1 minute he stopped when the boy next to him spoke to him. He did write some more but then tried to rub out one word with his finger. The other children on his table were also off task for some of the time and at one point for about 1 minute Simon was the only child on his table working. The teacher spoke to him more often during the half hour than to any other child, though always for a very short period. This was always to reprimand him, several times for his behaviour and a few times about his work.

Realistic intervention targets can be set by collecting information on the frequency of key behaviours for comparison pupils in the same teaching group who are making satisfactory progress. This recognizes, for example, that it would probably be unreasonable to expect a pupil *never* to call out without raising their hand. Indeed the importance of using systematic observation is illustrated by the finding that once teachers are concerned about the disruptive behaviour of particular pupils they will tend to overestimate its frequency. By collecting observations on a regular basis it is possible to obtain an indication of the success of interventions designed to reduce problem behaviour and increase positive behaviour. Scherer (1990) provides a clear and practical account of how this process of 'assessment by baselines' can be used by subject teachers in secondary schools to count and graph the number of disruptive incidents occurring with particular pupils while a series of intervention strategies are tried.

Event sampling involves recording each occurrence of a specified behaviour during a particular time period. For example, you might want a record of each time a pupil complies or fails to comply with a request from the teacher. This approach can be used whether or not a behaviour occurs frequently, and with event sampling it is possible to collect information on other pupils at the same time. Provided the number of behaviours and pupils to be observed is kept to a manageable number (and this will depend on the frequency of occurrence of the behaviour) this is a highly feasible approach for ongoing use by staff and pupils. Observations collected across different sessions may help to identify certain lessons or times of day the pupils find difficult and inform action planning.

Event sampling may also provide information about the environmental events surrounding the behaviour of concern. An 'ABC' outline is frequently used where the observer records:

A: antecedent events that precede the pupil's behaviour (e.g. 'teacher asks pupil to begin work');
B: behaviour engaged in by the pupil on that occasion (i.e. what exactly did the pupil do and say on this occasion when they swore at the teacher?);
C: consequences for the pupil that result from the behaviour (e.g. the reactions of the teacher and pupil, being sent out of class to the head of year).

One problem with observational approaches is that both children and the adults interacting with them may behave differently when being observed or when asked to carry out self-recording. If only a limited number of lessons are being observed a further concern is that these may not be representative and conclusions may be drawn that will not apply more generally.

Documentary sources such as report cards, records of attendance, detentions or other sanctions can be useful where they are sufficiently specific about the behaviour concerned. These sources can also be useful for monitoring the success of interventions over longer periods than is usually feasible with direct observations.

Cognitively-based methods

A variety of questionnaires and other techniques are available for use with pupils to assess particular cognitive constructs, such as self-perception (see Burden 1999), attributions (see Indoe 1999) and personal constructs (see Beaver 1996). For example, the Self-Perception Profile for Children (Harter 1985) is a paper and pencil questionnaire which was developed to assess the self-perception of children aged 8–14 years. It includes 36 items and covers five specific domains of competence: scholastic competence (assessing how clever the children think they are, how well they believe they are performing at school); social acceptance (assessing how popular the children feel they are and if they believe they have a lot of friends); athletic competence (assessing the children's perception of their athletic ability); physical appearance (assessing how attractive the children feel they are); and behavioural conduct (assessing how well the children feel they behave and if they like the way they behave). In addition there is a global

ACTIVITY 14.3   Observation case study, Part 2

(a) Read the behaviour support teacher's account of the structured observations they carried out with Simon and compare this with the account of the unstructured observations you read in Part 1.

(b) Could the difference be due to differences between the types of observation used – e.g. unstructured observations are likely to be less reliable and more open to bias?

(c) Assume that both observations are accurate. What does this tell you about the likely effect of context on behaviour?

(d) If you were advising this teacher, what further hypotheses or questions would you want to investigate about the apparent differences between Simon's behaviour in response to a writing task and a craft task?

(e) What issues might you want to discuss with the teacher about their use of positive recognition and negative comments?

(f) Would the information that Simon is an African-Caribbean pupil make you want to identify any additional hypotheses or questions?

(g) As you read the next section of this chapter consider what information you might want to collect about Simon's perceptions, attitudes and feelings.

Behaviour support teacher's notes on their structured classroom observations
I decided to investigate the frequency of five types of behaviour: name calling, poking/hitting, non-disruptive off-task behaviour, dropping pencil and wandering around the classroom. I planned to use time sampling to obtain an estimate of the percentage of time Simon spent on task and off task and engaged in either non-disruptive or disruptive behaviour. I decided to collect data on two other children also as I was interested in how Simon's behaviour compared to other children in the class. I asked the teacher to nominate another pupil about whom she had some concerns similar to those she had about Simon (Boy A), and a pupil about whom she had no such concerns (Girl B). I allocated 20 minutes for this observation. At the end of each ten-second period I looked at one of the three pupils (in the order: Simon, Boy A, Girl B) and recorded what I observed.

I also used event sampling to make a note of any positive or negative responses the teacher made to the three pupils I was observing, and whether they were made to social or academic behaviour.

During my unstructured observation session Simon had been attempting a writing task. On this occasion his teacher had planned a craft activity, very different from the writing task I had observed before. The children were supposed to be working in pairs but Simon had been unwilling to carry on with his partner and had been allowed to work on his own. The two children the teacher identified (Boy A and Girl B) were both working in pairs.

Time sampling: results
Key
T   inappropriate talking
P/H   poking/hitting
W   on task, working
O   off task, non-disruptive
D   off task, disruptive (e.g. dropping pencils, etc.)

Pupil	Sampling time									
	1	2	3	4	5	6	7	8	9	10
Simon	W	W	W	T	T	D	W	W	W	W
Boy A	W	W	T	T	T	W	O	O	W	W
Girl B	W	O	W	W	W	W	W	T	W	W

Pupil	Sampling time									
	11	12	13	14	15	16	17	18	19	20
Simon	O	W	O	W	W	T	T	W	W	W
Boy A	T	W	D	O	O	O	O	W	T	O
Girl B	W	W	W	W	W	W	W	T	W	W

	% time spent on				
	T	P/H	W	O	D
Simon	(4) 20	(0) 0	(13) 65	(2) 10	(1) 5
Boy A	(5) 25	(0) 0	(7) 35	(7) 35	(1) 5
Girl B	(2) 10	(0) 0	(17) 85	(1) 5	(0) 0

Event sampling

Pupil	Positive		Negative	
	Social	Academic	Social	Academic
Simon	1	0	2	0
Boy A	0	0	2	0
Girl B	2	0	0	0

Comparing two other children using this time sampling method enabled direct comparisons to be made and showed that Simon's behaviour was not extreme, or in the least inappropriate during the observation period. The teacher used positive recognition for social behaviour once in her remarks to Simon, who was on task for 65 per cent of the time and negative recognition twice. She also made two negative responses to social behaviour to Boy A, who was on task only 35 per cent of the time and used positive recognition twice to Girl B, who was on task 85 per cent of the time.

self-worth subscale, which assesses the extent to which children like themselves as people. For each item there are two statements which the child reads, or which can be read to them, 'Some children often do not like the way they behave *but* other children usually like the way they behave'. The child is first asked to decide which statement is most like him/her. Then the child is asked to decide if the statement selected is 'really true' or 'sort of true' for him/her. These responses are scored from 1 to 4, where a score of 1 indicates low perceived competence and a score of 4 indicates high perceived competence.

As Gibbs and Huang (1989) point out, cultural groups differ in the value attached to the different characteristics and abilities that become the sources of self-concept and self-esteem for the child. They highlight the importance of finding out about these differential values in order to properly interpret a pupil's criteria for self-evaluation. In this respect an advantage of the Harter measure is that an additional questionnaire is provided where the pupil rates the importance they attach to competence in each of the areas where self-perception is assessed. Children's priorities in self-evaluation are likely to change over time. These developmental changes may occur not only because of increasing psychological maturity but also when their personal circumstances change. This is perhaps seen most dramatically with those refugee children who have been exposed to traumatic life events before their migration (Hodes 2000).

One problem with self-report scales for children is that there is often a tendency for children to select the most socially desirable option, even if it is not really true for them. The structure of the Harter questionnaire attempts to overcome this by suggesting that each statement is chosen by some children and that both are therefore acceptable. Other questionnaires tackle the problem in a different way by including a 'social desirability' scale containing items such as 'I always tell the truth' and 'I am never unhappy'. That is a way of checking if the person completing the questionnaire is trying to give a good impression. The problem is that it does not eliminate the effects of that distortion from the other scales and the type of approach used by the Harter questionnaire is usually preferred.

Other problems sometimes encountered with pupil self-report scales relate to the pupil's understanding of the language used, and their perceptiveness and capacity for self-analysis. Approaches such as those based on personal construct psychology generally lack the data on reliability typically provided with standardized questionnaires. However they offer some relative advantages in that they use the child's own language and ways of categorizing their experience. This may be of particular value in the case of children whose cultural experience differs from that of the scale's authors. For further information about these techniques see Stoker and Walker (1996) and Ravenette (1997).

Psychodynamically-based methods

An individual interview is central to most psychodynamic approaches, sometimes deriving support from the use of projective techniques. The projective hypothesis is based on the assumption that when we respond to something outside ourselves our reactions are partly a reflection of our private inner world. When interviewers employ a projective technique they generally seek open-ended responses to stimuli designed to evoke inner conflicts of interest. For example, the Children's Apperception Test (Bellak and Bellak 1949) consists of black and white pictures of 'adult' and 'child' animals depicting scenes relating to various aspects of family life, such as food and mealtimes, toileting and bedtime. The child is asked to tell a story about each picture and their stories are interpreted as a projection of their inner conflicts. A child's perceptions of relationships within their family may be explored using a kinetic family drawing (Burns and Kaufman 1970). Children are asked to draw a picture showing themselves and everyone who lives at home with them in their family. Inferences about children's perceptions of their role in the family may be drawn on the basis, for example, of where they locate themselves in the picture or how large they draw themselves in relation to other family members.

One criticism of early uses of projective techniques was that insufficient attention was given to testing out in other ways the interpretations generated. It has been argued that the techniques may offer an interesting source of hypotheses but should not be accepted simply at face value. A further criticism is that the assessment information provided has only very limited applicability in generating practical intervention strategies for use in schools. On the other hand, these techniques may sometimes highlight an aspect of a child's problems that is otherwise likely to be ignored. The case study of Lesley (see Activity 14.4) illustrates this point. She completed another form of projective technique – a sentence completion task. In this method the child is presented with a series of sentence stems and asked to complete each sentence with the first words they think of. They are encouraged to work quickly and sometimes, if they do not write fluently themselves, dictate their responses to the interviewer. That is what Lesley did, as she had difficulty with all forms of literacy.

Systemically-based methods

Systemic assessment methods may be used to collate different perceptions about either organizational- or individual-level issues (see Chapter 8 for more information about the use of one such approach – SSM). At the organizational level, information about school rules and sanctions will generally be given in the school brochure. However, interviews with pupils, teachers and parents will often be necessary to identify the ways in which these rules and sanctions are perceived to operate in practice by different individuals. At the individual level, different perceptions of the behaviour of a particular pupil, perhaps collected by means of a round robin of their secondary school teachers, may be a starting point for identifying combinations of factors that are especially problematic for the pupil and those factors that are more successful in supporting appropriate behaviour. Department for Education Circular 9/94 (1994c: 17) advises:

ACTIVITY 14.4   Lesley's sentence completions

Lesley (aged 9) had severe difficulties with reading and writing. She seemed constantly
sad and subdued in school and rarely played with other girls during break times. For these
reasons she was referred to an educational psychologist. At the time she was living in
accommodation for the homeless with her mother. She had no siblings. There had not been
any contact with her father since shortly after she was born. Her mother rarely visited the
school but had agreed to the referral to the educational psychologist because she shared
the teacher's concern about Lesley's poor progress with reading. The sentence completion
task was one of a number of exercises that the psychologist employed to explore her
wide-ranging difficulties. In the text below the words in italics in each sentence are the
stem provided by the psychologist and the rest is what Lesley dictated in response.

Consider these questions:

(a) What, if anything, do you think Lesley's sentence completions indicate about her
    mood, state of mind, concerns and interests?
(b) What hypotheses might be formed about her feelings about key figures in her
    early life?
(c) Why do you think she kept coming back to the same themes – e.g. the dog, being
    nice? What purposes might this perseveration (excessive repetition) be serving for
    Lesley in this situation?

 1 *I like* the dog.
 2 *Father* sees the dog.
 3 *I wish* I had a dog.
 4 *When I am older* I will be by myself.
 5 *My school work* is great.
 6 *I hate* meat.
 7 *I dream that* of fairies.
 8 *I became shy when* uncle came.
 9 *I love* father very much but I wish that he wouldn't die.
10 *Other children* are playing.
11 *I try to get* out.
12 *In the dark* it is cold.
13 *What makes me angry is* boys.
14 *My brothers and sisters* is nice.
15 *School* is nice.
16 *Grown ups* are nice.
17 *I need* a father.
18 *Mother* cooks.
19 *I can't* read.
20 *I love my mother very much but I wish she wouldn't die.*
21 *I hope* uncle comes.
22 *My greatest worry is* that mummy isn't here.
23 *I secretly* hide in a hiding place.

The school should be particularly alert to patterns of behaviour during different activities, at different times of the day, on different days of the week, in working with different teachers or with different groups of children. This may provide important information about the particular circumstances in which the behaviour is more or less likely to occur. This in turn may inform the development of strategies to alleviate the child's difficulties.

The importance of the peer group social system in either supporting or undermining appropriate behaviour has also been recognized. Sociometric assessment questionnaires collect information from classmates (see Chapter 15) about the child's level of acceptance or rejection in the peer group. More recent questionnaires for monitoring bullying behaviour in school collect information from pupils not just about engagement in bullying or experience of victimization, but also about the range of roles that other members of the peer group play in relation to bullying incidents (see Sharp 1999). Because of the hidden nature of much bullying, assessment approaches such as this are very important in assisting headteachers to discharge their legal duty to introduce measures to prevent all forms of bullying (Department for Education and Employment 1998d).

Systemic assessment approaches typically collect information at a number of levels and may use cognitive or behavioural assessment strategies to do so. However, a characteristic of the approach is that it also focuses on collecting information about interactions between different levels and different individuals' perceptions. Techniques such as 'circular questioning' may be used to obtain information about relationships and differences in the perceptions of pupils, parents and teachers. Each person present may be asked to consider the thoughts, feelings and behaviour of the others and ways in which they may interact. For example, each person might be asked to choose, and give reasons for their choice of, the person who would be most pleased and the person who would be most disappointed if the pupil suddenly stopped presenting behavioural difficulties. Dowling and Osborne (1994: 23) point out that this style of questioning is 'intended to explore connections and effects rather than look for causes of behaviour' and makes 'it possible for the participants in the interview to develop a different view of the situation'.

'Reframing' involves putting forward an alternative interpretation of a situation. The use of circular questioning can indirectly lead participants to reframe events. Reframing may also be used directly to try out different possible interpretations of events that may enable all involved to shift their positions slightly and agree on action to move the situation on. For example, more opportunities for constructive action are likely to result if a parent's angry refusal to support a school's homework policy can be reframed as strong concern for their child's progress and about the possibility that the child may be disadvantaged if they don't feel they can help them with many aspects of homework. It is generally possible to challenge some constructions of events because they are inconsistent with aspects of the information that is available. Usually however, a number of alternative constructions of events are plausible so several 'reframes' are possible. This may be particularly important to acknowledge where different constructions of events relate to cultural differences. Ultimately we can only evaluate the success of this kind of systems analysis by asking whether it leads to improved outcomes, and this generally involves collecting data at the behavioural level. This applies whether the focus of work is with an organization or an individual.

Each of the commonly used assessment methods reviewed above has particular strengths, weaknesses and potential sources of bias. Greater confidence can be placed in conclusions reached when the results of different methods point in the same direction. This may be particularly important for pupils from certain racial or cultural groups. As was pointed out in Department for Education Circular 9/94 (1994c: 18): 'A relatively high proportion of pupils of African/African-Caribbean origin are referred for assessment. In observing and describing behaviour, it is clearly important to be impartial and objective, and to screen out any judgements which might be culturally-determined misinterpretations'.

Gray and Noakes (1994) stress the importance of checking out the accuracy of all information. For example, school staff may make inferences about the reasons for frequent family moves which become accepted within the school as fact. It is important to ask 'How do we know this?', 'How much reliance can we place on this source of information?' and 'Do we have supporting information from other sources?'

Given the identified importance of a multi-level systemic approach and an integrative orientation, the IF framework offers a means of representing assessment information about a particular pupil and their situation that has been collected using different assessment methods. The framework can accommodate a wide range of types of assessment information, irrespective of the theoretical perspectives employed. The framework can also be used to model the hypothesized effects of intervention strategies. Where problem behaviour is thought to be maintained by a number of interacting factors, it generally follows that a multi-pronged intervention approach will be required. This is a conclusion which emerges strongly from the following review of commonly-used intervention approaches for problem behaviour in schools.

Intervention strategies

The intervention strategies for EBD that are most commonly used in schools are drawn from behavioural, cognitive and systemic theories. Table 14.2 shows the frequency with which different types of strategies for pupils with EBD were recommended or implemented by educational psychologists in one county in a single term. In compiling this table, educational psychologists were first asked to identify all the strategies they had recommended in the past term and then to indicate the frequency (high, medium or low) with which each strategy had been recommended. It can be seen that behavioural strategies were the most frequently used, with almost half the psychologists reporting at least medium frequency of use. The psychologists were also asked in each case whether they had been working

Table 14.2 Percentages of each type of strategy recommended by educational psychologists in one LEA in one school term

Strategy	Frequency (%)		
	High	Medium	Low
Behavioural Based on behavioural approaches with the aim of increasing desirable behaviour and/or decreasing undesirable behaviour:	25.8	18.4	6.4
• Behavioural management work with school staff/involving pupil.			
• Family work on behavioural programmes with parent.			
Cognitive Based on a cognitive model addressing a child's problem solving skills, poor self-image etc. For example:	3.5	20.6	4.3
• Social problem solving and skills training (see Chapter 15).			
• Anger management – a set of approaches which helps clients analyse events that trigger anger for them, identify early signs in themselves, remain calm, think differently about the triggers, develop impulse control, learn adaptive strategies for expressing anger in an effective way (see Faupel et al. 1998).			
• Counselling – a collaboration between a helper and a client where clients 'through client-helper interactions, are in better positions to manage their problem situations and/or develop the unused resources and opportunities of their lives more effectively' (Egan 1994: 5).			
• Brief solution-focused therapy – consists of finding out where clients want to get to and helping them appreciate and build on what they are already doing which is likely to help them get there. The emphasis is on working towards solutions rather than exploring problems, and on helping clients find their own solutions or routes to their goals (see Rhodes and Ajmal 1995).			
Systemic Focusing on contextual interactions within the classroom (teacher and peer group), within the school at different levels, concerning home-school links, within the family/home environment. For example:	8.5	5.0	5.0
• Circle of friends – this approach attempts to support children who present EBD and other SEN by enlisting the help of the other pupils in their class and setting up a special group or 'circle' of friends. The special group helps to set, monitor and review weekly targets in a meeting facilitated by an adult. Group members also provide agreed support to facilitate the focus child's inclusion and to help them achieve their targets (see Newton et al. 1996).			
• Family systems work – this is a model for working jointly with both families and schools which draws on applications of systems theory to the fields of family therapy and consultative work in schools (see Dowling and Osborne 1994).			
• Conferencing with staff – this involves group consultation with teachers where the consultant acts as a non-directive interventionist who generates valid information that highlights the underlying issues; enables the teacher to make autonomous free and informed choices about the nature of the intervention; and fosters a climate of commitment to its implementation (see Hanko 1987).			
Suggested involvement of other agencies (e.g. pupil referral units, child guidance, play therapist)	0.7	0.7	2.1

with a primary or a secondary school. The use of behavioural strategies was reported about three times more often in primary than secondary schools, while counselling and other cognitive interventions were more frequently implemented in secondary schools. This is consistent with the finding of a national survey of educational psychologists' work which reported that counselling and therapeutic work in relation to behaviour had been provided in 50 per cent of secondary schools in the year of the survey but in only 15 per cent of primary schools (Department for Education and Employment 2000b).

Behavioural strategies

A brief outline of the range of behavioural strategies commonly used with pupils who present EBD is provided below. The reader is referred to Ayres *et al.* (1995) for a more detailed account.

Strategies aimed at increasing desirable behaviour include:

- *Positive reinforcement.* This is something which is given following the desirable behaviour and which increases the occurrence of the behaviour in future. For many pupils an opportunity to use the computer upon finishing their work would be an effective tangible reinforcer, while for most pupils a quiet word of praise from the teacher is an important social reinforcer. Houghton *et al.* (1988) found that a complimentary letter home to parents was regarded even by secondary pupils as a significant incentive. However, different things are experienced positively by different pupils. So it is advisable to consult the pupil concerned and to monitor the frequency of the desirable behaviour being targeted to ensure that it actually does increase.
- *Negative reinforcement.* This is something that increases a pupil's behaviour if it is removed as a result of the behaviour. Apologizing for disruptive behaviour is likely to be negatively reinforced by the lessening of teacher displeasure. While positive reinforcement is more commonly and appropriately used, teachers should be aware of ways in which they may unwittingly use negative reinforcement with the effect of increasing undesirable behaviour. For example, this may happen when a teacher removes or reduces work requirements because the pupil complains about them.

Strategies aimed at reducing undesirable behaviour include:

- *Extinction.* This involves withdrawing reinforcement from an undesirable behaviour. For example, the teacher may decide to withdraw their attention and start ignoring pupils who shout out answers instead of raising their hands.
- *Time out.* This involves removing the pupil for a brief period from all sources of reinforcement. There may be a chair in a screened-off section of the classroom or the pupil may be sent out of the classroom to a specially designated place supervised by a senior member of staff. This may be necessary when the disruptive behaviour is reinforced by other pupils or is behaviour which cannot be reasonably or safely ignored by the teacher.

- *Punishment*. This is something which will decrease an undesirable behaviour. For most pupils teacher reprimands or detentions will operate in this way. One of the problems with punishments are the negative emotions that they often arouse. Unless carefully handled there is the risk that they may damage the pupil–teacher relationship and make the teacher a less potent source of positive reinforcement and motivation for the pupil in future. These risks can be minimized by ensuring that the 'rules' relating to the use of punishments or sanctions are well known to all pupils, that they are applied consistently and in a way that is seen to be fair, and that they are administered in a calm and unemotional way by the teacher.

A problem with all approaches to decreasing undesirable behaviour is that if they are used on their own there is no guarantee that the pupils will learn what they should be doing instead. It is important therefore that they are only used in combination with approaches to increase the desirable behaviour that is wanted instead. This may not be as obvious to the pupil as it is to the teacher, and considerable support and encouragement may be needed for the pupil to make the change.

These approaches can be used with groups or whole classes as well as individuals, and Merrett and Houghton (1989) report a number of studies carried out in the UK in which behavioural techniques have been successfully implemented in secondary schools in a wide variety of interesting ways. For example, some studies have used novel game-type formats and some have utilized pupil self-recording.

In thinking about the examples we have given of commonly used reinforcers and punishments, it is important to bear in mind that a particular pupil's reactions to a particular reinforcer will depend on their previous experience. Teachers and other professionals should be cautious in making assumptions about what will constitute reinforcement for an individual pupil. This is particularly so when the pupil's background or culture differs from their own. From a behavioural perspective, problem pupils may be thought of as those for whom the reinforces normally used in the school are less effective for whatever reason or who have more difficulty in learning the associations between their behaviour and the events that follow as consequences. Behavioural contracts are often negotiated in these situations between pupils, teachers and sometimes parents and other professionals as well. They specify clearly what everyone will and will not do, and identify specific consequences that make success more likely for the individual pupil. Figure 14.8 shows an example of a contract for Carl.

In negotiating a behavioural contract it is important that everyone has a say in it and develops a commitment to it, recognizing that it will probably not be possible to get everything right at once and that some aspects may need to be renegotiated at the review meetings which are written into the contract. Similarly, the behaviours identified for the pupil need to be realistic and achievable. Where a pupil needs to make significant changes to their behaviour these will probably have to be achieved on a step-by-step basis over a number of contracts,

Contract

A *From today, 9 June until 7 July, Carl agrees:*
1 To arrive at lessons on time
2 To ensure that he has the equipment that he needs
3 To complete the tasks set by the teacher, without complaint

B *Carl's teachers agree:*
1 To provide support and positive comments when Carl is punctual and appropriately equipped
2 To check Carl's understanding of instructions and task demands with him individually
3 To tick Carl's contract card for each task successfully completed

C *Mr Williams, form tutor, will meet with Carl at the end of each school day to monitor his successes:*
1 He will arrange for Carl to spend a session in the computer room for every ten ticks achieved on his contract card
2 When Carl achieves an 80% task completion rate in a week, Mr Williams will inform Mr and Mrs Peters
3 He will arrange for incomplete work to be sent home along with relevant instructions as homework

D *Mr and Mrs Peters agree:*
1 To ensure Carl completes any tasks he brings home
2 Mr Peters will take Carl to watch City play at home when he achieves an 80% task completion rate

This contact will be reviewed by all concerned at 2 p.m. on 7 July.

Signed:

_____   Carl Peters
_____   Mr Williams
_____   Mr Peters
_____   Mrs Peters

each being reviewed after two to three weeks. When a satisfactory level of behaviour has been achieved it is important that the additional supports that have been put in place are phased out gradually. This will enable the need for any ongoing level of support to be accurately identified.

Department for Education and Employment Circular 10/99 (1999b) introduced 'pupil support programmes' which are school-based interventions for pupils who do not respond adequately to the approaches generally employed in school to combat disaffection and who are therefore likely to be at risk of exclusion. They share a number of features with the behavioural contracting approach reviewed above: 'The programme should set targets broken down into fortnightly tasks. It should identify the rewards that can be achieved for meeting the targets and the sanctions that will apply if certain behaviour occurs' (p. 29). In addition to involving parents, schools are encouraged to involve other relevant agencies including voluntary agencies and ethnic minority community groups, who may be able to support schools with mentoring programmes as well as offering advice and guidance.

In addition to looking at the consequences which follow behaviour, focusing on the antecedent conditions in the environment has also been considered important. Work has often been carried out at the whole-school level and has typically focused on developing whole-school behaviour policies, shared values, consistent expectations and reinforcement of these with sanctions. Some schools have supported this by introducing structured programmes such as 'assertive discipline' (Canter and Canter 1992). The focus is on making classroom rules and procedures clear and following through with associated rewards and sanctions. Nicholls and Houghton (1995) have shown that for some classes at least its introduction can result in an increase in on-task behaviour and a decrease in the frequency of disruptive behaviour.

Cognitive strategies

Cognitive strategies may be used to help children change their self-perceptions, the ways in which they attribute meaning to events in their environment or their ability to think and problem solve effectively about the situations they encounter. Some of these strategies are discussed in other parts of this book. Evidence that attribution retraining can have a positive impact on pupil behaviour and motivation is discussed earlier in this chapter (see pp. 392–3). Cognitive approaches to improve a child's social problem solving skills are described in Chapter 15 on social skills.

Other approaches listed in Table 14.2 such as counselling and solution-focused therapy require the development of an extended repertoire of skills, discussion of which is outside the scope of this book. Elliott and Place (1998) point out that counselling and solution-focused approaches are generally based on the premise that the pupil recognizes that they have a problem and wish to work with another to seek a solution. This may not necessarily be true where the disruptive behaviour is serving other purposes, such as securing status in the peer group. Hence the appropriateness of these approaches to a particular situation requires careful consideration. For detailed consideration of the application of these approaches in schools readers are referred to Rhodes and Ajmal (1995) in the case of solution-focused therapy, while in the case of counselling skills and approaches Bovair and McLaughlin (1994) and Cowie and Pecherek (1994) are recommended for further reading.

In the rest of this section we consider strategies that have been used to enhance children's self-esteem. Three types of approach to improving self-esteem have been identified by Beane (1991):

- personal development activities such as individually focused self-esteem courses;
- curriculum programmes that focus directly on improving self-esteem;
- structural changes in schools that place greater emphasis on cooperation, student participation, community involvement and ethnic pride.

In common with other authors, Beane (1991) argued that the third of these elements is crucial. He queried the relevance of interventions which are exclusively focused at the individual level and ignore 'the fact that having positive self-esteem is almost impossible for many young people, given the deplorable conditions under which they are forced to live by the inequities in our society' (Beane 1991: 27). Covington (1989) summarized research showing that programmes designed to promote self-esteem at an individual level alone, by making students feel better about themselves, are unlikely to improve academic outcomes. Such findings have readily been picked up by the media in articles such as 'Education: doing bad and feeling good' (Krauthammer 1990).

Beane (1991: 29) was a little more positive about curriculum programmes: 'there is a place for some direct instruction regarding affective matters, but this is not enough either'. In England and Wales, approaches utilizing the curriculum are likely to become more formalized following the introduction of the national framework for personal, social and health education and citizenship (Department for Education and Employment/Qualifications and Curriculum Authority, 1999a, 1999b). Key components of self-esteem are included – for example pupils should be taught:

- to think about themselves, learn from their experiences and recognize what they are good at (Key Stage 1);
- to recognize their worth as individuals by identifying positive things about themselves and their achievements, seeing their mistakes, making amends and setting personal goals (Key Stage 2);
- to reflect on and assess their strengths in relation to personality, work and leisure (Key Stage 3);
- to be aware of and assess their personal qualities, skills, achievements and potential, so that they can set personal goals (Key Stage 4).

Kahne (1996) agreed with the importance of a structural focus at the level of the school and classroom and argued that major threats to self-esteem are the narrow range of competencies that are valued in many schools and a focus on competition, where students make external comparisons of their achievements with those of other students. It can be appreciated that attempting to boost the self-esteem of a pupil who has SEN at an individual level with positive, affirming feedback might be unlikely to have a long-term impact in a school context where recognition and rewards focus on the highest levels of achievement, with effort or relative improvement being recognized in a more marginal or tokenistic way.

This is likely to become an increasingly important issue as more pupils who have SEN are included in mainstream classes. Renick and Harter (1989) found that pupils with learning difficulties who were included in mainstream classes tended to have lower academic self-esteem than those who were educated in separate special classes, while self-esteem in other areas (e.g. social, physical) did not show a difference across placements. However, they account for this finding by referring to social comparison theory, hypothesizing that individuals do not employ absolute standards in evaluating their own performance, but engage in a process of comparing their performance with an available reference group. In the case of the included pupils they appeared to be basing their self-evaluations on the performance of their mainstream peers, whose academic achievement was considerably higher. It could be argued that the special class pupils might have their self-esteem boosted by being in a selected special group. However, we would then expect pupils who are withdrawn to participate in special programmes for gifted pupils to show boosted self-esteem also, and this is not the case. Marsh *et al.* (1995) found that pupils who participated in gifted programmes tended to show declines in academic self-esteem compared to similar pupils who remained in mainstream classes, although self-esteem in other areas did not change.

It would seem therefore that an integrative focus on both individual- and organizational-level factors and strategies will be important in raising pupils' self-esteem. Gurney (1987) and Woolfolk (1998) each review a range of strategies supported by research that can be used to develop children's self-esteem. All of these relate to Beane's (1991) structural level in that they apply to pupils generally and would be appropriate to include in a school's behaviour policy for implementation within and across classrooms. However, a number of the strategies are also particularly applicable at the individual level in that they could be individualized for use with a particular student as part of an IEP. In Activity 14.5 you are asked to consider the applicability of these strategies in a school with which you are familiar and to identify those which appear particularly appropriate for use with individual pupils who are presenting EBD.

Strategies derived from psychodynamic theory

Ayres *et el.* (1995) describe a number of insights and strategies developed in this tradition which may be helpful to education service staff working in some situations. One of the approaches described is the use of metaphor. Through the construction and discussion with the child of a story relevant to their situation, it is hoped that they will identify with the characters in the story and be provided with a non-threatening opportunity to gain some insight into the ways in which their feelings and behaviours may be affecting their progress. Greenhalgh (1994) showed how this could be combined with sandplay in the setting of a small tutorial class for children with EBD. When George (aged 12) made a 'sandworld' in which there was some 'sinking sand', Greenhalgh asked him how the characters in that world felt when they were caught in the sinking sand. Moving in and out of the metaphor, the teacher and the child discussed depression and despair and how rafts might be made to overcome the problem: 'I said that I hoped that he would be able to take the concrete rafts away inside himself and be able to

ACTIVITY 14.5   Developing self-esteem

Listed below are a range of strategies (from Gurney 1987 and Woolfolk 1998) which are supported by research and can be used to develop children's self-esteem.

(a) Consider the applicability of each of these strategies in a school with which you are familiar.
(b) Identify those which would appear particularly appropriate for use with individual pupils where low self-esteem has been identified as a significant influence on the EBD they are presenting.

1 Value and accept all pupils for their attempts as well as their accomplishments.
2 Provide extra teacher help and attention on a planned systematic basis.
3 Avoid interacting most frequently with the more able, most rewarding pupils.
4 Create a climate that is physically and psychologically safe for students.
5 Make sure that your procedures for teaching and grouping students are really necessary, not just a convenient way of handling problem students or avoiding contact with some students.
6 Make standards of evaluation clear and help students learn to evaluate their own accomplishments.
7 Ensure that the curriculum is relevant and appropriate for each child and that learning support arrangements are in place for individual children who need them.
8 Avoid destructive comparisons and competition; encourage students to compete with their own prior levels of achievement.
9 Act as a role model for self-esteem enhancement – e.g. by using positive self-referent statements and by drawing attention to their own self-directing behaviour.
10 Aim to increase the frequency of children's positive self-referent statements by encouraging and commenting positively on them.
11 Encourage self-monitoring and self-reinforcing behaviour, since self-management appears to be productive in enhancing self-esteem.
12 Accept a student even when you must reject a particular behaviour or outcome. Students should feel confident, for example, that failing a test or being reprimanded in class does not make them 'bad' people.
13 Encourage students to take responsibility for their reactions to events; show them that they have choices in how to respond.
14 Set up support groups or 'study buddies' in school and teach students how to encourage each other.
15 Help students set clear goals and objectives; brainstorm about resources they have for reaching their goals.
16 Highlight the value of different ethnic groups, their cultures and accomplishments.

make good use of them if and when it might be necessary' (Greenhalgh 1994: 165).

Psychodynamic ideas about the importance of secure and trusting relationships with adults have also provided the theoretical basis for the development of nurture groups (Holmes 1995). These groups are designed to meet the needs of children who are seen as having missed crucial preschool experiences of adequate and attentive early nurturing care. As a result their emotional, social and cognitive development has been affected. Early nurture:

> is a many-stranded, intermeshing, forward-moving, unitary learning process that centres on attachment and trust and has its foundations in the close identification of parent and child, and the interaction and participation in shared experiences that stem from this. It is the first stage of a developmental process through which the child builds up adequate concepts and skills, learns to interact and share with others and feel concern for them.
>
> (Boxall 1996: 21)

'Nurture groups' are small special classes in primary schools of up to 12 children with a teacher and a special support assistant. Pupils do not normally attend for more than four terms. The aim is to provide 'a structured and predictable environment in which the children can begin to trust adults and to learn' (Department for Education and Employment 1997: 80). The nurture group team of a teacher and a special support assistant attempt to recreate the processes of adequate parenting within school. By creating a classroom setting in which elements of 'home' and 'school' interact they give children the opportunity to go through early learning experiences that they missed. In the home area of the classroom there is 'food, comfort, consistent care and support, and close physical contact seen in cradling, rocking, sensory exploration and communication by touch' (Boxall 1996: 22). Early basic experiences are offered within clear structures and routines that the teacher and assistant control. In contrast to the mainstream classroom, activities are taken slowly with a much greater emphasis on repetition, order and routine than is necessary for most children of this age. In contrast to the homes of the majority of children in the groups, strategies for managing their often uncontrolled behaviour emphasize consistency and clarity, as is needed by a younger child. Through these means it is intended that the child's experiences in the group will establish 'growth-promoting patterns' which were not encouraged in their earlier lives.

Holmes (1995) reports follow-up information on over 200 children who have attended nurture groups in London: 71 per cent had transferred to mainstream class without difficulty, while 17 per cent had transferred with additional support. The remaining 12 per cent transferred to special educational provision. Iszatt and Wasilewska (1997) pointed out that most children entering nurture groups in the London Borough of Enfield were at a point where their schools required help from an outside agency (Stage 4 of the SEN *Code of Practice* that was current at the time – Department for Education 1994a). Yet over four out of five returned to their mainstream classes after an average stay in a nurture group of just three terms. In two comparable schools where nurture group provision was not available the proportion of children requiring statutory assessments and special provision was almost three times greater, and 'the proportion of pupils requiring EBD school provision was almost seven times greater' (Iszatt and Wasilewska 1997: 69).

Systemic approaches to intervention and combating bullying

Systemic approaches are increasingly advocated by both researchers and practitioners. Reid (1993) considers the substantial body of literature that exists on
attempts to treat children who display antisocial behaviour patterns. He reported that
most of the more promising interventions focused on the *social interactional fabric*
in which the child's behaviour problems were embedded, dealing with the *behaviour* itself, the *social environment's reaction* to that behaviour, *social cognitions*,
and/or *skills*. Bear (1998) concludes from a review of the literature that effective
teachers can be characterized by their integrated use of three sets of strategies:

- classroom management and positive climate strategies for preventing behaviour problems;
- operant learning strategies for the short-term management and control of
  behaviour problems;
- decision making and social problem solving strategies for achieving the long-
  term goal of self-discipline.

In an evaluation of projects supported under the Standards Fund category
'Truancy, Disruptive and Disaffected Pupils' Hallam and Castle (1999) reported
that projects successful in reducing exclusions incorporated three levels of
intervention: whole-school development work, class-based work and work with
individual pupils. Elliott and Place (1998) argued that a whole-school behaviour
policy is unlikely to be sufficient for children who present particularly challenging behaviour. In these cases it is likely that additional measures will be needed,
such as: an analysis of interpersonal interactions at home and school; consideration of behavioural approaches; and analysis of the suitability of the educational
tasks with which the child is being presented. It is argued that intervention should
operate at all three levels and there are examples of programmes such as 'Building a Better Behaved School' (Galvin *et al.* 1990) where classroom management
approaches and behavioural approaches for managing the most disruptive pupils
are considered as part of a comprehensive whole-school approach.

'Framework for Intervention' (Daniels and Williams 2000) has been developed
as a systemic approach based on the understanding that 'problems in behaviour
in educational settings are usually a product of complex interaction between the
individual, school, family, community and wider society' (p. 222). The Framework offers an approach for tackling behaviour problems at a series of levels
analogous to the stages of the *Code of Practice*. However, at Level 1 rather than
developing individual programmes, intervention is focused on addressing environmental factors in the classroom and school. At levels 2, 3 and beyond, individual behaviour plans are introduced in addition to, not instead of, the behaviour
environment plans which continue.

Bullying in school

Systemic approaches have been identified as particularly important in dealing
with bullying following research that has highlighted its serious repercussions, its

disproportionate impact on minority groups, the extent to which it is usually hidden from staff, the complex influences of school ethos and peer group characteristics and the positive impact of whole-school approaches to tackling it (Smith 2000). Sharp (1999: 1) defines bullying as 'any behaviour which is deliberately intended to hurt, threaten or frighten another person or group of people. It is usually unprovoked and is often repeated and can continue for a long period of time. It always reflects an imbalance and abuse of power'. The guidance offered to schools in *Social Inclusion: Pupil Support* (Department for Education and Employment 1999b: 24) highlights different forms of bullying, 'be it racial, or as a result of a child's appearance, behaviour or special educational needs, or related to sexual orientation' and makes clear schools' responsibilities: 'Head teachers have a legal duty to prevent all forms of bullying among pupils' (p. 25).

Sharp (1999) highlights the influences on bullying of social dynamics at a range of environmental levels:

- *Peer and class culture*: prevalence of cliques and gangs; predominant mix of participant roles; bystander behaviour; pro-victim/pro-bullying attitudes.
- *School micro-culture*: playground supervision and environment; pastoral system; values, attitudes and behaviours of staff; policies and practice on behaviour, discipline, equal opportunities and bullying.
- *Home and society macro-culture*: values, attitudes and behaviours in the home; values, attitudes and behaviours in the community; media imagery and public opinion.

Sharp argues that intervention at the individual level, focused on assertiveness, self-esteem, social skills or coping strategies is unlikely by itself to be sufficient in the long term. Rather it is recommended that bullying should be tackled through quite intense intervention at the group and individual level. The most effective anti-bullying strategies include:

- Staff and students working together to develop a clear set of guidelines for everybody which specify what bullying is and what they should do when they know or suspect it is going on.
- Long-term curriculum work about bullying and other forms of antisocial behaviour, including teaching students how to manage personal relationships assertively and constructively.
- Peer-led approaches, such as peer counselling and buddying, to offer support to pupils who are new to the school or who are feeling lonely, rejected or victimized.
- Direct intervention strategies when bullying has occurred or is suspected of occurring. Problem solving approaches which involve all students, including those who have been indirectly involved, are most effective. Early involvement of parents is recommended. Follow-up over time is always needed to check that the bullying has not resumed (Sharp 1999: 5).

Further details of approaches to intervention are described in Sharp and Smith (1994).

Bullying and name-calling are a common feature of the experience of many children from ethnic and religious minorities in school. Teachers may not be aware of the scale of the phenomenon and may sometimes fail to appreciate its impact on the victims (Cohn 1987). Schools need to develop strategies for countering playground cultures that permit and foster such behaviour. Cohen (1998) has proposed a range of options, including the establishment of a student council where grievances about harassment may be taken up and weekly discussion times devoted to events in the playground. A crucial element of his approach is to ensure that racist bullies are helped to learn new ways of relating to their peers. An example is the use of stories with a narrative structure resembling a playground game in which children are encouraged in supervised surroundings to try out less stereotypical roles.

Conclusions

In this chapter we have highlighted the extent to which definitions of EBD must take account of interactions between the expectations, perceptions and behaviour of all those involved in a situation where a child's behaviour is considered to be problematic. There is evidence that there are often disparities in expectations and perceptions of parents and teachers – disparities that can be magnified by differences in culture. It is argued that an integrative framework is needed to properly understand the range and complexity of the interactive influences on behaviour. The IF framework which was introduced in Chapter 4 can be used to represent in an integrated way the theoretical approaches that are most commonly applied in attempting to understand situations in which EBD are identified.

Of the four commonly applied theoretical approaches, systemic approaches have proved particularly useful as they encompass influences at the cognitive, behavioural and environmental levels of the IF framework and interactions between factors at these different levels. However, each of the theoretical approaches can offer insights that may be valuable in particular situations. They each have also given rise to a range of assessment techniques and intervention approaches that have been described in this chapter. The IF framework can be used to represent the assessment information collected about a particular individual and their situation from any theoretical perspective. It can also help to highlight gaps in the available information (e.g. failure to consider the child's perspective), aspects that may have been overlooked (e.g. if a within-child perspective has been taken and possible environmental influences ignored) and conclusions that have been based on insufficient information (e.g. if information from a single source or assessment method has been accepted rather than being checked out).

The IF framework can also be used to model the likely effects of planned interventions and anticipate any knock-on effects in the school situation that may need to be accommodated. Most situations in which EBD are a concern require a multi-pronged intervention approach to address the interacting influences on the behaviour. Again, systemic approaches have the advantage in that they consider multi-level interactions and can incorporate techniques and strategies from other approaches in an integrated action programme. The advantages of systemic approaches are well illustrated by the research on effective interventions for bullying behaviour that were reported at the end of the chapter.

A final consideration must be evaluation. It is only through careful analysis of changes in the outcome measures specified in the objectives of the intervention programme that the appropriateness and success of the action taken can be judged. If the objectives are not satisfactorily achieved the evaluation information that has been collected will be crucial in helping all involved to look again at their understanding of the factors operating in the situation and to revise the intervention programme accordingly.

Chapter 15

Social skills

Objectives

When you have studied this chapter you should be able to:

1 Evaluate the different theoretical approaches that have been applied to the study of children's social skills.
2 Describe the range of techniques that are available for assessing different aspects of social skills.
3 Analyse social skills intervention programmes and suggest ways of improving their effectiveness.
4 Identify important implications for promoting social skills at school.

Contents

Introduction

What are social skills?

There is no commonly agreed definition of social skills. Many different definitions have been proposed. Here are three definitions, from the 1970s, the 1980s and the 1990s respectively:

> The complex ability both to emit behaviours that are positively or negatively reinforced and not to emit behaviours that are punished or extinguished by others.
>
> (Libet and Lewinshon 1973: 304)

> Social skills refer to children's ability to organise cognitions and behaviours into an integrated course of action directed towards culturally acceptable social or interpersonal goals. Also included is the propensity to continuously assess and modify goal directed behaviours so as to maximise the likelihood of reaching one's goals.
>
> (Ladd and Mize 1983: 127)

> On a general level social skills might be defined as socially acceptable behaviours that enable a person to interact effectively with others and avoid socially unacceptable responses from others.
>
> (Gresham and Elliott 1993: 139)

In the next section we will be looking at some of the ways in which these three definitions differ. However, for the present, it is useful to consider the main feature that they have in common. In all three cases desirable behaviour is defined in terms of the way in which others react to it. There are no absolute criteria that can be applied. Different societies, cultures and subcultures may approve of, and sanction, different behaviours. The relative, interactional, context-dependent nature of social skills make them particularly interesting from a multicultural perspective, and particularly challenging for many children with SEN to acquire. While the aspects of social skills which have been examined by researchers vary considerably from study to study there are a number that have been more consistently investigated. Caldarella and Merrell (1997) analysed 21 studies of social skills involving over 22,000 children and adolescents and identified the five major categories shown in Table 15.1.

Why are social skills important?

Growing attention has been paid to children's social skills in recent years. Influential research findings have shown that positive social adjustment and acceptance in school (which are assumed to be based on good social skills) are associated with other important short- and long-term outcomes. Social adjustment and acceptance in school have been found to be linked to school achievement (Wentzel 1991; Wentzel and Asher 1995) and low social acceptance in primary school has been

Table 15.1 The five most commonly occurring dimensions of social skills and the percentage of studies in which they occurred

Social skills dimension	Percentage of studies
Peer relationship skills (positive, prosocial behaviour with peers, empathy, sociability, and peer reinforcement and support)	52.38
Self-management skills (temper control, follows rules and limits, accepts criticism, reaches appropriate compromises and shows self-restraint)	52.38
Academic skills (shows independent and productive work habits in the classroom social context)	47.62
Compliance skills (gets on with others by appropriately sharing things and following rules and expectations)	38.09
Assertion skills (shows outgoing behaviour and exercises appropriate independence and social assertion)	33.33

Source: Caldarella and Merrell (1997).

linked with problems in adolescence and adulthood. When pupils who experienced social rejection by their peer group in primary school were followed up in secondary school they were found to have more academic problems, to present more discipline problems and to engage in more truancy (Parker and Asher 1987; Kupersmidt *et al.* 1990). Cowen *et al.* (1973) found that 8–9-year-old pupils who received negative ratings from peers were more likely to experience mental health problems in adulthood. So, the promotion of social adjustment is both an important educational objective in itself and a potentially important factor in raising achievement and reducing exclusions. It is therefore not surprising that the promotion of pupils' social adjustment is an important objective in LEA behaviour support plans and school behaviour policies.

The revised SEN *Code of Practice* (Department for Education and Skills 2001) has expanded the consideration traditionally given to EBD to include social development also ('Behaviour, emotional and social development' – p. 87). Draft guidance to schools in this area has emphasized the need to look beyond managing the pupil's behaviour and helping them to learn new skills: 'action will often focus on the management of the behaviour in the school and classroom. But this will need to be balanced against more targeted interventions aimed at overcoming the pupil's difficulties and at promoting learning' (DfEE 2000c: 24). The guidance goes on to describe a case study example where the development of social skills is targeted on the pupil's IEP and a specific intervention. The revised SEN *Code of Practice* indicates that greater attention is now being paid to the SEN of pupils who require:

- help with the development of social competence and emotional maturity;
- help in adjusting to school expectations and routines;

- help in acquiring the skills of positive interaction with peers and adults (DfES 2001, para. 7.60).

A new interest in the role of education in promoting the social development of all children can be seen in the National Curriculum handbooks (Department for Education and Employment/Qualifications and Curriculum Authority 1999a, 1999b). For the first time a national framework is provided from Key Stage 1 for the teaching of personal, social and health education, and citizenship. From September 2002 citizenship will become part of the statutory curriculum for secondary schools. The foreword to the primary National Curriculum handbook states that the incorporation of citizenship and of personal, social and health education 'reflect[s] the fact that education is also about helping pupils to develop the knowledge, skills and understanding they need to live confident, healthy, independent lives, as individuals, parents, workers and members of society' (1999a: 4).

Cross-cultural perspectives

There may be dangers in generalizing research findings between countries. For example, Chen et al. (1992) carried out a comparative study with 8- and 10-year-old children in Canada and China. In both samples sociability-leadership characteristics were associated with social acceptance in the peer group, and aggression-disruption characteristics with peer rejection. However shyness-sensitivity was negatively associated with measures of peer acceptance in the Canadian sample but positively associated with peer acceptance in the Chinese sample. The authors reported that in China children are encouraged to be dependent, cautious, behaviourally inhibited and self-restrained, so these behaviours are positively valued in Chinese culture. But they are negatively valued in western culture where they are seen as reflecting social immaturity and fearfulness. Of course, we cannot assume that similar findings would be found if Chinese children in Canada were studied, particularly for those living in highly acculturated communities. However, there is very little information on cross-cultural differences in children's social skills and as it is largely North American its main value is in alerting us to some of the issues we ought to be considering and questions we ought to be asking.

Merrell and Gimpel (1997) summarize available research findings on racial or ethnic differences in children's social skills, noting that these are sparse, complex and difficult to interpret:

- parents from different ethnic backgrounds appear to attach different value and importance to particular social skills;
- large nationwide data sets of children's social skills reveal only minimal ethnocultural differences.

Even if cross-ethnic differences are few, those that do exist may be significant and have important educational implications. Indeed, Townsend (1998) considers that cross-ethnic differences must be investigated and addressed because of the implications for schools. She argues that schools should explicitly examine the manner in which differences are perceived and the extent to which their practices, curricula and methods match children's varying characteristics and styles. She recognizes the dangers of overgeneralization and failure to acknowledge the diversity that exists within ethnic groups, but suggests that 'traditional social skills approaches, which fail to acknowledge or consider African and African-American cultural influences or social class differences, may have little relevance in the lives of African-American children' (1998: 226). A similar point might be made in relation to black and ethnic minority groups in UK schools.

Foster *et al.* (1996) discuss ethnically related differences in children's social behaviour along four dimensions:

- *Orientation towards the group*: an interdependent or cooperative orientation versus an individual and competitive orientation.
- *Attitudes towards authority*: deferential with a preference for hierarchically organized relationships as opposed to a more egalitarian outlook.
- *Communication style*: expressive versus constrained.
- *Coping style*: active, outcome-orientated versus passive, accepting.

They review research and locate different ethnic groups in the USA on these dimensions. For example, if African-American children are compared with white American children, African-Americans are found, on average, to be more towards the cooperative, interdependent end of the first dimension. On the second dimension African-American children's attitudes towards authority are described as more deferential. In general, African-American children are considered to display more expressive communication styles. It is reported that both African-American and white American children tend to adopt active coping styles compared with Asian or Hispanic-American children. There is great individual variation around these average scores and teachers need to be sensitive to different cultural expectations while not adopting rigid stereotypes in their own perceptions of their pupils.

Social skills: theory and practice

Different definitions of social skills reflect the different theoretical approaches to behaviour that were introduced in Chapter 14. The theoretical approaches are summarized in Table 15.2 and their influence on the definitions of social skills introduced on page 425 is illustrated by Activity 15.1.

It can be seen that the first definition has a behavioural basis in that it emphasizes the child's behaviour and the environmental contingencies operating on it. By contrast, the main emphasis of the second definition is on cognitions and goals; it therefore has a primarily cognitive basis. Greater systemic influence is apparent in the third definition which emphasizes effective interaction with others. The psychodynamic perspective is not represented here and has had little influence on conceptualizations of social skills. Psychodynamic theory focus on

Table 15.2 Theoretical approaches to behaviour

Theoretical approach	Definition
Behavioural	The primary focus is on behaviour that can be directly observed. It is assumed that behaviour is learned through what happens in a child's environment, so that well established patterns of behaviour can be changed by changing environmental consequences or other related events.
Cognitive	The primary focus is on cognitive processes – how the individual perceives events, thinks about them, plans and problem solves. It is assumed that the relationship between environmental events and a child's behaviour will depend on the child's interpretation of events. The primary focus is placed on individuals' perceptions and thoughts, rather than their behaviour or the environment
Systemic	The focus is on reciprocal interaction between individuals, their behaviour, thoughts and environment. The core features of a systems approach are the concept of mutual or interactive causality and the notion that a wholistic approach is important as in most situations the whole is greater than the sum of its parts.
Psychodynamic	Psychodynamic approaches are based on the assumption that many of the wishes, drives, anxieties and fantasies that determine our behaviour are unconscious. Children's behaviour problems are seen as outward and visible symptoms of internal and invisible conflict.

individual's unconscious wishes, drives and feelings and regards inappropriate social behaviour as but a symptom of underlying internal conflicts. Therapeutic approaches informed by this perspective would target an individual's inner world of wishes, beliefs and feelings, rather than their perceptions, overt behaviour and interactions in social situations. In this chapter we will argue that behavioural, cognitive and systemic approaches to the development of social skills each have a contribution to make and indeed that an integrated multi-dimensional perspective is to be preferred, particularly in a multicultural context.

Behavioural approaches to social skills

Behavioural approaches focus on teaching specific actions (e.g. smiling, eye contact) or sequences of actions (e.g. joining in games, refusing unreasonable requests). This is most important when the child knows what to do and really wants to do it, but just cannot seem to get it right. For example, Emma may know that 'asking nicely' is the best way to get let into a game but when she tries to 'ask nicely' she comes across to the other children as stuck up and bossy and is told she can't

ACTIVITY 15.1   Theoretical approaches in social skills research

Read the following definitions of social skills and identify the theoretical approach with which they are most closely associated.

Definition of social skills	Theoretical approach

1 'The complex ability both to emit behaviours that are positively or negatively reinforced and not to emit behaviours that are punished or extinguished by others' (Libet and Lewinshon 1973: 304).

2 'Social skills refer to children's ability to organise cognitions and behaviours into an integrated course of action directed towards culturally acceptable social or interpersonal goals. Also included is the propensity to continuously assess and modify goal directed behaviours so as to maximise the likelihood of reaching one's goals' (Ladd and Mize 1983: 127) .

3 'On a general level social skills might be defined as socially acceptable behaviours that enable a person to interact effectively with others and avoid socially unacceptable responses from others' (Gresham and Elliott 1993: 139).

play. Lucy may know that apologizing when reprimanded by a teacher is the best way to avoid getting into further trouble, but may often find herself in detention for insolence. Behavioural social skills training can help these pupils change what they say and the way they communicate – both verbally and non-verbally – so that they can more skilfully convey to other people what they *want* to convey.

However, behavioural approaches on their own are usually insufficient. Social competence requires a judgement about how much of a particular behaviour is appropriate in a given situation. This draws on cognitive components such as social perception and knowledge. Consider the use of eye contact as an example. Someone who makes insufficient use of eye contact when interacting with others presents as having poor social skills. They may be regarded as lacking in confidence, as a poor listener, as disinterested, etc. However it is clearly not the case that the more eye contact a person makes with others the better. In fact, others are likely to experience above average levels of eye contact as 'staring' and to consider it off-putting. Furthermore, the 'right' amount of eye contact varies from situation to situation, depending for example upon whether a child is talking to another child, or to a teacher; and whether the teacher is praising a child for exceptional work, reproaching them for failing to produce acceptable work or questioning them to check whether they have understood something.

In addition, the amount of eye contact which is considered appropriate in particular social situations may differ between different cultures. Sue and Sue (1990) report that on average white Americans make eye contact with another when they are listening for about 80 per cent of the time and make eye contact when they are speaking for about 50 per cent of the time. By comparison, African-Americans make more eye contact when speaking but less when listening, whereas Asian-Americans and Hispanics will tend to avoid eye contact altogether when speaking and listening to high-status people. If a child stares at the floor while being reprimanded this may be interpreted by white teachers as a sullen refusal to attend. However, in some cultures downcast eyes are a sign of respect, whereas making eye contact when being 'told off' would be regarded as a sign of defiance. While teachers may benefit from cultural sensitivity training, the child who is to become a successful social interactor in a multicultural society will need to be able to 'code switch' appropriately between different styles of social behaviour. This also requires cultural knowledge and complex social judgements. A purely behavioural approach to social skills training may teach people how to exercise a skill but not how to decide when it is appropriate.

Cognitive approaches to social skills

These approaches focus on social perception and problem solving skills. To be socially skilled the pupil needs to be able to:

- accurately judge the behaviour of other pupils and adults;
- understand the feedback from others and what it tells them about the way they are being perceived;
- think of a range of alternative ways of responding to another person;
- think of what the likely consequences of these different ways of behaving might be;
- decide exactly what to do or say.

At this point, when the child has thought through the options and decided what to do, they will need to draw on their behavioural social skills in actually carrying out the chosen behaviour. It is often found that children need help with some aspects of both cognitive and behavioural social skills: they may need to gain a greater understanding of what is happening in social encounters, as well as having help in improving their skills at performing certain behaviours. Therefore it is generally suggested that a combination of behavioural and cognitive approaches be used (Spence 1983; Beck and Forehand 1984). However, even combined behavioural and cognitive approaches leave out one important aspect of social competence – that it involves other people. Teachers are well aware that the performance of individual children is influenced by the other children with whom they are grouped. Masters and Furman (1981) conducted a study in which children's social skills were rated while they were playing a game with another child from the same class. They found that children were rated as more skilful when they were interacting with a child whom they liked than with a child whom they disliked. It is therefore important to take account of the social context in which children and their classmates are interacting.

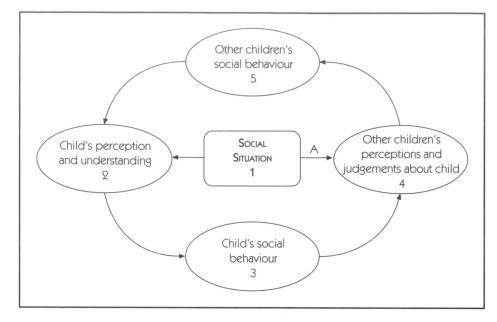

Figure 15.1
A model of social interaction in children
Source: Adapted from Dodge *et al.* (1986).

Interactive approaches to social skills

Figure 15.1 shows an interactive model of social competence in children which incorporates behavioural and cognitive approaches and which, in addition, includes circular chains of causality and interactions between individual and environmental influences.

Stage 1 at the centre of the model draws attention to the importance of the social situation in influencing children's perceptions of, and judgements about each other's behaviour. This was well illustrated by a study conducted by Dodge *et al.* (1982) which found that competent children made more social approaches than other children – but only in the playground, not in the classroom. On the other hand, children with low social competence made more social approaches in the classroom where they were likely to disturb children who were trying to work and hence attract the teacher's disapproval.

Stage 2 highlights the importance of the child's perception and understanding of the situation in which they find themselves. Dodge *et al.* (1984) have shown that problems may arise because children who have low social competence tend to interpret situations in a different way from their classmates. Children aged 5–10 years were shown a video containing a number of ambiguous situations in which one child did something that upset another. For example, in one scene two children were painting and one spilled paint on the other's picture. Compared to their classmates, children who had low social competence were more likely to jump to the conclusion that this had been done on purpose, rather than by accident.

Children's problem solving skills are also important at Stage 2. Dodge *et al.* (1986) have demonstrated that children who have low social competence are less likely to be proficient in one or more of the stages involved in processing information about a social situation and producing an effective response. These stages include: generating a range of possible responses (children who have low social competence tend to be able to think of fewer alternative possibilities for action) and evaluating the probable consequences of the responses generated (children who have low social competence tend to be inappropriately optimistic about the likely outcomes of aggressive behaviour).

At *Stage 3* the child produces the social behaviour selected at Stage 2. It may be skilfully or unskilfully executed but the effect on the child's acceptance or rejection by their classmates will depend on how their classmates interpret the behaviour at *Stage 4*. This will be influenced by:

- Whether the behaviour is perceived as fitting in with or offending peer-group norms which may vary in groups with different cultural values (Cartledge and Milburn 1996). Peer-group norms may also vary in some groups with SEN. Wright *et al.* (1986) described a group for pupils who have EBD in which aggressive interaction was the norm and where aggressive children, who are usually rejected by peers, were not rejected at all.
- Whether the behaviour is perceived as being appropriate to the situation. Coie and Benenson (1983) conducted a study where children were shown a video of child actors behaving aggressively. While unprovoked aggressive behaviour led to social rejection, aggressive behaviour in response to provocation led to social acceptance.
- Judgements which have been made about the child by their classmates. These may be based on prejudicial stereotypes with children giving higher acceptance ratings to same-sex classmates and, to a lesser extent, same-race classmates (Singleton and Asher 1979; Boulton and Smith 1992). Physical attractiveness has also been found to exert a strong influence on social acceptance (Dion and Berscheid 1974) which may have implications for children who have particular kinds of disability.

There is some evidence that prejudicial stereotypes can be influenced by situational factors (arrow A in Figure 15.1). Johnson *et al.* (1983) have demonstrated that cooperative learning experiences can lead to greater cross-ethnic acceptance in the classroom. However, Cowie *et al.* (1994) suggested that the effectiveness of cooperative group work may be lower outside special projects, when teachers are left to implement it with comparatively little support. These considerations are also relevant in trying to ensure that children who have SEN do not suffer severe social rejection because they lack competence in key areas accorded disproportionate status in school. Thus intelligence, academic achievement and skill at sport are all frequently associated with social acceptance. Yet these effects can be weakened and acceptance more equably distributed if the teacher acts to ensure that the apparent importance of difference between children in these respects is minimized while a range of other skills and contributions are also valued.

The way in which classmates interpret a child's behaviour is also influenced by their previous social experience with the child in question. Asarnow (1983) found that when boys with positive reputations behaved negatively towards others they were likely to receive a neutral response. But when boys with negative reputations behaved negatively towards others they were likely to receive a negative response. This suggests that children respond in a biased way to negative behaviour depending on the reputation of the child concerned. This helps to explain why teaching rejected children social skills is usually not enough. It is necessary also to change the perceptions and responsiveness of those rejecting them. The final stage in the cycle of social interaction shown in this model is the peers' behavioural response to the pupil (*Stage 5*). The peers' response in turn acts as a cue, which the pupil will process within the context of the ongoing social situation.

So current theory and research suggest that a pupil's social acceptance and competence are the result of an interaction between individual and environmental factors in a particular social situation at a particular time (Dodge *et al.* 1986; Newcomb *et al.* 1993). Practical application in schools of the full range of implications arising from the model in Figure 15.1 usually involves creating a situation:

- in which rejected children and their classmates can interact positively;
- where prejudices can be broken down;
- where differences in competence can be minimized by ensuring that everyone can make some valued contribution;
- where rejected children can be taught new skills;
- where their classmates can be helped to attend to change in the behaviour of the rejected child and interpret it appropriately.

Later in this chapter we will describe a range of programmes and strategies which can be used by teachers in helping children who are rejected in school settings. First we will look briefly at techniques that can be used to assess children's social competence and to evaluate programme success.

Ways of assessing social skills

Elliott and Busse (1991: 67) point out that: 'A standard battery of tests or methods for assessing social skills does not exist. Rather, hypotheses dictate the direction of assessment, the questions to be answered and the methods to be used'. The interactive model shown in Figure 15.1 is the basis for hypothesis generation. It is important in each case to consider the different facets of social competence and the assessment techniques described below are categorized according to the stage in this model on which they mainly focus. It is also important to collect further information over time about any aspects of a pupil's social skills that are identified as problematic so that the success of programmes used to help them can be evaluated.

Figure 15.2 describes available techniques for assessing each of the stages in the model of social interaction in children, with the exception of Stage 4 which is

ACTIVITY 15.2   Assessment techniques case study

As you read about the types of assessment technique described in this section, consider and note their potential advantages and disadvantages in assessing the needs of Ben.

Ben is 11 years old. He is one of seven children from a school for children with physical difficulties who were integrated 12 months ago into a mainstream middle school (for 8–12-year-old children). Ben was originally admitted to the special school with asthma, language delay, poor articulation and clumsiness – difficulties in each of these areas persist. In addition he has learning difficulties. Mathematics and spelling skills are at the equivalent level of a 7-year-old, although reading accuracy and comprehension are at a 9 and a half to ten year level.

The mainstream school feel that they are able to provide for Ben's learning needs from the resources which have been provided to support the integration programme. However, the school is seriously questioning the appropriateness of Ben's placement because he doesn't seem able to cope socially in mainstream. He is said to find peer relationships very difficult, tantruming when unable to get his own way.

Figure 15.2
Social skills assessment techniques appropriate to different stages in the interactive model

Stage 1: assessing the social situation

*Taxonomy of Problematic Situations (TOPS)** (Dodge *et al.* 1985): a teacher-completed rating scale which identifies the social situations that a pupil finds difficult.
Observations of the Classroom and School Environment: see Chapter 8 for approaches and techniques.

Stage 2: Assessing the child's perception and understanding

*Kusche Affective Interview – Revised (KAI-R)** (Kusche *et al.* 1988): an interview that identifies the cues pupils use to recognize emotion, their understanding of simultaneous and changing emotions and their knowledge of display rules for emotions.

Perceived Competence Scale for Children (Harter 1985): a questionnaire which has been widely used to assess children's global self-worth and their perception of their competence in the following areas: scholastic competence, social acceptance, athletic competence, physical appearance and behavioural conduct (assessing how well the children feel they behave and if they like the way they behave).

*Burnett Self Scale** (Burnett 1994): a questionnaire which provides information on pupils' thoughts and feelings about significant aspects of their lives – self-esteem, physical appearance, physical abilities, relationships with peers, reading, maths, learning.

*Children's Shyness Questionnaire** (Crozier 1995): this self-report questionnaire for 8–11-year-olds asks about feelings of shyness and embarrassment, about being nervous and quiet in social situations, about whether the child has a tendency to blush and whether they enjoy performing in front of others.

Figure 15.2
(cont'd)

Loneliness and Social Dissatisfaction Questionnaire (Asher *et al.* 1990): this assesses pupils' perception of loneliness and their dissatisfaction with their peer relationships at school. It has been used in a number studies in inclusive settings with pupils who have SEN.

Pre-school Interpersonal Problem Solving Test (PIPS) (Spivack and Shure 1974): an interview which uses pictures of children and toys to assess the ability of young children to think of alternative solutions to problems with peers and adults.

What Happens Next Game (WHNG) (Spivack and Shure 1974): an interview uses photographs of toys with which stick figures act out short stories to assess the ability of young children to think of likely consequences of actions in social situations.

Problem Solving Measure (McClure *et al.* 1978): assesses a number of social problem solving skills including the ability to generate alternative solutions.

Stages 3 and 5: assessing children's social behaviour

Observations in natural settings such as the classroom or playground: see Merrell and Gimpel (1997) for descriptions of different types of observational procedures, such as event recording, interval recording, time-sample recording, duration and latency recording and copies of forms that can be used to record observations.

Child Role-Play Measure* (Dodge *et al.* 1985): assesses pupils' social skills by asking them to imagine themselves in a number of social situations and to role-play their responses.

Child Behavior Profile (Edelbrock and Achenbach 1984) and the *Bristol Social Adjustment Guides* (Stott 1974): broader behaviour problem checklists *for teachers that have* relevant social skills subscales.

Mainstreaming Social Skills Questionnaires* (primary and secondary) (Salend and Lutz 1984; Salend and Salend 1986): obtain ratings of the social skills teachers consider necessary for successful performance in mainstream schools.

Social Skills Questionnaires (Spence 1995) and *Social Skills Rating System* (Gresham and Elliott 1990): questionnaire measures of children's social behaviour that contain versions for teachers, parents and the pupils themselves.

Guess Who Technique* (e.g. Hartshorne *et al.* 1929; Coie *et al.* 1982): descriptions (e.g. of cooperative and disruptive behaviour) are presented to a class who are asked to 'guess who?' from their classmates fits each description.

Class Play (Bower 1960): children are provided with positive or negative descriptions of characters in a play and are asked to nominate classmates who would be suited to play each of the characters.

considered separately below. Those marked with an asterisk are available to educational psychologists and schools in the *Psychology in Education Portfolio* (Frederickson and Cameron 1999).

Assessing other children's perceptions and judgements

This is a particularly important aspect as it is pupils' social adjustment and acceptance in school, resulting in part from their social skills, that are associated with other important short- and long-term outcomes. A variety of sociometric (social measurement) techniques are available to assess the perceptions and judgements of members of the peer group. Much of the research on the long-term effects of poor social competence in childhood has used one of the following kinds of sociometric measure.

Peer nomination

This type of approach was developed by Moreno (1934). Children are asked to nominate a certain number of classmates according to a specified criterion (e.g. best friend, especially liked). The majority of studies have used positive criteria but negative ones have also been employed (name three classmates you don't like much). The reliability of peer nomination measures over time is similar to that obtained for achievement tests and is found to increase throughout the primary age range. The approach can be adapted by using pictures of classmates for pre-school children.

Rating scale measures

Here children are provided with a list of all their classmates and asked to rate (on a scale from 1 to 5, for example) how much they like to play with them at school (Asher 1985). Versions for younger children include smiling, frowning and neutral faces instead of numbers and can include photos instead of names.

Forced choice group preference records

These methods appear similar to rating scale techniques but present and treat the alternative responses open to the child as separate categories that are totalled but not averaged. The Social Inclusion Survey (Frederickson and Graham 1999) is an example of a forced choice group preference record which can be used with whole classes of children aged 7 years and above. The method involves making up a worksheet like that shown in Figure 15.3, where a class of 9-year-olds are being asked about how much they like to play with each of their classmates. For older children it may be more appropriate to phrase the question in terms of who they like to 'hang around' with. It is generally good practice to use the children's own vocabulary in asking about free-time association. A second version of the questionnaire asks pupils to tick the face which shows how much they like to

Figure 15.3
A forced choice
group preference
record: The Social
Inclusion Survey
Source:
Frederickson and
Graham (1999).

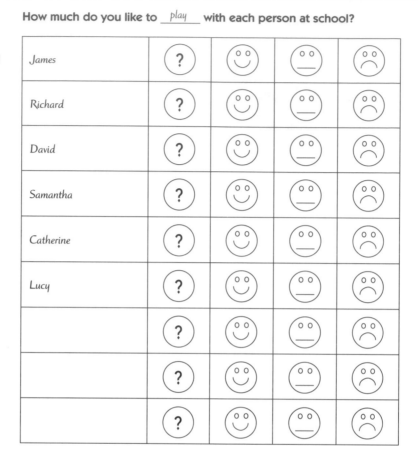

How much do you like to ___play___ with each person at school?

'work with' each person at school: the smiling face to indicate classmates with whom they like to work, the straight-mouthed face to indicate classmates with whom they don't mind whether they work or not and the frowning face to indicate classmates with whom they prefer not to work. Pupils are asked to use the question mark category to indicate any classmates they do not know well enough to decide how much they like to work with them. Good reliability and validity data on these measures are reported from studies carried out in schools in England with pupils who have SEN and their mainstream peers in inclusive school contexts (Frederickson and Graham 1999).

Teachers sometimes express concern about the possibility that sociometric assessment activities may implicitly sanction making negative statements about others or may influence children's attitudes towards classmates in undesirable ways. Connolly (1983) has argued that the dangers of highlighting unpopular children may be particularly pronounced in classes where children with learning difficulties are included. A number of studies have investigated this question but failed to find evidence of any negative effects (Hayvren and Hymel 1984; Bell-Dolan *et al.* 1989; Iverson and Iverson 1996; Iverson *et al.* 1997). Nevertheless, it is advisable to design procedures so as to minimize any possible risk. Frederickson and Furnham (1998a) argue that the forced choice group preference record approach can be particularly suitable for assessing the social acceptance or inclusion in mainstream schools of children with SEN because it avoids signalling out the included children in any way and does not require negative responses to be made. It also allows classmates to say if they don't know someone well enough to decide how much they like to play with them, which is important if children with SEN are integrated on a part-time basis.

It is important to appreciate that sociometric acceptance is also influenced by personal factors such as physical attractiveness, intelligence and academic success and by interactive factors such as similarities in gender and race (Hartup 1992; Foster *et al.* 1996). Within-race choice is less pronounced than is within-gender choice. No relationship has generally been found between race and rejected status. The few studies that have examined the behaviours associated with high peer rejection in predominately white and predominately black groups have reported similar findings, indicating that verbal and physical aggression and disruptive/inappropriate behaviour is similarly implicated in both populations.

Multi-method assessment in multiethnic contexts

Different assessment techniques have different advantages and limitations. A potential advantage of carrying out observations in natural settings is that comparison data from other pupils in the same situation can be collected and used to provide helpful context in interpreting the behaviour of the pupil targeted for observation. Where there are other pupils from the same ethnic or cultural group as the target child, comparative data can usefully be collected from them. However, observational approaches also have potential problems such as observer reactivity, where the presence of the observer has the effect of altering pupil behaviour. This is less likely to occur in a classroom if the observations are being carried out by a teaching assistant who is often present rather than by someone who is a stranger to the pupils.

Collecting observations in natural setting may also be time-consuming, especially if the behaviour being recorded is infrequent. In these cases teacher narrative records or the A-B-C record that was introduced in Chapter 14 may be more economical. Peer assessment is also sometimes preferred to direct observation because it is less intrusive and time-consuming. The social behaviour of older pupils, in particular, is relatively complex and private, making it difficult for adult observers to make reliable and representative observations. Peers may have better access to low frequency but psychologically meaningful events that lead to the establishment of social reputations.

Role-play measures can also be economical of time and can provide useful information for intervention planning, alongside other approaches. However, there are concerns about their validity. In a role-play, pupils may act out what they know they are supposed to do, even if this is not what they would actually do in a real life situation. So, a role-play test will show whether pupils know what behaviour is expected and whether they have the competencies to carry it out, but it cannot be assumed that the behaviour they choose to role-play is what they would actually do if the situation were real.

Because different approaches to assessment have different strengths and limitations it is desirable to have convergent evidence from a variety of approaches. As Maag (1989) points out, all the major reviews of social skills assessment and training call for multiple methods of assessment to be used. Assessment of a number of different stages in the model of social interaction will provide a better understanding of the process overall. The advisability of obtaining information from different respondents has also been highlighted by research findings. Whereas teacher ratings have been found to match closely with pupil self-report and observational data, parental reports tend not to correlate highly with other assessments (Cartledge and Milburn 1996). This probably reflects differences between children's behaviour at home and at school, and provides some support for the view that there is considerable situational specificity in social behaviour.

However, studies in the USA consistently report lower correlations between teacher and parent ratings when children are from racial and ethnic minority populations. For example Keller (1988) found higher correlations between parents' and teachers' social skill ratings of white 7-year-olds than were found between ratings of Hispanic or African-American children. This suggests the possibility of culturally or ethnically based differences in expectations and highlights the importance of parental involvement, if not in completing their own rating scale, then in discussing the assessment information collected in school and in contributing to the resulting intervention planning.

Cartledge and Milburn (1996) argue that the use of a variety of respondents and assessment procedures is particularly important when working with pupils from racial and ethnic minority groups. They report findings which suggest that culturally different behaviours by African-American and Asian-American pupils may be misperceived by teachers. A need is identified for educationists to seek advice and improve their cultural understanding so that they are able to accurately distinguish acceptable and problematic social skills, notwithstanding cultural differences in behavioural expression. Adding assessment information from parents and from classroom peers (with similar and different cultural backgrounds to the target child) may be valuable to teachers both in improving the appropriateness of their assessments and in developing their cultural understanding.

Interventions to improve social skills

A range of well researched intervention approaches are available for developing social skills and promoting social acceptance. The following commonly used intervention procedures will be outlined:

- reinforcement, shaping and modelling;
- coaching;
- social problem solving.

Reinforcement, shaping and modelling

Reinforcement involves the use of praise or other rewards when the child engages in the socially desirable behaviour being targeted (see Gresham and Elliott 1993). Shaping involves rewarding the child in a step-by-step fashion for increasingly accurate approximations to the target behaviour. Such approaches have been successfully used with isolated pupils by using adult attention as a reward, first for playing near peers, then for talking near them, then for participating in potential cooperative situations and finally for engaging in cooperative play. Praise or other rewards may also be given to peers for interacting with the target pupil. This approach, which has been widely used with preschool children has also been applied with older pupils.

When modelling is used the target pupil is provided with a step-by-step demonstration of all the behavioural components required. This may involve the person giving the demonstration 'thinking aloud' about what they are doing while they are doing it. Modelling may be either videotaped or live. With live modelling the pupil can be paired up with a socially skilled classmate for assistance in areas such as playing with peers, resisting aggression and engaging in conversations. The peer is trained in modelling techniques for the behaviours to be developed and in techniques for prompting and reinforcing the target pupil. The target pupil is told to observe the peer model and do as he or she does.

Coaching

Whereas in modelling you show the pupil what is required, in coaching you tell them in a step-by-step manner what to do. Oden (1986) provides a good example of a coaching approach to teaching social interaction concepts which might make playing games with other pupils more fun. The training procedure used is outlined in Figure 15.4.

Research has shown that the opportunity to practise with classmates is crucial to the success of coaching programmes in reducing social rejection (Bierman and Furman 1984). This also allows classmates to 'notice' the rejected child's different behaviour. In this way coaching can have an impact on other pupils' perceptions and judgements at Stage 4 of the Dodge *et al.* (1986) model, as well as the target child's understanding of the concepts being taught (Stage 2) and the social behaviour needed to put their ideas into practice (Stage 3). In some cases a class teacher may initially need the help of another member of staff to release them to spend time on Steps 1 to 5 of the coaching process and to set up the small group

Step 1   Teacher suggests a relevant social concept to child – e.g. 'Jamie, I want to talk about some ideas that make games more fun to play [or that help groups work better together]. Let's talk about cooperating.'

Step 2   Teacher probes child's understanding of concept by asking for specific examples: 'Do you know what cooperating means? Give me some examples.'

Step 3   Teacher repeats/rephrases child's example, or provides one if the child can't: 'Yes, sharing out the crayons and letting everyone have a turn with the bat are good examples of cooperating.'

Step 4   Teacher asks for specific counter-examples of the concept: 'Now give me some examples of not cooperating. What sort of things do children do when they are not cooperating?'

Step 5   Teacher asks child to evaluate whether each type of example (from Steps 3 and 4) should help make a game more fun to play: 'OK, suppose you share out the crayons, will that help to make the game more fun? Why's that? Suppose you won't stick to the rules, like you won't stand still when you are tagged, will that help to make the game more fun? Why's that?'

Step 6   Teacher asks the child to try out some of the ideas they have discussed. Especially when coaching is first used with the child, the teacher may set up an educational game for the child to play with a small group of classmates while they watch from a distance. This provides the child with an immediate opportunity to try out the ideas and to receive feedback at Step 7. Oden envisaged this small-group work being done outside the classroom and advised that once the child had got used to the procedure they should be asked to identify classroom or playground activities where the ideas could be tried out later. They would then be asked to try out the strategies which they had thought of and during the subsequent session a week later they would be asked if they had tried out the strategies and what the results had been.

Step 7   Teacher reviews with the child the helpfulness of the ideas: 'Did you try sharing during that game you've just played/when your group finished off their collage? How did things work out? Why do you think that happened?' If things have gone well: 'Well done for sharing, that was a good idea of yours.' If things have not gone well: 'What could you try next time? OK, give that a try and then tell me how it works.'

opportunities at Step 6. The case study description included in Activity 15.3 is typical of the inventive way in which class teachers have adapted the procedure so as to integrate it into ongoing group work in the classroom.

This technique can be adapted for use with any group, of whatever size, at any time that the group is about to engage in an activity that involves social interaction. Steps 1–5 can be run through by a teacher in a few minutes prior to starting the activity. For example, for a class about to engage in a group activity which involves discussion, the teacher could focus on the concept 'paying attention' in the following way:

ACTIVITY 15.3   Case study: Kelly's classroom coaching programme

This programme, described by Frederickson (1991), was implemented with Kelly, an attention seeking, domineering 9-year-old, by Mark, her class teacher. Mark first noted down a list of social concepts and skills which he felt that Kelly needed to learn in order to improve her social acceptance. He also thought about the complaints, which he frequently received from the other girls: 'Do we *have* to have Kelly in our group? She's so bossy/stuck up/nasty'. He reasoned that even if *he* didn't see Kelly as 'stuck up', work might have to be done to help the other children to see her in a different way.

At the start of each day Mark would review the activities involving a teaching input with a group containing Kelly and, if possible, would select one which lent itself to work on a relevant social concept. During his time with the group he would spend five minutes working through Steps 1 to 5 of the coaching procedure with the whole group, making sure that Kelly was actively involved. He would then ask the children to try out their ideas during the group work, letting them know that the implementation of the ideas would be reviewed briefly with the whole group when he came back to review their work on the activity with them.

Because Mark wished to discourage Kelly from being boastful, and encourage her to be positive and complimentary towards others, he asked pairs of children to try to notice each other using the ideas. In the feedback session children could only give positive examples, and only ones which involved others, not themselves. The children labelled this, 'telling nice tales' and it proved a very effective way of getting the other children to notice positive behaviour in Kelly. On the first few occasions that Mark used this approach he made sure before leaving the group to work on the activity that Kelly's partner would have something to say during the feedback. This was achieved by subtle prompting.

On days when there was no suitable teaching session with a group containing Kelly, Mark planned to prompt the group she was working with to apply ideas which had been worked on previously, and to ask them briefly how things had gone at the end of the session. As this took little more than the time required to walk past the group, the only difficulty was remembering to do it. In practice it often proved easier to do this with Kelly individually. Just before the start of each session Kelly would almost invariably come up to Mark to ask about something, despite his best efforts to discourage her. He now turned this to his advantage by asking her what idea(s) she was going to try out in the following session.

Mark chose to develop a coaching programme to help Kelly:

(a) Could he have used reinforcement and shaping, or modelling instead?
(b) If he had done so how might he have gone about it?
(c) What do think would have been the pros and cons of using each technique in this situation?

Now it is very important during this discussion to pay attention to whoever is speaking. What does paying attention mean? . . . Good. Can you give me an example of what you would be doing if you were paying attention? . . . Good. Paying attention means looking at a person, not interrupting, nodding and saying something about what they have said when they have finished speaking. Can you give me examples of what you might do if you were not paying attention? . . . Good. Examples of not paying attention are interrupting, reading, chatting to someone else. Which of these examples would make a discussion more interesting and enjoyable? . . . Now let's start the discussion, remembering the things that will help.

Many teachers have found that the coaching procedure provides a useful way of ensuring that the practical implications of school or class rules for acceptable social behaviour are clearly understood by all the children. Some children offer surprising examples of what they would be doing if they were 'being sensible' or 'being responsible'. Class rules are usually clearer and the children will ideally have been involved in developing them. However, it may be that most contributions to class discussion of rules are made by a small number of the most articulate children. It cannot simply be assumed that all the children really understand all the rules. This is a particularly important consideration in relation to children who have SEN and those from minority language communities and diverse ethnic backgrounds. The coaching procedure offers a flexible and efficient means of checking practical understanding and remedying any misunderstanding.

Social problem solving

Social problem solving (SPS) programmes focus on Stage 2 of the Dodge *et al.* (1986) model – on the target child's social perception and cognition. The primary use of such programmes has been for preventative/developmental purposes. A number of studies have attempted to evaluate the effectiveness of programmes of this kind, particularly with children who show early signs of social difficulties. While most studies report gains in trained problem solving skills, some have not found corresponding gains in broader adjustment measures such as changes in social behaviour or social acceptance in the peer group (Pellegrini and Urbain 1985).

The best-known examples of preventative/developmental SPS programmes are those developed by Spivack *et al.* (1976). They use the following steps:

1 Problem identification and goal setting.
2 Generation of alternative solutions.
3 Consideration of consequences and decision making.
4 Making plans and checking for success.

Class-based SPS programmes consisting of scripted lessons are available across the primary age range. As these are North American, some adaptations are necessary for use in UK schools. They typically use discussion, games and role-play to teach problem solving skills and support their application to real life situations. Shure's (1992) Programme for 4–6-year-olds, which consists of daily short group sessions over one term, makes extensive use of puppets and pretending. The skills taught in this North American programme are outlined in Figure 15.5.

Figure 15.5
I can problem
solve (ICPS)
programme for
4–6-year-olds
Source: Shure
(1992).

Prerequisite skills

- Language, listening and paying attention (and, some, or, is, not, some, different)
- Identifying emotions & rudiments of logic (if, then)
- Multiple attributes (revision of and, not)
- How can we tell? (identifying emotions)
- Do you like? (individual preferences)
- Emotional reactions
- Why? (because, connections)
- More about individual preferences
- A story – 'Will I have a friend?' (emotions/why-because)
- What might happen next?
- Puppet story (emotions & individual preferences)
- Review – How can I find out? Do you like? How can you tell?
- More why – because game
- Fairness

Problem solving skills

Section 1: Alternative solutions – 'What else can I do?'
Section 2: Alternative consequences – 'What might happen next if . . . ?'
Section 3: Pairing of solutions and potential consequences

The programme has been tried out in a number of UK schools where teachers have found it to provide a very useful basis for developing programmes of work in the early years of school.

In the UK, Thacker (1982) devised an SPS programme with a group of pupils in a school for boys with EBD. This programme has been developed into a published resource aimed at 11- to 13-year-olds, but has also been used extensively by educational psychologists with groups and individuals in primary schools (e.g. Daniels 1990). Thacker's programme involves the following components:

- instructions in the use of the problem solving sequence using cartoons and discussion;
- modelling of the steps involved, either live or videotaped;
- role-play, through which the group was able to explore alternatives and provide each other with feedback as to the consequences which might attach to the alternatives considered.

Pupils are taught to see problems as a normal part of life and are given a eight-point plan for dealing with them:

1 *Problem Identification*: watch out for signs of upset feelings.
2 *Impulse delay*: stop and think before you act.
3 *Problem definition*: pinpoint the problem and decide on your goal.
4 *Generation of alternatives*: think of as many solutions as you can.

5 *Consideration of consequences*: think ahead to what might happen next.
6 *Implementation*: when you have a really good solution, try it.
7 *Persistence*: if your solution doesn't work be sure to try again.
8 *Planning for success*: do you need to work out a step-by-step plan?

One advantage of SPS programmes is that most of the content and the examples used are drawn from the children themselves. Foster *et al.* (1996) challenge the idea that socially competent behaviours can be identified independently of the racial and ethnic context in which the child interacts. They highlight the necessity of considering the 'cultural fit' of the content of SPS programmes, particularly in multicultural settings where a set social skills programme is offered to a diverse group of pupils. By contrast, the flexibility of the problem solving approach enables diverse cultural perspectives to be represented.

If the advantages of SPS programmes are to be realized it is important that the problem solving approach to social skills training is used within a non-judgemental classroom ethos where all alternatives suggested are accepted, pending evaluation of their consequences by the pupils. Teachers may find this difficult as it sometimes means acknowledging as a possible solution behaviour that is not sanctioned by the school. For example, if a class are discussing a situation where Peter is teasing and laughing at Simon, they will usually identify beating Peter up as one of the possible options open to Simon. If the teacher expresses disapproval the pupils are likely to close down discussion of the consequences of this alternative from their point of view. However, if the teacher accepts the pupils' suggestion neutrally as one possibility and supports them in evaluating its consequences everyone may learn a great deal more. For example, in this kind of situation teachers have reported learning that:

- Children can usually identify more negative consequences of beating someone up than teachers can. (These include consequences that did not occur to the teachers, such as 'Your clothes might get torn, then your mum will be really angry and stop your pocket money'.)
- Although schools typically have rules and sanctions against fighting, inconsistent application by staff can create an ethos where pupils feel they can get away with it. (If pupils don't identify 'You get into trouble with the teachers' as an important negative consequence of beating someone up at school, then this is uncomfortable but important information for a school to have in reviewing the implementation of its behaviour policy.)
- In one school some boys from a particular group had been told by their fathers that they were to resolve their differences in a 'manly' way and not bring negative staff attention to their ethnic group by 'telling on' each other. (In this situation the teacher was able to help the boys identify a number of 'manly' ways in which they could resolve their differences that had more positive consequences than fighting with each other.)

At the same time it is also important to appreciate that a problem solving approach is not culturally neutral. Rotheram-Borus (1993) points out that SPS training is grounded in a world view that regards individuals as active shapers of their world. This contrasts with a 'wait and see' or 'trust to a higher power' type of philosophy that characterizes some cultures. One of the four dimensions along which Foster *et al.* (1996: 138) locate ethnically related differences in children's social behaviour is 'active, outcome orientated versus passive, accepting coping styles'. We might anticipate that problem solving approaches would be more congruent with the predominant approach in cultural groups located at the 'active, outcome orientated' end of this dimension.

Integrated social skills training programmes

As with social skills assessment, multi-method training programmes are generally recommended. Erwin (1994) examined 43 studies in order to evaluate the relative effectiveness of three methods: modelling, coaching and problem solving. He concluded that social skills training produced significant improvements in pupils' levels of social interaction, sociometric status and problem solving abilities, but that no particular training technique produced a significantly greater improvement than either of the others. It is generally recommended that intervention programmes combine different approaches in order to capitalize on the particular effects produced by each.

Spence (1995) provides a session by session guide to implementing programmes with children and adolescents which incorporates a number of different methods:

- Training in performance of specific basic social skills (e.g. eye contact). Techniques include: instructions and discussion, modelling, role-playing, giving feedback and setting homework tasks.
- Social perception skills training. Components include: learning about feelings, understanding and use of non-verbal social cues, relaxation training.
- Training in social problem solving skills.
- Training in the use of self-instructions to guide behaviour.
- Replacement of unhelpful thoughts with positive, helpful thinking.
- Application of these skills to specific social problems (e.g. making friends, dealing with teasing or dealing with disagreements).

Furnham and Argyle (1981: 131) identified generalization as 'the Achilles heel of social skills training'. They continued, 'There is a sizeable and largely depressing literature on the lack of generalisability of social skills training'. What this meant was that children from different schools would be brought together, say weekly in a clinic, and trained in specific social skills by a psychologist. Over the weeks video and other evidence would show that their social skills were improving in the clinic – they would be better at initiating conversations or responding assertively to teasing during the social skills training sessions. However, teachers and parents would report that at school and at home the children's behaviour hadn't changed at all. There was no evidence of generalization from the clinic training sessions to other contexts. More recent reviews (Gresham and Elliott 1993) have emphasized the need to train for generalization. Elliott and Busse (1991) suggest that generalization can be facilitated by including as many of the following strategies in the programme as possible:

- teach behaviours that are likely to be valued in everyday settings and so be naturally reinforced when they occur there;
- train across people and settings that the child encounters every day;
- gradually phase out any special rewards until they blend in with those generally available in the classroom or school;
- reinforce applications of skills to new and appropriate situations;
- include peers in training.

Bierman and Furman (1984) carried out a study which suggested that the outcomes obtained by social skills programmes are highly specific to the stage of the Dodge *et al.* (1986) model at which the intervention programme is targeted. Participants in their study were 10–12-year-old boys and girls who had low conversational skills and low peer acceptance. They were divided into four groups with seven boys and seven girls in each group. Group 1 received no intervention, and the other three groups each received a programme consisting of ten 30-minute sessions over a six-week period. Group 2 received an individual coaching programme, Group 3 received a programme of group experience with peers working towards shared goals and Group 4 received a programme of group experience combined with coaching. The results at the end of the intervention showed that both coaching groups had learned the conversational skills they has been taught and when the children were followed up six weeks later they were still using these skills. Both group experience groups were found to have improved in sociometric status at the end of the intervention. However, six weeks later their improved sociometric ratings had only been maintained among those classmates who had taken part in the group experience programmes with them. Only Group 4, who received both types of intervention, improved both their conversational skills and their social acceptance.

Interventions focused on the peer group

The importance of systematically considering and targeting for intervention each of the stages of the Dodge *et al.* (1986) model has been highlighted by other studies which also found that even when low-accepted pupils show changes in their behaviour following social skills training, classmates may be slow to grant them higher social status. Pellegrini and Urbain (1985) point out that well established friendship networks and a prior history of negative contact with the target pupil may both reduce the generalization of training effects from a social skills group to the classroom or playground. Because of this it has been suggested that other approaches, in addition to social skills training with the target pupil, may need to be implemented in order to change the perceptions, judgements and behaviour of their classmates.

ACTIVITY 15.4   Intervention programme case study

Read the following account of a social skills training programme that combined cognitively based SPS approaches and behavioural social skills training (Frederickson and Simms 1990).

(a) Think about the five stages of the Dodge *et al.* (1986) model and decide which stages are targeted by the programme and which are not.
(b) How could you change the programme so that the other stages are also targeted?

The programme involved a series of eight after-school sessions each lasting one and a half hours. It was run by psychologists in an out-of-school centre for a group of eight children from seven different schools. The children had all been referred by their schools to the educational psychology service, and difficulty in relationships with other children was a major area of concern in each case. During the sessions both behavioural social skills and problem solving strategies were taught to the children through games, discussion and role-play activities. Meetings were also held with parents and teachers to inform them about the programme, the skills that would be taught and follow-up work which could be done at home and school.

   At the end of the programme, assessment of children's SPS skills showed substantial gains and both parents and teachers noted improvements in the specific social skills that had been taught to their children. In addition, measures of social adjustment were completed by teachers, and sociometric measures were completed by classmates. These measures were completed on three occasions: before the programme started; just after it finished; and six months later (when most of the children had changed teacher). There was clear evidence of an improvement in teacher ratings of social adjustment following the programme that was maintained six months later. However, the children's acceptance by their classmates did not improve – despite their improved adjustment and newly-learned social skills.

'Circles of friends' is a recently developed approach that appears promising and warrants further research (Newton *et al.* 1996; Taylor 1996; Shotton 1998). It is an inclusive approach to support children experiencing emotional, behavioural or social difficulties in the educational setting by enlisting the help of the other children in their class and setting up a special group or 'circle' of friends. The special group helps to set, monitor and review weekly targets in a meeting facilitated by an adult. They also provide agreed support to facilitate the focus child's inclusion and to help them achieve their targets. Sapon-Shevin *et al.* (1998) express some concerns about 'techniques such as Circles of Friends', namely, 'a clear lack of reciprocity has been one of the major problems in such relationships, with the child with disabilities consistently being the one helped or supported, often with little attention given to the general social context of the classroom' (p. 105). However, circles of friends is an intervention that involves peers in helping a child change their behaviour and, at the same time, has the potential to change the peers' behaviour and attitude towards the child. It includes Stages 4 and 5 of the Dodge model and so provides a link that is missing in many behaviour change programmes.

'Peer mediation' is another strategy involving peers. Lane and McWhirter (1992) review research evidence that peer mediation results in greater pupil cooperation, more positive attitudes and reduced fighting. In particular there is some evidence of positive attitude change in pupils trained as peer mediators who were formerly frequently involved in conflict themselves. Where young people are notably orientated towards their peers, it may be that peer-mediated learning will be particularly beneficial for them (cf. Cartledge and Milburn 1996). Lane and McWhirter (1992) describe a process for introducing peer mediation to a school. It begins with staff commitment to the project and engagement in eight hours of training to develop their own mediation skills. Then the project is introduced to pupils in a way that will motivate them to volunteer as mediators, and five half-day training sessions are provided to the pupils selected as mediators. Trained peer mediators can then engage in a five-stage sequence:

1 Introduce themselves, outline their services and the conditions under which these services are offered.
2 Assist the pupils involved in the dispute to communicate their side of the argument to each other.
3 Help each disputing pupil to state what they want.
4 Help disputing pupils identify how each can help resolve the problem.
5 Ask each party to fill out a report on the peer mediation.

Interventions focused on the social situation

Interventions targeted on the social situation (Stage 1) have also received attention. For example, Johnson and Johnson (1991) have reported greater social acceptance of included special needs pupils if the classroom has been structured around cooperative group learning situations, and Siner (1993) describes a cooperative group-work approach to improving the social competence of Year 2 pupils. Cartledge and Milburn (1996) review evidence that cooperative classroom learning activities contribute to positive peer interactions, acceptance of SEN and racial differences, and academic achievement. They suggest that cooperative learning methods are particularly appropriate for ethnic groups such as African- Asian- and Hispanic-Americans whose cultural roots are in collectivist rather than individualistic societies. It could equally be argued that such methods are urgently needed where children have been prepared at home and in their community only for a competitive and individualistic model of behaviour.

Frederickson and Furnham (1998b) have demonstrated that both personal and environmental factors are associated with peer-group acceptance of integrated pupils who have MLD and that these factors differ when acceptance is assessed in relation to a play as opposed to a work context. Findings such as these suggest that the design of social skills programmes for particular pupils needs to be informed by knowledge both of their individual skills and peer-group interactions, and of broader situational factors such as the ethos and social organization of the classroom and school environment. Such factors were considered in detail in Chapter 8 on the learning environment.

Further issues and implications

Affective issues: social skills and emotional intelligence

The role of 'affect' or emotion has often been overlooked in discussions of social skills (Crick and Dodge 1994). However, there has been much interest in recent years in 'emotional intelligence'. The concept of emotional intelligence was introduced by Salovey and Mayer (1990) and popularized by Goleman (1995) who defined it as:

- knowing one's own emotions;
- managing emotions;
- motivating oneself;
- recognizing emotions in others;
- handling relationships.

If these five domains of emotional intelligence are compared with the five most commonly identified dimensions of social skills shown in Table 15.1, it is clear that there is considerable overlap. In particular, 'peer relationship skills' map closely onto 'handling relationships'; and 'self-management skills' onto 'motivating oneself'. The concept of emotional intelligence was initially criticized on the grounds that it added little to the concept of social skills and, in addition, that it was vague and loosely defined and there was no convincing reason for using the term 'intelligence'.

In response to these criticisms Salovey and Sluyter (1997: 10) revised the definition of emotional intelligence as follows: 'Emotional intelligence involves the ability to perceive accurately, appraise, and express emotion; the ability to access and/or generate feelings when they facilitate thought; the ability to understand emotion and emotional knowledge; the ability to regulate emotions to promote emotional and intellectual growth'. This definition focuses on 'emotional contributions to intelligence or intellectual understanding of emotion' (Salovey and Sluyter 1997: 16) and separates these processes from the collection of social skills and behavioural predispositions which had been included in earlier definitions. Salovey and Sluyter have elaborated their new definition into the two-dimensional cognitive model shown in Figure 15.6. The four branches of the model are organized in increasing order of psychological complexity, so that the lowest branch, 'Perception, appraisal and expression of emotion' is thought to contain the most basic processes, while 'Reflective regulation of emotions to promote emotional and intellectual growth' involves higher, more psychologically integrated processes. Along each branch there is a developmental progression from left to right, with the earlier emerging and more discrete skills in level 1 on each branch best illustrating the distinctions between the branches. A great deal of work has still

EMOTIONAL INTELLIGENCE

Reflective regulation of emotions to promote emotional and intellectual growth

LEVEL 1: Ability to stay open to feelings, both those that are pleasant and those that are unpleasant

LEVEL 2: Ability to reflectively engage or detach from an emotion depending upon its judged informativeness or utility

LEVEL 3: Ability to reflectively monitor emotions in relation to oneself and others, such as recognizing how clear, typical, influential or reasonable they are

LEVEL 4: Ability to manage emotion in oneself and others by moderating negative emotions and enhancing pleasant ones, without repressing or exaggerating information they may convey

Understanding and analysing emotions: employing emotional knowledge

LEVEL 1: Ability to label emotions and recognize relations among the words and the emotions themselves, such as the relation between liking and loving

LEVEL 2: Ability to interpret the meanings that emotions convey regarding relationships, such as that sadness often accompanies a loss

LEVEL 3: Ability to understand complex feelings – simultaneous feelings of love and hate, or blends such as awe as a combination of fear and surprise

LEVEL 4: Ability to recognize likely transitions among emotions, such as the transition from anger to satisfaction, or from anger to shame

Emotional facilitation of thinking

LEVEL 1: Emotions prioritize thinking by directing attention to important information

LEVEL 2: Emotions are sufficiently vivid and available that they can be generated as aids to judgement and memory concerning feelings

LEVEL 3: Emotional mood swings change the individual's perspective from optimistic to pessimistic, encouraging consideration of multiple points of view

LEVEL 4: Emotional states differentially encourage specific problem approaches, such as when happiness facilitates inductive reasoning and creativity

Perception, appraisal and expression of emotion

LEVEL 1: Ability to identify emotion in one's physical states, feelings and thoughts

LEVEL 2: Ability to identify emotions in other people, designs, artwork etc. through language, sound, appearance and behaviour

LEVEL 3: Ability to express emotions accurately and to express needs related to those feelings

LEVEL 4: Ability to discriminate between accurate and inaccurate, or honest versus dishonest expressions of feeling

Figure 15.6 A model of emotional intelligence
Source: Salovey and Sluyter (1997).

to be done in testing aspects of this model and investigating ways in which it might inform work in schools to promote children's emotional development.

Greenberg *et al.* (1995) describe an evaluation of one programme: PATHS (promoting alternative thinking strategies). The 35-lesson unit on 'Feelings and Relationships' which was the primary focus of the evaluation emphasized emotional and interpersonal understanding. Pupils were taught that all feelings are OK to have but that all behaviours are not OK. They were taught to attend to what their feelings are telling them and to use information from feelings in deciding what to do next. Labelling feelings was seen as an important basis for facilitating self-control and resolving problems effectively. Instruction was also provided on the use of cues in recognizing feelings in oneself and others, in managing feelings and deciding whether to show or keep them private and in gaining an empathetic realization of how one's behaviour can affect other people. The evaluation study found that the programme was effective for both mainstream and special needs pupils in Years 3 and 4 in:

- improving their vocabulary and fluency in discussing emotional experiences;
- enhancing their belief in their ability to manage emotions;
- developing their understanding of a number of aspects of emotions.

While the evaluation of this intervention addressed only two of Salovey and Sluyter's (1997) four branches of emotional intelligence it does represent a step forward. Greenberg *et al.* (1995: 134) point out that, to their knowledge, this study is the first clear demonstration that 'aspects of emotional fluency and understanding can be successfully taught in a school environment by classroom teachers'.

Implications for personal and social education in schools

Roffey *et al.* (1994) provide a wide range of activities for use by teachers in developing primary aged pupils' social competencies in school. These cover important areas for any personal and social education curriculum:

- developing social confidence;
- making friends;
- promoting inclusion;
- overcoming communication difficulties;
- celebrating difference;
- developing conflict resolution skills;
- tackling bullying;
- improving the playground environment;
- improving the social climate of the classroom.

Spivack and Shure (1974) describe ways in which teachers can use 'problem solving dialogues' to intervene in problem situations and help children resolve their difficulties for themselves. This approach can also be applied to incidents that the teacher has not seen, through having the children stage a re-enactment. Although this sounds potentially time consuming, it can in fact save much of the time which is typically wasted in fruitless interrogation of children involved in playground incidents.

This is how it works. If the children involved in a playground incident are upset, first wait until they are calm enough to talk. Then ask them to act out exactly what happened, the only proviso being that they must not actually make physical contact with each other. If rekindling of angry contact appears likely the children can be asked to replay the event 'in slow motion'. Primary aged children tend to find it difficult to 'stick to a story' when required to act out what happened with others. It is important at this stage that the teacher maintains a narrow and neutral focus on sorting out the practical detail of what happened. Sometimes a child will refuse to take part. In this case an onlooker can be asked to play their part and in practice most children soon start to join in, indignantly correcting inaccuracies in the acting.

Having quickly established what has happened the teacher can then take the children through the SPS steps, establishing:

- how each child perceived and interpreted the behaviour of others;
- how each child felt about it;
- what else they could have done and how things would then have been different;
- what can be done now and what consequences are likely to follow.

There are advantages to working through this process in the classroom, involving classmates in order to sensitize them to issues of fairness and increase their supportiveness towards children who are experiencing difficulties.

Implications for promoting inclusion

As discussed in Chapter 3, promoting the inclusion of pupils with SEN in mainstream schooling is a key government objective in the UK (Department for Education and Employment 1997). The central rationale for inclusion has involved human rights considerations with anticipated social benefits for the pupils featuring prominently (Roberts and Zubrick 1992; Vaughn *et al.* 1996). However, many studies have reported that integrated children with SEN have particular social difficulties compared to their mainstream peers (Kaufman *et al.* 1985; Taylor *et al.* 1987; Nabuzoka and Smith 1993) and a need for social skills training of such children has long been identified (e.g. Gresham 1982)

Merrell and Gimpel (1997) review available research on the social skills of children who have a variety of SEN (specific learning difficulties, MLD and SLD, speech and language difficulties and EBD). They conclude that children in all these groups are at heightened risk of social skills difficulties, with the risk being particularly high among pupils who experience EBD. They argue that social skills difficulties may present barriers to inclusion and suggest that social skills assessment and training represents an important means of promoting social acceptance and successful inclusion.

Conclusions

A growing appreciation of the importance of education in promoting children's social development is apparent in the new emphasis placed on this area in revisions to the National Curriculum and the SEN *Code of Practice*. In this chapter we have reviewed research on social skills in childhood which has been carried out from different theoretical bases and described related assessment techniques and intervention strategies. Some implications are highlighted both for general programmes of personal and social education and for targeted interventions to promote the inclusion of pupils who have SEN.

The importance of multi-method approaches to both assessment and intervention emerges as a consistent theme and one that is of particular relevance in multicultural school contexts. Cartledge and Milburn (1996) suggest that social skills trainers need to be aware of learners' cultural backgrounds and of culturally specific behaviours as different, rather than superior or inferior. It is suggested that social skills instruction should promote biculturalism which 'refers to the ability to negotiate two cultures simultaneously, with an awareness of the norms of both cultures' (Rotheram-Boras 1993: 182). This would involve helping pupils acquire the skills needed for success in the mainstream culture while retaining, valuing and applying, as appropriate, culturally specific behaviours.

References

Abreu, G. de (1995) Understanding how children experience the relationship between home and school mathematics. *Mind, Culture and Activity: An International Journal*, 2(2): 119–42.

Abreu, G. de, Cline, T. and Shamsi, A. (in preparation) Parents' representations of their children's mathematics learning in multiethnic primary schools.

Ackerman, D. and Howes, C. (1986) Sociometric status and after-school activity of children with learning disabilities. *Journal of Learning Disabilities*, 2: 416–19.

Adams, M.J. (1990) *Beginning to Read: Children Thinking and Learning about Print*. Cambridge, MA: MIT Press.

AFASIC (Association for All Speech-Impaired Children) (1990) *Checklists of Language Disability*. London: AFASIC.

Affleck, J.Q., Madge, S., Adams, A. and Lowenbraun, S. (1988) Integrated Classroom Resource Model Academic Viability and Effectiveness. *Exceptional Children*, 54: 339–48.

Ainscow, M. (1988) Beyond the eyes of the monster: an analysis of recent trends in assessment and recording. *Support for Learning*, 3(3): 149–53.

Ainscow, M. (1995) Education for all: making it happen. *Support for Learning*, 10(4): 147–54.

Ainscow, M. and Tweddle, D.A. (1979) *Preventing Classroom Failure: An Objectives Approach*. Chichester: Wiley.

Ainscow, M. and Tweddle, D. (1988) *Encouraging Classroom Success*. London: David Fulton.

Alders, C., Cava, M. and Tubbs, B. (1995) Assessing the learning environment: from multidimensional perspectives, in N. Frederickson and T. Cline (eds) *Assessing the Learning Environments of Children with Special Educational Needs*. London: Educational Psychology Publishing.

Alladina, S. (1985) Second language teaching through maths – learning maths through a second language. *Educational Studies in Mathematics*, 16: 215–19.

Allyn, B.A. and Boykin, A.W. (1992) African-American children and the educational process: alleviating cultural discontinuity through prescriptive pedagogy. *School Psychology Review*, 21: 586–96.

Alves, A.J. and Gottlieb, J. (1986) Teacher interactions with mainstreamed handicapped students and their nonhandicapped peers. *Learning Disabilities Quarterly*, 8: 77–83.

Anderson, J.A. (1995) Towards a framework for matching teaching and learning styles for diverse populations, in R.K. Sims and S.J. Sims (eds) *The Importance of Learning Styles: Understanding the Implications for Learning Course Design and Education.* London: Greenwood Press.

Anderson, L.W., Ryan, D.W. and Shapiro, B.J. (eds) (1989) *The IEA Classroom Environment Study.* Oxford: Pergamon.

Anthony, A., Bogle, D., Ingram, T.T.S. and McIsaac, M.W. (1971) *The Edinburgh Articulation Test.* Edinburgh: Churchill Livingstone.

Archbold, S. (1992) The development of a paediatric cochlear implant programme – a case study. *Journal of the British Association of Teachers of the Deaf*, 16(1): 17–26.

Archbold, S., Robinson, K. and Hartley, D. (1998) UK teachers of the deaf – working with children with cochlear implants. *Deafness and Education*, 22(2): 24–30.

Arens, L. and Molteno, C. (1989) A comparative study of postnatally acquired cerebral palsy in Cape Town. *Developmental Medicine and Child Neurology*, 31: 246–54.

Armitage, I.M., Burke, J.P. and Buffin, J.T. (1995) Visual impairment in severe and profound sensorineural deafness. *Archives of Disease in Childhood*, 73: 53–6.

Armstrong, D., Galloway, D. and Tomlinson, S. (1993) Assessing special educational needs: the child's contribution. *British Educational Research Journal*, 19(2): 121–31.

Arnold, L.E., Barnaby, N., Macmanus, J. *et al.* (1987) Prevention by specific perceptual remediation for vulnerable first-graders. *Archives of General Psychiatry*, 34: 1279–94.

Arter, J.A. and Jenkins, J.R. (1979) Differential diagnosis – prescriptive teaching: a critical appraisal. *Review of Educational Research*, 49(4): 517–55.

Artiles, A.J., Trent, S.C. and Kuan, L. (1997) Learning disabilities empirical research on ethnic minority students: an analysis of 22 years of studies published in selected refereed journals. *Learning Disabilities Research and Practice*, 12(2): 82–91.

Asarnow, J.R. (1983) Children with peer adjustment problems: sequential and non-sequential analysis of school behaviours. *Journal of Consulting and Clinical Psychology*, 51: 709–17.

Ashby, B., Morrison, A. and Butcher, H.J. (1970) The abilities and attainments of immigrant children. *Research in Education*, 4: 73–80.

Ashcraft, M.H., Kirk, E.P. and Hopko, D. (1998) On the cognitive consequences of mathematics anxiety, in C. Donlan (ed.) *The Development of Mathematical Skills.* Hove: Psychology Press.

Asher, S. (1985) An evolving paradigm in social skills training research with children, in B. Schneider, K. Rubin and J. Ledingham (eds) *Peer Relationship and Social Skills in Childhood: Issues in Assessment and Training.* New York: Springer Verlag.

Asher, S.R., Parkhurst, J.T., Hymel, S. and Williams, G.A. (1990) Peer rejection and loneliness in childhood, in S.R. Asher and J.D. Coie (eds) *Peer Rejection in Childhood.* Cambridge: Cambridge University Press.

Ashlock, R.B. (1982) *Error Patterns in Computation.* Columbus, OH: Merrill Publishing Co.

Ashton, C. (1996) In defence of discrepancy definitions of specific learning difficulties. *Educational Psychology in Practice*, 12(3): 131–40.

Askew, M. and Wiliam, D. (1995) *Recent Research in Mathematics Education 5–16.* London: HMSO.

Audit Commission (1992) *Getting in on the Act. Provision for Pupils with Special Educational Needs: The National Picture.* London: HMSO.

Audit Commission (1998) *Getting in on the Act: A Review of Progress on Special Educational Needs*. London: The Audit Commission.

Avramadis, E. and Bayliss, P. (1998) An inquiry into children with emotional and behaviour difficulties in two schools in the south west of England. *Emotional and Behaviour Difficulties*, 3(3): 25–35.

Ayers, H., Clarke, D. and Murray, A. (1995) *Perspectives on Behaviour*. London: David Fulton.

Baca, L.M. and Cervantes, H.T. (1989) *The Bilingual Special Education Interface*. Columbus, OH: Merrill Publishing Co.

Bagley, C. and Mallick, K. (1996) Towards achievement of reading skill potential through peer tutoring in mainstreamed 13 year olds. *Disability and Society*, 11: 83–9.

Baird, G. (1992) Assessment of hearing and management of hearing problems, in G.T. McCarthy and B.G.R. Neville (eds) *Physical Disability in Childhood: An Interdisciplinary Approach to Management*. Edinburgh: Churchill Livingstone.

Baker, C. (1996) *Foundations of Bilingual Education and Bilingualism*, 2nd edn. Clevedon: Multilingual Matters.

Baker, C. and Child, D. (1993) Communication approaches used in schools for the deaf in the U.K. – a follow-up study. *Journal of the British Association of Teachers of the Deaf*, 17(2): 36–47.

Baker, C. and Hinde, J. (1984) Language background classification. *Journal of Multilingual and Multicultural Development*, 5(1): 43–56.

Baker, E.T. (1994) 'Meta-analytic evidence for non-inclusive educational practices: Does educational research support current practice for special needs students?' Unpublished doctoral dissertation. Temple University, Philadelphia.

Baker, E.T., Wang, M.C. and Walberg, H.J. (1994–5) The effects of inclusion on learning. *Educational Leadership*, 52(4): 33–5.

Baker, J.M. and Zigmond, N. (1995) The meaning and practice of inclusion for students with learning disabilities: themes and implications from the five cases. *Journal of Special Education*, 29(2): 163–80.

Bakker, D.J. (1979) Hemispheric differences and reading strategies: two dyslexias? *Bulletin of the Orton Society*, 29: 84–100.

Ball, E.W. and Harry, B. (1993) Multicultural education and special education: parallels, divergences and intersections. *The Educational Forum*, 57: 430–7.

Ball, M.J. (2000) Problems of pragmatic profiling, in N. Muller (ed.) *Pragmatics in Speech and Language Pathology: Studies in Clinical Applications*. Philadelphia, PA: John Benjamins Publishing.

Ball, S.J. (1993) Education markets, choice and social class: the market as a class strategy in the UK and the USA. *British Journal of the Sociology of Education*, 14(1): 3–19.

Bamford, J. and Saunders, E. (1991) *Hearing Impairment, Auditory Perception and Language Disability*, 2nd edn. London: Whurr.

Bandura, A. (1977) *Social Learning Theory*. Englewood Cliffs, NJ: Prentice Hall.

Bangert-Drowns, R.L., Kulik, C.L.C., Kulik, J.A. and Morgan, M.T. (1991) The instructional effect of feedback in test-like events. *Review of Educational Research*, 61: 213–38.

Barker, I. (1989) *Multidisciplinary Teamwork: Models of Good Practice*. London: Central Council for Education and Training in Social Work.

Barnes, C. (1996) Theories of disabilities and the origin of oppression of disabled people in Western society, in L. Barton (ed.) *Disability and Society: Emerging Issues and Insights*. London: Longman.

Barrados, O. (1996) A study of the oral language proficiency of Portuguese bilingual children in London, in T. Cline and N. Frederickson (eds) *Curriculum Related Assessment, Cummins and Bilingual Pupils*. Clevedon: Multilingual Matters.

Barrett, M. and Trevitt, J. (1991) *Attachment Behaviour and the Schoolchild: An Introduction to Educational Therapy*. London: Routledge.

Barthorpe, T. and Visser, J. (1991) *Differentiation: Your Responsibility – An In-Service Training Pack for Staff Development*. Stafford: National Association for Remedial Education.

Bartlett, D. (1995) Educational performance in the early years in Birmingham LEA with particular reference to children with English as an additional language and those from minority ethnic groups. Paper presented at the Invitational Conference on Teaching and Learning English as an Additional Language, London, 27–28 April 1995. London: School Curriculum and Assessment Authority.

Batchelor, J. (2000) *Stepfamilies* (NCB Highlight No. 176). London: National Children's Bureau.

Baxter, C., Poonia, K., Ward, L. and Nadirshaw, Z. (1990) *Double Discrimination: Issues and Services for People with Learning Disabilities from Black and Ethnic Minority Communities*. London: Kings Fund Centre/CRE.

Beane, J.A. (1991) Sorting out the self-esteem controversy. *Educational Leadership*, 49(1): 25–30.

Bear, G.G. (1998) School discipline in the United States: prevention, correction and long term social development. *Educational and Child Psychology*, 15(1): 15–39.

Beaver, R. (1996) *Educational Psychology Casework: A Practical Guide*. London: Jessica Kingsley.

Beck, S. and Forehand, R. (1984) Social skills training for children: a methodological and clinical review of behaviour modification studies. *Behavioural Psychotherapy*, 12: 17–45.

Beech, J.R. and Keys, A. (1997) Reading, vocabulary and language preference in 7–8 year old bilingual Asian children. *British Journal of Educational Psychology*, 67: 405–14.

Bellak, L. and Bellak, S. (1949) *The Children's Apperception Test*. New York: CPS Co.

Bell-Dolan, D.J., Foster, S.L. and Sikora, D.M. (1989) Effects of sociometric testing on children's behaviour and loneliness in school. *Developmental Psychology*, 25: 306–11.

Bennett, J., Gash, H. and O'Reilly, M. (1998) Ireland: Integration as appropriate, segregation where necessary, in T. Booth and M. Ainscow (eds) *From Them To Us*. London: Routledge.

Bennett, N. (1991) The quality of classroom learning experiences for children with special educational needs, in M. Ainscow (ed.) *Effective Schools for All*. London: David Fulton.

Bennett, N. and Cass, A. (1989) *From Special to Ordinary Schools: Case Studies in Integration*. London: Cassell.

Bennett, N., Desforges, M., Cockburn, A. and Wilkinson, B. (1984) *The Quality of Pupil Learning Experiences*. London: Lawrence Erlbaum Associates.

Beresford, B. (1995) *Expert Opinions: A National Survey of Parents Caring for a Severely Disabled Child*. Bristol: The Policy Press.

Berger, A., Henderson, J. and Morris, D. (1999) *Implementing the Literacy Hour for Pupils with Learning Difficulties*. London: David Fulton.

Berk, R.A. (1984) Conducting the item analysis, in R.A. Berk (ed.) *A Guide to Criterion-Referenced Test Construction*. Baltimore, MD: Johns Hopkins University Press.

Berliner, D.C. (1987) Knowledge is power: a talk to teachers about a revolution in the teaching profession, in D.C. Berliner and B.V. Rosenshine (eds) *Talks to Teachers*. New York: Random House.

Bernstein, B. (1971) *Class, Codes and Control*. London: Routledge & Kegan Paul.

Bettle, S., Frederickson, N. and Sharp, S. (2001) Supporting schools in special measures: the contribution of educational psychology. *Educational Psychology in Practice*, 17(1): 53–68.

Beveridge, M. and Conti-Ramsden, G. (1987) *Children with Language Disabilities*. Milton Keynes: Open University Press.

Bierman, K. and Furman, W. (1984) The effects of social skills training and peer involvement on the social adjustment of pre-adolescents. *Child Development*, 55: 151–62.

Biggar, S. and Barr, J. (1996) The emotional world of specific learning difficulties, in G. Reid (ed.) *Dimensions of Dyslexia*, vol. 2. Edinburgh: Moray House.

Binder, C. (1993) Behavioural fluency: a new paradigm. *Educational Technology*, October, 8–14.

Bishop, D.V.M. (1989) *Test for Reception of Grammar*. Manchester: University of Manchester Age and Cognitive Performance Research Centre.

Bishop, D.V.M. (1997) *Uncommon Understanding: Development and Disorders of Language Comprehension in Children*. Hove: Psychology Press.

Bishop, D.V.M. (1998) Development of the Children's Communication Checklist (CCC): a method for assessing qualitative aspects of communicative impairment in children. *Journal of Child Psychology and Psychiatry*, 39(6): 879–92.

Bishop, D.V.M. and Butterworth, G.E. (1980) Verbal-performance discrepancies: relationship to birth risk and specific reading retardation. *Cortex*, 16: 375–90.

Black, P. and Wiliam, D. (1998) Assessment and classroom learning. *Assessment in Education*, 5(1): 7–74.

Blackledge, A. (ed.) (1994) *Teaching Bilingual Children*. Stoke-on-Trent: Trentham Books.

Blair, M. and Bourne, J. (1998) *Making the Difference: Teaching and Learning Strategies in Successful Multi-Ethnic Schools*. London: HMSO.

Blatchford, P. and Cline, T. (1992) Baseline assessment for school entrants. *Research Papers in Education*, 7(3): 247–69.

Blyth, E. and Milner, J. (1993) Exclusion from school: a first step in exclusion from society. *Children and Society*, 7(3): 255–68.

Board of Education (1943) *Curriculum and Examinations in Secondary Schools* (Norwood Report). London: HMSO.

Boder, E. (1973) Developmental dyslexia: a diagnostic approach based on three atypical reading patterns. *Developmental Medicine and Child Neurology*, 75: 663–87.

Booth, S.R. and Jay, M. (1981) The use of precision teaching technology in the work of the educational psychologist. *Journal of the Association of Educational Psychologists*, 5(5): 21–6.

Booth, S.R. and Jewell, T. (1983) Programmes for slow learners. *Journal of the Association of Educational Psychologists*, 6(2): 58–62.

Booth, T. (1986) Is integrating the handicapped psychologically defensible? Letter to the editor, *Bulletin of the British Psychological Society*, 39: 141.

Booth, T. (1993) Raising standards: sticking to first principles, in A. Dyson and C. Gains (eds) *Rethinking Special Needs in Mainstream Schools: Towards the Year 2000*. London: David Fulton.

Booth, T. and Ainscow, M. (eds) (1998) *From Them To Us: An International Study of Inclusion in Education*. London: Routledge.

Booth, T., Ainscow, M., Black-Hawkins, K., Vaughn, M. and Shaw, L. (2000) *Index for Inclusion: Developing Learning and Participation in Schools*. Bristol: CSIE.

Borkowski, J.G., Weyhing, R.S. and Carr, M. (1988) Effects of attributional retraining on strategy-based reading comprehension in learning-disabled students. *Journal of Educational Psychology*, 80: 46–53.

Bos, C.S. and Fletcher, T.V. (1997) Sociocultural considerations in learning disabilities inclusion research: knowledge gaps and future directions. *Learning Disabilities Research and Practice*, 12(2): 92–9.

Botting, N., Crutchley, A. and Conti-Ramsden, G. (1998) Educational transitions of seven-year-old children with specific language impairment in language units: a longitudinal study. *International Journal of Language and Communication Disorders*, 33(2): 177–219.

Boulton, M.J. and Smith, P.K. (1992) Ethnic preferences and perceptions among Asian and White British middle school children. *Social Development*, 1: 55–66.

Bourne, J. (1989) *Moving into the Mainstream: LEA Provision for Bilingual Pupils*. Windsor: NFER-Nelson.

Bourne, J. (1997) The continuing revolution: teaching as learning in the mainstream multilingual classroom, in C. Leung and C. Cable (eds) *English as an Additional Language: Changing Perspectives*. Watford: National Association for Language Development in the Curriculum.

Bourne, J., Bridges, L. and Searle, C. (1995) *Outcast England: How Schools Exclude Black Children*. London: Institute of Race Relations.

Bovair, K. and McLaughlin, C. (1994) *Counselling in Schools: A Reader*. London: David Fulton.

Bower, E.M. (1960) *Early Identification of Emotionally Handicapped Children in School*. Springfield, IL: Charles C. Thomas.

Boxall, M. (1996) The nurture group in the primary school, in M. Bennathan and M. Boxall (eds) *Effective Intervention in Primary Schools: Nurture Groups*, pp. 18–38. London: David Fulton.

Bradley, M. (1982) *The Co-ordination of Services for Children Under Five*. Windsor: NFER-Nelson.

Breen, M. and Littlejohn, A. (2000) *Classroom Decision-Making: Negotiation and Process Syllabuses in Practice*. Cambridge: Cambridge University Press.

Brennan, W.K. (1982) *Changing Special Education*. Milton Keynes: Open University Press.

British Psychological Society (BPS) (1996) *Attention Deficit Hyperactivity Disorder (ADHD): A Psychological Response to an Evolving Concept* (Report of a working party of the British Psychological Society). Leicester: British Psychological Society.

British Psychological Society (BPS) (1999) *Dyslexia, Literacy and Psychological Assessment*. Leicester: British Psychological Society.

Broadfoot, P., Dockrell, B., Gipps, C., Harlen, W. and Nuttall, D. (eds) (1993) *Policy Issues in National Assessment*. Clevedon: Multilingual Matters.

Brodie, I. (2000) Children's homes and school exclusion: redefining the problem. *Support for Learning*, 15(1): 25–9.

Brodie, I. and Berridge, D. (1996) *School Exclusion: Research Themes and Issues*. Luton: University of Luton Press.

Bronfenbrenner, U. (1979) *The Ecology of Human Development*. Cambridge, MA: Harvard University Press.

Brooks, P. and Weeks, S. (1999) *Individual Styles in Learning to Spell: Improving Spelling in Children with Literacy Difficulties and all Children in Mainstream Schools*. London: DfEE Publications.

Brophy, J. (ed.) (1998) *Advances in Research on Teaching*, vol. 7: *Expectations in the Classroom*. London: JAI Press.

Brophy, J.E. and Good, T.L. (1974) *Teacher-Student Relationships: Causes and Consequences*. New York: Holt, Rinehart & Winston.

Brown, A. and Campione, J. (1996) Communities of learning and thinking, or a context by any other name, in P. Woods (ed.) *Contemporary Issues in Teaching and Learning*. London: Routledge.

Brown, A.L., Campione, J.C., Webber, L.S. and Winnikur, D.W. (1992) Interactive learning environments: a new look at assessment and instruction, in B.R. Gifford and M.C. O'Connor (eds) *Changing Assessments: Alternative Views of Aptitude, Achievement and Instruction*. New York: Kluwer Academic Publishers.

Brown, E. (1996) *Religious Education for All*. London: David Fulton.

Brown, M. (1999) Swings of the pendulum, in I. Thompson (ed.) *Issues in Teaching Numeracy in Primary Schools*. Buckingham: Open University Press.

Brown, R., Hobson, R.P., Lee, A. and Stevenson, J. (1997) Are there 'autistic-like' features in congenitally blind children? *Journal of Child Psychology and Psychiatry*, 38: 693–703.

Bruininks, R.H., Rynders, J.E. and Gross, G.C. (1974) Social acceptance of mildly retarded pupils in resource rooms and regular classes. *American Journal of Mental Deficiency*, 78(4): 377–83.

Budoff, M. (1987) The validity of learning potential assessments, in C.S. Lidz (ed.) *Dynamic Assessment: An Interactional Approach to Evaluating Learning Potential*. New York: The Guilford Press.

Burden, R. (1978) School systems analysis: a project centred approach, in B. Gillham (ed.) *Reconstructing Educational Psychology*. Beckenham: Croom Helm.

Burden, R. (1981) Systems theory and its relevance to schools, in B. Gillham (ed.) *Problem Behaviour in the Secondary School*. London: Croom Helm.

Burden, R. (1999) Children's self perceptions, in N. Frederickson and R.J. Cameron (eds) *Psychology in Education Portfolio*. Windsor: NFER-Nelson.

Burden, R.L. and Fraser, B.J. (1993) Use of classroom environment assessments in school psychology: a British perspective. *Psychology in the Schools*, 30: 232–40.

Burnett, P.C. (1994) Self-concept and self-esteem in elementary school children. *Psychology in the Schools*, 11: 164–71.

Burns, R. and Kaufman, S. (1970) *Kinetic Family Drawings (K-F-D): An Introduction to Understanding Children through Kinetic Drawings*. New York: Brunner/Mazel.

Burt, C. (1917) *The Distribution and Relations of Educational Abilities*. London: King & Son.

Burt, C. (1937) *The Subnormal Mind*, 2nd edn. London: Oxford University Press.

Burt, C. (1957) *The Causes and Treatment of Backwardness*, 4th edn. London: University of London Press.

Burton, L. (1994) *Children Learning Mathematics: Patterns and Relationships*. Hemel Hempstead: Simon & Schuster Education.

Burwell, J., D'Sena, P. and Barrett, F. (1998) Accessing GCSE maths for 'bilingual' pupils, in P. D'Sena and F. Barrett (eds) *Raising Educational Achievement for All, LMU Education Papers No. 3*. Leeds: Leeds Metropolitan University.

Buxton, L. (1981) *Do You Panic About Maths?* London: Heinemann.

Byers, R. (1999a) Experience and achievement: initiatives in curriculum development for pupils with severe and profound and multiple learning difficulties. *British Journal of Special Education*, 26(4): 184–8.

Byers, R. (1999b) The National Literacy Strategy and pupils with special educational needs. *British Journal of Special Education*, 26(1): 8–11.

Cade, A. (1989) Listening to children – the young opinion formers on Earth. *Annual Review of Environmental Education*, 3: 10–11.

Caesar, G., Parchment, M. and Berridge, D. (1994) *Black Perspectives on Services for Children in Need*. London: Barnardo's/National Children's Bureau.

Caldarella, P. and Merrell, K.W. (1997) Common dimensions of social skills of children and adolescents: a taxonomy of positive behaviours. *School Psychology Review*, 26(2): 264–78.

Cameron, L. and Bygate, M. (1997) Key issues in assessing progression in English as an additional language, in C. Leung and C. Cable (eds) *English as an Additional Language: Changing Perspectives*. Watford: NALDIC.

Cameron, R.J. (1988) Enhancing the learning environment: psychology and curriculum management, in N. Jones and J. Sawyer (eds) *Management and the Psychology of Schooling*. London: Falmer Press.

Cameron, R.J. and Reynolds, A.R. (1999) Learning style and metacognition, in N.L. Frederickson and R.J. Cameron (eds) *Psychology in Education Portfolio*. Windsor: NFER-Nelson.

Cameron, R.J., Owen, A.J. and Tee, G. (1986) Curriculum management (Part 3): Assessment and evaluation. *Educational Psychology in Practice*, 2(3): 3–9.

Campione, J.C. (1989) Assisted assessment: a taxonomy of approaches and an outline of strengths and weaknesses. *Journal of Learning Disabilities*, 22(3): 151–65.

Cannella, G. and Reiff, J. (1989) Mandating early childhood entrance/retention assessment. *Child Study Journal*, 19: 83–9.

Canter, L. and Canter, M. (1992) *Assertive Discipline*. Santa Monica, CA: Lee Canter Associates.

Carlberg, C. and Kavale, K. (1980) The efficacy of special versus regular class placements for exceptional children: a meta-analysis. *Journal of Special Education*, 14: 295–309.

Carrasquillo, A.L. and Rodriguez, V. (1996) *Language Minority Students in the Mainstream Classroom*. Clevedon: Multilingual Matters.

Cartledge, G. and Milburn, J.F. (1996) *Cultural Diversity and Social Skills Instruction: Understanding Ethnic and Gender Differences*. Champaign, IL: Research Press.

Castle, R.L. (1976) *Case Conferences: A Cause for Concern?* London: NSPCC National Advisory Centre for the Battered Child.

Castles, F. and Parsons, C. (1997) Disruptive behaviour and exclusions from schools: redefining and responding to the problem. *Emotional and Behavioural Difficulties*, 2(3): 4–11.

Causey, V.E., Thomas, C.D. and Armento, B.J. (2000) Cultural diversity is basically a foreign term to me: the challenges of diversity for preservice teacher education. *Teaching and Teacher Education*, 16: 33–45.

Ceci, S.J. (1996) *On Intelligence*. Cambridge, MA: Cambridge University Press.

Centra, J.A. and Potter, D.A. (1980) School and teacher effects: an interrelational model. *Review of Educational Research*, 50: 273–91.

Central Advisory Council for Education (England) (1967) *Children and their Primary Schools* (the Plowden Report). London: HMSO.

Chall, J.S. (1983) *Learning to Read: The Great Debate*. New York: McGraw-Hill.

Chamba, R., Ahmad, W.I.U., Darr, A. and Jones, L. (1998) The education of Asian deaf children, in S. Gregory *et al.* (eds) *Issues in Deaf Education*. London: David Fulton.

Chapman, E.K. and Stone, J.M. (1988) *The Visually Handicapped Child in Your Classroom*. London: Cassell.

Chapman, J.W. and Tumner, W.E. (1995) Development of young children's reading self-concepts: an examination of emerging sub-components and their relationship with reading achievement. *Journal of Educational Psychology*, 87(1): 154–67.

Charles, R., Lester, F. and O'Daffer, P. (1987) *How to Evaluate Progress in Problem Solving*. Reston, VA: National Council for Teachers of Mathematics.

Chau, K.L. (1989) Sociocultural dissonance among ethnic minority populations. *Social Casework: The Journal of Contemporary Social Work*, 224–30.

Chaudhury, A. (1986) *ACE Special Education Advice Service for the Bangladeshi Community Annual Report 1986*. London: Advisory Centre for Education.

Chazan, M. (1964) The incidence and nature of maladjustment among children in schools for the educationally subnormal. *British Journal of Educational Psychology*, 35: 292–304.

Chazan, M. (1974) Children with learning difficulties, in M. Chazan, T. Moore, P. Williams and J. Wright (eds) *The Practice of Educational Psychology*. London: Longman.

Checkland, P.B. (1981) *Systems Thinking, Systems Practice*. Chichester: Wiley.

Checkland, P.B. (1986) A basic introduction to systems thinking, unpublished paper. University of Lancaster.

Checkland, P.B. and Scholes, J. (1990) *Soft Systems Methodology in Action*. Chichester: Wiley.

Chen, X., Rubin, K.H. and Sun, Y. (1992) Social reputation and peer relationships in Chinese and Canadian children: a cross cultural study. *Child Development*, 63: 1336–43.

Child, D. (1991) A survey of communication approaches used in schools for the deaf in the U.K. *Journal of the British Association of Teachers of the Deaf*, 15(1): 20–4.

Chinn, S.J. (1985) Learning difficulties in mathematics. *Learn*, 17: 26–35.

Chinn, S.J. and Ashcroft, J.R. (1998) *Mathematics for Dyslexics: A Teaching Handbook*. London: Whurr Publishing.

Chrispeels, J. (1996) Effective schools and home-school-community partnership roles: a framework for parent involvement. *School Effectiveness and School Improvement*, 7(4): 297–323.

Christenson, S.L. and Ysseldyke, J.E. (1989) Assessing student performance: an important change is needed. *Journal of School Psychology*, 27(4): 409–25.

Clark, C., Dyson, A. Millward, A. and Robson, S. (1999) Theories of inclusion, theories of schools: deconstructing and reconstructing the inclusive school. *British Educational Research Journal*, 25(2): 157–77.

Clarke, A.M. and Clarke, A.D.B. (1976) *Early Experience: Myth and Evidence*. Shepton Mallett: Open Books.

Clay, M. (1998) *By Different Paths to Common Outcomes*. York, ME: Stenhouse Publishers.

Clay, M.M. (1987) Learning to be learning disabled. *New Zealand Journal of Educational Studies*, 22: 155–73.

Clements, M.A. (1980) Analyzing children's errors in written mathematical tasks. *Educational Studies in Mathematics*, 11(1): 1–21.

Cline, T. (1989) Making case conferences more effective: a checklist for monitoring and training. *Children and Society*, 3(2): 99–106.

Cline, T. (1991) Professional constructions of the concept of moderate learning difficulties, in P.L.C. Evans and A.D.B. Clarke (eds) *Combatting Mental Handicap: A Multidisciplinary Approach*. Bicester: A.B. Academic.

Cline, T. (1992) Assessment of special educational needs: meeting reasonable expectations? in T. Cline (ed.) *The Assessment of Special Educational Needs: International Perspectives*. London: Routledge.

Cline, T. (1993) Educational assessment of bilingual pupils: getting the context right. *Educational and Child Psychology*, 10(4): 59–68.

Cline, T. (1995) The Code of Practice on Special Educational Needs: a short guide for those working with bilingual pupils. *NALDIC Occasional Paper*, 4: 17.

Cline, T. (1997a) Educating for bilingualism in different contexts: teaching the deaf and teaching children with English as an additional language. *Educational Review*, 49(2): 145–52.

Cline, T. (1997b) Special educational needs and language proficiency, in C. Leung and C. Cable (eds) *English as an Additional Language: Changing Perspectives*, pp. 53–64. Watford: National Association for Language Development in the Curriculum.

Cline, T. (1998) The assessment of special educational needs for bilingual children. *British Journal of Special Education*, 25(4): 159–63.

Cline, T. and Baldwin, S. (1994) *Selective Mutism in Childhood*. London: Whurr.

Cline, T. and Cozens, B. (1999) The analysis of aspects of classroom texts that challenge children when learning to read in their second language: a pilot study, in H. South (ed.) *Literacies in Community and School* (NALDIC occasional publications series). Watford: National Association for Language Development in the Curriculum.

Cline, T. and Frederickson, N. (eds) (1991) *Bilingual Pupils and the National Curriculum: Overcoming Difficulties in Teaching and Learning*. London: University College London, Department of Psychology.

Cline, T. and Frederickson, N. (eds) (1996) *Progress in Curriculum Related Assessment for Bilingual Pupils*. Bristol: Multilingual Matters.

Cline, T. and Frederickson, N. (1999) Identification and assessment of dyslexia in bi/multilingual children. *International Journal of Bilingual Education and Bilingualism*, 2(2): 81–93.

Cline, T. and Reason, R. (1993) Specific learning difficulties (dyslexia): equal opportunities issues. *British Journal of Special Education*, 20(1): 30–4.

Cline, T. and Shamsi, T. (2000) *Language Needs or Special Needs? The Assessment of Learning Difficulties in Literacy Among Children Learning English as an Additional Language: A Literature Review* (research report RR184). London: DfEE.

Cline, T., Frederickson, N. and Wright, A. (1990) *Effective Inservice Training: A Resource Pack for LEA INSET Providers*. London: Educational Psychology Publishing.

Coard, B. (1971) *How the West Indian Child is made Educationally Subnormal in the British School System*. London: New Beacon Books Ltd.

Cohen, O.P., Fischgrund, M.A. and Redding, R. (1990) Deaf children from ethnic, linguistic and racial minority backgrounds: an overview. *American Annals of the Deaf*, 135: 67–73.

Cohen, P. (1998) *Forbidden Games: Race, Gender and Class Conflicts in Playground Culture*. London: University of East London Centre for New Ethnicities Research.

Cohn, T. (1987) Sticks and stones may break my bones but names will never hurt me. *Multicultural Teaching*, 5(3): 8–11.

Coie, J.D. and Benenson, J.F. (1983) 'A qualitative analysis of the relationship between peer rejection and physically aggressive behaviour', unpublished manuscript. Duke University, Durham NC.

Coie, J.D., Dodge, K.A. and Coppotelli, H. (1982) Dimensions and types of social status: a cross-age perspective. *Developmental Psychology*, 18(4): 557–70.

Cole, N. and Moss, P. (1989) Bias in test use, in R. Linn (ed.) *Educational Measurement*, 3rd edn. New York: AERA/NCME, Macmillan.

Cole, N.S. (1973) Bias in selection. *Journal of Educational Measurement*, 10: 237–55.

Cole, T., Visser, J. and Upton, G. (1998) *Effective Schooling for Pupils with Emotional and Behavioural Difficulties*. London: David Fulton.

Condry, J. and Condry S. (1976) Sex differences: a study of the eye of the beholder. *Child Development*, 47: 812–19.

Condry, J. and Ross, D.F. (1985) Sex and aggression: the influence of gender label on the perception of aggression in children. *Child Development*, 56: 225–33.

Connolly, J.A. (1983) A review of sociometric procedures in the assessment of social competencies in children. *Applied Research in Mental Retardation*, 4: 315–27.

Conrad, R. (1979) *The Deaf School Child*. London: Harper & Row.

Cooper, D.H. and Valli, L. (1996) Designing classrooms for inclusion: beyond management, in D.L. Speece and B.K. Keogh (eds) *Research on Classroom Ecologies: Implications for Inclusion of Children with Learning Disabilities*. Hillsdale, NJ: Lawrence Erlbaum Associates.

Cooper, P. (1997) The myth of attention deficit/hyperactivity disorder. *British Psychological Society Education Section Review*, 21(1): 3–14.

Cooper, P., Smith, C.J. and Upton, G. (1994) *Emotional and Behavioural Difficulties: Theory to Practice*. London: Routledge.

Corbett, J. (1995) *Bad-Mouthing: The Language of Special Needs*. London: Falmer Press.

Corbett, J. (1998) *Special Educational Needs in the Twentieth Century: A Cultural Analysis*. London: Cassell.

Coupe, J. (1986) The Curriculum Intervention Model (CIM), in J. Coupe and J. Porter (eds) *The Education of Children with Severe Learning Difficulties: Bridging the Gap Between Theory and Practice*. London: Croom Helm.

Coupe, J. and Porter, J. (eds) (1986) *The Education of Children with Severe Learning Difficulties: Bridging the Gap Between Theory and Practice*. London: Croom Helm.

Covington, M.V. (1989) Self-esteem and failure in school: analysis and policy implications, in A. Mecca, N.J. Smelser and J. Vasconcellos (eds) *The Social Importance of Self-Esteem*. Berkeley, CA: University of California Press.

Cowen, E.L., Pederson, A., Babigian, H., Izzo, L.D. and Trost, M.A. (1973) Long-term follow up of early detected vulnerable children. *Journal of Consulting and Clinical Psychology*, 41: 438–46.

Cowie, H. and Pecherek, A. (1994) *Counselling Approaches and Issues in Education*. London: David Fulton.

Cowie, H., Smith, P., Boulton, M. and Laver, R. (1994) *Cooperation in the Multi-ethnic Classroom*. London: David Fulton.

Cox, T. and Jones, G. (1983) *Disadvantaged Eleven Year Olds*. Oxford: Pergamon Press.

CRE (Commission for Racial Equality) (1986) *Teaching English as a Second Language: Report of a Formal Investigation in Calderdale Local Education Authority*. London: Commission for Racial Equality.

Crick, N.R. and Dodge, K.A. (1994) A review and reformulation of social information-processing mechanisms in children's social adjustment. *Psychological Bulletin*, 115(1): 74–101.

Cripps, M. (1996) Sign Language and me, in *Sign Writing: Writing by a Group of Deaf People in Manchester*. Manchester: Ducie Adult Education Centre (Lloyd Street North, Moss Side, Manchester M14 4GA).

Critchley, M. and Critchley, E.A. (1978) *Dyslexia Defined*. London: Heinemann Medical.

Croll, P. and Moses, D. (1985) *One in Five: The Assessment and Incidence of Special Educational Needs*. London: Routledge & Kegan Paul.

Cross, L. and Walker-Knight, D. (1997) Inclusion: developing collaborative and co-operative school communities. *The Educational Forum*, 61: 269–77.

Crowther, D., Dyson, A. and Millward, A. (1998) *Costs and Outcomes for Pupils with Moderate Learning Difficulties in Special and Mainstream Schools* (research report RR89). London: DfEE.

Crozier, W.R. (1995) Shyness and self-esteem in middle childhood. *British Journal of Educational Psychology*, 20: 220–2.

Crutchley, A., Botting, N. and Conti-Ramsden, G. (1997a) Bilingualism and specific language impairment in children attending language units. *European Journal of Disorders of Communication*, 32: 267–76.

Crutchley, A., Conti-Ramsden, G. and Botting, N. (1997b) Bilingual children with specific language impairment and standardised assessments: preliminary findings from a study of children in language units. *International Journal of Bilingualism*, 1(2): 117–34.

Crystal, D. and Varley, R. (1998) *Introduction to Language Pathology*, 4th edn. London: Whurr.

Crystal, D., Fletcher, P. and Garman, M. (1989) *Language Assessment, Remediation and Screening Procedure (LARSP)*, 2nd edn. London: Cole & Whurr.

Cullingford, C. (1985) Teachers, parents and the control of schools, in C. Cullingford (ed.) *Parents, Teachers and Schools*. London: Robert Royce.

Cummins, J. (1984) *Bilingualism and Special Education: Issues in Assessment and Pedagogy*. Clevedon: Multilingual Matters.

Cummins, J. (1986) Empowering minority students: a framework for intervention. *Harvard Educational Review*, 56(1): 18–36.

Cummins, J. (1989) A theoretical framework for bilingual special education. *Exceptional Children*, 56(2): 111–19.

Cummins, J. (1996) *Negotiating Identities: Education for Empowerment in a Diverse Society* (California Association for Bilingual Education). Stoke-on-Trent: Trentham Books.

Cummins, J. and McNeely, S.N. (1987) Language development, academic learning, and empowering minority students, in S.H. Fradd and W.J. Tikunoff (eds) *Bilingual Education and Bilingual Special Education*. Boston, MA: College-Hill.

Cunningham, C. and Davis, H. (1985) *Working with Parents: Frameworks for Collaboration*. Milton Keynes: Open University Press.

Cunningham, C.C. and Sloper, P. (1984) The relationship between maternal ratings of first word vocabulary and Reynell Language scores. *British Journal of Educational Psychology*, 54(2): 160–7.

Cunningham, C.E., Cataldo, M.F., Mallion, C. and Keyes, J.B. (1983) Evaluation of behavioral approaches to the management of elective mutism. *Child and Family Behavior Therapy*, 5(4): 25–49.

Curnyn, J.C., Wallace, I., Kistan, S. and McLaren, M. (1991) Special educational need and ethnic minority pupils, in Scottish Education Department/Regional Psychological Services (eds) *Professional Development Initiatives 1989–1990*. Edinburgh: Scottish Education Department.

Curtis, S. (1992) Peer tutoring, 'entitlement', 'access' and 'equal opportunities'. *Multicultural Teaching*, 10(2): 15–18.

DaFontura, H.A. and Siegel, L.S. (1995) Reading, syntactic and working memory skills of bilingual Portuguese-English Canadian children. *Reading and Writing*, 7(1): 13–153.

DAHISS (1995) *Service Policy Document*. Leeds: Deaf and Hearing Impaired Service.

Dalton, P. (1996) When words fail: a personal construct approach to children's construing. *Educational and Child Psychology*, 13(4): 21–8.

Daniels, A. (1990) Social skills training for primary aged children. *Educational Psychology in Practice*, 6(3): 159–62.

Daniels, A. and Williams, H. (2000) Reducing the need for exclusions and statements for behaviour: The framework for intervention (Part 1). *Educational Psychology in Practice*, 15(4): 220–7.

Daniels, H. (1992) Dynamic assessment: pitfalls and prospects, in T. Cline (ed.) *Assessment of Special Educational Needs: International Perspectives*. London: Routledge.

Daniels, H., Hey, V., Leonard, D. and Smith, M. (1999a) Issues of equity in special needs education from a gender perspective. *British Journal of Special Education*, 26(4): 189–95.

Daniels, H., Visser, J., Cole, T. and de Reybekill, N. (1999b) *Emotional and Behavioural Difficulties in Mainstream Schools* (research report 90). London: HMSO.

Davidson, N. (1994) Cooperative and collaborative learning: an integrative perspective, in J.S. Thousand, R.A. Villa and A.I. Nevin (eds) *Creativity and Collaborative Learning: A Practical Guide for Empowering Students and Teachers*. Baltimore, MD: PH Brookes.

Davie, R. (1986) Understanding behaviour problems. *Maladjustment and Therapeutic Education*, 4(1): 2–11.

Davie, R. (1996) Raising the achievements of pupils with special educational needs. *Support for Learning: British Journal of Learning Support*, 11(2): 51–6.

Davie, R. and Galloway, D. (eds) (1996) *Listening to Children in Education*. London: David Fulton.

Davies, J. and Brember, I. (1995) Stories in the kitchen: reading attitudes and habits of Year 2, 4 and 6 children. *Educational Research*, 37(3): 305–13.

Davis, A. (1991) The language of testing, in K. Durkin and B. Shire (ed.) *Language in Mathematical Education: Research and Practice*. Buckingham: Open University Press.

Davis, A., Wood, S., Healy, R., Webb, H. and Rowe, S. (1995) Risk factors for hearing disorders: epidemiological evidence of change over time in the UK. *Journal of the American Academy of Audiology*, 6: 365–70.

Davis, A.C. (1983) A public health perspective on childhood hearing impairment, in B. McCormick (ed.) *Paediatric Audiology 0–5*, 2nd edn. London: Whurr.

Dawe, L. (1983) Bilingualism and mathematical reasoning in English as a second language. *Educational Studies in Mathematics*, 14: 325–53.

De Abreu, G., Cline, T. and Shamsi, A. (in preparation) Parents' representations of their children's mathematics learning in multiethnic primary schools.

De Gelder, B. and Vroomen, J. (1991) Phonological deficits: beneath the surface of reading acquisition. *Psychological Research*, 53: 88–97.

DeBlassie, R.R. and Franco, J.N. (1983) Psychological and educational assessment of bilingual children, in D.R. Omark and J.G. Erickson (eds) *The Bilingual Exceptional Child*. San Diego, CA: College-Hill Press.

Deforges, M. (1997) Ethnic minority communities and values and special education, in G. Lindsay and D. Thompson (eds) *Values into Practice in Special Education*. London: David Fulton.

Deforges, M. and Kerr, T. (1984) Developing bilingual children's English in school. *Educational and Child Psychology*, 1(1): 68–80.

Dehaney, R. (2000) Literacy hour and the literal thinker: the inclusion of children with semantic-pragmatic language difficulties in the literacy hour. *Support for Learning*, 15(1): 36–40.

Den Boer, K. (1990) Country Briefing: Special Education in the Netherlands. *European Journal of Special Needs Education*, 5(2): 136–50.

Deno, S.L. (1985) Curriculum based measurement: the emerging alternative. *Exceptional Children*, 52(3): 219–32.

Deno, S.L. (1989) Curriculum-based measurement and special education services: a fundamental and direct relationship, in M.R. Shinn (ed.) *Curriculum-based Measurement: Assessing Special Children*. New York: Guilford Press.

Deno, S.L. and Fuchs, L.S. (1987) Developing curriculum based measurement systems for data-based special education problem solving. *Focus on Exceptional Children*, 19(8): 1–16.

Department for Education (DfE) (1992) *Education (Schools) Act*. London: HMSO.

Department for Education (DfE) (1993) *Schools Requiring Special Measures* (Circular 17/93). London: HMSO.

Department for Education (DfE) (1994a) *Code of Practice on the Identification and Assessment of Special Educational Needs*. London: HMSO.

Department for Education (DfE) (1994b) *Pupil Behaviour and Discipline* (Circular 8/94). London: HMSO.

Department for Education (DfE) (1994c) *The Education of Children with Emotional and Behavioural Difficulties* (Circular 9/94). London: HMSO.

Department for Education (DfE) (1994d) *The Education of Children Being Looked After by Local Authorities* (Circular 13/94). London: HMSO.

Department for Education (DfE) (1995) *Key Stages 1 and 2 of the National Curriculum*. London: HMSO.

Department for Education and Employment (DfEE) (1996) *Education Act*. London: DfEE Publications.

Department for Education and Employment (DfEE) (1997) *Excellence for All Children: Meeting Special Educational Needs*. London: DfEE Publications.

Department for Education and Employment (DfEE) (1998a) *Numeracy Matters: The Preliminary Report of the Numeracy Task Force*. London: DfEE Publications.

Department for Education and Employment (DfEE) (1998b) *The Implementation of the National Numeracy Strategy: The Final Report of the Numeracy Task Force*. London: DfEE Publications.

Department for Education and Employment (DfEE) (1998c) *The National Literacy Strategy. Framework for Teaching*. London: DfEE Publications.

Department for Education and Employment (DfEE) (1998d) *School Standards and Frameworks Act*. London: DfEE Publications.

Department for Education and Employment (DfEE) (1999a) *Ethnic Minority Pupils and Pupils for whom English is an Additional Language: England 1996/97*. (Statistical Bulletin No. 3/99). London: DfEE Publications.

Department for Education and Employment (DfEE) (1999b) *Social Inclusion: Pupil Support* (Circular 10/99). London: DfEE Publications.

Department for Education and Employment (DfEE) (1999c) *The National Numeracy Strategy: Mathematical Vocabulary*. London: DfEE Publications.

Department for Education and Employment (DfEE) (1999d) *What the Disability Discrimination Act Means for Schools and LEAs* (Circular 20/99). London: DfEE Publications.

Department for Education and Employment (DfEE) (2000a) *SEN and Disability Rights in Education Bill. Consultation Documentation*. London: DfEE Publications.

Department for Education and Employment (DfEE) (2000b) *Educational Psychology Services (England): Current Role, Good Practice and Future Directions – The Research Report*. London: DfEE Publications.

Department for Education and Employment (DfEE) (2000c) *SEN Code of Practice on the Identification and Assessment of Pupils with Special Educational Needs and SEN Thresholds: Good Practice Guidelines on Identification and Provision for Pupils with Special Educational Needs*. London: DfEE Publications.

Department for Education and Employment (DfEE) (2001) *Special Educational Needs and Disability Act*. London: The Stationery Office.

Department for Education and Employment/Department of Health (DfEE/DH) (2000) *Guidance on the Education of Children in Public Care*. London: DfEE/DH.

Department for Education and Employment/Qualifications and Curriculum Authority (DfEE/QCA) (1999a) *The National Curriculum Handbook for Primary Teachers in England*. London: DfEE/QCA.

Department for Education and Employment/Qualifications and Curriculum Authority (DfEE/QCA) (1999b) *The National Curriculum Handbook for Secondary Teachers in England*. London: DfEE/QCA.

Department for Education and Skills (DfES) (2001) *Special Education Needs Code of Practice*. London: DfES.

Department of Education (1981) *Education Statistics of New Zealand*. Wellington: Department of Education.

Department of Education and Science (DES) (1964) *Slow Learners at School* (Education Pamphlet No. 46). London: HMSO.

Department of Education and Science (DES) (1978) *Special Educational Need* (Report of the Warnock Committee). London: HMSO.

Department of Education and Science (DES) (1981) *Education Act*. London: HMSO.

Department of Education and Science (DES) (1982) *Mathematics Counts* (Report of the Cockcroft Committee of Enquiry into the Teaching of Mathematics). London: HMSO.

Department of Education and Science (DES) (1983) *Assessments and Statements of Special Educational Need* (Circular 1/83). London: DES.

Department of Education and Science (DES) (1985) *Education for All: Report of the Swann Committee*. London: HMSO.

Department of Education and Science (DES) (1988) *Mathematics for Ages 5–16: Proposals for the National Curriculum*. London: HMSO.

Department of Education and Science (DES) (1989a) *Assessments and Statements of Special Educational Needs: Procedures within the Education, Health and Social Services* (Circular 22/89). London: HMSO.

Department of Education and Science (DES) (1989b) *The Education Reform Act 1988: The School Curriculum and Assessment* (Circular 5/89). London: DES.

Department of Health (DoH) (1989) *The Children Act*. London: HMSO.

Department of the Environment (1988) *Local Government Act*. London: HMSO.

Department of Trade and Industry (1995) *Disability Discrimination Act*. London: HMSO.

Deponio, P., Landon, J., Mullin, K. and Reid, G. (1999). An audit of the processes involved in identifying and assessing bilingual learners suspected of being dyslexic: a Scottish study. Paper presented at the Multilingualism and Dyslexia: BDA International Conference, Manchester, 17–19 June.

Desforges, M. (1995) Assessment of special educational needs in bilingual pupils: changing practice? *Schools Psychology International*, 16: 5–17.

Desforges, M., Mayet, V. and Vickers, M. (1995) Psychological assessment of bilingual pupils. *Educational Psychology in Practice*, 11(3): 27–35.

Dessent, T. (1992) Educational psychologists and 'the case for individual casework', in S. Wolfendale, T. Bryans, M. Fox, A. Labram and A. Sigston (eds) *The Profession and Practice of Educational Psychology*. London: Cassell.

Detheridge, T. (2000) Research involving children with severe learning difficulties, in A. Lewis and G. Lindsay (eds) *Researching Children's Perspectives*. Buckingham: Open University Press.

Dewart, H. and Summers, S. (1995) *The Pragmatics Profile of Everyday Communication Skills in Pre-school and School-aged Children*. Windsor: NFER-Nelson.

Dion, K.K. and Berscheid, E. (1974) Physical attractiveness and peer perception among children. *Sociometry*, 37: 1–12.

Dockrell, J. and McShane, J. (1992) *Children's Learning Difficulties: A Cognitive Approach*. Oxford: Blackwell.

Dockrell, J., Lewis, A. and Lindsay, G. (2000) Researching children's perspectives: a psychological dimension, in A. Lewis and G. Lindsay (eds) *Researching Children's Perspectives*. Buckingham: Open University Press.

Dodge, K.A., Coie, J.D. and Brakke, N.P. (1982) Behaviour patterns of socially rejected and neglected pre-adolescents: the roles of social approach and aggression. *Journal of Abnormal Child Psychology*, 10(3): 389–410.

Dodge, K.A., Murphy, R.M. and Buchsbaum, K. (1984) The assessment of attention-cue detection skills in children: implications for developmental psychopathology. *Child Development*, 55: 163–73.

Dodge, K.A., McClaskey, C.L. and Feldman, E. (1985) Situational approach to the assessment of social competence in children. *Journal of Consulting and Clinical Psychology*, 53(3): 344–53.

Dodge, K.A., Pettit, C.S., McClasky, C.J. and Brown, M.M. (1986) Social competence in children. *Society for Research in Child Development Monograph*, no. 213.

Dodge, K.A., Pettit, G.S., Bates, I.E. and Valente, E. (1995) Social information-processing patterns partially mediate the effect of early physical abuse on later conduct problems. *Journal of Abnormal Psychology*, 104: 632–43.

Dombey, H. (1998) A totalitarian approach to literacy education? *FORUM*, 40(2): 36–41.

Donald, D. (1994) Children with special educational needs: the reproduction of disadvantage in poorly served communities, in A. Dawes and D. Donald (eds) *Childhood and Adversity: Psychological Perspectives from South African Research*. Claremount, SA: David Philip (Publishing) Ltd.

Donaldson, M.L. (1995) *Children with Language Impairments: An Introduction*. London: Jessica Kingsley.

Douglas, J.W.B., Ingleby, J.D., Ross, J.M. and Tillott, J.M. (1972) Behavioural styles of four year old boys when responding to test demands. *Educational Research*, 14(3): 208–12.

Dowling, E. and Osborne, E. (1994) *The Family and the School: A Joint Systems Approach to Problems with Children*. London: Routledge.

Drillien, C. and Drummond, M. (1983) *Development Screening and the Child with Special Needs*. London: Heinemann Medical.

Dryden, R. (1997) A study of collaboration between the implant professionals and local educators in the rehabilitation of children with cochlear implants. *Deafness and Education*, 21(2): 3–9.

Dunlea, A. (1989) *Vision and the Emergence of Meaning: Blind and Sighted Children's Early Language*. Cambridge: Cambridge University Press.

Dunn, L.M. (1968) Special education for the mildly retarded – is much of it justifiable? *Exceptional Children*, 35: 5–22.

Dunn, L.M., Pantile, D. and Whetton, C. (1982) *British Picture Vocabulary Scale*. Windsor: NFER-Nelson.

Dyson, A. (1990) Special educational needs and the concept of change. *Oxford Review of Education*, 16(1): 55–66.

Dyson, A. (1991) Rethinking roles, rethinking concepts: special needs teachers in mainstream schools. *Support for Learning*, 6(2): 51–60.

Earl, L., Fullan, M., Leithwood, K. and Watson, N. (2000) *Watching and Learning: OISE/UT Evaluation of the Implementation of the National Literacy and Numeracy Strategies*. London: DIEE.

Edelbrock, C. and Achenbach, T.M. (1984) The teacher version of the Child Behavior Profile: 1. *Journal of Consulting and Clinical Psychology*, 52: 207–17.

Educable (2000) *No Choice, No Chance: The Educational Experience of Young People with Disabilities*. Belfast: Save the Children and Disability Action.

Edwards, A. (1998) Research and its influence on learning. *Educational and Child Psychology*, 15(3): 86–98.

Edwards, A.D. and Westgate, D.P.G. (1994) *Investigating Classroom Talk*, 2nd edn. London: Falmer Press.

Edwards, S., Fletcher, P., Garman, M., Hughes, A., Letts, C. and Sinka, I. (1997) *Reynell Developmental Language Scales III: The University of Reading Edition*. Windsor: NFER-Nelson.

Edwards, V. (1986) *Language in a Black Community*. Clevedon: Multilingual Matters.

Egan, G. (1994) *The Skilled Helper*, 5th edn. San Francisco, CA: Brooks/Cole Publishing Company.

Eiserman, W.D. (1988) Three types of peer tutoring: effects on the attitudes of students with learning disabilities and their regular class peers. *Journal of Learning Disabilities*, 21(4): 249–52.

Elliott, C.D. (1996) *British Ability Scale Word Reading Test*, 2nd edn. Windsor: NFER-Nelson.

Elliott, J. and Place, M. (1998) *Children in Difficulty: A Guide to Understanding and Helping*. London: Routledge.

Elliott, J.G. (2000) The psychological assessment of children with learning difficulties. *British Journal of Special Education*, 27(2): 59–66.

Elliott, S.N. and Busse, R.T. (1991) Social skills assessment with children and adolescents. *School Psychology International*, 12, 63–83.

Erwin, P.G. (1994) Effectiveness of social skills training: a meta-analytic study. *Counselling Psychology Quarterly*, 7(3): 305–10.

Farrell, P. (1997) The integration of children with severe learning difficulties: a review of the recent literature. *Journal of Applied Research in Intellectual Disabilities*, 10: 1–14.

Farrell, P., Balshaw, M. and Polat, F. (1999) *The Management, Role and Training of Learning Support Assistants* (research report RR161). London: DfEE.

Farmer, M. (1997) Exploring the links between communication skills and social competence. *Educational and Child Psychology*, 14(3): 38–44.

Faupel, A. (1986) Curriculum management (part 2): teaching curriculum objectives. *Educational Psychology in Practice*, 2(2): 4–15.

Faupel, A., Herrick, E. and Smith, P. (1998) *Anger Management: A Practical Guide*. London: David Fulton.

Fawcett, A. and Nicolson, R. (1996) *The Dyslexia Screening Test and Dyslexia Early Screening Test*. London: Harcourt, Brace & Company.

Ferri, E. and Smith, K. (1996) *Parenting in the 1990s*. London: Family Policy Studies Centre in association with the Joseph Rowntree Foundation.

Feuerstein, R. (1979) *The Dynamic Assessment of Retarded Performers: The Learning Potential Assessment Device*. Baltimore, MD: University Park Press.

Figg, J., Keeton, D., Parkes, J. and Richards, A. (1996) Are they talking about us? How EPs describe the views of children. *Educational and Child Psychology*, 13(2): 5–13.

Figueroa, R.A. (1989) Psychological testing of linguistic minority students: Knowledge gaps and regulations. *Exceptional Children*, 56(2): 145–52.

Fish, J. (1985) *Special Education: The Way Ahead*. Milton Keynes: Open University Press.

Ford, V. (1995) Assessing the learning environment: a classroom observation guide, in N. Frederickson and T. Cline (eds) *Assessing the Learning Environments of Children with Special Educational Needs*. London: Educational Psychology Publishing.

Foster, S.L., Martinez, C.R. and Kulberg, A.M. (1996) Race, ethnicity and children's peer relations, in T.H. Ollendick, and R.J. Prinz (eds) *Advances in Clinical Child Psychology No. 18*. New York: Plenum Press.

Foxman, D., Ruddock, G. and Thorpe, J. (1989) *Graduated Tests in Mathematics: A Study of Lower Attaining Pupils in Secondary Schools*. Windsor: NFER-Nelson.

Frankenberger, W. and Fronzaglio, K. (1991) A review of states criteria and procedures for identifying children with learning disabilities. *Journal of Learning Disabilities*, 24(8): 495–500.

Franks, D.J. (1971) Ethnic and social status characteristics of children in EMR and LD classes. *Exceptional Children*, 37: 537–8.

Fraser, B.J. (1982) Development of short forms of several classroom environment scales. *Journal of Educational Measurement*, 19(3): 221–7.

Fraser, B.J. (1984) Differences between preferred and actual classroom environment as perceived by primary students and teachers. *British Journal of Educational Psychology*, 54: 336–9.

Fraser, B.J. (1986) *Classroom Environment*. London: Croom Helm.

Fraser, B.J. (1987) Use of classroom environment assessments in school psychology. *School Psychology International*, 8: 205–19.

Fraser, B.J. (1991) Two decades of classroom environment research, in B.J. Fraser, and H.J. Walberg (eds) *Educational Environments: Evaluation, Antecedents and Consequences*. Oxford: Pergamon Press.

Fraser, B.J. (1998) Classroom environment instruments: development, validity and applications. *Learning Environments Research*, 1: 7–33.

Fraser, B.J. and Fisher, D.L. (1983a) Development and validation of short forms of some instruments measuring student perceptions of actual and preferred learning environments. *Science Education*, 67: 115–31.

Fraser, B.J. and Fisher, D.L. (1983b) Student achievement as a function of person-environment fit: a regression surface analysis. *British Journal of Education Psychology*, 53: 89–99.

Fraser, B.J. and Fisher, D.H. (1986) Using short forms of classroom climate instruments to assess and improve classroom psychosocial environment. *Journal of Research in Science Teaching*, 23(5): 387–413.

Fraser, B.J., Anderson, G.J. and Walberg, H.J. (1982) *Assessment of Learning Environments: Manual for Learning Environment Inventory (LEI) and My Class Inventory (MCI)*. Bentley: Western Australian Institute of Technology.

Fraser, B.J., Malone, J.A. and Neale, J.M. (1989) Assessing and improving the psychosocial environments of mathematics classrooms. *Journal of Research in Mathematics Education*, 20: 191–201.

Frederickson, N. (1990a) Systems approaches in educational psychology practice, in N. Jones and N. Frederickson (eds) (1990) *Refocusing Educational Psychology*. London: Falmer Press.

Frederickson, N. (1990b) Introduction to Soft Systems Methodology and its application in work with schools, in N. Frederickson (ed.) *Soft Systems Methodology: Practical Approaches in Work with Schools*. London: Educational Psychology Publishing.

Frederickson, N. (1991) Children can be so cruel – helping the rejected child, in G. Lindsay and A. Miller (eds) *Psychological Services for Primary Schools*. London: Longman.

Frederickson, N. (1993) Using Soft Systems Methodology to rethink special educational needs, in A. Dyson and C. Gains (eds) *Rethinking Special Needs in Mainstream Schools: Towards the Year 2000*. London: David Fulton.

Frederickson, N. (1997) Educational psychologists and the definition of dyslexia. Paper presented at the Annual Conference of the Association of Educational Psychologists, Bournemouth, 10 October.

Frederickson, N. (1998) Causal judgement and explanation: a practitioner response to Denis Hilton. *Educational and Child Psychology*, 15(2): 35–42.

Frederickson, N. (1999) The ACID test: or is it? *Educational Psychology in Practice*, 15(1): 3–9.

Frederickson, N. and Cameron, R.J. (1999) *Psychology in Education Portfolio*. Windsor: NFER-Nelson.

Frederickson, N. and Cline, T. (eds) (1990) *Curriculum Related Assessment With Bilingual Children*. London: Educational Psychology Publishing.

Frederickson, N. and Cline, T. (eds) (1995) *Assessing the Learning Environments of Children with Special Educational Needs*. London: Educational Psychology Publishing.

Frederickson, N. and Frith, U. (1998) Identifying dyslexia in bilingual children: a phonological approach with Inner London Sylheti speakers. *Dyslexia*, 4: 119–31.

Frederickson, N. and Furnham, A.F. (1998a) Use of sociometric techniques to assess the social status of mainstreamed children with learning difficulties. *Genetic, Social and General Psychology Monographs*, 124(4): 381–433.

Frederickson, N. and Furnham, A.F. (1998b) Sociometric status group classification of mainstreamed children who have moderate learning difficulties: an investigation of personal and environmental factors. *Journal of Educational Psychology*, 90(4): 1–12.

Frederickson, N. and Graham, B. (1999) Social skills and emotional intelligence, in N. Frederickson and R.J. Cameron (eds) *Psychology in Education Portfolio*. Windsor: NFER-Nelson.

Frederickson, N. and Monsen, J. (1999) The learning environment, in N. Frederickson and R.J. Cameron (eds) *Psychology in Education Portfolio*. Windsor: NFER-Nelson.

Frederickson, N. and Simms, J. (1990) Teaching social skills to children: towards an integrated approach. *Educational and Child Psychology*, 7(1): 5–17.

Frederickson, N., Webster, A. and Wright, A. (1991) Psychological assessment: a change of emphasis. *Educational Psychology in Practice*, 6(5): 23–32.

Frederickson, N., Frith, U. and Reason, R. (1997) *Phonological Assessment Battery*. Windsor: NFER-Nelson.

Frith, U. (1995) Dyslexia: can we have a shared theoretical framework? *Educational and Child Psychology*, 12(1): 6–17.

Frith, U. (1997) Brain, mind and behaviour in dyslexia, in C. Hulme and M. Snowling (ed.) *Dyslexia: Biology, Cognition and Intervention*. London: Whurr.

Fuchs, D., Fuchs, L.S. and Fernstrom, P. (1993) A conservative approach to special education reform: mainstreaming through transenvironmental programming and curriculum-based measurement. *American Educational Research Journal*, 30(1): 149–77.

Furnham, A. and Argyle, A. (1981) The theory, practice and application of social skills training. *International Journal of Behavioural Social Work*, 1: 125–43.

Fuson, K.C. and Kwon, Y. (1992) Korean children's understanding of multidigit addition and subtraction. *Child Development*, 63: 491–506.

Fuson, K.C., Smith, S.T. and Cicero, A.M. (1997) Supporting Latino first graders' ten-structured thinking in urban classrooms. *Journal for Research in Maths Education*, 28(6): 738–66.

Gadhok, K. (1994) Languages for intervention, in D. Martin (ed.) *Services to Bilingual Children with Speech and Language Difficulties: Proceedings of the 25th Anniversary AFASIC Conference, Birmingham, 1993*. London: AFASIC.

Gaine, C. (1995) *Still No Problem Here*. Stoke-on-Trent: Trentham Books.

Galaburda, A.M. (1989) Ordinary and extraordinary brain development: anatomical variation in developmental dyslexia. *Annals of Dyslexia*, 39: 67–79.

Galigan, J.E. (1985) Psychoeducational testing: turn out the lights, the party's over. *Exceptional Children*, 52(3): 288–99.

Gallaway, C. and Woll, B. (1994) Interaction and childhood deafness, in C. Gallaway and B.J. Richards (eds) *Input and Interaction in Language Acquisition*. Cambridge: Cambridge University Press.

Gallimore, R., Tharp, R. and Rueda, R. (1989) The social context of cognitive functioning in the lives of mentally handicapped persons, in D.A. Sugden (ed.) *Cognitive Approaches in Special Education*. London: Falmer Press.

Gallimore, R. (1996) Classrooms are just another cultural activity, in D.L. Speece and B.K. Keogh (eds) *Research on Classroom Ecologies: Implications for Inclusion of Children with Learning Disabilities*. Mahwah, NJ: Lawrence Erlbaum Associates.

Galloway, S. and Banes, D. (1994) Beyond the simple audit, in R. Rose, A. Fergusson, C. Coles, R. Byers and D. Banes (eds) *Implementing the Whole Curriculum for Pupils with Learning Difficulties*. London: David Fulton.

Galvin, P., Mercer, S. and Costa, P. (1990) *Building a Better Behaved School*. Harlow: Longman.

Gardner, H. (1993a) *Frames of Mind: The Theory of Multiple Intelligences*, 2nd edn. London: Fontana Press.

Gardner, H. (1993b) *The Unschooled Mind*. London: Fontana Press.

Geary, D.C. (1993) Mathematical disabilities: cognitive, neuropsychological and genetic components. *Psychological Bulletin*, 114(2): 345–62.

Gerber, M.M. (1995) Inclusion at the high water mark? Some thoughts on Zigmond and Baker's case studies of inclusive education programs. *Journal of Special Education*, 29(2): 181–91.

Gersch, I. (1992) Pupil involvement in assessment, in T. Cline (ed.) *The Assessment of Special Educational Needs: International Perspectives*. London: Routledge.

Gersch, I.S. (1987) Involving pupils in their own assessments, in T. Bowers (ed.) *Special Educational Needs and Human Resources Management*. London: Croom Helm.

Gersch, I.S., Holgate, A. and Sigston, A. (1993) Valuing the child's perspective: a revised student report and other practical initiatives. *Educational Psychology in Practice*, 9(1): 17–26.

Gersons-Wolfensberger, D.C.M. and Ruijssenaars, W.A.J.J.M. (1997) Definition and treatment of dyslexia: a report by the committee on dyslexia of the health council of the Netherlands. *Journal of Learning Disabilities*, 30(2): 209–13.

Gersten, R. and Woodward, J. (1994) The language-minority student and special education: issues, trends and paradoxes. *Exceptional Children*, 60(4): 310–22.

Geva, E. (1999) Issues in the assessment of reading disabilities in children who are working in their second language – beliefs and research evidence. Paper presented at the Multilingualism and Dyslexia: BDA International Conference, Manchester, 17–19 June.

Gibbin, K.P. (1992) Paediatric cochlear implantation. *Archives of Disease in Childhood*, 67(6): 669–71.

Gibbons, P. (1991) *Learning to Learn in a Second Language*. Newtown, Australia: Primary English Teaching Association.

Gibbs, J.T. and Huang, L.N. (1989) A conceptual framework for assessing and treating minority youth, in J.T. Gibbs and L.N. Huang (eds) *Children of Color: Psychological Interventions with Minority Youth*. San Francisco: Jossey-Bass.

Gickling, E.E. and Havertape, J.F. (1981) Curriculum based assessment, in J.A. Tucker (ed.) *Non-Test Based Assessment: A Training Module*. Minneapolis, MN: National School Psychology Inservice Training Network, University of Minnesota.

Gickling, E.E. and Thompson, V.P. (1985) A personal view of curriculum based assessment. *Exceptional Children*, 52(3): 205–18.

Gierl, M.J. and Bisanz, J. (1995) Anxieties and attitudes related to mathematics in grades 3 and 6. *Journal of Experimental Education*, 63: 139–58.

Gill, D., Mayor, B. and Blair, M. (eds) (1992) *Racism and Education: Structures and Strategies*. London: Sage Publications.

Gillborn, D. (1997) Ethnicity and educational performance in the United Kingdom: Racism, ethnicity and variability in achievement. *Anthropology and Education Quarterly*, 28(3): 375–93.

Gillborn, D. and Gipps, C. (1996) *Recent Research on the Achievements of Ethnic Minority Pupils*. London: HMSO.

Gipps, C. (1994) *Beyond Testing: Towards a Theory of Educational Assessment*. London: Falmer Press.

Gipps, C. and Murphy, P. (1994) *A Fair Test? Assessment, Achievement and Equity*. Buckingham: Open University Press.

Gipps, C. and Stobart, G. (1993) *Assessment: A Teacher's Guide to the Issues*. London: Hodder & Stoughton.

Glenny, G. (1996) Establishing children's views. *Educational and Child Psychology*, 13(4): 6–12.

Glutting, J.J., Oakland, T.A. and McDermott, P.A. (1989) Observing child behaviour during testing: constructs, validity and situational generality. *Journal of School Psychology*, 27: 155–64.

Goacher, B., Evans, J., Welton, J. and Wedell, K. (1988) *Policy and Provision for Special Educational Needs*. London: Cassell.

Godfrey, N. and Skinner, S. (1995) Investigating children's discourse in the primary classroom: the linguistic demands of classroom tasks, in M.K. Verma, K.P. Corrigan and S. Firth (eds) *Working with Bilingual Children: Good Practice in the Primary Classroom*. Clevedon: Multilingual Matters.

Goetz, L. and Sailor, W. (1990) Much ado about babies, murky bathwater and trickle down policies: a reply to Kauffman. *Journal of Special Education*, 23(3): 256–78.

Goh, S. and Fraser, B.J. (1998) Teacher interpersonal behaviour, classroom environment and student outcomes in primary mathematics in Singapore. *Learning Environments Research*, 1: 199–229.

Goleman, D. (1995) *Emotional Intelligence*. New York: Bantam Books.

Good, R.H., Simmons, D.C. and Smith, S. (1998) Effective academic interventions in the United States: evaluating and enhancing the acquisition of early reading skills. *Educational and Child Psychology*, 15(1): 56–70.

Gorrell-Barnes, G. (1985) Systems theory and family therapy, in M. Rutter and L. Hersov (eds) *Child Psychiatry: Modern Approaches*. Oxford: Blackwell.

Goswami, U. (1997) Learning to read in different orthographies: Phonological awareness, orthographic representations and dyslexia, in C. Hulme and M. Snowling (eds) *Dyslexia: Biology, Cognition and Intervention*. London: Whurr.

Goswami, U. (2000) Phonological representations, reading development and dyslexia: towards a cross-linguistic theoretical framework. *Dyslexia*, 6: 133–51.

Gottlieb, J. and Budoff, M. (1973) Social acceptability of retarded children in non-graded schools differing in architecture. *American Journal of Mental Deficiency*, 78(1): 15–19.

Gottlieb, J., Rose, T.L. and Lessen, E. (1983) Mainstreaming, in K.T. Kernan, M.J. Begab and R.B. Edgerton (eds) *Environments and Behaviour: The Adaptation of Mentally Retarded Persons*. Baltimore MD: University Park Press.

Graf, V.L. (1992) Minimizing the inappropriate referral and placement of ethnic minority students in special education, in T. Cline (ed.) *The Assessment of Special Educational Needs: International Perspectives*. London: Routledge.

Graham, S. (1997) Using attribution theory to understand social and academic motivation in African American Youth. *Educational Psychologist*, 32(1): 21–34.

Grant, D. and Brooks, K. (1996) Exclusions from school: responses from the black community. *Pastoral Care in Education*, 14: 20–7.

Grant, D. and Brooks, K. (2000) School exclusion of black pupils: an LEA response. *Support for Learning*, 15(1): 19–24.

Gravelle, M. (1996) *Supporting Bilingual Learners in Schools*. Stoke-on-Trent: Trentham Books.

Gravelle, M. (ed.) (2000) *Planning for Bilingual Learners: An Inclusive Curriculum*. Stoke-on-Trent: Trentham Books.

Gray, G., Smith, A. and Rutter, M. (1980) School attendance and the first year of employment, in L. Hersov and I. Berg (eds) *Out of School: Modern Perspectives in Truancy and School Refusal*. Chichester: Wiley.

Gray, P. and Dessent, T. (1993) Getting our act together. *British Journal of Special Education*, 20(1): 9–11.

Gray, P. and Noakes, J. (1994) Providing effective support to mainstream schools: issues and strategies, in P. Gray, A. Miller and J. Noakes (eds) *Challenging Behaviour in Schools*. London: Routledge.

Graziano, W.G., Varca, P.E. and Levy, J.C. (1982) Race of examiner effects and the validity of intelligence tests. *Review of Educational Research*, 52: 469–97.

Green, S. (1998) Inclusive education for pupils with English as an additional language: working with EAL teachers in a partnership framework. *NALDIC News*, 14: 9–12.

Greenberg, M.T., Kusche, C.A., Cook, E.T. and Quamma, J.P. (1995) Promoting emotional competence in school aged children: the effects of the PATHS curriculum. *Development and Psychopathology*, 7: 117–36.

Greenhalgh, P. (1994) *Emotional Growth and Learning*. London: Routledge.

Gregory, E. (1994) Cultural assumptions and early years' pedagogy: the effect of the home culture on minority children's interpretation of reading in school. *Language, Culture and Curriculum*, 7(2): 111–24.

Gregory, S. (1993) The language and culture of deaf people: implications for education. *Deafness*, 9: 4–11.

Gregory, S. and Bishop, J. (1991) The mainstreaming of primary age deaf children, in S. Gregory and G.M. Hartley (eds) *Constructing Deafness*. London: Pinter Publishers Ltd, in association with the Open University.

Gregory, S. and Hindley, P. (1996) Communication strategies for deaf children. *Journal of Child Psychology and Psychiatry*, 37: 895–906.

Gregory, S., Bishop, J. and Sheldon, L. (1995) *Deaf Young People and their Families*. Cambridge: Cambridge University Press.

Gresham, F.M. (1982) Misguided mainstreaming: the case for social skills training with handicapped children. *Exceptional Children*, 48(5): 422–33.

Gresham, F.M. and Elliott, S.N. (1990) *Social Skills Rating System*. Circle Pines, MN: American Guidance Service.

Gresham, F.M. and Elliott, S.N. (1993) Social skills intervention guide: systematic approaches to social skills training. *Special Services in the Schools*, 8(1): 137–58.

Grosjean, F. (1985) The bilingual as a competent but specific speaker-hearer. *Journal of Multilingual and Multicultural Development*, 6(6): 467–77.

Gross, J., Berger, A. and Garnett, J. (1999a) Special needs and the literacy hour: some general principles, in A. Berger and J. Gross (eds) *Teaching the Literacy Hour in an Inclusive Classroom*. London: David Fulton.

Gross, J., Jackson, S. and Atcliffe, J. (1999b) Managing behaviour difficulties, in A. Berger and J. Gross (eds) *Teaching the Literacy Hour in an Inclusive Classroom*. London: David Fulton.

Gross, R.D. (1987) *Psychology: The Science of Mind and Behaviour*. London: Edward Arnold.

Grossman, H. (1998) Linguistically appropriate special education. *Advances in Special Education*, 11: 41–54.

Grove, N. and Peacey, N. (1999) Teaching subjects to pupils with profound and multiple learning difficulties: considerations for the new framework. *British Journal of Special Education*, 26(2): 83–6.

Grugeon, E. (1992) Ruled out or rescued? A statement for Balbinder, in T. Booth, W. Swann, M. Masterton and P. Potts (eds) *Policies for Diversity in Education*. London: Routledge, in association with the Open University.

Gurney, P.W. (1987) Self-esteem in the classroom. *School Psychology International*, 8: 21–9.

Gutfreund, M., Harrison, M. and Wells, G. (1989) *The Bristol Language Development Scales*. Windsor: NFER-Nelson.

Guthke, J. (1993) Developments in learning potential assessment, in J.H.M. Hamers, K. Sijtsma and A.J.J.M. Ruilessenaars (eds) *Learning Potential Assessment: Theoretical, Methodological and Practical Issues*. Amsterdam: Swets and Zeitlinger.

Guthke, J., Beckmann, J.F. and Dobat, H. (1997) Dynamic testing – problems, uses, trends and evidence of validity. *Educational and Child Psychology*, 14(4): 17–32.

Gutierrez, K.D. and Stone, L.D. (1997) A cultural-historical view of learning and learning disabilities: participating in a community of learners. *Learning Disabilities Research and Practice*, 12(2): 123–31.

Hadow Committee (1924) *Psychological Tests of Educable Capacity*. London: HMSO.

Haertel, G.D., Walberg, H.J. and Haertel, E.H. (1981) Socio-psychological environments and learning: a quantitative synthesis. *British Journal of Educational Research*, 7: 27–36.

Haggard, M. and Hughes, E. (1991) *Screening Children's Hearing: A Review of the Literature and the Implications of Otitis Media*. London: HMSO.

Hagley, F. (1987) *Suffolk Reading Scale*. Windsor: NFER-Nelson.

Hall, D. (1995) *Assessing the Needs of Bilingual Pupils: Living in Two Languages*. London: David Fulton.

Hallam, S. and Castle, F. (1999) *Evaluation of the Behaviour and Discipline Pilot Projects (1996–1999) Supported Under the Standards Fund Programme*. Nottingham: DfEE Publications.

Hallett, C. and Stephenson, O. (1980) *Child Abuse: Aspects of Interprofessional Co-operation*. London: Allen & Unwin.

Hamers, J.H.M., Hessels, M.G.P. and Pennings, A.H. (1996) Learning potential in ethnic minority children. *European Journal of Psychological Assessment*, 12(3): 183–92.

Hammersley, M. (1997) Educational research and teaching: a response to David Hargreaves' TTA lecture. *British Educational Research Journal*, 23(2): 141–61.

Haney, M.R. and Evans, J.G. (1999) National survey of school psychologists regarding use of dynamic assessment and other non-traditional assessment techniques. *Psychology in the Schools*, 36(4): 295–304.

Hanko, G. (1987) Group consultation with mainstream teachers. *Educational and Child Psychology*, 4(3&4): 123–36.

Hanna, G. (1986) Sex differences in mathematics achievement of eighth graders in Ontario. *Journal for Research in Mathematics Education*, 17: 231–7.

Hannon, P. and McNally, J. (1986) Children's understanding and cultural factors in reading test performance. *Educational Review*, 38(3): 237–46.

Hargreaves, D.H. (1996) *Teaching as Research-based Profession: Possibilities and Prospects*. Teacher Training Agency Annual Lecture. London: Teacher Training Agency.

Hargreaves, D.H. (1997) In defense of research for evidence-based teaching: a rejoinder to Martyn Hammersley. *British Educational Research Journal*, 23(4): 405–19.

Haring, N.G. (1982) *Exceptional Children and Youth: An Introduction to Special Education*, 3rd edn. Columbus, OH: Charles E. Merrill Publishing Company.

Harlen, W. (1983) *Teaching and Learning Primary Science*. London: Paul Chapman.

Hart, S. (1996) *Beyond Special Needs: Enhancing Children's Learning Through Innovative Thinking*. London: Paul Chapman Publishing.

Harter, S. (1985) *Manual for the Self Perception Profile for Children*. Denver, CO: University of Denver.

Harter, S. and Renick, M.J. (1988) *Manual for the Self-Perception Profile for Learning Disabled Students*. Denver CO: University of Denver.

Hartshorne, H., May, M. and Maller, J. (1929) *Studies in the Nature of Character: II – Studies in Service and Self-control*. New York: Macmillan.

Hartup, W.W. (1992) Peer relations in early and middle childhood, in V.B. Van Hasselt and M. Hersen (eds) *Handbook of Social Development: A Lifespan Perspective*. New York: Plenum Press.

Hasbrouck, J.E., Wolbeck, T., Ihnot, C. and Parker, R.I. (1999) One teacher's use of curriculum-based measurement: a changed opinion. *Learning Disabilities Research and Practice*, 14(2): 118–26.

Haskey, J. (1996) The proportion of married couples who divorce: past patterns and present prospects. *Population Trends*, 83: 25–36.

Hastings, R., Sonuga-Barke, E.J.S. and Remington, B. (1993) An analysis of labels of people with learning disabilities. *British Journal of Clinical Psychology*, 32: 463–5.

Haworth, M. and Joyce, J. (1996) A resource for assessing the language skills of bilingual pupils, in T. Cline and N. Frederickson (eds) *Curriculum Related Assessment, Cummins and Bilingual Children*. Clevedon: Multilingual Matters.

Hayden, C. (1997) *Exclusions from Primary Schools*. Buckingham: Open University Press.

Haylock, D. (1995) *Mathematics Explained for Primary Teachers*. London: Paul Chapman Publishing.

Haynes, C. (2000) The outcome of speech and language impairment, in J. Law, S. Parkinson and R. Tamhne (eds) *Communication Difficulties in Childhood: A Practical Guide*. Abingdon: Radcliffe Medical Press.

Hayvren, M. and Hymel, S. (1984) Ethical issues in sociometric testing: impact of sociometric measures on interaction behaviour. *Developmental Psychology*, 20: 844–9.

HBPGE (Haringey Black Pressure Group on Education) (1984) *Black Critics of '81 Act*. London: Haringey Black Pressure Group on Education.

Hegarty, S. (1987) *Meeting Special Needs in Ordinary Schools*. London: Cassell.

Hegarty, S. (1993) Reviewing the literature on integration. *European Journal of Special Needs Education*, 8(3): 194–200.

Heim, A.W. (1970) *The Appraisal of Intelligence*. Slough: NFER-Nelson.

Heller, K.A., Holtzman, W. and Messick, S. (1982) *Placing Children in Special Education: A Strategy for Equity*. Washington, DC: National Academy Press.

Hembree, R. (1990) The nature, effects and relief of mathematics anxiety. *Journal for Research in Mathematics Education*, 21(1): 33–46.

Hernandez, R.D. (1994) Reducing bias in the assessment of culturally and linguistically diverse populations. *Journal of Educational Issues of Language Minority Students*, 14: 269–300.

Hessels, M.G.P. (1997) Low IQ but high learning potential: why Zeyneb and Moussa do not belong in special education. *Educational and Child Psychology*, 14(4): 121–36.

Hester, H., Ellis, S. and Barrs, M. (1988) *Guide to the Primary Learning Record*. London: Centre for Language in Primary Education.

Hewison, J. (1988) The long term effectiveness of parental involvement in reading: a follow-up study to the Haringey reading project. *British Journal of Educational Psychology*, 58: 184–90.

Hickson, J., Land, A.J. and Aikman, G. (1994) Learning style differences in middle school pupils from four ethnic backgrounds. *School Psychology International*, 15(4): 349–59.

Hiebert, J. and Lefevre, P. (1986) Conceptual and procedural knowledge in mathematics: an introductory analysis, in J. Hiebert (ed.) *Conceptual and Procedural Knowledge: the Case of Mathematics*. Hillsdale, NJ: Lawrence Erlbaum Associates.

Hieronymous, A.N. and Hoover, H.D. (1986) *Iowa Test of Basic Skills: Manual for School Administrators, Levels 5–14*. Chicago: Riverside Publishing Company.

Hill, J. (1994) The paradox of gender: sex-stereotyping within the statementing procedure. *British Education Research Journal*, 20(3): 345–57.

Hillage, J., Pearson, R., Anderson, A. and Tamkin, P. (1998) *Excellence in Research on Schools* (research report RR74). Suffolk: DfEE Publications.

Hind, S. (1998) Implications of otitis media for development, in S. Gregory, P. Knight, W. McCracken, S. Powers and L. Watson (eds) *Issues in Deaf Education*. London: David Fulton.

Hindley, P. (1997) Psychiatric aspects of hearing impairments. *Journal of Child Psychology and Psychiatry*, 38: 101–18.

Hinson, M. (ed.) (1998) *Surviving the Literacy Hour.* Tamworth: NASEN Publications.

Hitch, G.J. and McAuley, E. (1991) Working memory in children with specific arithmetical learning difficulties. *British Journal of Psychology*, 82: 375–86.

HMI (Her Majesty's Inspectorate of Schools) (1989) *Aspects of Primary Education: The Teaching and Learning of Mathematics.* London: HMSO.

Hodes, M. (2000) Psychologically distressed refugee children in the United Kingdom. *Child Psychology and Psychiatry Review*, 5(2): 57–68.

Holmes, E. (1995) Educational interventions for young children who have experienced fragmented care, in J. Trowell and M. Bower (eds) *The Emotional Needs of Young Children and their Families: Using Psychoanalytic Ideas in the Community.* London: Routledge.

Holt, J.A. and Allen, T.E. (1989) The effects of schools and their curricula on the reading and mathematics achievement of hearing impaired students. *International Journal of Educational Research*, 13: 547–62.

Holt, S. (1996) Reflecting light and shade: psychodynamic thinking in educational psychology in the 1990s, in C. Jennings and E. Kennedy (eds) *The Reflective Professional in Education.* London: Jessica Kingsley.

Hornby, G. (1995) *Working with Parents of Children with Special Needs.* London: Cassell.

Houghton, S., Merrett, F. and Wheldall, K. (1988) The attitudes of British secondary school pupils to praise, rewards, punishments and reprimands: a further study. *New Zealand Journal of Educational Studies*, 23: 203–14.

House of Commons (Select Committee on Education, Science and Arts) (1987) *Special Educational Needs: Implementation of the Education Act 1981.* London: HMSO.

Howitt, D. and Owusu-Bempah, J. (1994) *The Racism of Psychology: Time for Change.* Hemel Hempstead: Harvester Wheatsheaf.

Howlin, P. and Cross, P. (1994) The variability of language test scores in 3- and 4-year-old children of normal non-verbal intelligence: a brief research report. *European Journal of Disorders of Communication*, 29: 279–88.

Hughes, M. and Grieve, R. (1980) On asking children bizarre questions. *First Language*, 1: 149–60.

Hunt, P. and Goetz, L. (1997) Research on inclusive educational programs, practices, and outcomes for students with severe difficulties. *Journal of Special Education*, 31(1): 3–29.

Huss-Keeler, R.L. (1997) Teacher perception of ethnic and linguistic minority parental involvement and its relationship to children's language and literacy learning: a case study. *Teaching and Teacher Education*, 13(2): 171–82.

Hutnik, N. (1992) *Ethnic Minority Identity: A Social Psychological Perspective.* Oxford: Clarendon Press.

IDEA (Individuals with Disabilities Education Act) (1997) 20 US Congress. Chapter 33, Sections 1400–1491.

Indoe, D. (1999) Attribution and motivation, in N. Frederickson and R.J. Cameron (eds) *Psychology in Education Portfolio.* Windsor: NFER-Nelson.

Inner London Education Authority (ILEA) (1983) *A Policy for Equality: Race.* London: Inner London Education Authority.

Inner London Education Authority (ILEA) (1984) *Survey of Characteristics of Pupils in Inner London Special Schools.* London: Inner London Education Authority.

Inner London Education Authority (ILEA) (1985) *Educational Opportunities for All?* (Fish Report). London: Inner London Education Authority.

Inner London Education Authority (ILEA) (1990) *SMILE Mathematics*. London: SMILE Centre.

Iszatt, J. and Wasilewska, T. (1997) Nurture groups: an early intervention model enabling vulnerable children with emotional and behaviour difficulties to integrate successfully into school. *Educational and Child Psychology*, 14(3): 63–70.

Iverson, A.M. and Iverson, G.L. (1996) Children's long term reactions to participating in sociometric assessment. *Psychology in the Schools*, 33: 104–12.

Iverson, A.M., Barton, E.A. and Iverson, G.L. (1997) Analysis of risk to children participating in a sociometric task. *Developmental Psychology*, 33(1): 103–12.

Jefferies, E. and Donlan, S. (1994) Reluctant talkers in the early years: some key issues, in J. Watson (ed.) *Working with Communication Difficulties*. Edinburgh: Moray House Publications.

Jelly, M., Fuller, A. and Byers, R. (2000) *Involving Pupils in Practice*. London: David Fulton.

Jenkins, G.M. (1969) The systems approach. *Journal of Systems Engineering*, 1(1): 19–27.

Jensen, A.R. (1969) How much can we boost IQ and scholastic achievement? *Harvard Educational Review*, 39: 1–123.

Jensen, A.R. (1980) *Bias in Mental Testing*. London: Methuen.

Johnson, D.W. and Johnson, R.T. (1991) *Learning Together and Alone*, 3rd edn. Englewood Cliffs, NJ: Prentice Hall.

Johnson, D.W., Johnson, R.T. and Maruyama, G. (1983) Interdependence and interpersonal attraction among hetrogeneous and homogeneous individuals: a theoretical formulation and a meta-analysis of the research. *Review of Educational Research*, 53(1): 5–54.

Jones, D.V. (1993) Words with a similar meaning. *Mathematics Teaching*, 145: 14–15.

Jones, D.V. (1997) *The Assessment of Bilingual Pupils: Observations from Recent Welsh Experiences*. British Educational Research Association Annual Conference, York University, 11–14 September.

Jones, G.A. and Thornton, C.A. (1993) Children's understanding of place value: a framework for curriculum development and assessment. *Young Children*, 48(5): 12–18.

Jordan, L. and Goodey, C. (1996) *Human Rights and School Change: The Newham Story*. Bristol: CSIE.

Joseph, G.G. (1993) A rationale for a multicultural approach to mathematics, in D. Nelson, G.G. Joseph and J. Williams (eds) *Multicultural Mathematics*. Oxford: Oxford University Press.

Jowett, S. and Evans, C. (1996) *Speech and Language Therapy Services for Children*. Slough: NFER (for Department of Health and Department for Education).

Kahne, J. (1996) The politics of self-esteem. *American Educational Research Journal*, 33(1): 3–22.

Kampfe, C.M. and Turecheck, A.G. (1987) Reading achievement of prelingually deaf students and its relationship to parental methods of communication: a review of the literature. *American Annals of the Deaf*, 132: 11–15.

Kauffman, J.M. (1989) The Regular Education Initiative as Regan-Bush education policy: a trickle-down theory of the hard to teach. *Journal of Special Education*, 23(3): 256–78.

Kaufman, A.S. and Kaufman, N.L. (1983) *Kaufman Assessment Battery for Children*. Circle Pines, MN: American Guidance Service.

Kaufman, A.S. and Kaufman, N.L. (1993) *Kaufman Adolescent and Adult Intelligence Test*. Circle Pines, MN: American Guidance Service.

Kaufman, M., Agard, J.A. and Semmel, M.I. (1985) *Mainstreaming: Learners and their Environment*. Cambridge, MA: Brookline Books.

Kaul, S. (1992) The challenge of special educational needs: an approach to identification and assessment of individuals with cerebral palsy in a community setting, in T. Cline (ed.) *The Assessment of Special Educational Needs: International Perspectives*. London: Routledge.

Keller, H.R. (1988) Children's adaptive bahaviors: measure and source generalisability. *Journal of Psychoeducational Assessment*, 6: 371–89.

Kelley-Laine, K. (1998) Parents as partners in schooling: the current state of affairs. *Childhood Education*, 74(6): 342–5.

Kelly, B. (1999) Circle time: a systems approach to emotional and behavioural difficulties. *Educational Psychology in Practice*, 15(1): 40–4.

Kelly, G.A. (1991) *The Psychology of Personal Constructs*, vols 1&2; *A Theory of Personality; Clinical Diagnosis and Psychopathology*. Florence, KY: Taylor & Francis/Routledge.

Kenner, C., Wells, K. and Williams, H. (1996) Assessing a bilingual child's talk in different classroom contexts, in N. Hall and J. Martello (eds) *Listening to Children Think: Exploring Talk in the Early Years*. London: Hodder & Stoughton.

Keogh, B.K., Gallimore, R. and Weisner, T. (1997) A sociocultural perspective on learning and learning disabilities. *Learning Disabilities Research and Practice*, 12(2): 107–13.

Kerslake, D. (1982) Talking about mathematics, in R. Harvey, D. Kerslake, H. Shuard and M. Torbe (eds) *Language Teaching and Learning: Mathematics*. East Grinstead: Ward Lock Educational.

Kessissoglou, S. and Farrell, P. (1995) Whatever happened to precision teaching? *British Journal of Special Education*, 22(2): 60–3.

Kiernan, C. and Reid, B. (1987) *Pre-Verbal Communication Schedule*. Windsor: NFER-Nelson.

King, V. (1989) Support Teaching. *Special Children*, 33: 1–4.

Kirman, B.H. (1972) *The Mentally Handicapped Child*. London: Nelson.

Kistener, J.A., Osbourne, M. and LeVerrier, L. (1988) Causal attributions of learning disabled children: developmental patterns and relation to academic progress. *Journal of Educational Psychology*, 80: 82–9.

Knight, P. (1997) Bilingual nursery provision – a challenging start. *Deafness and Education*, 21(3): 20–30.

Knight, S.L. (1991) The effects of students' perceptions of the learning environment on their motivation in language arts. *Journal of Classroom Interaction*, 26(2): 19–23.

Knoff, H.M. (1984) The practice of multi-modal consultation: an integrating approach for consultation service delivery. *Psychology in the Schools*, 21: 83–91.

Knowles, M. (1990) *The Adult Learner: A Neglected Species*, 4th edn. Houston, TX: Gulf Publishing.

Koelle, W.H. and Convey, J.J. (1982) The prediction of the achievement of deaf adolescents from self concept and locus of control measures. *American Annals of the Deaf*, 127: 769–78.

Kolvin, I. and Fundudis, T. (1981) Elective mute children: psychological development and background factors. *Journal of Child Psychology and Psychiatry*, 22(3): 219–32.

Koontz, K.L. and Berch, D.B. (1996) Identifying simple numerical stimuli: processing inefficiencies exhibited by arithmetic learning disabled children. *Mathematical Cognition*, 2: 1–23.

Kratochwill, T. (1981) *Selective Mutism: Implications for Research and Treatment.* Hillsdale, NJ: Lawrence Erlbaum Associates.

Krauthammer, C. (1990) Education: doing bad and feeling good. *Time*, 135(6): 78.

Kupersmidt, J.B., Coie, J.D. and Dodge, K.A. (1990) The role of poor peer relations in the development of disorder, in S.J. Asher and J.D. Coie (eds) *Peer Rejection in Childhood.* New York: Cambridge University Press.

Kusche, C.A., Greenberg, M.T. and Beilke, B. (1988) 'The Kusche affective interview', unpublished manuscript. University of Washington, Department of Psychology.

Kyle, J.G. and Woll, B. (eds) (1983) *Language in Sign: An International Perspective on Sign Language.* London: Croom Helm.

Kyle, J.G. and Woll, B. (1985) *Sign Language: The Study of Deaf People and their Language.* Cambridge: Cambridge University Press.

Kysel, F. (1985) Characteristics of pupils in special schools and units, in F. Kysel (ed.) *Educational Opportunities for All? Research Studies for Fish Report*, vol. 2. London: ILEA.

Kysel, F. (1986) *Inner London Education Authority Statistics 1985: Language Census.* London: ILEA.

Labbe, E.E. and Williamson, D.A. (1984) Behavioral treatment of elective mutism: a review of the literature. *Clinical Psychology Review*, 4(3): 273–92.

Lacelle-Peterson, M.W. and Rivera, C. (1994) Is it real for all kids? A framework for equitable assessment policies for English language learners. *Harvard Educational Review*, 64(1): 55–75.

Ladd, G.W. and Mize, J. (1983) A cognitive-social learning model of social-skill training. *Psychological Review*, 90: 127–57.

Lam, T.C.M. (1993) Testability: a critical issue in testing language minority students with Standardized Achievement Tests. *Measurement and Evaluation in Counselling and Development*, 26: 179–91.

Landerl, K., Wimmer, H. and Frith, U. (1997) The impact of orthographic consistency on dyslexia: a German-English comparison. *Cognition*, 63: 315–34.

Lane, H. (1992) *The Mask of Benevolence.* New York: Alfred A. Knopf.

Lane, P.S. and McWhirter, J.J. (1992) A peer mediation model: conflict resolution for elementary and middle school children. *Elementary School Guidance and Counselling*, 27: 15–23.

Law, J. and Tamhne, R. (2000) The size of the problem, in J. Law, S. Parkinson and R. Tamhne (eds) *Communication Difficulties in Childhood: A Practical Guide.* Abingdon: Radcliffe Medical Press.

Lederberg, A.R. and Everhart, V.S. (1998) Communication between deaf children and their hearing mothers: the role of language, gesture and vocalisations. *Journal of Speech, Language and Hearing Research*, 41: 887–99.

Lee, T., Pappius, E.M. and Goldman, L. (1983) Impact of inter-physician communication on the effectiveness of medical consultations. *American Journal of Medicine*, 74: 106–12.

Leeds City Council Department of Education (1992) *Leeds Pupil Achievement Survey.* Leeds: Leeds City Council.

Lees, J. and Urwin, S. (1997) *Children with Language Disorders*, 2nd edn. London: Whurr.

Leung, C. (1996) An investigation of current practice in assessing stages of language acquisition, in *Collected Papers of the Invitational Conference on Teaching and Learning English as an Additional Language held in London on 27–28 April 1995.* London: School Curriculum and Assessment Authority.

Leung, C., Harris, R. and Rampton, B. (1997) The idealised native speaker, reified ethnicities and classroom realities. *TESOL Quarterly*, 31(3): 543–60.

Lewin, K. (1936) *Principles of Topological Psychology*. New York: McGraw Hill.

Lewis, A. (1995) *Primary Special Needs and the National Curriculum*. London: Routledge.

Lewis, A. and Lindsay, G. (eds) (2000) *Researching Children's Perspectives*. Buckingham: Open University Press.

Lewis, A. and Norwich, B. (2000) *Mapping a Pedagogy for Special Needs*. Monograph, University of Exeter, University of Warwick.

Lewis, C., Hitch, G.J. and Walker, P. (1994) The prevalence of specific arithmetic difficulties and specific reading difficulties in 9- to 10-year-old boys and girls. *Journal of Child Psychology and Psychiatry*, 35(2): 283–92.

Lewis, S. (1992) *Auditory processing*. Course documentation, Department of Psychology, University College London.

Libet, J. and Lewinshon, P. (1973) Concept of social skills with special reference to the behaviour of depressed persons. *Journal of Consulting and Clinical Psychology*, 40: 342–7.

Light, J. (1989) Towards a definition of communicative competence in individuals using augmentative and alternative communication systems. *Augmentative and Alternative Communication*, 5(2): 137–44.

Light, J.G. and DeFries, J.C. (1995) Comorbidity of reading and mathematics disabilities: genetic and environmental etiologies. *Journal of Learning Disabilities*, 28(2): 96–106.

Lim, T.K. (1995) Perceptions of classroom environment, school types, gender and learning styles of secondary school students. *Educational Psychology*, 15(2): 161–9.

Lindsley, O.R. (1992) Precision teaching: discoveries and effects. *Journal of Applied Behavioural Analysis*, 25(1): 51–7.

Linn, M.C., Benedictis, T.D., Delucchi, K., Harris, A. and Stage, E. (1987) Gender differences in National Assessment of Educational Progress science items: what does 'I don't know' really mean? *Journal of Research in Science Teaching*, 24: 267–78.

Lipsky, D.K. and Gartner, A. (1996) Inclusion, school restructuring, and the remaking of American society. *Harvard Educational Review*, 66(4): 762–95.

Liu, A. (1995) Full inclusion and deaf education – redefining equality. *Journal of Law and Education*, 24(2): 241–66.

Lokke, C., Gersch, I., M'gadzah, H. and Frederickson, N. (1997) The resurrection of psychometrics: fact or fiction? *Educational Psychology in Practice*, 12(4): 222–33.

Lovegrove, W. (1994) Visual deficit in dyslexia: evidence and implications, in A. Fawcett and R. Nicolson (eds) *Dyslexia in Children*. Hemel Hempstead: Harvester Wheatsheaf.

Lowe, M. and Costello, A. (1988) *Symbolic Play Test*, 2nd edn. Windsor: NFER-Nelson.

Lucas, T., Henze, R. and Donato, R. (1990) Promoting the success of Latino language minority students: an exploratory study of six high schools. *Harvard Educational Review*, 60: 315–34.

Lumb, D. and Lumb, M. (1989) *Early Mathematics Diagnostic Kit*. Windsor: NFER-Nelson.

Lynas, W. (1991) Deaf children with Usher's Syndrome. *Journal of the British Association of Teachers of the Deaf*, 15(2): 33–9.

Maag, J.W. (1989) Assessment in social skills training: methodological and conceptual issues for research and practice. *Remedial and Special Education*, 10(4): 6–17.

Macaruso, P. and Sokol, S.M. (1998) Cognitive neuropsychology and developmental dyscalculia, in C. Donlan (ed.) *The Development of Mathematical Skills*. Hove: Psychology Press.

McBrien, J. and Foxen, T. (1981) *Training Staff in Behavioural Methods*. Manchester: Manchester University Press.

McCallum, R.S. and Bracken, B.A. (1997) The Universal Nonverbal Intelligence Test, in D.P. Flanagan, J.L. Genshaft and P.L. Harrison (eds) *Contemporary Intellectual Assessment: Theories, Tests and Issues.* New York: Guilford Press.

McCarthy, G.T. (1992) Cerebral palsy: definition, epidemiology, developmental and neurological aspects, in G.T. McCarthy and B.G.R. Neville (eds) *Physical Disability in Childhood: An Interdisciplinary Approach to Management.* Edinburgh: Churchill Livingstone.

McClure, L., Chinsky, J. and Larcen, S. (1978) Enhancing social problem-solving performance in an elementary school setting. *Journal of Educational Psychology*, 70(4): 504–13.

MacDonald, A. and Rendle, C. (1994) Developing the foundations of communicative competence in children with severe physical disability, in J. Watson (ed.) *Working with Communication Difficulties.* Edinburgh: Moray House Publications.

MacDonald, I.M. (1996) Expanding the lens: student perceptions of school violence, in J. Ross Epp and A.M. Watkinson (eds) *Systemic Violence: How Schools Hurt Children.* London: Falmer Press.

McGee, R., Silva, P.A. and Williams, S. (1983) Parents' and teachers' of behavior problems in seven year old children. *The Exceptional Child*, 30(2): 151–61.

McKee, W.T. and Witt, J.C. (1990) Effective teaching: a review of instructional and environmental variables, in T.B. Gutkin and C.R. Reynolds (eds) *The Handbook of School Psychology.* New York: Wiley.

McKenna, P. (1990) Learning implications of field dependence-independence: cognitive style versus cognitive ability. *Applied Cognitive Psychology*, 4: 425–37.

McLaughlin, B. (1985) *Second Language Acquisition in Childhood*, 2nd edn, vol. 2. Hillsdale, NJ: Lawrence Erlbaum Associates.

McLaughlin, M.J. (1995) Defining special education: a response to Zigmond and Baker. *Journal of Special Education*, 29(2): 200–8.

McLaughlin, M.J. and Rouse, M. (ed.) (2000) *Special Education and School Reform in the United States and Britain.* London: Routledge.

MacLeod, F. (1996) Encouraging parents' involvement in their children's literacy development. *School Psychology International*, 17: 379–91.

McLeskey, J., Skiba, R. and Wilcox, B. (1990) Reform and special education: a mainstream perspective. *Journal of Special Education*, 24(3): 319–25.

MacMillan Test Unit (1985) *Graded Word Reading Test.* Windsor: NFER-Nelson.

Macpherson Committee of Enquiry (1999) *Report of the Stephen Lawrence Enquiry.* London: HMSO.

McWilliam, N. (1998) *What's in a Word? Vocabulary Development in Multilingual Classrooms.* Stoke-on-Trent: Trentham Books.

Madden, N.A. and Slavin, R.E. (1983) Mainstreaming students with mild handicaps: academic and social outcomes. *Review of Educational Research*, 52(4): 519–69.

Madhani, N. (1994) Working with speech and language impaired children from linguistic minority communities, in D. Martin (ed.) *Services to Bilingual Children with Speech and Language Difficulties: Proceedings of the 25th Anniversary AFASIC Conference, Birmingham, 1993.* London: AFASIC.

Maheady, L., Sacca, M.K. and Harper, G.F. (1988) Classwide peer tutoring programme on the academic performance of mildly handicapped students. *Exceptional Children*, 55: 52–9.

Male, D. (1996) Who goes to MLD schools? *British Journal of Special Education*, 23(1): 35–41.

Mallon, F. (2000) Peer and cross age tutoring and mentoring schemes, in H. Daniels (ed.) *Special Education Reformed: Beyond Rhetoric?* London: Falmer Press.

Manset, G. and Semmel, M.I. (1997) Are inclusive programs for students with mild disabilities effective? A comparative review of model programs. *Journal of Special Education*, 31(2): 155–80.

Markides, A. (1991) The teaching of speech: historical developments (extract from 1983 text), in S. Gregory and G.M. Hartley (eds) *Constructing Deafness*. London: Pinter Publishers Ltd.

Marschark, M. (1993) *Psychological Development of Deaf Children*. New York: Oxford University Press.

Marsh, H.W., Chessor, D., Craven, R. and Roche, L. (1995) The effects of gifted and talented programs on academic self concept: the big fish strikes again. *American Educational Research Journal*, 32: 285–319.

Martin, D. (1994) Towards a model of service delivery, in D. Martin (ed.) *Services to Bilingual Children with Speech and Language Difficulties: Proceedings of the 25th Anniversary AFASIC Conference, Birmingham, 1993*. London: AFASIC.

Martin, D. (2000) Communication difficulties in a multicultural context, in J. Law, S. Parkinson and R. Tamhne (eds) *Communication Difficulties in Childhood: A Practical Guide*. Abingdon: Radcliffe Medical Press.

Martin, D.S. (1997) Inclusion: time to rethink. *Educational Forum*, 61: 232–9.

Martin, E.W. (1995) Case studies on inclusion: worst fears realised. *Journal of Special Education*, 29: 192–9.

Mason, H. and Tobin, M.J. (1986) Speed of information processing and the visually handicapped child. *British Journal of Special Education*, 13(2): 69–70.

Masters, J.M. and Furman, W. (1981) Popularity, individual friendship selection and specific peer interaction among children. *Developmental Psychology*, 17: 344–50.

Mastropieri, M.A. and Scruggs, T.E. (1997) What's special about special education? A cautious view toward full inclusion. *Educational Forum*, 61: 206–11.

Mattes, L.J. and Omark, D.R. (1984) *Speech and Language Assessment for the Bilingual Handicapped*. San Diego, CA: College Hill Press.

Meadows, S. (1998) Children learning to think: learning from others? Vygotskyan theory and educational psychology. *Educational and Child Psychology*, 15(2): 6–13.

Meek, M. (ed.) (1996) *Developing Pedagogies in the Multilingual Classroom: The Writings of Josie Levine*. Stoke-on-Trent: Trentham Books.

Meherali, R. (1994) Being black and deaf, in C. Laurenzi and P. Hindley (eds) *Keep Deaf Children in Mind: Current Issues in Mental Health*. Leeds: NDCS Family Services Centre.

Mehrens, W.A. and Clarizio, H.F. (1993) Curriculum-based measurement: conceptual and psychometric considerations. *Psychology in the Schools*, 30: 241–54.

Merrell, K.W. and Gimpel, G.A. (1997) *Social Skills of Children and Adolescents: Conceptualisation, Assessment, Treatment*. Mahwah, NJ: Lawrence Erlbaum.

Merrett, F. and Houghton, S. (1989) Does it work with the older ones? A review of behavioural studies carried out in British secondary schools since 1981. *Educational Psychology*, 9(4): 287–309.

Merttens, R. (1999) Family numeracy, in I. Thompson (ed.) *Issues in Teaching Numeracy in Primary Schools*. Buckingham: Open University Press.

Merttens, R., Newland, A. and Webb, S. (1996) *Learning in Tandem: Parental Involvement in their Children's Education*. Leamington Spa: Scholastic Press.

Midgley, C., Eccles, J.S. and Feldlaufer, H. (1991) Classroom environment and the transition to junior high school, in B.J. Fraser and H.J. Walberg (eds) *Educational Environments: Evaluation, Antecedents and Consequences*. Oxford: Pergamon Press.

Miles, T.R. (1993) *Dyslexia: The Pattern of Difficulties*, 2nd edn. London: Whurr.

Miles, T.R. (1996) Do dyslexic children have IQs? *Dyslexia*, 2(3): 175–8.

Miller, A. (1996) *Pupil Behaviour and Teacher Culture*. London: Cassell.

Miller, N. (1984) Some observations concerning formal tests in cross-cultural settings, in N. Miller (ed.) *Bilingualism and Language Disability*. London: Chapman & Hall.

Mills, A.E. (1993) Visual handicap, in D. Bishop and K. Mogford (eds) *Language Development under Exceptional Circumstances*. Hove: Lawrence Erlbaum Associates.

Milroy, J. and Milroy, L. (1985) *Authority in Language: Investigating Prescription and Standardisation*. London: Routledge.

Ministry of Education (1945) *Handicapped Pupils and School Health Service Regulations*. London: HMSO.

Ministry of Education (1946) *Special Educational Treatment*. London: HMSO.

Ministry of Education (1955) *Report of the Committee on Maladjusted Children* (the Underwood Report). London: HMSO.

Ministry of Education (1963) *English for Immigrants*. Ministry of Education Pamphlet No. 43. London: HMSO.

Mischel, W. (1969) Continuity and change in personality. *American Psychologist*, 24: 1012–18.

Missiuna, C. and Samuels, M. (1988) Dynamic assessment: review and critique. *Special Services in the Schools*, 5(1,2): 1–22.

Mittler, P. (1985) Integration: the shadow and the substance. *Educational and Child Psychology*, 2(3): 8–22.

Mittler, P. (1986) Foreword, in J. Coupe and J. Porter (eds) *The Education of Children with Severe Learning Difficulties: Bridging the Gap between Theory and Practice*. London: Croom Helm.

Miura, I.T. (1987) Mathematics achievement as a function of language. *Journal of Educational Psychology*, 79(1): 79–82.

Miura, I.T. and Okamoto, Y. (1994) Comparisons of U.S. and Japanese first graders' cognitive representation of number and understanding of place value. *Journal of Educational Psychology*, 81(1): 109–13.

Moats, L.C. and Lyon, G.R. (1993) Learning disabilities in the United States: Advocacy, science and the future of the field. *Journal of Learning Disabilities*, 26(5): 282–94.

Molteno, C., Roux, A., Nelson, M. and Arens, L. (1990) Causes of mental handicap in Cape Town. *South African Medical Journal*, 77: 98–101.

Monaghan, F. (1999) *Defining a Role: The EAL Teacher in Maths*. Watford: NALDIC.

Moore, J. (1999) Developing a local authority response to inclusion. *Support for Learning*, 14(4): 174–8.

Moos, R.H. (1973) Conceptualisations of human environments. *American Psychologist*, 28: 652–65.

Moreno, J.L. (1934) *Who Shall Survive?* Washington: Nervous and Mental Disease Publishing Company.

Morgan, R. and Lyon, E. (1979) Paired reading – a preliminary report on a technique for parental tuition of reading-retarded children. *Journal of Child Psychology and Psychiatry*, 20: 151–60.

Morgan-Barry, R. (1988) *The Auditory Discrimination and Attention Test*. Windsor: NFER-Nelson.

Morris, J. (1998) *Don't Leave Us Out: Involving Disabled Children and Young People with Communication Impairments*. York: Joseph Rowntree Foundation.

Mortimore, P., Sammons, P. and Ecob, R. (1988) *School Matters: The Junior Years*. Salisbury: Open Books.

Morton, J. (1996) Helping children contribute to learning plans. *Educational and Child Psychology*, 13(2): 23–30.

Morton, J. and Frith, U. (1995) Causal modelling: a structural approach to developmental psychopathology, in D. Cichetti and D.J. Cohen (eds) *Manual of Developmental Psychopathology*. New York: Wiley.

Mosley, J. (1996) *Quality Circle Time in the Primary Classroom*. Wisbech: LDA.

Moss, H.A. and Susman, E.J. (1980) Longitudinal study of personality development, in O.G. Brim and J. Kagan (eds) *Consistency and Change in Human Development*. Cambridge, MA: Harvard University Press.

Mulford, R. (1988) First words of the blind child, in M.D. Smith and J.L. Locke (eds) *The Emergent Lexicon: The Child's Development of a Linguistic Vocabulary*. New York: Academic Press.

Murphy, R.L.J. (1982) Sex differences in objective test performance. *British Journal of Educational Psychology*, 52: 213–19.

Muter, V., Hulme, C. and Snowling, M. (1997) *Phonological Abilities Test*. London: The Psychological Corporation.

Nabuzoka, D. and Smith, P.K. (1993) Sociometric status and social behaviour of children with and without learning difficulties. *Journal of Child Psychology and Psychiatry*, 34(8): 1435–48.

Naglieri, J.A. (1999) *Essentials of CAS Assessment*. New York: Wiley.

Naglieri, J.A. and Das, J.P. (1997) *Cognitive Assessment System*. Itasca, IL: Riverside Publishing Company.

NALDIC (National Association for Language Development in the Curriculum) (1999) *The Distinctiveness of English as an Additional Language: A Cross-curriculum Discipline*. Watford: National Association for Lanuage Development in the Curriculum.

NALDIC Working Group (1998) *Provision in Literacy Hours for Pupils Learning English as an Additional Language*. Watford: NALDIC.

NALDIC/NASSEA (1999) *The Ethnic Minority Achievement Grant: Guidelines prepared by NALDIC and NASSEA*. Watford: NALDIC/NASSEA.

NAMH (National Association for Mental Health) (1969) *The Mentally Subnormal in England and Wales*. London: NAMH.

NASEN (National Association for Special Educational Needs) (2000) *Policy Document on Partnership with Parents*. Tamworth: NASEN.

National Curriculum Council (NCC) (1989a) *Implementing the National Curriculum – Participation by Pupils with Special Educational Needs* (Circular No. 5). York: NCC.

National Curriculum Council (NCC) (1989b) *A Curriculum for All: Special Educational Needs in the National Curriculum*. York: NCC.

National Foundation for Educational Research (NFER) (1998) *Code of Practice for the Development of Assessment Instruments, Methods and Systems*. Windsor: NFER.

Neale, M., Christophers, U. and Whetton, C. (1997) *Neale Analysis of Reading Ability*, 2nd revised British edn. Windsor: NFER-Nelson.

Nelson, D., Joseph, G.G. and Williams, J. (1993) *Multicultural Mathematics: Teaching Mathematics from a Global Perspective*. Oxford: Oxford University Press.

Nelson, K.E. (1998) Processes of facilitating progress by language-delayed children in special language-centred school units. *International Journal of Language and Communication Disorders*, 33: 208–10.

Newcomb, A.F., Bukowski, W.M. and Pattee, L. (1993) Children's peer relations: a meta-analytic review of popular, rejected, neglected, controversial and average sociometric status. *Psychological Bulletin*, 113(1): 99–128.

Newell, P. (1991) *The UN Convention and Children's Rights in the UK*. London: National Children's Bureau.

Newman, A. (1983) *The Newman Language of Mathematics Kit: Strategies for Diagnosis and Remediation*. Sydney: Harcourt Brace Jovanovich.

Newton, C., Taylor, G. and Wilson, D. (1996) Circles of friends: an inclusive approach to meeting emotional and behavioural difficulties. *Educational Psychology in Practice*, 11(4): 41–8.

Nicholls, D. and Houghton, S. (1995) The effect of Canter's Assertive Discipline Program on teacher and student behaviour. *British Journal of Educational Psychology*, 65(2): 197–210.

Nicholls, J.G. (1978) The development of the concepts of effort and ability, perception of academic attainment and the understanding that difficult tasks require more ability. *Child Development*, 49: 800–14.

Nicolson, R. and Fawcett, A. (1994) Reaction times and dyslexia. *Quarterly Journal of Experimental Psychology*, 47A: 29–48.

Nicolson, R. and Fawcett, A. (1995) Dyslexia is more than a phonological disability. *Dyslexia*, 1: 19–36.

Nicolson, R. and Fawcett, A. (1996) *Dyslexia Screening Test and Dyslexia Early Screening Test*. Sidcup: The Psychological Corporation.

Norman, R.D. (1963) Intelligence tests and the personal world. *New Mexico Quarterly*, 33: 153–84.

Norwich, B. (1999) The connotation of special education labels for professionals in the field. *British Journal of Special Education*, 26(4): 179–83.

Nunes, T. and Moreno, C. (1998) Is hearing impairment a cause of difficulties in learning mathematics? in C. Donlan (ed.) *The Development of Mathematical Skills*. Hove: Psychology Press.

Nunes, T., Schliemann, A. and Carraher, D. (1993) *Street Mathematics and Home Mathematics*. Cambridge: Cambridge University Press.

Nuttall, D., Goldstein, H., Prosser, R. and Rasbash, J. (1989) Differential school effectiveness. *International Journal of Educational Research*, 13(7): 769–76.

Oakhill, J. and Garnham, A. (1989) *Becoming a Skilled Reader*. Oxford: Basil Blackwell.

Oden, S. (1986) A child's social isolation: origins, prevention, intervention, in G. Cartledge and J.F. Milburn (eds) *Teaching Social Skills to Children*. Oxford: Pergamon Press.

O'Donnell, K. (1999) Lesbian and gay families: legal perspectives, in G. Jagger and C. Wright (eds) *Changing Family Values*. London: Routledge.

O'Donoghue, G.M. (1992) Cochlear implants in children. *Journal of the Royal Society of Medicine*, 85: 655–8.

O'Hare, A.E., Brown, J.K. and Aitken, K. (1991) Dyscalculia in children. *Developmental Medicine and Child Neurology*, 33: 356–61.

Ofsted (Office for Standards in Education) (1994) *Educational Support for Minority Ethnic Communities: A Survey of Educational Provision Funded Under Section 11 of the 1996 Local Government Act* (130/94/NS). London: Ofsted.

Ofsted (Office for Standards in Education) (1995) *Pupil Referral Units: The First Twelve Inspections*. London: Ofsted.

Ofsted (Office for Standards in Education) (1996a) *Exclusions from Secondary Schools 1995–1996*. London: Ofsted.

Ofsted (Office for Standards in Education) (1996b) *Successful Teaching of Literacy and Numeracy in Primary Schools: A Starting Point*. London: Ofsted.

Ofsted (Office for Standards in Education) (1997a) *The Assessment of the Language Development of Bilingual Pupils* (97/97/NS). London: Ofsted.

Ofsted (Office for Standards in Education) (1997b) *The Teaching of Number in Three Inner-Urban LEAs*. London: Ofsted.

Ofsted (Office for Standards in Education) (1998) *The National Literacy Project: An HMI Evaluation*. London: Ofsted.

Ofsted (Office for Standards in Education) (1999a) *Raising the Attainment of Minority Ethnic Pupils: School and LEA Responses*. London: Ofsted.

Ofsted (Office for Standards in Education) (1999b) *The National Literacy Strategy: An Evaluation of the First Year of the National Literacy Strategy*. London: Ofsted.

Ofsted (Office for Standards in Education) (2000a) *Evaluating Educational Inclusion: Guidance for Inspectors and Schools*. London: Ofsted.

Ofsted (Office for Standards in Education) (2000b) *The National Literacy Strategy: The Second Year*. London: Ofsted.

Ogbu, J.U. (1978) *Minority Education and Caste*. New York: Academic Press.

Okagaki, L. and Frensch, P.A. (1998) Parenting and children's school achievement: a multiethnic perspective. *American Educational Research Journal*, 35(1): 123–44.

Organization for Economic Cooperation and Development (OECD) (1981) *The education of the Handicapped Adolescent: Integration at School*. Paris: OECD.

Oritz, A.A. (1984) Texas: a state policy for Hispanic children with special needs, in P. Williams (ed.) *Special Education in Minority Communities*. Milton Keynes: Open University Press.

Ostad, S.A. (1997) Developmental differences in addition strategies: a comparison of mathematically disabled and mathematically normal children. *British Journal of Educational Psychology*, 67: 345–57.

Otterburn, M.K. and Nicholson, A.R. (1976) The language of CSE mathematics. *Maths in School*, 5(5): 18–21.

Padron, Y. (1991) Commentary, in M. Knapp and B. Means (eds) *Teaching Advanced Skills to At-risk Students: Views from Research and Practice*. San Francisco: Jossey-Bass.

Padron, Y. (1992) Instructional programmes that improve the reading comprehension of students at risk, in H.C. Waxman, J. Walker de Felix, J.E. Anderson and H. Prentice Baptiste (eds) *Students at Risk in At-Risk School: Improving Environments for Learning*. Newbury, CA: Sage.

Palazzoli, S.M., Cecchin, G., Prate, G. and Boscolo, L. (1978) *Paradox and Counter Paradox: A New Model of the Family in Schizophrenic Transaction*. London: Jason Aronson.

Palinscar, A.S. (1986) The role of dialogue in providing scaffolded instruction. *Educational Psychologist*, 21(1&2): 73–98.

Palinscar, A.S. and Brown, A. (1985) Reciprocal teaching: a means to a meaningful end, in J. Osborn, P. Wilson and R.C. Anderson (eds) *Reading Education: Foundations for a Literate America*. Lexington, MA: Lexington.

Parker, J.G. and Asher, S.R. (1987) Peer relations and later personal adjustment: are low-accepted children at risk? *Psychological Bulletin*, 102(3): 357–89.

Parry, G. (1996) Aetiology and prevalence of childhood hearing impairment in Bradford. *Audiens* (BACDA Newsletter), 20: 25–9.

Parsons, C. (1996) Permanent exclusions from schools in England in the 1990s: Trends, causes and responses. *Children and Society*, 10: 177–86.

Paulesu, E., Frith, U., Snowling, M., Gallagher, A., Morton, J., Frackowiak, R.S.J. and Frith, C.D. (1996) Is developmental dyslexia a disconnection syndrome? Evidence from PET scanning. *Brain*, 119: 143–57.

Peach, C. (1982) The growth and distribution of the black population in Britain 1945–1980, in D.A. Coleman (ed.) *Demography of Immigrants and Minority Groups in the United Kingdom*. London: Academic Press.

Pellegrini, D.S. and Urbain, E.S. (1985) An evaluation of interpersonal problem solving training with children. *Journal of Child Psychology and Psychiatry*, 26(1): 17–41.

Pema, S. and Pattinson, N. (1991) Developing bilingual assessment tasks, in G. Lindsay and A. Miller (eds) *Psychological Services for Primary Schools*. London: Longman.

Pennington, B.F. and Ozonoff, S. (1996) Executive function and developmental psychopathology. *Journal of Child Psychology and Psychiatry*, 27: 307–19.

Perez-Pereira, M. and Conti-Ramsden, G. (1999) *Language Development and Social Interaction in Blind Children*. Hove: Psychology Press.

Perrett, G. (1990) The language testing interview: a reappraisal, in J. de Jong and D.K. Stevenson (eds) *Individualizing the Assessment of Language Abilities*. Clevedon: Multilingual Matters.

Petersen, N.S. and Novick, M.R. (1976) An evaluation of some models for culture-fair selection. *Journal of Educational Measurement*, 13(1): 3–29.

Petito, L.A. and Marentette, P.F. (1991) Babbling in the manual mode: evidence for the ontogeny of language. *Science*, 251: 1493–6.

Peverly, S.T. and Kitzen, K.R. (1998) Curriculum-based assessment for reading skills: considerations and caveats for school psychologists. *Psychology in the Schools*, 35(1): 29–47.

Pickersgill, M. (1994) A bilingual policy in the education of deaf and hearing-impaired children. Paper Presented at a Study Day at University College London, 21 June.

Pielstick, N.L. (1987) Assessing the learning environment. *School Psychology International*, 9: 111–22.

Pietrowski, J. and Reason, R. (2000) The national literacy strategy and dyslexia: a comparison of teaching methods and materials. *Support for Learning*, 15(2): 51–7.

Pijl, S.J. (1995) The resources for regular schools with special needs students: an international perspective, in C. Clark, A. Dyson and A. Millward (eds) *Towards Inclusive Schools*. London: David Fulton.

Pomplun, M. and Capps, L. (1999) Gender differences for constructed response mathematics items. *Educational and Psychological Measurement*, 59(4): 597–614.

Potts, P. (1983) Medicine, morals and mental deficiency: the contribution of doctors to the development of special education in England. *Oxford Review of Education*, 9(3): 181–96.

Powers, S. (1996) Deaf pupils' achievements in ordinary schools. *Journal of the British Association of Teachers of the Deaf*, 20(4): 111–23.

Powers, S. (1998) An analysis of deaf pupils' examination results in ordinary schools in 1996. *Deafness and Education*, 22(3): 20–36.

Powers, S., Gregory, S. and Thoutenhoofd, E. (1998) *Educational Achievements of Deaf Children*. London: DfEE.

Pritchard, D.G. (1963) *Education and the Handicapped 1760–1960*. London: Routledge & Kegan Paul.

Pugh, G. (1988) *Services for Under Fives: Developing a Co-ordinated Approach*. London: National Children's Bureau.

Pumfrey, P.D. (1985) *Reading: Tests and Assessment Techniques*, 2nd edn. London: Hodder & Stoughton.

Pumfrey, P. (1986) Measuring attitudes towards reading, in D. Vincent, A.K. Pugh and G. Brooks (eds) *Assessing Reading: Proceedings of the UKRA Colloquium on the Testing and Assessment of Reading*. London: Macmillan Education.

Pumfrey, P.D. (1997) Assessment of affective and motivational aspects of reading, in J.R. Beech and C. Singleton (eds) *The Psychological Assessment of Reading*. London: Routledge.

Pumfrey, P.D. and Reason, R. (1991) *Specific Learning Difficulties (Dyslexia): Challenges and Responses*. London: Routledge.

Pyke, N. (1993) No room for blind pupils as deal ends, *Times Educational Supplement*, 23 July.

QCA (Qualifications and Curriculum Authority) (2000a) *A Language in Common: Assessing English as an Additional Language*. London: QCA.

QCA (Qualifications and Curriculum Authority) (2000b) *Curriculum Guidance for the Foundation Stage*, ref. QCA/00/587. London: QCA.

QCA (Qualifications and Curriculum Authority) (2001) *Curriculum Guidelines for Pupils with Learning Difficulties*. London: QCA.

Quilter, D. and Harper, E. (1988) Why we didn't like mathematics, and why we can't do it. *Educational Research*, 30(2): 121–34.

Quinton, D. and Rutter, M. (1988) *Parenting Breakdown: The Making and Breaking of Intergenerational Links*. Aldershot: Gower.

Rabinowitz, A. (1981) The range of solutions: a critical analysis, in B. Gillham (ed.) *Problem Behaviour in the Secondary School*. London: Croom Helm.

Rack, J.P. (1994) Dyslexia: the phonological deficit hypothesis, in A. Fawcett and R. Nicolson (eds) *Dyslexia in Children: Multi-disciplinary Perspectives*. London: Harvester Wheatsheaf.

Rafoth, M.A. (1997) Guidelines for developing screening programs. *Psychology in the Schools*, 34(2): 129–37.

Rampton, B. (1990) Displacing the 'native speaker': expertise, affiliation and inheritance. *ELT Journal*, 44: 97–101.

Ravenette, A.T. (1997) *Personal Construct Psychology and the Practice of an Educational Psychologist: Selected Papers*. Farnborough: EPCA Publications.

Ravenette, A.T. (1999) *Personal Construct Psychology and Educational Psychology: A Practitioner's View*. London: Whurr.

Raybould, E.C. and Solity, J. (1982) Teaching with precision. *Special Education Forward Trends*, 8(2): 9–13.

Rehal, A. (1989) Involving Asian parents in the statementing procedure – the way forward. *Educational Psychology in Practice*, 4(4): 189–97.

Reid, E. (1988) Linguistic minorities and language education – the English experience. *Journal of Multilingual and Multicultural Development*, 9(1–2): 181–91.

Reid, G. (1997) *Dyslexia: A Practitioner's Handbook*, 2nd edn. Chichester: Wiley.

Reid, J.B. (1993) Prevention of conduct disorder before and after school entry: Relating interventions to developmental findings. *Development and Psychopathology*, 5: 243–62.

Reid, M.K. and Borkowski, J.G. (1987) Causal attributions of hyperactive children: Implications for teaching strategies and self control. *Journal of Educational Psychology*, 79: 296–307.

Renfrew, C. (1997) *Renfrew Language Scales: Bus Story Test*. Bicester: Winslow Press.

Renick, M.J. and Harter, S. (1989) Impact of social comparisons on the developing self-perceptions of learning disabled students. *Journal of Educational Psychology*, 81: 631–8.

Rentoul, A.J. and Fraser, B.J. (1979) Conceptualisation of enquiry-based or open classroom learning environments. *Journal of Curriculum Studies*, 11: 233–45.

Reynolds, C.R. (1980) Differential construct validity of intelligence as popularly measured: correlation of age with raw scores on the WISC-R for blacks, whites, males and females. *Intelligence*, 4(4): 371–80.

Reynolds, C.R. and Kaiser, S.M. (1990) Test bias in psychological assessment, in T.B. Gutkin and C.R. Reynolds (eds) *The Handbook of School Psychology*, 2nd edn. New York: Wiley.

Reynolds, D. (1995) The future of school effectiveness and school improvement. *Educational Psychology in Practice*, 11(3): 12–21.

Reynolds, D. (1997) School effectiveness: retrospect and prospect. *Scottish Educational Review*, 29(2): 87–113.

Reynolds, D. and Farrell, S. (1996) *Worlds Apart? A Review of International Surveys of Educational Achievement Involving England*. London: HMSO.

Reynolds, D. and Muijs, D. (1999) Contemporary policy issues in the teaching of mathematics, in I. Thompson (ed.) *Issues in Teaching Numeracy in Primary Schools*. Buckingham: Open University Press.

Reynolds, M.C. (1989) An historical perspective: the delivery of special education to mildly disabled and at-risk students. *Remedial and Special Education*, 10(6): 7–11.

Reynolds, S., Martin, K. and Groulx, J. (1995) Patterns of understanding. *Educational Assessment*, 3: 363–71.

Rhodes, J. and Ajmal, Y. (1995) *Solution Focused Thinking in Schools*. London: BT Press.

Ribeiro, J.L. (1980) Testing Portuguese immigrant children – cultural patterns and group differences in response to the WISC-R, in D.P. Macedo (ed.) *Issues in Portuguese Bilingual Education*. Cambridge, MA: Evaluation, Dissemination and Assessment Center, Lesley College.

Richardson, S.A., Katz, M. and Koller, H. (1986) Sex differences in number of children administratively classified as mildly mentally retarded: an epidemiological review. *American Journal of Mental Deficiency*, 91(3): 250–6.

Riddell, S. (1996) Gender and special educational needs, in G. Lloyd (ed.) '*Knitting Progress Unsatisfactory': Gender and Special Issues in Education*. Edinburgh: Moray House Publications.

Riddell, S. and Brown, S. (1995) Special educational needs provision in the United Kingdom – the policy context, in S. Riddell and S. Brown (eds) *Special Educational Needs Policy in the 1990s*. London: Routledge.

Riddell, S., Brown, S. and Duffield, J. (1994) Parental power and special educational needs: the case of specific learning difficulties. *British Educational Research Journal*, 20(3): 327–45.

Riding, R.J. and Rayner, S. (1998) *Cognitive Styles and Learning Strategies*. London: David Fulton.

Ridley, J. (1991) The structure of the ear and the hearing system, *Education Guardian*, 25 June.

Rittle-Johnson, B. and Siegler, R.S. (1998) The relationship between conceptual and procedural knowledge in learning mathematics: a review, in C. Donlan (ed.) *The Development of Mathematical Skills*. Hove: Psychology Press.

Rivers, I. (2000) Social exclusion, absenteeism and sexual minority youth. *Support for Learning*, 15(1): 13–18.

Rizzo, J.V. and Zabel, R.H. (1988) *Educating Children and Adolescents with Behavioral Disorders: An Integrative Approach*. Boston, MA: Allyn & Bacon.

Roberts, C. and Zubrick, S. (1992) Factors influencing the social status of children with mild academic disabilities in regular classrooms. *Exceptional Children*, 59(3): 192–202.

Roberts, J.R. (1984) The relative development and educational achievement of ethnic minority children in a Midlands town. *Educational and Child Psychology*, 1: 14–22.

Robertson, A., Fisher, J., Henderson, A. and Gibson, M. (2000) *Quest*, 2nd edn. Windsor: NFER-Nelson.

Robertson, L. and Monsen, J. (2001) Issues in the development of a gay or lesbian identity: practice implications for educational psychologists. *Educational and Child Psychology*, 18(1): 13–32.

Robinson, V. (1993) *Problem-Based Methodology: Research for the Improvement of Practice*. Oxford: Pergamon Press.

Robson, A. (1989) Special needs and special educational needs. Unpublished paper, Inner London Education Authority.

Robson, A. (1995) The assessment of bilingual children, in M.K. Verma, K.P. Corrigan and S. Firth (eds) *Working with Bilingual Children: Good Practice in the Primary Classroom*. Clevedon: Multilingual Matters.

Robson, A. (1996) The application of Cummins' model to work with students with hearing impairment, in T. Cline and N. Frederickson (eds) *Curriculum Related Assessment, Cummins and Bilingual Pupils*. Clevedon: Multilingual Matters.

Roffey, S., Tarrant, T. and Majors, K (1994) *Young Friends: Schools and Friendships*. London: Cassell.

Rogers, M.R., Ingraham, C.L., Bursztyn, A. *et al.* (1999) Providing psychological services to racially, ethnically, culturally and linguistically diverse individuals in the schools: recommendations for practice. *School Psychology International*, 20(3): 243–64.

Rogers, U. and Pratten, A. (1996) The Cummins framework as a decision making aid for special education professionals working with bilingual children, in T. Cline and N. Frederickson (eds) *Curriculum Related Assessment, Cummins and Bilingual Children*. Clevedon: Multilingual Matters.

Ronning, J.A. and Nabuzoka, D. (1993) Promoting social interaction and status of children with intellectual disabilities in Zambia. *Journal of Special Education*, 27(30): 277–305.

Rothcram-Borus, M.J. (1993) Multicultural issues in the delivery of group interventions. *Special Services in the Schools*, 8(1): 179–88.

Rourke, B.P. (1988) Socio-emotional disturbances in learning disabled children. *Journal of Consulting and Clinical Psychology*, 56(6): 801–10.

Rourke, B.P. and Finlayson, M.A.J. (1978) Neuropsychological significance of variations in patterns of academic performance: verbal and visuo-spatial abilities. *Journal of Abnormal Child Psychology*, 6: 121–33.

Rowland, T. (1995) Between the lines: the languages of mathematics, in J. Anghileri (ed.) *Children's Mathematical Thinking in the Primary Years*. London: Cassell.

Roznowski, M. and Reith, J. (1999) Examining the measurement quality of tests containing differentially functioning items: do biased items result in poor measurement? *Educational and Psychological Measurement*, 59(2): 248–69.

Rubin, R.A. and Balow, B. (1978) Prevalence of teacher identified behavior problems: a longitudinal study. *Exceptional Children*, 45(2): 102–11.

Rudduck, J. and Flutter, J. (2000) Pupil participation and pupil perspective: 'carving a new order of experience'. *Cambridge Journal of Education*, 30(1): 75–90.

Rueda, R. (1989) Defining mild disabilities with language minority students. *Exceptional Children*, 56(2): 121–8.

Ruiz, N.T. (1995) The social construction of ability and disability II – Optimal and at-risk lessons in a bilingual special education classroom. *Journal of Learning Disabilities*, 28(8): 491–502.

Ruiz, N.T. and Figueroa, R.A. (1995) Learning handicapped classrooms with latino students: the optimal learning environment (OLE) project. *Education and Urban Society*, 27(4): 463–83.

Russell, R.L. and Ginsberg, H.P. (1984) Cognitive analysis of children's mathematics difficulties. *Cognition and Instruction*, 1: 217–44.

Rust, J. (1995) *Wechsler Objective Language Dimensions (WOLD)*. London: Psychological Corporation.

Rutter, M. (1989) Pathways from childhood to adult life. *Journal of Child Psychology and Psychiatry*, 30: 23–51.

Rutter, M., Tizard, J. and Whitmore, K. (1970) *Education, Health and Behaviour*. London: Longman.

Rutter, M., Yule, W., Berger, M. *et al.* (1974) Children of West Indian immigrants, 1: rates of behavioural deviance and of psychiatric disorder. *Journal of Child Psychology and Psychiatry*, 15: 241–62.

Rutter, M., Maughan, B., Mortimer, P. and Ouston, J. (1979) *Fifteen Thousand Hours*. London: Paul Chapman Publishing.

Rutter, M., Dunn, J., Plomin, R. *et al.* (1997) Integrating nature and nurture: implications of person-environment correlations and interactions for developmental psychopathology. *Development and Psychopathology*, 9: 335–64.

Rutter, M., Silberg, J., O'Connor, T. and Simonoff, E. (1999) Genetics and child psychiatry II: empirical research findings. *Journal of Child Psychology and Psychiatry*, 40(1): 19–56.

Ryan, J. (1999) *Race and Ethnicity in Multi-Ethnic Schools*. Clevedon: Multilingual Matters.

Sainsbury, M., Schagen, I. and Whetton, C. (1998) *Evaluation of the National Literacy Project, Cohort 1, 1996–1998*. Slough: National Foundation for Educational Research.

Salend, S.J. and Garrick Duhaney, L.M. (1999) The impact of inclusion on students with and without disabilities and their educators. *Remedial and Special Education*, 20(2): 114–26.

Salend, S.J. and Lutz, J.G. (1984) Mainstreaming or mainlining: a competency based approach to mainstreaming. *Journal of Learning Disabilities*, 17: 27–9.

Salend, S.J. and Salend, S.M. (1986) Competencies for mainstreaming secondary level learning disabled students. *Journal of Learning Disabilities*, 19: 91–4.

Salmon, P. (1988) *Psychology for Teachers*. London: Hutchinson.

Salovey, P. and Mayer, J.D. (1990) Emotional intelligence, imagination. *Cognition and Personality*, 9: 185–211.

Salovey, P. and Sluyter, D.J. (1997) *Emotional Development and Emotional Intelligence*. New York: Basic Books.

Sapon-Shevin, M., Dobbelaere, A., Corrigan, C.R., Goodman, K. and Mastin, M.C. (1998) Promoting inclusive behaviour in inclusive classrooms: 'You can't say you can't play', in L.H. Meyer, H-S. Park, M. Grenot-Scheyer, I.S. Schwartz and B. Harry (eds)

Making Friends: The Influences of Culture on Development. Baltimore, MD: Paul H. Brookes.

Sattler, J. (1988) *Assessment of Children*, 3rd edn. San Diego, CA: J. Sattler.

Sawyer, A. (1995) Developing early numeracy skills, in G. Moss (ed.) *The Basics of Special Needs*. London: Routledge.

Scarborough, H.S. (1990) Very early language deficits in dyslexic children. *Child Development*, 61: 1728–43.

Scarr, S., Caparulo, B.K., Ferdman, M., Tower, R.B. and Caplan, J. (1983) Developmental status and school achievements of minority and non-minority children from birth to 18 years in a British Midlands town. *British Journal of Developmental Psychology*, 1: 31–48.

Scherer, M. (1990) Assessment by baselines, in M. Scherer, I. Gersch and L. Fry (eds) *Meeting Disruptive Behaviour*. London: Macmillan.

Schiff-Myers, N.B. (1992) Considering arrested language development and language loss in the assessment of second language learners. *Language, Speech and Hearing Services in Schools*, 23: 28–33.

Schmidt-Rohlfing, B. (1993) Signing in class, in H. Claire, J. Maybin and J. Swann (eds) *Equality Matters: Case Studies from the Primary School*. Clevedon: Multilingual Matters.

Scruggs, T.E. and Mastropieri, M.A. (1994) Successful mainstreaming in elementary science classes: a qualitative study of three reputational cases. *American Education Research Journal*, 31(4): 785–811.

Scruggs, T.E. and Mastropieri, M.A. (1995) What makes special education special? Evaluating inclusion programmes with the PASS variables. *Journal of Special Education*, 29(2): 224–33.

SEAC (Schools Examinations and Assessment Council) (1990) *A Guide to Teacher Assessment, Pack C: A Source Book of Teacher Assessment*. London: Heinemann Educational.

Sebba, J. and Sachdev, D. (1997) *What Works in Inclusive Education?* Barkingside: Barnardo's.

Sebba, J., Byers, R. and Rose, R. (1993) *Redefining the Whole Curriculum for Pupils with Learning Difficulties*. London: David Fulton.

Semmel, M.I., Gerber, M.M. and MacMillan, D.L. (1994) Twenty-five years after Dunn's article: a legacy of policy analysis research in special education. *Journal of Special Education*, 27(4): 481–95.

Sepie, A.C. and Keeling, B. (1978) The relationship between types of anxiety and underachievement in mathematics. *Journal of Educational Research*, 72(1): 15–19.

Shackman, J. (1984) *The Right to be Understood: A Handbook for Anyone Working with, Employing and Training Community Interpreters*. Cambridge: National Extension College.

Shah, R. (1992) *The Silent Minority: Children with Disabilities in Asian Families*. London: National Children's Bureau.

Shah, T.A., Hall, W., Nelms, S., Parkes, J. and Richards, A. (1997) 'W(h)ither professionalism in assessment?' *Newsletter of the British Psychological Society Division of Educational and Child Psychology*, 79: 28–33.

Shalev, R.S., Manor, O., Amir, N., Wertman-Elad, R. and Gross-Tsur, V. (1995) Developmental dyscalculia and brain laterality. *Cortex*, 31: 357–65.

Shan, S-J. and Bailey, P. (1991) *Multiple Factors: Classroom Mathematics for Equality and Justice*. Stoke-on-Trent: Trentham Books.

Share, D.L. (1996) Word recognition and spelling processes in specific reading disabled and garden-variety poor readers. *Dyslexia*, 2(3): 167–74.

Share, D.L., Moffitt, T.E. and Silva, P.A. (1988) Factors associated with arithmetic-and-reading disability and specific arithmetic disability. *Journal of Learning Disabilities*, 21: 313–20.

Sharma, A. and Love, D. (1991) *A Change in Approach: A Report on the Experience of Deaf People from Black and Ethnic Minority Communities*. London: Royal Association in aid of Deaf People.

Sharman, C., Cross, W. and Vennis, D. (1995) *Observing Children: A Practical Guide*. London: Cassell.

Sharp, S. (1999) Bullying behaviour in schools, in N. Frederickson and R.J. Cameron (eds) *Psychology in Education Portfolio*. Windsor: NFER-Nelson.

Sharp, S. and Smith, P. (1994) *How to Tackle Bullying in Your School*. London: Routledge.

Shaywitz, S.E., Shaywitz, B.A., Fletcher, J.M. and Escobar, M.D. (1990) Prevalence of reading disability in boys and girls: results of the Connecticut Longitudinal Study. *Journal of the American Medical Association*, 264: 998–1002.

Sheil, G. and Forde, P. (1995) Profiling pupil achievement in language and literacy: current issues and trends, in B. Raban-Bisby, G. Brooks and S. Wolfendale (eds) *Developing Language and Literacy*. Stoke-on-Trent: Trentham Books.

Shepard, L., Camilli, G. and Averill, M. (1981) Comparison of procedures for detecting test item bias with both internal and external ability criteria. *Journal of Educational Statistics*, 60: 317–75.

Shields, M.M. and Steiner, E. (1973) The language of three- to five-year olds in pre-school education. *Educational Research*, 15(2): 97–105.

Shotton, G. (1998) A circles of friends approach with socially neglected children. *Educational Psychology in Practice*, 14(1): 22–5.

Shuard, H. and Rothery, R. (1984) *Children Reading Mathematics*. London: John Murray.

Shure, M.B. (1992) *I Can Problem Solve: An Interpersonal Congitive Problem Solving Programme [Pre-School]*. Champaign, IL: Research Press.

Siegel, L.S. (1990) IQ and learning disabilities: RIP, in H.L. Swanson and B. Keogh (eds) *Learning Disabilities: Theoretical and Research Issues*. Hillsdale, NJ: Lawrence Erlbaum Associates.

Siegel, L.S. (1992) An evaluation of the discrepancy definition of dyslexia. *Journal of Learning Disabilities*, 25: 616–29.

Siegel, L.S. and Ryan, E.B. (1989) The development of working memory in normally achieving and subtypes of learning disabled children. *Child Development*, 60: 973–80.

Sijtsma, K. (1993) Psychometric issues in learning potential assessment, in J.H.M. Hamers, K. Sijtsma and A.J.J.M. Ruilessenaars (eds) *Learning Potential Assessment: Theoretical, Methodological and Practical Issues*. Amsterdam: Swets and Zeitlinger.

Simmons, K. (2000) Parents: Legislation and Inclusion, in H. Daniels (ed.) *Special Education Re-formed: Beyond Rhetoric*? London: Falmer Press.

Simpson, M. (1997) Developing differentiation practices: meeting the needs of pupils and teachers. *The Curriculum Journal*, 8(1): 85–104.

Sinclair Taylor, A. (1995) 'Less Better Than The Rest': perceptions of integration in a multi-ethnic special needs unit. *Educational Review*, 47(3): 263–74.

Siner, J. (1993) Social competence and cooperative learning. *Educational Psychology in Practice*, 9(3): 171–80.

Singh, J. (1992) *Black Families and Respite Care: A Study of Minority Ethnic Families who have Children with Learning Disabilities in South Glamorgan*. Barkingside: Barnardo's.

Singleton, C. (1995) *Cognitive Profiling System*. Newark: Chameleon Education.

Singleton, L.C. and Asher, S.R. (1979) Racial integration and children's peer preferences: an investigation of developmental and cohort differences. *Child Development*, 50: 936–41.

Skemp, R.R. (1976) Relational understanding and instrumental understanding. *Mathematics Teaching*, 77: 20–6.

Skutnabb-Kangas, T. (1981) *Bilingualism or Not: The Education of Minorities*. Clevedon: Multilingual Matters.

Slate, J.R. and Saudargas, R.A. (1987) Classroom behaviours of LD, seriously emotionally disturbed and average children: a sequential analysis. *Learning Disabilities Quarterly*, 10: 125–34.

Sleeter, C. and Grant, C. (1987) An analysis of multicultural education in the USA. *Educational Review*, 57: 421–44.

Smith, B.R. and Leinonen, E. (1992) *Clinical Pragmatics: Unravelling the Complexities of Communicative Failure*. London: Chapman & Hall.

Smith, F. (ed.) (1973) *Psycholinguistics and Reading*. New York: Holt, Rinehart & Winston.

Smith, M.L. (1991) Put to the test: the effects of external testing on teachers. *Educational Researcher*, 20(5): 8–11.

Smith, P. (2000) *Bullying in Schools: National Children's Bureau, Highlight No. 174*. London: National Children's Bureau.

Smith, P. and Whetton, C. (1988) Bias reduction in test development. *The Psychologist: Bulletin of the British Psychological Society*, 7: 257–8.

Smith, P.K., Boulton, M.J. and Cowie, H. (1993) The impact of cooperative group work on ethnic relations in middle school. *School Psychology International*, 14: 21–42.

Snowling, M. (1995) Phonological processing and developmental dyslexia. *Journal of Research in Reading*, 18: 132–8.

Snowling, M. (1998) Dyslexia as a phonological deficit: evidence and implications. *Child Psychology and Psychiatry Review (CPPR)*, 3(1): 4–11.

Snowling, M., Stothard, S. and McLean, J. (1996) *Graded Nonword Reading Test*. Bury St Edmunds: Thames Valley Test Company.

Solity, J. (1991) Special needs: a discriminatory concept? *Educational Psychology in Practice*, 7(1): 12–19.

Solity, J. (1993) Assessment through teaching: a case of mistaken identity. *Educational and Child Psychology*, 10(4): 27–47.

Solity, J. (1995) Assessment through teaching and the code of practice. *Educational and Child Psychology*, 12(3): 29–35.

Solity, J. (1996a) Discrepancy definitions of dyslexia: an assessment through teaching approach. *Educational Psychology in Practice*, 12(3): 141–51.

Solity, J. (1996b) Reframing psychological assessment. *Educational and Child Psychology*, 13(3): 94–102.

Solity, J. and Bull, S. (1987) *Special Needs: Bridging the Curriculum Gap*. Milton Keynes: Open University Press.

Solity, J., Deavers, R., Kerfoot, S., Crane, G. and Cannon, K. (1999) Raising literacy attainments in the early years: the impact of instructional psychology. *Educational Psychology*, 19(4): 373–9.

Sparrow, S.S. and Davis, S.M. (2000) Recent advances in the assessment of intelligence and cognition. *Journal of Child Psychology and Psychiatry*, 41(1): 117–31.

Sparrow, S.S., Balla, D.A. and Cicchetti, D.V. (1984) *Vineland Adaptive Behavior Scales (Revised)*. Circle Pines, MN: American Guidance Service.

Speedy, J. (1986) Breaking down the barriers. *TALK*, 125: 12–14.

Spence, S. (1983) Teaching social skills to children. *Journal of Child Psychology and Psychiatry*, 24(4): 621–8.

Spence, S. (1995) *Social Skills Training: Enhancing Social Competence with Children and Adolescence*. Windsor: NFER-Nelson.

Spivack, G. and Shure, M.B. (1974) *Social Adjustment of Young Children*. San Francisco, CA: Jossey-Bass.

Spivack, G., Platt, J. and Shure, M. (1976) *The Problem-solving Approach to Adjustment*. San Francisco, CA: Jossey-Bass.

St George, R. (1987) Applying an internal criterion of test bias to Progressive Achievement Tests and the Test of Scholastic Abilities. *New Zealand Journal of Educational Studies*, 22(1): 117–19.

Stakes, R. and Hornby, G. (1996) *Meeting Special Needs in Mainstream Schools: A Practical Guide for Teachers*. London: David Fulton.

Stallings, J.A. and Freiberg, H.J. (1991) Observation for the improvement of teaching, in H.C. Waxman and H.J. Walberg (eds) *Effective Teaching: Current Research*. Berkeley, CA: McCutchan.

Stanovich, K.E. (1988) Explaining the differences between the dyslexic and the garden-variety poor reader: the phonological-core variable-difference model. *Journal of Learning Disabilities*, 21: 590–612.

Stanovich, K.E. (1996) Towards a more inclusive definition of dyslexia. *Dyslexia*, 2(3): 154–66.

Stanovich, K.E. and Stanovich, P.J. (1997) Further thoughts on aptitude/achievement discrepancy. *Educational Psychology in Practice*, 13(1): 3–8.

Staub, D. and Peck, C.A. (1994) What are the outcomes for non-disabled students? *Educational Leadership*, 52(4): 36–40.

Stein, J.F. (1994) A visual defect in dyslexics? in A. Fawcett and R. Nicolson (eds) *Dyslexia in children: Multi-disciplinary Perspectives*. London: Harvester Wheatsheaf.

Stein, Z. and Susser, M. (1960) The families of dull children: a classification for predicting careers. *British Journal of Preventive Social Medicine*, 14: 83–8.

Sternberg, R.J. (1985) *Beyond IQ: A Triarchic Theory of Human Intelligence*. Cambridge: Cambridge University Press.

Stobart, G. (1986) Is integrating the handicapped psychologically defensible? *Bulletin of the British Psychological Society*, 39: 1–3.

Stoel-Gammon, C. and Otomo, K. (1986) Babbling development of hearing impaired and normal hearing subjects. *Journal of Speech and Hearing Disorders*, 51: 33–40.

Stoker, R. and Walker, C. (eds) (1996) Constructivist approaches. *Educational and Child Psychology*, 13(4): 6–35.

Stone, J. (1995) *Mobility for Special Needs*. London: Cassell.

Stott, D.H. (1974) *The Social Adjustment of Children*. Sevenoaks: Hodder & Stoughton.

Stott, D.H. (1978) *Helping Children with Learning Difficulties: A Diagnostic Teaching Approach*. London: Ward Lock.

Stradling, R. and Saunders, L. (1991) *Differentiation in Action: A Whole School Approach for Raising Attainment*. Slough: National Foundation for Educational Research/Department of Education and Science.

Straker, N. (1988) Coping with shortage. *Mathematics Teaching*, 124: 44–5.

Street, B. (1995) *Social Literacies*. London: Longman.

Strickland, B.R. (1972) Delay of gratification as a function of race of the experimenter. *Journal of Personality and Social Psychology*, 22: 108–12.

Sue, D.W. and Sue, D. (1990) *Counselling the Culturally Different: Theory and Practice*, 2nd edn. New York: Wiley.

Suinn, R.M., Taylor, S. and Edwards, R.W. (1988) Suinn Mathematics Anxiety Rating Scale for elementary school students (MARS-E). *Educational and Psychological Measurement*, 48: 979–86.

Sur, D. and Sur, A. (1997) The mother's role in children's education. *NALDIC News*, 11: 8–9.

Sutherland, G. (1981) The origins of special education, in W. Swann (ed.) *The Practice of Special Education*. Oxford: Blackwell.

Sutherland, P. (1988) Dyscalculia, acalculia, dysgraphia or plain innumerate? A brief survey of the literature. *British Psychological Society Education Section Review*, 12(1): 11–12.

Swann, W. (1988) Integration or differentiation? in G. Thomas and A. Feiler (eds) *Planning for Special Needs: A Whole School Approach*. Oxford: Blackwell.

Swanson, H.L. (1993) Working memory in learning disability subgroups. *Journal of Experimental Child Psychology*, 56: 87–114.

Sweeney, T. (1995) Curriculum matters: using drama to extend the involvement of children with special educational needs, in P. Garner and S. Sandow (eds) *Advocacy, Self-Advocacy and Special Needs*. London: David Fulton.

Tallal, P., Miller, S.L., Jenkins, W.M. and Merzenich, M.M. (1997) The role of temporal processing in developmental language-based disorders: research and clinical implications, in B.A. Blatchman (ed.) *Foundations of Reading Acquisition and Dyslexia: Implications for Early Intervention*. Mahwah, NJ: Lawrence Erlbaum Associates.

Tauber, R.T. (1997) *Self-Fulfilling Prophecy: A Practical Guide to its use in Education*. Westport, CT: Praeger.

Taylor, A.R., Asher, S.R. and Williams, G.A. (1987) The social adaptation of mainstreamed mildly retarded children. *Child Development*, 58: 1321–34.

Taylor, G. (1996) Creating a circle of friends: a case study, in H. Cowie and S. Sharp (eds) *Peer Counselling in School*. London: David Fulton.

Terman, L.M. (1925) *Genetic Studies of Genius*, vol. 1. Stanford, CA: Stanford University Press.

Thacker, J. (1982) *Steps to Success: An Interpersonal Problem Solving Approach for Children*. Windsor: NFER-Nelson.

Tharp, R. and Gallimore, R. (1988) *Rousing Minds to Life*. Cambridge, MA: Cambridge University Press.

Tharp, R.G. (1989) Psychocultural variables and constants: effects on teaching and learning in schools. *American Psychologist*, 44: 349–59.

Tharp, R.G. (1994) Research knowledge and policy issues in cultural diversity and education, in B. McLeod (ed.) *Language and Learning: Educating Linguistically Diverse Students*. Albany, NY: State University of New York Press.

Thomas, G. (1992) *Effective Classroom Teamwork: Support or Intrusion?* London: Routledge.

Thomas, G., Walker, D. and Webb, J. (1998) *The Making of the Inclusive School*. London: Routledge.

Thomas, R.M. (1994) The meaning and significance of *ethnicity* in educational discourse. *International Review of Education*, 40(1): 74–80.

Thomas, W.P. and Collier, V. (1997) *School Effectiveness for Bilingual Students*. Washington, DC: National Clearinghouse for Bilingual Education.

Thorndike, R.L. (1971) Concepts of culture-fairness. *Journal of Educational Measurement*, 8: 63–70.

Thorndike, R.L., Hagen, E.P. and Sattler, J.M. (1986) *Cognitive Abilities Test (CAT)*, 2nd edn. Windsor: NFER-Nelson.

Thornton, K. (2000) Ministers claim exclusion credit, *Times Educational Supplement*, 12 May.

Tikunoff, W.J. (1985) *Applying Significant Bilingual Instruction Features in the Classroom*. Rosslyn, VA: National Clearing House for Bilingual Education (ERIC Document Reproduction Service No. 338 106).

Tindall, G.A. and Marston, D.B. (1990) *Classroom-Based Assessment: Evaluating Instructional Outcomes*. Columbus, OH: Merrill Publishing Company.

Tizard, B. and Hughes, M. (1984) *Young Children Learning: Talking and Thinking at Home and School*. London: Fontana.

Tizard, B., Blachford, P., Burke, J., Farquar, C. and Plewis, I. (1988) *Young Children at School in the Inner City*. Hove: Lawrence Erlbaum.

Todd, R. (1991) *Education in a Multicultural Society*. London: Cassell.

Tomblin, J.B., Spencer, L., Flock, S. and Gantz, B. (1999) A comparison of language achievement in children with cochlear implants and children using hearing aids. *Journal of Speech, Language and Hearing Research*, 42: 497–511.

Tomlinson, S. (1981) *Educational Subnormality: A Study in Decision Making*. London: Routledge & Kegan Paul.

Tomlinson, S. (1982) *A Sociology of Special Education*. London. Routledge & Kegan Paul.

Tomlinson, S. (1984) Minority groups in English conurbations, in P. Williams (ed.) *Special Education in Minority Communities*. Milton Keynes: Open University Press.

Tomlinson, S. (1988) Why Johnny can't read: critical theory and special education. *European Journal of Special Needs Education*, 3(1): 45–58.

Tomlinson, S. (2000) Ethnic minorities and education: new disadvantages, in T. Cox (ed.) *Combating Educational Disadvantage: Meeting the Needs of Vulnerable Children*. London: Falmer Press.

Tomlinson, S. and Craft, M. (eds) (1995) *Ethnic Relations and Schooling: Policy and Practice in the 1990s*. London: Athlone.

Tonnessen, F.E. (1997) How can we best define dyslexia? *Dyslexia*, 3: 78–92.

Tooley, J. and Darby, D. (1998) *Education Research: An Ofsted Critique*. London: Ofsted.

Topping, K.J. and Lindsay, G.A. (1991) The structure and development of the paired reading technique. *Journal of Research in Reading*, 15(2): 120–36.

Topping, K.J. and Lindsay, G.A. (1992) Paired reading: a review of the literature. *Research Papers in Education*, 7(3): 199–246.

Townsend, B.L. (1998) Social friendships and networks among African-American children and youth, in L.H. Meyer, H-S. Park, M. Grenot-Scheyer, I.S. Schwartz and B. Harry (eds) *Making Friends: The Influences of Culture on Development*. Baltimore, MD: Paul H. Brookes.

Townsend, H. (1971) *Immigrant Pupils in England: The LEA Response*. Windsor: NFER-Nelson.

Towse, J. and Saxton, M. (1998) Mathematics across national boundaries: cultural and linguistic perspectives on numerical competence, in C. Donlan (ed.) *The Development of Mathematical Skills*. Hove: Psychology Press.

Troike, R. (1978) Research evidence for the effectiveness of bilingual education. *NABE Journal*, 3: 13–24.

Tucker, J.A. (1980) Ethnic proportions in classes for the learning disabled: issues in non-biased assessment. *Journal of Special Education*, 14: 93–105.

Tucker, J.A. (1985) Curriculum based assessment: an introduction. *Exceptional Children*, 52(3): 199–204.

Tunmer, W.E. and Chapman, J.W. (1996) A developmental model of dyslexia: can the construct be saved? *Dyslexia*, 2(3): 179–89.

Turner, M. (1997) *Psychological Assessment of Dyslexia*. London: Whurr.

Turner, S. (1996) Meeting the needs of children under five with sensori-neural hearing loss from ethnic minority families. *Journal of the British Association of Teachers of the Deaf*, 20: 91–100.

Turner, S. and Lynas, W. (2000) Teachers' perspectives on support for under-fives in families of ethnic minority origin. *Deafness and Education International*, 2(3): 152–64.

UNESCO (United Nations Educational, Scientific and Cultural Organization) (1988) *The Review of the Present Situation of Special Education*. Paris: UNESCO.

UNESCO (United Nations Educational, Scientific and Cultural Organization) (1994) *The Salamanca Statement and Framework for Action on Special Needs Education*. Paris: UNESCO.

Upton, G. (1990) The Education Reform Act and special educational needs. *Newsletter of the Association for Child Psychology and Psychiatry*, 12(5): 3–8.

Uzzell, D. (1995) Ethnography and action research, in G.M. Brakewell, S. Hammond and C. Fife-Schaw (eds) *Research Methods in Psychology*. London: Sage.

Valdes, G. and Figueroa, R.A. (1994) *Bilingualism and Testing: A Special Case of Bias*. Norwood, NJ: Ablex Publishing Company.

Valsiner, J. (2000) *Culture and Human Development: An Introduction*. London: Sage.

Vaughn, S., Elbaum, B.E. and Schumm, J.S. (1996) The effects of inclusion on the social functioning of students with and without learning disabilities. *Journal of Learning Disabilities*, 29(6): 598–608.

Vellutino, F.R., Scanlon, D.M. and Tanzman, M.S. (1998) The case for early intervention in diagnosing specific reading disability. *Journal of School Psychology*, 36(4): 367–97.

Verhulst, F.C. and Akkerhuis, G.W. (1989) Agreement between parents' and teachers' ratings of behavioural/emotional problems of children aged 4–12. *Journal of Child Psychology and Psychiatry*, 30(1): 123–36.

Verma, G.K. (1986) *Ethnicity and Educational Achievement in British Schools*. Basingstoke: Macmillan.

Verma, G.K. and Pumfrey, P.D. (eds) (1994) *Cultural Diversity and the Curriculum*, vol. 4. Brighton: Falmer Press.

Vincent, C. (1996) *Parents and Teachers: Power and Participation*. London: Falmer Press.

von Bertalanffy, L. (1968) *General Systems Theory*. New York: Brazillier.

Vye, N.J., Burns, M.S., Delclos, V.R. and Bransford, J.D. (1987) A comprehensive approach to assessing intellectually handicapped children in C.S. Lidz (ed.) *Dynamic Assessment: An Interactional Approach to Evaluating Learning Potential*, pp. 327–59. New York: Guilford Press.

Vygotsky, L.S. (1978) *Mind in Society: The Development of Higher Psychological Processes* (edited and translated by M. Cole *et al.*). Cambridge, MA: Harvard University Press.

Wade, B. and Moore, M. (1993) *Experiencing Special Education: What Young People with Special Educational Needs Can Tell Us*. Buckingham: Open University Press.

Wade, J. (1999) Including all learners: QCA's approach. *British Journal of Special Education*, 26(2): 80–2.

Wadsworth, S.J., De Fries, J.C., Stevenson, J., Gilger, J.W. and Pennington, B.F. (1992) Gender ratios among reading-disabled children and their siblings as a function of parental impairment. *Journal of Child Psychology and Psychiatry*, 33: 1229–39.

Walberg, H.J. (1993) Learning 'disabilities' revisited. *European Journal of Special Needs Education*, 8(3): 289–302.

Walberg, H.J. (1995) Generic practices, in G. Cawelti (ed.) *Handbook of Research on Improving Student Achievement*. Arlington, VA: Educational Research Services.

Wang, M.C. and Baker, E.T. (1985–6) Mainstream programmes: design features and effects. *Journal of Special Education*, 19(4): 503–21.

Wang, M.C., Haertel, G.D. and Walberg, H.J. (1994) Educational resilience in inner cities, in M.C. Wang and E.W. Gordon (eds) *Educational Resilience in Inner-city America: Challenges and Prospects*. Hillsdale, NJ: Lawrence Erlbaum Associates.

Watkins, M.W., Kush, J.C. and Glutting, J.J. (1997) Discriminant and predictive validity of the WISC-III ACID profile among children with learning disabilities. *Psychology in the Schools*, 34(4): 309–19.

Watson, D.L., Omark, D.R., Grouell, S.L. and Heller, B. (1987) *Nondiscriminatory Assessment Practitioners' Handbook*. San Diego, CA: Los Amigos Research Associates.

Watson, J. (2000) Constructive instruction and learning difficulties. *Support for Learning*, 15(3): 134–40.

Watson, L. (1996) *Hearing Impairment*. Tamworth: NASEN.

Waxman, H.C. (1992) Reversing the cycles of educational failure for students in At-Risk school environments, in H.C. Waxman, J. Walker de Felix, J.E. Anderson and H. Prentice Baptiste (eds) *Students at Risk in At-Risk Schools: Improving Environments for Learning*. Newbury, CA: Sage.

Waxman, H.C. (1995) Classroom observations of effective teaching, in A.C. Ornstein (ed.) *Teaching: Theory into Practice*. Needham Heights, MA: Allyn & Bacon.

Waxman, H.C. and Huang, S-Y.L. (1996) Motivation and learning environment differences in inner-city middle school students. *Journal of Educational Research*, 90(2): 93–102.

Waxman, H.C. and Huang, S-Y.L. (1997) Classroom instruction and learning environment differences between effective and ineffective urban elementary schools for African American students. *Urban Education*, 32(1): 7–44.

Waxman, H.C., Wang, M.C., Lindvall, M. and Anderson, K.A. (1988) *Classroom Observation Schedule Technical Manual*. Pittsburgh, PA: University of Pittsburgh, Learning Research and Development Centre.

Waxman, H.C., Huang, S-Y.L., Anderson, L. and Weinstein, T. (1997) Classroom process differences in inner-city elementary schools. *Journal of Educational Research*, 91: 49–59.

Webster, A. (1987) Enabling language acquisition: the developmental evidence. *Division of Educational and Child Psychology Newsletter*, 27: 25–31.

Webster, A. (1988) The prevalence of speech and language difficulties in childhood: some brief research notes. *Child Language, Teaching and Therapy*, 4(1): 85–91.

Webster, A. and Wood, D. (1989) *Children with Hearing Difficulties*. London: Cassell.

Wechsler, D. (1944) *The Measurement and Appraisal of Adult Intelligence*. Baltimore, MD: Williams & Wilkins.

Wechsler, D. (1992) *The Wechsler Intelligence Scale for Children*, 3rd edn. New York: The Psychological Corporation.

Weiner, B. (1985) An attributional theory of achievement motivation and emotion. *Psychological Review*, 92: 548–73.

Weiss, L.G. and Prifitera, A. (1995) An evaluation of differential prediction of WIAT achievement scores from WISC III FSIQ across ethnic and gender groups. *Journal of School Psychology*, 33: 297–304.

Wentzel, K.R. (1991) Relations between social competence and academic achievement in early adolescence. *Child Development*, 62: 1066–78.

Wentzel, K.R. and Asher, S.R. (1995) The academic lives of neglected, rejected, popular, and controversial children. *Child Development*, 66: 754–63.

West, T.A. (1971) Diagnosing pupil errors: looking for patterns. *The Arithmetic Teacher*, 18: 467–9.

Wheale, A. (ed.) (2000) *Working with Parents*. Lyme Regis: Russell House Publishing.

White, D.R. and Haring, N.G. (1980) *Exceptional Children*. Columbus, OH: Merrill.

Wiig, E.H. (1988) *Clinical Evaluation of Language Fundamentals*, revised edn. London: Psychological Corporation.

Wiles, S. (1985) Language and learning in multi-ethnic classrooms, in G. Wells and J. Nicholls (eds) *Language and Learning: An Interaction Perspective*. London: Falmer Press.

Wiles, S. (1999) Evaluating additional grant funding for minority ethnic pupils. Paper presented at the NALDIC Annual Conference, Leicester, 20 November.

Wiliam, D. (1994) Creating matched National Curriculum assessments in English and Welsh: test translation and parallel development. *The Curriculum Journal*, 5(1): 17–29.

Wiliam, D. (1999) Formative assessment in mathematics, Part 1: rich questioning. *Equals: Mathematics and Special Educational Needs*, 5(2): 15–18.

Williams, A. (1996) Curriculum auditing: an accessible tool or an awesome task? *British Journal of Special Education*, 23(2): 65–9.

Williams, H. and Muncey, J. (1982) Precision teaching before behavioural objectives. *Journal of the Association of Educational Psychologists*, 5(8): 40–2.

Williams, P. (1993) Integration of students with moderate learning difficulties. *European Journal of Special Needs Education*, 8(3): 303–19.

Williams, R.L. (1971) Abuses and misuses in testing black children. *Counselling Psychologist*, 2: 62–77.

Williams, R.L. (1975) The BITCH-100: a culture specific test. *Journal of Afro-American Issues*, 3(1): 103–16.

Willingham, W.W. and Cole, N.S. (1997) *Gender and Fair Assessment*. Mahwah, NJ: Lawrence Erlbaum Associates.

Wilson, M. (1984) Why don't they learn? Some thoughts on the relationship between maladjustment and learning difficulties. *Maladjustment and Therapeutic Education*, 2(2): 4–11.

Wilson, M. and Evans, M. (1980) *Education of Disturbed Pupil*, Schools Council Working Paper 65. London: Methuen.

Winter, K. (1999) Speech and language therapy provision for bilingual children: aspects of the current service. *International Journal of Language and Communication Disorders*, 34(1): 85–98.

Wolfendale, S. (1989) *Parental Involvement: Developing Networks between School, Home and Community*. London: Cassell.

Wolfendale, S. (1990) *All About Me*. Nottingham: NES/Arnold.

Wood, D., Wood, H., Griffiths, A. and Howarth, I. (1986) *Teaching and Talking with Deaf Children*. Chichester: Wiley.

Wood, R. (1978) Sex differences in answers to English language comprehension items. *Educational Studies*, 4: 157–65.

Wood, R. (1991) *Assessment and Testing: A Survey of Research Commissioned by the University of Cambridge Local Examinations Syndicate*. Cambridge: Cambridge University Press.

Wood, S. and Shears, B. (1986) *Teaching Children with Severe Learning Difficulties: A Radical Reappraisal*. London: Croom Helm.

Woolfolk, A.E. (1998) *Educational Psychology*, 7th edn. London: Allyn & Bacon.

Wright, A.K. (1991) The assessment of bilingual pupils with reported learning difficulties: a hypothesis-testing approach, in T. Cline and N. Frederickson (eds) *Bilingual Pupils and the National Curriculum: Overcoming Difficulties in Teaching and Learning*. London: Educational Psychology Publishing.

Wright, A.K., Gallagher, S.P. and Lombardi, L.G. (1991) Investigating classroom environment in British schools. *Educational Psychology in Practice*, 7(2): 100–4.

Wright, J.A. (1993) Assessment of children with special educational needs, in J.R. Beech, L. Harding and D. Hilton-Jones (eds) *Assessment in Speech and Language Therapy*. London: Routledge.

Wright, J.A. and Kersner, M. (1998) *Supporting Children with Communication Problems: Sharing the Workload*. London: David Fulton.

Wright, J.C., Giamnarino, M. and Parad, H.W. (1986) Social status in small groups: individual-group similarity and the social misfit. *Journal of Personality and Social Psychology*, 50: 523–36.

Wyse, D. (2000) Phonics – the whole story? A critical review of empirical evidence. *Educational Studies*, 26(3): 355–64.

Yachnick, M. (1986) Self-esteem in deaf adolescents. *American Annals of the Deaf*, 131: 305–10.

Ysseldyke, J.E. and Christenson, S.L. (1987a) *TIES: The Instructional Environment Scale*. Austin, TX: Pro-Ed.

Ysseldyke, J.E. and Christenson, S.L. (1987b) Evaluating students' instructional environments. *Remedial and Special Education*, 8(3): 17–24.

Ysseldyke, J.E. and Christenson, S.L. (1993) *TIES-II: The Instructional Environment System-II: A System to Identify a Student's Instructional Needs*. Longmont, CO: Sopris West.

Yule, W. (1975) Psychological and medical concepts, in K. Wedell (ed.) *Orientations in Special Education*. London: Wiley.

Zigmond, N. and Baker, J.M. (1995) An exploration of the meaning and practice of special education in the context of full inclusion of students with learning disabilities. *Journal of Special Education*, 29(2): 1–25.

Zubrick, A. (1992) Child language impairment in Hong Kong, in P. Fletcher and D. Hall (eds) *Specific Speech and Language Disorders in Children*. London: Whurr.

Index